SOFIA TOLSTAYA, THE AUTHOR

SOFIA TOLSTAYA, THE AUTHOR

Her Literary Works in English Translation

by
Andrew Donskov

Translated from the Russian by
John Woodsworth and Arkadi Klioutchanski

UNIVERSITY OF OTTAWA PRESS
2022

University of Ottawa **Press**
Les **Presses** de l'Université d'Ottawa

The University of Ottawa Press (UOP) is proud to be the oldest of the francophone university presses in Canada and the oldest bilingual university publisher in North America. Since 1936, UOP has been enriching intellectual and cultural discourse by producing peer-reviewed and award-winning books in the humanities and social sciences, in French and in English.

www.press.uottawa.ca

Library and Archives Canada Cataloguing in Publication

Title: Sofia Tolstaya, the author: her literary works in English translation / Andrew Donskov.
Other titles: Works. English
Names: Tolstaia, S. A. (Sof'ia Andreevna), 1844-1919, author. | Donskov, Andrew, 1939- author.
Description: Series statement: Slavic studies | Includes bibliographical references and index. | Literary works translated from the original Russian. Critical analysis and literary interpretation in English.
Identifiers: Canadiana (print) 20210294639 | Canadiana (ebook) 20210304960 | ISBN 9780776629445 (softcover) | ISBN 9780776629476 (hardcover) | ISBN 9780776629452 (PDF) | ISBN 9780776629469 (EPUB)
Subjects: LCSH: Tolstaia, S. A. (Sof'ia Andreevna), 1844-1919. | LCSH: Russian literature—19th century—History and criticism. | LCSH: Russian literature—Women authors—History and criticism. | LCSH: Russian literature—19th century. | LCSH: Russian literature—Women authors.
Classification: LCC PG3470.T64 A2 2021 | DDC 891.78/309—dc23

Legal Deposit: First Quarter 2022
Library and Archives Canada

Production Team

Copy editing	Elizabeth Schwaiger
Proofreading	Tanina Dvrar and Robbie McCaw
Typesetting	Édiscript enr.
Cover design	Lefrançois, agence marketing B2B

Cover image

Sofia Andreevna Tolstaya (1901)

The University of Ottawa Press gratefully acknowledges the support extended to its publishing list by the Government of Canada, the Canada Council for the Arts, the Ontario Arts Council, the Federation for the Humanities and Social Sciences through the Awards to Scholarly Publications Program and the Social Sciences and Humanities Research Council, and by the University of Ottawa

To my love, Natalia,
and our wonderful children
Tatiana, Aleksandr, Adrian

Sofia Andreevna Tolstaya
Photo: Thiele and Opitz, Moscow, 1885

TABLE OF CONTENTS

PREFACE TO THE SECOND EDITION

THE PRESENT VOLUME — *Sofia Tolstaya, the author: Her literary works in English translation* — constitutes a second, expanded and updated edition of *Sofia Andreevna Tolstaya: Literary works*, first published in 2011 conjointly by the Slavic Research Group at the University of Ottawa and the State L. N. Tolstoy Museum in Moscow.

This new edition includes important updates in bibliographical references and an extended chronology, along with additional facts and the correction of a few typographical errors. Most significant, of course, is the translation into English of all Tolstaya's major literary works, which in the first edition appeared in their original Russian.

As I suggested in my Introduction to the first edition, the year 2010 heralded an increasing interest in the life and career of Sofia Andreevna Tolstaya (SAT) — none other than the lifelong spouse of the great Russian writer Lev Nikolaevich (Leo) Tolstoy (LNT). In that year, a number of important works appeared, namely:

- Alexandra Popoff's biography of SAT;
- Vitalij Remizov and Liudmila Gladkova's edition (in one volume) of LNT's *Kreutzer Sonata* and its 'rebuttals' — first by his wife's novella *Who is to blame?* and narrative *Song without words*, and then by their son Lev L'vovich's *Chopin's Prelude*.
- This was followed later in the year by the translation of the same volume into French by Michel Aucouturier and Eveline Amoursky and by Michael Katz's translation into English in 2014.
- Surely the most important publications in 2010 were the translations of SAT's major autobiographical memoir *My Life* into English, French and German (in Canada, France and Germany, respectively).

Since 2010 there has been a steadily increasing exploration of Tolstaya's life and works, right up until 2019, which marked 175 years since her birth and 100 years since her death. This included the first edition of the present volume, issued by the Slavic Research Group at the University of Ottawa in 2011, albeit with a rather limited tirage.

What has been missing to date is an English translation and substantive critical examination of a complete set of SAT's major works. Hence we were most happy when Lara Mainville, Director of the University of Ottawa Press, offered to publish this very combination in a single volume.

Mainville saw this as fitting in nicely with the Press's long-term plans for a whole series of books on Russian themes, beginning with Tolstoy. Four of these are already published: SAT's *My Life* (2010), *Tolstoy and Tolstaya: a portrait of a life in letters* (2017), *Leo Tolstoy in conversation with four peasant sectarian writers: the complete correspondence* (2019), and *Leo Tolstoy and the Canadian Doukhobors: a study in historic relationships* (2019). The first two of these are already available in audiobook format as well.

While the works themselves and the critical study are both presented in English, the reader will note that the bibliography contains many entries in Russian, for the benefit of Russian-speaking scholars who wish to access such sources in the original.

My acknowledgements in the earlier edition of this present volume mentioned a number of individuals and institutions to which I still owe a debt of gratitude and hold in great esteem. On the Russian side, I should like to re-extend my deep thanks to the State L. N. Tolstoy Museum in Moscow, the then Director, Vitalij Borisovich Remizov and the current Director, Sergej Aleksandrovich Arkhangelov, for allowing me access to their treasure-trove of archival materials, as well as to their colleagues — Senior Researchers Natalija Kalinina, Tat'jana Nikiforova, Bibliographer Valentina Bastrykina and, especially, Liudmila Gladkova, for their invaluable contribution, along with all the other scholars, whose help in anthologising the materials in Part II was instrumental. As usual, my thanks also go to Dr Marina Shcherbakova, Head of the Russian Classical Division of the Russian Academy of Sciences' Institute of World Literature in Moscow for her input and constant encouragement. I am equally grateful to Vladimir Il'ich Tolstoy — Director of the Yasnaya Polyana Tolstoy Museum Estate and great-great-grandson to Sofia Andreevna Tolstaya and Lev Nikolaevich Tolstoy — as well as the Museum Estate's Head of Research Galina Alekseeva and the Museum's Curator Tat'jana Komarova, herself an unquestioned authority on Sofia Tolstaya.

On the Canadian side, in particular I would like to reiterate in the strongest possible terms my deep appreciation for my friends, colleagues and collaborators John Woodsworth and Arkadi Klioutchanski, both of whom are not only accomplished scholars, but also distinguished translators. It was they who were the recipients of the 2010 Lois Roth award presented by the Modern Language Association of America for the best translation of a literary work (in this case, Tolstaya's *My Life*) into English. Several years later their translation of the Tolstoy-Tolstaya correspondence (with assistance from Tolstoy scholar Liudmila Gladkova) won second place at the 2018 Paris Book Festival.

Parts of my survey of Sofia Tolstaya's life and works have appeared in the two volumes mentioned, and I would like to thank the Press for allowing me to reproduce them here.

I am grateful to the University of Ottawa Press, especially its most capable director, Lara Mainville and her dedicated team, with special thanks to Maryse Cloutier, the remarkably diligent managing editor of the Press, as well as Caroline Boudreau, and Mireille Piché. My profound appreciation extends to Elizabeth Schwaiger — publishing consultant and editor. In my long career, I have never worked with anyone who was as erudite in her field and was better qualified to guide me so ably and patiently through the complexities of editing manuscripts. Her contribution was inestimable for this work, as well as the previous three volumes in the series, seeing the light of the day. Still, my greatest indebtedness goes to my wife of many years, Natalia Smirnoff-Donskov, for her unwavering selfless support and wise counsel.

Ottawa, Canada
September 2021

Andrew Donskov
Fellow of the Royal Society of Canada
Distinguished University Professor

EXPLANATORY NOTE

Transliteration of Russian words. This follows a modified academic system (for example, using *ju* and *ja* for the last two letters of the Russian alphabet, but *sh*, *ch* and *zh* in place of the variants with diacritics). An exception is made in the case of names and terms already possessing a well-established English spelling — e.g., *Tolstoy* (rather than 'Tolstoj'), *Yasnaya Polyana* (Jasnaja Poljana), *Dostoevsky* (Dostoevskij), *Tchaikovsky* (Chajkovskij). In line with the publication of Sofia Tolstaya's *My Life* in English, where she is identified as *Sofia Andreevna Tolstaya* (rather than Sof'ja Andreevna Tolstaja), it has been decided to include her (and all members of her family) in this group.

Calendar dates. Before February 1918, Russia operated on the old-style (O. S.) *Julian calendar*; by that time most Western countries had adopted the new-style (N. S.) *Gregorian calendar* proclaimed in 1582, designed to reflect more accurately the actual solar year by abolishing the date of 29 February (leap year) for those centenary years not exactly divisible by 400. As a result, by the nineteenth century the old-style calendar was 12 days behind the new-style (13 days in the twentieth century).

For example, Christmas Day (25 December) 1898 in the old-style calendar came on 6 January 1899 according to Western calendars, while on New Years' Day (1 January) 1899 in Russia, it was already 13 January new-style in the West.

In the year 1900, however, another day's discrepancy was added, since the day of 29 February, omitted that year from the Western calendar, continued to be observed in Russia according to the old Julian calendar. Hence New Year's Day 1901 old-style fell on 14 January new-style.

Unless otherwise noted, the dates in Tolstaya's text and the accompanying footnotes are cited according to the Julian (O. S.) calendar. However, in the case of encyclopaedic references (e.g., where the year of a birth or death differs depending on the calendar used), preference is given to the N. S. form.

Abbreviations. To avoid awkward repetition, I have abbreviated the names *Sofia Andreevna Tolstaya* and *Lev Nikolaevich Tolstoy* to *SAT* and *LNT,* respectively. Similarly, *War and peace* and *Anna Karenina* appear as *W&P* and *AK,* respectively. The initials *PSS* denote *Polnoe sobranie sochinenij* — that is, the Jubilee edition of Tolstoy's complete collected works (1928–58).

Bibliographical references. In the Bibliography, titles and publication information appear in the original language only, without translation. In the text and footnotes, bibliographical references are given in the usual academic style by author and year of publication. Text and footnote references to Russian titles also include the actual title, along with its English translation in square brackets; here publication information, where appropriate, is cited in English. Titles of both Tolstoy's and Tolstaya's works (including stories not published separately) in English are given throughout (except in the Bibliography) in *italics*. References to Tolstaya's text in the English edition of *My Life* (capitalised in this volume for ease of reading) are cited by Part and Chapter (e.g., IV.118 = Part IV, Chapter 118), references to her *Diaries* by volume and page number (e. g., II: 251).

Index of names. Names of historical persons (but not fictional characters) appear in the Index of names. Entries are listed under surname plus initials (first name and/or relationship included where necessary for distinction; other identification where initials are missing). Alternate surnames are given with cross-references if mentioned in the text.

For detailed explanations regarding Russian names and honorary titles, as well as terms designating currency, distances, area and weight, please see "From the Translators."

Those familiar with the Russian language who wish to read these works of Sofia Andreevna Tolstaya in their original form may still access the full Russian text in the first edition of the present volume — under the title *Sofia Andreevna Tolstaya: Literary works*, published jointly by the Slavic Research Group at the University of Ottawa and the State L. N. Tolstoy Museum in Moscow in 2011.

CHILDREN AND GRANDCHILDREN OF NIKOLAJ IL'ICH TOLSTOY
AND MARIJA NIKOLAEVNA TOLSTAYA

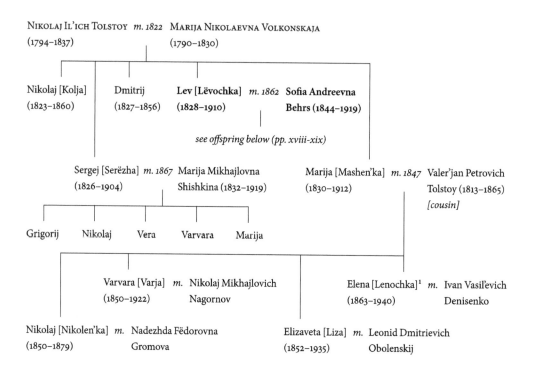

Nikolaj Il'ich Tolstoy *m. 1822* Marija Nikolaevna Volkonskaja
(1794–1837)   (1790–1830)

Nikolaj [Kolja]   Dmitrij   Lev [Lëvochka] *m. 1862* Sofia Andreevna
(1823–1860)   (1827–1856)   (1828–1910)   Behrs (1844–1919)

see offspring below (pp. xviii-xix)

Sergej [Serëzha] *m. 1867* Marija Mikhajlovna   Marija [Mashen'ka] *m. 1847* Valer'jan Petrovich
(1826–1904)   Shishkina (1832–1919)   (1830–1912)   Tolstoy (1813–1865)
                                                                                         [cousin]

Grigorij   Nikolaj   Vera   Varvara   Marija

Varvara [Varja] *m.* Nikolaj Mikhajlovich   Elena [Lenochka][1] *m.* Ivan Vasil'evich
(1850–1922)   Nagornov   (1863–1940)   Denisenko

Nikolaj [Nikolen'ka] *m.* Nadezhda Fëdorovna   Elizaveta [Liza] *m.* Leonid Dmitrievich
(1850–1879)   Gromova   (1852–1935)   Obolenskij

---

1   By her mother's extra-marital liaison (see *My Life* Part III, Note 435).

CHILDREN AND GRANDCHILDREN[2] OF ANDREJ EVSTAF'EVICH BEHRS
AND LJUBOV' ALEKSANDROVNA BERS

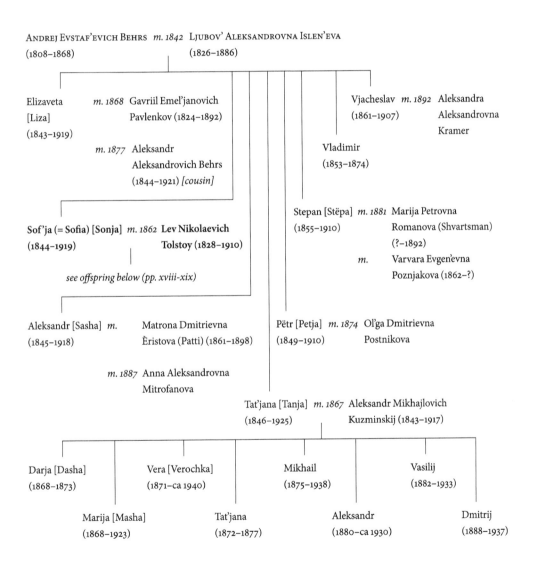

ANDREJ EVSTAF'EVICH BEHRS *m. 1842* LJUBOV' ALEKSANDROVNA ISLEN'EVA
(1808–1868)   (1826–1886)

Elizaveta   *m. 1868* Gavriil Emel'janovich   Vjacheslav *m. 1892* Aleksandra
[Liza]   Pavlenkov (1824–1892)   (1861–1907)   Aleksandrovna
(1843–1919)   Kramer

                 m. 1877 Aleksandr   Vladimir
                            Aleksandrovich Behrs   (1853–1874)
                            (1844–1921) *[cousin]*

Sof'ja (= Sofia) [Sonja] *m. 1862* **Lev Nikolaevich**   Stepan [Stëpa] *m. 1881* Marija Petrovna
(1844–1919)   **Tolstoy (1828–1910)** (1855–1910)   Romanova (Shvartsman)
                                                                                      (?–1892)

see offspring below (pp. xviii-xix)   *m.*   Varvara Evgen'evna
                                                                                      Poznjakova (1862–?)

Aleksandr [Sasha] *m.* Matrona Dmitrievna   Pëtr [Petja] *m. 1874* Ol'ga Dmitrievna
(1845–1918)   Èristova (Patti) (1861–1898)   (1849–1910)   Postnikova

          m. 1887 Anna Aleksandrovna
                     Mitrofanova

                              Tat'jana [Tanja] *m. 1867* Aleksandr Mikhajlovich
                              (1846–1925)   Kuzminskij (1843–1917)

Darja [Dasha]   Vera [Verochka]   Mikhail   Vasilij
(1868–1873)   (1871–ca 1940)   (1875–1938)   (1882–1933)

      Marija [Masha]   Tat'jana   Aleksandr   Dmitrij
      (1868–1923)   (1872–1877)   (1880–ca 1930)   (1888–1937)

2   Grandchildren listed only by Sofia Andreevna Tolstaya and Tat'jana Andreevna Kuzminskaja.

CHILDREN AND GRANDCHILDREN OF LEV NIKOLAEVICH TOLSTOY
AND SOFIA ANDREEVNA TOLSTAYA

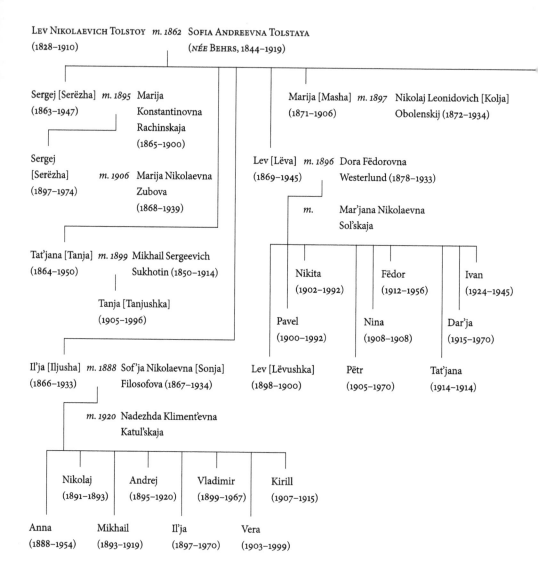

LEV NIKOLAEVICH TOLSTOY *m. 1862* SOFIA ANDREEVNA TOLSTAYA
(1828–1910)   (*NÉE* BEHRS, 1844–1919)

Sergej [Serëzha] *m. 1895* Marija
(1863–1947)   Konstantinovna
                             Rachinskaja
                             (1865–1900)

Sergej
[Serëzha]   *m. 1906* Marija Nikolaevna
(1897–1974)   Zubova
                           (1868–1939)

Tat'jana [Tanja] *m. 1899* Mikhail Sergeevich
(1864–1950)   Sukhotin (1850–1914)

Tanja [Tanjushka]
(1905–1996)

Il'ja [Iljusha] *m. 1888* Sof'ja Nikolaevna [Sonja]
(1866–1933)   Filosofova (1867–1934)

m. 1920 Nadezhda Kliment'evna
           Katul'skaja

Nikolaj   Andrej   Vladimir   Kirill
(1891–1893)   (1895–1920)   (1899–1967)   (1907–1915)

Anna   Mikhail   Il'ja   Vera
(1888–1954)   (1893–1919)   (1897–1970)   (1903–1999)

Marija [Masha] *m. 1897* Nikolaj Leonidovich [Kolja]
(1871–1906)   Obolenskij (1872–1934)

Lev [Lëva] *m. 1896* Dora Fëdorovna
(1869–1945)   Westerlund (1878–1933)

m. Mar'jana Nikolaevna
      Sol'skaja

Nikita   Fëdor   Ivan
(1902–1992)   (1912–1956)   (1924–1945)

Pavel   Nina   Dar'ja
(1900–1992)   (1908–1908)   (1915–1970)

Lev [Lëvushka] Pëtr   Tat'jana
(1898–1900)   (1905–1970)   (1914–1914)

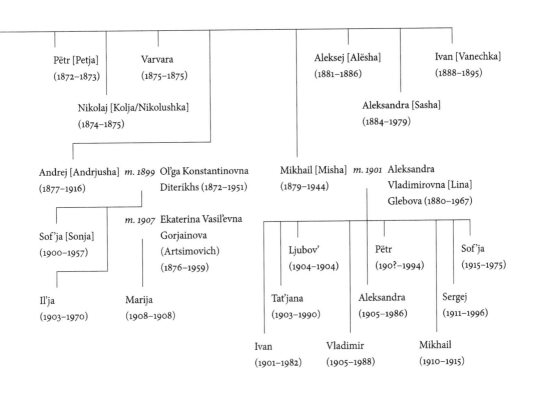

Pëtr [Petja]
(1872–1873)

Varvara
(1875–1875)

Aleksej [Alësha]
(1881–1886)

Ivan [Vanechka]
(1888–1895)

Nikolaj [Kolja/Nikolushka]
(1874–1875)

Aleksandra [Sasha]
(1884–1979)

Andrej [Andrjusha]   *m. 1899*   Ol'ga Konstantinovna
(1877–1916)   Diterikhs (1872–1951)

Mikhail [Misha]   *m. 1901*   Aleksandra
(1879–1944)   Vladimirovna [Lina]
                             Glebova (1880–1967)

m. 1907   Ekaterina Vasil'evna
            Gorjainova
            (Artsimovich)
            (1876–1959)

Sof'ja [Sonja]
(1900–1957)

Ljubov'
(1904–1904)

Pëtr
(190?–1994)

Sof'ja
(1915–1975)

Il'ja
(1903–1970)

Marija
(1908–1908)

Tat'jana
(1903–1990)

Aleksandra
(1905–1986)

Sergej
(1911–1996)

Ivan
(1901–1982)

Vladimir
(1905–1988)

Mikhail
(1910–1915)

PART I

SOFIA ANDREEVNA TOLSTAYA
A LITERARY LIFE

INTRODUCTION

Sofia Andreevna was endowed with considerable artistic talent, either by Nature or by the fact that she spent two quarters of a century living with Tolstoy.

— Ivan Alekseevich Bunin [1]

From my own observations during the time I was acquainted with the Tolstoy family, I must say that apart from all that she might have had in common with hundreds of other women — especially women in aristocratic circles with their positive and negative traits — she was in many respects a powerful and prominent individual, on a par with Lev Nikolaevich, thanks to the critical faculties which she applied to her study of works of art and which enabled her to help him in his literary endeavours... Sofia Andreevna herself was a powerful personality.

— Leonid Osipovich Pasternak [2]

Your life is chock-full of such lively interests on a high level that no matter what segment you might cut out of your everyday lives, that segment always turns out to be extremely interesting and not just for your friends.

— Afanasij Afanas'evich Fet [3]

---

1   I. A. Bunin, *Sobranie sochinenij v 9 tt.* [Collected works in 9 vols.] (Moscow, 1967): IX: 52.
2   L. O. Pasternak, *Zapisi raznykh let* [Notes from different years] (Moscow, 1975): 201.
3   A. A. Fet, personal communication to S. A. Tolstaya, quoted in *My Life* (Ottawa: University of Ottawa Press, 2010): IV.118 — Katkov. (*Note:* references to Tolstaya's *My Life* are cited by Part and Chapter — see Explanatory Note.)

SOFIA ANDREEVNA BERS was born 22 August 1844 at Pokrovskoe Glebovo-Streshnevo near Moscow. She received her education at home and in 1861, at the age of seventeen, passed the 'home-teacher' examination at Moscow University.

The following year, on 23 September 1862, she married Lev Nikolaevich Tolstoy, who had courted her while she was staying on her grandfather's estate (Ivitsy) near Tula, some fifty kilometres north of Yasnaya Polyana. The wedding took place at the Birth of the Virgin Mary Church [Tserkov' Rozhdestva Bogoroditsy] on the grounds of the Kremlin.

Sofia Andreevna quickly adapted not only to her role as Tolstoy's wife but also to that of his copyist and literary assistant, starting soon after the wedding with *Polikushka*, a story of peasant life, which was published the following year. It took her significantly longer to accustom herself to the duties of household manager and mother (of what eventually turned out to be a family of eight children — plus five more who did not survive to adulthood, and not counting several miscarriages). She fulfilled all these roles with a natural ability, efficiency and devotion. She took personal charge of her children's education during their younger years, even devising special readers and grammar books for them. Her busy home schedule left little time for leisure or travel, apart from the occasional trips to St. Petersburg, Kiev and the Crimean Peninsula. She never had the opportunity to travel outside Russia.

She was, however, quite active in community and social affairs, especially during her time in Moscow — most notably during the famine relief efforts of 1891 and 1892, when she set up and managed a campaign collecting funds for famine victims and purchasing needed food and other supplies.[4] She also found time to develop her artistic talent for music, painting, photography and writing. Among other painting activities, she would make copies of early portraits of her husband by well-known artists of the day.

One of her greatest legacies was her ongoing support of her husband's unique literary career. She authored the first biographical sketch of Tolstoy to appear in print.[5] During the 1870s she wrote a series of essays on certain aspects of his life (his conflict with Turgenev, for example), as well as his career as a novelist (in particular, his work on *War and peace* and *Anna Karenina*). During the periods of her husband's illness, she would issue press releases on the true state of his health in an effort to counteract widespread false rumours as to his 'arrest' or even 'death'. She publicly defended him from malicious attacks by his opponents and did her best to protect him from undesired visits to Yasnaya Polyana either by over-zealous supporters or by those interested primarily in personal gain. And despite her personal and

---

4   This is described in *My Life*, V.129.
5   Published in St. Petersburg by M. M. Stasjulevich in 1879 as part of his Russkaja biblioteka [Russian Library] series.

philosophical objections to his later writings such as *The Kreutzer Sonata,* she made a (successful) personal petition to the Tsar himself against their official censorship ban.

Fluent in French from childhood, and with a better-than-average knowledge of German and English, she frequently found herself translating Tolstoy's works into French as well as translating texts of interest to him from all three of these languages into Russian.[6]

Most importantly, particularly during the later years of their marriage, Tolstaya took an active role in the publication of her husband's writings. This included negotiations with printers and publishers, supervising the editing and proofreading process[7] and even maintaining a warehouse of his books in a wing of their home in the Khamovniki District in Moscow. A major turning point in this activity came in May 1883, when Tolstoy gave Tolstaya complete charge of the publication of all his writings published before 1881 (including royalties), while he himself renounced his rights to virtually all his later writings (as well as personal property). Between 1886 and 1891 she brought out eight different editions of his collected writings as well as republishing fifteen volumes of individual works.

Added to all this was her activity as archivist and documentary historian. It is in good measure thanks to Tolstaya that so many materials (including manuscripts, letters and diaries and a catalogue of her husband's library holdings at Yasnaya Polyana) have been preserved for future generations of scholars. According to senior museum researcher Tat'jana Nikiforova, the S. A. Tolstaya archive in the Manuscript Division of the State L. N. Tolstoy Museum in Moscow numbers 22,000 items,[8] including some 10,000 letters written by or addressed to her. Her correspondents included many prominent contemporary writers, artists, critics, philosophers, theatre people, lawyers and politicians.

6 In 1885–86, for example, she translated the book *Uchenie 12 apostolov* [Teachings of the twelve apostles] from German, and in 1888 her translation of Tolstoy's *O zhizni* [*On life*] was published in French.
7 This she did in close co–operation with Tolstoy's editorial adviser, Nikolaj Nikolaevich Strakhov, who enjoyed a relationship of mutual admiration and respect with both Sofia Andreevna and her husband. See A. Donskov (ed.), *L. N. Tolstoj i S. A. Tolstaja: Perepiska s N. N. Strakhovym / The Tolstoys' correspondence with N. N. Strakhov* (Donskov 2000). This volume contains the complete extant correspondence between Tolstaya and Strakhov: 40 letters written by Strakhov and 47 by Tolstaya, mainly discussing editing and proofreading questions.
8 These comprise documents relating to Tolstaya's biography; her writings (literary works and memoirs); household documents (various accounts, inventories of personal effects at the Moscow and Yasnaya Polyana residences, records of income and expenses, plans of the estate, records of payments to day-workers, orders for flower seeds and fruit-tree saplings for the Yasnaya Polyana orchard, etc.); publishing-related materials (order forms for publishing Tolstoy's writings, correspondence with print shop owners, subscription notices for regular editions, records of publication income and expenses, distribution lists for the volumes, along with their contents). See the first pages of the Bibliography for an extensive catalogue selection.

Sofia Andreevna Tolstaya's independent role as editor and publisher of Tolstoy's works is not to be underestimated. Indeed it features prominently in the writings of Tolstoy's biographers, who have provided a good deal of documentation on her life though sadly neglecting her own literary pursuits. She herself acknowledged the importance of this role in the 1904 preface[9] to her extensive autobiographical memoir *My Life* [*Moja zhizn'*], remarking that "the significance of my forty-two years of conjugal life with Lev Nikolaevich cannot be excluded from his life." Indeed, their conjugal experience served as a general catalyst for both Tolstoy's writing career and his inner spiritual development; in addition, more specifically, it was the basis for many of the scenes in LNT's novels.

Until recently, however, there were very few published objective portrayals of SAT's life and professional activity. The vast majority of recorded commentary can be divided into two diametrically opposed categories: on the one hand, comments by dedicated Tolstoyans and such like, who saw her as authoritarian, intellectually limited, offensive and coarse in her dealings with people; and, on the other, comments by visitors to her home and her own regular correspondents, who by and large came to appreciate her talents, her dedication to her family and her invaluable assistance to her husband's writing career. The latter group included many famous names, for example: artists Il'ja Repin and Leonid Pasternak, composers Sergej Taneev and Anton Arenskij, philosophers Nikolaj Grot and Pavel Bakunin, theatre directors Konstantin Stanislavskij and Vladimir Nemirovich-Danchenko, literary critic Nikolaj Strakhov and Vladimir Stasov; this group also comprised many writers and publishers — Afanasij Fet, Ivan Turgenev, Maxim Gorky, Zinaida Gippius, Nikolaj Leskov and Anna Dostoevskaja, to name but a few.

SAT's descriptions of these personalities serve as a chronicle of the times, affording a unique portrait of late-nineteenth and early-twentieth-century Russian society. Together with her other ventures, they also highlight her accomplishments as an author in her own right — a rarity in the largely male-dominated world of the time. Credit must be given to a number of Soviet-era and post-Soviet Russian scholars who have published some of Tolstaya's correspondence with such people in various journals — especially, Tat'jana Komarova, Tat'jana Nikiforova, Vladimir Porudominskij and Aleksandr Shifman. Museum researchers — notably, Ol'ga Golinenko, Irina Pokrovskaja and Berta Shumova[10] — have done some excellent editorial work

---

9   Quoted in full in the epigraph to the editor's introduction to Tolstaya's *My Life*, p. xix, and reproduced in Chapter 3.2 of the present volume.
10 See esp.: S. A. Tolstaja. *Dnevniki v dvukh tomakh* [*Diaries in two volumes*], comp. N. I. Azarova, O. A. Golinenko, I. A. Pokrovskaja, S. A. Rozanova and B. M. Shumova (Moscow, 1978).

in their Russian editions of SAT's diaries and selected passages from *Moja zhizn' [My Life]*.[11]

As these selected sources demonstrate, a considerable amount of documentation exists on Tolstaya. Still, to date no satisfactory *comprehensive* and *sustained* study of her life, and especially literary output, has been published. In his lengthy review of *My Life* and other publications on Tolstaya in the journal *Canadian Slavonic Papers,* Hugh McLean (2011) laments the fact that it has taken nearly century after her death to focus scholarly attention on Tolstaya, and that there has been no unified publication of her literary works, scattered as they are among dated journals or not published at all. We are indebted to Tolstoy Museum Director Vitalij Remizov for his publication in 2010 of Sofia Tolstaya's *Ch'ja vina? [Who is to blame?]* (earlier published in *Oktjabr'*) and *Pesnja bez slov [Song without words]*,[12] as well as, in 2011, *Moja zhizn' [My Life]* all in the original Russian.[13] Also to be recognized is Tat'jana Komarova, Curator of the Tolstoy Yasnaya Polyana Museum Estate, for her republication of *Kukolki-skelettsy [The skeleton-dolls]*.[14] SAT's letters to her son Lev L'vovich Tolstoy, indispensable to a study of her views on art, literature and social issues, are also being prepared for publication.

It is noteworthy that there was indeed an attempt in the early 1990s to publish most of SAT's writings in a single collection along with an introduction by Vladimir Porudominskij.[15] However, this initiative failed amidst the general pressure of economic and political unrest connected with the collapse of the Soviet Union. Years later, Porudominskij (2005) published his preface to the originally intended collection, under the title "Prizvanie i sud'ba" ["Mission and Fate"]:

> At the end of the 1980s and the beginning of the 1990s the collected works of S. A. Tolstaya were prepared for publication. The book included chapters from her notes to *Moja zhizn' [My Life]*, Sofia Andreevna's *Autobiography,*

---

11 S. A. Tolstaja, Excerpts from *Moja zhizn'*: (a) comp. I. A. Pokrovskaja and B. Shumova, *Novyj mir* N° 8 (1978): 34–135 and *Prometej* N° 12 (1980): 148–98; (b) comp. O. A. Golinenko and B. M. Shumova, *Oktjabr'* N° 9 (1998): 136–77 and in *Dom Ostroukhova v Trubnikah* (Moscow and St. Petersburg, 1998): 160–92.

12 In: V. B. Remizov and L. V. Gladkova, *Lev Nikolaevich Tolstoj, Sof'ja Andreevna Tolstaja, Lev L'vovich Tolstoj* (Moscow, 2010); see also: S. A. Tolstaya, "«Ch'ja vina?» Po povodu «Krejtserovoj sonaty» L'va Tolstogo", comp. O. A. Golinenko and T. G. Nikiforova, *Oktjabr'* N° 10 (1994): 3–59.

13 S.A. Tolstaja, *Moja zhizn'* (2 vols.). Moscow: Kuchkovo pole, 2011.

14 Published first as: S. A. Tolstaja, *Kukolki-skelettsy i drugie rasskazy* [Skeleton-dolls and other stories] (Moscow, 1910).

15 V. I. Porudominskij (1928–) — Russian writer and literary critic, author of a number of biographies and popular scientific works, contributor to the series *Zhizn' zamechatel'nykh ljudej [Lives of remarkable people]*. He emigrated to Germany in 1994, where he still carries on his literary activity.

the materials she had compiled for a biography of Lev Nikolaevich Tolstoy, as well as her literary writings — the major narrative *Ch'ja vina? [Who is to blame?]*, stories, and poems in prose. Unfortunately, the collection did not include Sofia Andreevna's second major narrative *Pesnja bez slov [Song without words]*. The theme of this narrative is significantly infused with the story of Sofia Andreevna's relationship with the composer Sergej Ivanovich Taneev, which served to complicate the Tolstoys' lives in later years. In spite of the discrepancies in plot, and the strict moral purity both in the description of all the participants in the 'love triangle' (which, in the accepted version, is not included in the narrative) and the whole unfoldment of the action, a few influential individuals still saw the work as a smear on the reputation of the great Russian writer's wife, as well as his own. In any case, interested readers will have no difficulty finding such descriptions outlined sincerely and trenchantly both in the correspondence between husband and wife and in recollections by family members.

The projected publication of Tolstaya's writings, however, was not to materialise: economic problems of the transitional period during the collapse of the Soviet Union] got in the way. Still, I am taking the liberty of independently offering readers my preface to the unpublished book. I would like to think that it will help give them not only a fuller understanding of the extraordinary complexity of Sofia Andreevna Tolstaya as an individual, but, in particular, an insight into Sofia Andreevna as a writer.

Recent years have seen a marked increase in interest on the part of current Russian scholars in SAT's life and works. The proceedings[16] of a 2005 conference devoted to the 160th anniversary of her birth contain papers more objective in nature than early accounts and are generally sympathetic to her point of view. Some of the more substantive studies in Russia along this line come

16 Vladimir Tolstoj and Ljudmila Gladkova (eds.), *Druz'ja i gosti Jasnoj Poljany, Materialy nauchnoj konferentsii, posvjashchennoj 160-letiju S. A. Tolstoj [Friends and guests of Yasnaya Polyana. Materials of a scholarly conference marking the 160th anniversary of S. A. Tolstaya's birth]* (Tula, 2006). Note especially the following articles: (a) T. V. Komarova, "...Gde vy, tam prazdnik" ["...Where you are, it's a holiday"], pp. 5–18; (b) V. A. Shenshina, "S. A. Tolstaja i A. A. Fet. Radost' tvorcheskogo obshchenija v Jasnoj Poljane" ["S. A. Tolstaya and A. A. Fet. The joy of creative communication at Yasnaya Polyana"], pp. 51–60; (c) N. G. Zhirkevich-Podlesskikh, "Sof'ja Andreevna i Lev Nikolaevich Tolstye na stranitsakh arkhiva A. V. Zhirkevicha" ["Sofia Andreevna Tolstaya and Lev Nikolaevich Tolstoy on the pages of the A. V. Zhirkevich archive"], pp. 87–100; (d) T. V. Nikitina, "S. A. Tolstaja i A. G. Dostoevskaja: «...Pokhozhie na svoikh muzhej»" ["S. A. Tolstaya and A. G. Dostoevskaja: '...Like their husbands'"], pp. 109–114; (e) I. K. Gryzlova, "Zhizn' sem'i Tolstykh v pis'makh S. A. Tolstoj i T. A. Kuzminskoj" ["The life of the Tolstoy family in the letters of S. A. Tolstaya and T. A. Kuzminskaja"], pp. 125–140; (f) O. V. Ulitina, "N. V. Davydov. Vospominanija i pis'ma" ["N. V. Davydov. Reminiscences and letters"], pp. 181–196; (g) E. G. Kornaukhova, "«Chudnye ljudi i chudnoe mesto Jasnaja Poljana dlja pamjati»" ["...Marvellous people and the marvellous place Yasnaya Polyana for remembering"], pp. 197–216.

from Pavel Basinskij,[17] Tat'jana Komarova,[18] Vladimir Porudominskij,[19] Inna Prussakova,[20] Vladimir Tunimanov and Aleksej Zverev.[21] Especially thorough are the numerous articles by Ju. G. Shumikhina (*née* Bajkova)[22] excerpted from her *kandidat* dissertation on SAT's stories.

In the West, too, SAT has been receiving more individual attention, notably in the form of special monographs concerning her biography and diaries. English-language publications on Tolstaya include contributions by Cynthia Asquith (1961), Anne Edwards (1981), Lily Feiler (1981), Tikhon Polner (1928, 1945), Alexandra Popoff (2010),[23] William Shirer (1994) and Louise Smoluchowski (1987),[24] as well as translations — quickly following the appearance of the originals: SAT's *Autobiography* [*Avtobiografija*], translated

17 Pavel Basinskij, *Lev Tolstoj: Begstvo iz raja* [*Leo Tolstoy: Flight from Paradise*] (Moscow, 2010).

18 Tat'jana Komarova has spent many years publishing on SAT; her articles tend to border on being too sympathetic, perhaps, but are extremely informative, based as they are on archival materials. Some of her more important ones are the following: (a) "Angel Jasnoj Poljany" [The angel of Yasnaya Polyana] (1992); (b) "Pometki S. A. Tolstoj na jasnopoljan-skom èkzempljare *Pisem grafa L. N. Tolstogo k zhene 1862–1910*" [Notes by S. A. Tolstaya on the Yasnaya Polyana copy of *Letters of Count L. N. Tolstoy to his wife 1862–1910*] (1999); (c) "S. A. Tolstaja — detjam" [S. A. Tolstaya to children] (1999–2000); (d) "Fet i S. A. Tolstaja" [Fet & S. A. Tolstaya] (2000); (e) "Fet v vospominanijakh S. A. Tolstoj «Moja zhizn'»" [Fet in S. A. Tolstaja's memoir *My Life*] (2003); (f) "Povest' Sof'i Andreevny Tolstoj *Ch'ja vina?* Kak otvet na *Krejtserovu sonatu* L. N. Tolstogo" [Sofia Andreevna Tolstaya's narrative *Who is to blame?* As a response to L. N. Tolstoy's *The Kreutzer Sonata*] (n. d.).

19 V. I. Porudominskij, "Iz zapisok daleveda" [Notes of a visisonary], *O Tolstom* [On Tolstoy] (St. Petersburg, 2005): 190–213.

20 Inna Prussakova, "O nekotorykh strannostjakh naivnosti" [On certain peculiarities of naïveté], *Neva* N° 7 (1995): 194–200. This article constitutes Prussakova's review of Tolstaya's *Ch'ja vina*, which was published a year earlier in *Oktjabr'* N° 10 (1994). This is no doubt the most vitriolic attack on SAT, both as a person and a literary figure.

21 Alekej Zverev & Vladimir Tunimanov, *Lev Tolstoj* (Moscow, 2006). See esp. the chapters: "Semejnye stseny. «Krejtserova sonata»" [Family squabbles: *The Kreutzer Sonata*], "Vanechka. Strannaja ljubov' Sof'i Andreevny" [Vanechka. Sofia Andreevna's eccentric love]; "Udirat', nado udirat'" [Escape, got to escape]. The whole book is a brilliant study, although often unduly critical of SAT's qualifications as a wife and a writer.

22 Julija Georgievna Shumikhina (*née* Bajkova) is surely the most serious scholar of SAT's works. In her articles she employs, very knowledgeably, a number of critical approaches in discussing Tolstaya's literary œuvre. See, especially, the following: (a) "Sof'ja Andreevna Tolstaja kak literator" [Sofia Andreevna Tolstaya as literator] (2005); (b) "Poètika prostranstva v sbornike detskikh rasskazov S. A. Tolstoj «Kukolki-skelettsy»" [The poetics of space in S. A. Tolstaya's collection of children's stories «The skeleton-dolls»] (2006); (c) "«Zhizn' nasha vroz'» (Dom i sem'ja Tolstykh v avtobiograficheskikh zapiskakh S. A. Tolstoj)" [«Our lives drifting apart» (The Tolstoys' home and family in S. A. Tolstaya's autobiographical notes)].

23 For a detailed, perceptive review article of Popoff's biography, see Nickell 2010.

24 I should point out that many of these works are either dated or inadequate, lacking a critical apparatus and dealing mainly with the Tolstoys' marital difficulties and SAT's conflicts with Vladimir Chertkov. For a succinct evaluation of the critical materials listed in this paragraph, including Tolstaya's own *My Life,* see McLean 2011.

by S. S. Koteliansky and Leonard Woolf (1922): SAT's *Diaries* [*Dnevniki*] in two volumes, translated by Cathy Porter (1985, 2009), which include an excellent overview of SAT's life; and *My Life* [*Moja zhizn'*],[25] translated by John Woodsworth and Arkadi Klioutchanski, under my editorship (2010). In 2009 French journalist and biographer Bertrand Meyer-Stabley published *La comtesse Tolstoï*. French translations of *My Life* [*Ma vie*] by Luba Jurgenson and Maria–Luisa Bonaque and SAT's novellas *Who is to blame?* [*À qui la faute ?*][26] and *Song without words* [*Romance sans paroles*] — both by Eveline Amoursky — were released in 2010, as were German translations of *Song without words* [*Lied ohne Worte*] by Ursula Keller[27] and *Who is to blame?* [*Eine Frage der Schuld*] by Alfred Frank and Ursula Keller.

In addition, a marvellous album of photographs taken by SAT, together with a selection of her diaries in English translation, was published by Leah Bendavid-Val (2007).[28]

In 2014, Michael Katz published his translation of *Kreutzer Sonata, Whose fault?* (Whose fault is Katz's version for the title Who is to blame), *Song without words*, and *Chopin's Prelude* (by Tolstaya's son Lev). In the same year, I published (as part of *V spore s Tolstym: na vesakh zhizni* [*Arguing with Tolstoy: on the scales of life*]) the complete correspondence between Tolstaya and Valentin Bulgakov (see pp. 227–299), consisting of 92 letters written between 1911 and 1918. This was followed in 2017 by my edition of selected correspondence (in English translation) between Tolstaya and her husband, published by the University of Ottawa Press.

Now is the time to share more of this remarkable woman's writings with the reading public. Such access to her original works will prove invaluable in any future comprehensive biographical study of SAT or, indeed, of her husband or any member of the Tolstoy clan. The task, though obviously worthwhile, is indeed daunting: it must take into account the sum total of her works (including her autobiographies, letters and diaries) and the reminiscences authored by almost all the members of her extended family and wide circle of acquaintances.

As a significant step toward this goal, all of Tolstaya's main literary works are gathered here in a single volume in an English translation. The brief analysis preceding them will help outline their history and content in relation to

---

25 It should be noted that *My Life* is based in large part on her diaries, which she kept during her whole married life. See two major review articles of this volume by G. M. Hamburg (2010) and Hugh McLean (2011).

26 It may be of interest to compare this rendition with another French translation of the same story by Christine Zeytounian-Beloüs (2010).

27 See also an important scholarly contribution to Tolstaya studies from a woman's perspective: Keller and Sharandak's *Sofja Andrejewna Tolstaja: Ein Leben an der Seite Tolstojs* [*Sofia Andreevna Tolstaya: A life at Tolstoy's side*] (2009).

28 *Song without* words: *the photographs and diaries of Countess Sophia Tolstoy*, Washington DC, National Geographic, 2007.

Tolstaya's writings and influence, while the detailed chronology — primarily from her own viewpoint, based largely on her diaries, *My Life*, letters and recent publications — will set them in the context of SAT's own eventful life and multi-faceted career: as spouse to one of the world's most famous novelists; mother to a large family; transcriber, secretary, literary advisor and 'co-author'; publisher, archivist, and historian; estate manager, fundraiser, photographer, artist, and musician; and — yes — as an author in her own right.

Finally, the comprehensive three-part bibliography will give the reader an idea not only of the extensive scope of her own writings, but also of the vast number of references to Tolstaya and her literary pursuits that have appeared — over the hundred or so years that have passed since these works first came to public attention — not only in scholarly articles and dissertations, but in a whole variety of books, plays and internet publications.

CHAPTER 1

Sofia Andreevna Tolstaya: a literary life in context

IN THE APTLY named chapter "Three significant periods" in *My Life* (Chapter III.39), Tolstaya describes the "considerable influence" they had as being her first acquaintance with Tolstoy's early works (which led to a subsequent interest in Russian and world literature), her platonic attraction to the Tolstoys' family friend Prince Leonid Dmitrievich Urusov, who introduced her to philosophy, and, finally, the death of her youngest son, Vanechka, and the subsequent comfort she found in music — in particular the music of pianist-composer Sergej Ivanovich Taneev. Tolstaya's platonic relationship with Taneev enriched and enhanced her life-long love of music and served as a catalyst for her novel *Song without words*. All three of these significant periods left their mark on Tolstaya's career as a writer and are worth exploring in some detail.

LITERATURE AND LEV NIKOLAEVICH TOLSTOY

In her youth, Tolstaya developed an interest in both Russian and world literature. She describes this experience in Chapter I.22 of *My Life* ("An atmosphere of love"):

> From the age of fourteen up to eighteen I read through the whole of Russian literature; […] I also read Grigorovich's *Rybaki* [*The fishermen*] and *Pereselentsy* [*The migrants*]. I was delighted to read Aksakov's *Semejnaja khronika* [*A family chronicle*]. I also read all of Tolstoy, and Goncharov's *Oblomov*, along with everything that came out in Russian translation — Dickens, and so forth.

We also read a good many French books at random: in the case of Molière, Racine and Corneille we just had to read *everything*. We read George Sand with great enthusiasm, as well as V[ictor] Hugo's *Notre Dame de Paris,* [Paul Henri] Féval's *Le Bossu* and many others.

[…] At the time, in German I was reading Goethe, Schiller and Auerbach, which I quite liked. I was particularly pleased with [Auerbach's] novel *Auf der Höhe* [On the heights].

She then goes on to recount her exploration of the whole history of Russian literature, likening it to "the growth of a living being" (*Autobiography*, Part II) and how she was particularly fascinated with Ivan Turgenev (1818–1883). As a university student she participated in a public reading of Turgenev's *Fathers and children*, finding "something very appealing and promising for the future" in the character of Bazarov (p. 141). She also had a special attraction to Charles Dickens' *David Copperfield* — which she initially read in Russian translation, although she would later become quite proficient in reading original works in English — growing very attached to the novel's characters, as though they were "the dearest and closest people to me" (*My Life*, I.7).

The greatest pleasure and impact of all, however, came from her reading of two autobiographical novels by Lev Nikolaevich Tolstoy, namely *Childhood* [*Detstvo*] and *Boyhood* [*Otrochestvo*], later to be supplemented by the third part of his well-known trilogy, *Youth* [*Junost'*]. When it came to Tolstoy, she "wasn't content with just reading — I would copy favourite passages and commit them to memory" (*My Life*, I.7).

It was in part her reading of these books that inspired her to write her first story, *Natasha*, which will be discussed at the beginning of Chapter 3 in this volume (see p. 58).

Here may be seen the very beginnings of a mutual literary attraction and interaction between Sofia Andreevna and Lev Nikolaevich, which preceded their personal relationship and romance.

After their marriage the newlywed Tolstaya took on the task of transcribing her husband's texts (penned in LNT's notoriously indecipherable handwriting) to make them legible for the typesetters. Because of the author's inevitable dissatisfaction with his initial drafts, this often meant copying the same stories over and over again to incorporate his many corrections and newly minted passages. While initially she found the task daunting — see her comment shortly after their marriage: "I have been transcribing Lëvochka's work for days on end, and am so tired" (*My Life*, II.6), — it is clear that she came to relish the opportunity for such close familiarity with her husband's creative process. In 1863 she confessed:

The transcribing of *War and peace* — and indeed, all Lev Nikolaevich's works — was a source of great aesthetic pleasure for me. I fearlessly looked forward to my evening labours, and joyfully anticipated just *what* I would derive from the delight of becoming further acquainted with his work as it unfolded. I was enthralled by this life of thought, these twists and turns, surprises and all the various unfathomable aspects of his creative genius. (*My Life*, II.14)

But Tolstaya's role in her husband's creative endeavours was not for long confined to simply transcribing. Her contribution to some of the descriptions (especially of women's clothing) in *War and peace* and *Anna Karenina* has been all too frequently left unsung. The eminent Tolstoy scholar Lidija Gromova-Opul'skaja (2005: 305), for example, states:

> It is well known that during the time *War and peace* was being created, Sofia Andreevna Tolstaya was not just a transcriber, but Tolstoy's first enthusiastic reader and even his assistant. According to È. E. Zajdenshnur, in both *War and peace* and *Anna Karenina* Sofia Andreevna would re-describe the clothing of Tolstoy's heroines. [For example,] Tolstoy wrote that Natasha and Sonja appeared at their first ball "in muslin dresses with roses on their corsages" [*v kisejnykh plat'jakh s rozami u korsazha*]. Sofia Andreevna changed this to: "in gossamer dresses with rose-coloured capes and roses on their corsages" [*v dymkovyx plat'jakh na rozovykh chekhlakh s rozami u korsazha*]. Tolstoy noticed this and agreed with Sofia Andreevna's wardrobe [descriptions].

There are in fact, several instances in which Tolstoy declined to describe his female characters' dress, happily leaving this task to Tolstaya as part of her transcribing duties.[1]

The writer Maxim Gorky, for one, recognised Tolstaya's contribution, declaring:

> We do not know what — or how — Leo Tolstoy's wife spoke to him in those moments when they sat eye to eye as he read to her (before anyone else) the book chapters he had only just finished writing. Mindful of the genius' monstrous intuitive insight, I still think that certain aspects of the images of women included in his great novel [*War and peace*] could only be perceived by a woman, who in turn suggested them to the novelist.[2]

Even earlier, just two years after their marriage, Tolstoy himself had acknowledged his wife's literary acumen in a letter he penned to her on 7 December 1864:

> What a smart girl you are in anything you put your mind to! [...] Like a good wife, you treat your husband as yourself, and I remember how you said to me that all the military and historical [stuff] I try so hard [to write] would turn out

---

1 For example, in one of the drafts of *AK* — see *PSS*, XX: 523 — LNT left a marginal notation: "Ask Sonja [= SAT] to describe the outfits."

2 Gorky 1973: XVI: 358–74, cited in the editor's Introduction to *My Life*, p. xxviii. See also *ML*, p. xxvi, where SAT is quoted as saying: "for some reason he actually believes and listens to my opinions (much to my pride)."

badly, while all the rest — family, character and psychological [development] — would turn out fine. If that isn't the truth, nothing is. And I remember your telling that to me, and I remember the whole of you like that.[3]

Indeed, the interaction between these two literary figures is perhaps most vividly recorded in the many letters Tolstoy and Tolstaya exchanged throughout their lifetime, beginning even before their marriage and despite the fact that one was obviously much more widely known. A good part of their correspondence centred on literary topics and was written in a superb literary style, with sensitive artistic descriptions of Nature, to the personal delight of Tolstaya. Her letters to him were replete with pithy and vivid psychological portrayals of people, capturing a whole image in the brushstrokes of a few sentences — not only providing for highly interesting reading, but making readers even today feel they are living part of her life along with her.

At times Tolstaya's letters contain opinions of her husband's works, some of which were occasionally critical. Overall, however, she was deeply appreciative of her husband's creative genius. She was particularly moved by his play *Vlast' t'my* [*The power of darkness*] and expressed enthusiasm over its performance in a number of theatres. She criticized *Voskresenie* [*Resurrection*] as "false, spicy, drawn out and even repulsive",[4] at the same time describing *Master and man* [*Khozjain i rabotnik*] as "fresh fruit" by comparison.

In a letter to her husband of 29 October 1895, she wrote with complete candour:

> I received your little letter before I left. It is brief, but again one that lets me feel the whole of you very close to me, and reachable, and kind, and understandable. Besides, I feel quite ashamed and sorry to tell you this, but for some reason I find joy in the fact that you've become disenchanted with your narrative [and early draft of *Resurrection* [*Voskresenie*]]. I've felt all along that it was *contrived*, and that it did not well up from the depths of your heart and talent. It was something you *composed*, but did not *live*. [...]
>
> How I would like to lift you higher so that when people read you, they might feel they, too, need wings to fly to you, so that their heart might melt, and so that whatever you wrote would offend no one, but make things better, and so that your work might have an *eternal character* and fascination.[5]

As much as she was put off by Tolstoy's post-1880 philosophical writings, she nevertheless remained a devoted supporter of his belletristic works and

---

3   Quoted in *My Life*, p. xxvii.
4   Letter to SAT's son Lev L'vovich Tolstoj, 12 August 1895 (L. N. Tolstoy Museum archives, unpublished).
5   See the exact statement in the comprehensive selection of their correspondence *Tolstoy and Tolstaya* (Donskov 2017, p. 249).

took every opportunity to encourage him to concentrate on the latter at the expense of the former. In a letter of 5–6 March 1882, for example, she wrote to him (quoted in *ML*, III.107):

> What a feeling of joy came over me as I read that you once more feel like writing in an *artistic genre*. You have felt something I've been waiting for and desiring for a long time. Herein lies our salvation and our joy — here is something that will bring us together once more, something that will comfort you and refresh our lives. It is the real work for which you were created, and outside this sphere there is no rest for your soul… May God grant you hold on to this vision, so that this Divine spark may flare up in you once more.

It is quite evident from her correspondence and diary entries that although SAT was aware of her own creative talent, she nevertheless felt herself consistently held back by the role dictated to her by society as a woman. She sensed that opportunities for manifesting that talent and devoting herself more fully to her literary pursuits were constantly being thwarted both by the overwhelming shadow cast by her world-famous husband's public profile and, perhaps above all, by the duties imposed on her as a wife and mother. In a diary entry of 12 June 1898 (*Diaries*, I: 388) she mused:

> I was thinking today: why are women not geniuses? There are no [women] writers, artists or composers. Because all the passion and abilities of energetic women are spent on their families, their love, their husbands — and, especially, their children. All other abilities have atrophied, and stay undeveloped in the womb. Once child-bearing and child-raising are over, then their artistic needs awaken — but by then it is already too late to develop anything within themselves.

Still, based on all the information presented both in this current volume and her own letters and writings, especially *My Life*, it is evident that SAT's own writing career did not completely atrophy, that she left to history a *remarkable* (given the constraints on her life) literary legacy worthy of study. Her early youthful jottings, her all too often neglected works of fiction, and above all her life-long interaction with her celebrated husband's belletristic creativity as described above — point to an observable development of her writing abilities far beyond "the womb". As devoted as she was to caring for the physical and educational needs of her husband and children, she did allow her own inherent genius to shine through, as much as her complex life circumstances would permit.

Indeed, her care of the educational needs of her children[6] also extended, on occasion, to the pursuit of writing and sculpture as a chosen profession. In a letter to Lev L'vovich dated 30 June 1897, she admits to an "excellent

---

6 For example, she compiled a Russian grammar for them, and composed a number of stories which she read to them during periods of extended travel.

understanding of the whole creative process," on the basis of which she willingly offered constructive literary advice to a son who had recently celebrated his 28th birthday:

> You write that you are continuing to write. I am afraid that you are taking a too light-hearted approach. Your story "Vorobejchik" [The little sparrow] is simply boring, and the public doesn't like that. It can't like it, and so that's why it was returned. You have to look at it from all sides and record, record, especially your direct impressions, or express your moments of inspiration in some kind of form, even if in the most compressed form. I am poor at expressing myself, but I have an excellent understanding of the whole creative process. (Archive of Lev L'vovich [Son] Tolstoy. L.N. Tolstoy Museum, Moscow, F. 303.N° 676)

To her eldest son Sergej L'vovich she wrote on 26 October 1917 on the difficulty of editing and arranging his father's literary manuscripts, along with the need for a collective approach:

> ...apparently you have clearly not appreciated the enormity and complexity of the task. For example, the manuscripts of *War and peace* were not only [damaged] in a ditch but then ended up being stuffed into a couple of drawers. These are all just clippings and fragments, and it's difficult to come up with a system to put everything in order. Working alone is unthinkable.[7]

Hence it may be seen that Sofia Andreevna's legacy as an author, albeit seemingly in competition with her family duties, is intricately bound together not only with her husband's writing pursuits, but those of her children as well. More than in the case of Tolstoy himself, who notoriously found it difficult to reconcile the ideals of his writing with real-life situations (at least in his later period),[8] the ideas underlying Tolstaya's brief writing career *grew out of* real life and were inseparable from it. From *Natasha* to *Who is to blame?*, each of her works may be found to be deeply rooted in her own life experience, which gives them a poignancy and an impression of realism that enhances their effect on the reader.

All of which only adds further weight to the significance of SAT's own pithy declaration in her brief preface to *My Life*: *"...the significance of my forty-two*

---

7 Quoted in *Diaries*, II: 597.
8 As I have frequently mentioned in other publications, even the peasants, with whom Tolstoy identified more than with any other social group, were generally represented in his writings as stereotypes or abstractions rather than as true-to-life individuals. See, for example, my 1979 article "The peasant in Tolstoy's thought and writings" in *Canadian Slavonic Papers*, where I argue that the *grace* that came to Tolstoy's characters in moments of their most intense spiritual anguish was in the form of peasants, not so much as true-to-life personalities than as the *symbolic qualities* they embody: qualities of sincerity, simplicity and naturalness. Over the course of Tolstoy's post-1880 writings, the peasants may be seen as evolving into vehicles through which, he hoped, everybody could learn a great deal about life.

years of conjugal life with Lev Nikolaevich cannot be excluded from his life." This is equally true if we substitute *literary career* for *life* in both instances in her statement. SAT sums up her debt to her husband in *My Life* (III.39) as follows: "...as for Lev Nikolaevich, who had opened up the treasure of literature to me through his *Childhood,* I naturally began to poeticise him, to love him as a human being. And, despite all the ups and downs in our lives, I have never stopped loving him."

PHILOSOPHY AND LEONID DMITRIEVICH URUSOV

"The second significant period in my spiritual life," Tolstaya continues in the same chapter of *My Life*, "was the time when I learnt to know the beauty of the philosophical thinking of the sages, who afforded me so much by way of spiritual development and even helped me live, simply through their wisdom."

Her reading list of philosophers is varied — both in terms of era and of language — and unquestionably impressive. Beginning with the Ancient World, she lists Greek and Roman classics, referring specifically to Socrates, Plato, Aristotle, Seneca the Younger, Epictetus and Marcus Aurelius, as well as the Chinese philosophers Confucius and Lao-Tse. The breadth of her reading then encompasses the canon of European thought from British philosopher William Angus Knight to Dutch philosopher Baruch de Spinoza and the French René Descartes, Étienne Vacherot, Charles Renouvier, Joseph Renan and Jean-Marie Guyau. Among philosophers of Germanic origin, her list ranges from the eighteenth to the turn of the twentieth century, although she does mention that "... the German thinkers no longer delighted or satisfied me" (*My Life*, III.116). This list comprised Immanuel Kant, Friedrich von Schiller, Friedrich Hegel, Artur Schopenhauer, Ludwig Feuerbach, Friedrich Büchner, Kuno Fischer, Friedrich Nietzsche and Georg von Gizicki, as well as the Swiss philosopher Henri-Frédéric Amiel. Among the Russian philosophers in her library (some of whom she knew in person) were Jurij Samarin, Pavel Bakunin, Boris Chicherin, Nikolaj Strakhov,[9] Nikolaj Fëdorov, Afrikan Shpir, Nikolaj Grot, Vladimir Solovëv, Lev Lopatin, Sergej Trubetskoj and Evgenij Trubetskoj.

For an idea of what some of these authors meant to her personally, note the following sample passage from SAT's *Autobiography* [*Avtobiografija*: 156]:

> The brilliant style and wealth of thinking of this philosopher [Marcus Aurelius] got me so carried away that I went over his writings twice. After this I read a number of philosophers one after the other, buying [their] books and writing out [their] thoughts and sayings which made an impression on me. I remember how I was struck by Epictetus' thoughts on death. I found Spinoza quite difficult

9   Nikolaj Nikolaevich Strakhov was one of the Tolstoy family's closest friends and associates, collaborating with both LNT and SAT on the editing, proofreading and publication of many of Tolstoy's works. See Donskov 2000, 2003.

to understand, but his *Ethics* interested me, especially his explanation of the concept of God. I was excited by Socrates, Plato and other philosophers (mainly Greek), and I can say that [such] sages went a long way toward helping me live and think. Later I tried reading newer philosophers, too: I read Schopenhauer and others, but I liked the ancient ones a whole lot better.

Interestingly enough, SAT immediately goes on to speak of the philosophical writings of her husband, Lev Nikolaevich, singling out her favourite, *On Life*. As another example of Sofia Andeevna's contribution to Tolstoy's literary career, in addition to those listed in the previous section, she translated this treatise into French, with the editorial help of a native French speaker surnamed Tastevin. In her *Autobiography* she also mentions seeking help with the translation from two philosopher friends, Nikolaj Grot and Vladimir Solov'ëv, as well as from Lev Nikolaevich himself.

However, there was more to SAT's philosophical attraction than the 'message' of philosophy itself. It turned out she was also deeply attracted to the 'messenger', in the form of a Tolstoy family friend, the Deputy Governor of Tula Gubernia, Prince Leonid Dmitrievich Urusov, who was largely responsible for introducing her to the study of philosophy. In the opening paragraphs to the chapter "Three significant periods," she elaborates on how she came to study philosophy (*My Life*, III.39):

> It was L. D. Urusov who set me and later guided me along this path. I became quite attached to him, and loved him for a long time because of this, — in fact, I have never really stopped loving him either, even though he has been dead a long time.

In the same passage, SAT repeatedly emphasises the *platonic* nature of her relationship with Urusov. Thus, after re-telling somewhat coarse remarks by Urusov's wife during a visit to Yasnaya Polyana, she insists unambiguously: "His relationship to me was gentlemanly and courteous, albeit occasionally on the ecstatic side. But we never, either in word or gesture, hinted at anything in the way of a romance between us."

Still, it is fair to say that she and Urusov came closer together on a philosophical level that satisfied their intellectual desires more fully than the 'spiritual' bonds they shared with their respective spouses at the time. As much as Tolstaya appreciated and was, on occasion, even enamoured by her husband's philosophical tendencies, she perceived them as largely taking him mentally away from her and their children. She yearned for an idea-based relationship where family duties played no part. At this point in her life, this is precisely what she found in Urusov. Conversely, Urusov, found little intellectual interest in common with his wife, Marija Sergeevna ('Monja', *née* Mal'tseva), whom SAT describes in the same chapter as highly materialistic, "a very unpleasant woman, who had lived almost all her life in Paris, and with a poor reputation to boot."[10] Not only that, but she had taken their four children to live with her in Paris, cutting them off almost completely from any family interaction with their father. It was not surprising, therefore, that the pursuit of common philosophical interests nudged both Tolstaya and Urusov into a special meeting of minds which transcended their respective personal situations.[11]

And this joint experience could not help but have its effect on Tolstaya's artistic and literary contributions.

MUSIC AND SERGEJ IVANOVICH TANEEV

Music had played a significant role throughout SAT's life, beginning with the final composition she wrote for her teaching certificate in 1861, simply entitled "Music".[12] During the early part of her marriage she often played four-handed piano pieces with Lev Nikolaevich.[13] Her diaries and letters mention regular attendance at concerts and musical evenings held at Yasnaya Polyana, along with commentaries about various composers and musicians. She was, in fact, familiar with about as many composers as philosophers (see list in the previous section). It was only in 1895, however, that Sofia Andreevna became fully aware of her absolute dependence on the comforting power of music to carry her through what must have been one of the worst ordeals of her life, namely, the death of her youngest son, Vanechka.[14] This experience she describes in the chapter on "three significant periods"[15] as follows:

> This was the time following the death of my little son Vanechka. I was in a state of extreme despair — the kind that happens only once in a lifetime. Such a state of sorrow is usually fatal, and those that survive are not in a condition to endure such heart-wrenching suffering a second time. But I did survive, and for that I am obliged to chance, as well as to the mysterious medium of… *music*.

10 Ironically, perhaps, as it turned out, Urusov's wife had a considerable appreciation and respect for Sofia Andreevna and her conjugal relationship to Tolstoy. In a letter to Tolstaya following Leonid Dmitrievich's death, she wrote: "*You* are your husband's best pupil — you have taken from him everything you need for the perfecting of your marvellous nature" (quoted in *My Life*, V.103 – Notes of a Mother).

11 It has been mistakenly assumed that the prototype for the character of the Duke's friend, Dmitrij Bekhmetev, in SAT's *Who is to blame?* was the poet Afanasij Fet. Clearly, the whole text, seen against the background of her letters, notes and diaries, points to Urusov as her model.

12 See Editor's Introduction to *My Life*, p. xxii.

13 See *My Life*, p. xxxi.

14 Her relation to Vanechka in itself inspired two of the stories in her collection *The skeleton-dolls* (see Chapter 3, p. 69 in PART I of this volume), and possibly had an influence on the writing of her final story for Tolstoy's *New primer* (see below).

15 Unless otherwise indicated, all the quotations in this section are from SAT's chapter "Three significant periods" (*My Life*, III.39).

Just as with SAT's earlier introduction to philosophy, the "medium" of music, too, arrived by way of a messenger, in the person of a prominent pianist and composer: "One day in May ... I was sitting on the balcony. It was a warm day, and the whole garden had already turned green. Sergej Ivanovich Taneev dropped by..."

As it happened, the well-known composer was looking for a place to live for the summer, and Sofia Andreevna offered to rent him the then empty annexe on the Yasnaya Polyana estate. She admitted she "was morally reaching out for anything that would take my mind off my life with Vanechka, and the presence of someone who was completely oblivious of my sadness to date — and was a pretty good pianist to boot — seemed quite desirable to me."

This situation continued for two summers, as well as for part of the intervening winter. Sofia Andreevna "became intoxicated by music and got so accustomed to hearing it" that she found herself "no longer able to live without it." She took out subscriptions to concerts and listened to music at every possible opportunity — not an easy task in an age when musical recordings were not nearly as readily available as they are today.

But it was Taneev's music which affected her most of all:

It was he who first taught me, through his marvellous playing, to listen to and love music. I made every effort to hear his playing wherever and however I could, and would arrange to meet him just for this purpose — just so that I could ask him to play. Occasionally, when I did not manage to do this for some time, I felt sad, tormented by the burning desire to hear him play once more, or even just to see him.

His presence had a beneficial effect on me whenever I started feeling a longing for Vanechka. I would weep and feel the energy drain from my life. Sometimes all it took to calm me down was to meet with Sergej Ivanovich and hear his quieting, dispassionate voice. I had already got accustomed to being calmed by his presence and especially his playing. It was a kind of hypnosis, an involuntary influence on my aching soul — one he was completely unaware of.

It was not a normal state to be in. It happened to coincide with my change of life. For all my moodiness I remained virtually unaffected by Taneev's personality....

For healing my sorrowful soul unintentionally through his music — he didn't even know about it — I have remained forever grateful to him, and I have never stopped loving him. He was the first to *open* the door for me to an *understanding* of music, just as Lev Nikolaevich led me to the understanding of the literary arts, just as Prince Urusov gave me an understanding of and love for philosophy. Once you enter upon these scenes of spiritual delight, you never want to leave them and you constantly come back to them.

As she had done on the topic of Urusov, SAT took pains to deny any kind of romantic relationship with her musical muse:

I refused to entertain such a thought. I would always deny it and was actually afraid of it, even though there was one time when the influence of Taneev's personality was very strong. Once that kind of feeling surfaces, it kills any sense of importance in the music and art. I wrote a long piece on that.

And this brings us back directly to Tolstaya's writing pursuits. The "long piece" she mentions was none other than her narrative *Song without words* [*Pesnja bez slov*],[16] which is based directly on her experience with the composer Taneev. Just as in real life, so too in her story, one of the distinguishing features of the relationship between composer and enchanted listener is that the music itself is its guiding principle, outweighing any feelings of romance or physical attraction. SAT's protests of innocence, however, did not serve to mitigate the real feelings of jealousy on the part of LNT over her obvious attention to Taneev. She sums up her own and her husband's viewpoints in Chapter VII.16 ["Crowds and life"] of *My Life*:

> Lev Nikolaevich also began to get irritated by Taneev's presence, even though in the evenings he continued to play chess with him and listen to his music. Whenever they talked, Lev Nikolaevich would get irritated and once even told Taneev: "Only peasants or very stupid people would ever reason like that!" Taneev got up and walked out without saying a word, and later Lev Nikolaevich apologised to him.
>
> Subsequently he wrote in his diary that he didn't like the fact that Taneev had become *le coq du village* in our home. Indeed, everybody liked him, and everybody had a good time with him. He studied Italian together with Tanja and Masha. We would all go for walks together or take a carriage ride. I was friendly with Taneev, too — I was very excited about his piano-playing.
>
> All this did not go over well with Lev Nikolaevich, and he was especially angry at me. I couldn't put it down to jealousy; at first that never even entered my head. I was already fifty-two, and men as such could not possibly exist for me. Besides, I was too firmly and fervently in love with my husband, and there was absolutely no point in comparing anyone with such a being as Lev Nikolaevich, who was unique in terms of his spiritual beauty and elevation.

Two preserved, albeit unsent, letters by LNT dating from May and July 1897, validate SAT's concerns over her husband's jealousy in this case, however overwrought her sensitivities might have been in other instances. "Your closeness with Taneev is not simply unpleasant for me — it's frighteningly tormenting," begins the letter from May, in which Tolstoy proposes several "ways out of this situation," including one in which they would "cease any kind of relations" and another where SAT would "cease all relations with Taneev, and you and I both go abroad."[17]

---

16 The title is taken from Mendelssohn's well-known collection *Songs without words* (see Chapter 3, p. 80 in PART I of this volume).
17 Donskov 2017, pp. 266–69.

In addition to the above, it should also be pointed out that, while always polite, understanding, cordial and appreciative of Sofia Andreevna, Taneev himself never experienced any romantic affection for her. He was, in fact, a homosexual, as was SAT's fictional composer hero (according to the author's unmistakable indications) in *Song without words*, as will be evident in the detailed exploration of the narrative in Chapter 3.

TOLSTAYA'S PUBLISHING AND EDITORIAL ACTIVITIES

Tolstaya was closely involved in the publication of Tolstoy's writings, negotiations with printers and publishers, supervision of editing and proofreading (much of which she did herself), and she even maintained a warehouse of his books in their Moscow home. A small glimpse of the intensity of her work along this line can be seen in this excerpt from a letter she wrote to LNT on 13 April 1887 (Tolstaya 1936b: 397):

> I have to work at a fearful pace to somehow finish the old edition. For two days I wrote out lists of who hasn't contributed [to the subscription], and it turned out that about 3,500 roubles were still owing on the old edition. I wrote memos, which was frightfully exhausting. I wrote 13 letters and I still have to write memos on 123 letters! [...] In the spring everything will always come together — both work and business. Tomorrow I shall be going round to the banks, and in the evening to a lecture. In the afternoon I shall be tutoring Misha and taking care of my affairs. I have found some proofreaders, but I still have to test them out. In the meantime I have been doing all the proofreading for three print shops.

In May 1883, when Tolstoy decided to renounce the copyright on his books, along with practically all his private property, he put his wife in charge of publishing all his pre-1881 writings and designated her the sole beneficiary of subsequent royalties therefrom.

But in 1891 Tolstoy published an announcement in the press stating that he was also renouncing his copyright on all of his works written after 1 January 1881, meaning that anyone who wished to do so might publish, re-issue, translate or stage any of these writings without paying a single kopek in royalties. Sofia Andreevna could, of course, include his later works in her own editions, but now had to share this right with other publishers. No longer able to sell rights to her husband's publications elsewhere, and holding the power of attorney to conduct her husband's financial affairs, she therefore set about publishing his later works herself.

From 1886 to 1911 she published eight different editions of Tolstoy's *Complete collected works* to date (110 volumes all told),[18] in addition to a fair number of individual re-issues.

18 The 5th and 6th editions, each consisting of 12 volumes, were published in Moscow in 1886, the 7th edition (also 12 vols.) a year later. The 8th edition appeared between 1889 and 1891, followed by the 9th edition (1893–98), each comprising 13 volumes. The 10th and 11th

To save money, she often took on the tiresome task of proofreading herself — this despite her chronic near-sightedness (in 1900 she lost sight in her left eye altogether).

The S. A. Tolstaya archives contain a large number of documents, including order blanks, receipts for the mailing of proofs, and samples of paper and type. The dates on these documents are very significant for tracing corrections, commentaries, clarifications and so forth, and have helped determine the sequence of the various drafts of Tolstoy's writings.

In 1872 Sofia Andreevna's participation in the publication of her husband's writings put her in touch with Nikolaj Nikolaevich Strakhov. This was the beginning of a relationship of mutual respect and friendship that lasted more than twenty years, practically up to Strakhov's death in 1896.

Strakhov soon turned out to be Tolstaya's closest collaborator in the publication of Tolstoy's writings. Her exchange of 87 letters with Strakhov (1872–95, published in Donskov 2000) is testimony to her tireless efforts in this field. This correspondence also offers a rare insight into both Lev Nikolaevich's and Sofia Andreevna's personal lives, as well as their thoughts on their family and acquaintances which they shared with one of their closest friends. Strakhov was a great admirer of Tolstaya's dedication, intellect and integrity, and appreciated her unique contribution to her husband's work — a subject that occupies fully a third of their epistolary exchanges and runs as a unifying thread throughout.

The primarily business-like nature of their correspondence may be seen in the following excerpts from three letters in late 1892. On 20 November 1892 SAT wrote to Strakhov (Donskov 2000: 242):

> My dear and deeply esteemed Nikolaj Nikolaevich,
>
> Finally, after ordering the paper and the photographs, as of 1 December I am undertaking the printing of Lev Nikolaevich's *Writings* [9th edition]. Recalling your [earlier] help in my project, I have decided to ask your advice as to how I should arrange his articles and stories in Volumes 2, 3, 12 and 13? In each edition I have been guided by different considerations, as for example: *The Kreutzer Sonata* was printed at the end of the volume for fear it might be banned by the censors, etc.
>
> Now I would like to be guided by higher considerations — simply, what is the best and wisest solution? I attach a sheet outlining my thoughts on what the arrangement should be. But I very much value your advice and thoughts for guidance in this matter. In a few days I'll send you the phototypes of the portraits and other pictures I plan on including in this edition.
>
> Here, too, I need your advice and approval: which ones should go into each volume? I'm not talking about the self-evident cases, but about those where I haven't yet reached a final decision. Only I would ask you not only

editions, each with 16 volumes, were released between 1897 and 1903. SAT's final (12th) edition of 20 volumes was published in 1911, the year after LNT's death.

not to let these phototypes out of your hands, but also to refrain from show-ing them to anyone else.

On 2 December 1892 Strakhov responded (250):

My deeply esteemed Sofia Andreevna, I am enclosing with this letter two proof-read [printer's] sheets and, if you like, I'll send you as many as you ask for. Your typing is very accurate, I came across only two or three mistakes…. [Strakhov proceeds to enumerate five specific points regarding his proofreading.]

On the whole I take great delight in this work and will get it done for you without delay.

I await your instructions. Are you in agreement with my outline for Volumes 2 and 3, as well as for 12 and 13? In what order will you be sending the volumes to the printer's? Starting with the first? Or several volumes at once?

Forgive me. God grant you health.

Your loyal and devoted

N. Strakhov

Finally, a couple of brief excerpts from SAT's reply dated 8 December 1892 (251):

I thought of getting two volumes printed right away at two printshops where I have already made an agreement concerning the terms. Now it's a question of getting the paper and the originals. […]

Concerning the arrangement of articles in Volumes 12 and 13, I quite agree as to the *thought*, but as far as the *size* goes, I shall have to do another page count. It seems that Volume 12 is too thick compared to 13. I'll take care of this today.

I've had Volumes 2 and 3 printed according to your recommendations.

Both LNT and SAT were immensely grateful for Strakhov's innumerable contributions to the editing and publishing process. A prime example of her appreciation is found in her letter to Strakhov of 20 February 1893: "It is impossible to *get* assistants anywhere in this world. They are sent by destiny … as God has sent you to me — an unselfish and industrious person, and, above all, a clever genius."[19] This was by no means flattery, as may be seen from the whole tone of their correspondence, which reveals SAT's genuine and unequivocal respect for this brilliant, albeit self-effacing, friend and edi-torial colleague.[20]

19 Donskov 2000: 268, as quoted in English in Donskov 2000: 9.
20 SAT's close personal friendship with Strakhov is indicated in his letter to her of 24 September 1893, whose opening paragraph reads: "I humbly thank you for sending the new edition [of Tolstoy's *Collected works*]; I was waiting for this favour, and it arrived at the very moment I was looking forward to it. A marvellous edition! I tried to find some mistakes, but didn't find any. What is especially exciting for me is that all my labour has been accepted and reflected in these pages. I swear to you that I had not great hopes for that. With the energy

The image of Sofia Andreevna that emerges from the correspondence with Strakhov is of an exemplary wife and mother — a woman well ahead of her time, an extremely intelligent and independent thinker, though rather set in her ways. And while the principal focus of the letters is undoubtedly the life and work of one of the most eminent writers of the world, they also explore in some depth the personalities of all three correspondents as individuals. Furthermore, the numerous references to Russian society of the day included in the letters offer a broad social canvas for depicting some of the country's best intellectual minds and creative thinkers of the last decades of the nineteenth century.

Another pertinent and most interesting correspondence took place between Tolstaya and Valentin Fëdorovich Bulgakov, who had been LNT's personal secretary during the final year of his life. Their correspondence began in 1911 and continued until her passing in 1919. Here, for example, is an excerpt from SAT's letter to Bulgakov dated 11 June 1911, encouraging him to accept a position in the Tolstoy Museum working with LNT's manuscripts:

> I've been thinking a lot about you — someone I've always regarded with sympathy. Living in the country and tilling the ground is not enough to satisfy you. You are a talented man — you're a good writer and a good thinker. Even if it takes some time, you should find a home in some intellectual milieu. Loving Lev Nikolaevich and his memory the way you do, you would do well to attach yourself to the State Museum and edit the deceased's manuscripts and other writings. That, by the way, is *my* dream, but everyone has their own life to live, and from the bottom of my heart I wish you all success and happiness. Write to me some time, especially when you change your address. My address will always be: *Zaseka*. My best greetings, as always, with brotherly affection and trust in your heart.

Bulgakov's letters to Tolstaya are for the most part responses to her requests regarding her husband's legacy. They give the reader an indication of the relations not only with each other, but with their contemporaries, too. Most of all, they testify to the close collaboration between them in the matter of promoting L.N. Tolstoy's works and maintaining his archive, along with Bulgakov's meticulous descriptions of his library. Running through their whole exchange of letters as a unifying thread are Tolstoy and his correspondents' relations to him. The letters also cover a host of burning social questions, profiles of various personalities, militarism and conscription, and the true meaning of freedom.

you have, it seemed to me you would spare no effort to exercise some control of your own. And yet you did everything exactly as I had indicated. I am very happy about that! After all, I was endeavouring to do my very best, in my labour of love over these precious writings. You understood that, you accepted it, and I thank you from the bottom of my heart" (Donskov 2000: 279).

In February 1885 Strakhov arranged a trip for Tolstaya to St. Petersburg to discuss publication procedures. He also put her in touch there with the writer Fëdor Mikhajlovich Dostoevsky's widow, Anna Grigor'evna Dostoevskaja (*née* Snitkina, 1846–1918), who already had considerable experience in publishing her own (late) husband's works.[21]

Prior to 1885, it had been Tolstoy's practice to sell the rights to publication of his works directly to publishers. In 1880, for example, the publishing firm known as *Nasledniki brat'ev Salaevykh* [Heirs of the Salaev brothers] released the fourth edition of LNT's collected works, comprising eleven volumes. But after his renunciation of copyright on his pre-1881 works, the compilation of the next edition fell to SAT. She describes her approach to this task in Chapter IV.25 of *My Life* (The mind-reader – end of 1884):

> It was getting near time to publish a new edition of Lev Nikolaevich's *Complete collected works*, and, upon learning that Dostoevsky's widow Anna Grigor'evna was selling her husband's works by subscription, I decided to go to Petersburg to study the book-publishing business, including printing and selling books by subscription.

Dostoevskaja provided SAT (in the latter's words) with "some very useful advice" on how to realise considerable profits from book sales. She was most happy to greet this new literary publisher and commented on their initial meeting as follows:

> I became acquainted with S. A. Tolstaya in 1885 (I had not known her before that) when on one of her trips to Petersburg she came to ask my advice on publishing. The Countess explained to me that to date the writings of her famous husband were being published by the Moscow bookseller Salaev, and that he was paying a relatively modest sum for the publication rights. After learning from her acquaintances that I was successfully publishing my husband's writings, she decided to try publishing Count Lev Nikolaevich's works herself, and came to find out from me whether book publishing entailed a great deal of trouble and problems. The Countess made an extremely good impression on me and I took genuine delight in sharing with her all the 'secrets' of my publishing activity.[22]

Sofia Andreevna and Anna Grigor'evna developed not just a professional relationship[23] but a personal friendship as well, which they continued to maintain

---

21 Anna Dostoevskaja put out seven editions of her husband's *Collected works*, in addition to a valuable bibliography and a volume of his letters. For more on Dostoevskaja, see: Shifman 1983; Nikiforova 2000 and 2004; and N. A. Nikitina 2010: 156–61.

22 Quoted in Tolstaya 1936b: 298.

23 The professional nature of their relationship is evident in this excerpt from Dostoevskaja's letter to Tolstaya dated 1 October 1885 (Nikiforova 2000: 294, as quoted in English in Donskov 2000: 20): "But now please allow me, esteemed Countess, to raise the question: do you wish to receive payment for Count Lev Nikolaevich's works in a lump sum, or through instalments? If I may be so bold, I should advise you to accept instalments. […] I speak from

through correspondence and occasional visits. Both these women aspired to preserve for posterity valuable archival materials as well as other representative samples of their husbands' personal effects.

Anna Grigor'evna was able to give her new friend many valuable insights into publication procedures. One of her early communications to Sofia Andreevna was particularly significant — an eight-page letter, dated 1 October 1885, outlining her experience with various publishers, most of whom she did not recommend. She also had useful advice on advertising the publications. Tolstaya recalls:

> I began making the rounds of paper merchants and printing shops, comparing cost estimates, studying paper quality, learning how to spot a large mixture of wood pulp in the paper, which made it unsuitable [for printing]. All this was challenging and complex for a novice. Besides, as regards financing, there wasn't even a kopek for the publication. I borrowed ten thousand roubles from my mother and more from the elderly Aleksandr Aleksandrovich Stakhovich, who kindly gave me 15,000 roubles on the spot at only 5% interest, and I was forever grateful to him for rescuing me on time.
>
> I then ordered the paper for the *Complete collected works* from Kuvshinov's firm. The first order was filled with no problem, but for the second order — of paper for the individual books *War and peace, Anna Karenina* and others — the paper the Kuvshinovs supplied me with was wretched, practically all wood pulp, which caused me never to deal with them again. (*My Life,* IV.27 "The publication of the *Completed collected works*")

Early the next year Tolstaya presented Dostoevskaja with a copy of her first publication venture: *Sobranie sochinenij Tolstogo v 12 tt.* [*Tolstoy's collected works in twelve volumes*]. In her thank-you letter written shortly thereafter,[24] Dostoevskaja responded:

> You don't know, dear Countess, how pleased and happy I was to receive your gift — the writings of Count Lev Nikolaevich, whom I hold in such high esteem. I have started to go through them and I realise how much genuine delight the reading of these truly great works can bring.

There are eight letters extant from Anna Grigor'evna Dostoevskaja to Sofia Andreevna Tolstaya,[25] although Sofia Andreevna's letters to her have unfortunately not survived. The overall tone of the letters is friendly and warm.

experience, as I know that it was only through instalments that I was able to sell 6,000 copies in two years at the relatively high price of 25 roubles per copy and realise 75,000 roubles of sheer profit."

24 Published in Nikiforova 2000: 298.

25 These letters were compiled with commentaries by Tat'jana Nikiforova (2000) in an article entitled "Pis'ma A. G. Dostoevskoj k S. A. Tolstoj" [A. G. Dostoevskaja's letters to S. A. Tolstaya].

One letter in particular — dated 7 November 1910, written to offer condolences on Lev Nikolaevich's passing — is especially moving and sums up the longstanding relationship of these two women (Nikiforova 2000: 305):[26]

> ...I could not help weeping as I read the account of the suffering and torture you felt at not being able to be at Count Lev Nikolaevich's deathbed. You were his kind genius throughout his life. After all, if your deceased husband managed to live to 83 [sic], then all of Russia is indebted to you, his guardian angel, for your untiring care and for your fervent love for him. And here during his last days you, his tenderly beloved wife who loved him all your life, were pushed aside by outsiders. They deprived you of the happiness of seeing him, and of the sad comfort you might have had in looking after him in his illness and calming him down.
>
> My heart is filled with revulsion and contempt for the people who did this. Could there be any justification for their contention that your arrival might have upset Count Lev Nikolaevich? His joy at seeing the one he had spent half a century with could only have had a beneficial effect on his recovery, and would have done him no harm.
>
> Such merciless treatment of you deeply saddens me, and I sympathise with this sorrow of yours with all my heart.
>
> I pray God He will give you strength to endure this trial sent from above.
>
> We have not seen each other for many years and it is possible you have forgotten me. But you have always remained in my recollections as one of the finest women I have ever met in my lifetime.

TOLSTAYA AND CENSORSHIP

In her efforts to publish the fifth edition, SAT immediately was confronted by almost insurmountable difficulties regarding censorship,[27] especially in Volume XII, where she dared include certain works by Tolstoy that had been previously banned — for example, *A confession* [*Ispoved'*] (written in 1879), *What then must be done?* [*Tak chto zhe nam delat'?*] (begun in 1882) and *What I believe* [*V chëm moja vera?*] (begun in the early 1880s). On more than one occasion, this involved personal confrontations between SAT and censorship officials — both government (from 1883 to 1896 in the person of Evgenij Mikhajlovich Feoktistov) and, especially, religious (in Konstantin Petrovich Pobedonostsev, who, as Senior Procurator of the Holy Synod of the Russian Orthodox Church between 1880 and 1905, served as censor-in-chief for the Russian Orthodox Church).[28]

In Part IV of *My Life*, SAT describes her meeting with both these gentlemen, one after the other, in St. Petersburg, on 26 November 1885, including her rendition of her dialogue with each of them. The following excerpts offer

---

26 See Illustration N° 36.
27 Hinted at in the excerpt from SAT's letter to Strakhov of 20 November 1892 (p. 25).
28 The government censor looked at concerns of 'political correctness' — i.e., texts which might be viewed as contrary to official policies — while the church censor was concerned with texts at variance with the Orthodox Church's accepted interpretation of Holy Writ.

some inkling of the rigid thinking she encountered as well as her sharp and skilful repartee, not to mention her powers of persuasion.

From her conversation with government censor Feoktistov (*My Life*, IV.59):

> Feoktistov received me graciously enough. He said that he could not allow *A confession* or *What I believe* to pass, and that I should put in an appeal to the religious censorship board.
>
> "But what about the article *What then must be done?* and *The tale of Ivan the fool?*" I asked him.
>
> "I didn't read them," replied Feoktistov.
>
> "Really?" I asked in surprise. "You don't feel obliged to read *Tolstoy* — how can you possibly relate to mere mortals?"
>
> I spoke fervently and, after a moment's pause, I added:
>
> "Where are *you*, Evgenij Mikhajlovich? The same Evgenij Mikhajlovich whom I knew back in Moscow as a fun-loving, out-and-out liberal, open to everything, interested in everything?"
>
> "Are you implying that I have corrupted myself, Countess?" he asked me with a kind of sickly smile on his impassive face.
>
> "It stands to reason you have, and what a pity!"
>
> "I'll tell you what, Countess: leave the book (Volume XII) with me until tomorrow. I'll read it myself and I'll indicate with pencil anything that has to be deleted from the articles."
>
> I thanked him and left. He kept his promise to me and marked in what seemed to be a haphazard fashion the passages [to be deleted] in the article *What then must be done?* He sent me back the book on the following day, along with a letter saying that it could be published in this form.

And from her dialogue the same day with Pobedonostsev, censor-in-chief for the Russian Orthodox Church (*My Life*, IV.60):

> …Pobedonostsev stopped directly in front of me, stared me in the face and said:
>
> "I have to say I am very sorry for you. I knew you in childhood. I had a great fondness and respect for your father, and I consider it a misfortune [for you] to be the wife of such a man [as Tolstoy]."
>
> "Now, that's news to me," I replied. "Not only do I consider myself fortunate, but everyone envies my position as the wife of such a talented and intelligent [*umnyj*] man."
>
> "I have to say," Pobedonostsev continued, "that I discern no significant intelligence in your husband. Intelligence is harmony, while your husband manifests only edges and extremes in every respect."
>
> "That may be so," I responded. "But Schopenhauer said that intelligence is a lantern which a man holds out in front of him, while *genius* is the sun which outshines all else."
>
> He had no response to this…

Another major battle with the censors came in 1891 with the first publication of Tolstoy's *Kreutzer Sonata*, although it had been circulating in manuscript form for two whole years prior to its appearance in print.

According to the plot, the protagonist recounts to a fellow traveller in a train compartment how he murdered his wife in a fit of jealousy. This story of lust, revenge, contempt of marriage ("legalised prostitution," as the author puts it) and misogyny, caused a furore among those who read it, and it was not cleared by the censorship board. Sofia Andreevna took great pains to counter the rumours that the story was based on the Tolstoys' own family life and to let people know that this was not a story she had lived herself. In preparing the manuscript for publication in Volume XIII of the next edition of her husband's works, she introduced some two hundred editorial revisions to the story (which she did not like at all), although later she decided to retract most of these.[29]

At the same time, however, she again lobbied both Feoktistov[30] and Pobedonostsev for the removal of the censure, believing in the principle of freedom of speech and appreciating her husband's sincerity in his treatment of the subject. But, as she wrote in her diary of 1 June 1891: "…I needed to try to get clearance of this story for the *public's* sake. Everybody knows that I *petitioned* the Tsar *in person*. If this whole story had been based on me and my relations with my husband, I would scarcely have petitioned for censorship clearance."

Indeed, Tolstaya was granted an audience with Emperor Alexander III, during which she managed to both make a personal impression on him and secure his permission for including *The Kreutzer Sonata* in her own edition of Tolstoy's *Complete collected works*. Her face-to-face meetings with both the Emperor and the Empress are vividly and engagingly described in *My Life* (V.92–94).[31]

There were many other occasions when Sofia Andreevna rallied to her husband's defence: notably, the police raid on the Tolstoys' home at Yasnaya Polyana to search for illicit propaganda; the Russian famine of 1891–92, in which she took a most active part; his activities surrounding his support of the Doukhobors; her resolute and sharp public attacks on the government and church hierarchy over her husband's excommunication (in 1901) from the Russian Orthodox Church, despite the religious differences between them.

29 SAT's editing of LNT's works will be further discussed below.
30 Feoktistov, for his part, informed SAT that *The Kreutzer Sonata* had been banned "by an order from the Tsar" (*My Life*, V.86 – "At the censorship board").
31 Pobedonostsev was quite nonplussed at SAT's daring and its successful result. SAT reports the censor blurting out to Strakhov: "Who does this Countess Tolstaya think she is, that over and above all the presentations and visits by society ladies and others she manages to worm her way into an audience with the Tsar and wangle *The Kreutzer Sonata* out of him?! When *I* suggested it should be cleared, nobody listened to me, but here a biddy asks, and he obliges" (*My Life*, V.95 – "Success").

All of this, however, proved to have a detrimental effect on her health, as evidenced by her letters to her husband, relatives and friends, her diary entries and, indeed, many passages in *My Life*. And her expressions of support for Tolstoy must be weighed against the many aspects of his teachings and activities that troubled her — his insistence on applying his abstract faith to everyday life (which she found impractical and insincere), his denigration of her and of women in general, and especially his too-cozy (as she saw it) relationship with Vladimir Chertkov and Chertkov's undue influence on him, especially after 1883. All this continued to provoke great dissatisfaction and depression in her right up to the time of Lev Nikolaevich's death in 1910.[32]

Yet, for all her defence of LNT's works before the censors, SAT was not above exercising a degree of editorial criticism over them herself. In *My Life* she makes clear her disapproval of what she considered too harsh a tone in some of his philosophical writings:

> His book *A criticism of dogmatic theology* was written in such a sharp manner that for the very first time I refused to transcribe one of Lev Nikolaevich's works. I was simply bothered by his cursings and railings at everything I was accustomed to hold dear. And in any case I did not understand philosophy in the form of coarse disgruntlement. A philosopher should lay out his thoughts calmly, concisely and wisely.
>
> I recall gathering all the sheets together, bringing them to my husband and declaring that I would no longer do any transcribing for him, that I did not relish criticising him, but it was impossible for me not to criticise this *Criticism of dogmatic theology*. Subsequently Lev Nikolaevich significantly softened his sharpness of expression in this book. (VI.62 – "Lev Nikolaevich's writings — From N. N. Strakhov's letters")

And on some occasions she herself acted as the 'softening agent,' as Gromova-Opul'skaja points out in discussing Tolstaya's editing of the 1891 edition of *The Kreutzer Sonata*:

> N. K. Gudzij's comparison of the last authorised manuscript of the narrative with the copy made by S. A. Tolstaya (typeset for the 1891 edition) and the edition itself reveals a considerable number of changes and deletions in the text. In a number of instances, these changes were introduced by S. A. Tolstaya deliberately — and, of course, without Tolstoy's knowledge, since she worked on preparing the edition, as well as the proofreading, all by herself, with the help of

---

32 It is noteworthy that no comprehensive study has been made to date of SAT's editions of her husband's works. A substantive article, if not a book, would be a welcome contribution to Tolstoy scholarship. The interested reader is referred, for starters, to Gudzij and Zhdanov 1953; Nikiforova 2004; the articles "Tvorcheskaja istorija povesti «Kholstomer»" ["The creative history of the narrative *The strider*"] in Gromova-Opul'skaja 2005: 76–92, and "Nekotorye itogi tekstologicheskoj raboty nad «Polnym sobraniem sochinenij L.N. Tolstogo" ["Some results of a textological study of L.N. Tolstoy's *Complete collected works*"], ibid.: 277–320.

[her sister] T[at'jana] A[ndreevna] Kuzminskaja. Apart from the inadvertent typographical errors, some of the changes were motivated by Tolstaya's efforts to avoid passages that were risky in terms of censorship (getting the narrative passed by the censorship board involved a tremendous effort), as well as to avoid what she considered expressions inappropriate for publication.

At this time Tolstaya was critical of the sharply accusatory content of Tolstoy's works and his concomitant 'sharpness' of style. It was quite natural that Tolstaya would introduce many softening corrections into the narrative text slated for *her* edition.[33]

Some examples of such 'softening' of 'inappropriate expressions,' often involving a change in a single word, are cited in Gudzij and Zhdanov's 1953 article "Voprosy tekstologii" ["Questions of textology"] — for example, the substitution of the singular form *polnuju grud'* [full breast] for LNT's original *polnye grudi* [full breasts], or her change of *publichnye doma* [public houses] to *izvestnye doma* [well known houses].[34]

It may be recalled from the beginning of this chapter that one of SAT's first joint literary tasks with her husband was to transcribe LNT's drafts into clear copies for him to work on. This more mechanical task from the early days of her marriage gradually evolved into proofreading and ultimately into editing his texts to make them more publicly acceptable: she finally came full circle.[35] It is instructive to ponder the significance of her notation in *My Life* in 1863 during her work on transcribing *War and peace*:

I would often ask myself: why did Lev Nikolaevich substitute a new word or phrase for one which appeared to be perfectly suitable already? It often happened that the galley proofs finally sent to Moscow for printing would be returned and corrected yet again. Sometimes he would telegraph an instruction to change some word or other — even just *a single word.*

Why were whole beautiful scenes or episodes deleted? Sometimes, in transcribing, I felt so terribly sad at deleting splendid passages he had crossed out. Sometimes he restored what he had crossed out, and that made me happy. It

---

33 Gromova-Opul'skaja 2005. Gromova-Opul'skaja goes on to point out that in the 1911 edition of Tolstoy's works, published after his death, Tolstaya restored Tolstoy's original wording in a number of passages which she had previously altered. And when it came to publishing the Jubilee Edition of Tolstoy's *Complete collected works*, in cases where there was a discrepancy between Tolstoy's last-known manuscript and Tolstaya's copy, the former variant was used. Note also Gromova-Opul'skaja's observations on SAT's contribution to clothing descriptions in her husband's major novels.

34 Gudzij and Zhdanov 1953: 233.

35 Some scholars have gone so far as to hint that the Tolstoy-Tolstaya collaboration was something along the lines of *co-authorship*. In reference to SAT's letter to her sister Tat'jana Kuzminskaja in December 1876, where she says: "We are finally writing *Anna Karenina* in a proper fashion", Svetlana Klimova (2010: 141) notes: "*We are ... writing* is no slip of the tongue, but [indicative of] the fact, of which Sofia Andreevna was fully aware, of their co-creative and co-participatory activity." Cf. also the quotation from Maxim Gorky above.

happens that you get so involved with all your heart and soul in what you're transcribing, and you become so familiar with all the characters that you yourself begin to feel you can improve it: shorten an overly long passage, for example, or rearrange punctuation marks for better clarity. […]

Lev Nikolaevich would explain to me why it had to be a certain way, or sometimes he would listen to me as though he were actually glad of my observation. (II.14 – "*War and peace*")

These are some of the questions, it seems to me, which Sofia Andreevna Tolstaya was obliged to ask herself — and *answer* — not only with respect to her editing of LNT's later texts, but also when it came to her own writing pursuits, both autobiographical and literary, as will be discussed (respectively) in the following two chapters.

CHAPTER 2

Autobiographical writings

SOFIA ANDREEVNA TOLSTAYA's works of non-fiction are all situated within the autobiographical genre and can be divided into three categories: her *Diaries* [*Dnevniki*] in two volumes, her extensive memoir *My Life* [*Moja zhizn'*] and her shorter so-called *Autobiography* [*Avtobiografija*].

DIARIES [*DNEVNIKI*]

The maintaining of diaries was one of the entrenched cultural traditions of the Russian nobility, including the Tolstoy family, throughout the nineteenth century. Diaries were kept by both Lev Nikolaevich and Sofia Andreevna, their children and relatives, Tolstoy's secretaries Nikolaj Nikolaevich Gusev (1882–1967), Valentin Fëdorovich Bulgakov (1886–1966), and the Tolstoy family doctor Dushan Petrovich Makovitskij (1866–1921) as well as their close friend, pianist and composer Aleksandr Borisovich Gol'denvejzer (1875–1961). Many Tolstoyans (that is, followers of Tolstoy's teachings) were similarly avid diarists.

Most valuable to scholars, have been SAT's own *Diaries*,[1] which she compiled independently of LNT's literary influence — a trait which, along with its recognised literary style, distinguished hers from the other diaries mentioned above.[2] With a few exceptions, she recorded entries more or less consistently

---

1 SAT's diaries were published in Russian in Golinenko et al. 1978 and in Cathy Porter's English translation (Golinenko et al. 1985), with an introduction by R. F. Christian. As mentioned, this translation was re-edited in 2009.

2 It must be remembered that in addition to her *Diaries*, SAT made use of two parallel record-books. One of these was entitled *Ezhednevniki* (perhaps best translated as "Daily

over a 55-year period beginning in her childhood at 11 years of age in 1855 and continuing until 1910, the year of her husband's death.[3]

Sofia Andreevna's *Diaries* reflect three distinct stages in her life: her youth before her marriage; the early, happy years of her marriage, when her husband was writing his major works of fiction and where we see her as an individual in her own right; and, finally, the latter part of her marriage after LNT's 'spiritual crisis' when he began to write mostly religious and philosophical treatises and where SAT's views on life took on a much greater seriousness and maturity.

Unfortunately, we can judge little about her early maidenhood diaries, since, when she married Lev Nikolaevich, she burnt these together with her story *Natasha*.

Her post-1862 diaries (especially those of the last stage mentioned above) reveal a complexity of thought, a forthrightness in description, a rich vocabulary, and an absolute confidence in the correctness of her position vis-à-vis that of her husband. Lev Nikolaevich constitutes the main focus of her attention, followed by her children and, after them, vivid descriptions of relatives, acquaintances, officials and other visitors to their residences in Khamovniki (Moscow) and Yasnaya Polyana. Many of these visitors, as was indicated in the preceding chapter, were prominent members of the Moscow arts community of their day — painters, sculptors, novelists, poets, musicians, composers, journalists and philosophers.

In the *Diaries* it is fascinating to read her accounts and insightful commentary on the books she read, through which we become familiar with her particular literary taste. Similarly, we read of concerts she attended, plays she saw, social gatherings she participated in and children's activities she organised, as well as the literary, musical and social evenings that frequently took place in her home.

But the *Diaries* are especially useful in showing the dynamics of the Tolstoys' conjugal relationship throughout the different phases of their life together. Witness the following examples — first, from the early part of their marriage, in 1868 (*Diaries*, I: 83):

> *31 July.* It's funny reading my [earlier] diaries. Such contradictions, such an unhappy woman I seemed to be [back then]. But is there another happier than I? Will you find any happier, more harmonious conjugal relationships? Sometimes you find yourself alone in your room and start laughing out loud for joy, and you cross yourself: God grant many, many more years like these. I always write my diary when we quarrel. And the days now are pretty

---

diaries"), in which she made brief notations about each day's events. There was also her *Zapisnaja knizhka* (Notebook), which she used for occasional jottings.

3 There are some gaps. Following Vanechka's death on 23 February 1895, there are no entries for almost two-and-a-half years, until 1 June 1897. Other years for which entries are sparse or absent are: 1868, 1880–81, 1884, 1888–89, 1893, 1898, 1905–07 and 1909.

quarrelsome; yet the quarrels arise from such delicate and emotional matters that if we weren't in love with each other there would be no quarrel. Soon I'll have been married a whole six years. And all I can do is love more and more. He often says that's no longer love, just that we've grown so accustomed to each other that we can't live without one another. And yet I still love him restlessly and passionately and jealously and poetically, and sometimes his restfulness makes me angry.[4]

And another example from the latter part of their conjugal life, dated 12 October 1904 (*Diaries*, II: 213):

> In the evening I showed Lev Nikolaevich his diary from 1862, which I had copied earlier, when he fell in love with me and proposed to me. He seemed surprised, and then said: "How difficult!"
>
> But I had one comfort left, namely, my past! Of course it was difficult for him. He has forsaken all that was bright, pure, true and happy for what was false, hidden, impure, evil and… weak. He suffers a great deal, dumps everything on me, casts me in the role of Xanthippe,[5] [observing] that I often said that everything would be easy for him, thanks to his popularity. But what role is he casting himself in — in the face of his conscience, God and his children and grandchildren? We shall all die, even my enemy will 'give up the ghost', but what will we all feel during our last moments [of life]? Will I forgive my enemy?
>
> I cannot consider that I am to blame, since I feel with all my heart that in taking Lev Nikolaevich away from Chertkov, *I am actually saving* him from the enemy — the devil. I pray God that His kingdom once again enter our house. "*Thy* (not the enemy's) kingdom come."

Tolstaya's *Diaries* are equally helpful in shedding light on her concern for her children, relatives and acquaintances. This is evident, for example, in the following entry:

> I transcribed *On life and death* [*O zhizni i smerti*] and now I've checked it carefully. I was intently looking for something new, I came across a number of concise expressions and fine comparisons, but the basic underlying thought is for me unmistakable — still the same — i.e., the rejection of a personal material life for the life of the spirit. One thing I find impossible and unjust, namely, that personal life must be rejected in the name of loving the whole world. I happen to think that there are unquestionable, God-given obligations, which nobody has the right to abdicate, and which are not a hindrance, but a help to the life of the spirit.
>
> My soul is despondent. I am very much annoyed by Il'ja and his secret and abominable life. Idleness, vodka, frequent lying, bad company and especially the absence of any kind of spiritual life. Serëzha's gone off again to Tula; tomorrow he has a meeting at their Peasant Bank. Tanja and Lëva keep playing vint,

---

4   All translations here and of all other *Diaries* extracts are by John Woodsworth.
5   *Xanthippe* — Socrates' reputedly ill-tempered wife.

which I also find annoying. As for the little ones I have lost any capacity to *bring them up*. I always feel terribly *sorry* for them, and I'm afraid of spoiling them. I feel a 'grandmotherly' fear for them as well as a 'grandmotherly' tenderness toward them. At the same time I still have a strong desire to educate them, and feel this is terribly important. I no longer have any point of support in life, but there are some magnificent moments in which I contemplate death, and occasionally a clear understanding of the dichotomy of the material and spiritual consciousness of myself, as well as the fact that life is undoubtedly eternal in both cases.

The *Diaries* are permeated with the same recurring moral theme found in SAT's literary works (indeed, the same theme which pre-occupied LNT during the latter part of his life) — namely, the multi-faceted interrelationship between spiritual life and earthly existence, and the frequent conflicts between the two.

In fact, the boundary between the autobiographical outline in the *Diaries* and the close-to-real-life fictional works such as *The skeleton-dolls, Who is to blame?* and *Song without words* is not as hard and fast as one might expect. SAT's diaries were frequently infused with exaggeration, frustration and anger, betraying a heightened emotional state at the time of writing (witness the first quotation above). The *Diaries* for Tolstaya, in their chronicling the life of her large family, served as a kind of *tvorcheskaja laboratorija* [creative laboratory] for her literary works, which may be seen to follow quite closely (only in a more poetic form) the realistic style of writing inherent in her *Diaries,* and with overlapping themes.

One might also point out, in connection with SAT's *Diaries,* a number of independently published autobiographical 'memoir sketches,' written at various times throughout her life. These include: *Poezdka k Troitse* [A trip to the Troitse-Sergiev Monastery], *Zhenit'ba L. N. Tolstogo* [L. N. Tolstoy's wedding], *O pervom predstavlenii komedii «Plody prosveshchenija»* [On the first performance of *Fruits of enlightenment*], *Vospominanija ob I.S. Turgeneve* [Reminiscences on Ivan Turgenev] and *Smert' Vanechki* [The death of Vanechka]. Many of these autobiographical accounts are also related in her *Diaries,* as well as in *My Life.* [6]

In view of the considerable range of critical materials already available on SAT's *Diaries* (as evident in the Bibliography in this volume),[7] I shan't dwell on further analysis of them here. As to their importance for Tolstoy studies, suffice it to cite the opinions of two prominent Tolstoy scholars: one in Russia and one in the West.

6 On SAT's published memoir sketches, see especially Shifman 1982: 51–53, Nikiforova 2004: 168–77 and Bajkova 2007b: 5–7.

7 See, esp., Rozanova 1978; R. F. Christian's Introduction to Golinenko et al. 1985: xiii– xviii; and Egorov 2002. See also Cathy Porter's Introduction to *The diaries of Sofia Tolstoy,* tr. Cathy Porter (UK: Alma Books, 2009), pp. xi–xxix.

In her introduction to the 1978 edition of SAT's *Dnevniki* [*Diaries*] (I: 10), S. A. Rozanova noted:

> S. A. Tolstaya's diaries belong to a documentary genre, but they reflect her literary talent and powers of observation, along with an ability to describe a person's external appearance and create a psychological portrait in two or three lines. They are also distinguished by a rich lexicon and a clearly expressed individual style.
>
> A prominent role in her diaries is taken by self-analysis, in the form of a thorough investigation of her soul — not just any soul, but a complex and broken soul, torn apart by contradictory feelings. They furthermore reveal a mastery of Russian prose as well as Tolstaya's accomplishments in the area of psychological analysis, [delving into] the inner world of the human being. From another point of view, the author's extremely laconic and expressive outlines of such a diverse variety of characters, her scenic landscapes sketched in an expressionistic style, her ability to portray inner mental conflicts, delicate shades of mood, the instability and changeableness of feelings and emotions, as well as her whole arsenal of descriptive devices — all lead to the conclusion that the author of these diaries was right in line with the poetic art of the beginning of the twentieth century.

Such appreciation is echoed by British scholar R. F. Christian's insightful comment in his introduction to Cathy Porter's English translation of her *Diaries* (Golinenko et al. 1985: xvii–xviii):

> …it would be unthinkable to write a serious biography of Tolstoy without drawing on them [the *Diaries*] extensively and … nobody except his wife could have written about him with such intimate knowledge and frankness.

***

One work of SAT's that grew directly out of both her and LNT's *Diaries* was an early biography of her husband. Indeed, she is credited with being Tolstoy's very first biographer. Even before her 26th birthday, Sofia Andreevna already had such a project in mind. Witness her entry for 14 February 1870 in the newly begun stage of her diary she entitled *Moi zapisi raznye dlja spravok* [My miscellaneous notes for [future] reference]:

> The other day, while reading a biography of Pushkin, it came to me that I could be of help to future generations interested in a biography of Lëvochka, writing not about his everyday life, but about his *inner* life, insofar as I am able to follow it. This actually came to me earlier, but I haven't had the time [to pursue it].[8]

---

8 *Diaries*, I: 495 (italics added by A. Donskov). Even at this time Tolstaya was much more interested in her husband's *thought,* his spiritual and artistic seekings, than his day-to-day activities. What SAT termed *Moi zapisi raznye dlja spravok* lasted from 1870 to 1881.

She did not attempt to start the biography until the autumn of 1876, and then soon gave up. In her diary entry of 17 September 1876 she states:

> I had Lëvochka's papers brought to me out of the gun-closet and immersed myself in the world of his literary works and diaries. It was with considerable excitement that I experienced a whole series of impressions. But I was not able to write the biography I had planned, because I could not be [sufficiently] impartial. But I shall try.

A second attempt that winter also failed. On 27 February 1877 she wrote in her diary:

> Today, having read over Lëvochka's old diaries, I convinced myself that I cannot write any "biographical materials" as I had wished. His inner life is so complicated and I get so emotionally wrought over the reading of his diaries that I become all confused in my thoughts and feelings, and no longer look at everything rationally. I feel bad about abandoning this dream of mine.

The following year, however, SAT managed to resume work on the biography. Her diary entry of 16 October 1878 reads:

> I have undertaken to compile a brief biography of Lëvochka for the next issue of *Russkaja biblioteka,* summarised from his works as selected by [Nikolaj Nikolaevich] Strakhov. This will be published by Stasjulevich. It turns out that compiling a biography is not an easy task. I have written a little, but it isn't very good.

On 28 November 1878 LNT sent the completed biographical sketch to Strakhov for his approval, explaining:

> Here is what *my wife and I* have put together, dear Nikolaj Nikolaevich, and are sending to you for consideration. If it is any good, submit it; don't add anything, but you are free to delete whatever you find superfluous.[9]

The importance of Tolstaya's work on LNT's biographical sketch cannot be overstated. Not only is it the first such account, valuable for the biographical study of both participants (individually and collectively), but it reveals significant details about the Tolstoys' life and home. As Serebrovskaja (1961: 498) puts it,

---

9 Donskov 2003: I: 484 (italics added by A. Donskov). The completed *Kratkaja biografija L. N. Tolstogo* [A brief biography of L. N. Tolstoy] was published in the journal *Russkaja biblioteka* [Russian Library], Nº 9 (1879), pp. iii–vii. On SAT's earlier redactions, see Serebrovskaja 1961: 497–98. It is evident from other correspondence, too, that the biography of LNT was very much a collaborative effort. Cf. also another of Tolstoy's letters to Strakhov dated 22…23 November 1878 (Donskov 2003: I: 480), where LNT uses the personal pronoun *we* in reference to their joint work on the project.

These sketches are the only source of certain valuable details about Tolstoy's life and career. It is only from these sketches that we learn about the article Tolstoy wrote in Kazan' on symmetry, about Tolstoy's reaction to the first positive review of his narrative *Childhood,* about the time and place [where] his work on *Polikushka* was begun, about new details concerning Tolstoy's reciting of Pushkin's poetry as a young boy, and so forth.

MY LIFE [*MOJA ZHIZN'*]

Tolstaya's *Diaries* may be regarded in one sense as a form of *journalism,* in that they present her life as a series of discrete events within the neat framework of specific months and days, with the benefit of immediate reporting. By contrast, her memoirs — *My Life* (begun in 1904) and *Autobiography* (penned during a relatively short period of time in 1913–14) — were written many years after the actual events. They did, however, have the benefit of hindsight, the opportunity to put connected events together in parts and chapters, and a perspective on the place each event described held in a whole lifetime of experiences. *My Life* is essentially a setting forth of reminiscences and personal feelings, and a retrospective on her inner life as well as outward events. And in contrast with her diaries, written largely on the spur of the moment, in *My Life* she describes her relationships with her husband and children with a full consciousness of documenting these for posterity. Indeed, one of her stated aims in initiating this memoir was to counteract misleading rumours and press reports on her family life, especially her relationship to LNT.

Her brief preface to this work is self-explanatory and deserves quoting in full:

> Last year Vladimir Vasil'evich Stasov asked me to write my autobiography for a women's calendar. I thought that was too immodest of me, and I declined.
>
> But the longer I live, the more I see the accumulation of acute misunderstandings and false reports concerning my character, my life, and a great many topics touching upon me. And so, in view of the fact that, though I myself may be insignificant, the significance of my forty-two years of conjugal life with Lev Nikolaevich cannot be excluded from his life, I decided to set forth a description of my life — based, at least for the time being, solely on reminiscences. If time and opportunity permit, I shall endeavour to include several additional details and chronological data drawn from letters, diaries and other sources.
>
> I shall try to be true and sincere throughout. Anyone's life is interesting, and perhaps there will come a time when my life will be of interest to some who wonder what kind of creature was the woman whom God and destiny found fit to place alongside the life of the genius and multifaceted Count Lev Nikolaevich Tolstoy.
>
> — *Countess Sofia Andreevna Tolstaya, Preface to* My Life
> 24 February 1904

From this preface it may be seen how much it meant to Tolstaya to tell her story from her own point of view. According to Shumikhina (*née* Bajkova), her deliberate use of the possessive pronoun *Moja* [My] in the title is highly significant.[10] As Ona Renner-Fahey (2009: 189) states: "How we view ourselves is not likely how we are viewed by others; autobiographical writing thus provides an opportunity to take some control of our reputation. And this reputation can of course only be re-formed through the presence of an audience."

It is interesting that Tolstaya was working on *My Life* at the same time that Tolstoy was working on his *Reminiscences* [*Vospominanija*], in which his principal aim was to examine his life "from the point of view of good and evil," in stark contrast to Tolstaya's aim stated in the last paragraph of her preface.

My Life, indeed, reveals its author as far more than just Tolstoy's wife. It shows her as his contemporary, a defender of women and their role in the professions, as well as a literary person.

The manuscript was not written in a single take, but intermittently over a period of twelve years, and the project continued for most of the remainder of her life, with a three-year hiatus — between 1912 and 1915 — due, she claimed, to a lack of available materials. By the spring of 1916 she had covered the events of her life only up to the end of the year 1901, which meant the last decade of her conjugal life with Lev Nikolaevich Tolstoy remained unchronicled.

All the way through *My Life*, Tolstaya drew heavily upon not only her own diaries, but also those of her husband and family members, as well as her exchanges of letters with the same, plus the extensive correspondence she maintained with numerous prominent (and not-so-prominent) acquaintances, many of them erstwhile visitors to the Tolstoy home.

The entire manuscript amounts to several thousand typewritten pages, which in the English edition were divided chronologically into eight parts as follows: Part I describes her life before her marriage (1844–62); Part II covers the years following the marriage up to 1875; Part III covers 1876–83; Part IV — 1884–88; Part V — 1889–91; Part VI — 1892–95; Part VII — 1896–99; Part VIII — 1900–01.[11] As a rule, each part comprises a hundred or more themed chapters, frequently very short and each centred around specific events, places, people or works of her husband's.

The process of writing this retrospective on her past was both a joy and an agony. In her diary entry of 30 March 1912, she noted: "My work on *My Life* serves a little to drown out the sorrow tugging at my heart, and it is good to relive the past, even though the past is beyond recovery."

---

10 See Bajkova 2007b: 79–80, especially the chapters "Zaglavie kak opredelenie avtorskoj intentsii" ["The title as an indicator of the author's intent"] (pp. 77–80) and "Prostranstvenno-vremennaja organizatsija povestvovanija" ["Space-time organisation of the narrative"] (pp. 80–87).

11 These divisions match SAT's own original typescript. The divisions between the parts were slightly altered in the Russian edition.

Indeed, many entries in her diaries reveal the seriousness with which she approached the writing of her memoirs. Here are just a few of them (in which the term 'autobiography' refers to the memoir *My Life* and not the shorter *Avtobiografija*):

> I spent all day on my autobiography and am happy with my work. (19 February 1906)
>
> All day I've been working on my autobiography. Lev Nikolaevich praises my work and approves it. I've been reading it to him. (2 February 1907)
>
> I've been writing my book, but it's a shame there are so few materials; I keep looking and use what I can. (9 February 1907)
>
> In the evening, as well as during the day, I spent a lot of time correcting my *notes* and dividing them into chapters. Lev Nikolaevich and Varja have been listening to a reading of my *notes* and are quite happy with them. (12 May 1907)
>
> I've been assiduously writing *My Life,* for 1895. I had many bitter bouts of crying as I described Vanechka's illness and death, and his life, and generally everything I felt so acutely back then. (7 January 1912)

During the time of her writing, she was aware of the biography of her husband undertaken by one of his followers, a Tolstoyan named Pavel Ivanovich Birjukov (1860–1931), but she felt it was too stylised and idealistic, almost icon-like, highlighting only the more gladsome aspects of Tolstoy's life. Moreover, she describes Tolstoy's own reaction to Birjukov's attempts at a biography as follows:

> I did not find it pleasant reading; it is just a millionth part of what I experienced. And still, everything he writes is insignificant, *random.* Anything really important is not described, it's missing. Instead, he describes trifling details which he has happened to pick up. It's all *out of proportion.* (Quoted in *My Life,* II.76 – "Alienation and quarrels")

By writing *My Life,* Tolstaya hoped to restore that sense of *proportion* and bring out *the whole truth* of their relationship, including what she perceived as its negative aspects. Indeed, in this endeavour she was supported by none other than Tolstoy himself, who once remarked that there was little point in writing only about the pleasant side of his life.

This more even-handed approach reflected in her writings is no doubt why this major work has been ignored or deliberately kept out of the public eye — first by the author's Tolstoyan contemporaries and for almost a century since. After Tolstaya herself published several chapters of *My Life* in 1912 and 1913, its public exposure, even in Russia, was until fairly recently limited to some two hundred pages at most, appearing in various journals (*Novyj mir, Prometej, Slovo, Oktjabr', Moskovskij komsomolets*) between 1978 and 1998, as well as (more recently) on the internet.

Pavel Birjukov, Vladimir Chertkov and other like-minded followers, while endorsing the publication of Tolstaya's diaries and correspondence (at least in part), were reluctant to bring any derogatory aspect of their mentor and idol to public attention. Then, throughout most of the remainder of the twentieth century, Soviet scholars dismissed SAT's description of the details of their everyday life as too mundane, and contrary to an ideology that by its very nature tended to promote historical stereotypes yet ignore historical facts, even where these were known. Under such official influence, Soviet researchers were, by and large, unable to acknowledge that it was precisely these everyday real-life details that were at the root of many of Tolstoy's literary portrayals — a fact that is only too evident from an investigation of Tolstaya's writings and her considerable epistolary legacy.

Some time after the collapse of communist ideology, scholars at the State L. N. Tolstoy Museum in Moscow began the laborious task of transcribing the lengthy typescript of *My Life* and preparing it for publication. It was only in 2011 that these memoirs were finally published in full by the Museum in their original language.[12]

These joint publications were timely, not only with respect to the centenary of Lev Nikolaevich's death in 2010, but also in view of the new 100-volume edition of Leo Tolstoy's works launched by the Russian Academy of Sciences. They also came at a time when increasing world tension prompted a renewed and heightened interest in Tolstoy as a writer, moralist and philosopher, including all the details of his life and work, his social, aesthetic, religious, moral and philosophical views. The questions of justice, conscience, war, revolution and terrorism that provoked his soul searching remain to torment our souls more than a hundred years later, and not only his religious and political treatises but also his works of fiction, especially when enhanced by Sofia Andreevna's constant critical participation, are instructive for our society today.

For twenty-first century Tolstoy scholars, the significance of Tolstaya's *My Life* (especially in combination with her *Autobiography*, diaries and correspondence) should prove considerable.

First, it is helping to fill some lacunae in the chronology of his works — the dates he started writing them, when he worked on revising them and when he completed his initial and subsequent drafts.

Secondly, Tolstaya's detailed descriptions of late nineteenth-century Russian society offers a fresh look at the writer's work in the broader context of this society, in both the aristocratic and peasant milieus which she and her husband had the opportunity to observe first-hand. And these observations are all the more remarkable, coming, as they do, not only from a participant

---

12 The Slavic Research Group at the University of Ottawa and the University of Ottawa Press here in the Canadian capital were fortunate, indeed, to have been granted exclusive rights to the translation and publication of these same memoirs in English (through an advance copy provided by the State L. N. Tolstoy Museum in Moscow) so that they may be shared with a much broader, worldwide readership.

in that society but a *woman* participant, whose perspective on life and events differed from that of her husband and other male observers of her time. Moreover, the society she was familiar with happened to include many of the prominent thinkers of her day: writers, poets, musicians, philosophers and scientists, including a number from Western Europe, Asia and the Americas. All this was set against a background of her formidable and broad self-education, including a high degree of fluency in French, German and English and an extensive acquaintance with philosophy, as we have seen.

Thirdly, and perhaps most importantly, *My Life* sheds light on the inner workings of both Tolstoy's and Tolstaya's minds as they faced their own individual spiritual development, on how they interacted not only with each other but also with both their immediate and extended families, on how they each perceived the day-to-day events — happy and tragic, major and minor — that formed the basis of many of Tolstoy's (not to mention Tolstaya's) literary works. Indeed, this is a chronicle of the whole Tolstoy family and their relatives and friends and offers a rich opportunity for further investigation by both young and seasoned researchers.[13]

In contrast to Sofia Andreevna's diaries and letters, which were written on the spur of the moment and focused primarily on contemporaneous events, the memoirs of *My Life,* written at a much later date, offer the benefit of hindsight and contemplation of the events of her life in a much broader historical context. It allowed her to reveal the interconnections between events from different time frames, as well as to comment on her life as a whole. It is also written from the point of view of the feelings of self-discovery which she experienced in the latter years of her life, including her ambivalent attitude to all her many years of coming up against her husband's wildly divergent moods, torn as he was between the normal human affection for his wife and family on the one hand and, on the other, his ascetic search for an abstract, otherworldly existence that seemed to be at irreconcilable odds with the demands of a practical, everyday family life.

Finally, Tolstaya's *My Life* sets forth many facts concerning Tolstoy's life and work to which she alone was privy. This is especially true during the early decades of their marriage — the 1860s and 1870s — when Lev Nikolaevich rarely made diary entries of his own, and details of his day-to-day life have been only scantily documented in other sources. Her description is all the more poignant in view of both Tolstoy's flourishing popularity as a novelist and the closeness of the family unit at Yasnaya Polyana during this period. It sheds light on the creative process behind many of Tolstoy's works, especially on how the details of his everyday life were translated into characters and scenes in his fictional work, also the interconnection between turning points

13 See G. M. Hamburg's (2010) excellent study, from an historian's point of view, on "Marriage, estate, culture and public life in Sofia Andreyevna Tolstaya's *My Life*" (based on the English translation published in 2010 by the University of Ottawa Press).

in his inner thought directions and corresponding turning points evident in his writings. All of this is reflected in the composition and chronology of Sofia Andreevna's narrative.

The fact that Sofia Andreevna Tolstaya was such an integral part not only of her husband's family and social life but also of his professional career as a writer makes her non-fiction works, *My Life* in particular, *the* most important documentary source for Tolstoy scholarship to be published in a great many years. It provides significant new information that is not to be found in any of her other writings. I can think of no better way to sum up this discussion of Tolstaya's major autobiographical work than to quote a review of the English translation written by the eminent Tolstoy scholar Hugh McLean in a 2011 issue of *Canadian Slavonic Papers* (2011: 74):

> We might call this huge volume SA's masterpiece, but perhaps it would be better to call it the literary record of her true masterpiece, which was the nurturing and support she gave for over five decades to one of the greatest literary talents the world has produced.
>
> [...] Reading it is an entrancing experience. Here is life, the real life as it was lived by a very intelligent, sensitive woman living in the second half of the nineteenth century and beginning of the twentieth, the life of a member of the Russian upper class, a countess, married to a man who was one of his country's greatest literary talents. It provides us a consistently fascinating view of that gentry world, seen both in the city, mostly Moscow, and the country, the famous Tolstoy family estate at Yasnaya Polyana...

AUTOBIOGRAPHY [*AVTOBIOGRAFIJA*]

If there is a disappointment in reading *My Life*, it may be that it extends only to the year 1901, which means that Tolstaya did not have the chance to describe in her customary detail the last decade of her conjugal life with Lev Nikolaevich Tolstoy.

Fortunately, this long and ambitious memoir, was not SAT's only attempt at recording the story of her life. As mentioned earlier, many events of her experience are set forth in her extensive diaries and numerous letters (particularly those addressed to her husband and other members of her family). Then, in 1913 she received a specific request to write her autobiography from none other than the distinguished biographer and literary historian, Semën Afanas'evich Vengerov (1855–1920), who over the period 1889–1904 had published six volumes of his *Critical biographical dictionary of Russian writers and scholars*[14] and was working on his *Sources of the Dictionary of Russian writers.*[15] In 1917 he would become the founding Director of the Russian Book Chamber

---

14 S. A. Vengerov, *Kritiko-biograficheskij slovar' russkikh pisatelej i uchënykh*, 6 vols. (St. Petersburg, 1889–1904, unfinished).

15 S. A. Vengerov, *Istochniki slovarja russkikh pisatelej*, 2 vols. (St. Petersburg, 1900–17, unfinished).

[*Russkaja knizhnaja palata*], destined to be Russia's principal national bibliographical research centre.

After receiving the request in July, Tolstaya completed the initial draft of the requested work in a period of slightly more than three months. She submitted the finished manuscript to Vengerov by the end of October of the same year.

Vengerov, however, was not happy with the result, feeling that there was something missing, and asked SAT to re-write parts of her manuscript, supplying additional material. Tolstaya obliged by sending him a completely re-worked Chapter III.[16] But Vengerov was still not satisfied. He had been expecting the author to reveal the 'juicier' details of what he thought must have been a serious disruption of LNT's family life brought on by the writing of his major novels. Vengerov's mistaken expectations were clearly evident in SAT's response to him dated 5 May 1914 (O.S.),[17] which begins as follows:

> My deeply esteemed Semën Afanas'evich,
> I received your letter, and in response to your partial dissatisfaction with the new chapter I would say this: you desired more *facts*, but where am I to get them from? Life [during the writing of LNT's major novels] was quiet, even-paced and solitary in the family.

Vengerov had apparently based his expectations on reports of other writers such as Gogol', Turgenev and Goncharov and the disruptive influence their writing had on *their* personal lives. But Tolstaya pointed out in reply that these were all bachelors with no families, "and that is quite a different matter." Their bachelor lives were reflected in their writings, she noted, just as Tolstoy's *family* life found expression in *his* writings. SAT concluded her letter by saying:

> And so, Semën Afanas'evich, in response to your closing words to the effect that from 1862 to 1870 Yasnaya Polyana gave the impression of a *home* in which literary interests were relegated to the back burner, I repeat once again that there was no such *home;* after all, I was a mere girl of eighteen years when I married, and did not yet have a clear understanding of the tremendous importance of my husband, whom I adored. That's all I have to say.

As the *Autobiography* is far less known than *My Life*, it is worth exploring its content in some detail. For one thing, it is significant that this work, unlike the latter, covered the entirety of her life up to and including her husband's

---

16 SAT's letters to Vengerov are included in the Introduction to her *Avtobiografija*, edited and published in 1921 by literary historian Vasilij Spiridonovich Spiridonov (1878–1952) (Spiridonov 1921: 131–36). All quotations from SAT's *Autobiography* are newly translated from this edition.

17 *Avtobiografija*, pp. 135–36.

death. Moreover, it was written in a fraction of the time it had taken to write the more voluminous memoir recounting events up to the end of 1901. This meant that earlier parts of her story must have been still fresh in her mind as she was writing the latter pages. It also meant that she was able to set forth (for the first time in a format intended for publication) the events of her husband's death as she perceived them, as well as her own subjective reaction to them. Indeed, as we shall see, much of the latter half of her *Autobiography* is devoted to personal observation and analysis, rather than merely factual description. An examination of both the similarities and distinctions between SAT's two autobiographical works will prove informative.

OVERVIEW OF CHAPTERS I TO V

As might be expected, it is apparent that in writing the first part of this shorter work, SAT drew heavily upon those parts of *My Life* she had already completed, only with an abbreviated and more concise re-telling. Indeed, there is considerable overlap in content between SAT's thirteen-chapter *Autobiography* and her more extensive memoir. This is especially noticeable in the first five chapters of the shorter work. Chapters I and II offer an outline of SAT's forebears and formative years (before marriage) with a few additions while Chapters III to V essentially summarise the events described in *My Life* with a number of new details added.

Brief and succinct, Chapter I of the *Autobiography* mostly reprises the family history presented in Chapter I.1 of *My Life* — namely, her birth in 1844 to a Russian Orthodox mother and a German Lutheran father, and their respective parental profiles. However, there are some additional details, such as the parentage of her paternal grandmother Elisaveta Ivanovna Vul'fert from an old noble German family in Westphalia, the killing in battle of SAT's paternal grandfather Evstaf Ivanovich Bers (German spelling: *Behrs*) at Zorndorf, and the fact that her maternal grandfather Aleksandr Islen'ev fought at Borodino, later to become an officer of the Preobrazhensk regiment. There is also a reference to the Bers coat-of-arms, featuring a bear and bees, which is not mentioned in *My Life*.

The two pages of Chapter II outline SAT's years of growing up in the intellectual atmosphere of the Bers household — basically the same information contained at greater length in Chapters I.3, I.7 and I.18–20 of *My Life*. However, it is here that we learn of LNT's reaction to SAT's story *Natasha*,[18] and SAT's own regret at having burnt this story and other childhood papers.

Of all the chapters in the *Autobiography*, Chapter III at six-and-a-half pages long shows the most overlap with *My Life*, covering some twenty-four topics touched upon in the longer work, mostly in Part II. These include the

---

18 This is mentioned in my introduction to the English translation of *My Life*, but not in SAT's text itself.

Tolstoys' relationship to Tat'jana Ergol'skaja (*My Life,* II.5), the transcribing of *Polikushka* (II.10, mentioned several times in the *Autobiography*), SAT's ambivalence regarding her transcribing activity (II.10, II.14, also mentioned repeatedly in the shorter work), her offering suggestions to her husband for changes in the text (II.14), LNT's research on the Masons (II.66), Turgenev's letter (in French) to Edmond About (II.75),[19] LNT's interest in writing legends (II.86) and the reading of his legends at the university (IV.72).

A number of the topics in this chapter touch specifically on LNT's first major novel *War and peace* [*W&P*]: LNT's reading of *W&P* to nieces Varja (Varvara Valer'janovna Tolstaya) and Liza (Elizaveta Valer'janovna Tolstaya) (II.44) as well as to *literati* (II.27); his fastidious corrections to *W&P,* along with SAT's helpful suggestions for improving the text (II.14); Strakhov's review of *W&P* (II.83); and finally the first editions of *W&P* and Shchedrin's criticism thereof.

Despite the substantive overlap with the content in *My Life*, Chapter III of the *Autobiography* also contains entirely new information: the friendship between LNT's sister Marija Nikolaevna Tolstaya and SAT's mother Ljubov' Aleksandrovna Islen'eva; an admission that LNT's writing came sometimes easily, sometimes slowly;[20] the influence of Yasnaya Polyana on LNT and his writing; and, interestingly, an indication that LNT began, and abandoned, ten attempts at a novel about Peter the Great.

Chapter III also offers new details related to LNT's major novels *War and peace* and *Anna Karenina*. Perhaps most notable among these is a description of the significant deterioration in family circumstances between the writing of the two novels. It is in the *Autobiography* that we learn of the date on which LNT began his work on *Anna Karenina*: 19 March 1872. Princess Irina Ivanovna Paskevich is described as making the first French translation of *War and peace*. Finally, LNT is described as reading *War and peace* to fellow writers Aleksej Mikhajlovich Zhemchuzhnikov and Ivan Sergeevich Aksakov, whereas in *My Life* (II.27) his audience is comprised of Zhemchuzhnikov and Aleksandr Nikolaevich Ostrovskij.

Chapter IV of SAT's *Autobiography* is less than two pages in length and details her positive experiences with visitors to Yasnaya Polyana, mostly during the 1860s and 1870s. Again, these all echo descriptions of people encountered in *My Life* — the writer Count Vladimir Aleksandrovich Sollogub (*My Life,* II.64), the poet Afanasij Afanas'evich Fet (II.26, III.104, IV.37), the novelist Ivan Sergeevich Turgenev (III.59) and the philosopher (and LNT's editorial

---

19 SAT correctly identifies the French writer Edmond About in her *Autobiography*. In *My Life* she mistakenly names the letter's addressee as "Michel About", who was Edmond About's son.

20 SAT writes: "Certain passages in *War and peace* and in his other writings I was obliged to transcribe over and over again, while others, like the description of the uncle's hunting in *War and peace,* spilled out all at once" (*Autobiography,* p. 146).

consultant) Nikolaj Nikolaevich Strakhov (VII.2). A description of LNT's fascination with another type of 'visitor', namely, *bees,* is also reminiscent of *My Life* (II.26), as is an expression of regret at not writing down LNT's conversations with visitors (VII.37). Two quotations from Fet's poems are included — "Your hand nestled into mine" and "And here, all filled with fascination" — also reproduced in *My Life* (II.26, IV.37).

The only 'new' (and yet perhaps not entirely new) information in this chapter is an expression of gratitude to "the dear, deceased *true* friends of ours for their invariably good and kind attitude toward me" (*Autobiography,* p. 150).

The first four paragraphs of Chapter V again show a considerable overlap with the longer memoir, describing: SAT taking more time for her family and less in assisting her husband (*My Life,* III.18), LNT's Greek studies (II.92), the Tolstoy couple's joint English studies (II.10), the move to Moscow, arising from the need to enrol the older children in a *gymnasium* (III.89–91) and SAT's treating the sick at Yasnaya Polyana (III.62).

In the remaining paragraphs of Chapter V SAT notes a gradual shift in LNT's views from the practical to the ascetic and philosophical, combined with a corresponding abandonment of his fatherly responsibilities toward his growing family. His new views on the meaning of life, which SAT finds disturbing, are sharply contrasted with her own principled devotion to the Tolstoy family's welfare. At this point we see a marked change in tone in SAT's writing from objective *description* and *summary* to subjective *observation* and *analysis*, a change that permeates the remaining chapters of her *Autobiography.*

The following excerpt (*Autobiography,* pp. 153–54) illustrates SAT's new authorial tone:

> The disagreement between my husband and myself came about not because I left him in my affections. I and my life remained as before. It was *he* who left *me,* not in everyday life, but in his writings, his sermonising to people on how they should live. There was no way I could bring myself to follow his teachings. Still, personal relations between us remained the same as before: we loved each other as before, we found parting as difficult as before [...]
>
> It was just that sometimes our happiness was darkened and our harmony disturbed by flareups of utterly unfounded mutual jealousy. Both of us being fervent and passionate people, we could not imagine anyone being able to come between us. However, this jealousy awakened in me with frightening force when I saw, toward the end of our life together, how my husband's soul, which had been open toward me for so many years, closed to me and opened, irrevocably and for no apparent reason, to an alien outsider.[21]

---

21 The reference here is to Vladimir Grigor'evich Chertkov (see below).

OVERVIEW OF CHAPTERS VI TO XIII

In the remaining chapters of her *Autobiography,* SAT's descriptions of events in her life are more frequently accompanied by her personal reaction, subjective observation and analysis, which tend to overshadow the actual depictions.

In Chapter VI (just over three pages) she comments on her husband's state of despair and threats of suicide, her own inability to accept his new views on religion, especially in light of her own deteriorating health and family burdens (cf. *My Life,* VI.95). With the encouragement of her close friend Leonid Dmitrievich Urusov, she seeks refuge in reading philosophy, including Marcus Aurelius, Seneca, Epictetus, Spinoza, Socrates, Plato and Schopenhauer (III.38, 116). She also speaks of her attraction to LNT's *On Life* (IV.102, 123). She then goes on to mention her own literary ventures, in particular her stories *Vorob'i* [*The Sparrows*], *Ch'ja vina?* [*Who is to blame?*], *Pesnja bez slov* [*Song without words*], *Kukolki-skelettsy* [*The skeleton-dolls*], her collection of 'poems in prose' entitled *Stony* [*Groanings*], as well as a grammar for children, described as being misplaced by a teacher "who had a high opinion of my work" (*Autobiography,* p. 156). As usual, however, she contrasts praise from others with her own negative self-evaluation: "I always regarded my own works with scornful irony, considering this activity an indulgence on my part" (p. 157).

Her list of her own writings includes three published articles alluded to in *My Life:* her appeal for donations to her family's famine relief efforts in 1891 (cf. *My Life,* V.129), her letter to the Metropolitans of the Russian Orthodox Church (VIII.16) and her reminiscences on Turgenev in *Orlovskij vestnik* (III.40). Finally, she speaks of *My Life* as her most significant accomplishment, though she laments the fact that she is now barred from accessing the materials which she herself donated to the Rumjantsev Museum (subsequently transferred to the Historical Museum).

SAT's commentaries in the page and a half comprising Chapter VII deal with her annoyance at LNT's insistence on performing physical labour helping the peasants in the fields (cf. *My Life,* IV.79), as well as his suicide threat that coincided with the birth of her last daughter Aleksandra (Sasha; IV. 14); this was followed by another suicide letter he wrote in July 1897 but never delivered (reproduced in full in *My Life,* VII.41). She then cites her negative reaction to LNT's attempts to legally transfer his property to her — first in 1883 (cf. III.135) and later in 1891 (V.68). This latter point is expressed in her *Autobiography* with a slightly different phrasing from *My Life.* In reply to LNT's justification that he regarded property as an evil, she declares: "So you want to transfer this evil to me, the person closest to you. I don't want it and I shan't take it" (*Autobiography,* p. 138; cf. *My Life,* III.135).

Chapter VII closes with a brief reference to her audience with Tsar Alexander III, which is described in great detail in *My Life* (V.92–95).

In Chapter VIII (three pages) SAT turns her attention to her family's relief efforts, noting how her own participation in this project was a source of comfort for her, helping to alleviate her worry over the safety of her older children on the 'front lines' of the relief project (cf. *My Life*, V.129 and 135). But she also notes that in her estimation LNT's participation only served to whet his appetite for an even greater 'heroic deed' [*podvig*] and increase his sense of being burdened by his family (VI.73). She was more compassionate toward what she saw as the more genuine suffering on the part of her son Lev (VI.1). But here, without so much as a sentence break, she immediately jumps to her worst tragedy of all (p. 160; cf. *My Life*, VI.109):

> But he [my son Lev] recovered, after being ill for more than two years, while in 1895 my youngest son Vanechka died at 7 years old. He was everyone's darling. He bore an extraordinary resemblance to his father; he was a clever and sensitive child, not a resident of this earth (as people say about such children [who pass on at a very young age]). This was the greatest sorrow in my life, and for a long time I couldn't even find comfort, let alone rest.

After a brief mention of her trip to Kiev with her sister Tanja (cf. *My Life*, VII.57), she reveals her greatest source of solace following Vanechka's death, namely, music — specifically in the person of the composer Sergej Ivanovich Taneev. Taneev spent three summers as a house-guest at Yasnaya Polyana, and exerted a musical influence on both LNT (VII.17) and especially SAT (VII.117) — the latter verging on a romantic (albeit platonic) attraction.[22] "Listening to his superb rendition of the miraculous sounds of Beethoven, Mozart, Chopin and others, I momentarily forgot my acute sorrow, and painfully waited for the evenings when I would once again get to hear this marvellous music" (*Autobiography*, p. 160).

The page-and-a-half comprising Chapter IX begins with a brief mention of two events described in Parts VII and VIII, respectively, of *My Life* — a visit with her husband to the Optina Pustyn' Monastery to see his sister Marija Nikolaevna (by this time a nun at the Shamordino Convent) and the Tolstoys' stay (on the advice of their doctors) at Gaspra in the Crimea over the winter of 1901–02, although neither of them found the trip medically beneficial.

At this point SAT has finished describing the happenings covered in *My Life* (which extends only up to the end of 1901) and turns her attention to subsequent events. Still in Chapter IX, she revisits the theme of her work on *My Life*, mentioning her long hours copying lengthy passages from her diaries and letters in the Historical Museum to which she still had access at the time. The remainder of the chapter is devoted to her pursuit of art and painting, including copying works by famous masters (such as Ivan Nikolaevich Kramskoj's portrait of LNT), as well as canvas depictions of the various flora and mushrooms of Yasnaya Polyana.

---

22 SAT's experience with Taneev, as discussed in the previous chapter, served as a basis for her novel *Song without words* (see also Chapter 3 in this volume).

Chapters X, XI and XII (five pages total) continue to cover what SAT has selected as the most noteworthy events of the last decade of her husband's life, including his death, along with her personal reaction to them. In Chapter X these include seeing her son Andrej off to the Russo-Japanese War in 1904, the birth of her granddaughter Tat'jana Mikhajlovna (Tanjushka) Sukhotina in 1905 (Tanja's daughter), her medical operation[23] and the death of her daughter Marija L'vovna (Masha) in 1906. She also complains about the increasing number of visitors to Yasnaya Polyana and their deleterious influence on her husband's health.

Over the course of Chapter XI we read of the increasing conflict in SAT's relationship with her husband, particularly with respect to one of his closest associates, Vladimir Grigor'evich Chertkov, with whom she fought over her husband's will, possession of his diaries and finally, at Astapovo, access to her husband on his deathbed. This latter event is the principal focus of Chapter XII. She depicts the climax of her sorrow in these words (p. 167):

> A new [round of] cruel sufferings began for me: here was my dying husband surrounded by a crowd of outsiders, alien people, while I, his wife, who had lived with him for 48 years, was not allowed to see him. They locked the doors on me, and when I tried to catch sight of my husband through the window, they pulled down the blind. Two field nurses assigned to me held me tightly by both arms and would not let me even move. In the meantime, Lev Nikolaevich called his daughter Tanja to his side, and when they were alone, he began enquiring about me, assuming I was back at Yasnaya Polyana. With each question he started to weep, and his daughter told him: "Let's not talk about Mama now, it's too upsetting for you." To which he replied: "Enough! That's more important than anything to me…" And he also told her, his voice now scarcely audible: "So much has fallen upon Sonja. We didn't manage things very well."

A very brief Chapter XIII (less than a page long) wraps up a few details of SAT's life following her husband's death. She describes her sadness at seeing the conflicts which developed among the peasants at Yasnaya Polyana after a good part of the estate lands was given to them, and their felling of many of the trees for commercial sale. She herself manages to retain 200 *desjatinas* [roughly 530 acres] and is grateful to the Tsar for a pension to help maintain the estate, but she is still obliged to offer financial assistance to the 38 members of her extended family. She wonders what will become of Yasnaya Polyana after her passing.

She concludes her *Autobiography* with a heartfelt appeal to the Divine:

---

23 In connection with her operation she sums up her life-credo in these words: "*What is important?* I seem to ask myself. Just one thing: if God placed us on earth and we are to live, the most important thing is to help one another in any way we can. Help each other to live. I still think that way." (p. 163)

Almost every day I visit [my husband's] grave. I thank God for the happiness vouchsafed to me earlier, and look upon the sufferings my husband and I endured as a trial and redemption of our sins before death. Thy will be done!

CHAPTER 3

Tolstaya's works of fiction

THIS CHAPTER offers a brief critical commentary on each of Sofia Andreevna Tolstaya's major works of fiction. In Part II, most of these works are presented for the first time in a single volume in English translation along with excerpts from *My Life* relating to her literary sources and a selection of SAT's poetry.[1]

These works of fiction comprise:

(1) *Natasha,* a story she wrote in her maidenhood;[2]

(2) SAT's contributions to her husband's anthology *A new primer* [*Novaja azbuka*];

(3) *The skeleton-dolls and other stories* [*Kukolki-skelettsy i drugie rasskazy*], a series of five stories published in 1910;

(4) *Who is to blame?* [*Ch'ja vina?*], a novella penned in the early 1890s partly as a response to LNT's controversial novel *The Kreutzer Sonata,* though not published in her lifetime;

(5) *Song without words* [*Pesnja bez slov*], a narrative written following the death of her youngest son Vanechka in 1895. This work also remained unpublished until 2010;

---

1   Available in their original Russian in the first edition of the present volume, published by the Slavic Research Group at the University of Ottawa in 2011, conjointly with the L. N. Tolstoy Museum in Moscow.

2   Since (as was mentioned in the previous chapter) the manuscript of *Natasha* was destroyed by the author before her marriage, we are unable to offer the complete story. Instead we are obliged to resort to a description of the work compiled by her sister, Tat'jana Andreevna Kuzminskaja.

(6) *Groanings* [*Stony*], which was crafted as a 'poem in prose' (a lyrical composition in poetic form but without traditional poetic devices such as metre or rhyme).

FIRST STORY *NATASHA*

One year before her marriage in 1861, Sofia Andreevna Bers was awarded a teaching certificate from Moscow University. The final composition she submitted to Professor Nikolaj Tikhonravov,[3] who apparently praised it highly for its literary qualities, was entitled "Music". This is an early indication of SAT's love for music, which kept growing in intensity right to the end of her life.

It was in this same period that the young Sofia made her first foray into literature, by writing a novella she entitled *Natasha*. Unfortunately for future generations, she decided to burn her manuscript just before her wedding in 1862, along with her youthful diary (which she had started writing at age 11). The content of this story, however, is known from a description given by Sofia Andreevna's sister, Tat'jana Andreevna Kuzminskaja (1846–1925), in her memoirs.[4] Both Kuzminskaja's description and SAT's elaboration on it in *My Life* (I.16) shed light not only on LNT's subsequent use of her novella (notably in shaping the character of Natasha in *War and peace*) but also on an analysis of SAT's later stories — *The skeleton-dolls, Who is to blame?* and *Song without words*. Consequently, these two pieces are deemed worthy of reproduction in this volume.

Indeed, it is not difficult to see how the various personages of SAT's early novella — Natasha, Zinaida, the mother and Smirnov — bear an unmistakable resemblance to characters in Tolstoy's first major novel *War and peace* — Natasha, Vera, the mother Rostova and Drubetskoj, respectively. LNT was truly impressed by his first reading of *Natasha,* noting in his diary: "She gave me her novella to read. What energy of truth and simplicity!"[5]

It was not long, however, before LNT began noticing the parallels between *Natasha* and real life — his own and that of the Bers family, whom he visited frequently. He later confided in Sofia Andreevna that he "had not slept the whole night and was very upset about [SAT's] condemnation of 'Prince Dublitskij', in whom he recognised himself, in that Dublitskij was 'a prince

---

3   Nikolaj Savvich Tikhonravov (1832–1893) — prominent Russian historian and philologist, who was appointed Professor of Russian Literary History at Moscow University in 1859. He later served as Rector of the University, from 1883 to 1889.

4   T. A. Kuzminskaja, *Moja zhizn' doma i v Jasnoj Poljane. Vospominanija* [*My life at home and at Yasnaya Polyana. Reminiscences*], 3rd ed. (Tula, 1960): 103–04. Reproduced in English translation in Part II, Chapter 1, p. 191 in this volume.

5   LNT diary of 26 August 1862 (*PSS*, XLVIII: 41), quoted in *My Life*, I.39. Tolstoy's diary entry continues: "She is tormented by any lack of clarity. I read everything without getting upset, with no trace of envy or jealousy, but [the phrases] 'with an extraordinarily unattractive appearance' and 'inconsistent in his opinions' touched a nerve. I calmed down. None of that is about me."

with an extraordinarily unattractive appearance' and that he was 'inconsistent in his opinions.'"[6]

What may be most interesting, however, is Tolstaya's own elaboration on her story, notably in her chapter entitled "Diary and novella" (I.16) in Part I of *My Life* (see also Illustration 39):

I had kept a diary from the age of 11 right up until I got married and, unfortunately, burnt all my papers before the wedding, including a long novella based on our life. In it I wrote about us three sisters, our flirtations, our family relations, various episodes. I was sixteen when I wrote the novella. Every evening I sat by the window of our classroom and wrote enthusiastically. I wrote about my sister Tanja with a special kind of love, calling her Natasha; I did a good job with her character, and when Lev Nikolaevich began describing his heroine in *War and peace*, he took a lot, including the name, from my novella. He read it a month before my wedding and was full of praise *for the pure demands on love,* as he later put it in his proposal that he wrote and handed to me. He took note of some other passages which I remember he especially liked in my novella, where I was describing a youth trip to Kuntsevo.

My sister Tanja was greatly interested in my novella and gave me daily encouragement. She asked me to read to her what I had written, and questioned me ahead of time: "And did you write about me?" She was delighted to recognise herself in the sweet character I portrayed in Natasha.

I should also mention *what* inspired me to write this novella. When I was fifteen, my cousin Ljuba Bers came to visit us, whose sister Natasha had just got married. In strictest confidence this Ljuba told me and my sister Liza all the secrets of marital relations. As a girl who idealised everything, this revelation was simply horrifying to me. I went into a fit of hysterics, I threw myself on the bed and began to cry so much that Mother came running, and to her questioning as to what was wrong with me, I could only reply: "Mamà, make me forget what I heard." I can't recall just how my mother calmed me down. I remember her cursing my cousin, and that after my tears, I fell asleep.

But somehow I had to cope with my inner feelings. I decided then and there that if I were to ever get married, it would have to be to a man who was just as chaste before marriage as I.

In my novella I described such a first, *pure* love between my hero and heroine.

In the same novella I wrote about the unattractive outward appearance of the hardened Prince Dublitskij, in whose personage I described to a small extent Lev Nikolaevich, and had him marry my elder sister Liza, who not just in the novella but in real life, too, was in love with Lev Nikolaevich and planned on marrying him. This came about because one time, in the presence of our German governess, Lev Nikolaevich said in the home of his sister, Marija Nikolaevna: "If the elder daughter in the family were all grown up, I would marry her, I like the whole Bers family so much."

---

6   Quoted in *My Life,* I.39. Note, too, the oblique references in the male characters' names: *Dublitskij* suggests duplicity, while *Smirnov* hints at the Russian word for 'meekness'.

The governess passed this along to Liza, and it set her head spinning, and she began to dream of marrying Lev Nikolaevich. I began drawing closer and friendlier to my brother's chum, [Mitrofan Andreevich] Polivanov. I idealised him as the boy who loved me *first* in his life. I wrote narratives about the ideal marriage of two poor spouses, whose home was complete with flowers and a singing canary.

For his part, LNT, despite his disclaimers to the contrary, could not seem to completely relinquish his initial self-identification with Dublitskij. The lingering effect of Sofia Andreevna's literary debut on Tolstoy is evident, first and foremost, in Lev Nikolaevich's written proposal of marriage to his intended:

Your novella has gone to my head, since in reading it, I have become convinced that it was unbecoming for me, Dublitskij, to dream of happiness, that your *distinct* poetic demands on love— that I have not been jealous and will not be jealous of those whom you love.[7]

Tolstoy's notorious penchant for *re*-writing touched even his marriage proposal. A preliminary draft penned a week earlier (which he did not show to Sofia Andreevna until later), closed with yet another reference to the novella:

I may be Dublitskij, but I can't simply marry a woman because I need a wife. I make terrible, impossible demands on marriage. I demand that I be loved the way I am capable of loving. But that is impossible.

If Lev Nikolaevich was at least in some respects Dublitskij, Sofia Andreevna was unequivocally not Elena, who declined the more difficult task of meeting Dublitskij's challenging demands in favour of marrying her own and younger first love, Smirnov. Unlike her literary alter ego, Sofia Andreevna *was* willing to take on impossible challenges, as long as she could reconcile them with her understanding of *destiny*. She closes her chapter on "Diary and novella" by citing the very characteristics of her future husband's that she attributed to Prince Dublitskij in *Natasha*:

…I am a firm believer in *destiny*, in the inevitability of everything that happens in our lives. I even learnt not to complain about anything, and not to rebuke anyone for anything, since both the kindest and most evil behaviour of people toward me were nothing but a *tool*, the *will* of that destiny that governs my life.
    It was this same destiny which threw me into the life of Lev Nikolaevich. His past, however — all the impure things that I learnt about and read in Lev Nikolaevich's past diaries — never *got erased from my heart and made me suffer my whole life*. My grandchildren, young men — everybody who ever reads this: know that the purity of your life will be a great happiness for the beloved women you meet, and a great satisfaction for your conscience.

---

7 This and the following excerpt are quoted in *My Life*, I.41.

60

As brief as Kuzminskaja's summary of *Natasha* may be, it is indicative of her sister's early artistic inclinations, along with her sense of practicality and entrepreneurial spirit in writing a story that would not fail to attract the attention of this larger-than-life family friend, already a famous writer himself. In his biographical account of Tolstoy and Tolstaya, Tikhon Polner (1928a: 48) points to Sofia Andreevna's apparent ulterior motives behind her first literary venture, claiming that "not everything is naïve in this child's story" and describing it as "a semi-confession, a call to openness, an unflattering portrait of her rival sister [Liza], and a provocation to a jealousy capable of arousing feelings of unease."[8]

Polner's description indeed points to one of the most significant aspects of *Natasha,* namely that its author was very much absorbed by the thoughts of the moment — to wit: her infatuation with Tolstoy as a famous writer competing with her earlier, simpler attraction to Polivanov as a decent, caring young man; her impressions of Tolstoy's frequent visits to the Bers' household and his presumed preference for her elder sister (recognisable as Zinaida in the story); the discrepancy in her relationship with her elder sister Liza (whom she did not get along with all that well) and her younger sister Tanja (whom she favoured throughout her life and honoured by her identification with the novella's title role). But it was her very ability to take the thoughts of the moment and translate them into written expression that would stand her in good stead in her future literary attempts — *The skeleton-dolls, Who is to blame?* and *Song without words,* as well as *Groanings.* And it was the same sense of practicality and entrepreneurial spirit that would enable her not only to meet the 'impossible demands' her husband imposed on the marriage, but also to act as transcriber, editor and publisher of his writings as well as manager of his estate, not to mention mother to an unusually large and extraordinary family.

CONTRIBUTIONS TO TOLSTOY'S *A NEW PRIMER*

In addition to her largely unheralded contributions to many of Tolstoy's fictional works,[9] Sofia Andreevna Tolstaya's most recognisable contribution to her husband's literary career may well be the stories she wrote, translated or re-worked for his educational children's primers.

Over his lifetime Tolstoy showed a lively interest in education and considered it essential to make it available to all social classes, especially the peasants, for whom he held the greatest respect and whose difficult lot he very much wanted to improve through education. He promised himself to do all he could toward this end — a promise he made valiant efforts to keep.

---

8   Tikhon Ivanovich Polner, *Lev Tolstoj i ego zhena. Istorija odnoj ljubvi* [Lev Tolstoy and his wife. A love story] (Moscow, 1928).

9   See the section entitled "Tolstaya's contribution to Tolstoy's creativity" in my Introduction to the English edition of *My Life* (pp. xxvii–xxviii).

He began by easing the peasants' living conditions on his own estate of Yasnaya Polyana. He established personal contact with them and eventually organised a school for peasant children, which operated from 1859 to 1863. In connection with this pedagogical experiment, he founded the educational journal *Yasnaya Polyana*, twelve issues of which were published over its brief lifespan in 1862–63.[10]

Tolstoy continued his involvement in education in the early 1870s with the publication of *A primer* [*Azbuka*] (1872) and later *A new primer* [*Novaja azbuka*] (1875). This laid the foundation for his own publishing house in 1885, which he established under the name *Posrednik* [Intermediary]. LNT's aim was to offer the more indigent classes of the reading public, literary works which were useful, edifying and at an affordable price.

A tremendous amount of work was devoted especially to the composition of his *Primer.*[11] In choosing the subjects — history, literature, sciences and natural phenomena (plants and animals) among others — he re-worked texts from the *Lives of Saints,* epic poetry, along with folk literature from various nations, and included Russian and foreign proverbs. The whole project was guided by the principles of clarity, simplicity, sincerity and beauty.

"The aim of the book," he stated, "is to serve as a guideline for the teaching of reading, writing, grammar, the Slavic tongue and arithmetic for Russian pupils of all ages and social classes and to present a series of good and well-written articles."[12]

LNT expressed his hope for the usefulness of his labours in a letter to Aleksandra Andreevna Tolstaya (1817–1904) dated 12 January 1872:

> My proud hopes for this primer amount to this: that this primer will be studied by two generations of *all* Russian children, from the Tsar's children to peasant children, that they will receive their first poetic impressions from them, and that having written this primer I shall be able to die in peace.[13]

The importance which Tolstoy attached to both his *Primer* of 1872[14] and his *New primer* of 1875 can also be seen from his extensive correspondence with his close friend and adviser, Nikolaj Nikolaevich Strakhov (1828–1896). The 1872 primer was mentioned in more than forty letters exchanged between the

---

10 See Donskov 1972: 37–65 and 117–158; also Donskov 1979.
11 *A primer* was comprised of four parts bound together in a single volume of some 750 pages, though in each part the page numbers began at 1. See Illustration 11.
12 *PSS*, LXI: 338.
13 *PSS*, LXI: 269.
14 Even though Tolstoy spent some three years working on his 1872 primer, it turned out to have little impact, and was severely criticised by various institutions. See Zverev and Tunimanov 2006: 272–77; also Gusev 1963: 57–113.

two in 1871–73,[15] dealing with questions of editing, source-materials, proof-reading and mistranslations.

Sofia Andreevna Tolstaya not only wrote stories for her husband's second primer[16] but was involved with their genesis and development right from the beginning. The idea of such an educational book for children was first presented to the Tolstoys by the American writer and translator Eugene Schuyler (1840–1890), who visited them at Yasnaya Polyana in 1868, telling them about the teaching of reading in America and about the educational materials being used there. Later he sent them a whole series of American primers (called *First reader, Second reader,* etc.) designed to follow a "strict progressive order of difficulty, both of reading itself and of understanding content" (*My Life,* II.81). According to Tolstaya, it was these books that "gave Lev Nikolaevich the idea for his *Primer,* as well as for the four *Readers,* which came out later." By comparison, she notes, the children's primers and textbooks then available in Russia were "quite inadequate." The Tolstoys envisioned together "a progressive series of readers for the children, along American lines — not only that, but these books should also be interesting, and not artificial and boring like almost all the existing children's readers" (II.89).

It must not be forgotten that Sofia Andreevna's own interest in producing children's literature of good quality was at least partially prompted by her personal situation of home-schooling a rapidly growing family of her own children. By the time of Schuyler's visit in 1868, they were already three in number — Sergej (b. 1863), Tat'jana (b. 1864) and Il'ja (b. 1866) — and all three had reached school age when Tolstoy's first primer was published in 1872. When *A new primer* was published in 1875 there were two more family members to be schooled — Lev (b. 1869) and Marija (= Masha, b. 1871). Hence it may be seen that the Tolstoys' own children were among the first beneficiaries of these particular works. In contemplating the need for such a publication, Sofia Andreevna noted in *My Life* under 1870 (II.89): "It turned out that our little world of children demanded more and more our personal attention and participation."

That both *A primer* and *A new primer,* as well as the subsequent *Readers,* were a joint production on the part of both Tolstoy and Tolstaya is clear from the following excerpt from *My Life* (from 1871, II.104):

That autumn Lev Nikolaevich and I worked assiduously on *A primer* and *Readers.* After reading a tremendous number of various books for background

---

15 See Donskov 2003: 14–96 (Letters 5–46).
16 Cf. her statement in *My Life* (II.14): "All throughout my long life with Lev Nikolaevich I offered him help in transcribing and later in proofreading, translating and composing sentences and stories for his *Primer* [*Azbuka*], the four *Readers* [*Knigi dlja chtenija*] and the *Cycle of readings* [*Krug chtenija*] as now, this year."

materials, Lev Nikolaevich either translated or set forth in his own words various stories and fairy tales from all sorts of different languages.

Lev Nikolaevich took such a conscientious approach to his work that even for the shortest story he would seek information from a specialist — a natural scientist in the case of physics, an expert on astronomy, a priest on religious matters, and so forth.

I also translated, condensed and even made up stories, as, for example, *Vorob'i* [Sparrows] or *Kak ja vyuchilas' shit'* [How I learnt to sew], and others. I also re-worked *Devochka i razbojniki* [The girl and the bandits] from the German [story *Das Mädchen und die Räuber*].

Whenever Lev Nikolaevich wrote or corrected something, I would immediately transcribe it with the help of [LNT's niece] Varja or my brothers. I helped a great deal in selecting the words and phrases in his *Primer*. We read through a lot of Russian proverbs.

Lev Nikolaevich needed a great deal of toil and inspiration to compile his *Primer* and four *Readers*.

SAT further describes her husband's work on *A primer* in Chapter II.109, mentioning in particular his inclusion of arithmetic, the Church Slavonic language and Russian epic folk tales known as *byliny*.[17]

Unhappy with the widespread criticism of his first primer in 1872, Tolstoy eventually decided to publish a second edition, entitled *A new primer* [*Novaja azbuka*], which appeared in 1875. This was a new and much more significant undertaking. For this LNT wrote some one hundred stories of progressive complexity. The first stories in the collection were composed mainly of simple, easy-to-understand words and combinations that were pronounced as they were spelled; the next set of stories introduced progressively more complex words and phrases. Finally, the children were presented with fables, fairy tales and more advanced stories.

It was specifically for the 1875 edition that SAT wrote or re-worked eight stories on her own. The titles are as follows (with page numbers from Volume XXI of *PSS*):

1) *Little girls have come to see Masha* [K Mashe prishli v gosti devochki] (p. 56);
2) *It was winter, but it was warm* [Byla zima, no bylo teplo] (p. 27);
3) *The cat was asleep on the roof* [Spala koshka na kryshe] (p. 27);
4) *The children went mushroom-picking in the woods* [Khodili deti po lesu za gribami] (p. 48);
5) *The nut-tree branch* [Orekhovaja vetka] (pp. 80–81);
6) *How Auntie told about how she learnt to sew* [Kak tëtushka rasskazyvala o tom, kak ona vyuchilas' shit'] (p. 108);

---

17 For further references to these works in Tolstaya's autobiographical memoir, see the Index of titles at the back of *My Life*, under *Primer*.

7) *A peasant's story about why he so loves his elder brother* [Rasskaz muzhika o tom, za chto on starshego brata ljubit] (pp. 129–30);

8) *How Auntie told about how she adopted a sparrow and named it Zhivchik* [Kak tëtushka rasskazyvala o tom, kak u neë byl ruchnoj vorobej — Zhivchik] (pp. 160–61).

In writing these stories, SAT was careful to follow Tolstoy's guidelines — namely, that the stories be written in a simple language, each one with increasing difficulty, starting with words already known to peasant children and gradually introducing new words. In terms of content, the first three stories, while just a few lines of large type in length, were designed to outline some basic rules of behaviour and the consequences entailed by violating these rules, always with a moral — showing the danger associated with carelessness or misperception.

In the first story, a little girl named Masha carelessly drops a teapot, but learns from her mistake. The lesson in the second is that in order to achieve something, one must be prepared to work hard and to sacrifice something. In the third, children learn to guard against outward appearances and potentially false initial impressions. The fourth story teaches children not to get too carried away by pleasant activities (in this case, mushroom-picking) and forget about lurking dangers (in the form of howling wolves).

SAT's fifth story, about the nut-tree branch, she defined as a fairy tale (*skazka*); its language, while still simplified, is somewhat more complex than that of the preceding stories. It is actually a re-working of a well-known folk tale. In Tolstaya's version a wealthy merchant, about to set off on a journey, asks his three daughters what kind of presents he should bring them. The two elder girls ask for manufactured goods — a necklace and a ring, respectively — while the third claims she "doesn't need anything," but says she wouldn't mind having "a branch from a nut-tree." On his way home, the merchant picks a nut-tree branch, only to be confronted by its owner, a fearsome bear. In return for sparing the merchant's life, the bear demands to be given the first family member to greet the merchant upon his return home. This turns out to be his youngest daughter (his favourite).

The family attempts to fool the bear by offering him a shepherd's daughter in place of their own, but the bear is even angrier when he discovers the ruse, and the family is forced to part with their own little darling.

However, when the merchant's daughter arrives at the bear's home, the bear turns out to be a prince who proposes marriage to her, and (this being a fairy tale) the couple, of course, 'live happily ever after'. Again, true to LNT's guidelines, *The nut-tree branch* celebrates the virtues of truth, modesty and simplicity, in addition to pointing out the dangers of neglecting these virtues. It is told in a simple fashion, but with just enough taste of adventure to keep young readers interested.

The sixth story by SAT (this one her own original composition) introduces young learners to sewing terminology, even as it inculcates the quality of patience with another's shortcomings and the need for loving guidance in bringing up one's own children. It is followed by a story of two brothers, one of whom is conscripted into the army just after getting married; his elder brother volunteers to enlist in his place, which earns him the younger brother's undying love and gratitude. The plot is reminiscent of Platon Karataev's sacrifice (in *War and peace*) to join the army in place of his younger brother, the actual recruit.

SAT's final story (the longest of the eight and, again, an original composition) takes up a mature and serious theme: three sisters adopt a family of five baby sparrows following the death of the birds' parents. But one by one four of the fledgelings die, apparently as a result of overfeeding by the girls. The last sparrow survives considerably longer than the others, but even it passes on somewhat prematurely. From this story the *Primer* readers learn that people's best efforts and intentions do not always guarantee desired results, especially when their hopes are tied too strongly to material things (such as food and creature comforts), and that love and other non-material elements are far more important, transcending human life and death.

In this particular narrative of SAT's, one cannot help but perceive an echo (or, as we shall see, even an omen) of very similar lessons she was already being forced to learn in her own life — namely, through the deaths of five of her children at a very early age. It is chilling to note the parallels in the relative timing involved:

- In the story, one of the fledgelings dies on the first day... The Tolstoys' son Pëtr [*Petja*], born in 1872, passed on the following year, in 1873.
- The same evening two more sparrows are dead... The next two Tolstoy infants, Nikolaj [*Kolja*] (born 1874) and Varvara [*Varja*] (born a year later), passed on within a year of each other in 1875.
  These first three deaths may be seen as echoes of events that had already taken place or were ongoing (Nikolaj and Varvara both died during the year *A new primer* was published). The remaining two deaths can only be considered *omens*.
- Two days later, in SAT's story, the fourth little bird succumbs, having lived more than twice as long as the previous three... In 1886 her son Aleksej [*Alësha*] died in his fifth year of life.
- The last remaining sparrow the sisters in the story name *Zhivchik* (from the word *zhiv* [alive]) because not only does it not die right off but it shows such courage and liveliness and zest for life that it comes to be dearly loved by all three girls. Indeed, it manages to survive much longer than the others, yet even Zhivchik passes on unexpectedly.... Similarly, the Tolstoys' last child, Ivan (known to everyone

as Vanechka, born 1888), displayed such lively and endearing qualities during his young life that he became the darling of the whole family (he was, by her own admission, Sofia Andreevna's favourite offspring). But even though he lived longer than the previous four unfortunate siblings, he, too, was eventually overcome by a fatal illness and died in 1895 just shy of his seventh birthday.

Tolstaya herself, as far as is known, did not connect her sparrow story with her children's deaths.[18] But it is apparent from a perusal of her diaries and autobiographies that her thought seemed to be frequently attuned to the potential for untoward events in her life, so it may not be surprising that this attitude was reflected in her writings as well as her life.

SAT continued to maintain a strong interest in both primers, especially since *A new primer* was approved by the Russian Ministry of Education for widespread use in the schools. It is significant that after the first edition, Tolstoy declined to involve himself in proofreading, correcting or revising any of the subsequent editions, giving this task completely over to his trusted wife and 'editorial consultant'. This occasionally meant fussy changes to suit the whims of the censorship board, who, for example, made her replace such 'undesirable' words as *vshi* [lice], *blokhi* [fleas], *chërt* [devil], *klop* [bedbug] with more acceptable euphemisms.[19] Although the work on the primers was but a small foretaste of her future role as editor and publisher of eight multi-volume editions of LNT's complete collected writings, it certainly foreshadowed her ability to hold her own as a member of the Tolstoy family literary team.

STORY COLLECTION: *THE SKELETON-DOLLS*
Much more interesting and engaging is Tolstaya's collection of short stories published in 1910 under the collective title *The skeleton-dolls and other stories* [*Kukolki-skelettsy i drugie rasskazy*], with illustrations by the artist Aleksandr Viktorovich Moravov (1878–1918), which were based on her outline and designs.[20] Earlier some of these stories had also appeared separately in children's magazines.

18 I am indebted to John Woodsworth, Research Associate with the Slavic Research Group at the University of Ottawa and translator of Part II in this volume, for drawing my attention to the parallels noted above.
19 Described in SAT's diary entry of 26 July 1891.
20 The first known mention of these stories was in SAT's diary of 14 February 1902 (II: 53): "Yesterday I read my unfinished children's story 'Skeletons' to the children. Varja Nagornova and the young ladies were also present. They seemed to like it." In another diary entry, dated 16 December 1909 (II: 298), SAT notes: "That evening I once again left for Moscow to wrap up some business, and to get my children's book published before the holidays." For further information on the stories, see Komarova's article (1999–2000) "S. A. Tolstaja — detjam" [S. A. Tolstaya to children].

It is not surprising that these stories show evidence of a deep understanding of the child psyche. In writing them, she was drawing upon a vast range of experience in several professional fields. First and foremost, she had personally organised and conducted the primary education of all eight of her surviving children. In her capacity as the only person in the neighbourhood of Yasnaya Polyana with any kind of medical expertise, she had spent years treating physical ailments of both the local peasant children and their parents. In 1900 and 1901 she worked as a volunteer at a Moscow children's shelter. She had purchased many books for her children (and, later, her grandchildren), some of which contained her very own drawings. She had organised many holiday parties over the years for both her own and the peasant children. With the help of her elder daughters, she had staged entertainment shows for these same children, and enlisted the children themselves as performers. And for some of these performances she and her daughter Tanja employed actual skeleton-dolls which they had bought and made costumes for themselves (described in *My Life*, II.70–71).

Sofia Andreevna shares that in fact the idea for the work arose out of a story of her husband's, which was in turn based on the skeleton-dolls she had purchased for the amusement of her own and the village children:

> Lev Nikolaevich used these skeletons as a basis for a children's story about how these skeleton-dolls were lying dead and then came to life and started living with the kids of Yasnaya Polyana. He used these dolls as a pretext to describe the reality of peasant life, especially the life of peasant children, in the hut where each recipient of one of the dolls lived. Unfortunately, the first part of this story was lost, and the story was never written.
>
> I tried using this theme to write a children's Christmas story, but I found myself quite unable to describe rural life, and so I left this story unfinished. (*My Life*, II.71)

Tolstoy felt the stories smacked too much of *charity*, a concept he had rejected throughout his life, and so he was perhaps too harsh in his criticism. There is little doubt, however, that these stories, especially now that they are translated into English, will be of considerable interest to children and adults alike in many parts of the world.

Sofia Andreevna's daughter Tat'jana L'vovna (Tanja), who helped her mother buy and costume the skeleton-dolls, describes them as follows:

> These were unclothed wooden dolls which bent only at the hip. Their heads with painted black hair and very rosy cheeks were of one piece with their torsos. Their legs were set into circular wooden boards so that they could stand up.
>
> Mamà bought a whole box of these 'skeletons', about a hundred altogether. They cost five kopeks each and were costumed and given out to each child who came to the Christmas party…

We costumed them as little girls and boys, and angels, as tsars and tsaritsas, and in various ethnic costumes — Russian peasant, Scottish, Italian boys and girls.

But Tolstaya's actual *Skeleton-dolls* story is only the first in a compilation of five short works published collectively as *The skeleton-dolls and other stories,* athough it does set the tone for the whole book. Two of the other stories are a 'legend' entitled *Grandmother's treasure-trove* [*Babushkin klad*] and a 'fairy tale' known as *The story of a grivennik* [*Istorija grivennika* (this word refers to a Russian coin in use at the time, worth ten kopeks)]. There is no evident link among the first three stories. The remaining two are taken from the real-life experiences of the Tolstoys' last-born son Vanechka, who passed on at an early age. They are entitled: *Vanechka: a real occurrence from his life* [*Vanichka: istinnoe proisshestvie iz ego zhizni*] and *The rescued dachshund: Vanja's story* [*Spasënnyj taks: rasskaz Vani*].

The major themes of the collection aimed primarily at younger readers are already evident in the very first story, *The skeleton-dolls,* which happens to be also the longest in the collection. The remaining pieces, whose length decreases in the order set forth in the book, develop, clarify and repeat the themes of the first, but raise no new themes of their own.[21]

THE SKELETON-DOLLS
The first story, which could well be considered a *novella* in itself, is divided into two parts: Part I — "The Christmas tree" [*Ëlka*] — describes Christmas festivities in the manor house of an estate, while Part II — "In the village" [*V derevne*] — depicts peasant life in the nearby village over the following winter. Part II, in effect, comprises a whole mosaic of episodes, each in turn composed of a number of scenes, including: children's games at *Maslenitsa* [Shrovetide]; other children's games over the winter season; the illness and death of one of the little peasant girls; a pilgrimage involving peasant women and a little boy; peasants' plans for the coming summer.

The plot opens in Sushkin's toy shop, where a shipment of dolls is being received, referred to ironically by one of the shop clerks as *skeletons*. But they do not sell well and are relegated to a crate in the stock room. Here the author endows them with suggested human qualities ("The dolls felt dark, stifled, awkward and bored lying in their crate..."), piquing the reader's curiosity as to the subsequent fate of these dolls. It is interesting to note that in contrast to her husband's story, SAT does not bring the dolls to life, but leaves this task to the reader's imagination with the occasional reference to their 'feelings'.

---

21 For a lucid discussion of the specific genres peculiar to the collection, see Bajkova 2006a: "Poètika prostranstva v sbornike detskikh rasskazov S. A. Tolstoj «Kukolki–skelettsy»" ["The poetics of space in S. A. Tolstaya's collection of children's stories *The skeleton-dolls*"].

Part I cannot be said to contain any plot-related surprises. It simply depicts events one would normally expect at the Christmas season in a Russian land-owner's home: going to the city to buy presents (for the landowner's children and tenant peasant kids), setting up the Christmas tree, and so on. But all these scenes serve to acquaint the reader with a gradually broadening cast of characters, mainly peasant visitors to the home who later take on greater significance in Part II. And the purchase of the skeleton-dolls by the landowner's wife at Sushkin's toy shop, which are later given to the peasant children as Christmas gifts, is another major element in setting the stage for the action of the second half of the story.

There is one small scene in the first half worth mentioning that does not seem to have any direct connection with the rest of the plot: on her way into the city the landowner's wife meets a poor widow who faces the prospect of being forced to sell her cow. The landowner's wife takes pity on her and offers her alms to meet her need.

The opening of Part II signals a complete turnabout in the plot line of the story. The focus shifts from the landowner's family to the peasant children and their unique relationship to the skeleton-dolls they received at the Christmas party. Tolstaya uses the simple theme of the dolls to broach a variety of impor-tant moral questions for her young readers and make them entertaining, thereby softening the underlying didacticism of the narrative and creating a delicate balance between fantasy and realism. It is interesting to note how the former gives way to the latter as Part II progresses, as the author makes her references to the dolls' 'feelings' less and less frequent, thereby helping wean the readers from the fantasy element to a pre-occupation with issues and ideas. This literary device is a stroke of genius.

This realism also extends to an authentic portrayal of the life of peasant children — indeed of peasant life in general — which, it may be conjectured, was Tolstaya's underlying purpose in writing the story, namely, to acquaint children from upper-class and middle-class families with a world wholly unfa-miliar to them. Only instead of introducing this life 'cold', as it were, where the shock of unfamiliarity might have put many would-be readers off, she first introduces the child 'heroes' of Part II in the much more familiar context of a manor-house Christmas party where they mingle freely with the children of the manor house itself, to which the majority of her readers could relate with ease. It is the peasant children and their interaction with their skeleton-doll presents that bring a sense of unity to the plot throughout.

It might be helpful to briefly consider the impact of this work on the modern reader. While the didactic elements (goodness, compassion, moral standards, etc.) are still just as recognisable in the twenty-first century as in the nineteenth, peasant life in the latter is as unfamiliar to the modern reader as it was to Tolstaya's own anticipated readership, and the setting of the nineteenth-century manor house along with the family customs of its inhabitants — especially their relationship to the local peasant class — are no longer familiar to a modern-day audience in either Russia or the West (except through the occasional historical novel or film). Hence Tolstaya's story offers today's readers a valuable added dimension, namely a realistic picture of a bygone era in Russian society. In this it is somewhat reminiscent of the 'physiological sketches' of the Natural School of the 1840s, designed to acquaint new readers with unfamiliar aspects of daily life.

Perhaps more than anything else, the story of *The skeleton-dolls* reminds one of a home movie comprising isolated segments captured over time, with seemingly minimal interconnection. It is difficult to overestimate the significance of a story which has unwittingly turned its plot and setting into documentary evidence of the times.

GRANDMOTHER'S TREASURE-TROVE

Grandmother's treasure-trove [*Babushkin klad*] is quite a different piece of writing from the first, set as it is against the background of historical events, namely, the War of 1812 and Napoleon's invasion of Russia. In addition, while easily recognisable in terms of genre, the plot is infused with a number of romantic details — the war itself, a treasure-trove dug out of the ground in the middle of the night, the characters' various attempts to gain access to it, each one accompanied by literary features that capture the imagination, such as the moon, thunder, nocturnal birds, a fire in the village, the hero's chronic illness confining him to bed and, finally, the happy recovering of the treasure trove, which offers relief to the poverty-stricken villagers. While the story is of little or no historical documentary value, given the temporal and cultural distance between the author and the events she describes, it does express more clearly the underlying didactic motif.

As in the previous story, here, too, one may observe the author's free-flowing style in her tendency to shift from one unrelated scene to the next and from one group of characters to the next with little attempt at a thematic connection between them. She also has no qualms about deliberately leaving certain plot lines incomplete: for example, when the old watchman departs from the estate following an unsuccessful attempt to steal part of the buried treasure, the reader is told that "nobody ever found out" what precisely happened that night. Such 'unfinished' episodes serve to bring the narrative on a closer parallel course with real life, which is similarly full of inconsequential meetings and partings with no opportunity to return to the past to tie up loose ends.

Compare this with Lev Nikolaevich's own employment of such a device — for example in Volume I, Part III, of *War and peace*, where the Russian army's foreign campaign is brought to a halt at Austerlitz. Among the many incidental characters presented to the reader are a couple of soldiers, one of whom teases the other by saying: "Titus, get busy threshing!", yet nothing is heard from them again. Tolstoy simply introduces them to show ordinary people caught up in a whirlwind of events, an example of random encounters, crossings and couplings which constantly happen in real life without further knowledge of or consequences to the observer. The author even resists the temptation to revisit this amusing pair of characters in subsequent parts of the novel, even where it might seem quite appropriate to do so. As in life, he allows them to pass by the perception of the reader in the role of observer, without further explicit reference and with any questions left unanswered.

This use of incomplete secondary plot lines to create the impression of a broader thematic perspective may be seen, then, as one particular device Tolstaya picked up from her long hours spent transcribing her husband's manuscripts and proofreading the finished product — tasks which she carried out most of the time not only with enthusiasm but with emotional involvement in the stories being told.

Her memories of this resurfaced with great intensity following Vanechka's death in 1895, when she hoped to find at least partial solace in reprising her transcribing work:

> When Lev Nikolaevich got down to work in earnest on his novel *Resurrection*, I remembered the joy that I had always derived from his belletristic works, which I had transcribed in my younger days — each one several times. What a lively interest was awakened in me by the mysterious flow of thoughts and creativity of such a writer as my husband was!
>
> After losing a child and feeling a great emptiness in my life, I wanted once more to get involved in Lev Nikolaevich's artistic life, and to be of service to him in his work. I timidly approached my husband with a request to give me once again his writings to transcribe. I was looking for deliverance from my sorrow. (*My Life*, VI.121)

She was bitterly disappointed when LNT refused her request on the grounds that "this always led to unpleasantries."

On other occasions she speaks of her emotional involvement in her proofreading tasks, for example:

> Occasionally, sitting up to three or four o'clock in the morning, I, too, would find myself hesitating and wondering whether it were right for me to be working so intensely, without a break. But to tear myself away from this work was something I wasn't prepared to do just yet, especially since reading Lev Nikolaevich's works over and over again gave me such tremendous pleasure. (*My Life*, VI.48)

THE STORY OF A GRIVENNIK

The same devices as applied in the first two stories may be seen at work, too, in the third component of the collection, *The story of a grivennik*. Once again we encounter unfinished plot lines, a shifting from one scene to another without a thematic transition, deliberately leaving unspecified details to the reader's imagination and, especially, tying the plot line together by means of a physical object passed from one character to another — in this case, a ten-kopek coin. This use of a particular object to tie various elements together, it may be noted, was frequently employed in the stories by the Danish children's writer Hans Christian Andersen (which, incidentally, Tolstaya mentions in *My Life* as stories she was in the habit of reading to her children — see, for example, VI.77).

The 'grivennik' story also echoes *The skeleton-dolls* in its detailed depiction of the life of ordinary people, reinforcing once again her attempts to educate her junior middle- and upper-class readership about the lives of people they might have little or no contact with, despite their geographical proximity.

From the didactic perspective, it might be noted that one of the issues highlighted toward the end of this particular story is the theme of death. Indeed, the subject of death surfaces a number of times throughout the collection. It was the author's deliberate intention to expose her young readers to significant issues of life and society, including death — through narratives leaning more toward the realistic than the sugar-coated. It may be noted that she also avoids the danger of over-dramatisation and the overwrought hysterics used by many writers in their 'exposition' of the more difficult aspects of life.

While Tolstaya may well be considered more of a realist than many of her turn-of-the-century contemporaries who laid claim to that title, her stories about common, everyday life still manage to attain a high degree of symbolism. This symbolism is manifest even in her simple endeavour to preserve a balanced outlook on life, unaffected by the temptation befalling many writers of the period to resort to extremes in their quest to put their point across or even capture their readers' attention.

This balanced outlook, among other things, served to give the lie to the not uncommon speculations of the time (notably on the part of Tolstoyans, for whom she had little or no love) as to her emotional imbalance. Such finely crafted plots with their delicately balanced composition of didactics, entertainment, realism and symbolism were hardly the product of a mentally disordered person. Indeed, it could be said that, much like her husband's writings, Tolstaya's stories are imbued with a significance that goes far beyond the interests of a strictly material sense of life.

VANECHKA'S LIFE

In examining the final two stories — *Vanechka: a real occurrence from his life*[22] and *The rescued dachshund: Vanja's story* — one must first draw attention to

---

22 It is very likely that the subject came from the occurrence described in Tat'jana L'vovna Sukhotina-Tolstaja's *Vospominanija [Reminiscences]* (1981: 419–20) as follows: "Our father [L. N. Tolstoy] was very much interested in the mentally ill. He would observe them attentively at any opportunity. He said that mental illness was selfishness taken to the extreme.

the author's literary sense of timing. As Tolstaya notes in *My Life*, the dachs-hund story was first published in the children's magazine *Igrushechka* [The Little Toy] (VI.107).

As in *The skeleton-dolls* and the other stories in the collection, once again she exercises a surprising and commendable degree of restraint, and does not resort to the melodramatic effects one might expect from a mother whose own real-life child died an untimely death. In fact, it is eminently noteworthy that Tolstaya does not impose her personal relationship to her hero upon the reader at all. Indeed, even though the theme of death is raised in both pieces (as it is at the close of *The story of a grivennik*), on each occasion it is in connection with a character other than Vanechka himself (a neighbour's child in the first story, a dog in the second). There is absolutely no indication in the story that this fine little boy, who unquestionably endears himself to the reader (as did the real-life Vanja to all who knew him), is about to perish. This is one of the many elements in the whole collection of stories that the author leaves readers to fill in for themselves — in this case, from the common knowledge in Russian society at the time concerning the real-life Vanechka's passing.

Reference was made above to the decreasing length of the stories through-out the collection. *The skeleton-dolls,* which opens the book, is indeed the longest, replete with many events both joyful and tragic. The subsequent sto-ries are in turn compressed tighter and tighter in length, with the final story being the shortest and most optimistic — truly, a story with a 'happy ending'. It is as though the author is conveying a message to her readers that life may be long and the understanding of it may prove a challenging quest, but finding happiness in life can be a relatively quick and easy task. And just as the griven-nik, after all the ups and downs of its adventures, is melted down into a new coin, as bright and glistening as at the beginning of the story, so man is not just resurrected to eternal life after death, but even on this plane of existence, life and happiness are constantly being renewed by new, bright souls coming into the world. The principal lesson is that people should not indulge in end-less complications, mostly of their own making, but instead, resolve to look for happiness, which they are then all the more likely to find.

The garden of our Moscow house was next door to a large park belonging to a clinic for the mentally ill, separated only by a board fence. Through the cracks in the fence we could see the patients strolling along the allées. We got to know some of them. They would offer us flowers and, when their monitors weren't watching, we would talk with them. One unfortu-nate fellow had lost his mind after the death of his only child, a boy about the age of my little brother Vanja [Vanechka]. This patient grew quite attached to Vanja. He would calmly wait for him to appear in the garden, and pick the most beautiful flowers for him that he could find in the park. Vanja was full of love and care for everything around him. And under the influence of my little brother's tenderness, the will to live was once again awakened in his soul. After leaving the clinic, he wrote my mother a touching letter. Vanja had taught him how much love and enchantment still remained in this world, and he was grateful to the one who had given life to such a delightful human being."

NOVELLA: *WHO IS TO BLAME?*

While her sometimes strained relationship with her husband was undoubtedly important, critics and biographers generally prefer to dwell on and even exaggerate her guilt and inability to comprehend her husband's seekings at the cost of focussing on her own remarkable individual talents — musical, literary and philosophical.

But Tolstaya did write both prose and poetry, and while much of her writing is confessional in nature, it deserves closer scrutiny than it has received to date.

Although she showed an early interest in belletristic writing (one need only consider *Natasha*), most of her literary output is associated with the last quarter-century of her life from the 1890s on and, indeed, is drawn from her own experience, from some issue in her family's life — although not exclusively, as is held by a number of critics.[23]

A most pertinent example is her novella *Who is to blame? (Regarding* The Kreutzer Sonata*)* [*Ch'ja vina? (Po povodu «Krejtserovoj sonaty»)*], which was written between 1891 and 1894, though not published until a century later. The following comments are taken from *My Life* (V.65), from the year 1891:

> While I was proofreading *The Kreutzer Sonata* for Volume XIII — a story I had never liked on account of its coarse treatment of women on the part of Lev Nikolaevich — it made me think about writing my own novel on the subject of *The Kreutzer Sonata*. This thought kept coming to me more and more frequently, to the point where I could no longer restrain myself...

The first mention of *Who is to blame?* is in her diary of 21 September 1891: "Yesterday I wrote an extensive outline for a story, which I should very much like to write, but shall not be able to" (Vol. I, p. 211).

In the manuscript of her story, she adds a subtitle: *Written by the wife of Leo Tolstoy,* while in the drafts she employs a number of variants of the title — e.g., *Davno ubita* [*Slain long ago*], *Kak ona ubita* [*How she was slain*], or *Vinovata li ona?* [*Is she to blame?*] — and this variant of the subtitle: *Dedicated to the hero of* The Kreutzer Sonata.

---

23 On this point, extant accounts are more or less negative in tone, needlessly defending Tolstoy and treating it as a conjugal polemic, a personal accusation against her husband. Especially derisive is Prussakova's (1995) article "O nekotorykh strannostjakh naivnosti" ["On certain peculiarities of naïveté"]; Zverev and Tunimanov's (2006) book *Lev Tolstoj* also betrays a strangely condescending attitude, failing to take into account either her significant literary talent or her own declaration: "If this whole story [i.e., *The Kreutzer Sonata*] had been based on me and my relations with my husband, I would scarcely have petitioned for censorship clearance" (SAT, Diary of 1 June 1881, as quoted in *My Life,* p. xxxiv). In fact, her dislike of *The Kreutzer Sonata* did not prevent her from taking her petition for censorship clearance to the Tsar himself (see V.92). A somewhat more balanced view is offered by Tat'jana Komarova, Tat'jana Nikiforova, Julija Shumikhina (Bajkova) and Pavel Basinskij, though even some of them tend to view it more as a valuable document for understanding the Tolstoys' family life rather than a work of literature deserving of critical analysis.

SAT offers several descriptions of her work on the story, perhaps most tellingly in *My Life* (VI.42) under the heading "My story and my son Lëva's reaction to it":

Just as in the country, so too in Moscow, where I was living, I filled my long, lonely evenings with writing the long story I had started in response to Lev Nikolaevich's *Kreutzer Sonata*. My son Lëva, upon hearing of its contents, strongly criticised me for it and even wrote to me from Petersburg on 27 November 1892:

As Papa's wife, as the mother of us all, someone who couldn't possibly carry out her appointed task better than she does and is still not finished with it, you have earned the right to high praise indeed. But if you should begin to corrupt this position of yours through various outpourings of your groundless and unfair annoyances in [the form of] a poorly written story, you will be departing from your chief, exalted purpose as a wife and mother, since there will no longer be any love here, and you will knock yourself off track.

I don't know whether my son was right or not. I do know that I began writing this story because, without any provocation, all eyes of the public, from the Tsar's right down to Lev Nikolaevich's brother Sergej Nikolaevich's, were focused on me. They began to feel sorry for me as the victim of a jealous husband, and a few of them began to suspect something. I wanted to give a more accurate portrayal of an honest woman and her ideals of love, in contrast to male materialism.

One of the central themes of *Who is to blame?* is the folly of allowing man's higher spiritual capabilities to be held hostage to the flesh.

The narrative consists of two parts. Part I describes how the young, idealistic, pure and innocent heroine, Anna Il'meneva, becomes acquainted with her future husband, Prince Prozorskij; it describes their courtship, marriage and early conjugal life up to the birth of their first child (an event dated approximately a year after the beginning of the story).

The action in Part II begins ten years later and covers the period of a year or so up to the death of the heroine at the hands of her husband. The narrative is told in the voice of an objective author-narrator, without any suggestion that the characters are drawn from real life. Almost twice her age (as was Lev Nikolaevich when he married Sofia Andreevna), the prince, who has imagined himself to be a great philosophical thinker, grows increasingly disappointed with his equally unhappy wife. The rift between the two increases with the birth of their children and a visit by the prince's friend Bekhmetev (evidently based on the author's close friend in real life, Prince Leonid Dmitrievich Urusov), whom he hasn't seen in twelve years. While previously Anna was racked by jealousy over her husband's earlier conquests of women, after Bekhmetev's visit it is the prince's turn to be jealous over his wife's relationship to this quiet, unassuming, artistic 'intruder'. In a fit of rage, he fatally wounds Anna, who, before she dies, proclaims her innocence and forgives the prince.

The few scholars that have made reference to Tolstaya's story in their studies tend to overemphasise the autobiographical association of Anna with the author and the many parallels between the two, as well as (naturally) the 'undeniable' similarity between Prince Prozorskij and Count Tolstoy.

Upon examining the details which distinguish the characters in the story from their real-life prototypes, however, one discovers not only that there are far more differences than similarities, but that the characters have a deeper significance in terms of understanding the narrative. What at first glance appears to be simply a feature of literary style eventually takes on a broader signification and opens up a whole new set of questions.

Above all, it becomes clear that Prince Prozorskij is no Lev Tolstoy. He turns out to be a man merely obsessed with writing, who enjoys pretending to be a great philosopher, writing "articles devoid of any kind of originality, comprising nothing but a rehash of old, worn-out themes and thoughts." The author herself reveals him to be quite indifferent to all the issues of public education which Tolstoy championed his whole life. Nor is the prince even close to being the husband of Sofia Andreevna Tolstaya. He is not even a caricature or a watered-down version of Tolstoy, but someone who is much simpler in his spiritual make-up.

This is significant in that the author, in effect, brings her character closer to reality by refusing to denigrate the image of her hero. Prince Prozorskij is not so much a specific individual as a generalised image which the author can associate with a great many men.

Here is a clear discrepancy between the heroine and her prototype, particularly in the former's somewhat exaggerated penchant for the quality of reverie and winsomeness, on which the reader is urged to side with Anna's mother and sister, as well as the prince. It is in some ways a reflection of SAT's own sense of self-irony when it comes to the frivolities of youth. Indeed, it may be seen that there is a somewhat closer relationship between Anna and the author than between the prince and LNT.

Yet the heroine is endowed with certain specific qualities which Tolstaya would scarcely associate herself with, especially in the eyes of others. There are frequent references in Part II, for example, to Princess Prozorskaja's unique physical beauty, even to the point of being a *femme fatale*. While her graceful and lively charms depicted in Part I may be seen as an innocent gift of her youth, in Part II she is prevented from realising her natural seductive potential only by her internal moral compass, along with her early marriage and move to the countryside. This portrayal is not so much reminiscent of Sofia Tolstaya with her firm adherence to moral standards as of Anna Karenina, who fails to come to grips with the passions in her soul — a failure that proves fatal to Tolstoy's unfortunate heroine.

In terms of ideological significance, *Who is to blame?* goes far beyond classification as a simple response to *The Kreutzer Sonata*. It is a polemic less about the battle of the sexes than about the nature of egotism. In *The Kreutzer Sonata*, Tolstoy's facile hand draws Pozdnyshev as a suffering and intelligent egotist, while in *Who is to blame?* Tolstaya declines to portray egotism in any broader connotations than its own kind of vice, thereby, apparently, refraining from complicating the matter further where a simple explanation is sufficient.

Not surprisingly, Tolstaya's polemic may be seen as extending beyond a single work of Tolstoy's, exploring themes such as the attempt at reconciliation between self-love and individual aspirations to unite with the world, or the search for intelligent compromise between natural self-interest and extreme dissatisfaction with the personality imprisoned in one's self. Perhaps Tolstaya is associating the character of the prince not so much with Tolstoy himself as with the (mainly male) major characters of his principal works. Her narrative, however, is far from idealising either women in general or her heroine in particular.

A few words about some obvious 'Tolstoy aspects' of the narrative might be in order here. Undoubtedly, certain thematic developments are justified to such an extent by the narrative's internal logic that any comparisons may be seen as completely co-incidental, and any analogies drawn therefrom might appear 'stretched'. This could be said, for example, of the prince's hunting trip in Chapter 1 of Part II, or of Anna's going off for a sleigh-ride with Bekhmetev in Chapter 6. Any analogies with the hunting scene or Nikolaj and Sonja's sleigh scene on the Svjatki in *War and peace* may appear superficial.

There are, however, certain aspects which would cause any reader familiar with Tolstoy's works to go immediately beyond an analogy with *The Kreutzer Sonata* and be reminded of his other works.

For example, the first sentence in Chapter 7 of Part II reads as follows: "As always happened with Anna, whenever she approached her house, she felt an increasing anxiety over whether she would find her children at home safe and sound." Assuming that the heroine had been living in the country for the past nine years or more (before this winter her husband "had never seen her in [Moscow's] high society"), the question presents itself as to how Anna could have experienced such a homecoming in the past. Perhaps the Prozorskijs would go to visit neighbours and stay overnight with them? It is by no means illogical to suppose that Anna's homecoming here echoes Nikolaj Rostov's first visit home from army service in *War and peace* and Tolstoy's description (which is now almost legendary) of the hero's increasing inner tension as his sleigh approaches his native home.

Another opportunity for comparison arises from the ballroom scene at the end of Chapter 4 of Part II. The 'Anna at the ball' scene speaks for itself, but the fact that her husband stays home only heightens comparisons with the conflicts in Tolstoy's second major novel.

There are more interesting, delicate moments, too. In Tolstoy criticism one rightly finds frequent comments on the writer's attention to details of the body. One example frequently cited is the case of "Bolkonsky's hand." It is interesting to note that when Prince Prozorskij is introduced right at the beginning of the whole narrative, the readers' attention is immediately drawn to his hand. Anna "looked askance at the outstretched masculine hand of the guest who had just risen from behind the tea-table, and then into his eyes...". One can observe many subsequent references to the author's attention to her character's various body parts throughout the narrative.

An important and rather obvious indication of the 'Tolstoy school' of writing is SAT's attention to her characters' inner state and the setting up of certain thematic collisions. These form the basis of both the conflict between the protagonist's inner state and outward circumstances and the failure of those around the heroine to understand her inner state, as well as the lack of correspondence between their behaviour and her expectations.

The confrontation with Dmitrij Ivanovich in Chapter 2 of Part I, or the couple's unsuccessful attempts at reconciliation in Chapter 8 of Part I illustrate this characteristic: "Anna realised that the reconciliation was not proceeding at all the way she fervently desired".

Naturally, all such aspects are a reflection of the broader concept of misunderstandings between people, upon which the whole conflict of the narrative is based. Yet one may still catch glimpses here of Tolstoy's creative approach.

Similarly, in Chapter 4 of Part II one can notice a purely Tolstoyan irony in the lack of correspondence between the thoughts of Prince Prozorskij and his resultant mood on the one hand and the perception of his behaviour by "a famous writer" on the other. This scene looks literally as though it had been taken right out of the pages of one of Tolstoy's works — not *The Kreutzer Sonata* with Pozdnyshev's nervous and angry voice, but specifically those works where Tolstoy makes no move to conceal his evident authorial presence.

One is especially reminded of the many times Tolstaya transcribed (and, of course, read and edited) episodes of *War and peace* in which Tolstoy gave full rein to his sense of irony. Still, such episodes are common enough in many of his other works.

There is no record of Tolstoy's own reaction to *Who is to blame?*. We do know that many of Tolstaya's acquaintances enjoyed it in manuscript form. Tolstaya herself did not show much interest in having it published. In *My Life* (V.65), she comments: "I did write this story, but it never saw the light of day and is now lying among my papers at the Historical Museum in Moscow." As mentioned earlier, the novella was finally published only in 1994 and reprinted in Remizov 2010.

NARRATIVE: *SONG WITHOUT WORDS*

Shortly after the death of her beloved youngest son Vanechka in 1895, Sofia Andreevna Tolstaya began writing her story *Pesnja bez slov* [*Song without words*], which remained unpublished until recently (in Remizov and Gladkova 2010). She worked on it fairly consistently up to 1898 and introduced some changes in the early 1900s.

Again, this project arose out of a personal circumstance — her tendency to seek refuge in music from the burdening thoughts and experiences that were driving her to despair. She would attend musical evenings when she could, but also relished sitting at the piano keyboard herself. Part of her much-needed solace after Vanechka's death and her ever-increasing conjugal conflicts came from an infatuation with the composer Sergej Ivanovich Taneev, a frequent visitor to the Tolstoy home, which provoked her husband's jealousy.

Both her diaries and many passages in *My Life* bear witness to her love of music and her intense interest in Taneev both as an artist and as a man. For example, in her diary entry of 4 June 1897 she wrote:

> I had a difficult conversation this morning with Lev Nikolaevich concerning S[ergej] I[vanovich] Taneev. The same intolerable jealousy.[24] I had throat spasms. I bitterly reproached my agonising husband and was tormented by depression the whole day. ... After going for a swim, I met with Taneev, and this turned out to be a sad reminder of the happy meetings the two of us enjoyed last year. After dinner he played some of his romances [on the piano] for Tanja. I love both his music and his character: calm, noble and kind. ... [Later] he kindly asked me to go for a walk with him, and we had a wonderful time...
>
> Taneev played two of the pieces from Mendelssohn's *Song without words*, which stirred the depths of my soul.[25]

Note also her entry of 7 June 1897: "I yearn for music, I yearn to play myself, but don't have the time. Just today I played two of the pieces from Mendelssohn's *Songs without words*. Oh, what songs those are! One of them in particular has left its mark on my heart."

Or, still another entry, this one from 23 July 1897:

24 For Tolstoy's reaction to his wife's infatuation with Taneev, see Basinskij 2010: 426–32 and Zverev and Tunimanov 2006: 530–40. There are 62 letters from SAT to Taneev, written between 1895 and 1910 (including 17 in 1897 and 18 in 1898). There is nothing in them to suggest anything beyond a platonic relationship between the two, along with SAT's concern over the pianist's health and activities. The letters do reveal a need on SAT's part to have Taneev close to her (witness the many pleas to come visit her). A few of SAT's letters were published in *Letopisi Gosudarstvennogo Literaturnogo Muzeja*, kn. 2 (Moscow, 1938): 247–54.

25 Over his brief lifetime Felix Mendelssohn (1809–1847) produced eight collections of what he called *Songs without words*, each comprising six short, lyrical, romantic piano pieces, many of which could be described as sentimental 'mood music'. It is not known exactly which 'songs' are referred to here in SAT's diaries.

They've been criticising me over Sergej Ivanovich, too. Well, let them! What this man has given me has been such a rich and joyful contribution to my life. He has opened the door for me into the world of music, where only after hearing his playing have I found any comfort and joy. His music has indeed brought me back to life — a life which vanished altogether after the death of Vanechka. And his meek and joyful presence has brought me spiritual tranquility. And now, each time after seeing him, I immediately feel so calm and comforted in my soul. And they all think I'm in love [with him]! Honestly, they really know how to demean everything! But I'm old, now, and such words and thoughts are not worthy of me.

In other diary entries from 1897 to 1900, she details the writing process and her special preoccupation with *Song without words*. Tolstaya preferred this story to *Who is to blame?*, considering it especially close to her heart. In her diary of 24 October 1897 (*Diaries*, I: 311), she wrote concerning *Song without words*: "In the evening I started the first chapter of the narrative. I feel it will turn out fine. But who can I give it to for an evaluation? I want to write and publish it with complete anonymity."

The process of writing this particular work shows Tolstaya's intense and serious approach to her writing — witness the following comments from her diaries:

> *18 June 1897* — I pondered the narrative and wrote out some notes (I: 251).
>
> *12 September 1897* — I played a bit in the evening and jotted down a few notes for the narrative which I really feel like writing (I: 296).
>
> *27 November 1897* — I read, i.e., I once again read over Parts I and II of Beethoven's biography, then worked on my own narrative which I'm not at all happy with (I: 322).
>
> *4 July 1898* — The other day I stayed up until three o'clock in the morning, working with pleasure on my narrative *Song without words* (I: 396).
>
> *31 December 1899* — I live from day to day; I have no goal, no seriousness of life either, and so I feel frightfully weary. I am writing a long novel, and that does interest me (I: 456).

Tolstaya kept working on (and correcting) her story until 1900. In *My Life* (VIII.6) she notes: "Among the activities which gave me pleasure was story-writing. I got really involved in this, correcting and revising, sometimes sitting up nights working on it. My basic underlying thought in writing a story was that the art should remain pure, unspoilt by any human passions or complications in one's personal life."

In her *Autobiography*[26] (1921: 156) she further elaborates the central idea of her work in these terms (the passage is also reproduced with some variation in *My Life*, VII.29):

---

26 Published in the journal *Nachala,* Nº 1 (1921).

I was drawn to write this story by an impression I had at a concert of some girls who displayed a rather strange treatment of a famous pianist [Józef Hofmann (1876–1957)]. They kissed his galoshes, tore his handkerchief to pieces and engaged in overall wild behaviour. Where was the music in all this? The point I'm trying to make is this, that one's attitude to art, just as to Nature, should remain virginal — i.e., pure, without interference from the baser human passions.

The plot of SAT's narrative *Song without words* is quite straightforward and draws upon her own platonic relationship with the composer Sergej Ivanovich Taneev.[27] Her heroine is Aleksandra Alekseevna (Sasha), married from a young age to a man named Pëtr Afanas'evich, who loves his wife, but seems not to understand her soul. They have a son named Alësha.

The story begins with the heroine, who is addressed and referred to mainly as Sasha, going to the Crimea to see her dying mother (an event the author experienced in real life). In the story, the death of her mother leaves the heroine utterly grief-stricken, even suicidal, far more so than might be expected over the death of someone so advanced in age. The reader suspects that the real cause of the grief lies deeper. One cannot help but be reminded of the author's own deep sorrow over the recent death of her favourite son, Vanechka, at the tender age of seven. Indeed, the whole opening scene is described so realistically, especially in the attention to small details, that one is obliged to conclude the author must have experienced it first-hand.

Throughout the text, the author portrays her heroine as a woman of extraordinary character, self-confidence and resilience — an assessment shared by the other personages in the story. Sasha is evidently a woman who knows what she wants and accustomed to giving orders she expects to be carried out, including to her husband. She is initially portrayed as "beautiful," but later also as "light-headed," "flighty," "passionate" and "powerful."

Her "tragic beauty" is noted even by the doctor treating her in hospital in the story's final scene. We learn that her husband cannot bear to live without his "cheery and clever Sasha," but she has also attracted the advances of two other men — a young fellow named Kurlinskij and a friend of her husband's named Mukhatov.

Yet Sasha's beauty is not merely on the surface, but extends to her inner nature as well. The quality of kindness is demonstrated, for example, in her

27 For a further elaboration of SAT's relationship with Taneev, see especially *My Life,* III.39, also the chapter on "Sergej Ivanovich Taneev" in S. L. Tolstoy 1956: 343–58. Here Sergej L'vovich writes (p. 350): "I can write about my mother's infatuation without hiding anything, as there is nothing to hide. She herself spoke about this several days before her death to her daughter Tat'jana. Neither I, nor my sisters or brothers ever had any doubt that our mother's words were true, and that in her relationship to Taneev they didn't even have 'a handshake that could not have been witnessed in public'. Still, this infatuation of our mother's was annoying to us, as it was very upsetting to our father."

invitation to Kurlinskij's mother to stay with her while visiting her son in Moscow. Not only that, but she herself summons up the courage to face her fears of mentally ill patients enough to pay a visit to Kurlinskij in hospital, attempting to convince him not to refuse military service.[28] Her success in doing so reveals the persuasive power of her personality. Other feats of competence include helping a deliveryman move a heavy barrel of water, helping out a pregnant mother by carrying her capricious little girl across the street, treating sick peasants[29] and expertly managing her household and financial affairs. All this time Sasha immerses herself, like the author, in philosophical study (Seneca and Epictetus, for example)[30] and meditation. Philosophical views on life and death become even more important to her following her mother's passing.

Sasha's role as mother to her son Alësha, however, is minimal. In contrast to the author's own lifetime of devotion to her children, motherhood does not figure prominently in the story, playing second fiddle to the much more prominent relationship with a composer she becomes infatuated with through his music, as well as her infatuation with music itself. Indeed, her son has little or no influence on any other aspect of the story.

Aside from suggesting a sense of artificiality, Sasha's portrayal as the 'ideal woman' is reminiscent of SAT's approach to a similar 'ideal woman' in her novella *Who is to blame?*. Her husband comes across as a kind and decent fellow, but she is irritated by his obsession with day-to-day earthly concerns (gardening, insurance companies) at the expense of any kind of spiritual life. His passionate attachment to his garden symbolises man's attraction to earthly rather than spiritual matters. His whole joy of life comes from raising plants, reaping a harvest and enjoying the fruits of his labours, in contrast to his wife's attraction to more intellectual and spiritual pursuits.

For example, on her journey to visit her dying mother, the rhythmic rumble of the train wheels evokes a particular melody in her head, which far outweighs any enjoyment of a meal when the train stops at a station — she simply "wolfed down some greasy cabbage soup without any real gusto."

As time passes, Sasha displays more indifference to her surroundings, she frets and cries. While this is mitigated for a time by her attraction to the beauty of Nature (for example, she gets a glimmer of hope by gazing at the planet Venus in the night sky), her depression inevitably returns.

Eventually the action moves to Sasha's country dacha, where it turns out that the neighbouring dacha is occupied by none other than a musician. Her first impulse, however, is to shy away from company and maintain her isolation.

28 Cf. SAT's visit to actor L. A. Sulerzhitskij in a mental hospital — *My Life*, VII.4.
29 Cf. SAT's treating sick peasants at Yasnaya Polyana — *My Life*, III.62.
30 Cf. SAT's philosophical studies described in *My Life*, III.38 and III.116.

One evening, while meditating on her sorrows on her balcony, she hears the sounds of one of Mendelssohn's *Songs without words* coming from next door and is immediately captured by the melody in a most unexpected way. The music "spoke to Sasha's despairing soul in tender, caressing tones and offered her both comfort and delight." For the first time in a long while she smiles and feels a sense of peace in her heart. In the ensuing improvisation she recognises the melody that was running through her head on the train. This frightens her, and she hurries into the house, where in a state of ecstasy she greets her husband.

This is a turning point in Sasha's life. She begins following her neighbour's every move in the expectation of hearing more of his music, which has now become for her the only channel of escape from her depression, enchanting her by its beauty, showing her a higher sense of life and affording her the strength to go on living.

There is where the leitmotif of the whole narrative begins, namely, Sasha's love for her dacha neighbour, the musician and composer, whose name is Ivan Il'ich. In the main, the story is told from the heroine's point of view, but the author also gives us some portrayal, albeit in brief brushstrokes, of the composer's reaction.

The neighbour befriends Sasha's husband, Pëtr Afanas'evich — a development which serves to exacerbate her feelings of guilt over her obsession with his music, even though there is nothing she can do about the situation.

The theme of *music,* which runs throughout the whole narrative, starts with the tune that runs through Sasha's mind on an earlier train trip to the Crimea. Ivan Il'ich's playing evokes in her some deep, prayerful, metaphysical feelings:

And Beethoven, where and how could he possibly sense these feelings in Sasha's heart? He understood everything, and the performer has understood Beethoven, and I understand both of them, I feel them, I love them… along with the thoughts of God, of spiritual joy, of eternity, of death and immortality, of everything outside of space and time; of my deceased mother, who has passed into this eternity. All these thoughts she accepted joyfully — the pain of loss, the chaos of nagging doubts as to human life and death, together with all the sufferings, temptations and evil — all of this became as clear to her as a bright sky after a storm, illuminating and refreshing Nature with the sun's own rays.

Undergoing a catharsis, she feels like kneeling before the man who has been able to bring about such a transformation in her soul.

Sasha realises that here at the dacha she is the only listener capable of truly understanding and appreciating the depths of his musical genius and power of expression:

… she literally opened her heart to perceiving new artistic impressions. She caught and took in everything offered by the collaboration of these two geniuses — the composer and the performer. It was a kind of bliss she had never before experienced in her life.

And of that there is no question in the reader's mind, so convincingly does the author describe her impressions of the various musical pieces. It is not so much a simple listening to somebody's playing, but becomes an actual existential experience, a reaching down into new, unexplored depths of being.

She acquires a new zest for life. She is no longer bothered by her former irritations. Quite to the contrary, she wants to be kinder to everyone. She lives in anticipation of the next time she hears him play and exults in her new-found love for music. It is during one of these times that Sasha suddenly comes to the realisation that "at that moment Ivan Il'ich had taken complete possession of her, and this possession of her soul was far stronger and far more significant than any possession of her body."

As the summer nears its end, she is obliged to contemplate her return to Moscow. Ivan Il'ich gets ready to go to the Crimea, but keeps putting it off. Sasha cannot bear to part from him. She has a nervous breakdown and decides to go off to a nunnery.

Sasha has loved monasteries and nunneries ever since childhood and dreamt of going off to one even before she made plans to enter the Conservatory. The narrative includes quite a number of references to religion. The heroine pays a visit to the Troitse-Sergieva Lavra to make confession and find spiritual peace. The author is particularly observant in her description here, and gives vivid and memorable details not only of the monastic scene (including a meal), but also of the journey there, riding in a horse-drawn cab through spring-time Moscow and encountering a crowd at the railway terminal. On the whole, however, the visit to the nunnery turns out to be just as mundane as the rest of the narrative and does not have much bearing on the heroine's principal focus as described above.

The same comment applies to the "Nunnery" chapter, where Tolstaya describes her visit to a charitable dinner at a convent.[31] The poetry of the monastic life appeals to her, the idea of service and contemplation of the Divine, renunciation of fleshly life and spiritual self-perfection. We are not told specifically what Sasha finds poetic in the monastic scene, but one gets the impression that it is rather the aesthetic view of an outsider, the view of one unable to comprehend the full significance of monastic life.

Indeed, it is plain that neither philosophy nor religion really works for Sasha. Her path toward divine enlightenment lies through more aesthetic

---

31 Cf. SAT's visit to such a dinner at the Novodevichij Nunnery in *My Life*, VI.100.

experiences. Hence the tremendous influence exerted on her by a talented composer and performer. For her he is more than just a talent, more than just a religious person, he is a "priest of art" (according to the title of one of the chapters). He is a servant of the Divine, capable of being perceived by the heroine, a spiritual leader and teacher, able to touch base with the higher world and lead others behind him — something she has never found in any church. This to her is a real priest, this is true religion! And in this misperception, it may be considered, lies her real tragedy.

Upon returning from the nunnery to the dacha, Sasha finds a farewell note from Ivan Il'ich, written "with cold and awkward expression," at the same time dedicating a romance to her. She stays on at the dacha until the end of the summer, absorbed by Nature and music, feeling herself free from wrong desire.

The days pass by in tedious monotony, but with a clear conscience and a sense of duty fulfilled. Several days later she decides to take a look at the composer's new romance, and discovers so much passion in it that it simply overwhelms her. Frightened by her own thoughts, she asks God to save her. In looking over some dried flowers which capture the essence of her whole summer, the heroine realises that she has fallen in love, and senses tragic consequences ahead. She bids farewell to the dacha life which has been so dear to her heart, and heads back to Moscow.

The titles of most of the remaining chapters are indicative of various stages of Sasha's tragedy and explain how everything happens: "Broken," "Resigned," "Symphony," "Jealousy," "The last sighs of the song," and "Oblivion".

Finally it happens: Ivan Il'ich returns from the Crimea, drops in to see Sasha in Moscow and ends up in her bedroom.

At one point, in an effort to retrieve a ball of yarn, Ivan Il'ich crawls under her bed and finds himself embarrassed by "the mysterious intimacies of the female psyche" — the bed and other objects in her room. He becomes withdrawn and stern. This time, while playing *Song without words,*

> she suddenly realised that the same sounds which initially gave her such peace and joy were now evoking fright and an emotion of pain and torture. They took over her whole body and facilitated his possession of her. Art had left the realm of the abstract, transformed into something quite earthy. It had lost its purity and virginity.

The author comments that in Ivan Il'ich's eyes, this evening with Sasha was a minor episode in his life, while it was a whole epoch in hers.

Following Ivan Il'ich's departure, Sasha reflects on the past summer's events and realises the extent of her obsession with him, along with her loss of genuine life and purity. At this point there is no use in struggling against it — she had no longer any choice but to give in to her passion. She does recognise that in the beginning it was a call to love through music:

And Sasha fell in love with music by virtue of this call. What she didn't know, and had not yet glimpsed, that this was also a call to life. It was only much later, after she had got to know the talented musician better, that she fell in love with him as a man. Any true, good and powerful love always begins in the realm of the abstract and only afterward carries over into the domain of passion.

So is she to blame for this? Wasn't it fate itself that inexorably and blindly led her step by step to the moment of Sasha's severe self-confession?

It is worthwhile to examine, in particular, Sasha's perception of Ivan Il'ich as a man. She is intrigued by him to the point of obsession. She very much wants to penetrate the soul of one who has the ability to reach such heights of spiritual creativity. Several times it is mentioned how "the heroine always had the desire to penetrate this mysterious, closed-in soul, but she never managed to do so."

Outwardly he is nothing to look at. He is described as having somewhat "darting eyes" and "a large head ... his hair thinning on top and greying around the temples." He doesn't seem all that young, in terms of age. The author describes him as a peasant recluse, accustomed to following a set pattern of activity each day.

We are given repeated hints that while Sasha is excited by Ivan Il'ich, he himself is a confirmed bachelor, and adheres to a strict routine in everything, taking pains to avoid any kind of excitement, preferring to confine his passions to his artistic endeavours. Upon learning that Sasha has gone off to a monastery, he attempts to find relief from his "sorrow" in musical creativity, composing a romance and dedicating it to Sasha.

Ivan Il'ich cherishes his peace and quiet above all else, which allow him to pursue his music uninterrupted. He shows no special interest in life itself. It is only during his playing that Ivan Il'ich is transformed: he becomes strong and powerful, and tunes out everything around him.... While playing, the author tells us, "Ivan Il'ich's face changed completely. His restrained excitement, seriousness and the determined expression on his face made him look almost handsome. It was as if he were conducting a whole orchestra with the powerful, precise movements of his splendid arms..."

But just as soon as he stops playing, everything goes back to the way it was before.

For Sasha, Ivan Il'ich remains a mystery to the end. He does not reveal to her either his feelings or his inner essence. It is only by his musical expression that the heroine has any idea of what he must be experiencing in the depths of his soul.

Following this, Sasha comes out of her period of suffering. Dreams of mutual co-operation in the service of music lift her spirits significantly.

After Ivan Il'ich's departure for St. Petersburg, however, Sasha is beside herself, she misses him so much. Her health deteriorates. In an effort to compensate for her loss, she takes to her piano-playing with a vengeance and makes good progress, but her feelings of longing persist. When they meet upon his return, she makes a scene when she learns that he was in the company of a female singer from the provinces on the night of his triumph.

Yet at the same moment she tells herself:

> No, I don't want to... I can't... start up a miserable romance with this man. I always love purity above anything else. Let him remain a pure priest of his art, let him serve it, let him keep his soul chaste and calm, permeated with that high art that he serves. And my life may perish, but it will perish unblemished either by illegitimate love or by the sin of his love, which may fetter and destroy this composer-genius's whole life!

From that time on the heroine resolves to overcome the feelings of love within herself and avoid any encounters with her beloved. Ivan Il'ich, on his part, takes this as a minor loss, with the added benefit of less distraction from his music. For her, life has completely lost its meaning. She dreams of her beloved, analyses his music, trying to feel the emotion he has put into the notes. Family life has become a nightmare for both spouses, and Sasha feels sorry for her husband. Finding her home-life unbearable, she runs away. Standing on a bridge, she glimpses the filthy water of the Moskva River, and begins spouting nonsense about the polluting of everything on earth.

The author infers that the heroine is going out of her mind as a result of this unhappy love. She sits beneath Ivan Il'ich's windows, listening to him play a Chopin *Nocturne*, which made "something break in her for all time." Sasha runs home through the streets with mournful cries, oblivious to everyone, and starts playing the piano. This is by no means a portrayal of real insanity; instead, it is the portrayal of a hysteric, drawn out by the heroine's own desire. She prefers to hide away in a hospital rather than live at home and struggle with an unhappy love. It appears that she is no longer aware of her surroundings or the people she talks with, and fidgets with her fingers as though playing the piano.

From that day forward Sasha abandons everything in her life. ... The *Song* of her love for Ivan Il'ich had been sung to the end without words, and this had torn her life apart. Having played out this song in her heart with all its tender and passionate phrasings, Sasha is still faced with the three final sighs marking the completion of Mendelssohn's *Song without words* in G Major,[32] with which her own beautiful young life must end... The first sigh is one of hopeless love, the second — a sigh of love on the part of a purified soul, while the third is a sigh of quiet joy. Then *pianissimo, morendo* — and everything is silenced for good...

---

32 Only two of Mendelssohn's *Songs without words* [Lieder ohne Worte] are listed as being written in G Major, both from Book 5, Opus 62 (1842–44). These are N° 1 (*Andante espressivo*) and N° 4 (*Allegro con anima*).

Sofia Andreevna seems to have crafted the whole narrative to bring out precisely these three stages: the soul is led to higher bliss through suffering and purification. The impression, however, is the exact opposite: in an effort to maintain her moral purity, yet at the same time finding herself unable to attain her desires, the heroine goes off into a world of infantile fantasy, allowing her husband to both take care of their child and pay for her stay at the clinic. Sasha takes absolutely no thought for how her son is going to live without his mother. All she knows is that she just can't go on living as before. In place of a suffering and purified heart we see uncontrollable egocentric hysterics. Overall, the descriptions of Sasha's insanity are theatrical and unconvincing, and represent the weakest element of the narrative.

As to Ivan Il'ich, the author attempts to create a portrayal of a 'priest of art' who lives only for music, but either consciously (as she herself has been humiliated by his prototype) or unconsciously ends up creating a rather unpleasant picture. Ivan Il'ich comes across as an indifferent egotist who shows not the least bit of human compassion for someone who was once quite dear to him. He cannot help but admit that perchance he was somewhat to blame for the tragedy in Sasha's life, but he comes away with no regrets and lifts not even a finger of concern over the state of her health. He remains aloof and utterly indifferent to the tragedy of the family whose hospitality he so recently enjoyed over the summer. It is hard to see this other than as a portrait of a man on the moral decline.

In stark contrast to this portrait of a 'cold genius' is the portrayal of the heroine's 'down-to-earth' husband, although the latter stays pretty much in the background throughout the narrative. The heroine rarely thinks about him. However, when he finds out his wife has fallen in love with another, he takes the news as a mortal blow:

> Pëtr Afanas'evich wept so much that it seemed everything he ever lived by had been torn away from him forever. He had *never* before been jealous for his wife: such feelings were foreign to him. Trustful, affectionate and kind, he naïvely loved only Sasha all his life, and he could not brook any suggestion that she could fall in love with anybody else.

Her husband refuses to make any scenes. He does not forbid his wife to see Ivan Il'ich, but perceives the situation as a trial sent from above which they must pass through together. He feels genuinely sorry for his wife and tries to support her. Such noble conduct and spiritual discernment tell us that Pëtr Afanas'evich is not the frivolous and earth-bound creature his wife takes him to be. His kind and noble demeanour, like his spirituality, is not expressed in art but in everyday life, his deep appreciation of Nature, his relations with others and his love for his wife.

Of all the characters in the narrative it is the heroine's husband who evokes the greatest sympathy and respect.

Of course, Ivan Il'ich is not married, and cannot bear the weight of respon-sibility for Sasha's fate. But it may be considered disappointing that all he is left with at the end of the story is a heightened sense of egotism stemming from an excited adorer's glorification of his talent. He is no doubt in need of such appreciation, aware that his talent, though on a relatively high level, does not reach the heights of pure genius and that he will never enter the ranks of the world-famous composers whose works he so masterfully performs. He even hints at this, telling Sasha that in St. Petersburg he did not receive the kind of grand ovation accorded him in Moscow, where his audiences included so many of his friends.

Each of the three protagonists, in their individual way, contributes to the theme of *misperception,* which runs throughout the work.

While it can be argued that the story does offer some insight into the psy-chological make-up of the characters as they are revealed through various dramatic collisions, rather than mere description, and while the author con-vincingly shows how music, even the perception of one particular piece, can have a decisive effect on one's worldview, it is also true that the story suffers from excessive sentimentality and verbosity. As was probably the case with the novella *Who is to blame?,* it is unlikely that Sofia Andreevna ever showed it to her husband. This arouses a certain suspicion — namely, that it was after all an essentially autobiographical venture, aimed in part at placing at least some of the burden of guilt for their shaky marriage on her husband's shoulders and at the same time finding solace in the actual process of writing the narrative. Her diaries show that even though she was more willing to publish this story than *Who is to blame?,* she did not make any serious effort to do so.

POEM IN PROSE: *GROANINGS*
Throughout her life, Sofia Andreevna wrote poetry — usually on special occasions or dedicated to her favourite people. Her archives contain some fifty unpublished poems. As an example I should like to focus on a collec-tion of so-called 'poems in prose', published in 1904 under the collective title *Stony* [Groanings] in *Zhurnal dlja vsekh* [Everybody's Magazine], which pub-lished almost exclusively works by women writers. According to literary critic Mikhail Leonovich Gasparov (1987: 425):

> A poem in prose is a lyrical composition in poetic form, possessing such char-acteristics as conciseness, heightened emotions, [...] an overall emphasis on the expression of a subjective impression or experience, but without devices such as metre, rhythm or rhyme. As such, a poem in prose is not to be confused with hybrid forms combining poetry and prose with characteristics of metre, rhyth-mic prose or free verse.

It is quite probable that Tolstaya adopted this popular Russian genre at least in part through her familiarity with Ivan Turgenev's *Poems in Prose,* created primarily in the period between 1877 and 1882. Tolstaya was well acquainted with Turgenev; his works were read aloud in the Tolstoy home. What appealed to her in Turgenev's *Poems in Prose* was the reflection of his innermost thoughts and feelings, and his use of the authorial *I* as the mirror of his soul.

The majority of Sofia Andreevna's nine poems comprising *Groanings* are sketches drawn from the author's life, where reality intertwines with thoughts and experiences, merging into a single flow of consciousness. With some degree of literary artistry, the author succeeds in drawing the reader into feeling her experiences and sensations from an inner point of view, using a wide range of adjectives and metaphors, a multitude of expressive details and a series of perceptions of surrounding circumstances through various sensory organs, all integrated into a single stream.

From the subjective, poetic element of these compositions the author is able to convey to the reader the impression of someone who has gone through a great deal in her life and is able to share her experiences, attitudes and interpretations of life directly with the reader. Throughout the collection, these impressions are tied to an underlying theme of *juxtaposition* and *contrast* — between the crudity, filth and monotony of earthly life on the one hand and the heroine's soul-searchings for a more ethereal, spiritual world on the other — a world which transcends earthly life and its burdens. Such searchings liberate the soul from its bodily prison and give a taste of the freedom associated with heaven.

"THE RIVER"
The first poem in the cycle, entitled "The River" ["Reka"] describes how the heroine, while bathing in the river and seeing the reflection of the sky in the water, is carried away by her imagination into a reflected, ethereal world. A sudden gust of fear threatens her with drowning, bringing her back to reality and forcing her to make a grab for the shore (or earthly filth) in an effort to avoid death. Desire for an ideal (escape from the earth) is contrasted with the impossibility of reaching it. The beauty of her body is contrasted with its function as a cunning and enslaving trap for the soul — a prison that must eventually be cast off.

"AT THE NUNNERY" AND "IN THE CAVES"
Two of the poems — "At the Nunnery" ["V monastyre"] and "In the Caves" ["V peshcherakh"] are associated with religious themes. The former of these depicts the heroine's visit to a nunnery, where she encounters a nun praying for the taking away of sins. The character of the nun symbolises people who are capable, even in this life, of taking steps into the realm of the spirit and breaking down earthly barriers, reflecting the author's own attempts along this line. Still, the description is abstract and impersonal — while we are given a physical description of the nun, we are not privy to the author's deeper

relationship to her as a character, or to the effect of the scene described on the author's attitude to her own transgressions. There is an indication, however, that the author is already somewhat acquainted first-hand with the object of her seeking through her own inner refinement and asceticism.

The latter poem describes the heroine's visit to the caves of the Kievo-Pecherskaja Lavra (the author's visit to the Lavra [Monastery] is noted in *My Life,* Chapter VI.115). As she journeys through the underground tunnels, she is prompted to examine the role of toil and suffering on the soul's path to Paradise. Again, however, she is overcome by a sense of fear and suffocation. An elderly monk presents to her an image not unlike the nun of the first poem — that is, one who is able to overcome earthly attraction and evil even before leaving this world, and prompts her to imagine herself having feelings in this direction. As in the preceding poem, the author manifests herself through the suggestion of aesthetic feelings and imagination.

"AUTUMN"

The poem "Autumn" ["Osen'"] focuses primarily on an expressive depiction of Nature rather than people. It is the only one in the cycle where the author does not put in a personal appearance. Instead, the emphasis is on Nature's autumnal dying, paralleled by the night-time felling of trees by an elderly peasant and enhanced by a rhythmical repetition of sounds: *"Temno, sero, teplo, tikho"* [Dark, grey, warm, silent]. Following a snowstorm, which results in an elderly man's death, the next morning reveals a contrasting reality: Nature is newly covered by "the maiden-like purity of a snowy covering" and even the dead old man himself is transfigured, all covered in white by snow. The poem concludes with the words: "man's soul is illuminated, renewed by eternal life."

"FROST" AND "MELANCHOLY"

The next two poems — "Frost" ["Inej"] and "Melancholy" ["Toska"] (also translatable as "Depression") — are drawn from the author's experiences in love. Again, in "Melancholy", we see juxtaposition and contrast: the love is sweet but impossible, and therefore tragic: "...I want to see the one I love but he is not there, he has left because we weren't able to love each other", and so the only solution must be sought through a contrasting ethereal (or aesthetic) perception of the world.

Some of the description of the heroine's feelings in these poems comes across as rather melodramatic, for example: "I continue to pray with melancholy, tears and a loss of emotional strength." As though in response to her prayer, she is visited by the soul of her beloved and, just for a moment, she can feel this soul's caressing and tenderness. But then the moment is gone and the soul along with it. Two other images are then presented in parallel with this experience: first, a moth, which flies off just like the soul of the heroine's beloved, and then flutters with sticky paper clinging to its wings, symbolic of our earthly captivity.

In "Frost" the heroine meets the object of her love at a concert, where she comes across as both an inner and an outer contrast to the crowd. During a performance of Beethoven's Fifth Symphony, she is carried away by the music into that same ethereal world of beauty and the spirit, only to be brought back to earth with a thud during the interval:

> All at once there was a whole lot of noise and movement, people were trying to get somewhere… What's all the fuss about?.. Yes, that's the *interval*. All these people have suddenly raised themselves up, and the stupid, crude and senseless expressions on the faces of most of these earthly creatures annoy me. I close my eyes….

The heroine is taken aback by this reality, while the concert-goers around her find themselves on a different plane of thought, unable to share or even comprehend her feelings. And even though the select few given access to her feelings include her beloved, he, too, "laughs stupidly and flirts with a plump, creepy singer in a yellow outfit" (although what makes the singer "creepy" is not specified). The crowd is portrayed indiscriminately as a surly mass, leaving a distasteful impression of pride and self-admiration, and this in sharp contrast to the portrayal of herself as a picture of beauty and refinement ("Wrapped in the soft skins of a fur coat, my nimble earthly being darts down the stairs…."). While the conduct of her lover, who does not measure up to her standards, traumatises the heroine, once again she finds solace in an aesthetic perception of reality, just as the frost, by covering the earth, transforms the outward picture of reality:

> Everything is turning silver, everything's shimmering and glistening: everything unclean, uneven, sinful and ugly has all been covered with a pure, white covering. …. And I forget about my earthly feelings, and my heart aspires to reach out along with these fuzzy white threads, into infinite space and the pure world of virgin Nature…. And once again I hear the strains of Beethoven's Fifth ringing in my ears, and in my soul the music — this great art — has merged with Nature and become so magnificent, pure and exalted, like the far-off sky with its frost flying in the starry, transparent ether…. The earth has disappeared, along with earthly human feelings. My soul has been cleansed and risen toward God.

"THE POET"

Of all Sofia Andreevna's friends and acquaintances, few captured her heart and interest more than the poet Afanasij Afanas'evich Fet. Over and over again in *My Life* she makes reference to her high regard for him as a poet and a person, as well as his not-too-concealed attraction to her, mitigated largely by the poet's respect and admiration for her husband. She frequently cites his poems, some of which were written about her or dedicated to her. Fet's passing and his funeral were a sad occasion in the Tolstoy household, and form the subject of the seventh poem in this collection, "The poet" [Poèt].

Here Tolstaya portrays the poet as yet another of those rare individuals endowed with a higher spiritual insight into the world of beauty and harmony, an ability to understand and appreciate the creative process. This group naturally includes the heroine herself, who is introduced in the poem rather ethereally as "the beautiful, pale, delicate and tall figure of a woman, in a cloud of black transparent fabric."

By way of contrast, this ethereal figure is juxtaposed against a variety of other people, all portrayed as spiritless and indifferent to the poet and his creations: "…the affected sorrowful faces of those present have, with their respective lies, caused [me] to avert [my] gaze," whereupon, having "authoritatively halted with her hand the coffin lid", she places a rose on the poet's breast.

> A single moment… a single impulse of love has exposed the depressing lie of respectability with its cold, artificial, thunderous colours, with the same cold and thunderous speeches the hypocrites use, and life has sparked into flame above the dead silence.

This is an echo of the author's real-life action, as described in *My Life* (VI.43), where she gives a detailed description of both Fet's passing and the ensuing funeral. In the framework of her poem, she alone is deemed capable of sincerely understanding and appreciating the poet, which she does "authoritatively", demonstratively and independently.

"THE VISION" AND "THE CHILD"
The final two poems in the cycle — "The vision" ["Videnie"] and "The child" ["Rebënok"] — are a poetic expression of the author's feelings upon the loss of her son Vanechka in 1895. "The vision", moreover, makes reference to her depression over a husband who no longer loves her. As she passes through places associated with people close to her heart, she pictures them so vividly in her mind, it is as though she can actually see them. A rare moment of spiritual union with her husband affords her a glimpse of happiness, while at the spot where her deceased child used to play she recites the Lord's Prayer. Submitting to God's will — which, as she saw it, had both given and taken away her son — she is carried away to an otherworldly place where her soul can meet not only with his, but with the souls of all her loved ones and with God Himself.

The closing poem, "The child" (again dealing with Vanechka's passing), is the most devoid of literary pretensions. It is a simple yet penetrating portrayal of events from the point of view of the mother as an observer: we do not see her from the sidelines, nor are we privy to her inner sensations or feelings.

What is portrayed for us is the child's death at the same moment as he perceives something very important, and the mother's illumination in conjunction with this moment:

> But at that instant the exhausted, suffering mother understood everything: the significance and the sacredness of God's will, the inevitability of what happened, the submission to that higher will, and the bliss experienced by the boy's pure, departed soul.

Once again we see an echo from previous poems: the child's pure soul is transported "into the heavenly spiritual realm, where there are no groanings, weepings or sufferings… nor sorrows from earthly evil". The mother herself is similarly transported along with her son, reflecting her hopes of being reunited with him, in time, in this spiritual reality.

At the very close of this final poem in the cycle, we find mention of the groanings which will have no place in the eternal, spiritual world which the soul strives to attain. It is most interesting to note how the author has consciously crafted each of these poems in prose, each of which in its own slightly different way contrasts the 'groanings' of the suffering and exhausted earthbound soul with the world of beauty and spiritual perfection it is so desperate to claim for its own. This contrast is reflected in the pseudonym *Ustalaja* [Weary woman] used by the author for this collection.

CONCLUDING REMARKS

TOLSTAYA was always concerned that her side be heard. The persistent intrusion into their family life and criticism of her on the part of Tolstoy's disciple Vladimir Chertkov and his followers was often more than she could bear. This is amply confirmed not only in individual letters to her husband and other correspondents and her diaries, but also in *My Life*. Note, in particular, her epigraph to the latter, in which she stated: "...the longer I live, the more I see the accumulation of acute misunderstandings and false reports concerning my character, my life, and a great many topics touching upon me. And so ... I decided to set forth a description of my life..."

Concern about "her side" and "her legacy" can be seen (again, in part) in her own ideas regarding Tolstoy's *Kreutzer Sonata* — by writing her two novellas and hastily responding (in 1913) to literary historian Semën Afanas'evich Vengerov's request to write an autobiography. Finally, there are the letters. Only a few years after Tolstoy's passing, she published his letters to her, appending hundreds of her own editorial annotations.

The first edition, issued in 1913, comprised 656 letters in chronological order, while the second edition (1915), including seven additional letters, was titled *Letters of Count L.N. Tolstoy to his wife, 1862–1910* [*Pis'ma grafa L.N. Tolstogo k zhene, 1862–1910*].

In her preface to the first edition she offered this explanation for the timing:

> Before I leave this life to join my beloved in the spiritual realm to which he has departed, I should like to share with those who love and admire him something he gave me that is very dear to me, namely his letters to me, including details of our conjugal life of forty-eight years together, which was happy almost to the very end....

I was prompted to publish these letters, too, by my concern that after my death, which is probably not far off, people will (as usual) misinterpret and write falsely about our mutual husband-wife relationship. So let them find interest in and base their judgements on true and living sources, and not on conjecture, gossip and invention.

And may they look with compassion on someone who took upon her delicate shoulders something she was possibly not quite ready for at such an early age, namely, the task of being the spouse of a genius and a great man.

One copy of the second edition preserved in the Yasnaya Polyana archives is, in fact, a dismantled printer's copy, with a fresh sheet of paper inserted between each page by Sofia Andreevna herself, containing her annotations and commentaries. She began these in January 1919 and continued work on them up to her death in November of that year. They clearly reveal remarkable editorial skills.

In summing up Sofia Andreevna Tolstaya's literary life, a few concluding remarks are in order.

While SAT herself referred to most of her literary works as *skazki* (equivalent to 'tales' or 'fairy tales'), it is quite evident that she was reasonably comfortable in more than one genre — children's stories, narratives, novellas, poems in prose, rhyming poems, legends and folk-tales.

Through all these diverse writings taken as a whole, we can readily recognise several recurring traits. One is the confessional nature of her authorship — most obvious, of course, in her autobiographical works but also evident as an underlying foundation for her belletristic pieces discussed in this chapter.

First and perhaps foremost, in contrast to the idealised and stylised characters of some of her contemporaries, hers are drawn from people in her own milieu and translated directly onto the page with little attempt to mask their prototypes or employ traditional approaches to fictionalisation. Secondly, her stories are clearly presented from a feminine point of view, not only in her narrator's commentaries but also in giving precedence to the ideas and opinions of her female characters over those of the men she portrays.

We have seen the roots of her very first story (*Natasha*) in her own early encounters with her future husband, told from a young girl's point of view. We have seen the parallels between her *New primer* contributions and her personal experiences with her children — especially in the 'sparrow' story, which prominently features three female characters (three sisters). We have seen how *The skeleton-dolls* was drawn from her activities in putting on plays (very much a motherly activity) for the benefit of her children as well as children from the village of Yasnaya Polyana. And how in a later story from the same collection, the wall between fiction and biography completely breaks down in her brief but potent piece *Vanechka's life,* vivifying in words her child's brief existence as only a mother could.

In *Who is to blame?*, there are justifiable grounds for linking the personage of Bekhmetev to her trusty friend (and frequent visitor to Yasnaya Polyana) Prince Leonid Dmitrievich Urusov. Indeed, many of the Bekhmetev episodes in the story can be compared directly with real-life descriptions of Urusov from *My Life*. At the same time, Bekhmetev's presence and function in the story are entirely credible from a literary standpoint. Not only that, but SAT does not miss the opportunity to drive home the woman's perspective — namely, that it is not enough to love a woman simply for the pleasure of the flesh, but a woman's spiritual and moral aspirations must be fulfilled — and on a higher level than the flesh.

It will be remembered from the above discussion that SAT's self-admitted platonic relationship with pianist-composer Sergej Ivanovich Taneev finds transparent expression in the character of the pianist-composer Ivan Il'ich in her narrative *Song without words*. Here, again, it is not difficult to posit a scene-by-scene comparison between novel and autobiography. And here, too, Tolstaya approaches the story as a woman, emphasising, for example, that affairs of the soul are far more meaningful and powerful than affairs of the body.

Both SAT's confessional approach and the woman's point of view are embodied in the pseudonym she attached to her 'poem in prose', *Groanings* — that is, *Weary woman*. In Russian it is even more concisely expressed in the single word *Ustalaja,* comprised of the stem *ustal* combined with a clearly feminine grammatical ending. Time after time in *My Life* we encounter references to the author's own weariness as a woman whose cherished hopes for her own literary career are unfulfilled, overshadowed by the demands of running an estate and looking after a large family without the degree of moral and physical support that might be expected from any dutiful husband and father. Like her other writings, *Groanings* finds its centre in the world of women, perceiving both family and social life through feminine eyes.

Perhaps it is Tolstaya's ability to render her characters and their surroundings in a natural, 'unsophisticated' manner — with truthfulness and spontaneity — that make her stories easily readable and appealing to readers at all educational levels. Even though her personages may lack the deep psychological traits with which those created by her more famous husband are imbued, they are replete with undeniable human emotions and characteristics and find themselves in individual predicaments common to most human beings in the kind of society familiar to Russians, Europeans and North Americans. Tolstoy's opinion of her first story, *Natasha* — *"What energy of truth and simplicity!"* — can be equally applied to most of her literary output.

All told, Sofia Tolstaya's life and substantive literary works help give voice to an important example of a woman's perspective on late-nineteenth-century Russian history and literature — the point of view of a woman who has most certainly earned the right to be known as something far more than a famous man's wife. She emerges indeed as a highly independent, cultured, intelligent, professional woman who was well in advance of her time. From a transcriber of her husband's writings to translator, editor, publisher, as well as social activist and correspondent — not to mention a devoted mother and loyal wife, Sofia Andreevna Tolstaya can be seen growing into a fully-fledged author in her own right.

Illustration 1: Andrej Evstaf'evich Bers — father to SAT
Photo: M. B. Tulinov, Moscow, 1862

Illustration 2: Ljubov' Aleksandrovna Bers (*née* Islavina) — mother to SAT
Photo: 1860s

Illustration 3: Sofia Andreevna [Sonja] Bers (left)
and her sister Tat'jana Andreevna [Tanja] Bers
Photo: 1861

Illustration 4: Lev Nikolaevich Tolstoy — groom
Photo: M. B. Tulinov, Moscow, 1862

Illustration 5: Sofia Andreevna Bers — bride
Photo: M. B. Tulinov, Moscow, 1862

Illustration 6: Yasnaya Polyana — entrance gates (autumn)
Photo: Tolstoy Yasnaya Polyana Museum Estate

Illustration 7: Yasnaya Polyana — main house (summer, from the south-west)
Photo: Tolstoy Yasnaya Polyana Museum Estate

Illustration 8: The Tolstoys' home in Khamovniki Lane, Moscow

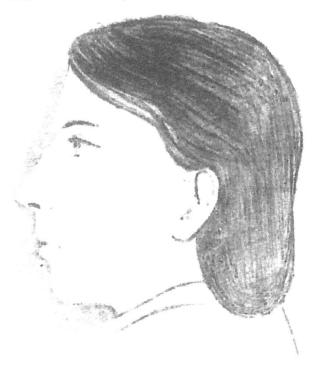

Illustration 9: Sofia Andreevna Tolstaya, pencil drawing by LNT, 1863

Illustration 10: SAT's desk at which she wrote and transcribed
Photo: N. V. Donskov, 2007

Illustration 11: *A new primer* (1875) and *A primer* (1872)
A new primer included several stories by SAT.

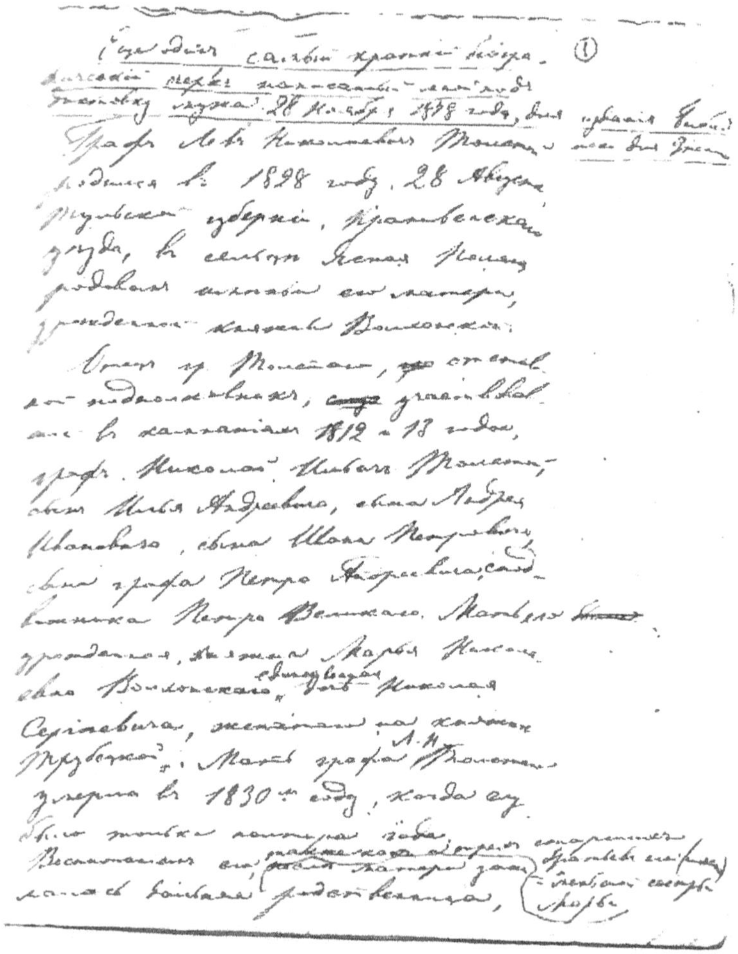

Illustration 12: A page from a draft of SAT's biographical sketch of LNT (1878) in her own handwriting

Illustration 13: Afanasij Afanas'evich Fet —
poet and close friend of the Tolstoy family
Photo: I. D'jagovchenko, 1880s

Illustration 14: Ivan Sergeevich Turgenev, 1879
Photo: K. A. Shapiro

Illustration 15: Nikolaj Nikolaevich Strakhov —
philosopher, editorial associate and close friend of the Tolstoys

Illustration 16: Prince Leonid Dmitrievich Urusov —
Deputy Governor of Tula Gubernia and a close friend of the Tolstoys
Photo: P. I. Birjukov, 1895

Illustration 17: Sergej Ivanovich Taneev —
composer, pianist and close friend of the Tolstoys

Illustration 18: Ivan L'vovich [Vanechka] Tolstoy (1888-1895)
Photo: Sherer, Nabgol'ts and Cº, Moscow, 1893-94

Illustration 19: Konstantin Petrovich Pobedonostsev —
Senior Procurator of the Holy Synod
Photo: G. Den'er, St. Petersburg, 1899

Illustration 20: Vladimir Grigor'evich Chertkov —
one of LNT's closest associates
Photo: K. A. Shapiro, St. Petersburg, mid-1880s

Illustration 21: LNT (left) and writer Maksim Gorky
Photo: S. A. Tolstaya, Yasnaya Polyana, 1900

Illustration 22: LNT (right) and writer Anton Pavlovich Chekhov
Photo: S. A. Tolstaya, Gaspra (Crimea), 1901

Illustration 23: Sofia Andreevna Tolstaya writing at Yasnaya Polyana, 1901
Photo: S. A. Tolstaya

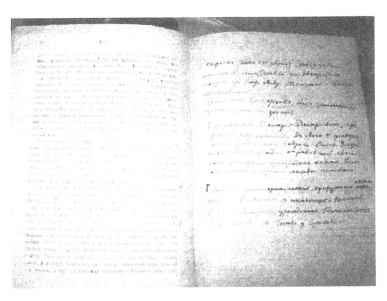

Illustration 24: SAT's commentaries from 1919 (on inserted pages) in a published volume of LNT's letters to SAT

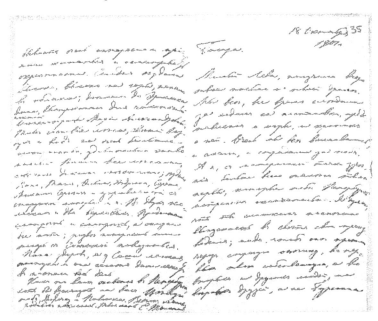

Illustration 25: Letter by SAT to her son Lev L'vovich [Lëva] Tolstoy, written from Gaspra in the Crimea, 18 October 1901

Illustration 26: Bas-relief of SAT and LNT in plaster-of-Paris, sculpted by SAT, 1902

Illustration 27: Self-portrait by SAT, Yasnaya Polyana, 1906

Illustration 28: The Tolstoy family at Gaspra, 1902
(left to right:)
Il'ja L'vovich [*Iljusha*], Andrej L'vovich [*Andrjusha*], Tat'jana L'vovna [*Tanja*],
Lev L'vovich [*Lëva*], Sofia Andreevna, Mikhail L'vovich [*Misha*],
Marija L'vovna [*Masha*], Sergej L'vovich [*Serëzha*], Aleksandra L'vovna [*Sasha*]
Photo: Sofia Andreevna Tolstaya, 1902

SOFIA ANDREEVNA TOLSTAYA
SELECTED CHRONOLOGY

THIS CHRONOLOGY is based primarily on both Sofia Andreevna Tolstaya's *My Life* [*Moja zhizn'*],[1] as the most recent source of pertinent information, and her diaries published in Russia in two volumes.[2] As in any other chronology, the aim here is to give the reader a broad idea of the overall course of her life, especially the later years, and, as much as possible, from her viewpoint and in her own words. For more details on a particular event or date, the reader is invited to consult the book itself. For a comprehensive list of Tolstaya's works, see Section I of the Bibliography in the present volume. For information on family relationships, please refer to the Selected Genealogy beginning on page xix of the present volume.

---

1   Note that dates prior to 1918 are cited according to the Old-Style Julian calendar (O.S.), as explained in the Explanatory note on p. xv in Part I of this volume. Details on how excerpts from *My Life* are cited in this work are also provided in the Explanatory note on p. xvi.

2   S. A. Tolstaja, *Dnevniki v dvukh tomakh.* 2 vols. Comp. N. I. Azarova, O. A. Golinenko, I.A. Pokrovskaja, S.A. Rozanova, B.M. Shumova. Intro. S.A. Rozanova. "Serija literaturnykh memuarov". Moscow: Khudozhestvennaja literatura, 1978. See also English translation by Cathy Porter: *The Diary of Sophia Tolstoy.* Ed. O. A. Golinenko, S.A. Rozanova, B.M. Shumova, I.A. Pokrovskaja, N. I. Azarova. Intro. R. F. Christian. New York: Random House, 1985. The excerpts from SAT's *Dnevniki* [Diaries] and *Ezhednevniki* [Daily diaries] presented below have been freshly translated by John Woodsworth from the 1978 Russian edition. Quotations from this publication are cited by volume and page number — e.g., "*Dnevniki,* II: 294" indicates Volume II, p. 294 of the 1978 Russian edition. Some of these page numbers may appear to be out of order. This is because certain excerpts were drawn from a separate compilation which SAT referred to as her *Ezhednevniki* [lit., 'Daily diaries']; these were included as a separate section in the same 1978 edition.

1844: 22 August — Sofia Andreevna Tolstaya [**SAT**] is born Sofia Andreevna Bers in the village of Pokrovskoe Glebovo-Streshnevo near Moscow into the family of a court physician, a doctor of the Moscow Court Administration, Supernumerary Physician to Moscow Theatres, Andrej Evstaf'evich Bers (1808–1868) and Ljubov' Aleksandrovna Islavina (1826–1886).

1855: 25 January — Sofia Andreevna's paternal grandmother, Elisaveta Ivanovna Bers (*née* Vul'fert, 1789–1855), dies of cholera at age 66. The year 1855 also sees the death of Tsar Nicholas I (1796–1855), who is succeeded by Alexander II (1818–1881, crowned 26 August 1856), as well as the continuation of the Russo-Turkish War in the Crimea (1853–56) and elsewhere, in which Lev Nikolaevich Tolstoy [**LNT**] serves.

1860s (beginning) — Sofia Andreevna writes the story *Natasha* and shows it to Lev Nikolaevich Tolstoy, who recognises himself in the ugly elderly hero Dublitskij, but nevertheless comments favourably on SAT's talent. She destroys the manuscript before their wedding. SAT is given a camera and taught how to use it; this kindles an interest in photography, to which she will return in the late 1880s. By the end of her life, she will have accumulated a portfolio of many hundreds of photographs capturing important events, landscapes and personalities (including self-portraiture) — truly, a family chronicle in photographs.

1861 — Sofia Andreevna passes the Moscow University Home Teachers' examination. As part of this requirement, she submits an outstanding composition in Russian Language, entitled "Music," to Professor Tikhonravov.[3]

1862 — Sofia Andreevna begins writing her *Diaries* [*Dnevniki*] which continue to 1910, albeit with significant gaps.[4]

1862: August — On her way (together with her family) to her grandfather's country estate of "Ivitsa" (Tula Gubernia), she stops over with LNT at Yasnaya Polyana.

1862: 16 September — LNT gives Sofia Andreevna a letter proposing marriage. He shows her his early diaries replete with accounts of his previous profligate life and conquests of peasant women. As late as December 1890, her diary entries reveal disappointment and suffering over her husband's behaviour (see entry under 8 December 1890 on p. 115).

1862: 23 September — Sofia Andreevna Bers marries Count Lev Nikolaevich Tolstoy (1828–1910), who is by that time already a famous writer. After their wedding at the Nativity of the Most Holy Mother of God Church in Moscow, she is taken by her husband to his Yasnaya Polyana estate. Although her early letters to her husband reveal excessive jealousy on her

3 *Nikolaj Savvich Tikhonravov* (1832–1893) — a prominent literary historian with Moscow University; Chair of Russian Literary History, later Dean of the Faculty of History and Philology; from 1877 to 1883 Rector of Moscow University.
4 There are practically no entries for the following years: 1868, 1880–81, 1883–84, 1888–89, 1893–94, 1896, 1905–07; 1909.

part, the couple remain happy during the first two decades of their married life (up to Tolstoy's religious conversion at the end of the 1870s).

1862: December — LNT starts writing a novel he initially calls *The Decembrists*, which eventually turns into *War and peace*. (See *My Life*, II.13–14)

1863: 28 June — Birth of the Tolstoys' first child Sergej L'vovich [*Serëzha*] Tolstoy (1863–1947).

1863–1864 — SAT's sister Tat'jana Andreevna [*Tanja*][5] carries on a romance with LNT's elder brother Sergej Nikolaevich Tolstoy (1826–1904) but he was also in love with a gypsy named Marija Mikhajlovna [*Masha*] Shishkina (1832–1919).

1864: 26 September — LNT falls from a horse and suffers a shoulder injury. After having no success with doctors in Tula, he goes to Moscow on 21 November to consult with doctors there. SAT is greatly concerned and writes almost daily letters to her husband.

1864: 4 October — Birth of the Tolstoys' second child Tat'jana L'vovna [*Tanja*] Tolstaja (1864–1950).

1864: 25 November — SAT writes in a letter to her husband concerning her ongoing transcribing of *War and peace*:[6] "What you have left me to copy — how good it all is! I do like everything [you've written] about Princess Mar'ja! One can just picture her. And such a glorious, likeable character. I'll still be your critic. — Prince Andrej, I would say, is still not clear. It's hard to tell what kind of person he is. If he's smart, how is it that he can't understand or explain to himself his relations with his wife? The old prince is very good, too. But the first one — the one you weren't happy with — I like better. On the basis of him I pictured to myself an ideal, which doesn't fit the present prince. The scene of Prince Andrej's departure is very good, and with the image of Princess Mar'ja — excellent. It was a real pleasure for me to transcribe this." SAT would later write in her *Autobiography*: "Before leaving Yasnaya Polyana he [LNT] would always leave me work to transcribe."[7]

1864: — SAT makes the acquaintance of an old friend of LNT's, acclaimed poet Afanasij Afanas'evich Fet,[8] who over his lifetime will dedicate several poems to SAT.

1866: 22 May — Birth of the Tolstoys' third child, Il'ja L'vovich [*Il'jusha*] Tolstoy (1866–1933).

---

5 *Tat'jana Andreevna Bers* (1846–1925) — SAT's younger sister, married in 1867 to jurist (later Senator) Aleksandr Mikhajlovich Kuzminskij (1843–1917), who is also a cousin to SAT and her sister.

6 By the time the novel was finished she had transcribed many parts of it several times.

7 *Nachala*, N° 1 (1921), p. 145.

8 *Afanasij Afanas'evich Fet* (real surname: Shenshin, 1820–1892) — Russian lyrical poet, accepted into the Petersburg Academy of Sciences in 1886. Many of his poems have been set to music.

1867: June — LNT's brother Sergej Nikolaevich marries the gypsy Marija Mikhajlovna Shishkina.

1867: 24 July — SAT's sister Tat'jana Andreevna marries Aleksandr Mikhajlovich Kuzminskij (1843–1917).

1868: 7 January — In Moscow SAT attends the wedding of her elder sister Elizaveta Andreevna [*Liza*][9] to a landowner from Rjazan', Gavriil Emel'janovich Pavlenkov, a colonel in the Hussars.

1868: spring — The Tolstoys spend a couple of months in Moscow to be near SAT's father, Andrej Evstaf'evich Bers (1808–1868), who is dying. Her father passes on 30 May 1868. (See *My Life*, II.77, 79, 80)

1869: 20 May — Birth of the Tolstoys' fourth child, Lev L'vovich [*Lëva*] Tolstoy (1869–1945).

1870 — SAT begins teaching her two eldest children to read and write — she will continue seeing personally to the primary education of all her children.

1870: 14 February — SAT writes under the heading *Moi zapisi raznye dlja spravok* [Various notes for future reference]: "The other day, as I was reading a biography of Pushkin, it came to me that I could be of service to my descendants, who might be interested in a biography of Lëvochka [=LNT], and make an account not of his everyday doings, but of his intellectual life, as far as I am able to keep track of it. This actually came to me earlier, but I didn't have enough time back then. / Now is a good time to start. *War and peace* is finished, and no major projects are underway." (*Diaries*, I: 495) Nine years later SAT will publish a brief biography of her husband (see entry under 1879 on p. 107).

1871: 12 February — Premature birth of the Tolstoys' fifth child, Marija L'vovna [*Masha*] Tolstaya (1871–1906). SAT nearly dies of postpartum fever.

1871: spring — Tolstoy takes a trip to Samara, accompanied by SAT's brother Stepan Andreevich [*Stëpa*] Bers (1855–1910), and purchases a 67,000-hectare tract of land in Samara's Buzuluk Uezd.

1871: August — Nikolaj Nikolaevich Strakhov's[10] first acquaintance with LNT and his family. Over the 25 years (from 1871 until Strakhov's death in 1896) both Tolstoy and Tolstaya will carry on extensive correspondence with Strakhov.[11]

---

9 *Elizaveta Andreevna* [Liza] *Bers* (née Bers, 1843–1919). Following a failed first marriage (in 1868) to Gavriil Emel'janovich Pavlenkov (1824–1892), in 1877 she married her cousin Aleksandr Aleksandrovich Bers (1844–1921).

10 *Nikolaj Nikolaevich Strakhov* (1828–1896) — Russian philosopher, librarian, literary critic and long-time editorial consultant to LNT and SAT. For his correspondence with both Tolstoys, see Donskov 2000 and 2003.

11 While not all the letters survived, a significant number were published (in Russian only) in Donskov 2000 and Donskov 2003. The former volume includes all extant letters exchanged between Strakhov and SAT, offering the reader a multitude of new insights into the relationship between them and their close co-operation in the matter of producing

1871: December — SAT organises a Christmas costume party for her own and the peasant children — a tradition which will continue over the years.

1872: April — In preparation for a new baby due in June, SAT fasts at a local nunnery, accompanied by her eldest son Serëzha.

1872: 13 June — SAT gives birth to a son, Pëtr [*Petja*], who dies of croup on 9 November of the same year.

1873: March — LNT begins writing *Anna Karenina*.

1873: summer — Samara Gubernia is plagued by a famine because of a poor grain harvest. SAT successfully pleads with Grand Duchess Marija Aleksandrovna Romanova (1853–1920) for aid in famine relief.

1873: autumn — Artist Ivan Nikolaevich Kramskoj[12] paints a portrait of LNT working on *Anna Karenina*. He does a second portrait of LNT for SAT.

1874: 22 April — SAT gives birth to a son, Nikolaj [*Kolja*], who dies of meningitis on 20 February 1875.

1874: summer — The Tolstoys are saddened by the death of 'Auntie' Tat'jana Aleksandrovna Ergol'skaja (1792–1874), a woman who after the death of her mother had been brought up in the home of LNT's paternal grandfather, Il'ja Andreevich Tolstoy (1757–1820).

1875: autumn — death of LNT's aunt Pelageja Il'inichna Jushkova (1801–1875), the youngest daughter of his grandfather, Il'ja Andreevich Tolstoy.

1875: 1 November — SAT gives birth to a daughter, Varvara [*Varja*], who dies immediately.

1876: spring — SAT remarks on the spring of 1876 as the beginning of LNT's 'moral transformation', first evident in a letter he wrote in mid-April 1876 to Countess Aleksandra Andreevna Tolstaya.[13] (See *My Life*, III.1 – "Beginning of Lev Nikolaevich's moral transformation")

1876: 12 September — SAT writes to her sister Tanja: "Lev Nikolaevich is in Orenburg. I've started teaching the children again with heartfelt intensity, as well as cutting out and sewing clothes, etc. Every hour it's a new subject: geography, history and such like. I'm going through it at a feverish pace because I'm concerned I shan't get through one or more of the subjects… In the evenings I've begun translating Lëvochka's composition *Al'bert* into French. Another thing I'm doing is compiling a grammar that will be easy for Il'ja to understand." (*My Life*, III.7 – "At home")

LNT's works — a subject that occupies fully a third of their letters and runs as a unifying thread through their whole correspondence.

12 *Ivan Nikolaevich Kramskoj* (1837–1887) — one of the most celebrated Russian artists of the nineteenth century. He was the first artist to persuade LNT to pose for a portrait.

13 *Countess Aleksandra Andreevna Tolstaya* (1817–1904) — daughter of Andrej Andreevich Tolstoy (1771–1844), whose brother, Il'ja Andreevich Tolstoy (1757–1820) was LNT's paternal grandfather. In 1846 she was appointed Lady-in-Waiting to the Imperial Court and in 1866 governess to Grand Duchess Marija Aleksandrovna Romanova (1853–1920).

1876: October — SAT begins writing what turns out to be the first biography of LNT; she continues working on it until April 1878.

1877: mid-January — On a trip to St. Petersburg SAT visits LNT's cousin Countess Aleksandra Andreevna Tolstaya, for whom she has a special affection. "I stayed in Petersburg less than four days. I went around to all my relatives. I went to see Countess Aleksandra Andreevna Tolstaya as well as her mother, Praskov'ja Vasil'evna.[14] I went to the Hermitage,[15] where they still had paintings by Russian artists, which were later transferred to the Alexander III Museum." (*My Life*, III.15 – "Trip to Petersburg – Botkin")

1877: spring — When the last part of *Anna Karenina* is published in *Russkij vestnik*, the editor, Mikhail Nikiforovich Katkov,[16] changes the ending without consulting LNT. LNT is then obliged to publish his original ending as a separate booklet. SAT finds Katkov "dry and unwelcoming." (*My Life*, III.15)

1877: summer — LNT begins to read a good many books on religion and starts writing religious treatises of his own.

1877: 6 December — Birth of the Tolstoys' sixth surviving child, Andrej L'vovich [*Andrjusha*] Tolstoy (1877–1916).

1878: 8 August — Ivan Sergeevich Turgenev[17] comes to visit Yasnaya Polyana to try to persuade LNT to take part in the Pushkin celebrations being organised in Moscow, but Tolstoy refuses. The two writers continue to meet infrequently up until July 1881.

1878: autumn — SAT makes the acquaintance of Prince Leonid Dmitrievich Urusov (1837–1885), whom she finds herself personally attracted to and who will have a far-reaching influence on her life. She speaks of the exposure to art and philosophy she gains from her relationship with Urusov as constituting "the second significant period of my spiritual life" (*My Life*,

14 *Countess Praskov'ja Vasil'evna Tolstaya (née Barykova, 1796–1879)* — wife of LNT's first cousin, twice removed.

15 *the Hermitage* [Russian: *Èrmitazh*] — one of the largest art museum complexes in the world, founded by Empress Catherine the Great in 1764 as her private collection, and opened for public viewing in 1852. It is housed in the Winter Palace and four adjacent palaces along the south bank of the Neva River in the heart of St. Petersburg. The gallery is restricted to foreign works of art; in 1898 all paintings and sculptures by Russian artists were transferred — by decree of Emperor Nicholas II — to the new Alexander III Russian Museum, which today (known as the State Russian Museum [*Gosudarstvennyj Russkij muzej*]) oversees many other public art galleries in the whole Russian Federation.

16 *Mikhail Nikiforovich Katkov (1818–1887)* — Russian thinker and writer, who alternately embraced progressive and conservative views; he was greatly enamoured of the British parliamentary system and British law. He became editor of *Russkij vestnik* in 1856.

17 *Ivan Sergeevich Turgenev (1818–1883)* — prominent Russian writer, Corresponding Member of the St. Petersburg Academy of Sciences. He is probably best known for his novel *Fathers and Children* [*Otsy i deti*].

III.39 – "Three significant periods") — the first being her reading of LNT's *Childhood* and *Boyhood* in her youth.[18]

1879 — SAT publishes her first biography of LNT, which is included in a volume of his works in the *Russkaja biblioteka* [Russian Library] series, Volume IX, *Graf Lev Nikolaevich Tolstoj* [Count Lev Nikolaevich Tolstoy], St. Petersburg, 1879. She prepares the fourth edition of LNT's *Complete collected works* [*Polnoe sobranie sochinenij / PSS*] which she publishes in eleven volumes the following year.

1879: summer — LNT works on his *Criticism of dogmatic theology.* SAT invites peasants from the estate and nearby village to come to her home where she offers them medical treatment. (See *My Life,* III.42 – "Hunting again")

1879: 20 December — Birth of the Tolstoys' seventh surviving child, Mikhail L'vovich [*Misha*] Tolstoy (1879–1944).

1880s — SAT's circle of interests and hobbies is seen in her notebook entries (see Illustration 30):

What I like:
Peace in my soul.
A dream in my head. People to like me.
I like children.
I like any kind of flowers. Sun and lots of light.
The woods.
I like gardening, pruning and caring for trees.
I like visual art — i.e., drawing, photography, role-playing; I like creating something, at least in sewing.
I like certain kinds of music.
I like clarity, simplicity and talent in people. Fancy dresses and jewellery.
Fun, having a good time, splendour, beauty. I like poetry. Tenderness. Sentimentality.
I like to work creatively.
I like straightforwardness, truthfulness…

What I don't like:
People's enmity and discontent.
Emptiness of soul and thought, even temporary. Autumn. Darkness and night.
Men (with rare exceptions). Games for money.
People darkened by alcohol and other vices. Secrets, insincerity, secrecy, untruthfulness. The steppes.
Dissolute, noisy people. The process of eating.
I don't like any domestic chores.

---

18 A 'third significant period' will be her attachment to her youngest son, Vanechka, who lives only a brief few years (1888–1895), and how she is helped after his death by another beloved friend — pianist and composer Sergej Ivanovich Taneev (1856–1915).

I don't like mediocrity or artifice, dissimulation or falsehood.

I don't like mocking or joking, parodies, criticism or caricatures.

I don't like idleness or laziness.

I can't stand any kind of misbehaviour.

(T. V. Komarova,[19] "Iz zapisnoj knizhki S. A. Tolstoj (Po materialam jas-nopoljanskikh memorial'nykh fondov)" [From S. A. Tolstaya's notebook (From the materials in the Yasnaya Polyana Memorial Collections)], *Jasnopoljanskij sbornik*, Tula, 2000: 158)

1880: 2–3 May — Ivan Sergeevich Turgenev comes for a visit to Yasnaya Polyana.

1881: January — SAT observes that LNT's obsession with studying the Gospels has made him "oblivious of life." (*My Life*, III.73 – "Studying the gospels – Lev Nikolaevich's difficult disposition")

1881: March — SAT is saddened at the news that Tsar Alexander II has been assassinated (1 March). He is succeeded by his son, Alexander III (1845–1894). (See *My Life*, III.76 – "The Assassination of Tsar Alexander II")

1881: June — LNT visits the Optina Pustyn' Monastery where he discusses the Gospels with the Venerable Father Ambrosius (1812–1891).

1881: summer — SAT devises a 'letter-box' game for her household, whereby members of her family and staff deposit brief anonymous writings in a 'letter-box', to be read by everyone together, the object being to guess who wrote what. One of LNT's entries relates to Sofia Andreevna: "Belongs to the non-aggressive ward but requires periodic isolation. Possessed by the mania termed *petulantia toropigis maxima*.[20] Particular craze: patient thinks that everyone is demanding everything of her, and that there is no way she can meet all these demands. Indicators: carrying out unassigned assignments, answering questions before they are asked, defending herself against allegations which have not been made, satisfying needs which have not manifested themselves. The patient suffers from the Blokhin-Bank mania.[21] Treatment: intense work. Diet: no communication with light-headed worldly people."[22] (*My Life*, III.84 – "Two families' lives at Yasnaya and *letter-box*") This game continues for several more summers.

---

19 *Tat'jana Vasil'evna Komarova* — chief curator, Yasnaya Polyana Museum estate.

20 *Translation from Latin:* "extreme lack of restraint".

21 *Note by SAT:* A peasant used to come to Yasnaya Polyana who was quite insane, but non-aggressive, with clear blue eyes and a soft smile which suggested guilt. He claimed to be His Highness the Prince Blokhin (from the Russian word *blokha*, meaning 'flea'). He had risen through all the ranks, and everywhere there was a bank *open* for him. Sometimes he called himself Romanov [the family name of the dynasty that ruled Russia from the seventeenth to the twentieth century] and said that he was expecting to receive funds from the Tsar.

22 See also: A. L. Tolstaya, *Otets* (2 vols., New York: Chekhov Publishers, 1953), Vol. I, p. 411.

1881: 2 August — SAT goes to Moscow to fix up an apartment she has rented for her family in the Volkonskij house in Denezhnyj Lane.

1881: 15 September — SAT moves with her family to Moscow, where tension increases over 'maternal concerns' between her and her husband; he threatens to leave. The Tolstoys enrol their sons Il'ja and Lev in a private *gymnasium* (school) run by Lev Ivanovich Polivanov.[23] They will continue to make frequent visits to Yasnaya Polyana, especially in the summer.

1881: 31 October — SAT gives birth to another son, Aleksej [*Alësha*].

1881: November — SAT falls ill. "About four weeks after the birth, tormented in body and spirit, I suddenly took seriously ill. I had such terrible pains in my right side and in the pit of my stomach that I fell to the floor, began crying out and was no longer able to get up. / In the middle of the night they sent word to the Society of Russian Physicians on the Arbat, where there was always a doctor on duty, and a Professor Belin was sent to me, who turned out to be a complete idiot. This Belin told me that I had cancer of the stomach and that I was incurable … After examining me, Chirkov[24] said I had gallstone colic and that I would have jaundice. And so I did. The pains in the pit of my stomach lasted a long time. I turned yellow all over, I drank Carlsbad water,[25] took bouillon only in small glasses, and, what with the painful breast-feeding besides, I was extremely exhausted." (*My Life*, III.95 – "Birth of Alësha")

1882: January — SAT becomes accustomed to 'high-society' life in Moscow.

1882: February — The Tolstoys receive a visit from prominent artist Nikolaj Nikolaevich Ge (1831–1894), who paints SAT's portrait. She, however, does not consider it a good likeness.

1882: spring — In Moscow SAT becomes acquainted with another Sofia Andreevna Tolstaya, widow of A. K. Tolstoy.[26] (See *My Life*, III.111 – "Count Aleksej Tolstoy's widow")

1882: May — Purchase of the I. A. Arnautov house with a large garden in Khamovniki Lane. (See *My Life*, III.114 – "Lev Nikolaevich at Yasnaya Polyana in the spring")

---

23 *Lev Ivanovich Polivanov* (1838–1899) — Russian educator and headmaster of a private gymnasium in Moscow emphasising classical education. He authored a number of books on teaching Russian language and literature.

24 *Vasilij Vasil'evich Chirkov* — a physician known to the Tolstoy family, who also served as a professor at Kiev University. He was an assistant to Dr Grigorij Antonovich Zakhar'in (1829–1895), a Moscow University professor who treated Tolstoy.

25 *Carlsbad water* — mineral water from the spa at Karlovy Vary in what is now the Czech Republic.

26 *Count Aleksej Konstantinovich Tolstoy* (1817–1875) — Russian novelist, dramatist, satirist and poet, known especially for his historical plays — e.g., his trilogy *Smert' Ioanna Groznogo* [*The death of Ivan the Terrible*] (1866), *Tsar' Fëdor Ioannovich* (1868) and *Tsar' Boris* (1870). To be distinguished from his better-known namesake Aleksej Nikolaevich Tolstoy (1882–1945).

1882: summer — LNT takes up the study of Hebrew, which concerns SAT; she considered that "this harnessing of his mental forces still had a bad influence on Lev Nikolaevich's health". (*My Life*, III.125 – "Hebrew")

1882: summer — Readings from Epictetus and Seneca at Yasnaya Polyana. "Apart from the wisdom that filled the pages of these philosophical books, I was enchanted by their conciseness, along with the high (albeit sub-conscious) religiosity of the pagans and of Epictetus — a slave [in his youth] — as well as the eloquence, brilliance and flexibility of expression with Seneca, the quiet wisdom of Cæsar Marcus Aurelius, and so forth. Then I tried reading the German philosophers too, including Schopenhauer, but the German thinkers no longer delighted or satisfied me." (*My Life*, III.116 – "Prince Leonid Dimitrievich Urusov and philosophy")

1882: 26 August — Yasnaya Polyana. A quarrel with LNT. "The quarrel was a very stormy one. Lev Nikolaevich yelled that his most passionate thought was to leave the family. [...] After his bout of yelling at me, Lev Nikolaevich left and didn't come back the whole night long. I sat down without getting undressed and wept." (*My Life*, III.121 – "Il'ja's typhoid fever – a bad quarrel")

1882: autumn — Moscow. "At first we drew from a plaster-of-Paris figure of Laocoön,[27] and then drew Antinous.[28] / As a lifelong lover of art, especially drawing, I joined the young people (despite my frightfully busy schedule) and drew with them. These young people comprised my [daughter] Tanja, alongside her first cousins Vera and Lenochka Tolstaya.[29] I remember how well my Antinous came out, and how I admired it! Unfortunately, however, these classes didn't keep up for very long." (*My Life*, III.126 – "Drawing from plaster sculpture – Prjanishnikov")

1883: 21 May — SAT receives a power of attorney from her husband and the right to publish his works written before the end of 1881. She competes with other publishers in publishing his works written after 1881. Over twenty-six years (1886–1911) SAT publishes eight editions of LNT's *Complete collected works* as well as many of his writings in separate editions. The large print runs and the moderately low prices contribute to the rapid circulation of LNT's works among the public at large.

27 *Laocoön* — Trojan priest of Apollo, who warned his fellow Trojans to destroy the wooden horse given them by the Greeks. His advice, however, went unheeded.

28 *Antinous* (ca. 100–130 CE) — male lover of the Roman Emperor Publius Aelius Hadrian (76–138 C.E), who declared him a god after his death.

29 *Vera Sergeevna* [Verochka] *Tolstaya* (1865–1923) — daughter to LNT's brother Sergej Nikolaevich Tolstoy (1826–1904) and *Elena Sergeevna* [Lenochka] *Tolstaya* (1863–1942) — daughter to LNT's sister Marija Nikolaevna Tolstaya (1830–1912) from her extra-marital liaison in Algiers with the Swedish Viscount Victor-Hector de Kleen. (See A. N. Wilson, *Tolstoy* (New York: Norton, 2001: 194.) In 1893 Elena Sergeevna married Ivan Vasil'evich Denisenko (1851–1916). On Lenochka's marriage see entry on **1893: 11 April** below.

1883: 3 August — SAT goes to visit her ill mother who lives with her son Vjacheslav Andreevich in Rjazhsk (Rjazan' Gubernia).

1883: 28 September — LNT is summoned to court to explain his refusal of jury duty on the grounds of his "religious convictions." (*My Life*, III.142 – "Refusal of jury duty")

1883: December — "In December I came down with a serious case of neuralgia, brought on [by] my exhaustion and my pregnancy." (*My Life*, III.147 – "Lev Nikolaevich's ten days at Yasnaya")

1884: January — Nikolaj Nikolaevich Ge paints a portrait of LNT which he eventually sells to the Tret'jakov Gallery in Moscow. A reproduction of this painting is acquired by Marija Aleksandrovna Shmidt (1844–1911), a former high-society lady who becomes "the most zealous devotee and follower of Lev Nikolaevich's new beliefs." (*My Life*, IV.1–2)

1884: spring — The Tolstoys make the acquaintance of Vladimir Grigor'evich Chertkov, who has embraced LNT's ideas in the extreme.[30] Over the years SAT will become increasingly concerned over what she sees as Chertkov's negative influence on LNT's life and decisions.

1884: 18 June — Birth of the Tolstoys' eighth (and youngest) surviving child, Aleksandra L'vovna [*Sasha*] Tolstaya (1884–1979).

1884: October — SAT is distressed to learn of her brother Sasha's[31] duel with Sergej Aleksandrovich Pisarev (ca. 1855–1909), for whom Sasha's wife Matrona Dmitrievna (a.k.a. Patti) has left him. Sasha seriously wounds Pisarev but does not kill him.

1884: beginning of December — In Moscow A. A. Fet brings his poem dedicated to SAT, entitled "Kogda stopoj slegka ustaloj…" [When with slightly weary step…]

1885: beginning of February — SAT travels to St. Petersburg with her daughter Tat'jana. "I very much wanted to make a more thorough study of the publishing business, especially publishing by subscription, to consult with Strakhov and Anna Grigor'evna Dostoevskaja,[32] who had already enjoyed some success with publishing her husband's works for some time. I had begun to correspond with her that autumn, and she gave me a good deal of helpful advice." (*My Life*, IV.31 – "My trip to Petersburg with Tanja") This is the start of a long friendship between the two writers' wives. While Tolstoy and Dostoevsky were never destined to meet in person, Tolstaya

---

30 *Vladimir Grigor'evich Chertkov* (1854–1936) — a close friend and adviser to LNT, who in exile set up his own publishing house in Britain known as *Svobodnoe slovo* [Free Word] to publish works by Tolstoy and his followers. He was also instrumental in helping the Doukhobors emigrate to Canada. The Doukhobor leader, Pëtr Verigin, stopped to see him in Britain on his way to Canada (see: Donskov 1995: 50).

31 *Aleksandr Andreevich* [*Sasha*] *Bers* (1845–1918), married to Matrona Dmitrievna Bers (*née* Princess Eristova, also known as Patti).

32 *Anna Grigor'evna Dostoevskaja* (née Snitkina, 1846–1918) — Russian memoirist, who also served as publisher of the works of her husband, Fëdor Mikhajlovich Dostoevsky (1821–1881).

and Dostoevskaja keep in contact through correspondence and occasional visits. In addition to publishing seven complete editions of her husband's works, Anna Grigor'evna prepares a bibliography thereof and edits a separate collection of his letters. / The eight letters written by A. G. Dostoevskaja to SAT are to be found in the Manuscript Division of the L. N. Tolstoy Museum in Moscow.[33]

1885: February — In St. Petersburg while visiting the Nicholas Institute (Orphanage), SAT is presented by Headmistress Ekaterina Nikolaevna Shostak[34] to Empress Marija Fëdorovna Romanova. SAT petitions the Empress for permission to publish LNT's banned works, but her petition is rejected.

1885: spring — LNT is intrigued by the writings of American economist Henry George (1839–1897), who proposes the nationalisation of private land.

1885: March — SAT proofreads LNT's collected works. "I was already up to my ears with the publication of Lev Nikolaevich's *Complete collected works,* and for five months I delved into the task of proofreading." (*My Life,* IV.38 – "Lev Nikolaevich's return to Moscow")

1885: spring — SAT sends a portrait of herself to Fet, and in return receives his poem "I vot portret, i skhozhe i ne skhozhe…" [And here's the portrait: so like you, yet unlike you…], dedicated to SAT.

1885: summer — "That summer I went for a brief visit to my brother's[35] in Orël, where he had bought a dacha near Pesochnaja Station." (*My Life,* IV.43 – "Work in the fields") A Jewish tailor named Isaak Borisovich Fejnerman begins to frequent Yasnaya Polyana; for a time, his unquestioning devotion to LNT's views irritates SAT.

1885: August — SAT goes with her daughters Tanja and Masha to the village of Djat'kovo in Brjansk Uezd, where Leonid Dmitrievich Urusov (gravely ill) and his wife are staying with his wife's brother, Nikolaj Sergeevich Mal'tsev. Urusov takes SAT on one last ride together. He dies of illness on 23 September 1885.

1885: ca 16 November — SAT goes to St. Petersburg, where she stays with her sister T. A. Kuzminskaja.

---

33 These were compiled with commentaries by Tat'jana Nikiforova in "Pis'ma A. G. Dostoevskoj k S. A. Tolstoj" ["The letters of A.G. Dostoevskaja to S.A. Tolstaya"] and published — for the first time (except for one previously printed) in: M. Shcherbakova & M. Mozharova (eds.), *Mir filologii.* Moskva: Nasledie, 2000: 290–306. The letters contain fascinating insights into the lives and personalities not only of their famous husbands, but also of the women themselves as professional publishers. They also comment on the publishing practices of the period.

34 *Ekaterina Nikolaevna Shostak* (née *Islen'eva,* ?—1904) — Director (1863–92) of the Nicholas Institute (Orphanage) in St. Petersburg and first cousin to SAT's mother.

35 *Aleksandr Andreevich* [Sasha] *Bers* (1845–1918).

1885: 20 November — In St. Petersburg SAT pays a visit to the Director of the State Office of Press Affairs, E. M. Feoktistov,[36] to petition the Censorship Board to allow publication of Volume 12 of LNT's *Complete collected works*. She also sees the Deputy Minister of Internal Affairs, V. K. Pleve.[37]

1885: 26 November — SAT receives from Feoktistov a written refusal to allow publication of Volume XII. He could not let pass *A confession* or *What I believe* and advises her to appeal to the church's censorship board. She goes for an appointment (granted the same day) with the head of the church's censorship board K. P. Pobedonostsev.[38]

1885: 27 November — SAT has an appointment with Chief of Staff Nikolaj Nikolaevich Obruchev,[39] at which she petitions, on behalf of her husband, for a young man named Aleksej Petrovich Zaljubovskij,[40] who has refused military service. (See *My Life*, IV.57 – "Zaljubovskij")

1886: 18 January — The Tolstoys' son, Aleksej [*Alësha*], dies of quinsy [an abscess near the tonsils] at age four.

1886: 4 April — With some concern, SAT sees LNT off on a trek on foot from Moscow to Yasnaya Polyana. He is accompanied by Mikhail Aleksandrovich Stakhovich[41] and Nikolaj Nikolaevich Ge Jr. He will do this twice more with different travelling companions.

1886: October — LNT begins writing his drama *The power of darkness*, which he completes the following January.

1886: early November — SAT goes to Yalta to visit her dying mother, Ljubov' Aleksandrovna Bers (*née* Isleneva, 1826–1886), who passes away 11 November 1886.

1887: 6 March — "I transcribed [LNT's] *On life and death* and then read it through carefully. Somewhat apprehensively I looked for something new,

36 *Evgenij Mikhajlovich Feoktistov* (1829–1898) — Russian writer who moved to St. Petersburg in 1862 and joined the Imperial government. From 1883 he served as Head of Press Affairs until his appointment as a senator in 1896.

37 *Vjacheslav Konstantinovich Pleve* [also spelt: *Plehve*] (1846–1904) — appointed Deputy Minister after serving three years as Head of the Ministry's Secret Police. He also served as a senator and in 1902 was appointed Minister of Internal Affairs. In 1904 he was assassinated by a social-revolutionary student named Egor Sazonov.

38 *Konstantin Petrovich Pobedonostsev* (1827–1907) — jurist, statesman and Senior Procurator of the Holy Synod of the Russian Orthodox Church between 1880 and 1905.

39 *Nikolaj Nikolaevich Obruchev* (1830–1904) — Chief of Staff and Chairman of the Military Scholarly Committee (1881–97).

40 *Aleksej Petrovich Zaljubovskij* (1863–?) — conscientious objector, imprisoned for refusing to take the oath of military service, and released two and a half years later. His refusal of military service in November 1884 was the first known case of such an action under LNT's influence.

41 *Mikhail Aleksandrovich Stakhovich* (1861–1923) — well-known poet and writer from Orël Gubernia, who switched from his liberal views to being an arch-conservative and in the 1900s participated in the first and second State Dumas as a right-wing deputy. Following the February 1917 revolution, he served as Governor-General of what was then the Russian gubernia of Finland for the Provisional Government.

came across some concise expressions and beautiful comparisons, but the basic underlying thought, for me, was still essentially the same — i.e., the rejection of one's personal life for the life of the spirit. One thing was impossible and unjust, as far as I was concerned, namely, any rejection of personal life should take place in the name of love for the whole world. I think that there are undoubted obligations put on us by God, which nobody has a right to reject, and in terms of the life of the spirit they are certainly not a hindrance, but actually a help." *(Diaries, I: 115)*

1887: 18 June — SAT continues treating local peasants' ailments (cf. entry under **1879: summer** above): "Every day a mass of sick people come to see me. I treat them all with the help of Florinskij's book.[42] But what a moral trauma I went through — I sometimes was at my wit's end trying to understand and diagnose the illness and what assistance I could render! Sometimes I just feel like quitting my attempts altogether, but then I go out and see this touching faith, these sick, pleading eyes, and I feel sorry, I feel a twinge of conscience. What can I do? Maybe I'm doing entirely the wrong thing. I dole out medicines and try not to think about these unfortunate ones." *(Diaries, I: 119)*

1887: 21 June — "In the afternoon, before going bathing, I gathered my young ones together and read them *A hero of our time* [Geroj nashego vremeni]. What remarkable thoughts it contains, and so mature already! I really like Lermontov.[43] If, as rumour has it, he was an acrimonious and unpleasant fellow, he was still so very smart and on such a high level compared to ordinary people. *He* was not understood, and yet *he* saw right through everyone and everything." *(Diaries, I: 120)*

1887: 1 September — SAT places LNT's manuscripts for the first time in the Rumjantsev Museum's Manuscript Division in Moscow.

1887: 23 September — The Tolstoys celebrate their silver wedding anniversary with just family present.

1887: autumn — The Tolstoys are distressed to hear of the broad circulation of copies of Repin's painting of LNT ploughing in the fields. (See *My Life,* IV.122 – "The reproduction of Repin's picture *The Ploughman*")

1888: 28 February — The Tolstoys' son Il'ja L'vovich marries Sof'ja Nikolaevna [*Sonja*] Filosofova (1867–1934). They settle at the family homestead Aleksandrovka in Chern Uezd.

1888: 31 March — SAT gives birth to a son, Ivan [*Vanechka*], who soon becomes her favourite child and the darling of the family. Sadly, he dies a month before his seventh birthday, on 23 February 1895.

---

42 *Vasilij Markovich Florinskij* (1834–1899) — author of the popular medical guide *Domashnjaja meditsina* [Home medicine], for which he was awarded the *Emperor Peter the Great* literary prize by the Ministry of Education's Academic Committee.

43 *Mikhail Jur'evich Lermontov* (1814–1841) — prominent Russian poet, prose-writer and dramatist. He wrote his best-known novel, *Geroj nashego vremeni,* in his mid-twenties.

1888: 17 April — Once again LNT sets out to walk from Moscow to Yasnaya Polyana, this time with Nikolaj Nikolaevich Ge Jr and Aleksandr Nikiforovich Dunaev.[44]

1888: 1 December — As a favour to Marija Aleksandrovna Shmidt's brother Vladimir, SAT buys from him a small nearby estate called Ovsjannikovo, which is eventually given to the Tolstoys' daughter Tat'jana L'vovna [*Tanja*].

1889: spring — LNT writes a comedy he calls *Themselves outwitted* [*Iskhitrilas'*], which eventually evolves into *The fruits of enlightenment* [*Plody prosveshchenija*].

1889: 2 May — LNT begins a third trek from Moscow to Yasnaya Polyana, this time with Evgenij Ivanovich Popov.[45]

1889: December — SAT stages a performance of LNT's comedy *The fruits of enlightenment* at Yasnaya Polyana. Three of the Tolstoys' children (Serëzha, Tanja and Masha) are in the cast.

1890: 5 August — A fire breaks out in one of the huts in the village of Yasnaya Polyana. Several members of the Tolstoy family render assistance.

1890: 8 December — "I'm still transcribing Lëvochka's diaries. Why have I never transcribed or even read them before? They've been in my dresser drawer for a long time. I believe the horror I experienced reading his diaries as a young bride and the sharp pain of a kind of jealousy and helplessness in the face of the horrors of male debauchery has never really healed. May God save all young souls from such wounds — they will never heal over." (*Diaries*, I: 127)

1890: 16 December — "This chaos of innumerable cares, one right after the other, often drives me mad, and I lose my equilibrium. It's easy to say, but at any given moment my attention is taken up with: children studying and ailing, my husband's state of physical and especially mental health, the older children with their activities and debts, children and [esp. military] service, the sale and plans of the Samara estate — they have to be obtained and copied for potential buyers, the new edition [of LNT's *Complete collected works*] and Volume XIII with the banned *Kreutzer Sonata*, the request for dividing [Tat'jana L'vovna's] property with the Ovsjannikovo priest, proof-reading Volume XIII, Misha's nightshirt, sheets and boots for Andrjusha; not to postpone payments on household expenses; insurance, taxes on the estate, passports for the staff, bookkeeping transcribing, etc., etc. — all of which invariably and directly ought to concern me." (*Diaries*, I: 131) On this date SAT is also working on transcribing LNT's treatise *The Kingdom of God is within you*.

---

44 *Aleksandr Nikiforovich Dunaev* (1850–1920) — close friend of the Tolstoys', sharing some of LNT's views; a director of the Moscow Torgovyj [Trade] Bank. Married to Ekaterina Adol'fovna Dunaeva (1851–1923).

45 *Evgenij Ivanovich Popov* (1864–1938) — a Tolstoyan characterised by LNT as "very pleasant, … kind and serious" (letter to SAT, 3 May 1889, *PSS*, 84: Letter 413).

1891 — SAT proofreads *The Kreutzer Sonata*.

1891: January — LNT takes the first steps to divest himself of personal property and gives SAT full power of attorney over his financial affairs.

1891: 12 February — "I don't know how or why *The Kreutzer Sonata* has been linked with our marital life, but it is a fact, and everyone, from the Tsar on down to Lev Nikolaevich's brother and his best friend [Dmitrij Alekseevich] D'jakov, has expressed their sympathies for me. In any case, what do others have to offer? In my own heart I have sensed that this story was aimed directly at me. Right from the start it wounded me, humiliated me in the eyes of the whole world and destroyed the last remaining love between us. And all this time I was not to blame for the slightest violation of my marriage vows, not even a sideways glance at anyone during all my married life!" (*Diaries*, I: 153)

1891: 25 February — The censorship board prohibits the publication of Vol. XIII of LNT's works, including *The Kreutzer Sonata*. "At the end of February, I myself went to Moscow, only to find to my great dismay that Volume XIII of Lev Nikolaevich Tolstoy's works with *The Kreutzer Sonata* which I had just printed was being held up in [M.G.] Volchaninov's print shop. A government order had been issued banning its release until a decision could be made by the Central Press Affairs Office." (*My Life*, V.76 – "Lev Nikolaevich writes — Young women")

1891: March — SAT reads Schopenhauer.

1891: 28 March — SAT leaves for St. Petersburg to petition for the removal of the prohibition on Volume XIII of LNT's *Complete collected works*.

1891: 13 April — SAT has a personal audience with Tsar Alexander III, where she obtains permission to include *The Kreutzer Sonata* in her edition of Tolstoy's *Complete collected works* (though not as a separate publication) as well as the Tsar's assurance that he will personally act as censor for LNT's future belletristic writings. She then has a separate meeting with Empress Marija Fëdorovna Romanova, conducted in French. (See *My Life*, V.92–94)

1891: June — LNT approves a plan for dividing his property among his family members. (See *My Life*, V.108 – "My activities and the property division")

1891: 21 July — SAT is saved from suicide by her brother-in-law Aleksandr Mikhajlovich Kuzminskij, thanks to the latter's encounter with a swarm of flying ants. (See *Diaries*, I: 201) In her memoir, this episode is related not only under 1891 (*My Life*, V.115 – "Flying ants") but also under August 1882 (III.121 – "In Moscow").

1891: 26 July — "I spent the whole day proofreading *A primer*. The censorship committee did not approve it on account of various words, such as: *vshi* [lice], *blokhi* [fleas], *chort* [devil], *klop* [bedbug], and because there were mistakes. They also proposed omitting certain stories — the one about the fox and the fleas, the silly peasant, etc., to which Lëvochka did not agree." [46] (*Diaries*, I: 204)

1891: 3 November — SAT's letter to the editor regarding the need for assistance to famine victims is published in *Russkie vedomosti* (N° 303). Later she helps LNT distribute food to famine-stricken peasants; her reports on charitable contributions to this cause appear in *Nedelja* (N°N° 47 and 50).

1892 — After a poor harvest and resulting famine in several gubernias, SAT appeals in the pages of the newspaper *Russkie vedomosti* for charitable contributions from the public. Later she helps LNT open food kitchens in Tula and Rjazan' Gubernias. In February of the same year, Sofia Tolstaya wrote the following about some of her experiences: (about these kitchens) "Lëvochka and I have been making the rounds about the kitchens in a sleigh. […] I was struck […] by the terrible poverty and amazed that people, and especially children, could still live in the face of such poverty. Twice we took a tumble, there were ravines everywhere, and I realised to my horror just what dangers and hardships all those going around to the kitchens were subjected to."

1892 — An article entitled "Countess S. A. Tolstaya's refutation of rumours of L. N. Tolstoy's arrest" is published in *Nedelja* (N° 13).

1892: April — At LNT's request, SAT's portrait is painted by artist Valentin Serov. [47]

1892: October — Reports on charitable contributions appear in *Nedelja* (N° 30) and in *Russkie vedomosti* (N°N° 48 and 109).

1892: 21 November — Afanasij Afanas'evich Fet, with whom SAT has had a long friendship, dies. He had dedicated a number of his poems to her: [48] She in turn dedicates her prose poem *The poet* [Poèt] to him. [49]

1892–1893 — SAT writes the novella *Who is to blame? [Ch'ja vina?]* in response to LNT's *Kreutzer Sonata*.

---

46 The stories mentioned were retained in subsequent editions of *A new primer*. The words 'fleas' and 'lice' were replaced by others. *A new primer* continued to be published in this form right through 1910.

47 *Valentin Aleksandrovich Serov* (1865–1911) — prominent Russian portrait artist, son of the famous composer Aleksandr Nikolaevich Serov (1820–1871) and pianist Valentina Bergman (1846–?).

48 Notably: "Kogda stopoj slegka ustaloj…" [When with slightly weary step…] (1864), "Kogda tak nezhno rastochala…" [When so tenderly your eyes radiated…] (1866), "I vot portret! i skhozhe… — i ne skhozhe…" [And here's the portrait: so like you, yet unlike you…] (1885), "Ja ne u Vas, ja obdelen…" [When not with you, I am deprived…] (1886), "Pora! po vlage krugosvetnoj" [It's time! through global dampness] (1889).

49 For the text of SAT's poem, see Part II page 421. See also, T. V. Komarova, "A. A. Fet i S. A. Tolstaja (Po materialam jasnopoljanskikh memorial'nykh fondov)" [A. A. Fet and S. A. Tolstaya (On the materials of the Yasnaya Polyana Memorial Collections)], in the anthology *A. A. Fet i russkaja literatura* [A. A. Fet and Russian literature], Kursk–Orel, 2000: 258.

1893 — SAT proofreads and publishes the Ninth Edition of Lev Tolstoy's works. In addition to her diaries, she begins writing what she calls *Ezhednevniki* [Daily diaries] to record the most salient details of her and her husband's lives.

1893: beginning of February — During Shrovetide SAT takes her children to a performance of *Ring of love* [*Kol'tso ljubvi*] at Moscow's Bolshoi Theatre. She pays a visit to the Grand Princess Elisaveta Fëdorovna.[50] She reads N. Ja. Grot's[51] article on LNT and Nietzsche.

1893: 11 April — The illegitimate daughter of LNT's sister Marija Nikolaevna, Elena Sergeevna (*Lenochka*, 1863–1942), marries Ivan Vasil'evich Denisenko (1851–1916). The wedding is held at the Tolstoys' home in Moscow.

1893: spring — SAT wraps up the division of family property. "I was by that time living with the younger children at Yasnaya Polyana, and they were all sick. Two major projects took up a great deal of my time: completing the property division and publishing [Lev Nikolaevich's] *Complete collected works*. Both were a source of irritation to Lev Nikolaevich. He wanted to give away both his land and his writings — the first to the peasants, the second to the public domain — i.e., renounce his copyright. With nine living children to care for at the time, I protested, of course, and there were times when my husband hated me for it and kept expecting me to change my mind." (*My Life*, VI.57 - "Another trip to Begichevka")

1893: 9 September — SAT takes her sons Andrjusha and Misha to a Moscow *gymnasium* [school]. She reads novels by Paul Margueritte.[52]

1893: 16 September — The new Ninth Edition of LNT's works goes on sale. "It was a beautiful edition, with portraits and illustrations, on high-quality paper, and meticulously corrected by N. N. Strakhov." (*My Life*, VI.66 - "New edition out, the ninth")

1894: beginning of January — SAT is involved in building an addition to the house at Yasnaya Polyana, on the side opposite from the drawing-room.

1894: winter — In Moscow SAT reads the narrative *Zarnitsy* [*Summer lightning*] by Lidija Ivanovna Veselitskaja (pseud. Mikulich),[53] the drama *Zhizn'* [*Life*] by Ignatij Nikolaevich Potapenko[54] and *Chërnyj monakh* [*The black monk*] by Chekhov, as well as the philosophical works of Plato.

---

50 *Grand Duchess Elisaveta Fëdorovna Romanova (1864–1918)* — granddaughter to Britain's Queen Victoria (1819–1901) and wife to Grand Prince Sergej Aleksandrovich Romanov. She was a devoutly religious believer, known for her charity work.

51 *Nikolaj Jakovlevich Grot (1852–1899)* — professor of philosophy at Moscow University, known especially for his work on the psychology of feelings.

52 *Paul Margueritte (1860–1918)* — French novelist born in Algeria, who often worked in collaboration with his brother Victor. Their joint works included an account of their father, General Jean-Auguste Margueritte, who died in combat at the Battle of Sedan in 1870.

53 *Lidija Ivanovna Veselitskaja (pseudonym: Mikulich, 1857–1936)* — Russian writer (especially of children's stories).

54 *Ignatij Nikolaevich Potapenko (1856–1929)* — Russian belletrist, playwright and literary critic.

1894: January–February — The Tolstoys' son Lev L'vovich [*Lëva*] goes abroad to Paris, where he falls ill. Their daughter Tat'jana Andreevna [*Tanja*] joins him in Paris and cares for him until she is able to bring him home.

1894: 12–13 May — SAT takes (for the second time) eight trunks of LNT's manuscripts to the Rumjantsev Museum[55] for preservation. "Before leaving for Yasnaya Polyana I packed up eight boxes of manuscripts and took them to the Rumjantsev Museum for safekeeping." (*My Life,* VI.90 – "Manuscripts off to the Rumjantsev Museum")

1894: mid-June — A play is performed at Yasnaya Polyana for the peasant children. LNT dictates to his daughter Masha a five-act play on a peasant theme. SAT is asked to come up with and put on some kind of dramatic ending. The performance goes well: "but I should say, without boasting, that the presentation I thought up had a much greater success with the audience" (*My Life,* VI.94 – "A performance"). SAT takes Vanechka and Misha to see her son Il'ja at Grinëvka, then to see her son Sergej at Nikol'skoe, and from there to her brother in Orël, where the Kuzminskij family is spending the summer at their dacha near Pesochnaja Station.

1894: 15 August — SAT reads the 1894 story "Zimnij den'" [Winter day] by Nikolaj Semënovich Leskov,[56] "after which I began to dislike this writer even more". (*My Life,* VI.98 – "Lev Nikolaevich at Yasnaya with the children") She does proofreading, sewing and housekeeping.

1894: 20 October — Tsar Alexander III dies of illness, to be succeeded by his eldest son, Nicholas II (1868–1918), who reigns until the Bolshevik revolution of 1917.

1895: January — Vanechka is ill. He dictates the story *Spasënnyj taks* [*The rescued dachshund*] to his mother. "One time, while lying on the daybed in the drawing-room, he said to me: / 'Mamà, I'm tired of everything. I want to write like Papà. I shall say the words to you and you write them down.' / And he dictated to me, in a rather artistic fashion, a little story from his life as a child entitled *Spasënnyj taks* [*The rescued dachshund*]. This story was published in the children's magazine *Igrushechka* [The Little Toy][57] and

55 *Rumjantsev Museum* — a museum of art works originally collected by Russian diplomat Nikolaj Petrovich Rumjantsev (1754–1826). Opened in 1862, the museum lasted until 1925. Its library served as the basis for the Lenin Library during Soviet times (now the Russian State Library [*Rossijskaja gosudarstvennaja biblioteka* / RGB], the repository of many documents relating to LNT and SAT).

56 *Nikolaj Semënovich Leskov* (1831–1895) — Russian writer, author of *Skazanie o Fëdore-khristianine i o druge ego Abrame-zhidovine* [A tale of Fëdor the Christian and his friend Abram the Jew], which instantly attracted LNT to Leskov.

57 *Igrushechka* — an illustrated magazine for children edited and published (beginning in 1888) by Aleksandra Nikolaevna Peshkova-Toliverova (1842–1918), a close associate of the writer Nikolaj Semënovich Leskov. Vanechka's story was published in issue N° 3 (1895): 39–43. Peshkova-Toliverova also put out a literary journal under the title *Zhenskoe delo*

later in my book *Kukolki-skelettsy* [*The skeleton-dolls*]."[58] (*My Life*, VI.107
– "They're back!")

1895: end of January, early February — SAT transcribes *Master and man*
[Khozjain i rabotnik] and publishes Volume XIII of LNT's works. LNT
submits *Master and man* to Ljubov' Jakovlevna Gurevich's *Severnyj vestnik*. SAT lays "down the law: either he give *Master and man* to both me
and Posrednik, or I commit suicide" (*My Life*, VI.108 – "The difficult circumstances surrounding *Master and man*"). LNT refuses, and SAT runs
out of the house into the frosty cold. Her daughter Masha follows her
and brings her back. The next day, she wants to go to the Kursk Railway
line and throw herself under the wheels of a train. She is stopped by her
children Serëzha and Masha. The younger children Sasha and Vanechka
are frightened. LNT weeps, kneels down and begs forgiveness. "After my
illness Lev Nikolaevich agreed to give his story to both me and Posrednik.
He even offered to withdraw it from *Severnyj vestnik*. But I didn't want
that — I didn't want to place him in the awkward position of someone who
goes back on his promises. I. I. Gorbunov[-Posadov] and I hastened to get
Master and man ready for the presses, and it came out — to the great disappointment of L.Ja. Gurevich — simultaneously in three editions." (VI. 108)

1895: 23 February — Vanechka dies. He is buried on 25 February in the village
of Nikol'skoe north-west of Moscow.[59] Sergej Ivanovich Taneev's[60] music
and friendship help mitigate SAT's sorrow over the loss of her favourite
child.

1895: April — SAT goes to visit her sister Tat'jana Andreevna Kuzminskaja in
Kiev, returning to Moscow on 2 May.

1895: spring — She offers Taneev a room for the summer in an annexe at
Yasnaya Polyana.

1895: 10 July — SAT goes to the wedding of her son Serëzha and Marija
Konstantinovna Rachinskaja.[61] "Lev Nikolaevich didn't go to the wedding,
but they persuaded me to go. The wedding was at Petrovsko-Razumovskoe
at Manja's father's estate." (*My Life*, VI.119 – "Serëzha's wedding")

[Women's Forum]. She first met LNT in 1892.

58 *Kukolki-skelettsy* — a collection of five stories by SAT for children, published in Moscow
in 1910 with illustrations by Aleksandr Viktorovich Moravov. See entry under **1910** below.

59 In 1932 his remains were transferred to the Tolstoys' family plot beside the Nikol'skaja
Church in Kochaki, not far from Yasnaya Polyana.

60 *Sergej Ivanovich Taneev* (1856–1915) — prominent Russian composer and a frequent visitor to Yasnaya Polyana. SAT is infatuated with his music and describes her relationship to
him in both *My Life* and her narrative *Pesnja bez slov* [Song without words].

61 *Marija Konstantinovna* [Manja] *Rachinskaja* (1865–1900) — daughter to the director of
the Moscow Agricultural Institute Konstantin Aleksandrovich Rachinskij (1838–ca. 1909)
and first cousin to Sof'ja Èmmanuilovna Dmitrieva-Mamonova (1860–1946 — an artist and
friend of Tat'jana L'vovna's). She became estranged from Sergej L'vovich soon after the marriage and passed on within five years.

1895: 20 September — SAT goes to Yasnaya Polyana after learning of LNT's illness.

1895: October — SAT takes her children Tanja and Misha to St. Petersburg. Two premières take place on the 17th and 18th of October. "We went to see two performances: Taneev's opera *Oresteia* and *The power of darkness* (also a première). We stayed at the Europa Hotel." (Letter to LNT, 22 October 1895)

1895: December — *Grandmother's treasure-trove: a legend* [*Babushkin klad: predanie*] is published in the children's magazine *Detskoe chtenie* [Children's Reading] (1895, N° 12). "They published my children's story in *Detskoe chtenie,* but I haven't seen it yet… I am doing quite a lot of transcribing now for Papà, and I'm happy to have found a way to make myself useful. This reminds me of the old days, when I was young and used to help him in his work." (Letter to Lev L'vovich Tolstoy, 12/24 December 1895)

1895: 19 December — A Czech quartet performs at the Tolstoys' Moscow home, brought in by Taneev.

1895–1900 — SAT writes the narrative *Song without words* [*Pesnja bez slov*].

1896: January — SAT goes to visit her son Andrej in Tver', who is serving in the armed forces.

1896: May — The Tolstoys' son Lev L'vovich [*Lëva*], in Sweden for treatment by Dr Ernest Westerlund (1839–1924), marries Dr Westerlund's daughter Dora,[62] who subsequently accompanies him back to Yasnaya Polyana.

1896: 18 May — In Moscow SAT witnesses the aftermath of the tragedy at Khodynka Field, where a crowd of people, under pressure from a militia unprepared to handle such a gathering, stampedes, and more than 2,600 people die or are wounded. (See *My Life,* VII.14 – "The Khodynka tragedy")

1896: June — "I just got back from my sons' yesterday. I stayed four days with Il'ja and Sonja and felt very much at home with them. There's a lot there that is not to my liking: it's dirty, poor, lots of flies, lots of dogs and horses and all sorts of animals, yet there is also a lot of love, friendship, geniality, along with charming, kind and healthy children. Sonja is pregnant again. / "I was also at Serëzha and Manja's and was very upset: their place is all very clean, neat and well-appointed, but there's no love or happiness, and no life at all. They are both bored, sluggish, unnatural, not busy. She really didn't give the appearance of a wife, but simply an old maid. They probably won't be having any children. They've been trying to live out some kind of *theories* on marriage, but the whole marriage is falling apart as a result of these theories." (Letter to Lev L'vovich Tolstoy, 2 July 1896)

---

62 *Dora Fëdorovna Westerlund* (1878–1933).

1896: summer — At Yasnaya Polyana LNT is writing *Outline of faith* [*Izlozhenie very*] [63] and *What is art?* [*Chto takoe iskusstvo?*], which SAT transcribes.

1896: summer — SAT accompanies LNT to the Shamordino Convent to see his sister Marija Nikolaevna. "From Shamordino Lev Nikolaevich and I paid a visit to Optina Pustyn'. We stopped in a hotel there, from where we went to see an elder [*starets*], Father Gerasim,[64] with whom I desired to take confession. We were met by his novitiate. Lev Nikolaevich stayed outside and did not go in. The novitiate led me through a narrow *seni*[65] into a small, low-ceilinged room, where several other women were already waiting." (*My Life*, VII.18 – "Taneev's departure — Lev Nikolaevich and I visit a nunnery")

1896: November — "On one of my visits to Yasnaya Polyana that November I asked Lev Nikolaevich to transfer his copyright on all his writings to me, to make it easier to look after all the publishing side and spare him from having to sign documents, money orders, cheques, and such like. He gave me a flat refusal with a tone of dissatisfaction. I got upset and accused him of not being true to his principles, on the grounds that I alone was doing the work while others were reaping the benefits of my labours. I went on for quite a bit on this subject." (*My Life*, VII.26 – "Our son Serëzha's misfortune and Lev Nikolaevich's mood")

1897 — In Moscow SAT works on publishing LNT's *Complete collected works.*

1897: February — SAT goes to St. Petersburg with LNT. "On leaving Moscow, I went [first] to Nikol'skoe, and Lev Nikolaevich and I went to Petersburg together, which was naturally quite a delight for me. We left on the 6th of February 1897. The Olsuf'evs had invited Lev Nikolaevich to stop over at their house on the Fontanka Embankment, where Count Aleksandr Vasil'evich Olsuf'ev[66] lived on the second floor and where there was a free room downstairs. As the Olsuf'evs had not extended the same invitation to me, I decided to stop at a hotel. However, after going around to seven hotels and not finding a room for myself, I timidly went back to the Fontanka and asked Lev Nikolaevich to allow me to stay with him these few days, to which he willingly agreed. [...] ...[I] wrote a letter to the

63 This eventually became his treatise *Christian teachings* [*Khristianskoe uchenie*].
64 *Father Gerasim* — apparently a reference either to the hieroschemamonk Gerasim (birth-name: *Martynov-Bragin*, ?–1898), who established the Women's Nicholas Community in Medyn' Uezd of Kaluga Gubernia, or to his pupil, the *Abbot Gerasim* (?–1918), who founded and built the Priory of the Venerable Sergij Radonezhskij near Kaluga.
65 *seni* — a covered but unheated entranceway between the main part of a house and the porch.
66 *Count Aleksandr Vasil'evich Olsuf'ev* (1843–1907) — a high-ranking officer in the Imperial Court, brother to the Tolstoy family's close acquaintance Count Adam Vasil'evich Olsuf'ev.

Minister of Internal Affairs Goremykin,[67] asking him for an appointment to find out whether anything would be censored in my new edition, or whether I could print everything according to the previous edition. With a censor like Solov'ëv,[68] it was all too frightening and I didn't want to risk [a confrontation]." (*My Life,* VII.33 – "My trip to Petersburg – Chertkov and Birjukov exiled")

1897: 1 March — SAT goes to visit her son Andrej in Tver'. "On the 1st of March I went to Tver' to visit Andrjusha, and I remember spending just one day with him and my nephew Andrjusha Bers."[69] (*My Life,* VII.35 – "Return to the Olsuf'evs' and to Moscow")

1897: 6 March — "At one time I, too, lived this clean, country, family life without any complications. I couldn't possibly do that now — something's broken inside me. I have never needed and do not need now, Lëva, a manager, but a friend — a quiet, tender companion, with whom I can calmly live out the rest of my days. But, as though it had been planned deliberately, I have been left lonely as I approach my old age, and instead of friendship and tender, happy relations, I have more of the same (which is now quite untimely) — a degrading, passionate and all-round stormy and complex life, which brings only new pain and new disappointments." (Letter to Lev L'vovich Tolstoy, 6 March 1897)

1897: March — In Moscow: "One time I went to a lecture at the Synodal Academy where a priest read an anti-Tolstoy paper 'On the oath.'"[70] (*My Life,* VII.36 – "Music and a lecture")

1897: April — "On the 15th of April Scriabin[71] paid us a visit and also played. I don't recall just what he played — perhaps it was his own compositions — but neither his personality nor his music made any kind of favourable impression on us." (*My Life,* VII.37 – "April in Moscow – Gusev's murder at Yasnaya Polyana")

67 *Ivan Logginovich Goremykin* (1839–1917) — served as Deputy Minister of Justice (1891–94) and senator (1894–95), before being appointed Deputy Minister, then Minister of Internal Affairs in 1895 (a post he held until 1899). From April to July 1906, he served as Chairman of the Council of Ministers, a position he held again from 1914 to 1916. Following the revolution, he and his family were assassinated in December 1917 at their dacha in Sochi on the Black Sea coast.

68 *Mikhail Petrovich Solov'ëv* (1841–1901) — head of the government's press affairs department; also an artist, specialising in miniatures.

69 *Andrej Aleksandrovich* [Andrjusha] *Bers* (1878–1939) — son to SAT's brother Aleksandr Andreevich [*Sasha*] Bers (1845–1918).

70 *the oath* — the oath of allegiance, to be sworn by every man enlisting in or drafted into the Russian armed forces, including a pledge to defend Russia and the Tsar by military means.

71 *Alexander Scriabin* [Russian: *Aleksandr Nikolaevich Skrjabin*] (1872–1915) — Russian pianist and composer, who pioneered an atonal musical language; he was considered to be the father of musical *serialism*.

1897: 18 April — SAT goes with her daughter Sasha[72] to visit the Troitse-Sergiev Monastery.[73]

1897: 5 June — After yet another visit with Sergej Ivanovich Taneev: "I feel so little guilt and so much in the way of quiet, peaceful joy from my pure, peaceful relations with this man that I cannot destroy them in my heart, any more than I can stop looking, breathing or thinking." (*Diaries*, I: 241)

1897: 8 June — "Today I proof-read *The Kreutzer Sonata,* and again that same weighty feeling: how much cynicism [there is] and naked exposure of the wretched human side!" (*Diaries*, I: 244)

1897: 19 June — "There was some unpleasant illegal timber-cutting today. A poor peasant from Grumont [near Yasnaya Polyana], dressed in rags, bowed to the ground as he asked forgiveness. I wanted to cry and was annoyed at whoever (I don't know who, exactly) had placed me against my will in this position of being in charge of a household and protecting the forests. And to protect them I had to punish such pitiful peasants as this fellow. I never liked and never had any skill for running an estate. That amounts to a struggle for existence with the common people, which is something I am not capable of doing." (*Diaries*, I: 252)

1897: 21 June — "I discovered something strange about myself: it's as though I'm looking for an excuse to commit suicide. I've been nurturing this thought within me for a long time, and it is fast maturing. I am terribly afraid of it, just as I fear madness. But I also love it, even though I am prevented [from carrying it out] by superstition and simple religious feeling. I believe it is a sin, and fear that as a result of suicide my soul will be deprived of communication with God and with the souls of the angels, including Vanechka. [...] Now each time I experience suffering, or reproach, or unpleasantness, I joyfully think: I'll go to Kozlovka [the closest railway station] and kill myself and you [can carry on] as you please. [...] And now to write out a menu: *soupe printanière* — ach! How boring! *Soupe printanière* — *every day* for thirty-five years.... I shan't write out any more *soupe printanière*.... I want to listen to the most difficult fugue or symphony. Every day I want to listen to the most complex, harmonious music, so that my attention and my efforts harness my soul to understand what the composer wanted to say through this mysterious, complex, mystical language that he lived by in the very depths of his soul as he was composing this piece." (*Diaries*, I: 254)

1897: 15 July — "I am passionately thirsting for music, I would like to play a bit myself. But either there is no time, or Lev Nikolaevich is working, or he's

---

72 *Aleksandra L'vovna* [Sasha] *Tolstaya* (1884–1979).

73 *Troitse-Sergiev Monastery* [Troitse-Sergieva Lavra] — a monastery about 70 kilometres northeast of Moscow, founded in the mid-14th century by Sergij Radonezhskij (ca. 1320–1392).

sleeping — and everything bothers him. Without the personal pleasure I now find in music, life is boring. I try to reassure myself, that there is joy in the fulfilment of *duty*. I make myself do the transcribing, along with everything that comprises my *duty,* only sometimes my will breaks — I have a desire for personal joys, a personal life, *my own* work, and not work on someone else's writings, as it has been my whole life, and then I become weak and don't feel very well." (*Diaries,* I: 265)

1897: summer — Yasnaya Polyana. SAT transcribes *On art,* feels weighed down by this work, plays the piano, continues work on her story *Song without words*. Brief visits by Sergej Ivanovich Taneev. An excruciating description of her relationship with LNT.

1897: October — SAT transcribes *What is art?* "For the seventh time I had to transcribe the 'Conclusion' to his article *On art,* and then I had to correct the mistakes in Chapter X, insert excerpts from various books, as well as the decadent verses which Lev Nikolaevich hated so much." (*My Life,* VII.43 – "Departure of our daughters – My trips to Yasnaya Polyana and back to Moscow")

1897: 30 October–6 November — "On the 30th of October Lev Nikolaevich invited me to go with him to see his brother[74] in Pirogovo. I wasn't all that happy about traversing the 35 versts over a bad road, but I was happy to have the chance to be together with my husband for several days, and so we went. Lev Nikolaevich, to my dismay, rode a horse, while I was in a simple *rozval'ni,*[75] since the road was neither in its autumn or winter state. Lev Nikolaevich paid a price for this trip: he caught cold, and developed a bad pain in his back." (*My Life,* VII.44 –"At Yasnaya Polyana – A trip to Pirogovo")

1897: autumn–winter — SAT reads *Beethovens Leben* by Ludwig Nohl,[76] takes piano lessons, goes to symphony concerts, meets with Sergej Ivanovich Taneev, listens to his and Gol'denvejzer's[77] piano performances in their home.

1897: December — SAT faces difficult emotional turmoil. "I recall that on the 5th of December I enquired of Lev Nikolaevich again as to when he would come and, receiving no reply, I left for the Yasenki Station, where I was a hair's breadth from [another] suicide attempt. It seemed as though Lev Nikolaevich wanted to completely abandon me, forever. As the train approached, I looked madly and longingly at the railway tracks, but at that

74 *Count Sergej Nikolaevich Tolstoy* (1826–1904).
75 *rozval'ni* — a kind of low, wide sleigh, drawn by horses.
76 *Ludwig Nohl* (1831–1885) — author of *Beethovens Leben* [Beethoven's life], originally published in German in 1867.
77 *Aleksandr Borisovich Gol'denvejzer* (1875–1961) — Russian pianist and composer, a pupil of Taneev's, who met Tolstoy in 1896 and became profoundly influenced by his ideas. He served two terms as rector of the Moscow Conservatory (1922–24, 1939–42).

point I couldn't bring myself to throw myself under the wheels. / After arriving in Moscow, I was tormented by my sin of desiring suicide. In addition, I was in a very difficult mental state, and I at once went off to Troitse-Sergiev, not telling anyone where I was going. I took a room there, went to the church, had nothing to eat and wept the whole time." (*My Life*, VII.45 – "Return of our daughter Tanja – *On Art* again")

1897: 4–6 December — Trip to the Troitse-Sergiev Lavra, confession and communion.

1897: 25 December — A letter is received with a threat to kill LNT on 3 April 1898. This letter, postmarked 20 December 1897, is reproduced in SAT's diary under the date 25 December 1897 as follows: "Count Lev Nikolaevich! / There is no doubt that your sect is growing and putting down deep roots. Groundless as it may be, with the help of the devil and people's stupidity you have quite succeeded in insulting our Lord Jesus Christ, who must be avenged by you. For the underground struggle against you and your underground [followers], we have formed a secret society of the 'Second Crusaders', whose aim is to kill you and all your followers — the leaders of your sect. We quite admit that this is not a Christian undertaking, but may the Lord forgive us and judge us in the life to come! As much as we regret [this], once a hand has been infected with gangrene it must be sacrificed.[78] We feel sorry for you, too, as a brother in Christ, but with your destruction evil must lose its power! The lot has fallen upon me, unworthy as I am: I am the one who must kill you! I name the day: the 3rd of April of the coming year, 1898. I do this because it is my mission, in the name of all that is sacred, and so that you can prepare for your transition to the life to come. / You may well ask me a logical question: why is this protest aimed solely at your sect? It is true that all sects are 'an abomination unto the Lord' [Deut. 17: 1], but their instigators are mere twits and no match for you, Count. Secondly, you are the enemy of our tsar and our fatherland. And so, 'til the 3rd of April. / Second Lot Crusader, First Lot. December 1897. Village of Smeloe." Following the text of this letter, SAT notes in her diary: "This letter disturbs me to the point where I cannot forget it for a moment. I am thinking of informing the Governor of Ekaterinoslav Gubernia and the local [Moscow] Police Chief [Dmitrij Fëdorovich] Trepov[79] so that they

---

78 Cf. Matth. 5: 30: "And if thy right hand offend thee, pluck it out, and cast it from thee: for it is profitable for thee that one of thy members should perish, and not that thy whole body should be cast into hell" (*Authorised King James Version*).

79 *Major-General Dmitrij Fëdorovich Trepov* (1855–1906) — son of former St. Petersburg mayor Fëdor Fëdorovich Trepov. In 1896 he was appointed Police Chief of Moscow, and in January 1905 became Governor-General of St. Petersburg. In May 1905 he took on the additional role of Russian Deputy Minister of Internal Affairs while still retaining the governor-generalship. See: Dmitrij Romanovich Martynenko, "Rol' gosudarstvennoj vlasti v gibeli Rossijskoj Imperii" [The role of state authority in the collapse of the Russian Empire], Referat, Moscow 2007.

can take some precautions. If they want to, they can be on the alert for dangerous people. / Lev Nikolaevich has shown no signs of alarm, saying that I shouldn't alert anyone and trust everything to God's will" (*Diaries*, I: 333).[80] (See *My Life,* VII.45, 48)

1898: 4 & 8 January — SAT goes to see the opera *Sadko* by Nikolaj Andreevich Rimsky-Korsakov (1844–1908) and enjoys it very much.

1898: February — "I, too, had to go to Petersburg then — it seems it was February by that time — in connection with my publication of Lev Nikolaevich Tolstoy's writings. At the Moscow censorship board I was warned that the edition, in the form in which it was being sold, would not be cleared. / I requested an audience with the then Minister [of Internal Affairs] Goremykin. He politely responded that he would come to me himself, which he did. I was told of no difficulties with the new edition and soon returned home." (*My Life,* Part VII.49 – "At Pobedonostsev's and Goremykin's")

1898: 6 February — "...I don't know where he has hid[den] his latest diary, and I'm afraid he might have sent it to Chertkov. I'm afraid to ask him about it, too. Oh my God! My God! We have spent our whole lives together — all my love, all my youth I gave to Lev Nikolaevich. And here — the result of our lives: I'm *afraid* of him! Even though I have nothing to be ashamed of before him, I'm afraid of him. And when I try to analyse this feeling of *fear,* I stop the analysing right away. As my life has developed over the years, I have come to understand a lot of things all too well. / The consistency and cleverness with which he has blackened my name, elucidating only my weak points with brief, poisonous strokes of the pen, shows how *cleverly* he has fashioned for himself a martyr's crown, and the scourge of a Xanthippe[81] for me. / Lord! You alone be our judge!" (*Diaries*, I: 350)

1898: 12 February — SAT is enraptured by the Gospel illustrations executed by the French artist Tissot.[82]

1898: March — "In addition to this work, I was proofreading Volume XV of L. N. Tolstoy's *Complete collected works,* which needed updating and, in some places, a whole new typesetting. For example, I asked that [Lev Nikolaevich's] Foreword to Carpenter's article '[Modern] Science' be included in my Volume XV — the article had been translated by our son Serëzha. However, Lev Nikolaevich had sent this Foreword behind my back

---

80 This incident, along with the letter, was incorporated into a 2001 Russian play by Èmil' Solomonovich Kotljarskij entitled *Chelovek po imeni Lev (p'esa dl'ja mysljashchikh)* [A man named Lev (a play for rational people)].
81 *Xanthippe* (5th century BCE) — wife of Socrates, infamous because of her bad temper.
82 *James Tissot* [also known as *Jacques-Joseph Tissot*] (1836–1902) — French painter and engraver whose works were also popular in Britain. He painted a variety of New Testament scenes following a trip to Jerusalem and Palestine.

to a journal I did not like, namely, *Severnyj vestnik*. After getting permission from the censorship board for inclusion of this article in Volume XV, I had to have the whole thing typeset again practically from scratch." (*My Life*, Part VII.51 – "Death of Liza Olsuf'eva — Lev Nikolaevich's articles — A. F. Koni's lecture")

1898: March — SAT visits St. Petersburg. "I ended up going to Petersburg in any case, stopping over at my elder sister's — Elizaveta Andreevna Bers (née *Bers*, 1843–1919) — and called upon Prince Ukhtomskij[83] to ask him, on Lev Nikolaevich's behalf, to publish something about the Doukhobors and their [need for] assistance. [...] I spent only four days in Petersburg..." (*My Life*, VII.51)

1898: 8 March — "There is a struggle going on in my heart between my passionate desire to go to Petersburg to hear Wagner and other concerts, and the fear of annoying Lev Nikolaevich and having this annoyance on my conscience. I cried out during the night from this difficult situation of *lack of freedom*, which weighs ever more heavily on me. In actual fact, of course, I am free: I have money, horses, dresses — everything. All I have to do is pack up, get into the carriage and set off. I am free to do proofreading, buy apples for Lev Nikolaevich, sew dresses for Sasha and shirts for my husband, take all kinds of pictures of him, order [the servants to make] dinner, run [the household] for the whole family. I am free to eat, sleep, keep quiet and submit. But I am not free to *think* for myself, *love* whatever and whomever I have chosen myself, walk or ride where I find it interesting and pleasing to my mind. I am not free to get involved in music. I am not free to chase those innumerable, useless, boring and often very wretched people out of my house and receive those who are good, talented, smart and interesting. We don't need such people in our house. One must *come to terms* with them and stand on an even footing, but in our house there are people[84] who like to enslave and admonish... / And I don't find any fun in life, only challenges. I can't even use the word 'fun' — that's not something I need. I need to live *purposefully* and *peacefully,* and here my life is tense, challenging, and hardly purposeful." (*Diaries*, I: 364)

1898: 9 March — SAT begins transcribing *Hadji-Murat*.

1898: spring — "In the spring of 1898, at our son Lëva's request, I purchased the Khamovniki house from him [Lëva] for 58,000 roubles, and right up to the time I sold it to the city, I felt at home there. I felt sorry about selling it after Lev Nikolaevich's death. I loved that house, but I was prompted to sell

83 *Prince Èsper Èsperovich Ukhtomskij* (1861–1921) — diplomat, poet, translator and specialist in Oriental studies, editor of *Sankt-Peterburgskie vedomosti* [St. Petersburg News] who supported LNT's move to help the Doukhobors emigrate to Canada. However, LNT at first accepted but then later rejected his initial suggestion that the Doukhobors be relocated to Mongolia (see Donskov 2005: 22).
84 This appears to be a disguised reference to LNT himself.

it by the thought that it would be turned into a Tolstoy museum." (*My Life*, VII.54 – "Trubetskoj — A bust of Lev Nikolaevich — Selling the house")

1898: 2 April — "My acquaintances ask me why I *have faded away*, become taciturn, quiet and sad. I replied: 'Look at my husband: see how sprightly, cheerful and content he is.' / And nobody will understand that when I was *alive* — i.e., was involved with art, fascinated by music, books and people — then my husband was unhappy, alarmed and angry. On the other hand, when I (as now) sew shirts for him, transcribe for him, and quietly, sadly fade away, he is happy and at peace, even cheerful. And here is my heart-break! For the sake of my husband's happiness [I had] to suppress everything living inside me, stifle my passionate nature, become dormant and not love, but *durer* [endure], as Seneca wrote in regard to a meaningless existence." (*Diaries*, I: 370, echoed in *My Life*, VII.54)

1898: 30 May — A notation on an evening spent with Sergej Ivanovich Taneev: "Then we sat and talked the way people talk who trust each other implicitly — seriously, sincerely, without any holding back, without any silly jokes. We talked only about what was of real interest to both of us. Not once was it awkward or boring. / And what an evening it was! Our last evening in Moscow — possibly the last evening of my life, too. / At nine o'clock he started getting ready to leave, and I didn't try to hold him back. In bidding me farewell, he just said quietly and sadly: 'Got to leave some time.' I didn't answer, I felt like crying. I saw him to the door and went out into the garden. After that I put everything away, cleaned things up, locked the doors, and at midnight we headed off to Yasnaya." (*Diaries*, I: 386)

1898: 14 June — "I read our son Lëva's story 'Preljudia Shopena' [A prelude of Chopin's] in *Novoe vremja*. He doesn't have a lot of talent, just a little — he's sincere and naïve." (*Diaries*, I: 390; see also *My Life*, VII.57)

1898: 12–22 July — "I left Yasnaya Polyana on the 12th of July. I headed first to the Maslovs at their Selishche estate in Karachevskij Uezd. […] I asked Sergej Ivanovich Taneev (who was also visiting the Maslovs) to play me something. And so once again I heard this marvellous playing, which I considered to have no equal. He played Chopin's *Polonaise in A-flat major*, Schubert's *Morgenständchen* and something by Händel. […] From the Maslovs' I went to see the Kuzminskijs in Kiev. […] My sister Tanja Kuzminskaja went with me to Yasnaya Polyana, which delighted me and everybody at Yasnaya. We arrived on the 22nd of July." (*My Life*, VII.57–58 – "Birth of Lëvushka — My trip to my sister Tat'jana Andreevna's in Kiev and to the Maslovs' in Selishche"; "Return to Yasnaya Polyana — Guests — *Father Sergius — Resurrection — Hadji Murat*")

1898: 15–20 July — SAT visits the Kuzminskijs at their dacha near Kiev. "I spent the whole time with the Kuzminskijs. We had a picnic with other dachniks on an island in the Dnieper; we all went to the Kitaev Folk Theatre. We bathed in the Dnieper. On the 20th Tanja and I went into Kiev itself, where we saw St-Vladimir's Cathedral. The best picture there was *Voskreshenie Lazarja* [The raising of Lazarus] by Svedomskij.[85] Vasnetsov's[86] paintings, especially his *Kreshchenie Vladimira* [Baptism of Vladimir] and *Kreshchenie naroda* [Baptism of the people], are beneath any criticism. Nowhere is there any refinement of form. Eve's legs in Paradise, for example, when she is being tempted by the serpent, are something awful. / The site of Vladimir's monument[87] is magnificent, with a very good view of the Dnieper. Overall, the classic monuments — for example, the one to Bogdan Khmel'nitskij[88] in Kiev — are much better than the modern ones — e.g., the ugly monument to Pirogov[89] in *Deviche pole* [Maiden's Field].

We also went to see the caves.[90] I decided to do it this time. I all at once became fearful after we had reached the point of no return in this airless, dark, underground space, which was lit only by the candles we held in our hands. And the thought crossed my mind that the devil was blocking my way. But the monk leading us was saying to me at the same time: 'What is it with you, my dear? How come you're shy? People lived down here, and you're afraid just to walk through. See, this is a church. Pray!' And I started crossing myself mechanically and began reciting the words of a prayer. And, indeed, all my fear completely left me and I walked on with interest. I was struck by the little round windows in the walled-in rooms of the cave, where saints had walled themselves in voluntarily, with little windows through which they received food once a day, and they eventually

85 *Pavel Aleksandrovich Svedomskij* (1849–1904) — Russian painter, whose work *Voskreshenie Lazarja* adorns the walls of St-Vladimir's Cathedral in Kiev. He and his elder brother Aleksandr Aleksandrovich Svedomskij (1848–?) spent a long time living and working in Rome.

86 *Viktor Mikhajlovich Vasnetsov* (1848–1926) — celebrated Russian artist, known especially for his landscapes on historical and folkloric themes. He, too, had an artist brother, Apollinarij Mikhajlovich Vasnetsov (1856–1933).

87 *Vladimir's monument* — erected in 1853 according to a design by the late award-winning Russian sculptor Vasilij Ivanovich Demut-Malinovskij (1779–1846), who had earlier produced sculptures for the Kazan' Cathedral in St. Petersburg.

88 *Monument to Bogdan Khmel'nitskij* — an equestrian statue of the celebrated Ukrainian hetman erected in 1888 in conjunction with the marking of the 900th anniversary of Christianity in Rus'. It was the work of prominent Russian sculptor Vladimir Nikolaevich Nikolaev (1847–1911). Khmel'nitskij was the leader of the Ukrainian (also known as Maloruss) war of liberation against the Polish-Lithuanian empire, which he won only by accepting Russian help (and subsequent domination). In January 1654 the Treaty of Pereyaslav proclaimed Ukraine's union with the Russian Empire.

89 *Monument to Pirogov* — an 1897 statue of the prominent Russian military surgeon Nikolaj Ivanovich Pirogov (1810–1881), designed by sculptor Vladimir Osipovich Shervud (1832–1897).

90 *The caves* [peshchery] — an extensive and complex network of narrow underground passages in the proximity of the *Kievo-Pecherskaja Lavra* [Kiev Monastery of the Caves], where religious hermits resided. One of the larger caverns was actually used as a church.

died in these confines — they were living graves." (*Diaries*, I: 398; see also *My Life*, VII.57)

1898: 28 July — "My sister left on the 28th of July, and I got down to business transcribing *Father Sergius*." (*My Life*, VII.58)

1898: August — SAT spends time copying Lev Nikolaevich's diaries, so that one copy may be preserved in the museum while the other remains at Yasnaya Polyana. She also transcribes *Father Sergius* and works on the proofreading of LNT's *Complete collected works*. She is concerned that her husband wants to sell three of his stories — *Hadji Murat, Resurrection* and *Father Sergius* — at a slightly higher price in Russia and abroad and donate the money to the Doukhobors' emigration to Canada.

1898: 28 August — SAT organises Jubilee celebrations at Yasnaya Polyana in honour of LNT's seventieth birthday. She is overwhelmed by the number of guests (thirty-six at lunch, forty at supper).

1898: 12 September — "In the evening Lev Nikolaevich read aloud the story he is currently working on: *Resurrection*. I have heard it before. He said he had re-worked it, but it is still the same. He read it to us three years ago, the summer after Vanechka's death. Both then and now I was struck by the beauty of the secondary episodes, the details and the falsehood of the novel itself, the relationship of Nekhljudov to the prostitute in prison, and the author's attitude to her. It's all some kind of sentimental play involving stretched, artificial feelings which don't really exist." (*Diaries*, I: 410)

1898: 13 September — On *Resurrection*: "This story has made me feel very depressed. All at once I decided I would go to Moscow, that I could not *love* this work of my husband's, that he and I had less and less in common…. He noticed my mood and began to rebuke me, saying I didn't love anything that he loved or was involved in. I replied that I loved his art, that I was in ecstasy from his *Father Sergius,* that *Hadji Murat* interested me as well, that I had a great appreciation for *Master and man.* I cried every time I read his *Childhood,* yet I found *Resurrection* repugnant.' / 'You don't like my involvement with the Doukhobors, either,' he reproached.' / 'I can't find any compassion in my heart for people who refuse military service themselves and thereby force poor peasants to enlist in their place, and at the same time demand millions of roubles to take them out of Russia…. / 'I did have compassion for the plight of the famine victims back in 1891 and 1892, and even now. I helped, worked myself and contributed money. And now, if I am going to help anyone financially, it will be only the meek and starving peasants, and not the proud Doukhobor revolutionaries.' / 'I feel very sad that we're not together in everything,' said Lev Nikolaevich. 'And what about me?! I have suffered so much from this disunity.' But *all* his life Lev Nikolaevich [worked] for people and purposes alien to me, while [I devoted] *all* my life to the family. I could not get it into my head and heart why this story, after Lev Nikolaevich had renounced copyright (and announced it in the papers), now for some reason wanted to sell it for a huge price to Marks'[91] *Niva*, and to give the money not to his grandchildren, who have no white bread, and not too poor [peasant] children, but to the Doukhobors, complete strangers, whom I could never love more than my own children. And yet the whole world will know of Tolstoy's involvement in helping the Doukhobors, and history and the press will write about that. And in the meantime, his grandchildren and the children are left to eat black bread!" (*Diaries*, I: 411)

1898: 23 October — SAT talks with her son Sergej L'vovich about LNT: "Serëzha says I should give away the copyright on his father's works. I say: 'Why? To reward the rich publishers? That's a lie.'" (*Diaries*, I: 419)

1898: 27 October — "I asked a lot of questions about *Resurrection* and approved the change in ending and other places. There's less and less *falsehood*. I am transcribing Lev Nikolaevich's diaries and I don't like the way he was. Debauchery without repentance, a lack of love for people, vainglory." (*Diaries*, I: 419)

1898: November — In Moscow SAT arranges an evening's literary reading. "For some time I had been interested in a proposed celebratory evening in Moscow on the occasion of Lev Nikolaevich's seventieth birthday. A Mrs Pogozheva[92] was doing a great deal of promoting toward this end. For a reading at this celebration I asked Lev Nikolaevich for an excerpt from *The story of a mother* [*Istorija materi*] he had planned to write, which I was obliged to submit to the censorship board. In order to get some idea of the impression the reading of this excerpt would have on the public, I called together a few close friends. I enthusiastically read to them this touching beginning of the story, and at the point where it left off, [people] wanted to know what came next? They wanted to peer [deeper] into the soul of this mother who was both likeable and interesting. / Unfortunately, this story was never written. / In return for my reading, my guests Taneev and Lavrovskaja[93] delighted me with a whole evening of marvellous music. In spite of her advanced years, Lavrovskaja sang with great enthusiasm,

---

91 *Adol'f Fëdorovich Marks* (1838–1904) — publisher of the weekly journal *Niva* (subtitled: *Zhurnal literatury, politiki i obshchestvennoj zhizni* [A journal of literature, politics and public life]) — an illustrated, middle-class family-oriented journal published in St. Petersburg from 1869 to 1918.

92 *Anna Vasil'evna Pogozheva* (1865–1908)— Assistant Chairman of the Moscow Educational Entertainment Society [*Moskovskoe obshchestvo sodejstvija ustrojstvu obshcheobrazovatel'nykh razvlechenij*], who was involved in organising lectures on popular science as well as literary and musical evenings.

93 *Elizaveta Andreevna Lavrovskaja* (*Princess Tserteleva* by marriage, 1845–1919) — Russian contralto, soloist of the Mariinskij Theatre in St. Petersburg, appointed professor of the Moscow Conservatory in 1888. She also sang abroad on the opera stages of London, Paris, Milan and Berlin.

accompanied by Taneev [on the piano]." (*My Life*, VII.62 – "Serëzha's departure with the Doukhobors — A Tolstoy evening")

1898: 19 December — "We arrived from the party at Korsh's Theatre, which was supposed to be an evening celebrating Tolstoy's seventieth birthday. What a pitiful, unsuccessful evening! Poor singing, poor reading, poor music, and repulsive live scenes, devoid of truth, beauty and art — they had nothing." (*Diaries*, I: 432; see also *My Life*, VII.62)

1898: 20 December — A Tolstoy evening is held at Korsh's theatre. [94]

1898: 22 December — Sergej L'vovich Tolstoy sets sail from Batoum with a party of some 2,200 Doukhobors bound for Canada. SAT is alarmed by the fact that the party was quarantined upon first arrival at Halifax.

1898: 26 December — "I'm reading a marvellous book on Buddhism entitled *The soul of a people*. [95] What marvellous and simple truths one finds in Buddhism. It's something one seems to know instinctively one's self, but to be reminded of them, with conciseness of expression, excites one's soul." (*Diaries*, I: 435)

1899: 8 January — The Tolstoys' son Andrej L'vovich [*Andrjusha*] marries Ol'ga Konstantinovna Diterikhs (1872–1951), sister to Vladimir Chertkov's wife, Anna Konstantinovna.

1899: 15 January — "I shall read your article. Yesterday I was reading *Jasha Poljanov* [96] and felt touched by this novella. So much of my life — i.e., our family life — and how do you remember it? I've forgotten a lot. I'm not one of these people who remembers things, and I'm glad of it. For some reason it is *painful* to recall everything, either the bad or the good, and I weep." (Letter to Lev L'vovich Tolstoy, 15 January 1899)

1899: 16 January — "Today I was with Tchaikovsky [97] at a rehearsal of the ballet *Sleeping beauty*. The music was charming; the production was splendid. But I have grown tired of ballet and found it boring, and so I left." (*Diaries*, I: 441)

1899: 26 January — "I transcribed the corrected proofs of *Resurrection* for Lev Nikolaevich, and I found the deliberate cynicism in his description of the Orthodox service repulsive. For example: 'The priest held out to the people

---

94 *Korsh's Theatre* — one of Russia's largest private theatres, founded in 1882 (after the abolition of the government monopoly) by theatrical entrepreneur Fëdor Adamovich Korsh (1852–1923) with a production of Gogol's *Revizor* [*The Inspector-General*].

95 *The soul of a people* (English title given) — an 1898 book by Harold Fielding Hall, which ran through four editions and six additional reprints between 1898 and 1911. Reprinted 1995 (Bangkok: Orchid Press).

96 *Jasha Poljanov* — a pseudonym adopted by Lev L'vovich [*Lëva*] Tolstoy, evidently based on the name *Yasnaya Polyana*. The work referred to here is *Vospominanija dlja detej iz detstva* [Reminiscences for children, from childhood] (Moscow, 1899).

97 *Modest Il'ich Tchaikovsky* [Russian: *Chajkovskij*] (1850–1916) — Russian dramatist, younger brother to the famous composer Pëtr Il'ich and their sister Aleksandra Il'inichna. He wrote librettos to his elder brother's operas.

a golden image of the cross on which Jesus Christ was executed *instead of a scaffold.*' He referred to the communion [bread and wine] as *okroshka*[98] in a cup. All this provocation, cynicism, and coarse teasing of believers I found terribly repugnant." (*Diaries*, I: 444; see also *My Life*, VII.64)

1899: 7 February — "...on the 7th of February, I received a telegram [informing me] that my sister [Tanja][99] had fallen dangerously ill in Kiev. I immediately started making preparations, said goodbye to my family and with a heavy heart headed off to be with my sick sister." (*My Life*, VII.66 – "My sister Tat'jana Andreevna Kuzminskaja's illness — My illness in Moscow")

1899: February–March — SAT falls seriously ill with the flu and is confined to bed for eight days.

1899: April — "I wasn't alive during this time, I was sick in soul and body. The doctors talked about a weakening of my heart-rate; my pulse sometimes reached only 48 beats per minute. I was fading away and felt a quiet sense of joy at this gradual departure from [earthly life]. There was a lot of love and care shown to me by the whole family, friends and acquaintances during my illness. But I didn't die. God willed that I should live on. For what? We shall see." (*Diaries*, I: 450, echoed in *My Life*, VII.67)

1899: 27 May — The Tolstoys' daughter Tat'jana L'vovna undergoes an operation in Vienna for frontal sinusitis.

1899: summer — "My everyday life was then full of photographic and musical activities. Sometimes I would play for four hours at a time. I would often retreat to the empty annexe [at Yasnaya Polyana] where even at night I would not fear loneliness, as I would get carried away studying a Beethoven sonata, or a Chopin scherzo, or Mendelssohn's *Song without words*. [...] My main activity that summer was the transcribing of *all* Lev Nikolaevich's letters to me over thirty-seven years. Later I added to this, transcribing all the rest he had written right up to the end of his life. And now they have all been published. [...] Ol'ga [*née* Diterikhs], Andrjusha's first wife, was living with us at the time. She and I were transcribing *Resurrection* for Lev Nikolaevich — a project he was still working on — and we often played four-handed [piano pieces]." (*My Life*, VII.70, 72 – "My activities and trips"; "Our daughter Tanja's decision — My life")

1899 — SAT requests her son Misha's assignment to the Sumsk cavalry regiment, after being granted an audience with Grand Prince Sergej Aleksandrovich.[100]

1899: 14 November — The Tolstoys' eldest daughter, Tat'jana L'vovna [*Tanja*] marries Mikhail Sergeevich Sukhotin (1850–1914).

---

98 *okroshka* — a cold soup made from kvass, cucumber and other vegetables.
99 *Tat'jana Andreevna* [Tanja] *Kuzminskaja* (1846–1925).
100 *Grand Prince Sergej Aleksandrovich* (1857–1905) — son of Tsar Alexander II, appointed Governor-General of Moscow in 1891 and Commander of the Moscow Garrison in 1896.

1899: 24 December — "…I'm tired of the city, especially the crowd of visitors that comes to see Papà. I asked him to allow me to have a rest from entertaining guests, at least for a couple of days, but he refused. He seems to be actually bored without any visitors, while I'm extremely bored with this whole crowd. I can't even choose people to talk with, but am obliged to chatter along with all of them. Sometimes I find the din of voices overwhelming, and I start feeling dizzy. If Papà continues to torment me with his visitors, I'm going to have a nervous breakdown like last time. Yesterday I rebelled, and shut myself off downstairs. I ordered tea brought to me in the dining room, while I left him upstairs with some ladies who sat for twelve hours annoying him. Today he's more humble, thank God. His health is much better, he's out walking, he's cheerful, he's playing chess either with Vasja Maklakov,[101] Taneev and Gol'denvejzer or Serëzha. A few days ago we had some music: Gol'denvejzer and Konjus[102] played sonatas by Mozart and Händel with violin. It was very good." (Letter to Lev L'vovich Tolstoy, 24 December 1899)

1900 — "I shan't count up the year's events. The most difficult thing was the weakening of my eyesight. There was a rupture in a fibre in the left eye, and, as I was told by a professor of ophthalmology, an internal hæmorrhaging, almost microscopic. There was a black ring constantly in front of my left eye, acute pains in the eye and my vision tended to cloud over. This happened on the 27th of May, and after that all reading, writing, work and any sort of tension was forbidden to me. I went through a difficult six months of inaction, purposeless treatment, without bathing [in the stream], without light, without an intellectual life." (*Diaries*, I: 456, 5 November 1900)

1900: January — SAT begins her service as a trustee for the children's shelter, which lasts until February 1902. (See *My Life*, VIII.2 – "Shaliapin — The shelter")

1900: January — "At that time I was unable to practise my music, since the whole house was full of guests, and instead of music I worked assiduously on my novel[103] and finished it. But it still had to be revised. I got ready to study Italian, all on my own, and had already bought a self-instructional textbook. I was never able to survive just on practical chores and material cares, and always sought out some kind of artistic activity or philosophical

---

101 *Vasilij Alekseevich Maklakov (1869–1957)* — a Moscow lawyer, later a member of the State Duma, and an acquaintance of the Tolstoys'.
102 *Georgij Èduardovich Konjus (1862–1933)* — Russian composer and music theoretician, appointed professor at the Moscow Conservatory in 1920. He worked out the so-called theory of metrotectonism, positing a single law of symmetry and proportion in the construction of musical works.
103 A reference to SAT's *Song without words,* a narrative she had been working on since 1895. She kept revising it all during the year 1900.

reading." (*My Life*, VIII.4 – "My children gone — *The power of darkness in New York* — Guests — Lev Nikolaevich takes notes on a dinner")

1900: 24 December — death of the Tolstoys' grandson Lev L'vovich [*Lëvushka*]. (See *My Life*, VIII.13 – "Death of Lëvushka — A mother's sorrow — Tanja's stillbirth at Kochety"))

1900: 27 December — news that the Tolstoys' daughter Tat'jana L'vovna [*Tanja*] has had a stillbirth. SAT hastens to visit both of her grieving children. (See *My Life*, VIII.13)

1901: 19 January — "I have been busy collecting and transcribing as many of my letters as possible to Lev Nikolaevich over my whole lifetime. What a touching account these letters hold of my love for Lëvochka and my life as a mother! One of them reveals my sorrow over my spiritual and intellectual life (so typical of me), for which I was afraid to wake up, so as not to let go of my duties as a wife, mother and household manager. The letter was written under the impressions of music (a melody of Schubert's) which Lev Nikolaevich's sister Mashen'ka[104] was learning to play at the time, as well as the sunset and religious meditations." (*Diaries*, II: 10)

1901: 28 January — news of a stillbirth from the Tolstoys' daughter Marija L'vovna [*Masha*].[105]

1901: 31 January — The Tolstoys' son Mikhail L'vovich [*Misha*] marries Aleksandra Vladimirovna [*Lina*] Glebova (1880–1967).

1901: 26 February — SAT writes a letter to the Senior Procurator of the Holy Synod, Konstantin Petrovich Pobedonostsev and the Metropolitan, who signed the decree excommunicating LNT from the Russian Orthodox Church two days earlier. (See *My Life*, VIII.16 – "Lev Nikolaevich's excommunication — My letter to Pobedonostsev and the Metropolitan — Ovations for Lev Nikolaevich on Lubjanka Square")

1901: 16 March — SAT notes concerning Metropolitan Antonius' response: "He didn't move me at all. Everything was correct and everything was soulless. And I had written my letter to him with a single breath of my heart, and it encircled the whole world and *infected* people with its insincerity. But for me all that has now retreated into the distance, and life is going forward, forward, irrevocably, complicatedly and challengingly." (*Diaries*, II: 17) Both SAT's letter and the Metropolitan's response are published in *Tserkovnye vedomosti*, N° 7 (1901). (See *My Life*, VIII.16)

1901: 17 March — A concert is organised as a benefit for the children's shelter of which SAT is patron. (See *My Life*, VIII.12 – "Lev Nikolaevich's illness — Letter to the Tsar — Trip to Yasnaya Polyana")

---

104 *Marija Nikolaevna* [Masha/Mashen'ka] *Tolstaya* (1830–1912) — younger sister to LNT.
105 *Marija L'vovna* [Masha] *Tolstaya* married Nikolaj Leonidovich [Kolja] Obolenskij (1872–1934) in 1897. She experienced a series of stillbirths before her death in 1906.

1901: 5 September — After LNT's serious illness over the summer, the Tolstoys leave for Gaspra in the Crimea, where they spend the winter at Countess Panina's[106] dacha. (See *My Life,* VIII.18 – "The move to the Crimea")

1901: 12 November — The Tolstoys' daughter Tat'jana L'vovna [*Tanja*] experiences a second stillbirth. (See *My Life,* VIII.19 – "At Gaspra — Grand Prince Nikolaj Mikhajlovich — Lev Nikolaevich's inflammation of the glands (testicles)")

1901: 2 December — "Lev Nikolaevich turned out just the way I had expected: on account of his advancing years he stopped behaving (quite recently) toward his wife as a lover, and this was replaced not by what I had vainly dreamt of all my life — a quiet, tender friendship — but by utter emptiness. / Every morning and evening he greets me with a cold, crafted kiss and bids me good-bye. He treats my caring for him as a duty. He is often annoyed and looks at life around him with indifference. The only thing that excites, interests and torments him on the material plane is *death,* and on the spiritual plane — his work. / I find myself more and more often indulging with quiet joy in the thought of death — the realm to which my children have departed — where I imagine things are more peaceful. In *this* life there can be no peace. If we *strive* for it, if we *try to work out for ourselves* a wise, objective attitude to everything, religious meekness and understanding — life is thereby brought to an end. Life is the vigorous, uninterrupted shifting of feelings, it is a struggle — the rise and fall of good and evil. Life is life. You cannot stop it, nor would you wish to stop it voluntarily. But when the time comes for it to stop on its own, then you must accept it peacefully and joyfully and, having glimpsed God, submitting to His will, join together with God through the spirit, and with Nature through the body. And there can be nothing but good in this." (*Diaries,* II: 28)

1901: 7 December — "I received a letter from Countess Aleksandra Andreevna Tolstaya. What an amazing spiritual harmony this magnificent woman expresses! What real love and compassion she gives people! / I feel myself more and more inclined to believe that sectarianism of any kind, including my husband's teachings, dry up people's hearts and make them proud. I am close to two different women: Lev Nikolaevich's sister Mashen'ka (a nun), and the above-mentioned Aleksandra Andreevna, and both of them, while still remaining in the church, have become kinder and more exalted." (*Diaries,* II: 29)

1902: January–June — The Tolstoys continue their stay at Gaspra. SAT devotes her time to caring for her husband in his serious illness. Their daughter Marija L'vovna [*Masha*] experiences a seventh stillbirth.

---

106 *Countess Sof'ja Vladimirovna Panina* (1871–1957) — a close family friend of the Tolstoys'. Her invitation to the Tolstoys was extended twice — in her letters of 25 July (received 3 August) and 13 August 1901.

1902: 27 June — The Tolstoys return to Yasnaya Polyana and decide to stay there for the winter.

1902: 2 September — "Personally speaking, I find living in Moscow *easier* — there are a lot of people around whom I like, and there is a lot of music as well as amusements (both meaningful and just for fun) — exhibitions, concerts, lectures, contact with interesting people, social life. With my poor eyesight I find long evenings difficult, but life in the country is simply boring. Nevertheless, I recognise that for Lev Nikolaevich living in Moscow is *unbearable* with all the visitors and the noise, and so I am happy and content to live at my beloved Yasnaya, and will take trips to Moscow whenever life here wears me down." (*Diaries*, II: 75)

1902: 25 November — SAT fervently expresses her displeasure over LNT's legend *The destruction of hell and its restoration* [*Razrushenie ada i vosstanovlenie ego*]: "This piece is infused with a truly devilish spirit of denial, anger and mockery of everything in the world, starting with the church. These supposedly Christian thoughts, which Lev Nikolaevich puts into negative conversations on the part of devils, are clad in such coarse and cynical forms that reading them caused me painful displeasure; I was completely thrown into a fever. I wanted to cry out and weep. I wanted to put my arms out in front of me to defend myself against this devilish hallucination. / And I fervently and emotionally expressed my displeasure. If the thoughts included in this legend are true, where is the need to dress up as devils, with pointed ears, tails and black bodies? Wouldn't it be better for a seventy-year-old man, who has the attention of the whole world, to speak in the words of the Apostle John, who in a state of decrepitude and unable to talk, said just one thing: 'Children, love one another'.[107] / Socrates, Marcus Aurelius, Plato, Epictetus — none these saw fit to put on devil's ears or tails to proclaim their truths. But perhaps mankind today, whom Lev Nikolaevich is so adept at catering to, does need this. / And the children — Sasha,[108] who is still immature, and Masha,[109] who is alien to me — echoed their father's evil laughter with their own hellish guffaws. As for me, I felt like sobbing. Was it worth living so long for a piece like *this*?! God forbid it should be his last! May God soften his heart!" (*Diaries*, II: 80)

1902: 18 December — "I first read *The Weavers* by Hauptmann[110] and thought: all we rich people — industrialists and landowners — are living in this exceptional luxury, and so often I don't go the village [of Yasnaya Polyana] so as not to feel that discomfort or even shame on account of my privileged

107 I John 3: 11.
108 *Aleksandra L'vovna* [Sasha] *Tolstaya* (1884–1979).
109 *Marija L'vovna* [Masha] *Tolstaya* (1871–1906).
110 *Gerhart Hauptmann* (1862–1946) — German playwright, recipient of the 1912 Nobel Prize for Literature. His 1892 play *The Weavers* [German: *Die Weber*] was based on the 1844 uprising of the Silesian weavers.

position of wealth amidst their poverty. And, truly, their meekness and lack of resentment toward us are something to wonder at. / Next I read the poems of A. Khomjakov.[111] There is a good deal of real poetry in them, and a lot of feeling. I especially liked 'Zarja' [The dawn], 'Zvëzdy' [Stars], 'Vdokhnovenie' [Inspiration], 'K detjam' [To the children] and 'Na son grjadushchij' [For the coming sleep]. 'To the children' simply poured forth from the heart truthfully and fervently. People who don't have children don't know that feeling of parenthood, especially on the part of mothers. / You go at night into the children's room where there are three or four cribs or little beds, you look around, and you feel a sense of fulness, pride and richness... You bend over each one and peer into their innocent, charming little faces, and from each of them emanates a sense of purity, holiness and hope. You make the sign of the cross over them either with your heart or your hand, you pray over them and you go away with a tender heart, and there's nothing you need ask God for — life is full. / And now they've all grown up and gone off... And it is not the empty cribs that make you sad, but the disappointments in the destinies and qualities of your beloved children, and for so long you don't want to see or believe them. And you don't ask the children to pray for themselves, but you go on praying for them, for the enlightenment of their souls and their inner happiness." (*Diaries*, II: 84–85)

1903: 2 January — News from the Tolstoys' daughter Tat'jana L'vovna of stillborn twin boys.

1903: 17 November — "Happy are those wives who live on friendly and participatory terms with their husbands right to the end! And unhappy and lonely are the wives of egotists, great people, whose wives their descendants later turn into modern Xanthippes! / There's nothing in this life that I like. There is nothing to which I can apply the energy of life seething inside me, there is no contact with people, no art, no business, nothing but utter loneliness all day long, while Lev Nikolaevich writes and plays vint in the evening for his own relaxation. [...] / [At vint there was] nothing but idle chatter, to which I could never accustom myself. I tried participating in this chatter, just so as not to be left out, but each time I caught myself feeling ashamed and even more depressed from this game of cards." (*Diaries*, II: 98)

1904: 12 January — Nine boxes of materials originally presented to the Rumjantsev Museum, together with autographs, are transported to the Historical Museum, where they are kept until the end of LNT's life. (See **1914: 18 December** below)

---

111 *Aleksej Stepanovich Khomjakov* (1804–1860) — Russian columnist, theologian and philosopher, elected a member of the Petersburg Academy of Sciences in 1856; a founder of the Slavophile movement.

1904: 18 January — "I went twice to Arenskij's[112] opera *Nal and Damayanti*; it was melodious and graceful, but no strength. But what a charming ideal of real womanhood there is in this epic poem! / I went everywhere with Sasha. We were at a symphony concert with Shaliapin.[113] He is the most talented and clever singer I have ever heard in my life. There was also a [piano] concert by Gol'denvejzer, who played with greater liveliness than usual. Then there was a rehearsal of Chekhov's *Cherry orchard*, which gave me great pleasure. Delicate, clever, with humour, interspersed with the real tragic elements of the situation — all this was good." (*Diaries*, II: 98–99)

1904: 24 February — SAT begins work on her memoirs entitled *Moja zhizn'* [My Life]. "Last year Vladimir Vasil'evich Stasov[114] asked me to write an autobiography for a women's calendar. I did not think this very modest of me, and I declined. / But the longer I live, the more I see the accumulation of acute misunderstandings and false reports concerning my character, my life and a great many topics touching upon me. And so, in view of the fact that though I myself may be insignificant, the significance of my forty-two years of conjugal life with Lev Nikolaevich cannot be excluded from *his* life, I decided to set forth a description of my life — based, at least for the time being, solely on reminiscences. If time and opportunity permit, I shall endeavour to include several additional details and chronological data drawn from letters, diaries and other sources. / I shall try to be true and sincere throughout. Anyone's life is interesting, and perhaps there will come a time when my life will be of interest to some who wonder what kind of creature was the woman whom God and destiny found fit to place alongside the life of the genius and multifaceted Count Lev Nikolaevich Tolstoy." (*My Life*, Preface)

1904: March — SAT publishes a collection of nine prose poems under the general title *Groanings* [Stony] in the magazine *Zhurnal dlja vsekh* [Everybody's magazine] (N° 3) under the pseudonym *Ustalaja* [Weary woman].[115]

---

112 *Anton Stepanovich Arenskij* (1861–1906) — Russian composer, pianist and conductor, appointed professor at the Moscow Conservatory in 1882, where one of his pupils was the famous composer *Sergej Vasil'evich Rakhmaninov* (1873–1943).

113 *Fëdor Ivanovich Shaliapin* [Russian: *Shaljapin*] (also spelt in English: *Chaliapin*, 1873–1938) — one of the most prominent Russian opera singers (a bass) of the early 20th century, born into a peasant family in Kazan'.

114 *Vladimir Vladimirovich Stasov* (1824–1906) — Russian art, literary and music critic (as well as archæologist, art historian and social activist), an Honorary Member of the Petersburg Academy of Sciences. He preferred a realistic approach to the arts over a purely academic one. He worked with several prominent Russian composers in developing a more nationalistic approach to Russian music. He had especially high praise for LNT's narrative *The death of Ivan Il'ich* [Smert' Ivana Il'icha].

115 Reproduced in English translation in Part II of the present volume. See also the discussion in Chapter 4 above.

1904: 5 August — SAT sees her son Andrej L'vovich [*Andrjusha*] off to fight in the Russo-Japanese War.

1904: 8 August — "Something has again broken in my heart. Another line of demarcation has distinguished one significant period of my life from the next — seeing my son off to war, and the terrible impression from the departure of the soldiers in general. What is war? Could one stupid person, Nicholas II (who is not evil, and possibly crying himself), have set so much evil afoot? / It suddenly seemed to me that war was like a storm, a spontaneous phenomenon. It is just that we don't see that evil force which so mercilessly and assuredly crushes so many human lives to death. When someone takes a stick and digs up an anthill, and the ants perish, dragging their eggs and all kinds of dirt along, they do not see either the stick, or the hand, or the person devastating them; so, too, we do not see the force that is behind the murder of war." (*Diaries*, II: 106–07)

1905: 11 January — Andrej L'vovich returns from the war.

1905: March — SAT sends an open letter (for publication) to Vladimir Chertkov in England with her views on the Russo-Japanese War in connection with the appearance of an article by her son Lev L'vovich in *Novoe vremja,* in which he supports the continuation of the war. SAT has heard rumours that she has inspired these views in her son. The letter counters these rumours and is published in *The Times.*

1905: summer–autumn — SAT continues to paint in oils. She copies her letters to LNT and goes on writing *My Life.*

1905: 6 November — The Tolstoys' daughter Tat'jana L'vovna [*Tanja*] gives birth to a daughter of her own, also named Tat'jana.[116]

1906 — SAT continues her oil painting and photography, helps look after her granddaughter Tat'jana, continues with *My Life,* works with papers at the Historical Museum. The Tolstoys' eldest son, Sergej L'vovich [*Serëzha*], marries for the second time, this time Marija Nikolaevna Zubova (1868–1939).

1906: 30 July — "Lev Nikolaevich read aloud his article *Two roads* [*Dve dorogi*]. [I keep having] dreams of a common Christian life. As always, the negative side is dominant, while the positive side is weak." (*Diaries*, II: 251)

1906: 22 August — SAT takes ill, experiences severe pain on the left side of her stomach.

1906: 1 September — "I took confession and communion, bade touching farewells to everyone and the staff. All the children except Lëva gathered. I saw death was near at hand. All my love for the children and Lev Nikolaevich came welling up in me with great strength." (*Diaries*, II: 253)

---

116 *Tat'jana Mikhajlovna* [Tanja/Tanjusha] *Sukhotina* (1905–1996) — daughter to Tat'jana L'vovna Sukhotina (*née* Tolstaya) and Mikhail Sergeevich Sukhotin. After managing the Yasnaya Polyana estate from 1917 to 1923, Tat'jana L'vovna emigrated with her daughter — first to France and later to Italy. In 1930 her daughter, Tat'jana Mikhajlovna, married an Italian named Leonardo Giuseppe Albertini (1903–1960). She died in Rome in August 1996.

1906: 2 September — SAT undergoes an operation performed by Dr V. F. Snegirëv.[117]

1906: 27 November — The Tolstoys' daughter Marija L'vovna [*Masha*] dies from inflammation of the lungs.

1907 — The Tolstoys' son Andrej L'vovich [*Andrjusha*] marries for the second time, this time Ekaterina Vasil'evna Gorjainova (Artsimovich) (1876–1959).

1907: 28 January — "In the morning I was at an Itinerant [*Peredvizhniki*] exhibition. The landscapes of E. Volkov's[118] and Dubovskoj's[119] were marvellous; those of Kiselev's[120] not so good. Vladimir Makovskij's[121] *Dve materi* [Two mothers] and especially his *Okhotniki* [Hunters] were excellent." (*Diaries*, II: 259)

1907: 25 February — "The whole day I spent running from exhibition to exhibition: the Union of Russian artists,[122] Borisov-Musatov,[123] Nesterov.[124] The last was the best of the three. Musatov is terrible in his decadence. Russian artists are on the wrong track and are of little interest." (*Diaries*, II: 261)

1907: 19 April — "I painted benches, taught Dorik,[125] read Lëva's drama *Landowner brothers* [Brat'ja pomeshchiki]. It's not bad, it stages well, and is lively, but it is contemporary, and that is always a mistake.

117 *Dr Vladimir Fëdorovich Snegirëv* (1847–1917) — professor of gynæcology at Moscow University, where he practised the methods of Dr Grigorij Antonovich Zakhar'in, who had earlier treated SAT.

118 *Efim Efimovich Volkov* (1843–1920) — Russian landscape artist. On 15 April 1887 SAT wrote LNT: "Today I was at the exhibition with Masha and the youngsters. ...everything's pretty monotonous. There is one landscape by Volkov, *Tishina* [Silence]. You know, if it hadn't been sold, I might have done something foolish and bought it. Amazing, how good it is! I would gaze at it in my disturbed moments, and oh how that *silence* would penetrate my soul." (S. A. Tolstaja, *Pis'ma k L. N. Tolstomu*. Moscow-Leningrad, 1936: 403)

119 *Nikolaj Nikanorovich Dubovskoj* (1859–1918) — Russian landscape artist. One of his best-known paintings, first presented at the 1903 exhibition, was *Na Volge* [On the Volga]. Volkov had already painted another scene with this same title in 1892.

120 *Aleksandr Aleksandrovich Kiselev* (1838–1911) — Russian painter; as a prominent member of the Itinerant school of Russian Artists, he specialised in peasant themes and was active in peasant education programmes.

121 *Vladimir Egorovich Makovskij* (1846–1920) — a founding member of the Itinerant school. He was known during the 1870s and 1880s for his humorous works on everyday social scenes; later he confined himself to more serious subjects. From 1895 to 1918 he served as Rector of the St. Petersburg Academy of the Arts. His elder brother — Konstantin Egorovich Makovskij (1839–1915) — was also a professional artist.

122 *Union of Russian artists* [Sojuz russkikh khudozhnikov] — a group that had just formed in February 1903, comprising the members of two former groups: *Thirty-six artists* and *The world of art*.

123 *Boris Èlpidiforovich Borisov-Musatov* (1870–1905) — Russian artist who often painted on the theme of man's harmony with Nature.

124 *Mikhail Vasil'evich Nesterov* (1862–1942) — Russian artist who was also known for his illustrations for Russian books, notably Pushkin's works.

125 *Fëdor Mikhajlovich* [Dorik] *Sukhotin* (1896–1921) — son of Mikhail Sergeevich Sukhotin (husband of Tat'jana L'vovna Tolstaya) by a previous marriage.

One ought to write about what is eternal and universal, and not arbitrary." (*Diaries*, II: 263)

1907: 20 May — SAT receives news about the murder of her brother Vjacheslav[126] by some workers.

1907: 8 August — "Our servant Aleksej told me a strange story about some hooligans questioning him about our house and offering him a hundred roubles for his collaboration. Everybody was afraid, nobody slept. I wrote to the Governor, and I sent out to buy a rifle." (*Diaries*, II: 268)

1907: September — Il'ja Efimovich Repin[127] comes for a visit and paints portraits of LNT and SAT.

1907: 27 November — "The day [= anniversary] of our daughter Masha's death. Exactly a year ago. How sad and often strange it seems that she is no longer with us. My life is quiet, lonely, depressed. I amuse myself by painting portraits — a big waste of attention and energy." (*Diaries*, II: 275)

1908 — The *Diaries of S. A. Tolstaya 1860–1891* are published by M. & S. Sabashnikov in Moscow, under the editorship of Sergej L'vovich Tolstoy.

1908: 28 August — celebration of LNT's 80th birthday.

1908: 16 September — "I feel burdened by all the bustle of household cares, which overshadow life itself, and I have thoughts about my approaching death. / It's as if everything is in preparation — what seems to be a *preparation* for life, but there is no life — i.e., there's no real, peaceful or leisurely life, no time for the activities which I really enjoy. This is where Lev Nikolaevich has been smart and happy his whole life. He has always worked at what *he* enjoys, and not because it was something he had to do. He would write whenever he wanted to. He would be out ploughing whenever he wanted to. Whenever he got tired of something, he would drop it. Would I ever try living like that? What would become of the children, or Lev Nikolaevich himself?" (*Diaries*, II: 114)

1908: 30 September — "I've given myself completely to household tasks. But this has been possible for me only because I've done it in conjunction with a constant communication with Nature and an admiration thereof. [...] Today I took a walk in the apple orchard. There are forty people out there clearing away moss, cutting up dried hay, smearing the tree-trunks with a clay, lime and cow-dung mixture. What beauty there is in these gaily coloured figures of girls against a background of still fresh green grass, the light-blue sky, the trees with their brown, red and yellow leaves! I long admired a particular apple tree, bearing Oporto apples. Such a symphony of colours — tender yellow, pink and bright green — would be difficult to reproduce [in words]; the whole figure of the apple tree is precious. [...]

---

126 *Vjacheslav Andreevich Bers* (1861–1907).

127 *Il'ja Efimovich Repin* (1844–1930) — celebrated Russian artist and memoirist. Repin was a close friend of LNT's, had many discussions with him about art, and did quite a few portraits of the writer using various media.

During all this time I read articles about Lev Nikolaevich, about us, in all different languages. Nobody really knows or understands him. I know the actual essence of his nature and mind better than anybody else. But no matter what I write, people will not believe me. Lev Nikolaevich is a man of tremendous intellect and talent, a man of extraordinary imagination, sensitivity and artistic instinct. Yet he is also a man without a real heart or genuine kindness. His kindness is *conceptual,* not *direct.* [...] I am depressed and lonely in my soul; nobody loves me. Apparently, I am unworthy. There is a good deal of passion within me, an unmitigated compassion for people, — but there's not much kindness in me, either. My best qualities are a feeling of duty and motherhood." (*Diaries*, II: 116–17)

1909: 12 March — SAT raises a protest in the newspapers against the exile of Vladimir Grigor'evich Chertkov out of Tula Gubernia.

1909: July — SAT takes ill with neuralgia in her left hand and inflammation of her left lung. LNT prepares to go to a world congress in Sweden. SAT is opposed to the trip.

1909: 1 July — "I amuse myself by painting roses in oils, but nothing comes of it. I get paid for haycutting, while peasants' money burns my hands." (*Dnevniki*, II: 288)

1909: 8 November — "Today I wrote my last will and testament, but only in draft form and with no witnesses for the time being. Then I finished making a list of materials for my *Notes*. My right eye is almost completely blind, and that is painful." (*Diaries*, II: 296)

1910 — SAT's collection of children's stories is published under the title *Kukolki-skelettsy* [*The skeleton-dolls*] (with eight colour illustrations painted by artist Aleksandr Moravov).[128] It includes not only her stories *The skeleton-dolls, Grandmother's treasure-trove* [*Babushkin klad*] and *The story of a grivennik* [*Istorija grivennika*], but also a story composed by her youngest son Ivan, called *The rescued dachshund, Vanja's story* [*Spasënnyj taks. Rasskaz Vani*], as well as *Vanechka: a real occurrence from his life* [*Vanechka: istinnoe proisshestvie iz ego zhizni*].

1910: 20 May — "I spent about three hours walking around Yasnaya Polyana. While I was picking flowers and admiring Nature, the sky and everything, it was fine. But at the peak of its flourish the orchard was attacked by weevils; the harvest was scanty, the earth was not fertile. There was a struggle with the peasants over wood, over the meadowlands damaged by the cattle, and managing the estate is one big headache." (*Diaries*, II: 319)

1910: 29 May — "I had a difficult conversation with Lev Nikolaevich... He reproached me for our aristocratic lifestyle and for my complaining about the difficulties in managing the household. He chased me out of Yasnaya

---

128 *Aleksandr Viktorovich Moravov* (1878–1951) — a member of the *Peredvizhniki* [Itinerant] group of artists.

Polyana [and said I should go] live in Odoev, or Paris, or somewhere else. I went (out of the house). It was hot, my foot was hurting, my pulse was beating fearfully, I lay down in a ditch and lay there until someone was sent with a horse to look for me. I spent the rest of the day in bed, ate nothing, and wept." (*Diaries*, II: 321)

1910: 26 June — "My life with Lev Nikolaevich is becoming more unbearable by the day because of his heartlessness and cruelty towards me. And this is all the fault of Chertkov, gradually and consistently over a period of time. He has taken hold of this unfortunate old man any way he can, he has separated us from each other, he has killed the spark of artistry in Lev Nikolaevich and kindled the condemnation, hatred and denial which I have sensed in Lev Nikolaevich's articles these past few years, which he had written under the influence of a stupid evil genius." (*Diaries*, II: 119)

1910: 1 July — SAT writes a letter to Chertkov as well as tells him verbally to return LNT's diaries: "Chertkov peppered our whole conversation with obscenities and coarse thoughts. For example, he would cry: 'You're afraid that I will expose you through the diaries. If I wanted to, I could throw as much smut (quite an expression for a supposedly decent man) at you and your family as I liked.' [...] Chertkov also snapped that if he were married to a wife like me he would have either shot himself or run off to America. Later, on coming down the stairs with our son Lëva, Chertkov maliciously said regarding me: 'I don't understand a woman who has been involved all her life in murdering her husband.' / It must have been a pretty slow murder, if my husband's already 82. And he persuaded Lev Nikolaevich that this was so, and that is why we are unhappy in our senior years. [...] I have lost my long-time influence and love for ever, unless the Lord has mercy on me." (*Diaries*, II: 127)

1910: 7 July — "Evening. No, Lev Nikolaevich has not yet been taken away from me, thank God! All my sufferings, all my energy of fervent love for him have broken the ice that was separating us these past days. Nothing can stand up to the heartfelt link between us; we are tied together by a long life and a solidly grounded love. I went up to see him as he was going to bed and said to him: 'Promise me that you will never slip away from me quietly, on the sly.' He responded: 'I have no plans to do that, and promise you that I shall never leave you; I love you' — and his voice trembled. I started crying. I embraced him, saying how afraid I was of losing him, that I fervently loved him, and despite the guilty and silly distractions over the course of my life, I never for a moment ceased loving him more than anyone else in the world, right into his old age. Lev Nikolaevich said that the feeling was mutual, and that I had nothing to worry about, that the link between us was too great for anyone to break. And I felt that this was true, and I began to feel happy. I went to my room, but returned once more to thank him for lifting the stone from my heart." (*Diaries*, II: 134)

1910: 14 July — "Lev Nikolaevich came in, and I told him with fearful emotion that the return of the diaries hung in one side of the balance, my life in the other. It was up to him to choose. And he chose — thank God he did — to get the diaries back from Chertkov. [...] For three days straight I had had nothing to eat, and that for some reason alarmed everyone, but that was the least of it... The crux of the matter was in [my] passion and strength of [my] irritation. I very much regret and repent that I also irritated my children, Lëva and Tanja — especially Tanja. Once again she was so loving, compassionate and kind toward me! I love her very much. I need to allow Chertkov to visit us, even though to me he is very, very difficult and unpleasant. If I don't permit these meetings, there will be a whole litany of secret, fraternal correspondence, which is even worse." (*Diaries*, II: 144–45)

1910: 22 July — Behind his wife's back LNT signs a codicil to his will giving rights to his inheritance to his daughter Aleksandra.

1910: 27 July — "Morning. Again, I didn't get any sleep all last night. My heartache keeps festering from the horrible uncertainty as to some kind of conspiracy with Chertkov and a paper which Lev Nikolaevich signed yesterday. (Apparently, this was a codicil to his will, drawn up by Chertkov and signed by Lev Nikolaevich.)[129] This paper was his revenge on me for [my complaining about] the diaries and Chertkov. Poor old man! What kind of legacy is he preparing to leave?! His heirs will not yield to Chertkov *one bit*, and they *all* will contest [the will], since they all hate Chertkov and they all see his sly evil influence. *Non-resistance*, as might have been expected, has turned out to be an empty word." (*Diaries*, II: 159).

1910: 3 August — "I wanted to explain to Lev Nikolaevich the reason for my jealousy of Chertkov and showed him a page from a diary he had written in his youth, back in 1851, where he said that he had never fallen in love with women, but had many times fallen in love with men. I thought that he, like P.I. Birjukov[130] and Dr Makovitskij,[131] would understand my jealousy and calm me down, but instead he went all white and displayed such a fury that I had not seen in a long, long time." (*Diaries*, II: 166)

1910: 12 October — "Today I told Lev Nikolaevich that I knew about his arrangement. He had a pitiful, guilty look and was evasive the whole time.

---

129 This parenthesis was a later addition to SAT's diary.
130 *Pavel Ivanovich* [Posha] *Birjukov* (1860–1931) — social activist and political commentator, as well as a friend, follower and biographer of LNT. Of noble birth, Birjukov was a graduate of the Page Corps and the naval academy. In 1895 he went to the Caucasus to study the Doukhobor movement and report back to Tolstoy; he later spent time with the Doukhobor émigrés in Canada. He was also instrumental in establishing the Tolstoy Museum in Moscow and served as the first curator of its manuscript division.
131 *Dushan Petrovich Makovitskij* (1866–1921) — a Slovak immigrant and friend of the Tolstoys, who served as their personal physician from 1904 to 1910. Dr Makovitskij accompanied LNT on many of his trips and outings during that time, as well as on his final departure from Yasnaya Polyana in 1910.

I said that it was wrong for him to sow evil and contention, that the children would not give up their rights without a fight. And it was painful for me to see that over the grave of a loved person could arise so much evil, reproaches, court cases and difficulties! Yes, it was an evil spirit that was arming the hand of this Chertkov — he wasn't named after the devil for nothing!"[132] (*Diaries*, II: 212–13)

1910: 13 October — "The thought of suicide is growing in me again, and more forcefully than before. Now it feeds on silence. […] Life is becoming unbearable. It's like living under bombs dropped by Mr Chertkov. […] And it is this despotism that has enslaved an unfortunate old man. Besides, back in his youth, when he wrote in his diary that he was in love with one of his chums, the main thing was that he tried to *please* him and not irritate him. In fact one time he spent eight months of his life in Petersburg for this very reason… He's doing the same thing now. He thinks he has to *please* this idiot's emotions and obey his every whim." (*Diaries*, II: 213–14)

1910: 9 November — "What happened on the 26th and 27th [of October] was not recorded, but on 28 October, at 5 o'clock in the morning, Lev Nikolaevich stole out of the house along with [his doctor] D. P. Makovitskij. The excuse for his flight was that I had supposedly gone through his papers at night, but even though I did drop into his study for a moment, I did not touch a single paper; indeed, there were *no* papers on his desk. In a letter to me (for the whole world), his excuse was [to extricate himself from] a luxurious lifestyle and a desire to escape to *solitude* — to live in a hut like the peasants.[133] […] / Having learnt of Lev Nikolaevich's flight from Sasha and the letter, I threw myself into the pond in despair. Alas, Sasha and Bulgakov[134] pulled me out. After that I did not eat for five days, but on the 31st of October at 7.30 in the morning I received a telegram from the offices of *Russkoe slovo*: LEV NIKOLAEVICH SICK AT ASTAPOVO STOP FORTY DEGREE FEVER. Our son Andrej and daughter Tanja and I went by emergency train from Tula to Astapovo.

132 The word *Chertkov* includes the word *chert* (lit., 'devil').
133 LNT himself wrote in his farewell letter: "I can no longer live in such luxurious conditions as I did, and I am doing what old men of my age usually do: they forsake worldly life to live out their remaining days in solitude and quietude." (*PSS*, 84: 404; also *Dnevniki*, II: 509, Note 155)
134 *Valentin Fëdorovich Bulgakov* (1886–1966) — a devoted Tolstoyan who served as LNT's personal secretary during the last year of the writer's life. He was personally responsible for preventing SAT from committing suicide after her husband's death. He stayed on for several years at Yasnaya Polyana and helped SAT sort what remained of LNT's papers. He also published two books of his own memoirs — *L. N. Tolstoj v poslednij god ego zhizni* [L. N. Tolstoy during the last year of his life] and *Zhizneponimanie L. N. Tolstogo v pis'makh ego sekretarja* [Tolstoy's world view in the letters of his secretary] — which were quickly translated into a variety of languages. See, for example: Bulgakov 2012, 2014.

I was not permitted to see Lev Nikolaevich; they were holding him by force; they had locked the doors, tearing my heart.[135] On 7 November at 6 a.m. Lev Nikolaevich passed on. On 9 November he was buried at Yasnaya Polyana." (*Diaries*, II: 225–26)

1910: 10 November — SAT falls ill herself; her illness lasts until the end of November.

1910: 15 November — "My son Serëzha, Mar'ja Aleksandrovna, [M. V.] Bulygin and [N.N.] Ge spent the day with me. [My daughter] Sasha came, and she and I got along well. I did a lot of crying. My final separation from Lev Nikolaevich was unbearable." (*Diaries*, II: 330)

1910: 16 December "The whole village of Yasnaya Polyana — peasant men, women and children — gathered today at the grave on the fortieth day of Lev Nikolaevich's passing, which we fixed up and decorated with fir branches and wreaths. Three times they fell to their knees, doffed their caps and sang 'Eternal memory' [*Vechnaja pamjat'*]. I found myself crying and suffering a lot, but at the same time I was heartened by the people's love. And how affectionate they all were toward me. I wrote my sister Tanja, my daughter Tanja, Il'ja and Andrjusha. [I felt] lonely and burdened!" (*Diaries*, II: 330)

1911 — SAT publishes a twenty-volume edition of LNT's works, in which she attempts to correct a series of earlier works by carefully checking the text against LNT's original manuscripts (*Childhood, The raid, The Kreutzer Sonata*).

1911: January — The Tolstoys' daughter Aleksandra, acting on her late father's wishes, sends out a notarised document forbidding SAT access to the room in the Historical Museum containing family documents and ordering her to cease publication of the latest edition of LNT's works. SAT files a countersuit. SAT goes to her husband's grave, where she prays and asks his forgiveness. (See entry under **1914: 18 December** below)

1911: 4 January — "My sons Il'ja, Andrej and Misha came rushing in and asked for 1,500 roubles. They were going to send Il'ja off to America to sell Yasnaya Polyana, which was sad and repugnant to me. I didn't go along with it. I wanted to see Yasnaya Polyana [remain] in Russian and public hands." (*Diaries*, II: 333)

1911: 17 February — Volumes XVI, XIX and XX of LNT's *Complete collected works* are detained by the censors. SAT writes a number of letters on this.

135 At this point LNT was in the company of his daughters Tat'jana [*Tanja*], Aleksandra [*Sasha*] and his son Sergej [*Serëzha*]. His doctor, Dushan Makovitskij — along with two colleagues — made the following statement in "Medical conclusions regarding the death of L. N. Tolstoy": "At a family consultation, in agreement with the doctors' advice, it was decided that no other relative would be allowed to see Lev Nikolaevich, since there was reason to believe that the appearance of new people would upset Lev Nikolaevich, which could have a fatal effect on his life, which was hanging by a thread." (*Diaries*, II: 509–10, Note 157)

1911: 10 May and 18 November — SAT twice petitions the Tsar with an appeal to have Yasnaya Polyana be acquired as State property. In her first appeal she writes as follows: "The passing of my husband, Count L. N. Tolstoy, and his will, have so impoverished his large family, consisting of seven children and twenty-five grandchildren, that some are no longer in a position either to bring up or even to feed their children. It is with heartfelt pain that we recognise the necessity of selling the valuable estate the deceased willed to us before his death — an estate near the village of Yasnaya Polyana consisting of 885 desjatinas. We no longer have any possibility of maintaining it in our family. In any case, even though selling off the land in small lots would be financially advantageous to us, we find that prospect exceedingly distasteful, as the birthplace and burial site of a man so dear to us could easily fall into obscurity. It is our fervent wish to hand over his 'cradle and grave' to the protection of the State. It is this motivation, along with our cramped financial status, that emboldens us to resort to the mercy of your Imperial Majesty in petitioning you to allow the acquisition of Yasnaya Polyana as State property. Through such mercy granted by you, Your Majesty, my many grandchildren would be afforded the opportunity to receive an education. They would grow up conscious of their undying gratitude to our benevolent Tsar who has generously extended his hand to assist them and their parents, as well as an aggrieved and impoverished widow." (T.V. Komarova, "Angel Jasnoj Poljany" [The angel of Yasnaya Polyana]. *Pamjatniki Otechestva*, N° 28 (1992): 91)

1911: 13 May — SAT goes to the Moscow City *Duma* [Council] to see Guchkov[136] about selling the Khamovniki house to the city. On 28 May it is announced in the press that the Council of Ministers has decided to purchase Yasnaya Polyana for 500,000 roubles.

1911: 28 August — "Lev Nikolaevich's birthday. There were about 300 visitors to the house and many of them at the gravesite. I didn't go. It was hard for me to see so many policemen and at the same time so little genuine feeling for Lev Nikolaevich." (*Diaries*, II: 355)

1911: 7 November — "A sad day — the day Lev Nikolaevich died [one year ago]. All my sons came, except Lëva. We had a flood of reporters, members of the Tolstoy Society — about 500 visitors in all. Our peasants came to see me, and sang 'Eternal memory' over the grave. My granddaughter Tanjushka Sukhotina was with me. There was a lot of bustle, talk about selling Yasnaya Polyana, and heaviness on my heart." (*Diaries*, II: 363)

1912 — SAT's article *L.N. Tolstoy's marriage* is published in *Russkoe slovo* (N° 219) and *Reminiscences (The power of darkness)* in *Tolstovskij ezhegodnik* [Tolstoy annual]. She publishes an article *Pervoe predstavlenie komedii*

---

136 *Nikolaj Ivanovich Guchkov* (1860–1935) — Moscow entrepreneur and politician. He was the elected head of the Moscow city *Duma* from 1905 to 1912.

L.N. Tolstogo «Plody prosveshchenija» [First performance of LNT's comedy "The fruits of enlightenment"] in *Solntse Rossii* (N° 145). In addition, she continues her work on *My Life,* reads all the articles she can about LNT, receives visitors.

1912: 21 April — SAT sells all her unsold edition copies to I. D. Sytin[137].

1912: 28 August — "My deceased Lëvochka's birthday. I went with my little granddaughter Tanechka Sukhotina to his grave. This was the best moment of the whole day." (*Diaries,* II: 378)

1912: October — SAT goes to see the Minister of Internal Affairs on the matter of the official banning of the film *Ukhod velikogo startsa.*[138]

1912: 7 November — "The day of Lev Nikolaevich's passing [two years ago]. From early morning there were all sorts of visitors to the house and the grave, [including] police, cinematographers, reporters and the general public. My son Andrjusha came, later Serëzha. Toward evening, after everyone had gone, I walked to the grave with Andrjusha. Serëzha went on his own." (*Diaries,* II: 382)

1912: 13 December — "Today I got down to a difficult task — the transcribing and editing of all the letters written to me by my late husband Lëvochka. This task will take some time. It will be hard on me reading the letters from my whole married life. Very challenging at times." (*Diaries,* II: 383)

1913 — SAT prepares and publishes *Pis'ma grafa L. N. Tolstogo k zhene 1862–1910* [LNT's letters to his wife 1862–1910], with commentaries. A second edition appears in 1915.

1913 — In a reply to the reminiscences of Aleksej Moshin,[139] SAT publishes corrective information in *Zhizn' dlja vsekh* (N° 7) on Agaf'ja Mikhajlovna (a maid in the employ of LNT's grandmother) and LNT's nurse.

1913 — SAT publishes *Chetyre poseshchenija gr. L. Tolstym monastyrja Optina pustyn'* [Four visits by Count L. Tolstoy to the Optina Pustyn Monastery] in *Tolstovskij ezhegodnik.*

1913: January — SAT compiles *An inventory of live and dead stock...* and *A report on the state of the livestock on the estate of Countess S.A. Tolstaya near the village of Yasnaya Polyana for 1913,* both of which attest to SAT's untiring efforts on the household scene. On 1 January 1913 the estate includes a large inventory: "27 horses, 26 cows, 1 bull, 24 calves, 11 pigs, 9 sheep, 78 fowl". On 20 December 1912 Yasnaya Polyana's storage barns are

---

137 *Ivan Dmitrievich Sytin* (1851–1934) — Russian printer and publisher, who printed the books for Posrednik, a publishing firm set up in 1884 jointly by LNT and Chertkov.

138 *Ukhod velikogo startsa* [Departure of a grand old man] (also known as *Zhizn' L. N. Tolstogo* [The life of L. N. Tolstoy]) — a 1912 film directed by Jakov Protazanov and Elizaveta Thiman. SAT's son Lev L'vovich Tolstoy and her sister Tat'jana Andreevna Kuzminskaja were at the first showing in Petersburg and protested against further showings (see *Diaries,* II: 567, Note 55). It was the first film in Russian history to be banned outright by the censors.

139 *Aleksej Nikolaevich Moshin* (1870–1928) — a writer and acquaintance of Tolstoy's.

preserving: "Oats: 880 poods, Rye: 800 poods 10 funts; Rye flour: 6 poods 36 funts; Field hay: 5 stooks, approx. 1200 poods; Oats on wagons: 2 wagons = 150 stacks; Potatoes: approx. 400 poods" (T. V. Komarova, "Samaja luchshaja na svete…" [The best in the world…]. *Zhizn' v usad'be,* N° 2: 4 [2004]: 39). Cabbage is also grown, along with cucumbers, raspberries, white and red currants, a variety of greens, melons, turnips. One can get an idea of the area devoted to cucumbers from the purchase of 3 funts of seeds for 1914. During these years SAT has two assistants: a field manager named Koring and a gardener-beekeper named Soans. Twenty hired people carry out the work in the home and on the estate.

1913: March — SAT buys from her sons the portions of Yasnaya Polyana belonging to them: 200 desjatinas.

1913: 22 March — "I went to Gaspra with Julija Ivanovna.[140] It was very pleasant, even the recollections of Lev Nikolaevich's illness, since it was we — *his own family* — who took care of him then, with love, and he was *all mine,* and not Chertkov's![141] And how beautiful it is there!" (*Diaries,* II: 389; see also *My Life,* VIII.18)

1913: July — At the request of Semën Afanas'evich Vengerov, Director of the Russian Book Chamber [*Rossijskaja knizhnaja palata*], SAT agrees to write a short Autobiography, which she completes by the end of October 1913. Vengerov then asks her to elaborate on life at Yasnaya Polyana during LNT's work on *War and peace* and *Anna Karenina,* which she does. To his further complaint that certain 'facts' were missing, she responds on 5 May 1914: "You wanted more *facts,* but where should I get them from? Life was quiet, even-paced and lonely in the family." She goes on to explain how life went on pretty much as usual during her husband's years of novel-writing, that much of her time was taken up with looking after her children and other household duties. She rejects Vengerov's comparisons of Tolstoy with other 'professional' writers ([N. V.] Gogol', [I. S.] Turgenev, [I. A.] Goncharov, for example) on the grounds that they were bachelors and did not share Tolstoy's family commitments. But regarding her husband, she has this to say in particular: "That Lev Nikolaevich was altogether a *human being* and not just a writer is completely accurate. But it is *not* accurate (forgive me) to say that writing was *easy* for him. Indeed, he experienced the 'pains of creativity' in large measure; his writing was arduous and time-consuming; he was continually revising; he doubted his own abilities, denied his own talent and was in the habit of saying: 'Creating is like giving birth: until the fœtus matures, it won't come out, and when it does come

---

140 *Julija Ivanovna Igumnova* (1871–1940) — an artist and friend of Tat'jana L'vovna Sukhotina (*née* Tolstaya). She lived at Yasnaya Polyana for a time and served as LNT's secretary.

141 A play on words here. The Russian word translated 'Chertkov's' is *chertkovskij,* which is very close to the word *chertovskij* (meaning 'the devil's').

out, it is with hardship and suffering."' SAT concludes by saying the image of the Tolstoy home imagined by Vengerov simply doesn't exist. (Preface to SAT's *Autobiography*)

1913: 27 September — "Last night I stayed up to 3.30 a.m. writing my 'Autobiography', and today I read it to [daughter Tat'jana's husband Mikhail Sergeevich] Sukhotin and Tanja. I am trying to be truthful, to write reservedly and interestingly, which isn't easy." (*Diaries*, II: 397)

1913: 7 November — "The day of Lev Nikolaevich's death. It's been three years now, and still painful! The day went well. As soon as I got up I went to the grave, where a variety of visitors had already gathered. Later about a hundred people came to the house, mostly young people. Four of my sons came: Serëzha, Il'ja, Andrjusha and Misha." (*Diaries*, II: 400)

1913: 21 December — SAT writes of Dostoevsky, whose novel *The Idiot* she has been reading, that he is "coarse, and I don't like him". (*Diaries*, II: 402)

1914: May — SAT compiles an inventory of books and objects room by room, cupboard by cupboard, which she records in an oilcloth-covered notebook. On the inside front cover she writes in black ink: "List compiled and checked by S.A. Tolstaja, May 1914." (See also **1918: May–June** below.)

1914: Summer — SAT's daughter Aleksandra goes off to war as a nurse. Her son Lev becomes a Red Cross representative. Her son Il'ja becomes a correspondent for the paper *Russkoe Slovo* [The Russian Word], while her son Mikhail goes off to war.

1914: 9 August — A telegram is received concerning the death of SAT's son-in-law Mikhail Sergeevich Sukhotin. SAT goes to Kochety to comfort her daughter Tat'jana.

1914: 18 October — SAT receives word about a settlement in her favour of the conflict over her manuscripts in the Historical Museum.

1914: 31 October — SAT publishes a letter in *Novoe vremja* on the police interrogation of Tolstoy's last secretary Valentin Fëdorovich Bulgakov.

1914: 18 December — SAT's access to LNT's manuscripts which were transferred to the Historical Museum in 1904 (see **1904: 12 January** above) is restored by a Senate decree; access was cut off after his death as a result of a dispute which had broken out between SAT and her daughter Aleksandra L'vovna, to whom LNT had left them in his will. (See entry under **January 1911** above)

1915: 28–29 January — SAT once again gives Tolstoy's manuscripts to the Rumjantsev Museum for preservation. Pursuant to her appeal to the Museum's director on 26 January and his reply the next day, SAT organises a special room in the Museum called "Tolstoy's Study".

1915: 7 June — SAT receives word about the death of her composer-friend Sergej Ivanovich Taneev.

1915: July — SAT re-reads the Gospels.

1916: 11 February — SAT receives word about her son Andrej's illness. He dies on 24 February.

1916: 23 March — "It's sad that Lëva's family life has fallen apart. Personally, it is so much easier and more pleasant for me to live with him than all by myself…" (*Diaries*, II: 434)

1916: November — SAT's son Il'ja goes to America to give lectures on LNT; her son Lev heads to Japan for the same reason. SAT ceases writing *My Life* (which at this point has reached the end of 1901).

1917: 5 March — "A red-letter day for Yasnaya Polyana. Workers came from cast-iron foundry at Kosaja Gora,[142] bringing red flags and pins to do reverence to Tolstoy's house and widow. Carrying portraits of Lev Nikolaevich, they walked to his grave through deep snow and biting winds. My two Tat'janas walked with them. The workers sang, made speeches, all about *freedom*. In response I made a brief speech, too, about Lev Nikolaevich's legacy. At the grave they sang *Vechnaja pamjat'* [Eternal memory] and took snapshots." (*Diaries*, II: 443)

1917: 16 April — "The thought came to me that a person's life is like that of a leaf: first the bud, then the fresh green leaflet, next the mature leaf; after that it withers, life dies, the leaf yellows, dries up and falls off. Just so, all my capacities and brain are drying up and dying. I see this, I feel it, but to stop this dying is impossible." (*Diaries*, II: 444–45)

1917: 30 April — "There have been a tremendous number of visitors to the house and the grave — all soldiers. They have been interested in everything and treated both my daughter Tanja and me very kindly. There is no feed for the cattle, and that disturbs me a great deal. Our own provisions are running out." (*Diaries*, II: 445)

1917: 25 August — "It's sad that my relations with my sister [Tat'jana Andreevna] have turned sour. She gets irritated quickly by everything. She complains and calls me *God's blessed fool,* since I give the appearance of bearing everything calmly, but nobody can see what is in my heart." (*Diaries*, II: 449)

1917: 11 September — "There are events going on in government circles which are impossible to comprehend! Evidently, Kerensky[143] will soon be gone. So many intrigues, failures, so much lust for power and neglect of what is important for the people and the country!" (*Diaries*, II: 450)

1917: 17 October — "…They've brought in ten or twelve (I don't remember exactly how many) soldiers for our protection, for whom they somehow

142 *Kosaja Gora* — the administrative centre of the Privoksal'nyj District of Tula Gubernia, situated 4 km from the Kozlovka-Zaseka railway station near Yasnaya Polyana.
143 *Alexander Kerensky* [Russian: *Aleksandr Fëdorovich Kerenskij*] (1881–1970) — Minister of Justice, then War Minister, then Prime Minister in the Provisional Government, which lasted from 3 March to 26 October (O.S.) 1917, when it was overthrown by the Bolsheviks.

managed to find lodgings. The whole southern part of Krapivna Uezd is burning with incendiary fires." (*Diaries*, II: 452)

1917: 23 October — "There's a rumour been going round that we'll be burnt out of our home. Policemen have come for the night to protect us. Nobody's slept, or even undressed." (*Diaries*, II: 452)

1917: 29 December — Valentin Bulgakov writes in a newspaper article: "The preservation of the historic estate is now guaranteed more than ever before. [...] The protection of Yasnaya Polyana is under the direct care of Tula political organisations, which have appointed a special constant guard to keep watch over the estate... The inhabitants of the estate are being supplied with food provisions... Just a few days ago a telephone was installed, connecting Yasnaya Polyana with Tula and Moscow... The shadow of Lev Nikolaevich is covering it and, hopefully, protecting it." (*Diaries*, II: 593, Note 2)

1918: 4 January — "Sergeenko[144] went to Tula for kerosene. We are using one lamp or a wax candle. One pood of poor-quality kerosene costs 60 roubles." (*Diaries*, II: 454)

1918: 15–20 April (N. S.)[145] — On the basis of a decision by the Sovnarkom[146] of 30 March, the Gubernia Conference on Land Apportionment adopted a resolution "on the recognition of L.N. Tolstoy's Yasnaya Polyana estate as not being subject to apportionment among the citizens of neighbouring village and its function as an historical treasure to be used only for cultural and educational purposes". At first the local peasants accepted this decision, then decided to take over the land in any case, but later changed their minds again. (*Diaries*, II: 594–95)

1918: May–June — SAT reviews her May 1914 inventory and adds to it. "I.e., what has not been surreptitiously pilfered from me. S. Tolstaya. 30 May. 12 June." (T.V. Komarova, "Gde vy, tam prazdnik" [Where you are, there is a holiday], in *Druz'ja i gosti Jasnoj Poljany* [Friends and guests of Yasnaya Polyana] Tula, 2007).

1918: 3 September — "I wrote a new will to include my daughter Sasha among my inheritors. I had excluded her earlier on account of her horrible treatment of me after the death of her father. I have now forgiven her." (*Diaries*, II: 463)

1919: 1 February — "I spent the whole day writing a commentary to [LNT's] *Letters to my wife* [*Pis'ma k zhene*]. I became very depressed reading some

---

144 *Pëtr Alekseevich Sergeenko* (1854–1930) — Russian writer and literary critic, who was acquainted with LNT for many years. He authored several books on Tolstoy and was the first to publish a compilation of LNT's correspondence.

145 Dates from this point on will be given according to the New Style (Gregorian) calendar, adopted by the new Bolshevik régime in February 1918.

146 *Sovnarkom* — an abbreviation of *Sovet Narodnykh Komissarov* [Council of People's Commissars].

of the letters he had written to me, in which I could feel his sufferings caused by my reproaches, my demands for him to stay with me, and so forth. My desire not to separate from my husband grew, after all, out of my love for him! I loved him very much, right to the end of his life." (*Diaries*, II: 468–69)

1919: 2 February — SAT and her daughter Tat'jana L'vovna appeal to the board of the educational Yasnaya Polyana Society with a request to transfer the management of the estate and its buildings to this same Society. Their request is granted, and the management is entrusted to N. L. Obolenskij.[147] (See *Diaries*, II: 599, Note 8).

1919: 14 July — SAT wrote a letter to be read after her death: "Apparently the circle of my life is closing, I am gradually dying, and I wanted to tell everyone with whom I have been living recently and before, Farewell and forgive me. / Farewell, my dear, beloved children, especially my daughter Tanja, whom I love more than anyone else in the world, whom I ask forgiveness for all the difficulties she had to endure on account of me. / Forgive me, my daughter Sasha, that I did not give you sufficient love, and I thank you for your kind treatment of me these last times. / Forgive me, too, my sister Tanja, for not being able, despite my immeasurable love for you, to make your life easier and comforting you in your lonely and difficult situation. I ask Kolja [= Nikolaj Leonidovich Obolenskij] to forgive me for being sometimes unkind to him. No matter what the circumstances might have been, I ought to have better understood his difficult and challenging situation and treated him more kindly. Forgive me, too, all of you who have served me over my lifetime; I thank you all for your service. I have a special relationship with you, my dear, fervently beloved granddaughter Tanjushka. You made my life especially joyful and happy. Farewell, my darling! Be happy; I thank you for your love and tenderness. Do not forget your grandmother who loves you, S. Tolstaya." (*Diaries*, II: 600, Note 18)

1919: 14 August — "There have been rumours going around concerning the dastardly rule of the Bolsheviks. Everybody is happy, and I am grateful to them [the Bolsheviks] for their constant service and care." (*Diaries*, II: 475)

1919: 8 October — In a memo to the Sovnarkom adopted at a special session of the Yasnaya Polyana Society, the Society warns about the danger of the estate falling into a war zone in view of the advance of General [Anton Ivanovich] Denikin's army onto the southern front. The VTsIK issues a

---

147 *Nikolaj Leonidovich Obolenskij* (1872–1934) — son of Leonid Dmitrievich Obolenskij and Elizaveta Valer'janovna Obolenskaja (*née* Tolstaya). In 1897 he married his first cousin, once removed — the Tolstoy's daughter Marija L'vovna [*Masha*] (1871–1906). Yasnaya Polyana was under the Society's management up until 1921, when the *VTsIK*— an acronym for All-Russian Central Executive Committee [*Vserossijskij Tsentral'nyj Ispolnitel'nyj Komitet*] decided to nationalise the estate.

corresponding order and the Red Army troops which have gathered in the village of Yasnaya Polyana are withdrawn from there.

1919: 4 November — SAT dies at Yasnaya Polyana from inflammation of the lungs. She is buried in the family cemetery at Nikol'skij Church in the neighbouring village of Kochaki.

1920 — The Tolstoys' son Il'ja L'vovich marries for the second time, this time Nadezhda Kliment'evna Katul'skaja.

1921 — SAT's brief autobiography, which she had written at the request of Professor S. A. Vengerov,[148] is published in the journal *Nachala* (N° 1) by V. S. Spiridonov.

1923: 11 February — SAT's wide-ranging letter to Anatolij Fëdorovich Koni of 4 December 1910, describing LNT's departure from Yasnaya Polyana, is published for the first time by Charles Salomon in *Le Figaro* (11 February) under the title "Les derniers jours de Tolstoï".

1928–2009 — Three volumes of SAT's diaries from the years 1860 and 1862–1909 are published by M. and S. Sabashnikov and C° ("Sever") under the title: *Dnevniki S.A. Tolstoj, 1928, 1929 i 1932 gg.* [*Diaries of S. A. Tolstaya, 1928, 1929 and 1932*]. Her most complete diaries are published (in Russian) in two volumes in 1978 (Moscow: Khudozhestvennaja literatura), edited by: V. È. Vatsuro et al., compiled by: N. I. Azarova, O. A. Golinenko, I. A. Pokrovskaja, S. A. Rozanova, B. M. Shumova. In 1985 they are published in an English translation by Cathy Porter, with an introduction by Reginald F. Christian (New York: Random House, 1985). A newly-edited version of the same translation, with a Foreword by Doris Lessing, is published in 2009 (London: Alma Books, 2009). Excerpts from Cathy Porter's translation, together with a number of SAT's photographs), compiled by Leah Bendavid-Val, are published by the National Geographic Society in Washington (D. C.) in 2007.

1936 — Excerpts from Tolstaya's diary of 1910, with a preface by her eldest son, Sergej L'vovich Tolstoy, are published in Aylmer Maude's English translation by Allen and Unwin in London.

1974 — Excerpts from Tolstaya's diaries are published in English translation by Random House in New York, edited by Mary J. Moffat and Charlotte Painter. A Vintage (paperback) edition appears the following year.

1980–81 — A two-volume French translation (*Sophie Tolstoï. Journal intime*) of Tolstaya's diaries by Daria Olivier and Frédérique Longueville is republished in Paris by Albin Michel (first published in 1931 by Plon et Nourrit).

1997: January — The Alberta Theatre Project in Calgary premieres a play (in English) by Frank Moher entitled *Tolstoy's wife*.

---

148 *Semën Afanas'evich Vengerov* (1855–1921) — literary historian, critic and bibliographer, a close acquaintance of LNT's.

2009: May — Èmil' Kotljarskij's 2001 play (in Russian), *Chelovek po imeni Lev (p'esa dlja mysljashchikh)* [*A man named Lev (a play for rational people)*], focusing on the Tolstoys' marital relationship, is published on the Internet.

2009 — *The last station,* a feature film about the last few months of Tolstoy's life, is released under the direction of Michael Hoffman, based on the 1990 biographical novel of the same name by writer Jay Parini. The starring role of Sofia Andreevna Tolstaya is played by British actress Helen Mirren, herself of Russian background, who wins the Best Actress award at that year's Rome International Film Festival. Both she and Christopher Plummer (in a 'supporting role' as Lev Nikolaevich Tolstoy) are nominated for Oscars for their performances in this film in their respective categories.

2010 — Saskatchewan journalist Alexandra Popoff's biography of SAT (*Sophia Tolstoy. A biography*) is published by Free Press in New York.

2010: summer — Tolstaya's *Song without words* [*Pesnja bez slov*] and *Who is to blame?* [*Ch'ja vina?*] are published in Russian (the former for the very first time) by Vitalij Remizov and Ljudmila Gladkova at the State L. N. Tolstoy Museum in Moscow. The volume also includes a republication of her husband Lev Nikolaevich Tolstoy's *Kreutzer Sonata* [*Krejtserova sonata*] and her son Lev L'vovich Tolstoy's *A prelude of Chopin's* [*Preljudija Shopena*].

2010: September — An unabridged English translation of SAT's *My Life* is published in Canada by the University of Ottawa Press. The translation is carried out by John Woodsworth and Arkadi Klioutchanski under the editorship of Andrew Donskov, who provides a critical introduction thereto. This translation wins that year's Lois Roth Award presented by the Modern Language Association of America for the best translation of a literary work into English. Shortly afterward, a French translation (*Ma vie*) by Luba Jurgenson and Maria-Luisa Bonaque is published in Paris by Éditions des Syrtes.

2010: autumn — Two French translations of Tolstaya's *Who is to blame?* (À qui la *faute?*) are published in Paris. Eveline Amoursky's translation is released by Éditions des Syrtes, the one by Christine Zeytounian-Beloüs by Albin Michel. A German translation of the same novel (*Eine Frage der Schuld*) by Alfred Frank and Ursula Keller is published by Manesse Verlag in Zürich.

2010: autumn — Tolstaya's *Song without words* is published in a French translation (*Romance sans paroles*) by Eveline Amourski at Éditions des Syrtes, as well as in a German translation (*Lied ohne Worte*) by Ursula Keller at Manesse Verlag in Zürich.

2011 — Tolstaya's *My Life* is finally published in its original Russian under the overall editorship of Vitalij B. Remizov and Ludmila Gladkova, produced by the publishing house Kuchkovo Pole. The Slavic Research Group at the

University of Ottawa and the State L. N. Tolstoy Museum publish *Sofia Andreevna Tolstaya: Literary works.*

2012 — Tolstaya's *The skeleton-dolls and other stories* [*Kukolki-skelettsy i drugie rasskazy*], originally published in Moscow in 1910, is issued in a reprint by the Tolstoy Museum at Yasnaya Polyana.

2014 — A compilation of excerpts from SAT's diaries [*Dnevniki*] is issued by A. Zhuravlëv through the ACT publishing house, under the title *My husband Lev Tolstoy* [*Moj muzh Lev Tolstoj*].

2014 — Michael Katz publishes *The Kreutzer Sonata Variations. Lev Tolstoy's Novella and Counterstories by Sofiya Tolstaya and Lev Lvovich Tolstoy.* New Haven, London, Yale University Press 2014.

2014: 27 August — A special exhibit is held at the L. N. Tolstoy Museum in Moscow to mark the 170th anniversary of Sofia Tolstaya's birth, featuring a display of rare photos, needlework and manuscripts of her compositions.

2014–2020 — Exhibits of 'skeleton-dolls' inspired by Sofia Tolstaya's stories are held in various parts of Russia — in museums, municipal centres, children's hospitals, facilities for gifted children. Special attention is devoted to SAT's story *The Christmas tree* [*Ëlka*] and her Christmas activities over the years at Yasnaya Polyana.

2017 — SAT's novella *Who is to blame?* [*Ch'ja vina?*] published (in Russian) in audiobook form by LitRes, read by Marina Livanova.

2017 — A book featuring SAT's recipes is published under the title *Sofia Andreevna Tolstaya's cookbook* [*Kulinarnaja kniga Sof'i Andreevny Tolstoj*] through Tsentropoligraf in Moscow.

2017 — A volume titled *Materials for a biography of L.N. Tolstoy and details about the Tolstoy family and especially Count Lev Nikolaevich Tolstoy* [*Materialy k biografii L. N. Tolstogo i svedenija o semejstve Tolstykh i preimushchestvenno gr. L'va Nikolaevicha Tolstogo*] is published in St. Petersburg and Moscow.

2017 — A volume of selected correspondence between SAT and LNT in English translation (edited by Andrew Donskov, translated by John Woodsworth, Arkadi Klioutchanski and Liudmila Gladkova) is published by the University of Ottawa Press under the title *Tolstoy and Tolstaya: a portrait of a life in letters.* Runner-up for the Non-fiction Prize at the 2018 Paris Book Festival.

2019: 17 May — Opening of an exhibit at the Tolstoy Centre in Moscow (a branch of the L. N. Tolstoy Museum) to mark the 175th anniversary of Sofia Tolstaya's birth, titled *The life of his wife* [*Zhizn' ego zheny*].

2020: 27–30 July — *Exposition de photos de Sofia Tolstoï,* Institut d'Études Slaves, Paris.

2020: 6 February — Tolstaya's play *Ma vie dans l'art* [*Moja zhizn' v iskusstve*] is performed in French translation at the "Centre de Russie pour la science et la culture à Paris," with prominent comedienne Anne Lefol in the starring role.

2020: summer — Russian writer/Tolstoy scholar Pavel Basinskij, together with poetess Ekaterina Barbanjaga (from St. Petersburg) publish a biography: *Sonja ujdi! Sof'ja Tolstaja: vzgljad muzhchiny i zhenshchiny. Roman-dialog* [*Sonja, go away! Male and female perspectives. A novel in dialogue*]. The format of the book is an ongoing dialogue featuring two differing points of view.

BIBLIOGRAPHY

THE SOFIA ANDREEVNA TOLSTAYA ARCHIVE in the Manuscript Division of the State L. N. Tolstoy Museum in Moscow comprises some twenty-two thousand separate documents. These include: (a) biographical documents; (b) Sofia Andreevna's writings (literary and memoirs); (c) materials pertaining to her household activities (various invoices, descriptions of objects in the family homes in Moscow and at Yasnaya Polyana, income and expense statements, plans of the estate, notes on payments to day-workers, orders for flower seeds and fruit-tree saplings for the garden at Yasnaya Polyana etc.); (d) materials pertaining to her publishing activities (order blanks for the publication of Leo Tolstoy's works, correspondence with owners of printing houses, announcements of subscriptions to various editions, records of publishing income and expenses, prospecti for various editions, distribution lists for various volumes etc.).

Sofia Andreevna's poems, written over the years, number more than fifty. Most of them were written for the "Yasnaya Polyana *letter-box*". See: S. L. Tolstoj, *Ocherki bylogo* [Sketches from the past] (4th ed., revised and expanded; Tula: Priokskoe knizhn. izd., 1975), pp. 388–406. Sofia Andreevna's poems *Po griby, Angel, Plach neuteshnoj dushi nashej teten'ki, Allegorija,* are to be found on pp. 397–400 of *Ocherki bylogo* (a few are reproduced in Tat'jana Komarova's papers). The rest of her poems are preserved in the S. A. Tolstaya Archive but remain unpublished.

A great many materials written by or relating to Tolstaya can be found in the Tolstoy Museum at Yasnaya Polyana. These comprise:

1. Her personal notebook
2. Letters and postcards

3. Her unpublished annotations on the collection *Dni nashej skorbi* [*Days of our sorrow*]
4. Her unpublished annotations on *Pis'ma grafa L. N. Tolstogo k zhene 1862–1910 gg.* [*Letters of Count Tolstoy to his wife, 1862–1910*]
5. Her captions for various exhibits, telling their history
6. Descriptions and book catalogues compiled by her
7. Typescript variant of her reminiscences *Moja zhizn'* [*My Life*], with author's corrections
8. Menu compiled by her for 1910
9. Herbarium
10. Her drawings for her grandchildren
11. Her book for children *Kukolki-skelettsy i drugie rasskazy* [*Skeleton-dolls and other stories*] (Izd. Kushnerev, 1910)
12. Icons and other religious objects
13. Last wills and testaments

The epistolary section of the Tolstaya Archive, comprising more than ten thousand items, is of special interest. Her correspondents included: writers I. S. Turgenev, A. A. Fet, L. N. Andreev, V. V. Rozanov and Z. N. Gippius; artists I. E. Repin and L. O. Pasternak; composer S. I. Taneev; critics N. N. Strakhov and V. V. Stasov; philosopher N. Ja. Grot; theatre director K. S. Stanislavskij (real name: Alekseev); Moscow Art Theatre actress M. F. Andreeva (wife of Maxim Gorky); the famous legal expert A. F. Koni; the prominent revolutionary activist V. D. Bonch-Bruevich and many others.

To date there is no anthology or comprehensive bibliography of Sofia Andreevna's works, either published or unpublished. The following list, though not exhaustive, will give at least some idea of the research opportunities for scholars. It consists of three sections:

Section I comprises a list of her works, both published (in Russian) and unpublished, as well as a few of her known translations. The published items include some of her shorter pieces, together with commentaries by Tat'jana Komarova, Tat'jana Nikiforova, Liudmila Gladkova, Ol'ga Golinenko, as well as her sons Sergej L'vovich Tolstoy and Il'ja L'vovich Tolstoy.

Section II details documents to be found in various Russian archives, including some of her works, letters written by and to Sofia Andreevna, as well as a number of critical references to her life and works.

Section III lists general critical materials on Sofia Andreevna's life and works.

Note: For the purposes of the bibliography, Sofia Andreevna Tolstaya is listed under the original Russian variant of her name: *Tolstaja, Sof'ja Andreevna*. The designation *PSS* [= *Polnoe sobranie sochinenij*] refers to the Jubilee Edition of Tolstoy's collected works (Moskva–Leningrad: Goslitizdat, 1928–1958). Also, no English translations are provided for entries in Russian (except for those published in English translation). These entries are provided here mainly for scholars interested in further archival research.

I. Works, Translations & Major compilations by Sofia Andreevna Tolstaya (née Bers)

I.a. Works by Sofia Andreevna Tolstaya

Bers, S. A. [= S. A. Tolstaja]. "Muzyka" [examination composition, Moscow University, "dlja poluchenija zvanija domashnej uchitel'nitsy"]. 1861. Destroyed by Sofia Andreevna before her marriage.

—. *Natasha* [story]. 1861–1862. Lost.

Tolstaja, S. A. "Pis'ma k L. L. Tolstomu". Collection of Gos. muzej L. N. Tolstogo, Moskva, Unpublished (N.d.)

—. [Stories written for L. Tolstoy's *Novaja azbuka* and published in Tolstoy's *PSS* (vol. 21)]: "Byla zima, no bylo teplo" [21: 27]; "Spala koshka na kryshe" [21: 27]; "Khodili deti po lesu za gribami" [21: 48]; "K Mashe prishli v gosti devochki" [21: 56]; "Orekhovaja vetka" [21: 80–81]; "Kak tëtushka rasskazyvala o tom, kak ona vyuchilas' shit'" [21: 108]; "Rasskaz muzhika o tom, za chto on starshego brata ljubit" [21: 159]; "Kak tëtushka rasskazyvala o tom, kak u neë byl ruchnoj vorobej — Zhivchik" [21: 160–61].

—. "Pis'mo v gazetu «Novoe vremja»". *Novoe vremja* N° 463 (1877).

— (ed. L. N. Tolstoj). "Graf Lev Nikolaevich Tolstoj". In: M. M. Stasjulevich (ed.). Ser. "Russkaja biblioteka", IX, *Graf Lev Nikolaevich Tolstoj*. Skt-Peterburg, 1879.

—. "Svoi i chuzhie mysli. 24 nojabrja 1882". Inv. N° 4050. Jasnaja Poljana (Fondy Doma-muzeja L. N. Tolstogo "Jasnaja Poljana"). Unpublished.

—. "Pis'mo v gazetu «Russkie vedomosti» ob okazanii pomoshchi golodajushchim". *Russkie vedomosti* N° 303 (3 November 1891).

—. "Spasënnyj Taks. Rasskaz Vani". *Igrushechka: Dlja maljutok* N° 3 (1895): 39–44.

—. "Babushkin klad: Predanie". *Detskoe chtenie* N° 12 (1895).

—. *Pesnja bez slov* [story, 1895–1898, 122 pp.]. Published in Remizov & Gladkova (2010).

—. "Vospominanija o Turgeneve S. A. Tolstoj". *Orlovskij vestnik* N° 224 (1903). [Also: Vospominanija o Turgeneve grafini Tolstoj". *Literaturnyj vestnik* Kniga 6 (1903): 160–62]

—. "Pis'mo v gazetu «Novoe vremja»". *Novoe vremja* N° 9666 (31 January 1903).

—. "Stony" [short poems in prose]. *Zhurnal dlja vsekh* N° 3 (1904): 168–71.

—. *Kukolki-skelettsy i drugie rasskazy*. Illustr. A. V. Muravov. Moskva: Tipo-litografija T-va I. N. Kushnereva i K°, 1910.

—. *Iz zhizni L. N. Tolstogo: Snimki raboty iskljuchitel'no grafini S. A. Tolstoj*. Moskva, 1911.

—. "Vospominanija. Vlast' t'my. Otryvok iz neizdannoj knigi gr. S. A. Tolstoj «Moja zhizn'»". *Tolstovskij ezhegodnik* (1912): 17–25.

—. "Pervoe predstavlenie komedii grafa L. N. Tolstogo «Plody prosveshchenija». Iz zapisok gr. S. A. Tolstoj pod zaglaviem «Moja zhizn'»". *Solntse Rossii* N° 145 (1912): 9–11.

—. "Zhenit'ba L. N. Tolstogo". *Russkoe slovo* N° 219 (1912). [Also: *L. N. Tolstoj v vospom-inanijakh sovremennikov*. Vol. 1. Moskva, 1978: 153–73.

—. L. D. Opul'skaja (comp.). *Tolstoj L. N. Povesti. Vospominanija sovremennikov.* Moskva: Pravda, 1990: 267–86]

—. "Iz zapisok grafini Sofii Andreevny Tolstoj pod zaglaviem «Moja zhizn'». Chetyre poseshchenija L. N. Tolstogo monastyrja «Optina pustyn'»". *Tolstovskij ezhegodnik* 3 (1913): 3–7.

—. (comp.). *Tolstoj, L. N. Pis'ma k zhene. 1862–1910.* 2 vols. Izd. 1-e. Ed. A. E. Gruzinskij. Moskva: A. A. Levenson, 1913.

—. (Comp.). Tolstoj, L. N. Pis'ma k zhene. 1862–1910. 2 vols. Izd. 2-e, ispravlennoe i dopolnennoe. Moskva: Tipo-litografija I. N. Kushnerev, 1915.

—. *Avtobiografija grafini S. A. Tolstoj.* Ed. V. S. Spiridonov. *Nachala* N° 1 (1921): 131–85.

—. *The autobiography of Countess Sophie Tolstoi,* with preface and notes by Vasilii Spiridonov. Trans. S. S. Koteliansky & Leonard Woolf. USA: Hogarth Press, 1922.

—. "Zapiski S. A. Tolstoj". In: *Dve zheny: Tolstaja i Dostoevskaja (Materialy, kommentarii Ju. I. Ajkhenval'da).* Berlin: Arzamas, 1925: 5–56.

—. *Dnevniki S. A. Tolstoj. 1860–1891.* Ed. S. L. Tolstoj. Intro. M. A. Tsjavlovskij. Moskva: Izdatel'stvo M. i S. Sabashnikovykh, 1928. Ser. «Zapisi proshlogo».

—. *Dnevniki S. A. Tolstoj. 1891–1897. Chast' vtoraja.* Ed. S. L. Tolstoj. Intro. M. A. Tsjavlovskij. Moskva: Izdatel'stvo M. i S. Sabashnikovykh, 1929. Ser. "Zapisi proshlogo".

—. *Dnevniki S. A. Tolstoj. 1897–1909.* Ed. S. L. Tolstoj. Moskva: Sever, 1932. Ser. "Zapisi proshlogo".

—. *Dnevniki S. A. Tolstoj. 1860–1891.* Ed. S. L. Tolstoj. Moskva: Sovetskij pisatel', 1936a. Ser. "Zapisi proshlogo".

—. *Pis'ma k L. N. Tolstomu 1862–1910.* Ed. A. I. Tolstaja & P. S. Popov. Intro. P. S. Popov. Moskva & Leningrad: Akademija, 1936b.

—. "Pis'ma k raznym litsam". *Letopisi gosudarstvennogo literaturnogo muzeja.* Book 2: *L. N. Tolstoj.* Moskva, 1938: 247–54.

—. "Tri biograficheskikh ocherka Tolstogo. Ocherki, sostavlennye Sof'ej Andreevnoj so slov Tolstogo i im vypravlennye". Comp. E. S. Serebrovskaja. *Literaturnoe nasledstvo* 69: 1: *Lev Tolstoj.* Moskva: Akademija Nauk, 1961: 497–518.

—. "Pis'ma k T. A. Kuzminskoj 1876–1897". Comp. A. I. Popovkin. *Jasnopoljanskij sbornik.* (Tula: Izd. dom. "Jasnaja Poljana", 1962): 80–104.

—. "Pis'ma k V. F. Bulgakovu 1911–1918". In: V. F. Bulgakov. *O Tolstom.* Tula, 1964: 280–312.

—. "Po griby!", "Angel", "Plach neuteshnoj dushi nashej teten'ki", "Allegorija" [short poems]. In: S. L. Tolstoj. *Ocherki bylogo.* Tula: Priokskoe knizhnoe izdatel'stvo, 1975: 397–400.

—. *Dnevniki v dvukh tomakh.* 2 vols. Comp. N. I. Azarova, O. A. Golinenko, O. A. Pokrovskaja, S. A. Rozanova, B. M. Shumova. Intro. S. A. Rozanova. "Serija literaturnykh memuarov". Moskva: Khudozhestvennaja literatura, 1978.

—. "V kanun ukhoda" [Letters by S. A. Tolstaja and T. L. Sukhotina-Tolstaja to L. L. Tolstoj: 25 April & 11 September 1910]. *Zvezda* N° 8 (1978): 138–141.

—. Excerpts from "Moja zhizn'". I. A. Pokrovskaja & B. M. Shumova (eds.). *Novyj mir* N° 8 (1978): 34–135.

—. Excerpts from "Moja zhizn'". I. A. Pokrovskaja & B. M. Shumova (eds.). *Prometej* N° 12 (1980): 148–98.

—. "Perepiska S. A. Tolstoj s G. P. Georgievskim 1911–1918". Comp. G. I. Dovgallo. In: *Gosudarstvennaja biblioteka SSSR im. Lenina. Zapiski otdela rukopisej.* Vypusk 47 (Moskva: 1988): 151–64.

—. "Vanechka: Istinnoe proisshestvie iz ego zhizni". Comp. B. S. Svadkovskij. *Sem'ja i shkola* N° 6 (1991): 38–39.

—. *Povarennaja kniga S. A. Tolstoj.* Tula: Priokskoe knizhnoe izdatel'stvo, 1991.

—. "Moja zhizn'". *Slovo* N° 9 (1992): 5–8.

—. "S. A. Tolstaja. Neopublikovannye pis'ma iz «stal'noj komnaty». *Sovershenno sekretno,* N° 3 (1992): 8.

—. "Pis'mo S. A. Tolstoj k V. F. Snegirëvu ot aprelja 1911 g." *Sovershenno sekretno,* N° 3 (1992): 9.

—. "Ob otluchenii L'va Tolstogo: Po materialam semejnoj perepiski". Comp. & intro. L. V. Gladkova. *Oktjabr'* N° 9 (1993): 184–90.

—. "Pis'ma S. A. Tolstoj i M. L. Obolenskoj k I. I. Gorbunovu-Posadovu". Comp. Z. I. Ivanova. In: *Neizvestnyj Tolstoj v arkhivakh Rossii i SShA.* Moskva: AO Tekhna-2, 1994: 183–93.

—. "Ch'ja vina? Po povodu «Krejtserovoj sonaty» L'va Tolstogo". Comp. O. A. Golinenko & T. G. Nikiforova. Intro. V. I. Porudominskij. *Oktjabr'* N° 10 (1994): 3–59.

—. "Pis'ma k A. L. Tolstoj v Moskvu ot 16 nojabrja 1916, 24 fevralja, 28 marta, 12 ijunja 1917". *Slovo* N° 11/12 (1994): 45–49.

—. "Pis'mo grafini S. A. Tolstoj Mitropolitu Antoniju ot 26 fevralja 1901 g.". Collection of State Tolstoy Museum, Moscow.

—. "Pis'ma k L. O. Pasternaku: 22 sentjabrja 1908, 1 oktjabrja 1911". *Pamjatniki kul'tury: Novye otkrytija. Pis'mennost'. Iskusstvo. Arkheologija: Ezhegodnik 1995.* Moskva, 1996: 346–49.

—. Excerpts from "Moja zhizn'". Ed. O. A. Golinenko & B. M. Shumova. Intro. V. Porudominskij. *Oktjabr'* N° 9 (1998): 136–77.

—. "Moja zhizn'". In: O. A. Golinenko & B. M. Shumova (eds.). *Dom Ostroukhova v Trubnikakh.* Moskva & Skt–Peterburg, 1998: 160–92.

—. "Iz zapisnoj knizhki S. A. Tolstoj". Ed. T. V. Komarova. *Jasnopoljanskij sbornik 2000* (Tula: Izdatel'skij dom "Jasnaja Poljana", 2000): 154–58. [Various short poems and thoughts: "K 28-mu avgustu" (Tolstoy's birthday), "Akrostikh"; "Iz zapisok D. P. Makovitskogo; slova gr. L'va Nikolaevicha Tolstogo v 1906-m godu"; "Chto ja ljublju"; "Chto ja ne ljublju"; "K kartine I. N. Kramskogo *Neuteshnoe gore*"; "Starost'"; "Pravilo dlja zhizni"].

—. "«Zhila s bespokojstvom v serdtse o L've Nikolaeviche»: Pis'ma S. A. Tolstoj k E. F. Junge [1902–1907]". *Jasnopoljanskij sbornik 2000* (Tula: Izdatel'skij dom "Jasnaja Poljana", 2000): 162–69.

—. "Perepiska s N. S. Leskovym [1890–1894]". *Literaturnoe nasledstvo.* Vol. 101: *Neizdannyj Leskov. V 2-kh knigakh.* Kn. 2. Moskva: RAN. Institut mirovoj literatury im. A. M. Gor'kogo, Nasledie, 2000: 373–82.

—. "Pis'ma k A. L. Tolstoj 1914–1919". In: S. V. Smetana-Tolstaja & F. E. Smetana (comp.). *Neizvestnaja Aleksandra Tolstaja.* Moskva: 2001: 21– 24, 26–27, 33–36.

—. "Zhit' stalo nevynosimo tjazhelo v Rossii" [three unknown letters]. Comp. T. V. Komarova. *Jasnopoljanskij sbornik 2002* (Tula: Izdatel'skij dom "Jasnaja Poljana", 2002): 372–78.

—. "Stikhotvorenija v proze Stony". Comp. T. V. Komarova. *Litsej na Pushkinskoj* N° 18–20. Tula: 2004: 178–81.

—. "Pis'mo k mitropolitu Antoniju". 26 fevralja 1901. [Pribavlenie k N⁰ 12 neofitsial'noj chasti «Tserkovnykh vedomostej», izd. pri Svjatejshem Sinode]
—. "Pis'mo k V. G. Chertkovu". 18 March 1905. [For publication in *The Times,* although it is not clear whether it was published or not; a copy of the original is in the editor's possession].
—. *Moja zhizn'*. Ed. L. V. Gladkova, V. B. Remizov. 2 vols. Moskva: Kuchkovo Pole, 2011.
—. *Kukolki-skelettsy i drugie rasskazy* (Moskva, 1910). Reprinted: Tula: Muzej-usad'ba L. N. Tolstogo «Jasnsaja Poljana», 2012.
—. *Moj muzh Lev Tolstoj.* Comp. A. Zhuravlëv. Serija: «Velikie biografii». Moskva: «ACT», 2014.
—. *Kulinarnaja kniga Sof'i Andreevny Tolstoj: obed dlja L'va.* Moskva: Tsentrpoligraf, 2017.
—. *Materialy k biografii L. N. Tolstogo i svedenija o semejstve Tolstykh i preimushchest-venno gr. L'va Nikolaevicha Tolstogo* (24 oktjabrja 1876 goda). 2 vols. Skt-Peterburg/Moskva, 2017. Vol. I: 7–21.
—. *The autobiography of Countess Sophie Tolstoi.* Trans. S. S. Koteliansky & V. Woolf. Richmond: Hogarth, 1922.
—. *The Diary of Tolstoy's wife: 1860–1891.* Trans. Alexander Werth. London: Gollancz, 1928. [Also: New York: Payson & Clarke, 1929]
—. *The Countess Tolstoy's later diary, 1891–1897.* Trans. Alexander Werth. London: Gollancz, 1929.
—. *Sophie Tolstoï. Journal intime.* Traduit du russe par Daria Olivier et Frédérique Longueville. 2 vols. Paris: Plon et Nourrit, 1931. Réédité: Paris: Albin Michel, 1980–81.
—. *The final struggle: being Countess Tolstoy's Diary for 1910, with extracts from Leo Tolstoy's diary of the same period.* Preface by S. L. Tolstoy. Trans. Aylmer Maude. London: Allen & Unwin, 1936.
—. "Sophie Tolstoy". In: *Revelations: Diaries of women.* Ed. Mary J. Moffat & Charlotte Painter. New York: Random, 1974: 138–48. [Also: New York: Vintage, 1975]
—. *The Diaries of Sophia Tolstoy.* Ed. O. A. Golinenko, S. A. Rozanova, B. M. Shumova, I. A. Pokrovskaja, N. I. Azarova. Trans. Cathy Porter. Foreword: R. F. Christian. New York: Random House, 1985.
—. *The Diaries of Sofia Tolstoy.* Trans. & Intro.: Cathy Porter. Foreword: Doris Lessing. London: Alma Books, 2009.
—. "*Song without words*". *The photographs & diaries of Countess Sophia Tolstoy.* Comp. Leah Bendavid-Val. Washington: National Geographic, 2007.
— *The Diaries of Sofia Tolstoj.* Trans. Cathy Porter. Foreword by Doris Lessing. Abridged edition. London: Alma, 2009.
—. *My Life.* Trans. John Woodsworth & Arkadi Klioutchanski. Ed. Andrew Donskov. Ottawa: University of Ottawa Press, 2010; audiobook 2019.
—. *Ma vie.* Trans. Luba Jurgenson & Maria-Luisa Bonaque. Paris: Éditions des Syrtes, 2010.
—. *Romance sans paroles.* Trans. Eveline Amoursky. Paris: Éditions des Syrtes, 2010.
—. *À qui la faute?* Trans. Eveline Amoursky. Paris: Éditions des Syrtes, 2010.
—. *À qui la faute?* Trans. Christine Zeytounian-Beloüs. Paris: Albin Michel, 2010.
—. *Lied ohne Worte.* Trans. Ursula Keller. Zürich: Manesse Verlag, 2010.
—. *Eine Frage der Schuld.* Trans. Alfred Frank & Ursula Keller. Zürich: Manesse Verlag, 2010.

—. "Whose fault?" and "Song without words". Trans. Michael Katz. Published together with Leo Tolstoy's "Kreutzer Sonata" in: *The Kreutzer Sonata Variations*. Ed. & Intro.: Michael Katz. Princeton, N.J. USA: Yale University Press, 2014.

—. *Tolstoy and Tolstaya: a portrait of a life in letters*. Ed. A. Donskov. Trans. J. Woodsworth, A. Klioutchanski, L. Gladkova. Selected correspondence. Ottawa: University of Ottawa Press, 2017.

I.b. Translations by Sofia Andreevna Tolstaya

Lehre der zwölf Apostel. Russian translation from German: *Uchenie dvenadtsati apostolov*. Unpublished manuscript, State L. N. Tolstoy Museum archives.

Sabatier, Paul. *Vie de Saint François d'Assise*. Russian translation from French: *Zhizn' Frantsiska Assizskogo*. Moskva: Posrednik, 1895.

Sprague, Sydney. *A year with the Bahais in India and Burma*. Russian translation from English: *Istorija dvizhenija Bakhai. Vsemirnoe veroispovedanie*. Published (without translator credit) in: L. N. Tolstoj, *Kalendar' dlja kazhdogo na 1911 god*. Moskva: Posrednik, 1911: 125–32.

Tolstoj, L. N. *O zhizni*. French translation from Russian by S. A. Tolstaja and M. M. Tastevin: *De la vie*. Paris: Marpon et Flammarion, 1889.

I.c. Major compilations by Sofia Andreevna Tolstaya

L. N. Tolstoj. *Polnoe sobranie sochinenij*. All published: Moskva: A. I. Mamontov or I. N. Kushnerëv i Kº.

—. 5th ed. (Vols. I–XII), 1886.

—. 6th ed. (Vols. I–XII), 1886.

—. 7th ed. (Vols. I–XII), 1887.

—. 8th ed. (Vols. I–XIII), 1889–91.

—. 9th ed. (Vols. I–XIV), 1893–98.

—. 10th ed. (Vols. I–XVI), 1897–1900.

—. 11th ed. (Vols. I–XIV), 1903.

—. 12th ed. (Vols. I–XX), 1911.

II. Lists of texts by or relating to Sofia Andreevna Tolstaya in Russian archives
I.a. Sofia Andreevna Tolstaya's letters in RO IRLI [= Rukopisnyj otdel / Institut russkoj literatury] (Pushkinskij dom, Skt-Peterburg), written to the following addressees [listed in Russian alphabetical order]:

Abamelek-Lazarev, S. S., Prince. Two letters. 27 August 1888 & [1888]. F. 400. Nº 13. Arkhiv Abamelek-Lazarevykh.

Antonij, Mitropolit [printed variant]. 16 March 1901. F. 302. Op. 3. Ed. khr. 697. Sobranie Tolstovskogo muzeja.

Bertenson, L. Four letters. June–December 1902. F. 302. Op. 3. Ed. khr. 698. Sobranie Tolstovskogo muzeja.

Bulanzhe, P. A. 6 January 1902. F. 302. Op. 3. Ed. khr. 699. Sobranie Tolstovskogo muzeja.

Bunin, I. A. 20 October 1893. F. 123. Op. 1. Ed. khr. 139. Sobranie Burtseva.

Fortunato, S. V. 22 January 1902. F. 704. Nº 140. Arkhiv S. V. Medvedevoj-Petrosjan.

Gintsburg, I. Ja. 25 November 1897. F. 123. Op. 3. Nº 127. Sobranie Burtseva.

Grigorovich, D. V. 6 February 1894. F. 82. Nº 153. Arkhiv Grigorovicha.

Grot, K. Ja. Two letters. 12 October 1909. F. 302. Op. 3. Ed. khr. 700 & 8 May 1885. F. 302. Op. 3. Ed. khr. 701. Sobranie Tolstovskogo muzeja.

Koni, A. F. Sixteen letters. 21 August 1902—30 March 1913. F. 134. Op. 13. Ed. khr. 30. Arkhiv Koni.

—. Telegram. 12 February 1903. F. 134. Op. 13. Ed. khr. 31. Arkhiv Koni.

—. Envelope for letter. 2 July 1904. F. 134. Op. 3. Ed. khr. 2267. Arkhiv Koni.

Kotljarevskij, N. A. 15 April 1911. F. 302. Op. 3. Ed. khr. 72. Sobranie Tolstovskogo muzeja.

Lemke, M. K. Two letters. 7 March 1908 & 20 February 1909. F. 661.N° 1118. Arkhiv Lemke.

Men'shikov, M. O. 22 May 1902. F. 302. Op. 3. Ed. khr. 703. Sobranie Tolstovskogo muzeja.

Neljubin. Two letters. 14 April 1912 & 8 January 1917. F. 123. Op. 3.N° 128. Sobranie Burtseva.

Neizvestnyj adresat [= Unknown addressee]. Letter concerning the arrest of V. G. Chertkov [2nd typed copy]. 1909. F. 302. Op. 3. Ed. khr. 713. Sobranie Tolstovskogo muzeja.

Neizvestnyj adresat. 29 January 1912. F. 123. Op. 3. N° 129. Sobranie A. E. Burtseva.

Rejnbot, V. E. 22 January 1911. F. 302. Op. 3. Ed. khr. 705. Sobranie Tolstovskogo muzeja.

Romanov, K. K. N.d. F. 137. Ed. khr. 88. Arkhiv Romanova.

—. 1910. F. 134. Op. 13. Ed. khr. 41. Arkhiv Koni.

Shljapkin, I. A. 1911. F. 341. Op. 1 N° 2185. Arkhiv Shljapkina.

Svjatejshij Synod i K. P. Pobedonostsev. 26 February 1901. F. 231. N° 286. Arkhiv M. I. Pisareva.

Sverbeev, A. D. 18 April 1891. F. 598. Op. 1. N° 781. Arkhiv Sverbeeva. Sluchevskij, K. K. [editor of Pravitel'stvennyj vestnik]. 8 & 12 February 1892. F. 302. Op. 3. Ed. khr. 706. Sobranie Tolstovskogo muzeja.

Sreznevskij, V. I. Telegram. "23" [no precise date]. F. 302. Op. 3. Ed. khr. 1040. Sobranie Tolstovskogo muzeja.

—. 1916. F. 302. Op. 3. Ed. khr. 707. Sobranie Tolstovskogo muzeja.

Stasjulevich, M. M. Three letters. 1 January 1901—4 May 1904. F. 293. Op. 1. Ed. khr. 1440.

Stakhovich, M. A. Telegram. 1911. F. 302. Op. 3. Ed. khr. 1039. Sobranie Tolstovskogo muzeja.

—. Twenty-five letters and two telegrams. 1891–1914. F. 302. Op. 3. Ed. khr. 708. Sobranie Tolstovskogo muzeja.

Tolstaja, A. A. [LNT's cousin]. Thirty-four letters. 1873–1902. F. 302. Op. 3. Ed. khr. 709. Sobranie Tolstovskogo muzeja.

Tolstaja, Dora F. [wife of Lev L'vovich Tolstoj]. Five letters. 1916–1917. F. 302. Op. 3. Ed. khr. 710. Sobranie Tolstovskogo muzeja.

—. Five letters. 8/21 September 1902—5 May 1914. F. 303. N° 881. Arkhiv L. L. Tolstogo.

Tolstoj, L. L. [LNT's son]. Arkhiv L. L. Tolstogo (except as noted):

—. 21 letters and 1 telegram. 8 May—26 December 1895. F. 303. N° 674.

—. 20 letters. 6/18 January—23 December [1896]. F. 303. N° 675.

—. 8 letters. 25 January—30 June/12 July 1897. F. 303. N° 676.

—. 20 January 1898. F. 303. N° 677.

—. 19 letters. 15 January—24 December 1899. F. 303. N° 678.

—. 8 letters. 7/19 January—11 November 1900. F. 303. N° 679.

—. 21 letters & 2 telegrams. 6 January—30 December 1901. F. 303. N° 680.

—. 22 letters. 24 January—1 December 1902. F. 303. N° 681.

—. 2 letters. 18 May 1903 & 14 April 1908. F. 302. Op. 3. Ed. khr. 131.

—. 14 letters. 24 May—21 December 1903. F. 303. N° 682.

—. 17 letters. 16 January—26 November 1904. F. 303. N° 683.

—. 13 letters and a telegram. 7 January—18 November 1905. F. 303. N° 684.

—. 14 letters. 23 January—24 December 1906. F. 303. N° 685.

—. 9 letters. 1 January—7 December 1907. F. 303. N° 686.

—. 17 letters. 24 January—27 September 1908. F. 303. N° 687.

—. 17 letters. 11 June—22 December 1909. F. 303. N° 688.

—. 18 letters. 8 January—12/25 October 1910. F. 303. N° 689.

—. 2 letters. N.d. [before 1910] & 17 January 1910. F. 303. N° 690.

—. 11 letters. 19 January—28 November 1911. F. 303. N° 691.

—. 11 letters. 21 January—12 December 1912. F. 303. N° 692.

—. 17 letters. 1913–1914. F. 302. Op. 3. Ed. khr. 711. Sobranie Tolstovskogo muzeja.

—. 4 letters. 30 May 1913—17/30 August 1914. F. 303. N° 693.

—. 13 February 1915. F. 303. N° 694.

Tolstoj, L. N. [fragment of letter, hand-written copy]. 4 September 1869. F. 302. Op. 2. Ed. khr. 303. Sobranie Tolstovskogo muzeja. Tolstovskij muzej [= Tolstoy Museum]. Two letters. 1911 & 9 January 1916. F. 302. Op. 3. Ed. khr. 712. Sobranie Tolstovskogo muzeja.

Veselitskaja, L. I. [Fragment with signature]. N.d. F. 44, N° 22. L. 48 (23). Arkhiv Veselitskoj.

Vestnik Evropy (to the editor). 2 September 1908. F. 293. Op. 3 Ed. khr. 218. Arkhiv Stasjulevicha.

I.b. Other letters by and to Sofia Andreevna Tolstaya in IRLI (Pushkinskij dom)

S. A. Tolstaja to S. A. Vengerov. F. 377 (S. A. Vengerov).

S. A. Tolstaja to N. N. Vrangel'. F. 60 (N. N. Vrangel').

S. A. Tolstaja to L. Ja. Gurevich. F. 89 (L. Ja. Gurevich).

S. A. Tolstaja to K. D. Kavelin [historian]. F. 119 (K. D. Kavelin).

K. K. Pavlova to S. A. Tolstaja. F. 134 (A. F. Koni).

S. A. Tolstaja to A. F. Marks. F. 175 (A. F. Marks).

S. A. Tolstaja to *Novoe vremja*. F. 303 (L. L. Tolstoj).

S. A. Tolstaja to V. V. Stasov. F. 294 (Stasovy).

N. N. Strakhov to S. A. Tolstaja. F. 287 (N. N. Strakhov).

S. A. Tolstaja to I. S. Turgenev. F. 241 (Ja. P. Polonskij).

I. S. Turgenev to S. A. Tolstaja. F. 306 (I. S. Turgenev).

S. A. Tolstaja to A. A. Fet. F. 377 (A. A. Fet).

II.c. RGIA [= Rossijskij gosudarstvennyj istoricheskij arhkiv] (Skt-Peterburg)

M. G. Savina. Letters to S. A. Tolstaja. F. 869 (M. G. Savina).

S. A. Tolstaja. Letters to S. S. Tatishchev [historian]. F. 878 (S. S. Tatishchev).

II.d. TsIAM [= Tsentral'nyj istoricheskij arkhiv Moskvy] (Moscow)

Perepiska S. A. Tolstoj s Ljuboshchinskimi [relatives of V. I. Vernadskij]. F. 2049 (Fokiny).

Perepiska S. A. Tolstoj s Tolstovskoj komissiej. F. 634 (Russkoe bibliograficheskoe obshchestvo pri Moskovskom universitete).

II.e. RGB [= Rossijskaja gosudarstvennaja biblioteka] (Moscow)
S. A. Tolstaja's letters to the following addressees:
Kerzin, A. M. 27 October 1903. F. 124. III. 100.

Kerzina, M. S. Three letters. 8 April 1905; 12 July 1907; 20 December 1908. F. 124. III. 99.

Krasheninnikov, N. A. 24 August 1908. F. 452. 1.40.

Korolenko, V. G. 2 September 1908. F. 135. Razdel II. 34. 80.

Pobedonostsev, K. P. 26 February 1901. F. 230. 1 dop. 3.

Russkoe slovo. Five letters. 16 November 1910—17 July 1913. F. 259. 22. 27a ("Russkoe slovo").

Sytin, I. D. 12 August 1912. F. 259. 22. 29 ("Russkoe slovo").

Chernogubov, N. N. 1 June 1901. F. 328. 6. 2.

Darstvennaja nadpis'. 17 March 1901. Litvinovu Aleksandru Aleksandrovichu na titul'nom liste knigi *Sochinenija gr. L. N. Tolstogo,* vol. 1. Moskva: 1893. 466. 59. 36 (Sobranie Egereva).

Otzyvy o knige: Tolstaja S. A. *Dnevnik. Ch. 1, 1860–1891.* Moskva: Izd-vo M. I. S. Sabashnikovykh, 1928. [Also: *Dnevnik. Ch. 3, 1897–1909.* Moskva: Kooperativnoe izdatel'stvo «Sever», 1932. F. 261. 23. 66]

II.f. RGALI [= Rossijskij gosudarstvennyj arkhiv literatury i iskusstva] (Moscow)
Texts by or relating to Sofia Andreevna Tolstaya (*née* Bers):
"Vospominanija o L. N. Tolstom" [typescript]. Tezisy vystuplenija v TsDRI. 1950, VII, 23. F. 3002 (Filippov). Op. 1. Ed. khr. 535.

"Zhenit'ba L. N. Tolstogo". Memoirs. From *Russkoe slovo.* 28 May 1912. F. 2167 (Prugavin A. S.). Op. 1. Ed. khr. 52. L. 18.

"Kratkaja biografija L. N. Tolstogo" [handwritten]. 28 November 1878. F. 508 (Tolstovskoe sobranie). Op. 1. Ed. khr. 324.

"Moi zapisi raznye dlja spravok". 1870–1881. F. 508 (Tolstovskoe sobranie). Op. 1. Ed. khr. 326.

"Pochemu Karenina Anna i chto povlijalo na mysl' o podobnom samoubijstve". 1881. F. 508 (Tolstovskoe sobranie). Op. 1. Ed. khr. 322.

"Primirenie grafa L. N. Tolstogo i I. S. Turgeneva". 1978. F. 508 (Tolstovskoe sobranie). Op. 1. Ed. khr. 325.

"Ssora L. N. Tolstogo s I. S. Turgenevym" & "Primirenie L. N. Tolstogo s I. S. Turgenevym". 22 January 1877 & 12 August 1878. F. 436 (Sreznevskij). Op. 1. Ed. khr. 2187.

[Otvet M. O. Men'shikovu]. Article from a newspaper [1908]. F. 278. (Lazarevskij). Op. 1. Ed. khr. 5. L. 175.

"Dnevniki". 1897–1907 [fragments copied by A. N. Tikhomirov]. [1939–1940 (?)]. F. 2163 (Tikhomirov). Op. 1. Ed. khr. 54. Ll. 1–2.

"Dnevniki" [typed copies]. 1893–1902, 1906, 1910. F. 2532 (Rodionov). Op. 1. Ed. khr. 53, 54.

"Vypiski iz «Dnevnikov S. A. Tolstoj za 1876–1878 gg.»" [typescript]. 1910s. F. 436 (Sreznevskij). Op. 1. Ed. khr. 2144.

"Vypiski iz «Dnevnika» S. A. Tolstoj" [typed copy]. 1919. F. 1365 (Basov, Verkhojantsev). Op. 1. Ed. khr. 131.

"Oglavlenie k al'bomu «Jasnaja Poljana», podarennomu V. A. Shchurovskomu". 1909. F. 508 (Tolstovskoe sobranie). Op. 2. Ed. khr. 148.

"Pravka na stat'e L. N. Tolstogo «O narodom obrazovanii»" (1875). 29 March 1886. F. 508 (Tolstovskoe sobranie). Op. 1. Ed. khr. 76.

"Privetstvie organizatoram chital'ni g. Ivano-Voznesenska. Litografija s avtografa". 9 November 1908. F. 90 (Vashkov). Op. 1. Ed. khr. 28. L. 8.

"Vyskazyvanija ob èksponatakh Tolstovskoj vystavki". From *Russkie vedomosti* Nº 249 (29 October 1911). F. 2167 (Prugavin A. S.). Op. 1. Ed. khr. 51. L.149.

"Pis'mo mitropolitu Antoniju po sluchaju otluchenija L. N. Tolstogo ot tserkvi" [print copy]. 1901. F. 508 (Tolstovskoe sobranie). Op. 1. Ed. khr. 327.

Seven letters to P. I. Birjukov. 9 April 1904—25 September 1915. F. 41 (Birjukov). Op. 1. Ed. khr. 103.

Letter to P. I. Birjukov. N.d. F. 41 (Birjukov). Op. 2. Ed. khr. 17.

Letter to Ja. G. Broner. 6 March 1913. F. 508 (Tolstovskoe sobranie). Op. 1. Ed. khr. 328.

Letters to V. F. Bulgakov [published by V. F. Bulgakov]. Fragment from: V. F. Bulgakov. *Na chuzhoj storone*, vol. II (Prague: 1923). F. 2226 (Bulgakov). Op. 1. Ed. khr. 102. L. 3–16.

—. Thirty-five letters [published; typed copies]. 11 June 1911—13 May 1918. F. 2226 (Bulgakov). Op. 1. Ed. khr. 102. L. 3–16.

Letter to E. L. Gedgovd. 22 April 1903. F. 508 (Tolstovskoe sobranie). Op. 1. Ed. khr. 329.

Letter to I. Ja. Gintsburg. 1891. F. 733 (Gintsburg). Op. 2. Ed. khr. 2.

—. 29 July 1891. F. 733 (Gintsburg). Op. 2. Ed. khr. 2. L. 2.

Letter to O. A. Golenishcheva-Kutuzova. [1890s]. F. 143 (Golenishchev-Kutuzov). Op. 1. Ed. khr. 275.

Letter to E. E. Gorbunova-Posadova. 20 September 1914. F. 122 (Gorbunov-Posadov). Op. 1. Ed. khr. 1945.

Letters to I. I. Gorbunov-Posadov. 18 March 1892 [letter addressed simultaneously to E. E. Gorbunova-Posadova] & 5 April 1892. F. 122 (Gorbunov-Posadov). Op. 1. Ed. khr. 1352.

Letter to G. K. Gradovskij [typed copy]. 16 October 1910. F. 508 (Tolstovskoe sobranie). Op. 1. Ed. khr. 330.

Letters to A. E. Gruzinskij. 27 October 1911—16 March 1914 (37 pp.). F. 126 (Gruzinskij). Op. 1. Ed. khr. 293.

Three letters to N. V. Davydov. 19 January—30 May 1919. F. 1166 (Savodnik). Op. 1. Ed. khr. 101.

Letter to N. M. Ezhov. 4 December 1915. F. 189 (Ezhov). Op. 1. Ed. khr. 34.

Letter to N. M. Zhdanov. 4 June 1913. F. 201 (Zhdanov). Op. 1. Ed. khr. 29.

Two letters to E. A. Zhemchuzhnikova. 1875 & N.d. F. 639 (Zhemchuzhnikov). Op. 2. Ed. khr. 109.

Letter to A. A. Izmajlov. 27 June 1907. F. 227 (Izmajlov). Op. 1. Ed. khr. 168.

"Pripiska na pis'me L. N. Tolstogo" to K. A. Islavin [photocopy]. N.d. F. 228 (Islavin). Op. 1. Ed. khr. 201.

Eleven letters to K. A. Islavin. 2 March 1896—30 October 1902. F. 228 (Islavin). Op. 1. Ed. khr. 202.

Letter to A. M. Kalmykova. 30 June 1901. F. 258 (Kalmykova). Op. 3. Ed. khr. 134.

Letter to A. F. Koni. 11 September 1902. F. 508 (Tolstovskoe sobranie). Op. 1. Ed. khr. 330a.

Letters to N. O. Lerner. 1903 (3 pp.). F. 300 (Lerner). Op. 2. Ed. khr. 4.

Letter to N. S. Leskov. 7 July 1892. F. 275 (Leskov). Op. 1. Ed. khr. 306.

Two letters to E. V. Molostvova. 13 June 1907 & 30 October 1917. F. 508 (Tolstovskoe sobranie). Op. 5. Ed. khr. 42.

Four letters to O. N. Novikova [in French]. 6 March 1867 & N.d. F. 345 (Novikova). Op. 1. Ed. khr. 755.

Two letters to I. K. Parkhomenko [handwritten & authorised typescripts]. 11 July–1 September 1909. F. 508 (Tolstovskoe sobranie). Op. 1. Ed. khr. 332.

Letter to I. K. Parkhomenko [typed copy]. 1 September 1909. F. 612 (GPM). Op. 1. Ed. khr. 1573. L. 24.

Two letters to I. D. Petrov [handwritten & handwritten copy]. 6 August 1910 & 6 August 1911. F. 508 (Tolstovskoe sobranie). Op. 2. Ed. khr. 113.

Letter to K. P. Pobedonostsev ("po povodu otluchenija L. N. Tolstogo ot tserkvi") [typed copy]. 26 February 1901. F. 331 (Nelidova). Op. 1. Ed. khr. 421.

Two letters to V. A. Rachinskaja. 6 August 1907 & N.d. (4 pp.). F. 427 (Rachinskie). Op. 1. Ed. khr. 1267.

Notes on N. Sergievskij's letter to V. G. Chertkov. 1891–1915. F. 552 (Chertkov). Op. 1. Ed. khr. 2520.

Letter and telegram to O. P. Smirnova [in French]. 29 December 1874 & N.d. F. 485 (Smirnova). Op. 1. Ed. khr. 655.

Two letters to P. P. Sojkin. 1910. F. 468. Op. 1. Ed. khr. 31.

Letter to D. V. Stasov [typed copy from 1910s]. 28 June 1907. F. 436 (Sreznevskij). Op. 1. Ed. khr. 2223.

Letters to A. S. Suvorin. 1877–1911. F. 459 (Suvorin). Op. 1. Ed. khr. 4251.

Two letters to M. F. Superanskij. 1912. F. 488 (Superanskij). Op. 1. Ed. khr. 83.

Letters to L. N. Tolstoy [with editing and notes by A. I. Tolstaja and P. S. Popov; incomplete collection, typed with editing notes and correction]. 1935–1936. F. 629 (Academia). Op. 1. Ed. khr. 1555.

Letter to M. N. Tolstaja. 1863–1864. F. 508 (Tolstovskoe sobranie). Op. 1. Ed. khr. 335.

Letter to E. M. Feoktistov [handwritten copy with a note by V. S. Sreznevskij, after 1926]. 18 May 1862. F. 436 (Sreznevskij). Op. 1. Ed. khr. 2224.

Two letters to F. F. Fidler. 6 January 1903 & 13 October 1909. F. 518 (Fidler). Op. 3. Ed. khr. 10.

Two letters to Isabel Florence Hapgood [photocop.; in English]. 22 June 1892 & 1 July 1893. F. 508 (Tolstovskoe sobranie). Op. 2. Ed. khr. 114.

Letter to V. G. Chertkov. 19 February 1892. F. 552 (Chertkov). Op. 1. Ed. khr. 2694.

Letter to M. P. Shenshina. N.d. F. 515 (Fet). Op. 1. Ed. khr. 68.

Three telegrams to V. A. Shchurovskij. 17 January–7 December 1902. F. 508 (Tolstovskoe sobranie). Op. 2. Ed. khr. 145.

Letter to A. I. Juzhin. 10 December 1897. F. 878 (Juzhin). Op. 1. Ed. khr. 2012.

Two letters to S. A. Jur'ev. 5 December 1886 & 6 January 1887. F. 638 (Jur'ev). Op. 1. Ed. khr. 489.

Letter to unknown addressee. 27 October 1909. F. 508 (Tolstovskoe sobranie). Op. 2. Ed. khr. 115.

Letters to unknown addressee [handwritten copies]. 22 January 1911 (2 pp.). F. 122 (Gorbunov-Posadov). Op. 1. Ed. khr. 2030.

Letter to relatives and friends [typed copy]. 1 July 1919. F. 122 (Gorbunov-Posadov). Op. 1. Ed. khr. 2030.

Last letter to relatives and friends [typed copy]. 1/14 July 1919. F. 122 (Gorbunov-Posadov). Op. 1. Ed. khr. 2030.

Letter to society "Khudozhestvennaja beseda v Prage" [thanks on behalf of L. N. Tolstoy for books sent to him; typed copy]. 12/24 March 1895. F. 669 ("Khudozhestvennaja beseda v Prage"). Op. 1. Ed. 4.

Letter to *Russkaja mysl'*. 20 July 1903. F. 508 (Tolstovskoe sobranie). Op. 1. Ed. khr. 334.

Letter to "Nachal'nik stantsii goroda Sevastopol'". 22 January 1902. F. 508 (Tolstovskoe sobranie). Op. 2. Ed. khr. 115.

Letter to Holy Synod [about the excommunication of L. N. Tolstoy; copy by R. M. Glier in his letter to M. M. Glier]. 1901. F. 2085 (Glier). Op. 1. Ed. khr. 387.

"Tsirkuljarnoe pis'mo" v Svjatejshij Synod [about the excommunication of L. N. Tolstoy; handwritten and typed] by K. A. Islavin. 26 February 1901. F. 228 (Islavin). Op. 1. Ed. khr. 14.

Letter "v Ministerstvo vnutrennikh del ob okhrane Jasnoj Poljany i o golode, grozjashchem zhivushchim v usad'be". 3 September 1917. F. 95 (Volynskij). Op. 1. Ed. khr. 1095.

"Darstvennaja nadpis'" V. F. Bulgakovu na foto mogily L. N. Tolstogo". 4 March 1913. F. 2226 (Bulgakov). Op. 1. Ed. khr. 1518.

"Zapiska na vizitnoj kartochke A. I. Juzhinu". N.d. F. 878 (Juzhin). Op. 1. Ed. khr. 132. L. 121.

Letter from Mitropolit Antonij [in reply to S. A. Tolstaja's letter about the excommunication of L. N. Tolstoy; print copy]. 1901. F. 508 (Tolstovskoe sobranie). Op. 1. Ed. khr. 327.

Letters from A. E. Bers to S. A. Tolstaja and L. N. Tolstoj [typed copies]. 1862 (34 pp.). F. 508 (Tolstovskoe sobranie). Op. 1. Ed. khr. 196.

Fragment of E. A. Bers's letter to S. A. Tolstaja. 1868. F. 126 (Gruzinskij). Op. 1. Ed. khr. 186.

Telegram from L. B. Bertenson to S. A. Tolstaja. 8 February 1902. F. 508 (Tolstovskoe sobranie). Op. 5. Ed. khr. 34.

Letter from P. I. Birjukov to S. A. Tolstaja [typed copy]. 1 November 1905. F. 41 (Birjukov). Op. 1. Ed. khr. 62.

Letter from F. I. Borodin to S. A. Tolstaja. 5 December 1909. F. 508 (Tolstovskoe sobranie). Op. 2. Ed. khr. 117.

Letter from I. I. Gorbunov-Posadov to S. A. Tolstaja. 4 February 1911. F. 122 (Gorbunov-Posadov). Op. 1. Ed. khr. 173.

Letter from K. Kjugel'gen to S. A. Tolstaja. 18 March 1897. F. 508 (Tolstovskoe sobranie). Op. 6. Ed. khr. 20.

Letter from N. S. Leskov to S. A. Tolstaja. 2 July 1892. F. 275 (Leskov). Op. 3. Ed. khr. 11.

Letter from K. Marsden to S. A. Tolstaja [in English]. 12 June 1892. F. 345 (Novikova). Op. 1. Ed. khr. 1107.

Letter from M. V. Rundal'tsev to S. A. Tolstaja. 28 October 1908. F. 508 (Tolstovskoe sobranie). Op. 2. Ed. khr. 118.

Letter from M. G. Savina to S. A. Tolstaja. 3 January 1886. F. 853 (Savina). Op. 2. Ed. khr. 190.

Letter from F. A. Strakhov to S. A. Tolstaja. 27 May 1899. F. 508 (Tolstovskoe sobranie). Op. 1. Ed. khr. 226.

Letter from M. F. Superanskij to S. A. Tolstaja [draft]. 9 October 1912. F. 488 (Superanskij). Op. 1. Ed. khr. 58a.

Letter from Tokutomi Kendziro to S. A. Tolstaja [trans. from Japanese by N. I. Konrad; typed]. 3 July 1912. F. 622. Op. 1. Ed. khr. 161. Ll. 157–65.

Telegrams from L. N. Tolstoy to S. A. Tolstaya [typed with V. I. Sreznevskij's notes (before 1926)]. 1864–1880s. F. 436 (Sreznevskij). Op. 1. D. 2165zh.

Letters from L. N. Tolstoj to S. N. Tolstoj [175 documents, some with additions by S. A. Tolstaja ("pripiski"); typed copies]. 13 May 1849–1903. F. 122 (Gorbunov-Posadov). Op. 2. Ed. khr. 264. Ll. 1–199.

Letter from K. M. Fofanov to V. A. Tikhonov. 28 August 1908. F. 525 (Fofanov). Op. 1. Ed. khr. 484. Ll. 1–2.

Letter from V. G. Chertkov to S. A. Tolstaja. 27 October 1904. F. 522 (Chertkov). Op. 1. Ed. khr. 74.

Letter from an unknown person to S. A. Tolstaja [with a typed copy]. 1911. F. 598 (Tolstovskoe sobranie). Op. 2. Ed. khr. 119.

"Pis'mo Soveta Moskovskogo khudozhestvennogo obshchestva s soboleznovaniem v svjazi s konchinoj L. N. Tolstogo". 1910. F. 680 (Uchilishche zhivopisi, vajanija i zodchestva). Op. 1. Ed. khr. 749. L. 148.

Tolstaja, S. A. "Dukhovnoe zaveshchanie. Notarial'naja kopija". 19 November 1875 & 21 December 1884. F. 591 (Litfond). Op. 1. Ed. khr. 61.

"Udostoverenie, vydannoe L. N. Tolstym S. A. Tolstoj v tom, chto on razreshaet ej prozhivat' vo vsekh gorodakh Rossii v 1886 g." [typed copy]. 5 November 1886. F. 508 (Tolstovskoe sobranie). Op. 2. Ed. khr. 109.

"Svidetel'stvo, vydannoe T. I. Miljaevu" [autographed copy]. 26 November 1911. F. 508 (Tolstovskoe sobranie). Op. 1. Ed. khr. 323.

"Dogovor s izdatel'stvom I. D. Sytina o prodazhe emu soch. L. N. Tolstogo izd. 1910–1911 gg." [typescript]. February 1912. F. 508 (Tolstovskoe sobranie). Op. 5. Ed. khr. 51.

"Dogovor S. A. Tolstoj s «Tovarishchestvom pechatanija, izdatel'stva i knizhnoj torgovli I. D. Sytina» o prodazhe «Tovarishchestvu…» izdannogo eju sobranija sochinenij L. N. Tolstogo". N.d. F. 41 (Birjukov). Op. 2. Ed. khr. 20.

"Zajavlenie v pravlenie Tolstovskogo obshchestva o svoem soglasii na peredachu veshchej i rukopisej L. N. Tolstogo iz Rumjantsevskogo muzeja v Tolstovskij muzej" [typed copy]. 18 September 1917. F. 508 (Tolstovskoe sobranie). Op. 3. Ed. khr. 35.

"Spisok chlenov Moskovskogo gorodskogo obshchestva vzaimnogo strakhovanija" [brochure]. 1 January 1909. F. 674 (Stroganovskoe uchilishche). Op. 1. Ed. khr. 156. Ll. 236–77.

"Vizitnaja kartochka". N.d. F. 453 (Sollogub). Op. 2. Ed. khr. 10. "Postanovlenie fondovoj komissii GLM o priobretenii ot S. A. Maklakovoj portreta S. A. Tolstoj, vdelannogo v kryshku derevjannoj korobki" [typescript]. 29 March 1933. F. 612 (GLM). Op. 1. Ed. khr. 3034. L. 28.

"Postanovlenie polnomochnoj komissii GLM o priobretenii u V. E. Maslovoj 2-kh pisem S. A. Tolstoj s pripiskoj L. N. Tolstogo" [typescript]. 27 July 1924. F. 612 (GLM). Op. 1. Ed. khr. 3035. L. 58.

Letters to V. E. Maslova "o priobretenii u nee 2-kh pisem S. A. Tolstoj". 15 September 1934—29 December 1937. F. 612 (GLM). Op. 1. Ed. khr. 2396. Ll. 40, 41.

"Spisok raznochtenij v mashinopisnom i pechatnom tekstakh «Dnevnikov S. A. Tolstoj»" [typescript]. 1959. F. 2226 (Bulgakov). Op. 1. Ed. khr. 624. Ll. 95–101.

"U Sof'i Andreevny" [newspaper article by unknown author]. 1910. F. 637 (Jazykov). Op. 1. Ed. khr. 68. L. 125.

Bulgakov, V. F. "Pis'ma S. A. Tolstoj k V. F. Bulgakovu". Predislovie k publikatsii [manuscript; typed with author's editing]. 1956–1960. F. 2226 (Bulgakov). Op. 1. Ed. khr. 96. Ll. 216–236.

Val'be, B. S. [typed with author's editing]. "Dnevniki S. A. Tolstoj". Ocherk. N.d. F. 613 (MKhL). Op. 8. Ed. khr. 2241. Ll. 329–38.

Gorbov, D. A. "Sof'ja Andreevna i L. N. Tolstoj" [article]. Pages from Oktjabr' (June 1935). F. 2242. Op. 1. Ed. khr. 9. Ll. 95–106.

Grushvitskij, A. N. "Perepiska s GLM o prodazhe muzeju rukopisnogo spiska pis'ma S. A. Tolstoj" [4 letters]. 28 August—26 September 1938. F. 612 (GLM). Op. 1. Ed. khr. 756.

Zhdanov, V. A. "Pis'mo v GLM o peredache v muzej 2-kh pisem S. A. Tolstoj, odno s pripiskoj L. N. Tolstogo". 26 July 1934. F. 612 (GLM). Op. 1. Ed. khr. 883. L. 18.

Zloukin, A. I. "Predlozhenie o peredache v GLM pis'ma S. A. Tolstoj". 1935. F. 612 (GLM). Op. 1. Ed. khr. 3049. L. 209.

Lerner, N. O. "Perepiska s GLM o peredache v muzej pis'ma S. A. Tolstoj, drugikh materialov" [44 letters]. 3 December 1932—15 June 1934. F. 612 (GLM). Op. 1. Ed. khr. 1252.

Maslova, V. E. "Predlozhenie o peredache v muzej 2-kh pisem S. A. Tolstoj". 1934. F. 612 (GLM). Op. 1. Ed. khr. 3045. L. 251.

Molostvov, N. G. & P. A. Sergeenko. "L. N. Tolstoj: Kritiko-biograficheskoe issledovanie". Vypusk VI. "Grafinja S. A. Tolstaja" [typed with corrections by S. A. Tolstaja]. 1909. F 508 (Tolstovskoe sobranie). Op. 1. Ed. khr. 261.

Nita Ara. "K kharakteristike S. A. Tolstoj" [article; typed with editing]. [1938]. F. 634 (Redaktsija "Literaturnoj gazety"). Op. 1. Ed. khr. 770. Ll. 42–46.

Novgorodtsev, A. I. "Predlozhenie o peredache v GLM pis'ma S. A. Tolstoj i kopii pis'ma 3-kh studentov L. N. Tolstomu". 5 November 1933. F. 612 (GLM). Op. 1. Ed. khr. 3042. L. 110.

Parkhomenko, I. K. "Perepiska s GLM o peredache pis'ma S. A. Tolstoj i drugikh materialov" [19 letters]. 28 February 1934—21 December 1939. F. 612 (GLM). Op. 1. Ed. khr. 1573.

Perel'man, M. A. "Podrugi velikikh. Z. N. Nekrasova, O. S. Chernyshevskaja, S. A. Tolstaja. Obrazy i kharakteristiki: Issledovanie-trilogija. Chast' III. «Sof'ja Tolstaja»" [typed with author's editing]. [1935–1949; 857 pp.]. F. 2242 (Perel'man). Op. 1. Ed. khr. 59.

Rejzov, B. G. "Perepiska s GLM o pis'me S. A. Tolstoj i portretakh L. N. Tolstogo raboty Kh. K. Gusikova" [two letters]. 20–26 March 1937. F. 612 (GLM). Op. 1. Ed. khr. 1739.

Rozanov, V. V. "O pis'me gr. S. A. Tolstoj" [article; proofs]. N.d. F. 419 (Rozanov). Op. 1. Ed. khr. 172.

Saranchin, M. M. "Predlozhenie o peredache v GLM rukopisi S. A. Tolstoj". N.d. F. 612 (GLM). Op. 1. Ed. khr. 3056. L. 78.

III. General criticism

Afanas'ev, A. Ju. Velikie pisateli. Moskva: Astrel', 2002: 238–66.

Aichenval'd, Julij I.: Dve zheny. Tolstaja i Dostoevskaja. Berlin, 1925. Also in German translation: *Zwei Frauen. Die Gräfin Tolstaja und Frau Dostojewskij.* Berlin, 1926.

Andrew, Joe, (ed.). *Russian women's shorter fiction: an anthology, 1835–1860.* Oxford & New York: Oxford University Press, 1996.

Arbuzov, S. P. *Vospominanija S. P. Arbuzova, byvshego slugi L. N. Tolstogo.* Moskva, 1904.

Asquith, Cynthia. *Married to Tolstoy.* Boston: Houghton-Mifflin, 1961.

Bajkova [= Shumikhina], Ju. G. "Sof'ja Andreevna Tolstaja kak literator". *Obraz zhizni i obraz myslej: materialy nauchnykh chtenij (7 sentjabrja 2005).* Ul'janovsk: Simbirskaja kniga, 2005a: 14–21.

—. "Motiv stranstvija v skazke S. A. Tolstoj «Istorija grivennika». *Mirovaja slovesnost' dlja detej i o detjakh.* Moskva, 2005b. Vyp. 10, Ch. 2: 251–53.

—. "Zhenskij vzgljad (Povest' S. A. Tolstoj «Ch'ja vina?» kak polemicheskij otklik na povest' L. N. Tolstogo «Krejtserova sonata»). *Ljubov' kak universalija bytija. Materialy XIII Vserossijskoj nauchno-prakticheskoj konferentsii «Chelovek v kul'ture Rossii».* Ul'janovsk: UIPKPRO, 2005c. Vyp. 1: 75–77.

—. "Poètika prostranstva v sbornike detskikh rasskazov S. A. Tolstoj «Kukolki-skelettsy»". *Jasnopoljanskij sbornik* (Tula: Izd. dom «Jasnaja Poljana», 2006a): 232–41.

—. "Obraz materi v sbornike detskikh rasskazov S. A. Tolstoj «Kukolki-skelettsy»". *Mirovaja slovesnost' dlja detej i o detjakh.* Moskva, 2006b. Vyp. 11: 260–61.

—. "Zhanr svjatochnogo rasskaza v tvorchestve S. A. Tolstoj". *Literatura XI–XXI vv. Natsional'no-khudozhestvennoe myshlenie i kartina mira: materialy mezhdunarodnoj nauchnoj konferentsii (20–21 sentjabrja 2006 g.).* V 2-kh chastjakh. Ul'janovsk: UlGTU, 2006c. Ch. 1: 357–62.

—. "«Zhenskij ser'ëznyj mir» (Khudozhestvennoe tvorchestvo S. A. Tolstoj)". *Vestnik BashGU.* Ufa, 2007a. Vyp. 3: 55–57.

—. "S. A. Tolstaja kak literator". Dissertatsija na soiskanie uchënoj stepeni kandidata filologichestikh nauk, Ul'janovskij gos. un-t. Ul'janovsk, 2007b.

—. "«Zhizn' nasha vroz'» (Dom i sem'ja Tolstykh v avtobiograficheskikh zapiskakh S. A. Tolstoj)". *Jasnopoljanskij sbornik* (Tula: Izd. dom «Jasnaja Poljana»), 2008: 305–13.

Barker, Adele M., (ed.). *Consuming Russia: popular culture, sex, and society since Gorbachev.* Durham, NC: Duke University Press, 1999.

Basieva, A. S. "S. A. Tolstaja i N. D. Solzhenitsyna: paralleli i perpendikuljary odnoj sud'by". *Materialy Vserossijskoj nauchnoj konferentsii (9–11 oktjabrja 2018 g.).* Lipetsk: LGPU, 2018: 14–18.

Basinskij, Pavel. *Lev Tolstoj: Begstvo iz raja.* Moskva: Astrel', 2010.

Basinskij, Pavel & Ekaterina Barbanjaga. *Sonja ujdi! Sof'ja Tolstaja: vzgljad muzhchiny i zhenshchiny.* Moskva: Molodaja gvardija, 2020.

Birukoff, Paul [= P. I. Birjukov]. *The Life of Tolstoy.* London: Cassel & Co., 1911.

Birjukov, P. I. *Biografija L'va Nikolaevicha Tolstogo.* 2 vols. Moskva & Petrograd: Gosizdat, 1923.

Bonch-Bruevich, Vladimir. "K istorii russkago dukhoborchestva". *Obrazovanie* (St-P.), N°N° 9, 10, 11/12 (1905): 27–56; 145–203; 52–80.

Bulgakov, V. F. *U L. N. Tolstogo v poslednij god ego zhizni. Dnevnik.* Moskva: I. D. Sytin, 1911. [English translation:] *The last year of Leo Tolstoy.* New York: Dial Press, 1971.

—. "V osiroteloj Jasnoj Poljane: Vospominanija. Ijul'–dekabr' 1912 g.". Ed., intro., comm. S. Romanov. *Slovo* N° 5 (2002): 41–49.

—. *Kak prozhita zhizn'. Vospominanija poslednego sekretarja L. N. Tolstogo.* Red. i stat'ja: A. A. Donskov. Comp. L. V. Gladkova, J. Woodsworth, A. Klioutchanski. Ottawa: Slavic Research Group at the University of Ottawa & Moskva: Rossijskij gos. arkhiv literatury i iskusstva & Moskva: Gos. muzej L. N. Tolstogo. Moskva: Kuchkovo Pole, 2012.

—. *V spore s Tolstym: Na vesakh zhizni.* Red. i stat'ja : A. A. Donskov. Ottawa: Slavic Research Group at the University of Ottawa & Moskva: Rossijskij gos. arkhiv literatury i iskusstva & Moskva: Gos. muzej L. N. Tolstogo. Moskva: Kuchkovo Pole, 2014.

Bunin, I. A. *Osvobozhdenie Tolstogo.* Paris, 1937.

—. *Sobranie sochinenij v 9 tt.* Moskva, 1967.

Bursov, B. I. *L. N. Tolstoj. Seminarij.* Leningrad: Gosudarstvennoe uchebno-pedagogicheskoe izdatel'stvo ministerstva prosveshchenija RSFSR, 1963.

Cain, Thomas G. S. "Tolstoy in letters". *Queen's Quarterly* N° 86 (1979): 273–80.

Cheauré, Elisabeth. "«Po povodu Krejtserovoj sonaty...» Gendernyj diskurs i konstrukty zhenstvennosti u L. N. Tolstogo i S. A. Tolstoj". In: Cheauré, E. & C. Heyder (eds.). *Pol. Gender. Kul'tura. Nemetskie i russkie issledovanija.* Moskva, 1999: 193–212.

Chertkov, V. G. *Ukhod Tolstogo.* Moskva: Komitet imeni L. N. Tolstogo po okazaniju pomoshchi golodajushchim, 1922.

Christian, R. F. *Tolstoy: a critical introduction.* Cambridge: Cambridge University Press, 1969.

Clyman, Toby W. & Diana Greene, (eds.). *Women writers in Russian literature.* Westport, Connecticut: Greenwood Press, 1994.

Correspondance entre Romain Rolland et Maxime Gorki 1916–1936. Cahier 28. Paris : Édition Albin Michel SA, 1991.

Davis, Fumiko. *Kovcheg. Sem'ja Tolstykh.* Trans. from the Japanese: T. L. Sokolova-Deljusina. Moskva: Rus'-Olimp, 2010.

Dolgina, L. (ed.). *Druz'ja i gosti Jasnoj Poljany.* Comp. L. V. Gladkova, T. V. Komarova. Materialy nauchno–prakticheskoj konferentsii, posvjashchennoj 170-letiju so dnja rozhdenija S. A. Tolstoj, 1–2 ijunja 2014. Tula: Izd. dom «Jasnaja Poljana», 2017.

Donskov, Andrew. *The changing image of the peasant in nineteenth-century Russian drama.* Helsinki: Suomalainen Tiedeakatemia, 1972.

—. "The peasant in Tolstoy's thought and writings". *Canadian Slavonic Papers* 21: 2 (1979): 183–96.

—. (ed.). *L. N. Tolstoj—P. V. Verigin: perepiska.* S-Peterburg: Izd. «Dmitrij Bulanin», 1995. Also published together with an English translation by John Woodsworth: *Leo Tolstoy—Peter Verigin: correspondence.* Ottawa: Legas, 1995.

—. (ed.). *Sergej Tolstoj and the Doukhobors: a journey to Canada.* Comp. Tat'jana Nikiforova. Trans. John Woodsworth. Ottawa: Slavic Research Group at the University of Ottawa & Moskva: Gos. muzej L. N. Tolstogo, 1998.

—. (ed.). *L. N. Tolstoj i S. A. Tolstaja: perepiska s N. N. Strakhovym / The Tolstoys' correspondence with N. N. Strakhov.* Comp. L. D. Gromova & T. G. Nikiforova. Ottawa: Slavic Research Group at the University of Ottawa & Moskva: Gos. muzej L. N. Tolstogo, 2000.

—. (ed.). *L. N. Tolstoj i F. A. Zheltov: perepiska.* Comp. L. Gladkova. Ottawa: Slavic Research Group at the University of Ottawa & Moskva: Gos. muzej L. N. Tolstogo, 1999. English edition: *A Molokan's search for truth: the correspondence of Leo Tolstoy and Fedor Zheltov.* Trans. John Woodsworth. Ed. Ethel Dunn. Berkeley (Calif.): Highgate Road Social Science Research Station & Ottawa: Slavic Research Group at the University of Ottawa, 2001.

—. (ed.). *Novye materialy o L. N. Tolstom: iz arkhiva N. N. Guseva / New materials on Leo Tolstoy: from the archives of N. N. Gusev.* Ottawa: Slavic Research Group at the University of Ottawa and Moskva: Gos. muzej L. N. Tolstogo, 2002.

—. (ed.). *L. N. Tolstoj—N. N. Strakhov: polnoe sobranie perepiski / Leo Tolstoy & Nikolaj Strakhov: complete correspondence.* 2 vols. Comp. L. D. Gromova & T. G. Nikiforova. Ottawa: Slavic Research Group at the University of Ottawa & Moskva: Gos. muzej L. N. Tolstogo, 2003.

—. *L. N. Tolstoj i N. N. Strakhov. Èpistoljarnyj dialog o zhizni i literature.* Ottawa: Slavic Research Group at the University of Ottawa & Moskva: Gos. muzej L. N. Tolstogo, 2006.

—. *Leo Tolstoy and Russian peasant sectarian writers: selected correspondence.* Correspondence trans. John Woodsworth. Ottawa: Slavic Research Group at the University of Ottawa, 2008a.

—. *Leo Tolstoy and Nikolaj Strakhov: a personal and literary dialogue / L. N. Tolstoj i N. N. Strakhov: èpistoljarnyj dialog o zhizni i literature.* Ottawa: Slavic Research Group at the University of Ottawa & Moskva: Gos. muzej L. N. Tolstogo, 2008b.

—. (ed.). *My Life: Sofia Andreevna Tolstaya.* Trans. John Woodsworth and Arkadi Klioutchanski. Ottawa: University of Ottawa Press, 2010.

—. *Sofia Andreevna Tolstaja: Literary works.* Ottawa: Slavic Research Group at the University of Ottawa and Moscow: State L. N. Tolstoy Museum, 2011.

—. (ed.) *Tolstoy and Tolstaya: a portrait of a life in letters.* Trans. John Woodsworth, Arkadi Klioutchanski and Liudmila Gladkova. Ottawa: University of Ottawa Press, 2017.

—. *Leo Tolstoy and the Canadian Doukhobors: a study in historic relationships.* Expanded and revised edition. Ottawa: University of Ottawa Press, 2019.

—. *Leo Tolstoy in conversation with four peasant sectarian writers: the complete correspondence.* Trans. John Woodsworth. Ottawa: University of Ottawa Press, 2019.

Edwards, Anne. *Sonya: the life of Countess Tolstoy.* London: Hodder & Stoughton, 1981.

Egorov, O. G. "Dnevniki kruga L. N. Tolstogo: S. A. Tolstaja". In: *Dnevniki russkikh pisatelej XIX veka: Issledovanie.* Moskva: Nauka, 2002: 193–229.

Eguchi, Mahoko. "Music and literature as related infections: Beethoven's Kreutzer Sonata Op. 47 and Tolstoi's novella, «The Kreutzer Sonata»", *Russian Literature* 40 (1996): 419–32.

Emerson, Caryl. "Tolstoy and music". In: Donna Tussing Orwin (ed.), *Anniversary essays on Tolstoy.* Cambridge: Cambridge University Press, 2010: 1–32.

Feiler, Lily. "The Tolstoi marriage: conflict and illusions". *Canadian Slavonic Papers* 23: 3 (1981): 245–60.

Eikhenbaum, Boris [= B. M. Èikhenbaum]. *Tolstoi in the sixties.* Trans. Duffield White. Ann Arbor: Ardis, 1982.

Fet-Shenshin, A. A. *Moi vospominanija. 1848–1889.* Moskva, 1890.

—. *Liricheskie stikhotvorenija.* Skt-Peterburg, 1894.

—. *Sochinenija v 2 tt.* Moskva, 1982.

—. Stikhotvorenija, poèmy, perevody. Sost., vstup. st. i komment. A. Tarkhova. Moskva: Pravda, 1985.

Freeborn, Richard. "The long short story in Tolstoy's fiction". In: Donna Tussing Orwin, (ed.). *Anniversary essays on Tolstoy*. Cambridge: Cambridge University Press, 2010: 127–41.

Gasparov, M. L. *Literaturnyj* èntsiklopedicheskij *slovar'*. Red. V. M. Kozhevnikov i R. A. Nikolaev. Moskva, 1987.

Gertè, K. Ju. "Sof'ja Bers: stat' zhenoj genija". *Mezhvuzovskie VII tolstovskie studencheskie chtenija s mezhdunarodnym uchastiem*. Tula: TGPU, 2016 : 43–46.

Gillès, Daniel. "Noces d'or ou la vie de Sonia et Léon Tolstoï". In: *Tolstoï aujourd'hui*. Paris: Institut d'Études Slaves, 1980: 41–50.

Gladkova, L. V. "Ob otluchenii L'va Tolstogo. Po materialam semejnoj perepiski". *Oktjabr'* 9 (1993): 184–190.

—. *On i Ona: Istorija knigi i ljubvi*. Moskva: M., 2011.

—. (ed.). *On i Ona (Lev Tolstoj i Sof'ja Andreevna)*. Preface by N. A. Kalinina. [Catalogue of materials from the collections of the State L. N. Tolstoy Museum.] Tula: IPO «Lev Tolstoj», 2011.

Golinenko, O. A. (intro., comp. & notes). "Vy kazhetes' mne v sto raz vyshe Petra I!" *Oktjabr'* N° 11 (1997): 177–83.

Golinenko, O. A. & B. M. Shumova, (eds.). Excerpts from "Moja zhizn'". Intro. V. Porudominskij. *Oktjabr'* N° 9 (1998): 136–77.

Golinenko, O. A. et al., (eds.). *S. A. Tolstaja. Dnevniki v dvukh tomakh*. 2 vols. Intro. S. A. Rozanova. "Serija literaturnykh memuarov". Moskva: Khudozhestvennaja literatura, 1978.

Gor'kij, Maksim [= Maxim Gorky]. "O S. A. Tolstoj". *Polnoe sobranie sochinenij*, 16: 358–374. Moskva: Nauka, 1973.

Goscilo, Helena & Beth Holmgren, (eds.) *Russia, Women, Culture*. Bloomington: Indiana University Press, 1996.

Green, Dorothy. "The Kreutzer Sonata: Tolstoy and Beethoven". *Melbourne Slavonic Studies* 1 (1967): 11–23.

Gromova-Opul'skaja, L. D. *Lev Nikolaevich Tolstoj. Materialy k biografii s 1886 po 1892 god*. Moskva: Nauka, 1979.

—. *Lev Nikolaevich Tolstoj. Materialy k biografii s 1892 po 1899 god*. Moskva: Nasledie, 1998.

—. *Izbrannye trudy*. Ed. M. I. Shcherbakova. Moskva: Nauka, 2005.

Gruzinskij, A. E. (ed.). *Pis'ma grafa L. N. Tolstogo k zhene*. Moskva, 1913.

Gryzlova, I. K. "Zhizn' sem'i Tolstykh v pis'makh S. A. Tolstoj k T. A. Kuzminskoj". In V. Tolstoj & L. Gladkova, 2006: 125–39.

Gudzij, N. K. & V. A. Zhdanov. "Voprosy tekstologii". *Novyj mir* 3 (1953): 232–42.

Gurevich, L. Ja. "S. A. Tolstaja". *Zhizn' iskusstva* (N°N° 299–303, 1919).

—. "Pervye vpechatlenija ot S. A. Tolstoj". RGALI. F. 131. Op. 1. Ed. khr. 15.

Gusev, N. N. "K istorii semejnoj tragedii Tolstogo (po neizdannym istochnikam)". *Literaturnoe nasledstvo*. 37–38: *L. N. Tolstoj*. Moskva, 1939: 674–97.

—. *Letopis' zhizni i tvorchestva L. N. Tolstogo. 1828–1890*. Moskva: Gos. izd. khudozhestvennoj literatury, 1958.

—. *Lev Nikolaevich Tolstoj. Materialy k biografii s 1855 po 1869 god*. Moskva: Izd. AN SSSR, 1958.

—. *Letopis' zhizni i tvorchestva L. N. Tolstogo. 1891–1910*. Moskva: Gos. izd. khudozhestvennoj literatury, 1960.

—. *Lev Nikolaevich Tolstoj. Materialy k biografii s 1870 po 1881 god.* Moskva: Izd. AN SSSR, 1963.

—. *Lev Nikolaevich Tolstoj. Materialy k biografii s 1881 po 1885 god.* Moskva: Nauka, 1970.

Hamburg, G. M. "Marriage, estate culture and public life in Sofia Andreyevna Tolstaya's «My life»". *Tolstoy Studies Journal* N⁰ 22 (2010): 122–135.

Heier, Edmund. *Religious schism in the Russian aristocracy 1860–1900. Radstockism and Pashkovism.* The Hague: Nijhoff, 1970.

Ioann, arkhiepiskop San-Frantsisskij [= D. A. Shakhovskoj]. "Zhena". In: *K istorii russkoj intelligentsii (Revoljutsija Tolstogo).* Moskva: Lepta-Press, 2003: 381–412.

Ivanova, L. N. (comp.). "Pis'ma S. A. Tolstoj k L. L. Tolstomu". *Zvezda* 8 (1978): 138–41.

Johansen, D. S. & Peter Ulf Møller. "Perepiska S. A. Tolstoj s P. G. Ganzenom". *Scando-Slavica* 24 (1978): 49–62.

Jurovitskij, V. *Sof'ja Andreevna. Drama v chetyrëkh dejstvijakh s prologom.* http://www.yur.ru/art/drama/sofia.htm

Kagal, Ayesha & Natasha Petrova (eds.). *Present imperfect: stories by Russian women.* Oxford & Boulder, Colorado: Westview Press, 1996.

Katz, R. Michael. "'Though this be madness'. Sofia Tolstaya's second response to Kreutzer Sonata". *Tolstoy Studies Journal* 25 (2013): 67–71.

—. (trans. and ed.). *The Kreutzer Sonata Variations. Lev Tolstoy's Novella and Counterstories by Sofia Tolstaya and Lev Levovich Tolstoy.* New Haven & London: Yale University Press, 2014.

Keller, Ursula & Sharandak, Natalja. *Sofja Andrejewna Tolstaja: Ein Leben an der Seite Tolstojs.* Frankfurt am Main & Lepizig: Insel Verlag, 2009.

Kelly, Catriona (ed.). *An anthology of Russian women's writing. 1777–1992.* Oxford & New York: Oxford University Press, 1994.

—. "Women's writing in Russia". In: Neil Cornwell, (ed.). *The Routledge companion to Russian literature.* London and New York: Routledge, 2001: 150–162.

—. *A history of Russian women's writing. 1820–1992.* Oxford & New York: Clarendon Press, 1994.

Khitajlenko, N. N. (comp.), T. P. Rjukhina (ed.). *Lev Tolstoj v Khamovnikakh.* Moskva: Planeta, 1994.

Khrabrovitskij, A. V. (comp.). "V. G. Korolenko i S. A. Tolstaja". *Jasnopoljanskij sbornik* (Tula: Priokskoe kn. izd., 1978): 287–89.

Klimova, S. M. "Priroda tvorcheskogo myshlenija v perepiske Tolstogo i Strakhova". In: S. M. Klimova et al. (eds.), *N. N. Strakhov v dialogakh s sovremennikami. Filosofija kak kul'tura ponimanija.* Skt-Peterburg: Aletejja, 2010: 135–52.

Komarova, T. V. "Ob ukhode i smerti L. N. Tolstogo". *Jasnopoljanskij sbornik 1992* (Tula: Posrednik, 1992): 213–18.

—. "Angel Jasnoj Poljany". *Pamjatniki Otechestva: Al'manakh.* Moskva: Russkaja kniga, 28 (1992): 91–94.

—. "Pometki S. A. Tolstoj na jasnopoljanskom èkzempljare *Pisem grafa L. N. Tolstogo k zhene 1862–1910 gg.*". *Jasnopoljanskij sbornik 1998.* Tula: Izdatel'skij dom «Jasnaja Poljana» (1999): 155–58.

—. "S. A. Tolstaja — detjam". *Litsej na Pushkinskoj* N⁰ 13–14. Tula, 1999–2000: 141–48.

—. "Fet i S. A. Tolstaja". In: *A. A. Fet i russkaja literatura.* Kursk & Orël: Kurskij gos. universitet & Orlovskij gos. universitet, 2000: 255–59.

—. *Semejnye relikvii roda grafov Tolstykh*. Tula: Izdatel'skij dom «Jasnaja Poljana», 2000.

—. "Fet v vospominanijakh S. A. Tolstoj «Moja zhizn'»". In: *A. A. Fet i russkaja literatura*. Kursk: Kurskij gos. universitet, 2003: 216–23.

—. *Odna iz Shamordinskikh monakhin'. Marija Nikolaevna Tolstaja*. Tula: Izdatel'skij dom «Jasnaja Poljana», 2003.

—. "Samaja luchshaja na svete…". *Zhizn' v usad'be* N° 2 (2004): 38–39.

—. "…Gde vy, tam prazdnik". In: V. Tolstoj & L. Gladkova, 2006: 5–17.

—. "Povest' Sof'i Andreevny Tolstoj *Ch'ja vina?* Kak otvet na *Krejtserovu sonatu* L. N. Tolstogo" [manuscript (7 pages)].

—. "«Detskaja kniga» S. A. Tolstoj. K stoletiju so dnja vykhoda v svet". *Mansurovskie chtenija*, Kaluga, sentjabr' 2011.

—. "S. A. Tolstaja — popechitel'nitsa detskogo prijuta. Iz istorii odnoj memorial'noj fotografii". In: L. V. Gladkova (ed.). *Materialy Tolstovskikh chtenij 2013 g. i Gorokhovskikh chtenij 2013 g. v Gos. muzee L. N. Tolstogo.* Comp. L. G. Gladkikh, Ju. V. Prokopchuk. Moskva, 2014: 227–230.

—. "Sof'ja Tolstaja: muza grafa Tolstogo i dusha Jasnoj Poljany". *Myslo Tula,* 9 aprelja 2014.

—. "Sof'ja Andreevna Tolstaja: sposobnost' k risovaniju". *Mansurovskie chtenija: Jasnaja Poljana,* sentjabr' 2014. Tula, 2016. 6: 176–180.

Kornaukhova, E. G. "…Chudnye ljudi i chudnoe mesto Jasnaja Poljana dlja pamjati". In: V. Tolstoj & L. Gladkova, 2006: 197–216.

—. "S. A. Tolstaja (1844), D. G. Burylin (1914, 1924), S. N. Tolstaja (1934)". *Mansurovskie chtenija: Jasnaja Poljana,* sentjabr' 2014. Tula, 2016. 6:188–191.

Kosov, Aleksej. "Papina dochka. Aleksandra Tolstaja". *Stolichnaja gazeta* N° 10 (49) (2005): 16–18.

Kotljarskij, Èmil' Solomonovich. *Chelovek po imeni Lev (p'esa dl'ja mysljashchikh).* http://zhurnal.lib.ru/k/kotljarskij_e_s/levtolstoy.shtml

Krylova, R. N. "L. N. Tolstoj i ego pomoshchniki na golode v Dankovskom uezde Rjazanskoj gubernii v 1891–1893 godakh". *Tolstovskij ezhegodnik 2002.* (Tula: Izd. dom «Jasnaja Poljana», 2003): 242–54.

Kulov, T. K. "L. Andreev i M. Gor'kij". *Uchenye zapiski Moskovskogo oblastnogo pedagogicheskogo instituta im. N. K. Krupskoj,* vol. 129. Moskva: Sovetskaja literatura, 1963: 115–44.

Kuzminskaja, G. N. *Kuzminskie rodstvenniki S. A. Tolstoj.* Sbornik statej, napisannykh po istoriko-genealogicheskim materialam. SPb: Znanie, 2018.

Kuzminskaja, T. A. *Moja zhizn' doma i v Jasnoj Poljane.* 3-e izd. Tula: Tul'skoe kn. izd., 1960.

Lazurskij, V. "L. N. Tolstoj i N. N. Strakhov: iz lichnykh vospominanij". *Russkaja byl'* 3 (1910): 148–56.

Ledkovsky, Marina, Charlotte Rosenthal & Mary Zirin. *Dictionary of Russian women writers.* Westport, Connecticut: Greenwood Press, 1994.

Makovitskij, D. P. *U Tolstogo. 1904–1910. Jasnopoljanskie zapiski* N° 1–4. Moskva: Nauka, 1979.

Mandelker, Amy. *Framing "Anna Karenina". Tolstoy, the woman question and the Victorian novel.* Columbus: Ohio State University, 1993.

Martynenko, D. R. "Rol' gosudarstvennoj vlasti v gibeli Rossijskoj Imperii". http://www.dmr2.ru/files/2/1-history_ref.doc

Matveev, P. "L. N. Tolstoj i N. N. Strakhov v Optinoj Pustyni". *Istoricheskij vestnik* 4 (1907): 151–57.

McLean, Hugh. "The Tolstoy marriage revisited — many times". *Canadian Slavonic Papers* 53 (2011): 65–80.

Mejlakh, B. *Ukhod i smert' L'va Tolstogo.* Moskva & Leningrad: Gos. izd. khudozhest-vennoj literatury, 1960.

Meyer-Stabley, Bertrand. *La Comtesse Tolstoï.* Paris: Payot, 2009.

Meza, E. "Mirren, Plummer to star in 'Station'. Tolstoy biopic costars McAvoy, Giamatti." Internet, 2008. https://variety.com/2008/film/markets-festivals/mirren-plummer-to-star-in-station-1117983229/

Mirsky, Dmitry. *Uncollected writings on Russian literature.* Edited, with an introduction by G. S. Smith. Berkeley: Berkeley Slavic Specialties, 1989.

Moher, Frank. *Tolstoy's wife* [play premiered by Alberta Theatre Project, Calgary, January 1997]. Gabriola Island, BC: Single Lane, 1997.

Müller, Peter Ulf. *Postlude to the Kreutzer Sonata. Tolstoj and the debate on sexual morality in Russian literature in the 1890s.* Trans. from the Danish by John Kendal. Leiden, New York, København, Köln, 1988. [Esp. pp. 172–77]

Nickell, William. "Tolstoy wars". *Tolstoy Studies Journal* N° 22 (2010): 136–46.

—. *The death of Tolstoy. Russia on the eve, Astapovo Station, 1910.* Ithaca & London: Cornell University Press, 2010.

Nikiforova, T. G. "«...chto mozhet byt' polezno ljudjam». K istorii sobiranija rukopis-nogo nasledija L. N. Tolstogo". *Oktjabr'* N° 11 (1997): 171–77.

—. "Pis'ma A. G. Dostoevskoj k S. A. Tolstoj". In: M. Shcherbakova & M. Mozharova (eds.), *Mir filologii.* Moskva: Nasledie, 2000: 290–306.

—. "S. A. Tolstaja" [manuscript, 13 pp.].

—. "Nachalo izdatel'skoj dejatel'nosti S. A. Tolstoj". In: *Tolstoj — èto tselyj mir.* Moskva, 2004: 168–77.

Nikitina, N. A. *Povsednevnaja zhizn' L'va Tolstogo v Jasnoj Poljane.* Moskva: Molodaja gvardija, 2007.

—. *Sof'ja Andreevna Tolstaja.* Moskva: Molodaja gvardija, 2010.

Nikitina, T. V. "S. A. Tolstaja i A. G. Dostoevskaja: «Pokhozhie na svoikh muzhej»". In: V. Tolstoj and L. Gladkova, 2006: 109–14.

—. "Odin èpizod iz moskovskoj vstrechi (S. A. Tolstaja i A. G. Dostoevskaja)". In: *Lev Tolstoj i Obshchestvo ljubitelej rossijskoj slovesnosti.* Moskva: Akademija, 2008: 219–76.

Panchenko, N. T. "Iz perepiski S. A. Tolstoj s E. M. Feoktistovym i I. N. Durnovo". *Russkaja literatura* N° 4 (1960): 167–72.

Paperno, Irina. "Who, what is I? Tolstoy in his diaries". *Tolstoy Studies Journal* 2 (1999): 32–54.

—. *"Who, what am I": Tolstoy struggles to narrate the self.* Ithaca: Cornell University Press, 2014.

Parini, Jay. *The last station.* New York: Holt, 1990. Pasternak, L. O. *Zapisi raznykh let.* Moskva, 1975.

Persky, Serge. *Trois épouses : Nathalie Pouchkine, Anna Dostoïevsky, Sophie Tolstoï.* Paris: Payot, 1929.

Pinkham, Sophie. "Sofiya Tolstoy's defense". *The New Yorker,* 21 October 2014.

Pokrovskaja, I. A. & B. M. Shumova (eds.). "Excerpts from «Moja zhizn'»". *Novyj mir* N° 8 (1978): 34–135.

—. "Excerpts from «Moja zhizn'»" *Prometej* N° 12 (1980): 148–98.

Poljakova, T. V. "Istorija sozdanija V. A. Serovym portreta S. A. Tolstoj".*Jasnopoljanskij sbornik 2000* (Tula: 2000): 343–49.

Polner, Tichon [= Tikhon Polner]. *Tolstoj und seine Frau. Die Geschichte der Liebe.* Berlin, 1928.

—. *Lev Tolstoj i ego zhena. Istorija odnoj ljubvi.* Moskva, 1928. Republished: Moskva-Ekaterinburg, 2000.

—. *Tolstoy and his wife.* Trans. Nicholas Wreden. New York: Norton, 1945.

Popoff, Alexandra. *Sophia Tolstoy. A biography.* New York: Free Press, 2010.

—. *The wives. The women behind Russia's literary giants.* New York & London: Pegasus Books, 2012.

Popov, P. "Pis'mo Tolstogo k S. A. Tolstoj (Novoe o semejnykh otnoshenijakh L. N. Tolstogo)". *Literaturnoe nasledstvo 37–38: L. N. Tolstoj.* Moskva: Akademija Nauk, 1939: 665–73.

Popovkin, A. (comp.). "Iz pisem T. A. Kuzminskoj k S. A. Tolstoj". *Jasnopoljanskij sbornik* (Tula, 1960): 191–94.

Porudominskij, V. I. "Iz zapisok daleveda". *O Tolstom.* Skt-Peterburg: Aletejja, 2005a: 190–213.

—. "Prizvanie i sud'ba". *O Tolstom.* Skt-Peterburg: Aletejja, 2005b: 160–75.

Prugavin, A. S. *O L've Tolstom i tolstovtsakh. Ocherki, vospominanija, materialy.* Izd. 2, 1911. Reprint: Moskva: Librokom, 2012.

Prussakova, Inna. "O nekotorykh strannostjakh naivnosti". *Neva* (1995): 194–200.

Puzin, N. P. "Tolstaja Sof'ja Andreevna". *Kratkaja literaturnaja èntsiklopedija.* Vol. 7. Moskva, 1972: 537.

—. "Iz perepiski A. A. Feta s L. N. i S. A. Tolstymi". In: N. P. Puzin & T. N. Arkhangel'skaja. *Vokrug Tolstogo.* Tula: Priokskoe knizhnoe izdatel'stvo, 1988: 18–42.

—. "Potomstvo L. N. Tolstogo". In: N. P. Puzin & T. N. Arkhangel'skaja. *Vokrug Tolstogo.* Tula: Priokskoe knizhnoe izdatel'stvo, 1988: 159–79.

—. *Kochakovskij nekropol'.* Tula: Izdatel'skij dom "Jasnaja Poljana", 1998.

—. *Dom-muzej L. N. Tolstogo v Jasnoj Poljane.* Tula: Izdatel'skij dom «Jasnaja Poljana», 1998.

Rachmanowa, Alja. *Sonja Tolstoj. Tragödie einer Liebe.* Stuttgart, 1953.

Rak, Julie. *Negotiated memory: Doukhobor autobiographical discourse.* Vancouver: University of British Columbia Press, 2004.

Rancour-Laferriere, Daniel. *Tolstoy on the couch: misogyny, masochism and the absent mother.* New York & London: New York University Press & Macmillan, 1998.

—. "Lev Tolstoy's moral masochism in the late 1880s". In: Michael C. Finke & Carl Niekerk, (eds.). *One hundred years of masochism.* Amsterdam: Rodopi, 2000: 155–70.

Rancour-Laferriere, Daniel (ed.). *Russian literature and psychoanalysis.* Amsterdam: John Benjamins, 1989.

Remizov, V. B. "Lev Tolstoj pered sudom zheny". Afterword to: S. A. Tolstaja: *Moja zhizn'.* Moskva: Kuchkovo Pole, 2011. T. 2: 591–605.

Remizov, V. B. & L. V. Gladkova (eds.). *Lev Nikolaevich Tolstoj, Sof'ja Andreevna Tolstaja, Lev L'vovich Tolstoj.* 2 vols. Moskva: Gos. Muzej L. N. Tolstogo, Izd. dom «Porog», 2010.

Renner-Fahey, Ona. "Diary of a devoted child". *Slavic & East European Journal,* 53: 2 (2009): 189–202.

Reznikov, K. Ju. "Ukhod Tolstogo: vzgljad iz Severnoj Ameriki. I. Literaturovedy SSha i Kanady ob ukhode Tolstogo iz Jasnoj Poljany". Report for scholarly grant RGNF N° 09-04-00493 a/R "L. N. Tolstoj v russkom i mirovom soznanii: pereklichka na rubezhe vekov (100 let posle ukhoda)", 2009. Moskva: Samizdat online journal, 2009. http://zhurnal.lib.ru/r/reznikow_k_j/tolstoysflightviewfromnorthamerica.shtml

—. "Ukhod Tolstogo: vzgljad iz Severnoj Ameriki. II. Semejnaja zhizn' L. N. i S. A. Tolstykh v amerikanskoj khudozhestvenno-biograficheskoj literature i kino". Report for scholarly grant RGNF N° 09-04-00493 a/R "L. N. Tolstoj v russkom i mirovom soznanii: pereklichka na rubezhe vekov (100 let posle ukhoda)", 2010.

Roberts, Spencer E. (ed. & trans.). *Russian memoirs: writers through the eyes of their contemporaries.* Vols. I & II. USA: Xlibris Publishing, 2009. (see chapter on Tolstoy in Volume II.)

Rozanova, S. A. Introduction to Golinenko et al. (eds.). *S. A. Tolstaja. Dnevniki v dvukh tomakh.* "Serija literaturnykh memuarov". Moskva: Khudozhestvennaja literatura, 1978: I: 5–34.

Safonova, O. Ju. *Rod Bersov v Rossii.* Moskva: Èntsiklopedija sel i dereven', 1999.

Samofalova, E. A. "Samoidentifikatsija lichnosti zhenshchiny v vospominanijakh Sof'i Andreevny Tolstoj". *Uchenye zapiski: èlektronnyj nauchnyj zhurnal Kurskogo gos. universiteta,* N° 2, 2014.

Serebrovskaja, E. S. "Tri biograficheskikh ocherka Tolstogo". *Literaturnoe nasledstvo,* Moskva 1961, kn. 1: 497–518.

Shcherbakova, M. I. (ed. & intro.). *I. S. Aksakov — N. N. Strakhov: Perepiska / Ivan Aksakov — Nikolaj Strakhov: Correspondence.* Ottawa: Slavic Research Group at the University of Ottawa and Moskva: Institut mirovoj literatury im. L. M. Gor'kogo, 2007.

Shengelija, M. (ed.). *L. N. Tolstoj. Dokumenty, fotografii, rukopisi.* Moskva: Planeta, 1995.

Shenshina, V. A. "S. A. Tolstaja i A. A. Fet. Radost' tvorcheskogo obshchenija v Jasnoj Poljane". In: V. Tolstoj & L. Gladkova, 2006: 51–60.

Shestakova, E. G. "Svet iz detskoj komnaty". *Tolstovskij ezhegodnik 2002.* (Tula: Izd. Vlasta, 2003): 218–40.

—. "S. A. Tolstaja. Uzory zhizni: vystavka v Muzee-usad'be L. N. Tolstogo «Khamovniki»". In: L. V. Gladkova (ed.). *Khamovniki* [booklet]. Moskva, 2014.

Shestakova, E. G., N. A. Zubkova & È. N. Anan'eva. *Uzory zhizni Sof'i Tolstoj v Khamovnikakh.* Red. L. V. Gladkova, M. K. Tjun'kina. Moskva, 2020.

Shifman, A. "Vanechka". *Moskva* 9 (1978): 55–65.

—. "Izdatel'nitsa L'va Tolstogo". *V mire knig* (1982): 51–53.

—. "Iz perepiski S. A. Tolstoj i A. G. Dostoevskoj". *Neva* N° 2 (1983): 162–67.

Shirer, William L. *Love and hatred: the troubled marriage of Leo Tolstoy.* New York: Simon & Shuster, 1994.

Shirma, T. E. *V gostjakh u L'va Tolstogo.* Moskva: Slovo, 2012.

Shklovskij, V. *Lev Tolstoj.* Moskva: Molodaja gvardija, 1963.

Shore, Elizabeth. "Po povodu *Krejtserovoj sonaty.* Gendernyj diskurs i konstrukty zhenstvennosti". In: *Pol. Gender. Kul'tura.* Moskva: Rossijskij gosudarstvennyj gumanitarnyj universitet, 1999: 193–211.

Shumikhina, Ju. G. — see: Bajkova [= Shumikhina], Ju.G.

Smoluchowski, Louise. *Lev and Sonya: the story of the Tolstoy marriage.* New York: G. P. Putnam's Sons, 1987.

Snegirëv, V. F. "Operatsija (iz zapisok vracha)". In: P. Sergeenko (comp.). *Mezhdunarodnyj tolstovskij al'manakh: o Tolstom.* Moskva: Kniga, 1909: 332–340.

—. "Kopija s rukopisnogo pis'ma V. F. Snegirëva k S. A. Tolstoj ot 10 aprelja 1911 g." / F47, KP 8375, Inv. N° 30853. Moskva: L. N. Tolstoy Museum.

—. "«Chast' moej dushi istrachena na Vas...» (pis'ma V. F. Snegirëva v Khamovniki i Jasnuju Poljanu)". *Vrach,* 4 (1992): 56–58.

—. "V. F. Snegirëv v Khamovnikakh i Jasnoj Poljane". *Jasnopoljanskij sbornik* Tula, 1992: 114–26.

Strakhov, N. N. "Zhenskij vopros". *Zarja* 2 (1870): 107–49.

Stroganova, E. N. "Zhena pisatelja Sof'ja Andreevna Tolstaja". In: L. V. Gladkova (ed.). *Tolstaja segodnja: Materialy Tolstovskikh chtenij 2012 g.* Moskva, 2014: 210–26.

Sukhotina-Tolstaja, T. L. *Vospominanija.* Moskva: Khudozhestvennaja literatura, 1981.

Svadkovskij, B. S. "«Ja ponjal ètot ... vopl' dushi» (pis'mo V. F. Snegirëva k S. A. Tolstoj ot 10 aprelja 1911 g. ob ukhode i smerti Tolstogo)." *Meditsinskaja gazeta,* 28 April 1989.

—. "Neizvestnoe pis'mo: Vrach D. Nikitin o zhene L'va Tolstogo". *Meditsinskaja gazeta* 5 March 1993.

Taneev, S. I. *Dnevniki v 3 kn.* Moskva: Muzyka, 1985.

Tjurina, N. "Tri uroka Sof'i Tolstoj, ili Otvet «nesovremennoj chitatel'nitse»". *Federatsija* 4 (September 1993): 5.

—. "Ona dala nam obraz jasnoj zhizni". *Rabochaja tribuna,* 28 October 1993.

Tolstaja, A. L. *Otets: Zhizn' Tolstogo.* 2 vols. Moskva: Kniga, 1989. [esp. Ch. 25: "Esli by ja kogda-nibud' zhenilsja": 143–52; Ch. 26: "Zhenat i schastliv": 152–59]

Tolstoj, I. L. *Reminiscences of Tolstoy.* Trans. George Calderon. London: Chapman & Hall, 1914.

—. *Moi vospominanija.* Moskva: Khudozhestvennaja literatura, 1969: 254–68.

—. *Tolstoy. My Father. Reminiscences.* Trans. Ann Dunnigan. Chicago: Cowles, 1971.

Tolstoj, Il'ja & Svetlana Svetana-Tolstaja. *Puti i sud'by. Iz semejnoj khroniki.* Moskva: Izdatel'stvo IKAR, 1998.

Tolstoj, L. L. [= Jasha Polenov] *Vospominanija dlja detej iz detstva.* Moskva, 1899.

—. "Preludija Shopena". In: L. L. Tolstoj. *Preljudija Shopena i drugie rasskazy.* Moskva. 1900: 3–52. Republished in Remizov & Gladkova 2010.

—. *Le prélude de Chopin.* Trans. Eveline Amoursky. Paris: Éditions des Syrtes, 2010.

Tolstoj, L. N. *Polnoe sobranie sochinenij.* Jubilejnoe izdanie. Moskva: Goslitizdat, 1928–1958. [Vols. 83 (1938) & 84 (1949) contain Tolstoy's letters to Sofia Andreevna]

Tolstoï, S. [= S. L. Tolstoj]. "Les derniers jours de ma mère. Fragment inédit d'un journal intime". *Europe* N° 67 (1928).

Tolstoj, S. L. *Ocherki bylogo.* Ed. K. Malysheva. Moskva: "Khudozhestvennaja literatura", 1956. See esp. "Konchina moej materi": 272–76.

Tolstoj, S. M. *Deti Tolstogo.* Trans. from the French [*Les Enfants de Tolstoï,* Paris, 1989] by A. N. Polosina. Tula: Priokskoe knizhnoe izdatel'stvo, 1994.

Tolstoj, Vladimir & Ljudmila Gladkova (eds.). *Druz'ja i gosti Jasnoj Poljany. Materialy nauchnoj konferentsii, posvjashchennoj 160-letiju S. A. Tolstoj.* Tula: Izd. dom. «Jasnaja Poljana», 2006.

Tomei, Christine D. (ed.). *Russian women writers.* 2 vols. New York: Garland, 1999.

Ulitina, O. V. "N. V. Davydov. Vospominanija i pis'ma". In: V. Tolstoj & L. Gladkova, 2006: 181–96.

Van de Stadt, Janneke. "Narrative, music and performance: Tolstoy's «Kreutzer Sonata» and the example of Beethoven". *Tolstoy Studies Journal* 12 (2000): 57–70.

Vasil'eva, S. A. "Vs. S. Solov'ëv o Tolstom". In: V. Tolstoj & L. Gladkova, 2006: 115–23.

Velikanova, N. & R. Vittaker [= Robert Whittaker]. *L. N. Tolstoj i SShA. Perepiska.* Moskva: IMLI RAN, 2004.

Vengerov, S. A. *Kritiko-biograficheskij slovar' russkikh pisatelej i uchënykh*, 6 vols. (St. Petersburg, 1889–1904, unfinished).

—. *Istochniki slovarja russkikh pisatelej*, 2 vols. (St. Petersburg, 1900–17, unfinished).

Volzhanin, O. "Pravda o S. A. Tolstoj". *Vestnik literatury* N° 6–7 (1921): 2–5; N° 8 (1921): 2–4.

—. "«Opal'naja» S. A. Tolstaja". *Molva* [newspaper] (Warsaw), N° 90 (July 1932).

Vronskaja, Ju. (ed.). *Povarennaja kniga S. A. Tolstoj.* Tula: Izd. dom «Jasnaja Poljana», 2011.

Wattlen, Margaret (trans.). *Reminiscences of Lev Tolstoi by his contemporaries.* Moscow: Foreign Languages Publishing House: N.d.

Zhdanov, V. A. *Ljubov' v zhizni L'va Tolstogo.* Moskva: Planeta, 1993.

—. *Tolstoj i Sof'ja Bers.* Moskva: Algoritm, 2008.

Zhirkevich-Podlesskikh, N. G. "Sof'ja Andreevna i Lev Nikolaevich Tolstye na stranitsakh arkhiva A. V. Zhirkevicha". In: V. Tolstoj & L. Gladkova, 2006: 87–100.

Zverev, Aleksej & Vladimir Tunimanov. *Lev Tolstoj.* Moskva: Molodaja gvardija, 2006.

PART II

SOFIA ANDREEVNA'S
LITERARY WORKS
IN ENGLISH TRANSLATION

FROM THE TRANSLATORS

FOR MY CO-TRANSLATOR AND ME, this volume is already our third journey into the fascinating world of Sofia Andreevna Tolstaya — author, editor, publisher, spouse of one of the world's most talented writers of all time, and the mother of their thirteen children.

Our first journey introduced us to Tolstaya's many careers and activities through the autobiographical memoir *My Life* (2010). The second gave us a more personal insight into her intimate relationship with her husband, Lev Nikolaevich (Leo) Tolstoy, through hundreds of examples of their shared correspondence in *Tolstoy and Tolstaya: a portrait of a life in letters* (2017). This present, third journey explores a hitherto less documented aspect of her extraordinary career — namely, as an author in her own right.

From the start, we were faced with a critical decision in our task as translators. We could have chosen an academic translation style, rendering Sofia Andreevna's words and phrasal structures into English as faithfully as possible to the original Russian text. While this might have been useful to those few Tolstoy scholars less familiar with the Russian tongue, the remainder who know the language already have access to Tolstaya's works in their original form in the Slavic Research Group's 2011 publication *Sofia Andreevna Tolstaya: Literary works* (now also under the imprint of the University of Ottawa Press). In other words, an academic approach to translation would have deprived English-speaking readers of a more enjoyable reading experience, not to mention an appreciation of Sofia Andreevna's rich talent as an international writer, capable of touching the hearts of people (whether scholars or not) in many parts of the world.

And so, instead, with Andrew Donskov's agreement, we decided to opt for a translation in a more literary style. This meant revising the translated text to make it sound more natural to the anglophone ear. Given that the English Sofia Andreevna studied and spoke in the cultural milieu of her time would have reflected more British than North American norms of the language, we have tended (for the most part) to use British spelling and phraseology throughout.

It will be seen that Sofia Andreevna's stories include words and phrases in French — a language with which she was also familiar (indeed, a knowledge of French was common among the privileged classes of nineteenth-century Russian society). These terms have been left in French.

Other terms that have been left in their original form (through the lens of transliteration) are *Russian names, units of currency and measurement*, and *calendar dates*.

It is worth recalling that *Russian names* in their standard form have three parts: (a) *imja* — a first name, given by one's parents at birth (e.g., *Sofia*); (b) *otchestvo* — a patronymic, derived from one's father's first name (e.g., *Andreevna*, from *Andrej*), and (c) *familija* — one's family name (or the family name of one's husband), passed down through the generations (e.g., *Tolstaya*, the feminine form of *Tolstoy*). Finally, there are numerous diminutives of any Russian first name, especially common in reference to children — for example, *Sasha* (from *Aleksandra*), *Alësha* (from *Aleksej*), and *Petja* (from *Pëtr*).

In the category of *units of currency and measurement*, the following should be noted especially: The Imperial Russian *rouble* in 1899 was worth approximately one-tenth of a pound sterling, or about 50 cents (Canadian or American), at the time. A *kopek* was a hundredth part of a rouble. The *grivennik* was worth ten kopeks (i.e., one-tenth of a rouble), while the *pjatak* (or *pjatachok*) referred to a five-kopek copper (or, occasionally, silver) coin.

For other measurements, we might note the *funt*, which at 409.5 g was slightly less than a pound (453.6 g); 40 Russian funts made a *pood* (16.38 kg). Distance was calculated by the *verst* (1.07 km), the *sazhen'* (2.1 m), and the *arshin* (0.71 m). Area was measured by the *desjatina* (1.09 ha).

For *calendar dates*, please see the author's "Explanatory Note" at the beginning of this volume.

I should like to conclude by paying special tribute to my co-translator, Arkadi Klioutchanski — not only as a native speaker of Russian and a Tolstoy expert to boot, but also as an academic with a remarkable knowledge of English literary style — in fact, I accepted his stylistic suggestions in preference to my own on a number of occasions. I look forward to working with him on future literary translations.

Ottawa, May 2021   John Woodsworth
Member, Slavic Research Group
at the University of Ottawa
Member, Literary Translators
Association of Canada

CHAPTER 1

Natasha
(Sonja's story) [1]

AFTER MY BROTHER AND KUZMINSKIJ LEFT A WEEK LATER, the house became quiet. I kept myself busy with music, reading and mushroom picking. Sonja would often head upstairs to do some writing. I found out she was writing a novella.

What kind of novella? I thought. *After all, she's always been good at writing compositions.* And I became quite interested in her story.

Each evening I would come to her, and she would always delight in reading me aloud what she had written.

"And did you write about me?" I would ask. "I did," she would reply.

I don't recall the details of the story too well, but the plot and the main characters have remained in my memory.

There are two main characters in the story: Dublitskij and Smirnov. Dublitskij is middle-aged, not terribly attractive, energetic and clever, with inconsistent views on life. Smirnov is young, about twenty-three, with high ideals, of a calm and positive nature, trustworthy and making a career for himself.

The story's heroine is Elena, a young girl, beautiful, with large dark eyes. She has an elder sister, Zinaida, who is a cold and unfriendly blonde,

---

1 Editor's note: Among Tolstaya's literary works presented here in English translation for the first time, "Natasha" is the only work of which no copy survived. As Tolstaya stated, she destroyed the story on the eve of her wedding. The translation that follows is based on the reminiscences of Tolstaya's sister, Tat'jana Andreevna Kuzminskaja, who recalls the storyline and circumstances of the creation of the original work. It is a valuable document of Tolstaya's early interest in writing.

SOFIA TOLSTAYA, THE AUTHOR

as well as a younger sister, the fifteen-year-old Natasha, a delicate and high-spirited lass.

Dublitskij rides over to her house without any thoughts of love. Smirnov is in love with Elena, and she is attracted to him. He proposes to her, but she is hesitant about accepting; her parents are against this marriage because of his youthful years.

Smirnov goes off to do military service. There is a description of his heart-wrenching soul-searching. There are many peripheral characters. There is a description of Zinaida's attraction to Dublitskij, along with Natasha's various capers, and her attraction to her cousin.

Dublitskij continues to visit Elena's family. She is in a state of bewilderment and cannot sort out her feelings. She doesn't want to admit to herself that she is starting to love Dublitskij. She is tormented by the thought of her sister and Smirnov. She struggles with this feeling, but the struggle is too much for her. Dublitskij seems to be attracted to her more than to her sister, and this makes him all the more appealing to her.

She realises that his constantly changing views on life are wearing her down. She feels constrained by his observant mind. She consciously compares him to Smirnov and tells herself: *Smirnov is simple and loves me with a pure heart, he doesn't demand anything of me.*

Smirnov arrives. Upon seeing his mental agonising and at the same time feeling an attraction for Dublitskij, she thinks of entering a convent.

I don't remember any further details at this point, but the story ends with Elena seeming to arrange a marriage between Zinaida and Dublitskij and, much later, she marries Smirnov.

This story is interesting in that Sonja is describing the situation of her own soul at the time, and our family in general. Pity that my sister burnt her story, because in it there is a clear presentation of what seems to be the beginnings of the Rostov family [in *War and peace*] — the mother, Vera and Natasha.

Tat'jana Andreevna Kuzminskaja, *My life at home and at Yasnaya Polyana. Reminiscences.* 3rd edition. Tula: Tul'skoe knizhnoe izdatel'stvo, 1960, pp. 103–04.

CHAPTER 2

Sofia Andreevna's contributions to Tolstoy's A new primer *(Stories)*

SOME LITTLE GIRLS CAME TO SEE MASHA...

SOME LITTLE GIRLS CAME TO SEE MASHA FOR TEA. Masha, the hostess, took her seat at the tea table to pour. But the 'hostess' was little herself. She took hold of the teapot. The handle was hot. Masha dropped the teapot and it broke, burning herself and her friends.

It was winter, but the weather was mild. There was a lot of snow. The children went to the pond. They gathered up some snow and made a snowman. — Their hands were freezing. Still, the snowman turned out splendidly. They put a pipe in its mouth. The snowman's eyes were two lumps of coal.

A cat was sleeping on the roof, her paws folded in front of her. A little bird sat beside her. Don't sit too close, little birdie — cats are crafty.

The children went into the woods to hunt for mushrooms. They gathered several baskets full. Then they headed out into a meadow and sat down on a haycock to count their harvest. All at once wolves started howling behind the bushes. The children forgot about the mushrooms, threw them on the hay and headed for home.

THE LITTLE HAZELNUT TREE BRANCH
(A FAIRY TALE)

ONCE UPON A TIME there lived a wealthy merchant who had three daughters. He was about to take a trip to a local market. He asked his daughters what he could bring back for them. The eldest asked for a string of beads, while the second girl asked for a ring. The youngest said: "I don't need anything. But if you happen to think of me, bring me a little branch with nuts."

The merchant went off, took care of his purchases and bought beads and a ring for his two elder daughters. He was already on his way home through a large, wooded area when he remembered that his youngest daughter had asked for nothing but a little nut-bearing tree branch. He stepped down from his carriage and went to tear off a branch from a hazelnut tree. All at once he noticed that he was looking at no ordinary nut branch, but one covered with nuts of gold. The merchant thought: "Here's a fine present for my youngest smart little girl!" So he bent the branch and broke it off.

Suddenly out of nowhere came a huge bear. He grabbed the merchant's arm and said: "How dare you break off my branch?! Now I shall eat you!" The merchant took fright and said: "I wouldn't have taken the branch, except my youngest daughter asked me to."

Then said the bear: "All right, go home, but remember this: you must give me the first person to greet you when you get home." The merchant gave his word and the bear let him go. The merchant went on his way and arrived home.

The moment he rode into the courtyard, who should rush to greet him but his favourite daughter — his youngest! The merchant remembered that he'd promised to give the bear whoever would be the first to greet him and was momentarily taken aback.

The merchant told his family everything that had happened, and how he had to give his youngest daughter to the bear. Everyone started to cry. But the mother said: "Don't cry — I know what we'll do. When the bear comes for our little girl, we'll dress up the shepherd's daughter in fancy clothes and hand *his* daughter over in place of our own."

Soon after, everyone was sitting at home when they noticed a carriage entering the courtyard. They looked closer. They saw a bear climb out of the carriage. The bear came into the merchant's house and said: "Give me your daughter."

The merchant didn't know what to do. But his wife knew. She dressed the shepherd's daughter in fancy clothes and brought her to the bear. The bear put her in his carriage and left. No sooner had they driven off than the bear let out a huge roar and wanted to eat the shepherd's daughter. Then the girl confessed that she was not the merchant's daughter, but the shepherd's.

The bear went back to the merchant and said: "You deceived me; give me your real daughter." Everyone wept. They got their daughter dressed, said their goodbyes, and handed her over to the bear. The bear put her in his carriage and left.

They rode and rode. At last they came to a large forest and stopped. The bear climbed out of the carriage and said: "This is our home. Follow me." The bear crawled into a pit, the girl after him. Then the bear opened a large door and led the girl into a dark cellar, saying: "Follow me." The girl trembled with fear, thinking that her end was at hand. But she kept following the bear.

Suddenly she heard a loud cracking noise, like thunder. Everything became bright, and the girl saw that she was not in a cellar, but in a magnificent palace: all was bright, there was music playing, people in fancy clothes greeted her and bowed to her. And right next to her appeared a young prince. The prince went up to her and said: "I'm not a bear, but a prince, and I want to marry you."

Then they sent for the girl's father and mother, invited a number of guests, and proceeded with the wedding. They lived happily ever after, and forever cherished the original nut-bearing branch.

WHAT AUNTIE TOLD ME ABOUT HOW SHE LEARNT TO SEW
WHEN I WAS SIX YEARS OLD, I ASKED MY MOTHER TO LET ME SEW. She said: "You're still too little, you'll only prick your fingers." But I kept pestering her.

Finally, she took out a red-coloured rag from a trunk. Then she threaded a piece of red thread into a needle and showed me how to hold it. I began to sew, but couldn't make even stitches; one stitch came out big, the next happened to fall at the very edge and tore right through the material.

Before long I pricked my finger. I tried not to cry, but when my mother asked me what the matter was, I couldn't help myself and burst into tears. Then Mother told me to go and play.

When I went to bed that night, I couldn't stop dreaming about stitches; I kept thinking about how I could learn as fast as possible to sew, and it seemed so hard that I thought I would never learn.

Now that I'm all grown up, I don't remember how I learnt to sew. And now when I'm teaching my little girl to sew, I marvel at the trouble she has just holding a needle.

A *MUZHIK*'S STORY ABOUT WHY HE LOVES HIS ELDER BROTHER
NATURALLY I LOVE MY BROTHER, but I love him most of all for taking my place as an army conscript. Here's how it happened.

A lottery was held, and the lot fell on me. I was drafted into the army, and I had just got married the week before. I didn't want to be parted from my new bride.

My mum started sobbing and said through her tears: "How can Petrusha go — he's so young!" But there was nothing anyone could do, so they started to get me ready. My wife sewed me some shirts, collected money for me, and the next day I was to report to the conscription office in town. Mum was crying, beside herself with grief. As for myself, every time I thought about going, my heart was crushed as though I were heading straight for my death.

That evening we all gathered around the supper table. Only nobody felt like eating. My young wife was in tears. Father was angry. Mum put the *kasha* on the table, but no one touched it. Mum began to call my brother Nikolaj to supper.

He came in, crossed himself, sat down at the table and said: "Don't fret, Mum. I'll take Petrusha's place in the draft. After all, I'm the older brother. Hopefully, I'll survive. I'll serve my term and come home. And you, Pëtr, take care of Mum and Dad while I'm gone, and treat my wife with respect." I was delighted. Mum, too, stopped crying. We began to get Nikolaj ready to go.

When I awoke the next morning and thought about how my brother was taking my place, I began to feel sick to my stomach. And I said to my brother: "Don't go, Nikolaj. It's my turn, and I'll go." But he kept mum and went on getting himself ready. As did I. We're both strong solid lads, so we are standing there and waiting: there's no way they would reject either of us from serving. My older brother looked at me, gave a laugh and said: "Enough, Pëtr. You go home. And don't be sad for me. I'm going of my own free will." I burst into tears and started home. And today, whenever I think of my brother, I feel I would be ready to die for him.

WHAT AUNTIE TOLD ME ABOUT HER PET SPARROW ZHIVCHIK
BEHIND ONE OF THE WINDOW SHUTTERS IN OUR HOME a sparrow made a nest and laid five little eggs. My sisters and I watched as the sparrow carried a single straw or feather at a time and wove its little nest. And later, when she laid her eggs, we were truly delighted. The sparrow stopped coming in with feathers and straw and began to sit on the eggs. A second sparrow — we were told they were husband and wife — brought worms and fed them to his wife.

Several days later we heard chirping sounds from behind the shutter and looked to see what was happening in the nest. In it were five tiny naked birdies with no wings or feathers; their beaks were soft and yellow, and they had rather large heads.

They seemed quite ugly to us, and no longer a source of delight. Only from time to time would we look to see how they were doing. The mother-bird would often fly off in search of food, and when she returned, the wee little sparrows would open their yellow beaks and the mother would reward them with little pieces of worms.

By the end of the week the little sparrows had increased considerably in size, grown all downy and more pretty, and we then decided once more to keep a watch on them. One morning we came for a look at our sparrows and saw the mother sparrow lying dead under the shutter. We guessed that she had fallen asleep the night before on top of the shutter and that she had been crushed when the shutter was closed.

We picked up the old bird and tossed her onto the grass. The little ones chirped, lifted up their heads and opened their beaks, but there was no one to feed them.

Our older sister said: "Now they don't have a mother, no one to feed them; why don't we feed them ourselves?"

We responded with delight. We got a large box, laid some cotton down on the bottom, put the nest with the birds into it, and carried it upstairs to our room. Then we dug up some worms, moistened pieces of bread with milk and began to feed the little sparrows. They ate well, shook their heads from side to side, and cleaned their beaks on the walls of the box — all very happily.

And so we enthusiastically fed them all the day long. But upon looking into the box the next morning, we noticed that the smallest bird was lying lifeless, his feet entangled in the cotton fabric. We tossed him out and removed all the cotton, so that the other birds would not get caught in the same way, and laid grasses and moss in the box. But by evening two more sparrows splayed their feathers and opened their beaks, closed their eyes and also died.

Two days later the fourth sparrow died, and only one was left. We were told we had overfed them.

My elder sister wept over her sparrows and took to feeding the last one all on her own, while we merely looked on. The remaining (fifth) sparrow was cheerful, healthy and full of energy; we named him *Zhivchik* (the lively one).

This Zhivchik lived so long that he soon started to fly and responded when his name was called.

Eventually he grew up and began to feed himself. He lived upstairs with us. Sometimes he would fly out the window but would always return to spend the night in his own little box.

One morning he didn't fly off anywhere. His feathers were damp and he splayed them out, as the others had done when they were dying. My sister never left Zhivchik's side; she stayed to care for him, but he wouldn't eat or drink.

He languished for three days; on the fourth day he died. When we saw him lying dead on his back with crumpled claws, all three of us broke into such tears that Mother came running up the stairs to find out what was going on. No sooner did she enter the room than she caught sight of the dead sparrow on the table and understood our grief. My sister would not eat or play for several days; all she did was cry.

We wrapped Zhivchik in our best pieces of cloth, put him in a little wooden box and buried him in a pit in the garden. Then we made a burial mound over his grave and placed a little stone on top.

CHAPTER 3

The skeleton-dolls and other stories

3.1 THE SKELETON-DOLLS (A CHRISTMAS STORY)

THE CHRISTMAS TREE

RIGHT ON THE MAIN STREET OF THE TOWN OF T. was a small toy store owned by an elderly gentleman by the name of Sushkin. This kindly old man, his shaven face all covered in wrinkles, would often sit on a little bench in front of his shop, graciously bowing to the children he knew and inviting them to buy something or just to look at the toys and start talking about them.

He didn't do any selling himself, but he had behind the counter a resourceful and sly shop assistant named Sasha. Sasha would demonstrate the various toys, wrap them up, and deal with customers. He would first name a high price and then bargain with them; he liked chatting with the clientèle. When there were hardly any customers in the store, or when the shop-owner was not around, Sasha would take down the best accordion and play a wide variety of pieces. The local children strolling along the main street with their governesses or nannies loved to stop in at the toy store and listen to Sasha's music.

"Play the *Trepak*, Aleksandr Ivanovich!" the children would ask, or *Barynja*, or *Seni moi seni*. And Sasha would play, wagging his head and stomping his feet in time with the music. He would play the *Hungarian polka*, or *The distant troyka*, along with many other pieces.

Christmas was coming. The elderly Sushkin ordered special toys for the holidays, and gradually populated his shop with toys brought in on trains, from factories, from the countryside (some expensive and others cheap),

199

decorated cardboard boxes, lanterns, finely crafted wooden dolls, little horses made of cardboard and other materials.

The shop assistant Sasha had no more time to play the accordion. He was busy all day long spreading out all the nice new toys on the shelves and in the store display cases. Drums, stuffed animals, boxes of dishes, and toy bricks went on the shelves; the floor he covered with horses (with or without manes), along with saddles and harness sets; another spot he filled with all sorts of little carriages, wagons and tiny doll beds. Whistles, lanterns, toy rifles, whips and other things he hung on the wall.

"Well, thank God, I at least got something sorted out," said Sasha to the elderly Sushkin. "Now I'll put the labels on."

"And what is *that*?" asked the shop owner.

"Gosh, I quite forgot. This is something a *muzhik* brought from the countryside, and I bought these dolls from him at a penny a piece — you see, they're simply undressed skeletons, sheer junk. I'm just going to toss them in here, into this empty drawer."

And Sasha threw several dozen wooden dolls into an empty drawer under a shelf and closed it. The 'skeletons' made quite a clatter as they piled one on top of another. Their shiny black wooden heads struck against each other; their arms, fastened to their bodies with rags, got mixed up; their straight wooden legs with their decorated pink boots stuck out awkwardly in all directions. The skeletons felt dark, stuffy, bored and awkward lying in the drawer. Before long they were completely forgotten about.

Not far from the town of T., in the village of Krasnye Polja, there was a great commotion, not just among the owners of the manor house, but also among the servants, and in the village. Into the manor house they brought a beautiful tall tree, and they invited all the servants' children and many of the village children in to see it. The *barynja* [lady of the manor] herself, Ol'ga Nikolaevna, got ready in the morning to go to the town of T. Everything she needed for the tree she wrote out on a long sheet of paper. Her children ran through the house, noisily declaring that Mamà would be buying a thousand toys for the whole village, along with *prjaniki* [spice cake], candy and nuts. Presently, she was on her way into town.

"And we'll get to gild the nuts and put them in cardboard candy boxes," piped up the chubby little boy Il'ja, who loved sweets.

"But you can't, you're too small, you'll just eat them," retorted little Tanja, the mischievous nine-year-old.

Next the little boy Lelja spoke up:

"But Miss Hannah promised to make flowers — that would be very nice."

"Masha, Masha," Miss Hannah addressed Masha in English, "go to Mamà and tell her that for the flowers we need multicoloured paper, and glue, and wires."

"She gets everything mixed up," interjected the agile, dark-eyed Tanja, and she herself ran through all the rooms to reach her mother's bedroom.

The diligent Sergej, who was practising scales on the piano in the parlour, caught his sister out of the corner of his eye as she brushed past him, and muttered under his breath: "What's all the commotion about? I don't even like Christmas parties, they're just a lot of fuss and bother."

But he got up and went to look out the window. In the driveway stood a *troyka* of bay horses. The old coachman Filipp Rodivonych, wearing a sheepskin over a half-length fur coat with warm mittens, and a large astrakhan hat over his ears, was waiting for his *barynja*.

There was a heavy frost out, around minus twenty [Celsius].

The sun hung low in the sky and offered little heat during these short December days. The horses shivered, twitching their ears and impatiently pawing on the hard frozen ground.

At long last Serëzha [= Sergej] waited until his mother made an appearance, likewise wearing two fur coats. He saw how the housekeeper Dunechka packed the grocery bags away into the corners of the sleigh, at the same time giving some instructions to the coachman Rodivonych. Then, after knocking with his fingers on the window-frame, waving out the window to his mother, and watching the sleigh as it creaked over the frost-covered ground, Serëzha once more sat down at the piano.

Ol'ga Nikolaevna turned onto the main road and was soon passing peasant wagons. The frozen peasants, seeking to warm up from their walking, clapped their hands (protruding from long leather mittens) as they walked alongside their sleighs, goading their frost-covered, shaggy horses carrying oats to sell in town to hurry their pace.

"They, too, have to buy something for the holidays," the coachman Rodivonych observed. "See — they're taking oats to sell."

They passed one convoy of wagons and drew level with another. One of the sleighs had a mangy old cow attached to it; a peasant woman was sitting in the sleigh.

"Looks like Ivanovna is taking her cow to sell in town," Rodinovych went on talking aloud. "Not able to feed her through the winter — there wasn't enough feed."

"Is she a widow?" asked Ol'ga Nikolaevna.

"Yes. Sidor, her husband, died last summer, of consumption. Three small children are left."

Ol'ga Nikolaevna felt in her bag for her money-purse. She had brought along a hundred roubles for gifts and holiday purchases, as well as for a Christmas tree, and she started to feel awkward and dejected in her heart.

"Stop, Rodivonych!" she suddenly said.

The wagon with the cow drew level with Ol'ga Nikolaevna's sleigh.

"Ivanovna, come here. Are you taking your cow to sell?"

"What else can I do, Ol'ga Nikolaevna? Nothing to feed her with!"

"Don't sell your cow. Here you are," said Ol'ga Nikolaevna, as she pulled out her money-purse with frostbitten fingers and handed Ivanovna a twenty-five-rouble note.

"Take it, Ivanovna, and go home to your children. This is my gift to you for the holidays," she added, as she hid her purse and her hands in her muff. "Go on now," she told Rodivonych.

"And that brings holiday joy to my heart," Ol'ga Ivanovna quietly whispered. She remembered how just the other day her old nanny had given a coin to a beggar and crossed herself right afterward.

Ivanovna in her ragged old half-length fur coat and torn headscarf was completely frozen. Now, on account of all the surprise, the joy and the cold — she could not utter a word.

By the time she was able to thank the *barynja*, the latter was already far off in her bay *troyka*, and Ivanovna crossed herself and thanked God.

Folding the twenty-five-rouble note into a corner of her headscarf, she turned her horse around and headed for home, all the while thinking of how happy the kids would be when she got home. They had cried so much that morning when they said goodbye to their cow.

Upon arriving in town, Ol'ga Nikolaevna warmed herself up in a familiar shop, where crowds of people were stocking up on all sorts of provisions for the holidays and ordered her purchases from the clerks bustling about. She took off her outer fur coat and ordered the horses unharnessed and fed.

Then she went to Sushkin's toy store. The young clerk (the one named Sasha) took pains to bow properly to the wealthy lady and began to show her a number of toys. Ol'ga Nikolaevna spent a long time choosing just the right ones — a doll, a set of dishes, musical instruments, decals and stickers — ensuring that each child would get something they liked. Iljusha [= Il'ja] loved horses — she bought him a toy stable complete with horses, along with a pellet gun and accessories. Little Masha would receive two dolls and a little carriage; Lelja — a watch on a chain, somersaulting clowns, and a music box.

Serëzha was a serious boy, and for him Ol'ga Nikolaevna bought an album with lots of decals and stickers, along with a real knife set which included nine different tools: a file, a screwdriver, an awl, scissors, a corkscrew and so forth. In addition, from Moscow she ordered a book about birds. For the dark-eyed Tanja, Ol'ga Nikolaevna chose a real tea service with a pink floral design, a deck of playing cards and a fancy-looking tool-drawer, into which she placed scissors, bobbins, needles, ribbons, hooks, buttons — everything necessary for women's work, including a fine silver thimble with a glittering red decal at the bottom.

"Well, thank God, I've got everyone's presents chosen!" said Ol'ga Nikolaevna. "Now, Sasha, give me a variety of toys for the peasant children, and all sorts of decorations for the Christmas tree."

Sasha brought out a large box and they began to fill it with firecrackers, cartons, lanterns, wax candles, glittery things, beads and such like. For presents for the peasant kids, Ol'ga Nikolaevna asked for toy horses and dolls. She was obliged to choose simpler and cheaper toys both for her own children and the village kids; twenty-five roubles had already been given to Ivanovna, and now she was obliged to cut down on her purchases. She chose thirty toy horses on wheels, and asked for some dolls.

At this point a young *muzhik* [peasant-man] arrived at the shop. He went up to Sasha and with a cheerful smile asked him for a five-kopek toy for his boy.

The young clerk rummaged through the toy horses, picked out one and handed it to the *muzhik*.

"Aren't those the ones you had set aside for me?" enquired Ol'ga Nikolaevna.

"No, Madame, this one isn't suitable for you."

"Why not?"

Sasha didn't answer.

Ol'ga Nikolaevna took the toy horse out of the *muzhik*'s hands and saw that one of the legs was broken and that one of the little wheels had fallen off completely.

"Shame on you, Sasha, palming off a clearly broken toy horse on this poor *muzhik*!"

Sasha went red in the face and started to make excuses, saying he hadn't noticed. His puckish eyes darted about; he exchanged the broken horse for a healthy one, handed it to the *muzhik* and took his five-kopek coin. The *muzhik* gave Sasha a courteous 'thank-you', smiled again and exited the store.

"I'm buying forty roubles' worth from you, and you think a broken horse is not good enough for me, but is good enough for a poor person? Shame, Sasha, shame on you!" Ol'ga Nikolaevna went on berating the lad. "Now give me some of those inexpensive undressed dolls."

"There aren't any, Madame," Sasha replied.

"That's not possible... Oh, hullo, Nikolaj Ivanovich!" Ol'ga Nikolaevna turned to greet the shop's owner, an old acquaintance of hers, who had just walked in.

"My deepest respects to you," replied the elderly man.

"I was just asking, don't you have any dolls which my children could dress themselves? We need a lot of them for the peasant boys and girls."

"Sasha, go and show the *barynja* the 'skeletons' we have," said Nikolaj Ivanovich; "she might like them."

"I know she won't," said Sasha scornfully. "They're not merchandise for the manor house. But maybe they'll do for the village..."

Whereupon Sasha pulled out the drawer, reached in with both hands picked up a whole fistful of undressed wooden dolls, which he scornfully called *skeletons*. The skeletons started squirming, their faces and shiny little heads all illuminated by the bright light of a lamp. They began to feel cheerful, bright and at ease. By this time, they were quite bored lying in the drawer, and very much wanted someone to buy them and give them life.

Ol'ga Nikolaevna counted them and purchased all forty of them.

"Well, that's everything," she said. "Write up the bill; in the meantime, I'll go buy nuts, candy, *prjaniki*, apples and various sweets. Then I'll come back for the toys and pay you."

The resourceful and sly Sasha set about packing everything up; he filled two baskets full, and once again stuffed the skeletons into a cramped space, wrapping them tightly in thick, grey paper, tying them up with string and tossing them into a basket.

Ol'ga Nikolaevna finished all her shopping, picked up her purchases at the toy store, and finally headed for home.

In the town of T. the lanterns had been lit, the frost had settled in, and already the iron runners of sleighs and sledges could be heard creaking over the hard-packed snow. As Ol'ga Nikolaevna was leaving the town and paying the toll at the gatehouse, she happened to glance up at the sky and marvelled at the beauty of the bright stars. The trees were all white with frost, whole fields were covered with white, and the frost had given the very air a silvery sheen. How pure, spacious and serene the fields seemed! Not at all like in the town.

Ol'ga Nikolaevna arrived home around six, just in time for supper. Her children had been impatiently waiting for her, and rushed downstairs to greet their mother in the entrance hall.

"Cold, everything's cold," she called out from down below. "Don't come down — there's nothing for you to see yet."

"Mamà, Mamà, what did you buy? Did you buy a lot? What did you get me?" the children cried.

"We'll take a look at everything after supper, but now go away! Go away, d'you hear, or I won't show you anything before it goes under the tree."

Five pairs of children's feet stomped across the drawing-room's parquet floor, but the noise and the excitement did not cease.

"Hurrah! Mamà's arrived!"

"Such huge baskets! I saw."

"I'm sure Mamà bought me a pistol…" said one of the boys.

"Run, I'll catch up to you," cried lively little Tanja, giving Iljusha a shove in the backside, and both laughingly ran around the table, which was already set for supper.

In trying to outrun Tanja, chubby Iljusha inadvertently caught a corner of the tablecloth, pulled it along and caused the whole table setting to come clattering to the floor. Plates, knife, fork, spoon and salt-shaker — all came noisily crashing down. And just at this moment who should walk in but the father of the family!

"What's all this?!" he asked in a severe tone. Everyone suddenly fell silent. Tanja began to pick up the fallen dishes, but Miss Hannah forbade her to touch the broken pieces; these she picked up herself. Tanja quietly approached her father from behind (he had already taken his seat at the table). Giving him a quick kiss on the crown of his head, she whispered: "I'm the one to blame, Papà."

Father smiled at his favourite daughter and stroked her dark hair.

The supper proceeded quietly. Ol'ga Nikolaevna described her trip into town, complained about the cold, and told the girls that after supper they should pick out pieces of fabric and start dressing the 'skeletons'.

"What skeletons?" enquired Tanja with a smile.

"These are the dolls that the store-clerk Sasha called *skeletons*. You'll see. They were lying in a drawer in the toy counter, not on display, but I discovered them and brought them to light. We'll do such a job of dressing them up, it'll seem like a miracle!"

After supper they brought out the warmed-up skeletons and immediately laid them out on the big table.

"How ugly!" the father remarked. "God only knows what rubbish! Some kind of freaks. Such ugliness will only serve to spoil children's tastes," Father muttered as he sat down to read the paper.

"Just wait — once we dress them up, they won't look that bad," said Mother.

"Ha, ha, ha!" laughed Tanja. "Just look at those legs, like sticks with pink slippers…"

"And that snub-nosed one, with the shiny dark head, silly face and clayish coloration — phew!" Serëzha observed with a tone of disgust.

"Well, dance, you corpses!" exclaimed Iljusha, grasping hold of two of the dolls and making them jump up and down.

"Give *me* one," begged wee little Masha, stretching out her delicate white hands.

The skeletons were very happy. They felt warm, bright and cheerful with the children. They had been sleeping a sleep of death in the dark drawer in the toy shop, cold and bored. But here they were called to life. Their little wooden bodies began to warm up and come alive. They were about to be all dressed up and placed by a Christmas tree on a large round table, in the centre of which was a little tree with candles and decorations. How joyful!

"Well, girls, let's go pick out some pieces of fabric for their clothes!" Ol'ga Nikolaevna called to Tanja and Masha.

In the bedroom she pulled out the lower chest of drawers and got out several bundles of old fabric pieces. There was so much to discover! Here was a remnant from Tanja's red dress, and a striped piece from Iljusha's Russian pantaloons; strips of ribbon from Mamà's hat, some velvet, remnants from a pale-blue pillowslip, and so much more. Tanja and Masha, truly two 'little women,' set upon the pieces of fabric with considerable enthusiasm. They gathered a whole bundle of scraps and ran to the main hall.

The cutting and fitting began; they made all sorts of costumes for the skeletons. Miss Hannah, Ol'ga Nikolaevna, Tanja and the nanny they had called upon to help — all set themselves to work. Tanja sewed and cut out skirts and sleeves, Miss Hannah and the nanny sewed little shirts, jackets and trousers for the boy-dolls, while Ol'ga Nikolaevna made caps, hats and various decorations.

The first and best-looking of the skeletons they dressed as an angel. They gave her a fancy white muslin shirt, put a gold paper halo on her head, and two muslin wings stretched over a thin frame behind her wooden back.

"How charming!" Tanja sweetly admired as she took the doll from her mother's hands. "Oh, Mamà, what an adorable little angel! She'll be sure to please someone!"

And still admiring the fancily clothed skeleton, Tanja carefully put it to one side.

"And look at the *muzhik* Nanny dressed — a real marvel!" exclaimed Iljusha, holding up the doll in the red shirt and round black cap.

Ever the innovator, Tanja made a Turk in a white turban with a red base. They stuck a moustache and beard on it and made a long gaily coloured caftan with wide pantaloons. Then they dressed up another skeleton as an army officer with gold epaulettes and a sabre of silver paper.

They also costumed a wet-nurse in a nurse's cap, an old woman with white hair made of cotton batting, a gypsy girl with a red shawl across her shoulder, a ballerina in a tutu with flowers in her hair, two soldiers in blue and red uniforms, a jester wearing a pointed cap with a little bell sewn into its peak. There was a cook all in white, and a baby in a bonnet, and a tsar with a golden crown.

The work went smoothly and cheerfully. The once ugly, naked skeletons evolved more and more into beautiful, fancy and gaily dressed dolls. The tsarina turned out especially well. Ol'ga Nikolaevna cut her a crown out of gold paper, made her a long, velvet gown, and placed a tiny fan in her wooden hand.

The children were in ecstasy over the skeletons. They worked on them for three evenings straight, and finally all forty dolls were ready, standing on the table in rows, comprising a most striking motley throng.

Emboldened, Tanja ran to fetch her father and brought him to the dining room.

"Look, Papà, would you call that rubbish now?"

"Can those be the same ugly pieces Mamà brought home? That's not possible! This is such an absolutely charming picture!"

"What did I tell you, Papà? Give us some praise now — we worked on them three days!"

"It's true, you really have brought these wooden corpses to life. A whole people — a beautiful, elegant people to boot!"

The children were so delighted to hear Papà himself praise the skeletons, and on the next day a new task ensued. They began to gild the nuts, make flowers, glue boxes together, but the dolls were relegated to a cupboard. The revived skeletons could no longer stomp about. Confined to a large cupboard, dressed in costume, they patiently waited for the Christmas tree, and spent a happy time among the other toys — the animals, the cartons and the rest of the pretty things.

***

At long last Christmas Day arrived. What excitement could be felt in the air right from early morning! The children in their best clothes ran through the whole house, wishing everyone a merry Christmas. Ol'ga Nikolaevna thoughtfully went through all the rooms, even the kitchen, handing out Christmas gifts and money to her help. In addition to the money, she had prepared a present and a packet of sweets for each one.

The whole family gathered in the dining room. Miss Hannah, that kind and cheerful Englishwoman, had made a scrumptious raisin-currant cake for the morning meal. For dinner she prepared a huge plum-pudding. Wrapped in pudding cloth, it had been boiling all day on the stove under the watchful eye of the elderly cook Nikolaj; after dinner it would be doused with rum and set alight, to burst into flames.

My God, how exciting it all was! The frosty sun glistened through the patterns traced on the frozen windows, and illuminated the gigantic, decorated tree in the main hall. The skeletons were displayed on the round table, each one more beautiful than the next. On the other side of the room could be seen the horses, concertinas and other toys for the peasant kids.

On a different table were set out five sections of various gifts, each one marked with a note indicating the intended recipient. Off to one side lay a present for Hannah: a gold brooch and some cambric handkerchiefs in a flat little box, tied with a pink ribbon.

Ol'ga Nikolaevna covered everything with a long muslin cloth, so that the children would not see the presents 'til evening.

After breakfast the village priest Vasilij Ivanovich arrived with a cross in his hands. He usually gave Serëzha and Tanja lessons in Scripture. Whenever he told them something, he was wont to ask: "Got it?", which greatly amused the children. This time he brought with him a red-haired deacon, along with the always cheerful sexton Alësha, who during the service exchanged glances with Iljusha, and both broke into uncontrollable laughter. The deacon, stroking his long red hair on both sides of his face, gave them a stern look and started singing a prayer in his bass voice.

Everyone reverently approached the cross, Nanny kissed the priest's hand, Ol'ga Nikolaevna slipped some money into Vasilij Ivanovich's hand, asked after his wife and children, and wished them all pleasant holidays.

But how long it still seemed until evening! The children ran out of patience altogether — both those who lived in the house and those who had gathered outdoors on the porch. There was a whole crowd there, practically the whole village; children chattered away, pushed each other, peered in the windows, reporting their impressions.

Finally, the supper was over. The pudding, which had flamed up bright as a hearth, had been eaten. They had set aside a piece for Nanny, but to wee Masha's amazement, it turned out that Nanny did not like the pudding at all, saying she thought that *molochnaja lapsha* [milk noodle soup] was by far tastier.

Then at long last the doors of the main hall were locked tight, and Ol'ga Nikolaevna, Hannah and the servant Pëtr put wax candles on sticks and began to light the tree. On the other side of the living-room doors gathered Ol'ga Nikolaevna's children as well as some of the servants' children.

The playful minx Tanja shoved the laundress's daughter Varja to a crack in the door, saying:

"Look there, Varja, over by the tree, there's a bear sitting."

"Absurd!" Serëzha seriously objected. Lelja, a dreamy litte boy, observed that the beautiful tree was best of all, and he didn't want anything to spoil it as long as possible. Little Masha kept on chattering in English with no let-up about what dolls and other things she would have. Stout Iljusha was happy most of all to know that there would be sweets available all week long, if only he could restrain himself and not eat everything at once.

At the other door, which gave out onto a spacious veranda and down a staircase, stood the village children, warmly dressed in half-length fur coats and bast shoes; whatever they were chattering about was not discernible, only that their voices were all happy ones. The nanny was tasked with letting the children into the hall when the bell sounded.

Finally, the bell sounded, both doors swung open, and from both sides crowds of children poured into the spacious hall of the large country house with white walls, with a large dark green, brightly lit and glistening Christmas tree.

For the first minute all the kids fell silent, simply gazing at the tree, their eyes blinded by the light and glitter. Little by little they became bolder and started walking around the tree.

"I see a white bunny hanging there!" shrieked little Pet'ka.

"Ooh, apples and gold nuts!" admired the girls. "And the beads, d'you see?!"

"Look, Parashka, the bird hanging over there, almost as if it were alive, only it doesn't sing," remarked Akul'ka Ershova.

"Such a bright horsie!" said Fed'ka Fokanov, touching one of the silver horses.

"Come over here," Ol'ga Nikolaevna called the young boys and girls, leading them to the skeleton-dolls.

Some of the children even shrieked with joy and surprise.

The elegantly dressed skeletons stood in a circle around a small Christmas tree, which was similarly decorated and lit with candles. They seemed so joyous and cheerful.

"They made a tree for the dolls!" Tanja exclaimed. "Hurrah! That's a real marvel!"

"They deserve to have a good time, too," remarked Lelja, all smiles.

"Well, time to give them out," announced Ol'ga Nikolaevna after a moment's wait. "Tanja, you help me."

They began to present the village children with toy horses and whistles. The older ones got little books and concertinas, the younger ones — the skeleton-dolls. Tanja took a bunch of them in hand, and, judging by each one's character, placed a skeleton-doll in each one's rosy hand.

"This one's for you," she said as she handed the Turk to little Vlas with his weak eyes and impish smile.

"You, Fed'ka, get the army officer, and you," addressing Mishka, the widow Ivanovna's son, "take the tsar." The ragged orphan, Mishka, stretched out his frail little hand and took the tsar doll.

Lelja gazed intently at the whole scene and his eyes lighted upon the thoughtful whitish-looking face of six-year-old Akul'ka Ershova. He silently chose out of the row of skeletons the angel with the tiny wings which his mother had so easily, tenderly and beautifully costumed, and gave this doll to Akulja. She immediately broke into a radiant smile and kissed the doll.

When all the toys had been given out to the village children and many of them were biting into the hardy red Crimean apples which were constantly falling from the tree with a loud bang onto the floor, all five of Ol'ga Nikolaevna's happy and contented children began looking at their own toys and other gifts and ran off to thank their mother.

The tree candles burned for a long time, and they had the boys and girls start singing. They struck up a rousing dancing song; the weak-sighted Vlaska boldly leapt out to the middle of the floor and started dancing, repeating over and over: "*Ja vot kakoj!*" [This is who I am]. The cheerful Fed'ka Fokanov, watched for a while; then he, too, began to execute various dance steps with his feet, to the general laughter of the children.

"Undress yourself a bit, take your caftan off," advised Nanny.

Fed'ka threw his caftan on the floor, and, holding up the officer-skeleton in the red uniform, set himself dancing once again. The children laughed even louder in approval. Someone got out a concertina and pointed out another girl who was a terrific dancer.

"All right, Dashka, dance!" the kids encouraged.

Dashka hesitated at first, but then, passing her tsarina doll to Matrësha, who was standing beside her, she took off her mother's red shawl, put on a serious face, and smoothly, like a peasant woman, clapping her hands over her head, gracefully swept around the room, executing delicate dance steps, whooping from time to time in a high-pitched voice.

"Way to go, Dashka, love that!" Tanja cried with delight, jumping up and down with bright eyes.

But it was getting late. Hannah led wee Masha off to bed; all the children were tired. Nanny called the village kids together and told everyone it was time to leave.

Soon children's feet could be heard clattering down the main staircase: the front doors opened with a creak and a crack, letting a burst of frosty air into the house, and a throng of peasant children made their way with noise and chatter down the old birch allée, which showered the happy youngsters' shiny faces with a dusting of frosty snow from its cold, bare branches.

The tree candles were snuffed out. Serëzha leafed through his stickers, admiring the Chinese, Indian and other nationalities depicted on them. Then he opened the Kajgorodov book [Dmitrij Nikiforovich Kajgorodov, Russian ornithologist, 1876–1924] and saw marvellous pictures of all sorts of birds; all this really took his fancy.

A pensive lad who loved music, Lelja quietly turned the crank on his music-box and tried to understand the theme of the piece he was listening to. Then he wound his new watch and put the chain around his neck.

Iljusha was especially delighted with the box of accessories, along with the real knife and rifle. The toy stable with horses he placed under his bed. He was already munching on his fifth apple. A large *prjanik* in the shape of a fish had also disappeared. They took away the rest of the sweets to hide for another day, so that he wouldn't eat too much and get a tummy ache.

Most radiant of all was Tanja. She had so many things that she couldn't carry them all to the children's room on her own. Tomorrow she would have real tea in the new teacups; she would invite the nanny, and the laundress's daughters and the dolls, and she would have a magnificent feast.

Softly but resonantly the large grandfather clock on the stairway landing struck midnight. The house was absolutely quiet — everyone was asleep. Lying about on the cold, empty floor were scraps of *prjaniki*, shells of gilded nuts, broken cartons and ashes from wax candles. In the middle of the hall two mice were persistently gnawing on something — they, too, were enjoying themselves after the Christmas party.

In the children's room frail little Masha kept constantly waking up and whimpering, calling out for Nanny. Next to her pillow lay two fine porcelain dolls — white, like her own skin.

The lights had gone out in the village, too. Bright stars twinkled in the distant sky. In the Ershovs' hut a special lamp burned before the icons and the Virgin's suckling child shed tears. Pale and delicate, Akulja, wrapped in a calico blanket, slept soundly on a bench, while on a ledge above her stood her new angel doll.

The widow Ivanovna spent a long time that evening cleaning her hut and preparing something in the corner. Her three children slept right with her, and the youngest, Mishka, held the tsar skeleton firmly clenched in his fist. The tsar's crown of gold paper had got crumpled. Ivanovna quietly extracted the doll from her boy's hand, smoothed out the crown and placed the doll on the table. From outdoors could be heard the mooing of the cow which Ivanovna didn't sell, and today in honour of the holiday they had enjoyed *molochnaja kasha* [milk porridge] and tea with milk.

The jovial Fed'ka Fokanov, who lived on the edge of the village, made his army officer do so much dancing that his arm got torn off. Tossing the 'skeleton' under a bench, he lay down beside his grandfather Mikhajla [= Mikhail] to sleep.

And so from this night on the skeletons began a new life in the huts of Krasnye Polja village.

IN THE VILLAGE

MASLENITSA [Shrovetide] came. The village kids fashioned wooden benches and poured water over them to use for downhill sledding. School classes were cancelled for a time, and once again it was a holiday everywhere. *Muzhiks* and the womenfolk went into town to buy flour and butter for *bliny* [pancakes]; those with a little more money bought smelt and herring, too.

The weather was marvellous. After a thaw came more frost and sunshine, the roads were smooth and slippery, which was just what the kids needed for sledding.

Out of almost every house where children lived came boys and girls towing 'benches' and toboggans behind them. Climbing aboard in twos or threes, they flew down the long, fairly steep hill. See, there's Fed'ka Fokanov with his older brother Ivan, towing a long, large bench-sled, all covered with ice.

"Hey, Mishka!" Fed'ka called out to the orphan Mishka (Ivanovna's son), "You don't have a sled. Come and sit with us."

"You, too, Vlaska! More people come join us, there's enough room for everyone. But what's *that*?" Fed'ka asked Vlas.

All at once the kids broke out into gales of happy laughter. Sticking out from the pocket of Vlaska's half-length fur coat was the head of a skeleton-doll dressed as a Turk in a white turban. Its painted face had all but disappeared, and the turban was by now quite dirty.

"We'll take the Turk sledding, too!" Fed'ka solemnly announced.

The large bench-sled set off and quickly flew down the hill to the kids' happy, animated cries.

In the Matveevs' hut they were eating *bliny*, and the two boys Kolja and Sasha also hurried outdoors, still licking their buttery fingers as they put on their half-length fur coats. Under the table lay a skeleton-soldier in a blue uniform, with little gold beads sewn on in place of buttons. They had forgotten about him as he lay there all bored in the dust and darkness.

Then the door of the hut opened, and together with the neighbour, the boy Pet'ka, the neighbours' puppy flew in. He at once spied the doll and rushed to have some fun with it.

"No, wait! Leave it alone!" shouted the boys, trying to get hold of the doll, and they all rushed at the shaggy grey pup with the wrinkled muzzle. But it was too late: the officer doll was all in tatters, its cap had flown off to the side, the hand with the sabre of silver paper was torn off, while its little head, chewed as it was by the pup's saliva-covered teeth, was actually repulsive. Little Sasha started crying, while his older brother Kolja took the doll outside and threw it as far as he could into a snowbank.

Within a few minutes, though, grief was forgotten, and all three were flying down the hill, while the guilty shaggy puppy, sticking out his tongue to one side, rushed headlong after the sled, trying to catch up to the kids.

Out of a little hut at the corner of a village sidestreet came Akulja. She dragged behind her a tiny self-made sled on a rope, which caught on the door, and she turned around and looked at her mother.

"Akuljushka, don't go out," said Mother. "Your head has been aching and a wind has come up. Don't go out, little one."

"It's okay, Mamushka, it's passed now," Akulja replied. "I'll do a bit of sledding with Matrësha."

Whereupon Akulja went outside. Mother gave a sigh. Going back into the hut, she sat down on the bench and looked up at the ledge where the angel-clad skeleton-doll was standing. The white dress and wings had become grey with soot, and the doll's face had also darkened. Akulja loved her little angel a great deal and cherished it, and her mother knew this. She took the doll, brushed off the dust and soot, and put it back in place. Then she went and lay down. But something was weighing on her mind that kept her from getting to sleep.

Akulja returned an hour later. She was shaking all over, her face was pale. Tossing the sled aside, she dashed over to her mother and lay down beside her.

"Mamushka, I'm frightfully cold," she said, her teeth chattering.

"What did I tell you, child? — you shouldn't have gone out sledding. Let me fix you a cup of tea."

Whereupon Akulja's mother, whose name was Marfa, went out into the *seni* [covered outdoor passageway], and started up a rather leaky samovar. Taking down from a cupboard a small paper packet, she extracted a tiny thimbleful of tea and poured hot water over it after the samovar came to a boil. She slipped Akulja a piece of sugar and began feeding her the tea.

But Akulja couldn't even drink. Her whole head felt it was burning, her large blue eyes were inflamed, her little rosy hands shook and couldn't hold the saucer. Soon she fell asleep, and the fever kept intensifying. From time to time, she would jump up and cry out: "I'm afraid, I'm afraid, someone has got hold of me…"

Towards morning she became quiet and lost consciousness. Akulja never came to again. A doctor was sent from the manor house to treat her. Nevertheless, on the evening of the next day Akulja died.

Weeping bitter tears, Marfa dressed her beloved daughter in a white shirt and rose-coloured *sarafan*, covered her little face with a white muslin cloth, and lit a candle.

A soft light fell on dear Akulja's angelic little face, and her angel doll stood on the ledge above her head.

"Take your dear little toy with you to the grave," said Marfa, as she took the little angel down from the ledge and placed it next to Akulja.

Akulja was buried together with her beloved doll, leaving her poor, grieving mother alone in the world.

Easter was late that year, and spring came during Lent. The melting snow caused broad currents of brooks to run in all directions down the Krasnye Polja hill. The kids threw sticks and woodchips into the water and ran after them with enthusiastic cries. Fed'ka Fokanov, a bold and clever boy, made a real boat by carving out a log with a knife. He put two little sticks he had carved into the bottom and attached to them like flags pieces of red calico cloth he had asked his mother for.

When Fed'ka brought out his little boat, all the kids gathered round him with excitement and curiosity.

"Well, put the boat in the river!" one of them called out.

"It'll float away, you won't catch it," cried another.

"No doubt," they cheered Fed'ka on.

When they launched the little boat, it swiftly floated downstream. and the kids ran after it. But upon encountering an obstruction, the boat caught onto something and came to a stop. Fed'ka grasped hold of it.

"Wait, chaps," he said. "Enough of the funny stuff!" And he ran back all the way to his hut. A few minutes later he returned with the army officer doll in the red uniform, only without one arm. He placed the toy officer in the boat and tied it with thread to the sticks with the red flags.

"That's really good!" said the house servant Mit'ka with the thin but handsome face and dark eyes. "Well then, one-armed officer, go to sea again and make war!"

"He has nothing to fight with," Vlaska poined out. "He's lost his arm with the sabre."

"He'll strike with a single hand," the kids joked.

They launched the boat in a pond, and the current carried it even faster, because of the added weight of the officer doll.

Twisting and jumping, the little boat went more and more swiftly, and it wasn't long before the kids could not keep up with it. Flowing downhill, the water poured under a bridge, then farther into a tributary, and from the tributary into a river... The red uniform and red flags could hardly be seen any more, and soon they disappeared altogether... Farewell, little boat, farewell, officer! Whether they ended up in a large river, or someone picked up the boat with the doll — this will forever remain a mystery.

"Farewell, officer! Come back from the war!" the kids joked, but they were all sadly quiet as they trudged up the hill back to their village.

"Lulla-by, by..." A high-pitched voice could be heard from the hut belonging to Agaf'ja, who walked with a limp, and right after that the cry of a newborn baby. The village kids were surprised and listened attentively and stopped to look through the windows.

"Hey, where did this baby suddenly come from?" asked one of the older boys, the house servant Mit'ka, as he started to go into the hut.

"Mashka, oh Mashka!" he greeted a little four-year-old girl. "What are you doing there?"

"I'm rocking my doll, putting her to sleep," the girl answered, showing her skeleton-doll clothed in a bonnet, wee shirt and vest, like a tiny baby.

"But I heard a real baby cry — what was that?"

"Mamushka had a baby girl last night... Mamushka's been rocking her baby, and I — mine," the girl added, as she wrapped her doll in some rags.

"Lulla-by, by..." Masha intoned again, rocking her doll and climbing onto a bench with it.

"Oh, dear! why are you letting cold air into the hut?" growled the sick mother, Agaf'ja.

"The cripple Agaf'ja's had a baby girl!" Mit'ka solemnly announced as he came out of the house and told the news to the kids outside.

It was starting to get dark. The tired kids dispersed to their huts; someone drove their two-horse sleigh through the village street with jingling bells. Still later, after supper, lights began to go out all over, and only in homes where there was somebody ill or a suckling child, could be seen a light dimly glowing through windows which had already frosted up for the night.

On the sixth week of Lent the poor widow Ivanovna got together with her son Mishka and Akulja's grieving mother, Marfa, for a pilgrimage to Mtsensk, where, she was told, there was an icon of Nikolaj the Miracle-worker which was said to have crossed the river to Mtsensk on a rock. Ivanovna left Grandmother Natal'ja at home, entrusting her to look after the other two children and the cow.

The women got their bags together, dried out a supply of rusks from rye bread, took a few coins with them, and early in the morning on the Palm Sabbath they set out on their journey.

The roads had not yet dried out, there were fresh morning frosts, but the sun shone so cheerfully; first, spring birds flew in and sang as they busied themselves in the bushes, looking for convenient places to weave their nests.

When Ivanovna came out with Akulja's mother, Marfa, they crossed themselves and had taken but a few steps from the hut when her son Mishka suddenly turned around and went back to his hut to look for something. Finding it, he hid it in his jacket.

"Why did you turn back, Mishka?" his mother asked. "Or did you forget something?"

"Nothing..." Mishka answered curtly, feeling inside his jacket for his beloved tsar doll.

And so Ivanovna, Marfa and Mishka walked for one day, then a second day. From village to village they would be offered a piece of bread, or a kopek, or something else. When the women got tired, along with Mishka; they would rest in some sort of little hut and sleep so sweetly without cares or sorrows. They were going to be praying, so there was no heaviness in their soul. Whenever Mishka felt bored, he would take out the tsar doll and play with it: he would put it astride a stick, and pretend the tsar was riding a horse. Or he would seat it next to him and 'feed' it with bread, sugar or something else.

The pilgrims, along with Mishka, stayed overnight in the town of Mtsensk. They visited a magnificent cathedral, kissed the icon of Nikolas the Miracle-worker, placed two thin candles in front of it, at mass they took a piece of *prospheron* [holy bread] for their health. Another woman-pilgrim undertook to show them the rock on which the icon of Saint-Nikolas was said to have crossed the river. They went to have a look at it. After spending the night somewhere in the barn of a local hostelry, they began their journey home.

Mishka had never been in a town before; everything was a big surprise for him — the shops that sold all sorts of good treats and sweets; the cabbies with their droshkies; the churches, and the elegantly dressed people. But his feet ached, his bast shoes were falling apart, and he really wanted to go home.

And here they were again — Mishka with his mother and Marfa — walking on the main road in the opposite direction. There was no bread or sugar left, and no money either.

Marfa bade farewell to them, saying she was going to see her sister in one of the villages along the way.

"Well, now, somehow, son, we'll make it home!" Ivanovna said with a sigh, glancing at the exhausted Mishka.

Mishka felt hungry and gloomy. His feet hurt; since morning he had had only a small piece of bread, and all he had left to eat was one tiny slice.

Around nightfall they arrived at a village. Ivanovna timidly went up to a hut on the edge of the settlement and asked if they could stay the night. They let her in.

"But don't ask for any bread," said the hut's owner as she was clearing the table. "We have very little, and we've used up what we were holding 'til spring. No doubt you have some with you."

Ivanovna didn't say a word. Giving Mishka the last slice, she was ready to lie down for the night. But Mishka broke it in two and gave half back to his mother.

"Oh, my precious! You're so hungry yourself, but you're sharing it with your mother."

Ivanovna crossed herself and began to chew the bread through her dry lips. Then she got up and asked where she could get some water. After drinking a mugful, she gave some to her son and lay down on a bench, yawning and making the sign of the cross over her mouth.

Dawn came. Cocks throughout the village competed with their crowings. Villagers carried their buckets downhill to fetch water from the well. Ivanovna got up, awoke Mishka, and prepared to set out. Home was still twenty-five versts away, and they had neither bread nor money left.

Thanking the owner of the house for their lodging, they set off for home on an empty stomach. Ivanovna felt sorry for her son, and Mishka, too, felt uneasy when he looked at his exhausted, starving mother.

They walked and walked. In their fatigue they sat down at the side of the main road near a bridge. Mishka took off his shoes, got out his tsar doll and sat it down beside him.

All at once came the sound of sleigh-bells — a fancy carriage was approaching. A little black dog with an elegant looking collar began barking at Ivanovna and Mishka, but, upon spying the doll, gave it a look of surprise and ran over and sniffed it.

"Give alms, kind sirs," Ivanovna dared to beg the gentleman sitting in the carriage.

"What are you begging for?!" exclaimed the gentleman with evident annoyance and started to have his horse walk across the bridge, offering nothing to Ivanovna.

"Stop, Papà!" suddenly cried a fine-looking young lad from the carriage. Well dressed in a blue sailor outfit, his attention was focussed on the dog sniffing the doll. "I want to take a look at what kind of doll Jack was sniffing. Look, Papà, it's sitting there right next to the boy."

"Now where did you see a doll? We've no time to stop."

But the boy in the sailor outfit was already eager to jump out of the carriage. The coachman stopped the horses, and the well-dressed lad went over to Mishka.

"Where did you get the tsar?" he asked.

"It was a Christmas present from our masters."

"Lemme see it! Lemme hold it in my hands!"

"Viktor, what's going on? Come here at once!" the father cried to the well-dressed boy from the carriage.

"I'm coming, Papà! What a fine-looking tsar!" the young lad admired, examining the doll. "Sell it to me for ten kopeks. I've only got one *grivennik*."

Mishka felt very badly about the doll. He took it back from the lad in the sailor jacket and hid it behind his back.

"Vitja!" cried his father.

"Coming! I'm coming!" called Vitja anxiously. "Now, my dear fellow, sell it! I'll even throw in a *prjanik* along with some caramel bonbons."

"Ple-ea-se!" he added, as he rummaged in his bag.

"Oh, dear!" groaned Ivanovna.

Mishka looked at his mother, remembering that neither of them had had anything to eat that day. Then all at once he handed his beloved tsar skeleton to the well-dressed Vitja.

"Here, take it," he said. "Gimme the money and the *prjanik*."

The lad Vitja handed him the money, the *prjanik* and the caramel bonbons, took the doll and raced back to the carriage.

The sleigh bells sounded again, and all in a flash the carriage sped up the hill and disappeared from view, while Misha put on his dilapidated shoes and dejectedly trudged along with Ivanovna to the next village. Here they bought bread, had a bite to eat, and cheerfully made it home by evening. The *prjanik* and the caramel bonbons Mishka shared with his two brothers, who were overjoyed at the treats.

"Well, praise God," Ivanovna said to the elderly Natal'ja, "we said our prayers, went to see Nikolaj the Miracle-worker, everything's fine at home, thank God." And once again she settled into her lonely, arduous routine of life.

At long last came a real, joy-filled spring. The village boys and girls no longer played with their dolls, and even forgot about them. Farm chores started up, the kids had to help their fathers and mothers; one summer task followed another: ploughing, sowing, harvesting hay, tending to the horses at night, bringing the cattle in, bringing grain in from the field to the village, digging potatoes, threshing grain, etc., etc.

For some people summer is a fun time, but for country folk it is nothing but work.

3.2 GRANDMOTHER'S TREASURE TROVE: A LEGEND

PART I

IN 1812 THERE WAS A WAR BETWEEN THE RUSSIANS AND THE FRENCH. The French came to Russia, and got as far as Moscow itself, which they began to burn and lay waste. Many residents fled with their whole families, taking their precious possessions with them; some families, however, were unable to flee, and to prevent their treasures from falling into the hands of the enemy, they buried their money and valuables in the ground.

At that time, in the settlement of Elisavetino, not far from Moscow, lived a rather wealthy lady — a *barynja* by the name of Elizaveta Fëdorovna Glebova.

She possessed a lot of money, gold, silver dishes, expensive things and precious stones.

When she heard rumours that the French were already in Moscow, she became frightened and set about fleeing her estate and taking her treasures with her. But the fright made her ill, and she had to spend a long time in bed. By the time she recovered, travelling would be very dangerous, at least for an elderly lady. On all the roads and in all the forests round about Moscow were wandering starving Frenchmen in tattered uniforms, who would attack and rob whomever they could.

Elizaveta Fëdorovna initially thought to stay in Elisavetino and hide her treasures, but everyone warned her that she might be killed by the French, and so she decided to bury a trunk full of her treasures in the ground and flee to her estate in Rjazan' Gubernia.

It was a dark, cold night. Elizaveta Fëdorovna quietly rose from her bed and called her faithful old servant Mar'jushka, who had been with her since childhood.

Mar'jushka was frightened; she thought the *barynja* might have taken ill, or that the French had come; she came running in a hurry and asked what Elizaveta Fëdorovna might want.

"Look, Mar'jushka, lock the door with the key, and let's pack as quickly as possible."

The elderly *barynja* opened all the closets and commodes. She had a large trunk brought out to the middle of the room and, together with Mar'jushka, began gathering from all around the room money, along with gold and silver things and other valuables. They put them all in the trunk, which the *barynja* locked with a large padlock. She gave the key a double turn, which made a loud noise in the quiet room.

Then Elizaveta Fëdorovna ordered Mar'jushka to have the wagon harnessed at once and brought to the back porch.

"We'll bury the trunk, Mar'jushka," she said. "Have them fetch a lantern and shovels."

Mar'jushka woke the coachman Nikita and the caretaker Pëtr and told them of the *barynja*'s command.

"Quieter, lads, so that none of the other servants hear or know what we're up to."

"An' just what *are* we up to?" asked Nikita.

"Whatever the *barynja* orders," replied Mar'jushka, as she walked off.

Nikita and Pëtr began harnessing the horse. A thaw prevailed; from the sky came a mixture of snow and rain.

As the coachman and the concierge got busy around the stable, mud stuck to their heavy boots: everything was wet and slipped out of their hands, it was quite a challenge, pitch-black darkness reigned everywhere. Even up close, their eyes could scarcely make out the bare tree branches in the large garden.

Finally, everything was ready. The wagon noiselessly pulled up to the back porch of the manor house, and Nikita and Pëtr, feeling puzzled, awaited their orders. When Mar'jushka told the elderly *barynja*, the latter put on warm boots and a long cloak, and all at once started to feel ill at ease.

All her life she had lived in her dear, quiet Elisavetino, and now, such an alarming situation! She devoutly crossed herself before the only image left in its icon-holder, where an icon-lamp was still burning, and quietly entered the room of her one and only, dearly beloved grandson, Fedja [Fëdor], who was sound asleep at the time.

Fedja was ten years old. He had been left an orphan, without a father or mother, and was being raised by his grandmother. There were no close relatives, and the two of them lived a happy and harmonious life together.

"Fedja! Get up, my darling!" said the grandmother as she tried to wake her grandson.

Still not quite awake, Fedja whispered something that sounded like a question, then turned himself to the wall and fell asleep again.

"Oh, my God! Fedjushka! Get up. It's urgent… Fedja! I'm doing this for you, you're a big boy now, wake up, help your Granny," the old woman pleaded, in a tizzy and almost in tears.

Fedja jumped up distractedly, rubbed his eyes, his dishevelled hair stuck out in all directions; he sat silently on the bed, his feet dangling over the side. He stared straight ahead with a blank look of non-comprehension. Finally, he woke up.

"What is it, Granny, what?!… Is it the French?"

"No, Fedja, it's not the French, thank God!… But they could still come… We need to flee as soon as possible, and so as to leave nothing behind for them, I want to bury all our treasures in the ground. Everything's ready, we'll go now and hide the trunk in the woods. You see, Fedjushka, I'm already old, I don't need anything, this is all for you. You come with us, and see where we bury our trove, and when you're older, and need some money or treasures, you'll be able to find them."

It was hard for Fedja to raise himself out of bed in the middle of the night. He kept trembling, and wanted to go back to sleep, but he was glad that his grandmother was addressing him as a grown-up, and that he would have a treasure trove in the ground to draw upon. He hastily pulled on his boots, donned a hat and a half-length fur coat and went out to the porch with Granny and Mar'jushka.

Never before had Fedja got up so early. But last year his grandmother had taken him to morning prayers on Easter Sunday. It had been dark then, too, as now, and he had felt like sleeping, too, but back then it was a warm spring night, in the distance you could hear the church bells pealing out the good news, while the people, cheerful and dressed in their Sunday best, were hurrying to the church. Everything was so joyous then, while now it was all so frightening, cold and damp.

Following the *barynja*'s orders, Nikita and Pëtr carried out the heavy trunk and placed it on the wagon. All around silence reigned; the only sounds to be heard were the bell-tower chime and the watchman beating on his cast-iron gong.

Pëtr touched the reins; Nikita used one hand to keep the trunk in place while holding a lantern in the other; the horse gave a stretch and, breathing heavily, started out along the muddy road. Mar'jushka led the *barynja* by the hand; Fedja timidly held on to his grandmother's long cloak with his freezing fingers; they all moved forward together and disappeared into the night-time fog. They had to make their way down a steep icy slope; both the people and the horse skidded; the trunk was heavy, tilting the wagon to one side, Nikita could barely keep it in place. It was all Grandmother could do to put one foot in front of the other. Fedja couldn't help trembling with fear. Finally, they made it to the bottom of the hill; ahead lay a smoother road straight along the stream.

"To the left, to the left!" cried Grandmother breathlessly.

Pëtr jerked on the reins, and the wagon, making a sharp turn to the left, creaked as it headed into the old oak forest.

"Stop!" commanded Elizaveta Fëdorovna.

She ordered another lantern to be lit, peered all around, and, pointing to the place where a huge, age-old oak was growing right at the edge of the forest, quickly snapped:

"Dig a pit here… look alive!"

Nikita and Pëtr set to work. The digging was very difficult. The tree roots criss-crossed each other in the damp earth, and sticky, clay-like mud stuck to the shovels.

Fedja watched with horror the ever-deepening black hole, and suddenly it seemed to him as though they were really digging graves for himself and his grandmother. The whole time a crow, scared by the lantern flame, cawed sharply and plaintively over the heads of those standing at the edge of the open pit.

"Oh, that's a bad sign," said Pëtr with a heavy sigh.

"We have the power of the cross," declared Mar'jushka, crossing herself.

Grandmother sat on the trunk and let out a moan. Mar'jushka tenderly covered her with a warm scarf and kept encouraging:

"Mamushka, dear, you'll catch your death of cold, please go home. We'll clear things away without you."

But Grandmother went on sitting there for an hour, even two hours, waiting for the pit to be dug. When the task was finished, Elizaveta Fëdorovna fumbled around for the huge padlock. Bringing it forward, she inserted the key, and once again opened and closed the trunk. The lock rang with a strange sound amidst the silence of the forest. Fedja gave a shudder. Confident that the trunk was now locked securely, Elizaveta Fëdorovna commanded that it be lowered into the pit.

Nikita and Pëtr managed to hoist the heavy iron-clad trunk full of treasures and lower it on ropes into the pit. Then they picked up shovels and began to cover it with earth.

"What's that?" everybody cried in horror.

In the nighttime silence hoofbeats could be heard, carriages could be seen flitting by in the distance, while, from time to time, faint sounds of human activity could be heard of people running, shouting and making a commotion at the manor-house.

"What's all that? The French? My God! Faster, faster!" Elizaveta Fëdorovna kept urging them on.

After Nikita and Pëtr had tossed a few more shovelfuls of earth, brushwood and moss, they brought the pit up to ground level, and began placing their shovels and ropes into the wagon.

Everyone started for home. Fedja sat with Pëtr in the empty wagon, while Grandmother was escorted by Nikita and Mar'jushka. The closer they got to home, the more distinct became the voices and noises in the manor-house courtyard.

"My God, what is going on there?" Mar'jushka kept repeating with a sigh.

When they arrived at the house, everyone perked up their ears. The voices were Russian — that meant, it wasn't the French they were hearing. This was a relief to all. By the time they had come still closer, they could tell that in the driveway of the manor-house stood a large carriage with a team of six horses: running out to greet Elizaveta Fëdorovna was no Frenchman, but an old friend, a colonel, surrounded by Russian soldiers.

"Where did you disappear to, dear lady, Elizaveta Fëdorovna? We've been looking for you for two hours," said the colonel. "I learnt in Moscow that you were at the estate, and I came for you. There's no time to waste — not even a minute! Cold and hungry French soldiers are roaming nearby, they're plundering, even killing people, and you can't possibly remain here, it's too dangerous. We must go right now, Elizaveta Fëdorovna, everything's ready! Quick, Mar'jushka, get yourself ready."

"Heavens! You haven't forgotten this old woman! Mar'jushka, hurry! Oh, Lord!... Nikita, Pëtr, pack up, tomorrow you all should head off to our Rjazan' estate. Fedja, where are you? Take rifles and axes. The French, they'll kill, my dears, they'll kill!" said Grandmother, all flustered.

She was completely beside herself. But no matter how many times the colonel asked her where she had been during the night, the old woman said nothing, offering only: "I'll tell you after, my dear, later..."

They hastily got a few things together, along with provisions for the trip. The colonel helped Grandmother into the carriage; she was joined by an exhausted and terribly frightened Fedja. Mar'jushka took the seat opposite; then the colonel climbed in, and the carriage set off, surrounded by soldiers mounted on horseback. They headed up the muddy main road, past the forest.

Several hours later, toward morning, a crowd of hungry French soldiers in tattered uniforms and armed with various weapons, stormed into the manor house at Elisavetino and plundered it. People barely escaped with their lives — some managed to flee, others hid in the woods. The house was completely abandoned, and nobody lived there for a long, long time after that.

PART II

Several years passed. The war ended, the French made peace with the Russians, Moscow was rebuilt better than before, and residents began once again to move in and settle in their new houses.

Only the manor house in Elisavetino stood on its estate empty and desolate, awaiting its owner.

Soon after her departure from her beloved Elisavetino, Elizaveta Fëdorovna fell ill and died. She had caught cold that same night that she and her grandson Fedja buried the treasure. Her fright, along with her hasty nighttime departure, also ate away at her frail health, and no sooner had she arrived at her Rjazan' estate than she fell ill and was confined to bed.

Fedja, who slept in the room next to Grandmother's, would often hear her groan and pray in the middle of the night: "Lord, have mercy upon me, a sinner! Lord, do not abandon my orphan grandson, Fedja!"

And he would feel sad and uncomfortable. He felt like crying, and the thought came to him: "Why did Granny have to go out and bury the trunk in the middle of the night? And look, she caught her death of cold! Who needs that trunk, anyway? And Granny might actually pass on. I need Granny, I can't live without her, I love her!" And Fedja hid his face in a pillow and wept. He kept on weeping, gradually getting tired, until sleep finally brought his tear-swollen eyes to a close.

Grandmother continued to grow worse with each passing day. Death was near; the elderly woman summoned Fedja to her side, and softly, with intermittent breaths, began confiding to him:

"Fedja, I've grown worse. Apparently, it's pleasing God to take me from you... soon you'll be left all alone... don't cry, my little friend... Listen to me, remember my last will..." Grandmother coughed and fell silent for a few moments... "You remember, Fedja," she continued, "how you and I buried a treasure... Well, my little friend, I ask you not to open the treasure until you need it for some good cause."

Grandmother again fell silent. Fedja looked at her emaciated face, and tears rolled down his cheeks.

"Fedjushka, remember: if you dig into the treasure out of greed, to give yourself greater riches, it won't bring you any happiness... Farewell, my darling, may the Lord bless you for any good deeds you may do, and remember Grandmother's words..."

From under her pillow, she took out a small icon and blessed Fedja.

Fedja could not bring himself to say anything. He sobbed and kissed Grandmother before he was led away. By evening Grandmother quietly passed away.

Fedja was left all alone in the world. His trustee, some distant relation, came for him, and took him off to an élite boarding school in Moscow. Fedja grew up a lonely child — there was no one to love him or show him affection, and even on holidays there was nowhere for him to go.

Several more years went by. Fedja grew up. He finished his schooling and went to live in Elisavetino, where he had lived in his childhood with his grandmother. Now he was the full owner of his ancestral home. The house needed to be renovated and cleaned up, the pathways in the garden had become overgrown with grass; the service buildings had become dilapidated — everything had to be put in order. Fedja started to manage the estate and before long became quite wealthy. Not even once did he think about the treasure buried in the woods. He didn't like recalling the trunk which caused the death of his beloved grandmother. Sometimes, when out for a walk, he would approach the old oak tree with the wide trunk, now grown even larger, where they had buried the treasure and fled soon afterward; this reminded him of his dying grandmother's words; it made him frightened and gave him a shudder, and he went home as fast as he could.

No one except Fedja and the elderly Nikita now knew where the treasure was buried. Mar'juška, Grandmother's maid, lived but a few years longer than her *barynja*. Pëtr was conscripted into military service and disappeared without a trace. The elderly Nikita now served as a night watchman and set up quarters in the garden, in a grotto not far from the buried treasure.

One of his duties was to start up the fountains whenever people from the city came to take a stroll in the marvellous Elisavetino park. Sometimes children would slip a coin into 'Uncle' Nikita's hand and ask him to start up the fountains. Nikita would get up, go to the stream, turn on some sort of tap, and, lo and behold, out of the open mouth of a winged marble dragon would rise a tall, thin jet of water, and the round marble basin would be filled with a bubbly white foam.

And just beyond was another fountain — a fish, all silvered, and from the fish's mouth a torrent of water gushed forth with a roar and splashed the children as they squealed with delight. Later 'Uncle' Nikita made another trip to the stream, turned the tap off (to the children it seemed like magic), and the fountains ceased flowing. A great silence ensued, and with weary footsteps the old man went back to his dark, cool grotto, where he lay down on a bench to rest.

Lying there, he must have often thought of the buried treasure, saying to himself: "All that wealth is going to waste in the ground, while we have become like paupers, without a cow, and a poor horse, nobody has any decent shoes or clothes, a disaster! Not enough bread to last 'til Christmas, our pay is small, what can we do?! If only we could get our hands on a few coins... we could dig up that trunk again and tie up all the loose ends." And Nikita remembered the elders saying: "Whoever finds the treasure buried here, the same will die within a year."

Nikita did not want to die. Crossing himself, he chased away the bad thoughts and said to himself: "Save me, Lord, we don't need anyone else's goods — even without them God will still help us, we'll get by somehow." This calmed him down.

But over the last while Nikita was visited more and more often by the thought of how nice it would be to dig up the earth, secretly break open the trunk, scoop out a little money before closing it and burying it again. This thought gave Nikita no peace at night and banished sleep; during the day, sitting alone in his dark stone grotto, moment by moment he would picture before him the large trunk filled with treasure. Several times he would go up to the old oak tree, which looked as though it was zealously standing guard over Grandmother's treasure, but then once more retreated, crossing himself and repeating: "Sinful! Such a temptation! God have mercy on me!..."

So passed the summer. Autumn came again, and the dwellers of the manor house stopped coming to Elisavetino. Nikita stopped sitting by the fountains and kept watch over the manor house at night. Nikita had been a watchman for a very long time. He was a bold old fellow, wasn't afraid of anything, and all night long he could be heard making his rounds and banging on a resonant cast-iron gong.

But now, all of a sudden, a change came over Nikita. Starting from the moment the thought first came to him to dig up the treasure, he was overcome by fear. As always, he would make his rounds of the house, the stables, the barns, the servants' quarters and other buildings, only now he began to imagine that from all sides someone was ready to attack him, grasp hold of him and capture him. Or he imagined that someone was running up to the oak tree and beckoning him to follow. Then Nikita would hurry to the house, where there were people; he would sit down on a bench and for a very long time was unable to return to his watchman's duties.

It was the same kind of dark autumn night as the one long ago when Nikita, Pëtr and Grandmother buried her treasure. Nikita took supper, put on his caftan and belt, crossed himself in front of the icon hanging in the corner of his hut, and set out on his rounds. It was drizzling, part rain, part snow; the wind was howling, tearing roofs off houses.

It was very dark, though from time to time the Moon peeked through and floated out from the covering clouds.

All that day, from morning on, Nikita was not himself. He decided that he would go that night, dig up the treasure and take a little cash from the trunk.

He was so convinced of this decision that without further thought he took up his spade and headed straight for the oak tree.

The old man walked cheerfully, as if he were going to do a good deed. He had so encouraged himself that even his timidity left him. He walked up to the oak, looked all around, lit a match, focused his gaze on the little mound beneath which the trunk had been buried, and with a strong arm began to dig up the earth, shovelling it to one side.

Nikita worked long and steadily; all at once his spade struck iron. Nikita gave a shudder, but he continued digging. "That can't be the trunk, we buried it deeper," Nikita muttered to himself.

He carefully lowered the spade and again struck something. He then began to dig with his hands, wondering what it could be, and, picking up something iron, brought it to the surface. It was the padlock from the old trunk, broken off together with the clasps. The lock had caught on a root of the oak tree, had broken off and thus remained near the surface while the weighty trunk had sunk lower.

No sooner Nikita had grasped hold of the lock than he suddenly remembered his deceased *barynja*, how she herself had locked the trunk with this very padlock, how he had not seen her since that time, and took fright. He again lit a match, causing a frightened owl perched in the oak tree to ruffle her wings and utter sharp cries over Nikita's head. It stopped raining, and all at once the Moon peeked out from behind the clouds and illuminated the old oak with its gnarled branches.

Immediately Nikita felt his bravery vanishing. Disturbed, he began to focus his gaze on the oak tree where the frightened owl was perched, and it seemed to him that, from behind the branches, some of which were still covered here and there with dried brown leaves, his old *barynja* was reaching out to him and handing him the key to the lock.

Nikita cried out at the top of his voice. His own ageing, croaking voice sounded frightening to him in the night-time silence and the echo scared him even more. This unfortunate old man, holding the spade in one hand and the padlock in the other, ran, slipping and falling, to the servants' quarters. Upon reaching the door, he forced it open and ran inside like a madman, terrifying the other servants as they were preparing to go to bed.

"Uncle Nikita, what's the matter with you? Were you attacked by bandits?" asked the coachman.

"The *barynja*! The *barynja*! Fetch the key from her!" spluttered Nikita, still not himself.

"Christ be with thee, Grandpa! The devil's got a hold of him!" declared the lady cook.

"He's not well, by God! Lie down, Grandpa, I'll do your rounds for you," piped up a young worker.

Nikita didn't say anything more. He tossed the spade and the lock into a corner and lay down, pulling the covers over his head.

"What's this about a padlock?" enquired the cook. "It's huge!" she exclaimed as she examined the lock. "We have to show it to the foreman."

Nikita kept muttering to himself all night long. He became feverish. First, he dreamt about his *barynja* with the key, next he prayed and asked God to forgive his sins, and then it seemed he was buying some cows and horses in town. He developed a high fever and stayed ill for a long time.

After Uncle Nikita recovered from his illness, he prepared for a pilgrimage and started to wander. He would return home no more, and so nobody ever knew why Uncle Nikita took ill and why, all at once, after asking his master's permission to go on a pilgrimage, he decided to spend the rest of his life in a monastery.

PART III

When Fedja arrived at Elisavetino in the spring, he was told that Uncle Nikita had gone away. The same night he took ill, Nikita had brought in some sort of padlock, which they showed to Fedja. Fedja recognised the padlock and surmised what Nikita had wanted to do, and how terribly he had suffered as a consequence. Now Fedja was the only one who knew where the treasure was buried. And still, Fedja would never breathe a word about to anyone else, so afraid was he that someone would want to steal it like Nikita.

From childhood Fedja had been a warm-hearted boy, he loved to do good and never held back. As he began to mature and found himself all alone in the world, his heart became less sensitive; there was no one to love him, and no love for him to reciprocate.

At first, at the élite boarding school which he attended, he became very attached to a certain boy who was poor and weak, and shared everything he had with him. But this boy later left the boarding school, and once more Fedja felt completely alone. When Fedja grew up, he became miserly, stopped doing good deeds, stopped helping the poor and tried to accumulate as much money as he could. However, he still refrained from digging up his grand-mother's treasure, remembering her words: "Do not open the treasure until you need it for some good cause."

It seemed to Fedja that there would never be an occasion for such a good deed, and so he began to reason: "What's the use if the money stays lying stu-pidly in the ground? Better to take it and get interest on it, and that will make me richer still. Besides, the trunk is not even locked, the padlock broke off, it should at least be closed…"

Fedja thought for a long time and decided to dig up the trunk. In Moscow he bought himself a new large iron shovel. One night he headed out to the place where the chest was buried. The earth dug up by Nikita lay in a small mound to one side.

Fedja did not want to bring the whole treasure into the house at once. Without taking the trunk itself out of the ground, he planned to bring home a few pieces each night. He started digging, but after a short time Fedja got so exhausted that he gave up and went home.

The next night, too, he could not sleep, his thoughts were so concentrated on the oak tree. He picked up the lock, inserted the key which he always kept on his person, locked it and opened it again; after that he took the key out and put it in his pocket. Furtively and quietly Fedja set out on his misdeed and started to dig again. He was unaccustomed to such work and quickly became exhausted. His arms and legs hurt worse than the day before, but still he kept on digging.

All at once he had the impression he was under attack; his legs suddenly gave out, and he staggered and fell. He could no longer feel his legs, nor budge from the spot. Fedja was frightened, but he soon recalled that he had a lot of money, and that doctors, or even a trip abroad could cure him. Most importantly, he did not want to be discovered here, by the treasure, and so, taking a spade under his arm, he crawled on his hands away from the oak tree, painfully dragging his legs behind him, attempting to get out onto the road.

For a long time, he dragged himself through the forest, through trees and undergrowth. From time to time, he would stop to rest, and then once again crawl further to get to the road. Finally, he made it, where he waited patiently for the morning.

Around five o'clock in the morning a young man happened to pass by carrying a barrel of water. Fedja called out to him. The water carrier took fright at first, and then became shocked to discover his master lying helplessly on the road in the wee hours of the morning.

Fedja began to think about what he should say, but he got his words mixed up and ended up saying that he couldn't sleep, that he wanted to dig up young oak trees from the forest and to transplant them to the garden early in the morning, but he had had an accident, his legs had given out, and he was unable to walk.

Fedja was brought home and put to bed. Doctors began coming to see him, but no matter what treatment they tried, nothing helped. He could no longer walk and needed to be pushed around in a wheelchair.

It pained Fedja to find himself so miserable and helpless at such a young age. He became quite restless and declined to get involved in anything. His whole estate fell into decay, his affairs into disorder, and he quickly became more and more impoverished. Still, he was now afraid to touch the treasure and did not like even to think about it. Finally, he ran completely out of money. All that was left was Elisavetino, that small estate near Moscow where Fedja lived.

Then came summer, the time for work. As soon as dawn broke, all the servants would head off to the field. At night the men and boys pastured the horses, while the exhausted women caught whatever sleep they could, but only until dawn, when they had to start work again.

One time on a holiday night, around two o'clock, Fedja was awakened by dreadful cries of "Fire! Fire!" A few minutes later the alarm was sounded, and the chime of the bell was accompanied by the despairing screams of women and children. Fedja wanted to jump out of bed, but his legs could not move, and he fell back on the bed. Through the lowered window blind, he could see the red glow of fire and began to call loudly for his servant. The servant who cared for him woke up, but, on seeing the glow of the fire through the window, he abandoned his master and ran to the village to help his relatives drive out the cattle and carry out their belongings.

It was frightful for Fedja to be alone; the village was right there, close to his estate — well, what if his house caught fire, but he would not be able to get up or get out and would probably burn to death without help?

He began praying to God.

Suddenly he heard something strike the roof of his house with a thud, but then bounced off and fell somewhere out of sight.

What fell was a firebrand, carried from the village by a strong wind, and it set fire to the manor house. Fedja began to listen attentively. From the village he could hear frightening screams, as well as the terrible crack of falling roofs and burning huts.

For the first time in a long time, Fedja felt compassion for someone else's misfortune, and he began to feel sorry for the people. "How miserable! What will they do now? Everything they have will burn down; where and how will the old people live — those old women, like my grandmother…"

Suddenly from the next room smoke began to waft in his direction; then a cracking sound was heard, and the neighbouring room was engulfed in flames.

"Oh my God! I'm on fire!" thought Fedja. "I can't run away, and I'll burn a horrible death!"

Fedja tried to get up, but could not. In despair, he lowered his head to the pillow, closed his eyes and began to pray. "Thy will be done!" he cited. He recalled his sins, recalled how little good he had done in his life, and he was terribly afraid of dying. Still praying, he promised God that if he were saved, he would devote his whole life to doing good.

Meanwhile, the room became filled with smoke and hot with fire. Somewhere over to one side, something began to crack…

Then, at that very moment, someone's strong fist broke the window, the frame fell away, and Fedja's servant bounded into the room.

He grasped Fedia with his strong arms, lifted him from the bed and the next moment carried him out to the garden where he put him in a wheelchair which had been left the night before in the gazebo.

"Ivan, is that you? Thank you, my dear chap, you saved me from death! You alone remembered me." A few moments later he enquired: "Over there, in the village, did everyone escape? Did the children and old people managed to get out?… Oh my God, what a disaster!"

"God is merciful," came Ivan's reply. "Everyone's out. And all at once I looked and saw the manor house on fire! I dropped everything and ran, fearing that our master was in danger."

"Well, what are you going to do now? I suppose all your possessions are gone."

"What will I do?! Whatever is God's will. 'The Lord giveth, the Lord taketh away.' It's over."

The master was taken to the servants' quarters, which had escaped the fire, and put to bed.

The fire claimed the whole village, as well as the manor house. Very little was saved. The next day Fedja asked to be taken out in his wheelchair to the site of the fire. Nothing had been cleaned up yet: trunks, barrels, wheels, cups, samovars, rags, benches, tables — everything was lying in the street. Women were howling, little children were screaming in their unaccustomed surroundings. Cows, most of them tied to wagons, were mooing. Chickens trotted about distractedly. The peasants were trying to drag away the still burning pieces of wood with long hooks and dousing charred beams. Some burnt-out huts with blackened chimneys sticking out of them were still smouldering.

Fedja took in the whole scene and wept bitterly. He had known all these peasants from childhood. They had all grown up with him. His eyes fell on Pëtr, with whom he once had got lost in the forest as a child; now he was a man with a beard, he had children of his own, and here he was walking sadly around his burnt-out hut, evidently looking for something. And then Fedja spied Taras; Taras had been a cheerful lad, dark-eyed, lively, who loved to do funny dances that left Fedja's grandmother in stitches of laughter, and Fedja was glad that his grandmother was fond of his friend. Taras's house had also burned down; this man, who suffered from consumption, had four children, all of them small. And Fedja's gaze then lighted upon Avdoshka, the village fool, who was running and blowing assiduously on something and looked very surprised; but his face was pitiful — where was he to go now with his ageing mother?

"How can I help? How can I help?" Fedja was thinking, and he remembered the words of his grandmother:

"Open the treasure when you need it for some good cause."

Fedja's face suddenly lit up, his heart beating with joy. "Yes, now I can dig up the treasure and give it to those unfortunate people; I can help them and do a good deed."

Fedja called the village elder along with several other men he knew and said:

"Do not grieve, my friends, God will send us help. Listen here: take shovels, spades, whoever has ones in good condition, and follow me. I'll tell you where to go."

The peasants were frightened, they initially thought that their master had gone mad from grief or fright. But Fedja gave them a kind smile and continued:

"See here, brothers, I'm not joking; I haven't gone out of my mind, thank God. Take me where I tell you and follow me."

The peasants collected spades and shovels from wherever they could and went after their master, pushing him in the wheelchair while he led the way.

Finally, they arrived at the old oak tree.

"Dig, chaps, as fast as you can!! There's treasure buried here. Back in '12, my late grandmother and I buried her treasures to hide them from the French, and now they'll bring benefit to all of us after the fire."

The men set to work with a vigour. Soon the spades rattled against something hard, and at last they spied the whole large, red trunk, bound with iron straps, tarnished with time. There was no lock on it; the padlock had come off when Nikita found it.

Fedja told them to open the lid. The men did so and gasped. The trunk contained a treasure worth thousands of roubles! They took everything out and loaded it onto a wagon which they had sent for. Fedja said that everything should be sold, and all the money given to the peasants. He forgot about himself; he was just so happy that he could help others.

However, first of all, the peasants built a house for Fedja, right where the old one had stood, and only then did they rebuild their village. Fedja remembered the promise to God that he had made that night when he was about to be burned to death, and began to make friends with people, delighting both in his own life and in the happiness he had brought into the lives of everyone around him.

3.3 THE STORY OF A *GRIVENNIK*: A FAIRY TALE

IN PETERSBURG THERE IS A LARGE BUILDING KNOWN AS THE MINT. This is where they make silver and gold coins. Every year they release full bags of them and send them all over Russia — large silver roubles, small five-kopeck pieces, and *grivenniks* [ten-kopeck pieces], along with gold coins — all these begin to circulate from hand to hand, from one coin purse to another.

One particular *grivennik* stood out from a large pile of new coins; it was so bright and shiny that it attracted everyone's attention. All white and pure, dumped into a large bag with other *grivenniks*, it started to wonder: "Where shall I go when I get out of this bag? Where will I live? What will people buy with me? I'm so small!"

One time it heard the jangling of keys. Someone was approaching. The jangler came close, unlocked the trunk, pulled out one bag and began to rummage his hands through it. He pulled out a fistful of coins and counted them; then a second, and a third. The third fistful contained the same shining *grivennik* described above. It looked at the man who was holding it and saw a grey-haired old fellow with a serious face and severe-looking eyes. The *grivennik* did not want to stay in this old fellow's possession, and it was glad when he handed over all the money, including our *grivennik*, to a kind and poor official who had come to receive a payment.

The official slipped the coins into his pocket with a smile and set out on a brisk walk home. Along the way he stopped into a stationery store, where he spent a long time looking at the merchandise. Finally, he bought a fine looking coin purse that was outfitted with a tricky little lock. He put our *grivennik* (the shiniest one) into his new purse and went home.

When he rang the doorbell, three small children rushed out into the entrance hall; two of them cried out:

"Papà, today is Misha's name day, what are you going to give him?"

Misha, the elder boy, was standing next to them with a happy, expectant face, waiting for greetings and a name-day gift from his father. His father kissed him and gave him the new purse.

It took the children a long time to figure out how to open the tricky lock; they got it, finally, and the shiny little *grivennik* fell out onto the floor. It rolled across the floor right under the paws of a huge dog called Sport. Sport was intrigued, sniffed the coin and turned away when he realised that it was not edible. The children then hurried to pick up the *grivennik*.

"Now you are rich, Misha, you have money!" said Misha's little sister Vera. "What are you going to buy with it?"

"I'll buy everything!" said Misha, who never had had money before and did not know its value; but this was already the third coin he had been given today — "including a sledge, and a toy horse, and candies, and oranges; I'll buy everything, everything…"

Misha was very happy; he ran to his nanny to show her the gift and asked her to go with him at once to buy something. But there was a heavy frost out, the windows were so frozen that they could not see through them to the outside. The sledges passing by the windows made a squeaking noise with their runners; and the people outside were so cold, they were almost running down the street. Mother refused to let Misha go shopping but told him he could go when it got warmer out. Misha was upset, but there was nothing he could do; he put all the money, including the *grivennik*, into his new coin purse and locked it in a drawer.

In the meantime, he had some visitors, boys his own age; they had chocolate after breakfast, and afterward they played various games, running through the whole house.

In the evening, when all the guests had gone, Misha was tired and went to see his nanny in the children's room. He sat down on a small bench and began to ask Nanny what he could buy with his money. But Nanny was not listening to Misha; a laundry woman was visiting her; over tea they engaged in some gloomy conversation.

Misha couldn't help overhearing. Spiridonovna (the laundry woman) was telling about her son, that now he had no job, as his employers had let him go and left the country. His family lived in a cold, little room; his young boy kept crying because his little arms and legs were so cold, they had become all stiff. The mother of this child washed floors for twenty kopeks, while her boy kept crying for his mother, he was so hungry. His mother bought him some *baranki* [a kind of pretzel] for ten kopeks, moistened them and gave them to her son. She herself ate another *grivennik*'s worth.

Then came a day when she was no longer able to wash floors; she had got a splinter in her hand which was inflamed and developed an abscess.

The next day, again they would have nothing to eat, and again the boy would spend the whole day in tears. The nanny took a knife and cut a large white roll in half, put with it four lumps of sugar, which she then offered to Spiridonovna.

"Take this to the boy; and don't be angry — we give what we can."

"Thank you, my dear nanny," said Spiridonovna, and she wrapped up the bread and sugar in a cloth and began to set out for home.

Misha initially listened to his nanny's conversations with the laundry woman; but quickly became bored. He was tormented by the image of the crying boy with cold hands. He went off to bed and dreamt about some boy crying and reaching out to him.

The next morning Misha woke early, jumped out of bed and ran to the window to see what the weather was like. No sooner had he lifted the blind than a bright ray of sunlight fell on him. The weather was clear and calm, and Nanny said that today they could go and buy something with Misha's money.

After breakfast Misha put on a fur coat, cap, *bashlyk* [a type of hood] and warm boots, and Nanny went with Misha to the toy store. As they passed a familiar cab driver, Misha shouted out to him:

"Nikita, yesterday was my name day!"

He also declared the same in the toy store and started to look at what he might buy. Mother had added a little extra money. Nanny chose for him a tilting doll known as *Van'ka-Vstan'ka*, also a whistle, and a porcelain dog. With the remaining money Misha bought two oranges and gave the fruit vendor his shiny *grivennik*. There was no more money left, and all at once Misha recalled yesterday's conversation between Spiridonovna and his nanny and asked her:

"Nanny, did Spiridonovna buy her grandson a *baranka*?"

"I dunno, Misha; they probably don't have bread at home, much less a *baranka*."

Misha became bored again. When he got home, he gave the oranges to his brother and sister instead of eating them himself. He put the new toys on the table without even opening them.

Nanny asked him why he wasn't playing with his new toys.

"I don't feel like it, take them away, Nanny," said Misha. He hid his face in Nanny's apron, and started crying, only he wouldn't tell anyone what he was upset about.

In the meantime, the fruit vendor who had sold Misha the oranges, put the shiny *grivennik* in his dirty palm, gave it a shake, admired how it glistened in the sun, and tossed it into his large leather moneybag. The *grivennik* was not happy in its new home; it was dirty there and smelled of tobacco, herring and leather, and there were a lot of copper coins which pressed in on the pure, brightly shining *grivennik*.

"Oranges! Good oranges!" cried the fruit vendor, whose name was Ignat. "Oranges! Buy my oranges!" he urged passers-by as he walked about quickly, scraping his boots on the frosty pavement. He peered into the shop windows along the street and approached a number of sleighs. He desperately wanted to sell all his oranges today so tomorrow he could go to the village where his mother, wife and children lived.

By evening Ignat's desire was fulfilled; all his oranges had been sold and Ignat began to get ready for the next day's trip to his village. He counted his money and put the silver *grivennik* in a separate matchbox for his little son. Then from under the bed he took out a small chest, storing his vendor's tray away in its place. His chest contained gifts which he had bought at different times: a warm headscarf for his elderly mother, a *sarafan* for his wife, and a warm toque for his little son, along with earrings and a small apron for his daughter. In addition to that, he had sweets for them — *baranki* and tea with sugar.

It was a treat for Ignat to go home; it had been a long time since he had seen his family. That evening he prayed and went to bed. Early in the morning he jumped out of bed, put his shoes on, along with a half-length fur coat and warm hat, picked up his chest and headed off to the railway station. The train was already standing there and whistling. It was very crowded; everyone was in a frantic hurry, pushing each other, dragging their trunks and bags. A long queue of people stood at the ticket counter, waiting their turn to buy a ticket.

At last, everything was done; Ignat dragged his chest into the railway carriage and, after crossing himself, sat down in his seat.

The locomotive whistled and snorted, the third warning bell sounded, and the train started moving. After passing through the city, an endless vista of snow-covered fields opened up. Occasionally Ignat glimpsed villages, forests and carts along the road. Ignat loved the countryside and enjoyed looking out the window. He did not like living in Moscow but lived there because there was too much poverty back home. But now he really wanted to fix up his hut and purchase a horse by the following summer.

For two years in a row, some unsavoury people had stolen Ignat's horses during the night. At first Ignat had hired himself out as a concierge and later started selling oranges to make money.

Towards evening Ignat arrived at his stop. It was already dark. But still, when he stepped out of his stuffy carriage, everything seemed to him so spacious, cheerful and fresh. He looked all around and then upward: the sky was deep blue, with many, many bright stars.

"Thank God, I've arrived!" said Ignat with a sigh and went to have a look in the station courtyard, to see if he could spot any familiar faces. Three sleighs were there, and Ignat spied the bay horse belonging to 'Uncle' Vlas, who before long came out of the station and recognised Ignat at once.

"Well, a fellow-villager! Is that you?" the local man exclaimed. "How are you doing, my friend, or have you missed us?"

"Hello, Uncle Vlas! I *have* felt lonely, such a pity! Could you please give me a ride, Uncle, as I didn't call anyone from home; I thought I'd just show up."

"Get in, get in, I'll take you."

Uncle Vlas's horse looked well fed, and his sleigh was in good shape. They loaded Ignat's chest and climbed into the sleigh. Soon they were driving along a smooth country road — first through fields, then through forest, and finally their native village came in sight. Whenever they went uphill, Ignat climbed out to make it easier for the horse, but his heart was pounding, and he was terribly eager to get home. Suddenly the bay horse gave a start, and something black could be seen flitting away in a distance. They stopped the horse and took a look around.

"A wolf!" both men exclaimed.

It was indeed a large old wolf. With broad, bouncing leaps, it bounded across the field straight for Vlas and Ignat, who quickly jumped back into the sleigh. Uncle Vlas struck his exhausted bay with a whip, but the horse was not able to sustain speed for any length of time. The wolf was fast approaching, and the situation became frightening. The men started shouting, thinking to scare the wolf. But the wolf was not afraid of anything, and they could already see its white teeth — indeed, its whole profile.

Vlas struck his poor horse with all his might while Ignat threw his chest at the oncoming wolf. As the horse took a sudden leap forward, the wolf stopped in its tracks, looking at the chest with some surprise. Before long, the beast lost interest and lumbered slowly off into the forest. The men went back and picked up the chest which had opened upon falling; some of the contents had fallen out, which they had to retrieve in the dark using matches.

At long last they arrived at Ignat's house. Ignat was the first to jump out of the sleigh.

"Thank you, Uncle Vlas," he said. "You and I had a good scare back there."

"We did, didn't we? Take care, now," Vlas replied, as he headed for his own home.

Ignat did not go into his house immediately. First, he tried looking in the window, but it was covered with frost. Then he quietly opened the door and went inside. His wife, who was sitting at the table, initially took fright. Who could be coming in the door so late at night?

"Ignat!" she suddenly exclaimed and joyfully rushed to embrace her husband. His elderly mother, who was sleeping on the peasant stove [a common custom in Russian winters], turned over and, still half asleep, could not fathom for a long time what was going on. When she recognised her son, even though she felt like getting to her feet, she could only give a deep sigh, whereupon Ignat climbed onto the bench beside the stove and kissed his mother. The children did not even wake up.

The next morning brought them a lot of joy. Ignat handed out all the presents he had brought, including *baranki* for tea, and started telling about his life in the city. At this point, he remembered the *grivennik* which he had hidden in a matchbox and went to look for it in his chest. But neither matchbox nor *grivennik* was to be found.

"Obviously my *grivennik* fell out of the chest when I threw it at the wolf and the chest broke open. Pity! It was a good coin! Now we'll never find it in the snow."

Ignat felt sorrowful but soon forgot about the incident. He started to work on repairing the hut, insulating it with straw to make it warmer. One Sunday he borrowed a horse and sleigh from a neighbour and went to the market in town, where he bought a horse for himself. He took his son Petja with him. The boy put on his new cap, imagining himself a hero, and even asked his father if he could take over the reins.

Ignat settled in into his new life, taking care of the house, managing all his affairs.

Spring came early, the snow melted, the roads turned into mudpuddles, and it was hard to get anywhere.

One of the residents of the village was an elderly woman named Praskovja Timofeevna, the widow of the local priest. She had a daughter, no longer young, as well as a dog, a mongrel, as old as Praskovja Timofeevna herself, who had once saved the mongrel from death. She had been walking alongside a ditch when she heard a squeal. Upon looking, she spied a puppy with a broken paw, all cold and wet.

The old woman picked up the dog and took it home. She covered it with a woollen scarf, gave it some warm milk and bandaged the paw. The puppy recovered, grew up and became very attached to Praskovja Timofeevna. Wherever she went, the little mongrel followed her. And it guarded the house so well that nobody could approach it unnoticed.

One day the priest's widow started out to visit a neighbour who lived in the next village — the same village where her favourite goddaughter, Natasha, lived. She walked for a long time, her boots got all muddy, and it was difficult to make any headway. The little mongrel ran ahead. All at once it stopped and started digging in the mud with its paws. Praskovja Timofeevna bent down and saw a matchbox all waterlogged and washed out.

"Leave it, little mongrel, leave it, it's only rubbish, no need to stop."

But all of a sudden Praskovja Timofeevna spotted something glistening amidst the dirt. It turned out to be the shiny *grivennik* which had fallen out of Ignat's chest.

"See, someone must have dropped it," said the old woman as she put the coin in her purse.

After her visit, Praskovja Timofeevna returned home very tired. She took the *grivennik* out of her purse, admiring it and, after putting it on the table, sat down to knit a stocking. The mongrel lay at her feet, and both of them dozed off. Suddenly the dog jumped up, started barking and rushed helter-skelter to the dresser. As it pushed aside the little table, the *grivennik* fell off, rolled across the floor and ended up in a crack in the floor.

That very moment, a huge rat scampered out from underneath the dresser. The old woman screamed and started to call for help. Her daughter came running, along with the caretaker, who was carrying a big stick. Upon learning that the old woman had been frightened by a rat, they began to chase it away. As the rat scampered off, it was struck by a blow from the caretaker's stick, but survived, and with incredible speed scurried over to the large icon of the Saviour.

"Oh, damn, it's crawled onto the icon!" screamed the daughter, as she smacked the rat again, this time with a mop. The rat tumbled to the floor where the concierge dealt it yet another blow. Without thinking, the wounded rat rushed straight at Praskovja Timofeevna and the next moment jumped from behind into her voluminous jacket.

"Holy Fathers! Help! Oh, you, bugger!" cried the old woman, her hands grasping the rat together with the edge of her jacket.

The caretaker helped pull off the rat and threw it to the floor. He was going to kill it, but the rat escaped, and no matter how hard they looked for it, they could not find it anywhere.

The old woman then remembered the *grivennik* which she had put on the table. They began looking for it; her daughter moved the furniture around, crawled under the sofa, and swept some dirt from under the dresser, but the *grivennik* was nowhere to be found.

Several days later they noticed such a bad smell that nobody could stand being in the same room. They all realised that they were smelling a dead rat. They then called in a carpenter, lifted some floorboards and found the dead rat, which they quickly threw out.

"Bugger!" exclaimed the carpenter. "The rat has evidently accumulated some capital. See, right next to it is a shiny *grivennik*."

The carpenter picked up the coin; after admiring it, he gave it to the old lady.

"I found it under the floor, ma'am; it must have fallen through a crack."

"Indeed! We were looking for it, but did not find it, and here it turned up all on its own… Keep it as an extra little thank-you."

"Thank *you*, ma'am."

Whereupon the carpenter popped the *grivennik* into his coin-purse, collected his tools and went home.

Many other experiences awaited our *grivennik*! By and by it fell into the hands of a little Tatar girl. This is how it happened.

One time in Samara Province a Tatar man was on his way to work. He had a wife and two children: a little boy two years old whose name was Nagim — a healthy, chubby and cheerful boy — and a little girl called Alifa, who was four years old; her eyes were infected, she was sorrowful, often hungry and always dirty. The boy was heavy to carry, and they had a long way to walk. So his father made a little wagon with four wooden wheels and put Nagim into the wagon. His big sister walked on her own.

At last, they arrived in a large village, where they hired themselves out to a rich peasant to work in his field. They built themselves a small lean-to, where they lodged the whole summer. The Tatar and his wife worked during the day, while their daughter looked after her little brother. In the evenings the man would sing sorrowful Tatar songs and play his peasant flute, while the children and their mother slept.

The ever-hungry girl often ran to the village. She hardly spoke any Russian but learnt to ask for bread, which she called *lepëshka* [flatbread]. Approaching a wealthy-looking dwelling, she saw children eating; she would stand by the porch or a window and ask in a pitiful voice: "Auntie, give me a *lepëshka*!" They would give her a piece of brown bread which she would take in her grubby little hand before running off. She used her other hand and dirty sleeve to rub her infected eyes.

She was noticed by a lady doctor who had moved to the village to treat ill peasants. She took pity on the girl and undertook to help her. First of all, she washed her whole body, and then began to give her milk and treat her eyes. The little Tatar girl made a complete recovery, became filled out and even pretty. She grew quite fond of the doctor and spent a lot of time with her.

The girl's father wanted to pay the doctor for her treatment and dropped several *grivenniks* onto the table, including the one we know about. But the kind doctor did not take the money. Calling the girl over to her, she took measurements of her thin neck and set about making a hole (with the aid of a nail) in each coin. After she did this, she sewed all the *grivenniks* together with a ribbon and put the ribbon around the little girl's neck.

"Let's have a look in the mirror, shall we?" suggested the doctor, handing the girl a small looking glass.

Alifa broke into a joyful smile while her father looked gratefully at the doctor. Tatar women always wear coins around their neck or on their braids, and the father was very glad to have his daughter so adorned.

By the time the summer was over, the family had earned some money and went home. The *grivennik* stayed a long time on Alifa's ribbon, but eventually the ribbon broke and the coins scattered in all directions.

Our favourite *grivennik* also rolled away. It was eventually picked up by a passing boy, who took it home. He wanted to buy something with it, but nobody would take a coin with a hole. They finally gave it to a merchant in return for several kopeks. The merchant happened to be a dealer in old silver. Thus our *grivennik*, old, darkened, dirty and pierced through with a nail, once again found itself in a large cauldron, where old silver was melted down before it was once more turned into new silver objects and coins.

Thus it is, too, in our lives: we are born new and bright, like pure infants. We go through various changes in life, and then, once again, go back to where we came from, only to begin to live a new life in the next world.

3.4 VANECHKA: A TRUE STORY FROM HIS LIFE

IN A REMOTE CORNER OF MOSCOW STANDS A YELLOW WOODEN HOUSE amidst a large garden with a linden allée, a mound of earth, a gazebo and even apple trees. It is especially nice in this garden in the springtime: lilacs are in bloom, pathways are covered with sand, here and there are seen blossoming tulips and fragrant daffodils. Next door to this garden, on the other side of the fence, there is another garden, even bigger and more beautiful.

In this yellow wooden house lived a large family; their youngest son was named Vanechka. He was thin, pale, with curly golden hair, very smart, with tender eyes, carefree, cheerful, and beloved by everybody. He was six years old, and he was so sensitive that he could not stand to hear anybody cry, or get upset, or get angry, or quarrel. He often became anxious and melancholic, and he would ponder how he could reconcile quarrels, how to comfort the sorrowing or the weeping or how to cheer up anyone who was angry. If he did not succeed, he himself would burst into such bitter tears that everyone around took pity on him and became kinder.

One time his nanny took him for a walk, but it was cold out; his mother started to reprimand Nanny, but Vanechka began to cry and asked his mother not to scold her as he would rather die than see Nanny offended.

At Christmas time they planned a party. Vanechka asked his mother not to invite rich guests, but to ask in the poor and give them presents. Mother agreed; she invited the children of a poor schoolteacher, a certain hunchbacked boy, and the children of the family's servants. Vanechka was ecstatic. He was especially glad to see the five-year-old hunchbacked Igor drive his little wagon and keep looking at it, laughing with delight. Vanechka clapped his hands and burst into laughter himself.

They gave out a lot of presents — cardboard boxes, nuts and party poppers with surprises — to everybody, including the children of the valet and care-taker; it was more than the children could carry home.

Vanechka also laughed when they broke open the party poppers; all the children put on a variety of paper hats and walked around the Christmas tree, tasting the flavourful red Crimean apples and the *prjaniki* in different shapes.

But all at once Vanechka turned sad, sat down on a chair with his frail legs hanging; his sparkling eyes silently followed the servants passing by as they prepared tea; he also kept looking at his nanny and other members of the staff who had come to see the tree.

"Why are you so sad, Vanechka? Don't you like your toys?"

"You know, Mamà, I really like the music box, and the toy horse, and everything; only you know, dearest Mamà, you really ought to do something fun for our servants. They are always serving us, but they don't have any fun. Please do something for them."

And Vanechka's mother began to feel remorse that such a thought had not come to her, that Vanechka was right, and she began to think of what kind of entertainment she might arrange for the staff — maybe take them to her box in the theatre or set up some kind of treat for them.

Vanechka very much liked to give away his things, his pictures, his boxes and toys. Even though he was only six years old, he already knew how to write. He would cut up pieces of paper and write: "From Vanja to Masha," and attach the note to his gift before entrusting it to one of the maids. And when it was the cook's name day, he bought him a matchbox and wrote: "From Vanya with love."

He especially liked to celebrate Nanny's name day; he called it *keeping one's name day*. For several days he was very excited, he kept asking who was plan-ning to give what to Nanny; he himself prepared to give her a cup, a headscarf, a jewellery-box or something else.

Nanny bought sausages, mint cakes, halva and marmalade to treat every-one, and Vanechka was delighted.

Vanechka was especially fond of his garden; in winter there was a snow hill which he could slide down with his sister Sasha, along with the workers' children. Then they bought him skates and made him a small skating rink; Vanechka learnt how to skate and really loved it.

But it was even better in the springtime; he could run around every-where — to the earthen mound, to the gazebo, to the brick wall with multi-coloured stones and also to the well which offered pure, fresh water.

One time, Vanechka went out into the garden all by himself. He was curi-ous to find out what was happening in the large garden next door on the other side of the fence. He climbed onto a stump, found a hole in the clay fence and began to peer through. He saw a lot of men strolling in the garden, or singing, or just chatting away; others were sitting on benches and drawing something in the sand with sticks.

One of these people came close to the fence. His hair was getting a little grey, though he had kind, sorrowful eyes. Noticing someone was peering through the hole, he, too, bent down and started to stare back. Vanechka took fright and ran home. He told his nanny about the people strolling, and how he ran away upon seeing someone stare back at him.

"Oh!" exclaimed Nanny. "What are you saying, Vanechka? Can you really look through the fence? There are only ill and crazy people there. It's terrible, they'll frighten you."

But Vanechka was not frightened. The next day, when Nanny had gone for lunch, he called over his sister Sasha. They walked down the linden allée right to his hole in the fence.

The sorrowful patient he saw yesterday was again strolling in the garden.

"Hello!" Vanechka rasped through the hole in his thin voice.

"Hello!" answered the patient with a smile. "What's your name?"

"Vanechka. What's yours?"

"I'm Vanja, too — Ivan Vasil'evich."

"Are you ill?" asked Vanechka.

"Yes, I'm ill, and I'm very miserable. You see, I had a little boy, just like you, and he died. It made me lonely, and I became ill."

Vanechka gave a sigh, closed his eyes, fell into deep thought and then said:

"I'll love you, and we'll talk every day, okay?"

Sasha began to call her brother home; she was worried that he was talking with a mentally ill person. But Vanechka did not listen to her; he was bent on carrying out his favourite deed — comforting the unfortunate — which absorbed him completely.

"What was your boy's name?"

"Vanechka, just like yours. One day he went fishing and fell into the water; they lifted him out and brought him home all wet. He caught cold, fell ill and died, and now I have no family left."

"So now he's an angel," Vanechka comforted.

"Yes, but I am still lonely."

"I'll come here every day, every day! I'll bring you my little book, and I have lots of pictures, and we can talk about everything and about your Vanechka."

"D'you have a mamà and papà?"

"Yes, I have."

"And who do you love more?"

Vanechka gave the stranger a stern look and calmly said:

"I love everyone. And I love you."

The patient also reflected for a while.

"Yes, we have to love everyone, and then things will be better…"

240

Vanechka changed the topic and started talking about his nanny, about how she would write letters and pray to God, about how he loved going mushroom hunting, and so on.

The family and the nanny no longer interfered with Vanechka's conversations with the patient through the hole in the fence. Nothing bad came of it; indeed, there was a lot of good.

One day the patient brought Vanechka a piece of chocolate. Vanechka became very anxious and asked his mother whether it was okay to eat if a crazy person had given it to him.

Vanechka was terribly fond of sweets and was overjoyed when they told him that it was all right for him to eat the chocolate.

Another time, when blue snowdrops appeared, the patient picked a large bouquet and passed it through the fence. Vanechka took it, thanked him and brought the bouquet to his mother. With a winsome smile he explained to her that poor Ivan Vasil'evich had passed the bouquet to him through the hole in the fence.

Thus it went on all springtime, until it came time for Vanechka to leave with his family for the country. Everything was packed up, they took down all the curtains, they cleaned all the carpets and furniture in the yard; the maid Dunechka ran through the yard with jars and other things, shaking out dresses to get rid of dust. The caretaker Nikita put boxes together. Wagons arrived. They tied a reddish-brown moo-cow to one of them, then they brought the sorrel Sultan along with old Chestnut out of the stable and also attached them to wagons. Soon the whole convoy started moving.

Vanechka also set out on the road, carrying a carpetbag. The bag contained everything he needed for the trip — candies, an orange, a little notebook with a pencil, a comb, a mug, a real conductor's whistle, a little bronze dog and a *prjanik*.

Before he left, Vanechka ran to say goodbye to his friend, the patient Ivan Vasil'evich. He walked up to the hole in the fence and started calling his name in loud voice.

Ivan Vasil'evich came up to the fence and cheerfully said to Vanechka:

"I'm going home, too. I'm healed now and feel much better."

"Really? I'm so glad!" Vanechka exclaimed. "Farewell!"

"Farewell, my dear little friend. You comforted me, you're a kind, good boy… I love you very, very much… and now I also love *everyone* — most of all, I will love *all* children and not just my late son."

Vanechka didn't quite understand what Ivan Vasil'evich had said, but he realised that everything was all right, that Ivan Vasil'evich had recovered and was determined to love — everyone, and this made Vanechka ecstatic.

"Here's a letter to give to your mamà," added Ivan Vasil'evich.

"Yes, of course," said Vanechka. He loved letters, both writing and receiving them, and he was happy to take this letter to his mother.

Ivan Vasil'evich gave Vanechka two large chocolate candies before he walked away, and Vanechka ran to give his mother the letter. Here is what the letter said:

"Madam, I am going away, but I wanted to tell you how heavy my soul used to be — it was in agony over the loss of my only son. I was sick with grief. I thought that I would never be able to return to life. Now I am healthy, but it wasn't the doctors who healed me. God sent your Vanechka to comfort me. This angel gave me the happiness of a new love for him and through him for all children and people. And I was healed through him and now I am able to leave the hospital. I bless the proximity of your house. God bless your little son and your whole house. Farewell. I. T."

3.5 THE RESCUED DACHSHUND: VANECHKA'S STORY

ONE DAY MY BROTHER MISHA WAS GIVEN A LITTLE DOG NAMED DACHS. He had short legs, long ears and was black all over. He was rather boring, trotting quietly about the house, and did not play with anyone. All day long he lay curled up in a corner and only got up to have something to eat or drink. He ate very little and was quite a challenge for us; we had to force bits of meat into his mouth. Finally, we decided that he was ill.

Mamà was unhappy that they had taken such a boring and frail dog into the house and was going to return him to his former owner, but Misha took pity on him and would not part with him.

Somehow Dachs managed to disappear. Mamà was glad, but Misha looked for him everywhere. Eventually he learnt from the concierge that Dachs had been seen at the brewery next door.

Three boys lived there, the sons of the head brewmaster. They liked this short-legged dog; they fed him and kept him in their house. But several days afterward Dachs came back to us. Indeed, he continued to wander back and forth between us and our neighbours.

It was early spring. The snow had melted on Moscow's streets, streams were flowing, though in our garden there were still piles of snow here and there. We cleared it away with our little shovels and took it in wheelbarrows to a far corner of the garden.

During this time Dachs was missing again. In fact, he had been missing for several days already. We checked at the brewery, but he was not there, either. We thought that somebody must have taken him, or that he had simply died. Misha decided to keep looking for him everywhere. We searched through all the bushes, swept up wet leaves, looked into the well, by the fence, in the barns, stables, and basements, but he was nowhere to be found.

Then we decided that he was gone for good and started cleaning up the space in front of the house where we had been skating during the winter. It was where we played croquet and other games in the spring. When the work was finished and all the snow had been cleared away, Mamà reminded us of the flower beds, where the pointed tips of hyacinths, tulips and narcissi could be seen poking up above the wet leafy earth.

"You see, all this will soon be in bloom," said Mamà.

We all enjoyed the garden, and didn't feel like going home, but it was time for breakfast. We put our shovels, rakes and wheelbarrows into the gazebo, where we stored our sledges in the wintertime and our garden tools during the summer.

Suddenly, I spied in the corner of the gazebo, where I was about to store my shovel, something small, round and black. I showed it to Mamà, but she was short-sighted and didn't notice anything.

"Go home, children," she said, "as fast as you can; everyone's waiting for us."

Then I said to her:

"Mamà, bend down and look — isn't that our Dachs?"

"What are you saying, Vanechka, where do you see Dachs?"

Then my sister Sasha, who was short-sighted, like Mamà, got down on her knees and, bending quite low, also noticed the unfortunate Dachs — curled up into a ball right in the corner, lying motionless on the moss on which the flower bulbs had been laid and which had remained there in a corner of the gazebo since the previous autumn.

"Good God, he's dead!" Mamà screamed, and I saw her starting to pity the little dog. At that moment I reached out and patted Dachs, and he moved just the teensiest bit.

Mamà called out to me:

"Don't touch Dachs, Vanechka, he's gone."

"No, no, he's alive, really, alive," I cried, "He's breathing."

Sasha and I carefully lifted Dachs's muzzle, and he opened his eyes a wee bit. He was terribly thin; it was evident that he was suffering horribly from disease, weakness and hunger. Mamà sent Sasha to the kitchen to fetch some food for little Dachs.

Sasha brought some soup in an old bowl.

Mamà tried to press Dachs's muzzle into the bowl, but he hesitated, screwed up his eyes and wouldn't eat for a long time. Finally, Nanny came and said:

"Why are you not having breakfast? Papà and the young ladies are waiting, Andrjusha's come from school, but *you* are missing…"

"Holy Father!" Nanny exclaimed in surprise, "What have you there, Vanechka?"

"Our dear little Dachs," I replied. "I happened to spot him when I was putting away my shovel. Look, Nanny, how pitiful he is!"

"Well, God be with him, forget him — phew! He's quite gone, and there you go patting him."

But I felt such pity on the little dog that I didn't feel like eating myself, and I could not bear to leave him. Once I found him, I wanted to rescue him and I again tried to press his muzzle into the soup. Suddenly he stuck out his dry tongue and started to lap up the soup.

"Hurrah!" we all cried, joyfully clapped our hands, and hurried off to our breakfast.

On the way back to the house, Mamà said to me:

"Well, Vanechka, you saved this little dog's life; if you hadn't spotted him, he would no doubt be dead, since he was too weak and ill to look for food on his own."

I was very happy; Misha and Sasha also praised me.

From that day on, we began to really look after Dachs and feed him. He recovered, started to catch rats and mice and grew very attached to all of us. He no longer visited the brewery. Most surprising of all, Mamà started loving him from that day on.

Illustration 29: LNT and SAT
on their 43rd wedding anniversary, 23 September 1905
Photo: S. A. Tolstaya

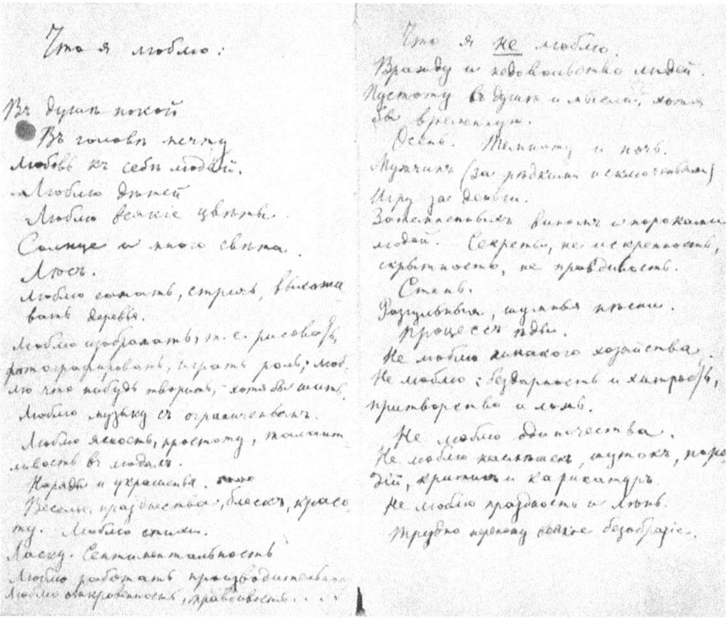

Illustration 30: SAT's outline *Chto ja ljublju* [What I like]
and *Chto ja ne ljublju* [What I don't like] in her own handwriting

Illustration 31: Front cover of SAT's published story collection *The skeleton-dolls and other stories* [«Kukolki-skelettsy» i drugie rasskazy], 1910

Illustration 32: Illustration by artist Aleksandr Viktorovich Moravov for SAT's story "Grandmother's treasure-trove" ["Babushkin klad"] published in the collection *The skeleton-dolls and other stories*, 1910

Illustration 33: Fëdor Mikhajlovich Dostoevsky.
Photo: K. A. Shapiro, St. Petersburg, 1879

Illustration 34: Anna Grigor'evna Dostoevskaja (*née* Snitkina) —
stenographer and second wife to F. M. Dostoevsky
Photo: Moscow Historical Museum, 1916

Illustration 35: Envelope for Anna Grigor'evna Dostoevskaja's letter to SAT at Yasnaya Polyana, postmarked at St. Petersburg, 8 November 1910

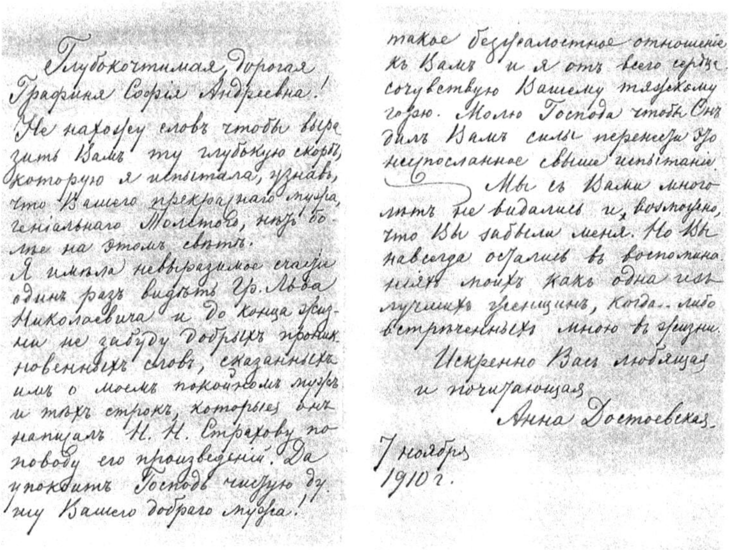

Глубокочтимая, дорогая
Графиня Софія Андреевна!
Не нахожу словъ чтобы выра-
зить Вамъ ту глубокую скорбь,
которую я испытала, узнавъ,
что Вашего прекраснаго мужа,
геніальнаго Толстого, нѣтъ бо-
лѣе на этомъ свѣтѣ.
Я имѣла невыразимое счастіе
одинъ разъ видѣть Гр. Льва
Николаевича и до конца жизни не забуду добрыхъ проник-
новенныхъ словъ, сказанныхъ
имъ о моемъ покойномъ мужѣ
и тѣхъ строкъ, которыя онъ
написалъ Н. Н. Страхову по
поводу его произведеній. Да
упокоитъ Господь чистую душу Вашего добраго мужа!

такое безжалостное отношеніе
къ Вамъ и я отъ всего сердца
сочувствую Вашему тяжкому
горю. Молю Господа чтобы Онъ
далъ Вамъ силы перенести это
ниспосланное свыше испытаніе.
Мы съ Вами много
лѣтъ не видались и, возможно,
что Вы забыли меня. Но Вы
навсегда остались въ воспомина-
ніяхъ моихъ какъ одна изъ
лучшихъ женщинъ, когда-либо
встрѣченныхъ мною въ жизни.
Искренно Васъ любящая
и почитающая
Анна Достоевская.
7 ноября
1910 г.

Illustration 36: First and last pages of letter from Anna Grigor'evna Dostoevskaja to SAT, dated 7 November 1910, expressing her sympathy for SAT's exclusion from her husband's dying moments at Astapovo Station

Illustration 37: SAT looking in the window of the Astapovo stationmaster's house (after being prevented by Tolstoy's followers from seeing her husband on his deathbed), November 1910

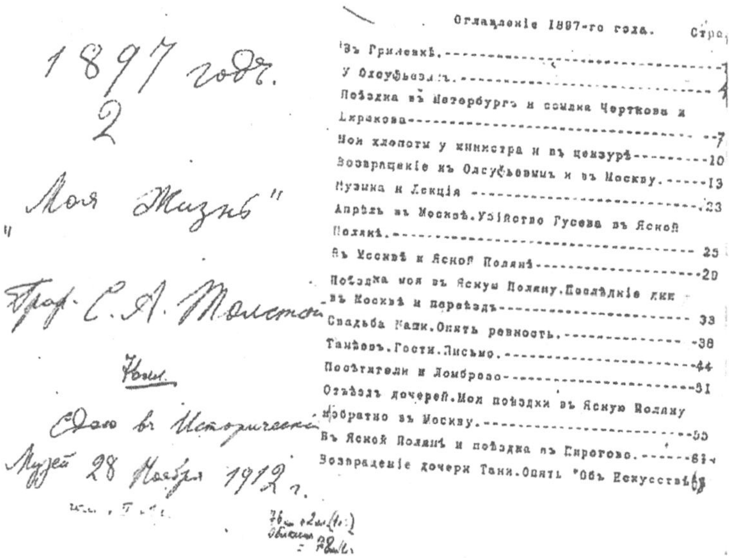

1897 годъ.
2
„Моя Жизнь"
Граф. С. А. Толстой
Отдано въ Исторический Музей 28 Ноября 1912 г.

Оглавленіе 1897-го года. Стр.

Illustration 38: Chapter outline for *My Life*,
showing the year 1897, with notations in SAT's own handwriting

Дневники и письмо.

Въ началѣ Октября я была опять въ Ясной Полянѣ, соскучившись въ долгой разлукѣ съ мужемъ. Поѣхалъ какъ то разъ Левъ Ник. верхомъ въ Тулу. Оставшись одна, я пошла въ его кабинетъ, тогда еще въ низу подъ сводами, и увидавъ, что вездѣ пыль и плохо убрана комната, я взяла щетку, полотенце я стала сама все убирать и чистить. Когда я двинула большой письменный столъ , откуда то упалъ ключъ отъ стола. Убравъ комнату, я отперла столъ и стала читать дневники Льва Никол. Право на это онъ мнѣ далъ разъ на-всегда, также, какъ и я ему. По мѣрѣ того какъ я читала, меня охватывалъ холодъ и ужасъ. Не вѣрилось во многихъ мѣстахъ, что это писалъ мой мужъ, человѣкъ котораго я любила больше всего на свѣтѣ, съ которымъ, казалось, мы жили столько лѣтъ одной жизнью, не измѣняя другъ другу. Сколько несправедливой злобы, сколько горькихъ мнѣ упрековъ. Какое мѣстами презрѣніе ко мнѣ. За что. А я и безъ того была такъ несчастна!

Перелиставъ дневники, я положила ихъ обратно въ столъ, заперла и положила ключъ на то мѣсто, гдѣ я предполагала онъ былъ спрятанъ. Я ничего не сказала мужу, но опять горько плакала и витосковала еще больше. Левъ Никол. внимательно всматривался въ меня и спрашивалъ что со мной? Тогда я рѣшилась написать ему письмо, которое перепишу въ эту книгу,

Illustration 39: SAT's typescript of the first page of a chapter from *My Life*, entitled "Diaries and a letter"

1901 годъ.

„Моя Жизнь"

Графини Софіи Андреевны

Толстой

Кончила писать въ 1916 году.

весной

Illustration 40: Notation by SAT at the end of *Moja zhizn'*: "The year 1901. My life. By Countess Sofia Andreevna Tolstaya. Finished writing, spring 1916."

Послесловие

Кончаю писать свои записки, и вероятно не придется их продолжить. Не имея никогда намеренья их писать, я не готовила материалов, а когда начала эти записки, материалы оказались скудны и даже мало интересны. Но за то без предвзятой подготовки, все здесь правдиво и искренно.

Дневников Льва Николаевича последних лет его жизни – я не имела в руках, они у дочери Саши. Есть мой дневник, Крымский 1901 и 1902 года; он может служить продолжением этих моих записок.

Illustration 41: SAT's Afterword [Posleslovie] (in computer transcription) to the whole of *My Life*

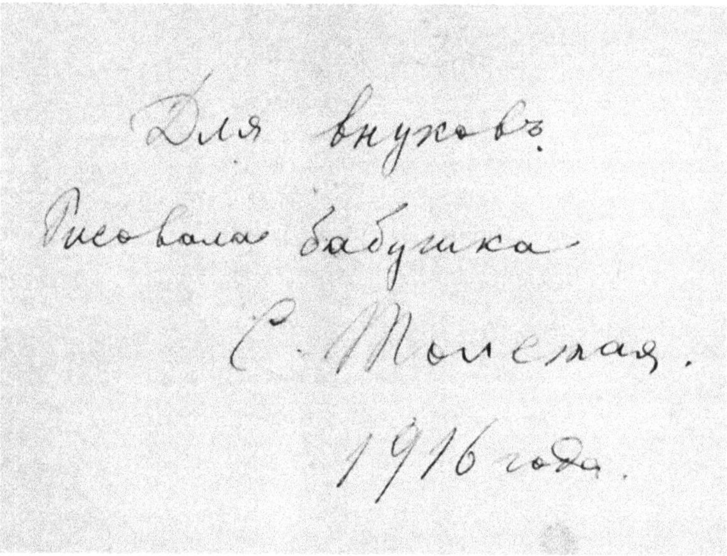
Для внуковъ.
Рисовала бабушка
С. Толстая.
1916 года.

Illustration 42: SAT's dedicatory message for her illustrations.
The message reads: "For [my] grandchildren.
Drawn by Grandmother S. Tolstaya, 1916."

Illustration 43: SAT's illustrations for her grandchildren, 1916

Illustration 44: Valentin Fëdorovich Bulgakov, LNT's last secretary, 1961

CHAPTER 4

Who is to blame?
(A novella)

PART I

CHAPTER 1

IT WAS A MARVELLOUS, CLEAR AND DELIGHTFUL DAY. A real feast of summer bloom. How beautiful and joyous appeared the clear, pale blue sky, the hot rays of the sun, the plethora of chattering, motley-coloured birds in all the luxuriant trees and flowering bushes! And, in the distance, the deep blue waters of the lake all glistening, reflecting the sky and the bright, vivacious, rich vegetation along its shores.

The same festive, blooming and vivid appearance was presented by two girls running from the lake along the path to a large white stone house. They both ran barefoot, carrying their shoes in their hands; the towels draped over their shoulders were wet, their hair unkempt. Their little pale feet, unaccustomed to treading directly on dew-laden grass, tripped timidly and lightly, almost trembling. The girls were laughing loudly.

"Careful, somebody might be watching," one of them said.

"So what, is that bad?" questioned the other, her eyes wide open in surprise. "Don't all the peasant women go barefoot?"

"But it's prickly and painful walking."

"Never mind, start running — it's easier!"

And the thin dark-eyed girl ran as fast as she could to the house. She soon found herself on the porch, breathless, red-faced and excited. Taking a look around, the girl suddenly remembered her surroundings; painfully embarrassed, she froze, rooted to the spot.

"What's with you, Anna?" asked her surprised mother sternly, as she looked her red-faced daughter up and down.

"Natasha and I were bathing and … and … we tried walking barefoot. We didn't know…" said Anna, trying to hide her feet.

Out of the corner of her eye she spied a man's hand reaching out to her. It belonged to a guest seated at the tea-table. She then looked into the man's eyes and, with a guilty smile, offered him her own hand.

"I was unaware you had come. Hello, Prince… Just a moment, I'll be right back."

And with that the young woman disappeared into the house. Another girl quickly followed suit without stopping.

The man who offered his hand to Anna was an old acquaintance of their mother's, Prince Prozorskij. He was about thirty-five years old and occasionally dropped by the Il'menev family on his way to or from his distant estate. He had known these 'children' since the day they were born. He loved the whole simple, delightful, family atmosphere of the entire household and would often find the growing young girls most appealing.

After the two sisters disappeared inside the house, Prozorskij continued to smile with delight for a long time. Travelling abroad, he hadn't visited the Il'menevs in quite a while and, as often happens, was unaware of the changes taking place as the girls matured. They were no longer little girls but had all at once (or so it seemed) turned into grown women.

Not realising the full picture, the prince was only vaguely aware of this. In his mind he still had the impression of Anna's pretty bare feet, her head tossed back, showing off her dark unkempt hair, her strong, lithe figure flitting past under her flowing, white morning dress.

"My God, how good it is here!" exclaimed the prince, his eyes still fixed on the door where the girls had gone in. He sensed within himself a hint of a young, uplifted spirit. "How joyful everything is, how bright!… Oh, youth!" he added with a sigh. "Our youth has gone, Ol'ga Pavlovna, but nobody can stop admiring it."

"Well, if we always had youth, we would never have appreciated it…" Ol'ga Pavlovna calmly reasoned. "D'you think they notice it or appreciate it? Not on your life!"

After chatting a while longer, she excused herself, saying that she had some household tasks to take care of, but that they would all meet for breakfast.

"Here are some newspapers, Prince, for you to take a look at in the meantime. There is an interesting article there about the riots in France."

Ol'ga Pavlovna left, and the two sisters soon returned. They had changed into dark-coloured, plain and simple dresses, combed their hair and presented an altogether prim and proper appearance.

"Too bad that you changed," said the prince. "You've become proper young ladies, but before, you were prettier, more natural."

"But this is more proper," said Natasha, as she poured herself a cup of coffee.

"Nothing but prejudice," Anna noted tersely. "What is proper depends on what you're accustomed to," she added, as she started to eat the berries, pecking at them from the saucer one by one, like a bird.

"Are you having fun?" asked the prince.

"Terribly!" Anna replied. "Natasha and I keep pretty busy. I am currently reading philosophy and am writing a story. Natasha says it's good; every evening I read to her what I wrote that morning."

"And what sort of philosophy are you reading?"

"Recently Dmitrij Ivanovich gave me some books by Büchner and Feuerbach. He says they are necessary for start of my education. And everything has become so much clearer! I realise that such unmistakable evidence could easily turn one into a materialist."

"And how old are you?"

"I'll soon be eighteen."

"Forget Büchner and Feuerbach, don't spoil your delicate soul that way. You aren't able to understand them, and you'll only get mixed up."

"By reading philosophy? That will never happen! On the contrary, I'm sure to come to terms with myself and my doubts. I've also read your articles, but they're difficult; I still can't fully understand them."

"And what is your story about?" enquired the prince, changing the subject.

"It's about how to love. You won't understand. Natasha here, well, she comprehends perfectly."

"It's not hard to understand," said Natasha, "but Anna, after all, is very sentimental. She dreams of a kind of love which must be pure and ideal, practically a prayer."

"But how to reconcile that with materialism, Anna Aleksandrovna?… Aha, I've got you there…"

"Oh, there's that butterfly — the one Misha was looking for to add to his collection," Anna suddenly cried. With her quick, strong legs, she leapt onto the porch railing in an attempt to catch a large dark-winged butterfly.

The sight of Anna's gracious figure made the prince blush. Jumping down from the porch railing, butterfly in hand, she flitted before him like a shadow.

"Let's go for a walk, a long walk, and take Misha with us," suggested Natasha.

All agreed and went to fetch their hats. Calling upon little Misha to join them, they decided to go visit Misha's wet-nurse in the neighbouring village.

The road through the fields was hot and dusty. Everyone felt lazy, and real conversation was fleeting.

Anna started walking ahead. Catching up with her, the prince said with a smile:

"How plain and simple everything is in your life! And no matter how often you try to ask them, you simply have no questions to ask — indeed, you can't have any. You yourself — with your youth, clarity and faith in life — you yourself are the answer to all doubts. God, how I envy you!"

"No, you need not envy. I'm actually full of doubts, and, besides... I am so immature," she added ruefully. "Since I learnt that everything in the world boils down to the motion and relation of atoms, I can't really tell if there is a God. You see, there's Dmitrij Ivanovich — you know, that student who comes to us from Sosnovka — he says that God is a fantasy, that there is no such thing as the will of God, that everything is governed by the laws of Nature... However, that's only the words of an unbeliever. Maybe, he's right, but I still can't understand everything. There are times when I really feel like praying — but to whom?"

"Don't you listen to anyone. Dmitrij Ivanovich will only confuse you, and that's bad," said Prozorskij, as he examined the delicate skin on Anna's temples, drawing attention to her pale blue veins.

Anna blushed.

"I don't deny that he confuses me. But he's trying so hard to educate me!"

"Misha! Misha! Where are you going?" Anna suddenly yelled out.

But it was already too late. Misha, whom they had forgotten, had not crossed the bridge like the others, but went a roundabout way, straight into a swamp, where he got bogged down up to his knees. The prince reached out to him with a stick and pulled him out.

But Misha was now wet all over. Natasha, who had been picking flowers a little ways away, came running and began to dry Misha off with grasses and handkerchiefs, all the while muttering angrily at him. Anna laughed. But to go any further was unthinkable; they had to return home.

That evening, Dmitrij Ivanovich — a neighbour, a pale, blond, bespectacled student with crude manners — arrived. Unembarrassed by anyone's presence, Dmitrij Ivanovich didn't leave Anna's side the whole evening. They sat together on the terrace porch, reading some sort of philosophical book, Dmitrij Ivanovich constantly interrupting with his own enthusiastic interpretation of Darwin's theory.

The prince was, perforce, left in the company of Ol'ga Pavlovna, who had shown up for tea. She kept looking askance at Anna and her companion. Natasha, too, was out of sorts and for some reason didn't feel like talking to the prince.

The prince left late that evening, saying that he would be sure to drop by the Il'menevs again on his way back from Petersburg to his estate. Bidding farewell, he gave Dmitrij Ivanovich an angry look and refrained, as though unintentionally, from offering him his hand.

"Yes, he's got youth on his side," thought the prince. As he left the Il'menevs' house, his gaze turned towards the black, starry sky, the darkened lake and the mysterious distant forest around its shores. It seemed to him that the whole world had been extinguished, that all happiness had been left far behind in the past, drowning in this mysterious night, and it terrified him.

"This girl, who only recently was a child whom I carried in my arms, I... No, that's not possible!" His breath failed him.

"Not possible! What does it mean? Again ... for the umpteenth time ... everything's the same! But this is not the same, it's something new!" And once again he saw Anna before him, and in his imagination he mentally undressed her slender legs along with her curvaceous, powerful, virginal waist.

"Ah, those eyes! Dark as night, limpid, honest... What kind of a creature are you? Something quite unique. But when did all this happen? Why do I suddenly feel that I cannot live without those limpid eyes, without that pure, delightful, and precious look in her eyes? Indeed, it seems only recently I was looking at these girls calmly and joyously... But now? All at once I see that she is a woman, that there is nobody beside her, and it is my duty (in fact, I can't do otherwise) to possess this child..."

Blood rushed to the prince's head. He closed his eyes to remember Anna more clearly. His carriage was moving, jolting, along the bumpy country road — a ride which made him sleepy, increasing his feeling of languor and his need of pleasure on this marvellous summer night.

CHAPTER 2

The following day the two sisters were seated at a table in a bright, spacious upstairs room. Natasha was sewing while Anna read aloud from her story, her voice full of excitement. The large Italian window was wide open, the air outside was noisy and tense; frogs were croaking by the lake, nightingales were trilling in the garden, and peasants' voices could be heard singing in the nearby village. Anna's voice quivered slightly as she read.

"In a small, sparsely furnished room sat a young woman, eagerly sewing something large and white. She occasionally glanced out the window and sighed, as she listened — through the song of the bird in a cage above her head — to the footsteps along the sidewalk outside. The young woman had recently married and was waiting for her husband to return from classes. Both were poor, both worked, but..."

"And that's your ideal, Anna?" her sister interrupted. "Oh, don't go so wrong! After all, you can't live just with flowers and birds, let alone poverty! Life also has its prose elements: diseases, kitchen work, deficiencies, quarrels... On these you are intentionally silent — in both your life and your story."

"There should be nothing of that sort in there, at least nothing that should attract attention. One ought to live one's life purely spiritually; everything else is by the way. I feel that I am capable of reaching such a spiritual plane that I shan't want to eat ever again. After all, is not a piece of bread sufficient for life? Yes? Well, that will be given. You know, Natasha, it sometimes seems to me that the more I run, the stronger my feet are planted in the earth, and the next moment I'll be flying. That's the way it is with my soul, too; yes, especially my soul, it should always be ready to fly, far away, to infinity… That's what I know and how I feel! And for some reason nobody understands that!"

"But how can one live an unearthly life on the Earth?" asked Natasha. "You were saying just yesterday how important it is to get married. Well, if you're married with children and are concerned with household cares, you won't get very far on a handout of bread and you'll certainly never fly."

Anna thought for a moment.

"True, if you look at marriage the usual way, it's better not to get married at all. First of all, you need love, and this love must be higher and more ideal than anything earthly… I can't describe it, I can only feel it…"

"That's enough, Anna. Let's go downstairs. Dmitrij Ivanovich has already come. Anna, do you love him?"

"I dunno. I love talking with him, but when I shake his hand to say good night, he has a particular way of squeezing it, and his hand is so sweaty — all at once he seems so repulsive! But I think he has a good understanding of everything, he is educated and smart, and he has his ideals."

The sisters went downstairs. There was nobody on the porch except Dmitrij Ivanovich and Misha's teacher. They were talking about university regulations and drinking tea. Anna asked Dmitrij Ivanovich whether he had brought her anything special to read.

"What do you call *special*?" he asked, and pulled out of his pocket a book of Tjutchev's verse. "Here's something I happen to have in my pocket," he said.

Anna opened it and began to leaf through it.

"I know this book. And how I love his poetry! *Human tears*," she read. "I know these poems by heart. 'You're pouring forth invisible and inexhaustible.' Yes, they are tears most painful. I'll be shedding a lot of those tears in my lifetime."

"But it always seems to me that you, in particular, don't have to shed them. You are always so bright and cheerful. Only you're too much of a dreamer, Anna Aleksandrovna. That won't get you by."

"And what will, if I may ask?"

"You have to get used to living more with social and earthly interests in mind, you have to participate in all mankind's affairs, and not bother with your own human weaknesses."

"And what do I need to do for that?"

"At the very least, don't stay in the clouds, but act. Try it, Anna Aleksandrovna, try to live a healthier life, without prejudice and — most importantly — without pathetic religious falsehoods."

"Well, I could try it," Anna responded with a tinge of sadness. "But what do you mean by *pathetic religious falsehoods*? Don't you have any religion?… Can you live without it?… Tell me, do you believe in God?"

Dmitrij Ivanovich gave her a mocking and condescending smile.

"Why are you so fond of the word *God*?"

"It's not the word I need, but the *idea* of Deity. And I am not going to surrender this idea, d'you hear?…" Anna suddenly exclaimed with fervour. "If there is no God, there is no *me* either, there is nothing, nothing… No life!…"

Anna blushed, her eyes glistened, her voice quivered with tears; she turned away and fell silent. Dmitrij Ivanovich once more tried an ironic smile, but when he looked at Anna, he felt uneasy and lowered his eyes.

Night came. The moon had risen a long time ago and was now illuminating the meadow by the lake, near the house. The contours of the dark green trees surrounding the meadow stood out even darker against the bright moonlit sky. This light shining out of the darkness was also alluring and, after everyone had gone to bed, Anna stood for a long time on the terrace, still looking at this meadow. All this mental chaos which had obsessed her from her reading of philosophical books and conversations with Dmitrij Ivanovich, began, as it were, to explain itself, and gradually left her mind.

A rustling noise from the garden made her shudder. Dmitrij Ivanovich was approaching from the garden. He was coming from the annexe (where Misha's teacher lived) on his way home through the garden. However, upon seeing Anna, he went up to the terrace and approached her. She was annoyed that he interrupted her mood and silently, paying no attention to him, she continued to gaze at the bright meadow and the depths of the lake beyond.

"What an inspiring look you had when you were talking about God, Anna Aleksandrovna!"

Anna, angered, did not say a word.

"Anna Aleksandrovna, how much fire and energy you have within you! You could turn into a beautiful, energetic woman, if only you could trust an educated person, if only you submitted to his influence, if only you could fall in love with him…"

Dmitrij Ivanovich quietly crept close to Anna and unexpectedly kissed her hand.

What happened at that moment with Anna he could in no way foresee. This thin and tender girl suddenly turned into one of the Furies. Her dark eyes cast such a spate of angry lightning at Dmitrij Ivanovich that he froze on the spot.

She pulled her hand away, turning her palm upward in disgust, and wiping it on her dress.

"How dare you!" she exclaimed. "Phew, how horrid! I *de...spise* you!"

Shame, despair, anger over the violation of her prayerful, contemplative mood, disgust and pride — all this arose in her, and all at the same time. She ran straight to her mother's bedroom and threw herself onto the settee, sobbing loudly.

Ol'ga Pavlovna, who was preparing for bed, was terribly frightened.

"What happened? What's the matter with you?"

"Mamà, how dare he! Just now on the terrace Dmitrij Ivanovich kissed my hand. What a horrid thing to do!"

Still snivelling, Anna took a bottle of eau-de-cologne from the dresser and began to wipe the spot where Dmitrij Ivanovich had kissed her hand.

"Where was it you saw him?"

"He ... no, I was on the terrace, I was looking at the moon, he approached me, I got irritated, he said something, but I wanted to be alone. Then all of a sudden he grabbed my hand and kissed it." Anna gave a shudder and once again ran her thin hand over her dress.

"Well, it's your own fault," muttered Ol'ga Pavlovna. "What a strange thing for a girl to stay out on the terrace when everybody else is sleeping! Now calm down," she went on, softening her voice. "I'll write Dmitrij Ivanovich a note and ask him to stop coming over."

"Please do, Mamà!"

"All right then, go to bed. I really didn't like your conversations. Good night! Your sister went to bed quite a while ago."

It took a long time for Anna to calm down. After she made her way upstairs, she sat for a long time in silence at her dressing table, soothing her turbulent heart. Finally, she opened her diary and began to write:

"Yes, this love was a big mistake, a trick of my imagination. What do I want? What am I unhappy about? Why is my soul so torn apart? Either my youth is demanding more life when there is no real life, or maybe I am simply feeling sorry for all who are unhappy. And all happy people are selfish. Where does people's happiness come from? From fate?... But what is fate? A law of Nature, the movement of the universe, the will of God? God's will, yes, undoubtedly. It's good to pray to God! Or is prayer only a toy for those who are bitter in spirit? But I can't break it. I can't admit that everything in the world is but the motion of atoms, that I am good or evil only because of good or bad weather, that people are moral because their blood circulates more slowly, making them passionless, that a certain combination of material particles is turning people and their fate upside down... My God, my head is filled with chaos! Everything in the world is so mysterious! How pitiful I am, how immature, powerless and confused... My God, help me, enlighten me!..."

Anna tossed her diary into a drawer. She then got down on her knees and prayed for a long time. She hadn't done this for quite a while. People experience such a prayerful state either in moments of great sorrow or in moments of great moral growth. So it was with Anna.

When she finally rose to her feet, exhausted and mentally beaten, she felt that some kind of transformation had taken place within herself and that everything would be different from now on.

She lay down on the bed. Undoing the pink ribbons of her white muslin bedcurtains, she let them fall around her.

Everything at once became still; not a sound could be heard from the window. The pale summer sky looked sad; it was illuminated in the west only by the waning moon, in the east — by the not-yet-risen sun.

Anna looked out the window, trembling nervously, and fell into an uneasy sleep.

CHAPTER 3

For Anna, a brand-new chapter of her maiden life had silently begun. It was as though she had cast off all quests and doubts, along with the questions and mental burdens which she had attached to life. Youth had claimed its own. The carefree, cheerful Anna began to look God's world in the eye with such bold transparency, as though she had discovered therein some new delightful aspects previously hidden from view.

"Natasha, I am putting everything in order now," she told her sister one day as she was gathering her art tools together. "While it is still light, I want to portray the whole autumn in oils and work at it every day. I'll take a walk after lunch, do some reading and write in my diary. When you start teaching school, I'll help you."

"Well, I don't believe that. I know *your* kind of help: you'll run in for five minutes, have a little chat, read something useless — and that's it."

"Oh, Natasha, you believe all you need is arithmetic. But in my opinion, moral development is an even greater need."

"Well, that is something neither you nor I will achieve in a few weeks. After all, we have only two months left before we leave for Moscow. God willing, we'll start with the ABCs, and there won't be any chance to think about development."

"If only we could stay here for the whole winter!"

"You've got to be kidding! No way. Mamà is restless, and Misha is about to enter grammar school."

"And when does your school start?" asked Anna.

"The older girls will be coming tomorrow evening, and I promised to read something to them. I'll be opening the school starting Monday. I only have to get it started, make sure everything is in order, and then hand it over to the teacher."

"I'd better get going while it's still light," and then Anna picked up a small canvas, a box of paints and an umbrella, walked out into the garden and headed for the lake. She chose a spot which she had long noted as especially picturesque, stuck her umbrella in the ground and started to work. She painted easily and cheerfully: the patch of blue sky among the hanging tree branches turned out so well that Anna herself started admiring her picture. She kept moving her hand nervously from the palette to the canvas and back and got so carried away with her work that she did not notice Prince Prozorskij approaching from behind. He had stopped to visit the Il'menevs on his way back from Petersburg.

"So, I found you here," he greeted Anna. "Oh, how well you paint! How talented you are, I hadn't realised."

"Really? I plan on doing a lot of work. But if *you* say so, so much the better. After all, you understand everything," added Anna, as she trustingly and tenderly kept looking into the eyes of the prince. She was accustomed to treating him that way ever since her childhood, but without realising why.

Probably because everyone in the house — beginning with the old nanny, Ol'ga Pavlovna, and Misha, — everyone was accustomed to showing love to the prince who had been so long a familiar and regular visitor to the Il'menev family. He had known Ol'ga Pavlovna ever since childhood; they were neighbours. And when Ol'ga Pavlovna got married and received by way of a dowry the very estate where she had lived in her youth, the prince continued to visit her occasionally. Then she became a widow and for a long time did not return to her estate. For several years the prince did not see her, nor did he meet with her until the girls were all grown up and Ol'ga Pavlovna's hair started turning grey.

Prince Prozorskij was not so much handsome as he was elegant and refined. His broad education and significant personal wealth opened doors for him everywhere. He travelled a lot, and after leading a wild and fun-filled youth, he became tired of it all. He ended up settling in the country, studying philosophy and imagining himself to be a deep thinker. This was his weakness. He wrote articles, and it seemed to many that he was very clever indeed.

Only the keenest scholars discerned that in essence the prince's philosophy was rather pitiful and even ridiculous. The articles he wrote and published in journals were completely unoriginal; they were simply a regurgitation of old, outmoded themes and thoughts of a host of ancient and modern thinkers. The regurgitation was done so expertly that the majority of readers even reacted to them with a degree of enthusiasm — a minor success which brought the prince no end of pleasure.

But this was not the reason Anna treated Prince Prozorskij with trust and tenderness.

Anna simply loved in him his inherent sympathetic kindness — the product of his considerable success in the world. It was a quality the prince showed to all women and which made him attractive to them all. Natasha and Anna also fell under this spell of adoration, and the prince's visits were celebrated by the whole family. He was able, as they said jokingly, to *raise* interesting questions, to carry on the most engaging conversations; he was able to give timely help to Ol'ga Pavlovna in the game of patience; he taught Misha how to assemble collections of butterflies and bugs; he joked with the old nanny and gave generous tips to the servants.

'Have you been in the house yet, Prince?" asked Anna.

"I was, I saw everyone and was looking for you. They directed me here. After all, without you everything in the house would be dark and boring, like a lantern without a flame."

"D'you really think so? What have I to offer?…" she asked with a blush. It seemed to bring her such amazing happiness that this attractive prince, who was beloved by everyone, was talking about *her*, a mere girl whom he had known as a child. And she remembered what a bad, mischievous, lazy and tactless child she had been. She also remembered how the prince used to hold her back so carefully and delicately in situations where her natural vivaciousness and decisiveness verged on the extreme. Anna always thought that he despised *her* while he approved of Natasha. For some reason, when today he suddenly praised her painting and claimed he was bored without her, her heart was filled with unexpected joy.

Anna continued to paint. She couldn't take her eyes off the marvellous weeping birch tree bending over the lake. Its white trunk looked unnatural on her canvas but turned out surprisingly well against the background of the fresh autumn colours. But she could feel the prince staring at her. Her hand trembled, and her heart beat faster.

"That's enough, I can't do anymore," Anna said.

"Why is it I feel so emotional? Surely, it's because he praised me!" she thought.

It began to get dark, the cool night air gradually set in. Anna folded her umbrella, and collected her things, which the prince at once took out of her hands, and both headed to the house.

The prince walked a few paces behind, his face intense. With an air of a connoisseur of women, he admired her strong, easy gait — an inevitable sign of a healthy inner constitution. He admired the surprising tilt of her small head on her delicate, round neck, whose every turn was so picturesque and gracious, as well as her elegant waist, girdled by a ribbon. The wind blew back her ribbons along with her dress which constantly hugged her legs; her exquisite dark hair with its barely perceptible golden sheen made her face and neck look even more pale and tender.

As they approached the house, Anna turned and looked at the prince. She was disturbed by his appearance.

"What's the matter with him?" she thought. "He just praised me so kindly, and now his eyes are completely different, even beastly… What for?"

Indeed, what for? The only thing she was guilty of was that her waist, her hair, her youth, her exquisitely sewn dress and slender legs — all this was an arousing source of temptation for this confirmed bachelor — a temptation so foreign to Anna's child-like innocence. He could feel in this girl a rare type of woman who, underneath her innocent, child-like manner, betrayed all the hallmarks of a fervent, complex, artistic and passionate feminine nature. And even though, in contrast to this nature, the ideals of religion and chastity were firmly (albeit unconsciously) implanted in her soul, the prince did not appreciate these latter qualities, but felt the former ones with his whole being. As a result, he presented an almost animal appearance, which proved so disturbing and frightening to Anna.

CHAPTER 4

Although the prince was supposed to return home and even said that he was in a hurry to see his mother, he could not force himself to leave. Instead, he began to make daily visits to the Il'menevs. He pretended that he had some business in the nearby district town and asked Ol'ga Pavlovna's permission to come and take a break from his affairs in her dear family. Everyone was happy to see their beloved guest, and the prince started coming every day.

He had a distinct feeling that for him there was no turning back. His passion for Anna was growing stronger day by day and so obsessed him that he could not sleep nights, was tormented with doubts and, most of all, was afraid that his proposal to her would be met with surprise instead of love.

Staying in a dingy room in the district town, he was bored and tormented. He wrote letters to Anna. He carried them around in his pocket but could not decide what to do with them. This went on for a fortnight.

In the meantime, Anna continued to lead her carefree, cheerful life; she kept busy in her own way. What could be more enjoyable for a young lady than this leisure time, which smart, sensible girls know how to use in various ways effectively, but which disordered ones waste, and simply end up sharpening their nervous system.

Besides busying herself with painting, Anna (together with the gardener and the servant girls), planted exotic bushes and trees that she had ordered and wished to acclimatise. She wrote in her diary, taught music to Misha, and herself practised some rather difficult Bach fugues. In addition, she often ran over to the village, Florinskij's book of cures in hand, to visit sick peasants. She devoted her undivided attention and strength to this endeavour, in an effort to at least partially compensate for her ignorance and inexperience in medical matters.

Every day proved fruitful and joyful. Moreover, the prince's constant presence, along with the troubling awareness that he was romantically attracted to her, gave Anna an added energy and interest in everything. The days when he, feeling guilty about his frequent visits, did not come to the Il'menevs, seemed to her unfulfilled, even boring, and every activity somehow lost its significance. She would eagerly wait for him to tell him about everything that had happened to her in his absence; she enthusiastically introduced him to her own interests, all the while mistaking his excitement for genuine compassion, not realising that he was simply reacting to her external appearance and youth.

Natasha opened her school and held evening readings for groups of peasant girls. She gave her whole effort to this activity, repressing her envy over Prozorskij's preference for her sister, given that she loved the prince as much as anyone else in the family. She was surprised at the prince's enthusiasm for life and Anna's activities, which she herself derided as useless.

It was Sunday. In the little annexe used by the school, about twelve peasant girls sat at a simple wooden table. Some of them seriously and carefully read aloud syllable by syllable as they followed the printed text with their fingers, while others diligently and beautifully copied down individual words, sounding them out loud as they wrote. Sitting beside Natasha, tall and gorgeous Ljubasha confidently read a story from peasant life. The atmosphere in this small, bright room was cozy and inviting, although everyone looked rather bored and exhausted. Natasha conducted her classes in good conscience but was still unable to infuse her work with the animation it needed.

The door opened quietly, and in walked Anna. She carefully made her way to a corner of the room, sat down and began to listen. The prince had been absent all day. Anna missed him sorely, though she couldn't bring herself to admit it. There was a copy of the Gospels lying on the table; she picked it up and began to open it at random, seeking answers to a multitude of questions.

Going over her imagined replies, she eventually got carried away with perusing the sacred book that aimed to offer blanket solutions to the most complex doubts about life.

All of a sudden she got the desire to find out just where these girls were in their spiritual development. At this point she remembered the prince's story about how peasants responded to questions about the Holy Trinity, and she asked:

"Tell me, girls, who comprises the Holy Trinity?"

Ljubasha answered forthrightly:

"The Lord God, the Mother of God, and Saint Nicholas."

"Look what she is saying," the quiet, serious Marfa interrupted. "The Trinity means: God the Father, God the Son and the Mother of God."

"And the Holy Spirit," Natasha corrected sternly.

"And have you read the Gospels?" asked Anna.

"We've heard them in church. And then our teacher, Mistress Natalja Aleksandrovna, read to us last year during Passion Week about the sufferings of Christ."

"Well, now I am going to read to you about Christ's teachings."

Anna found her favourite passage and began reading the Beatitudes and the Sermon on the Mount. Her sonorous, distinct voice, with its unique sensitivity, imparted a special expression to what more than anything else touched human hearts. When she finished the chapter, she began to explain it.

The peasant girls made a circle around her. Even though some of them had trouble understanding her, it was Anna's religious enthusiasm that got her message across to her naïve listeners.

"More, more!" they begged.

Next, Anna read to them about Peter's denial, the prayer in the Garden of Gethsemane and Judas's betrayal. She showed pictures and gave explanations, all excited herself. Many of the girls wept. Quietly the thoughtful Marfa grasped Anna's hand and held it in hers; the bold and fervent Ljubasha put her arm around Anna's delicate little neck and kissed her noisily on the lips.

In the meantime, from the porch of the manor house could be heard the sound of an approaching carriage. Anna jumped up, her face full of joy.

"It's the prince," announced Natasha. "Well, go to him, you're not doing much good to us here. I thought he might not even come."

"What's the matter with you?" asked Natasha, looking at her excited sister.

"*Je crains d'aimer le prince,*" Anna muttered quickly. She clasped her hand to her breast, as though wishing to stop the beating of her heart and fled out of the room.

All excited, with a quick and light step, she ran into the spacious hallway, where the prince was taking off his coat. On looking at her, he was struck by the beauty of this energetic girl, her face full of fresh inspiration from what she had just experienced. Her dark eyes sparkled, she looked at him joyfully and tenderly, and for the first time he felt that she was happy to see him, and that it was even possible that she reciprocated his love. But at the same time he could not help feeling that this magnificent creature, which he had only recently got to know so well — one with a poetic and pure approach to life and with a religious bent and elevated ideals — would eventually come crashing down against his selfish, fleshly love and his past lifestyle.

"All the same, there's no other way, and so be it," a voice whispered to him, a voice that was always ready to tempt people who thought only about themselves and cherished their own happiness and pleasures.

"Mine, mine…" the prince instinctively mused as he kissed Anna's hand.

That evening, everything was supposed to happen the way he wanted. This was something he felt himself, and Anna felt it too. Some sort of common awkward tension prevailed; they were both waiting for a solution to what had lately been troubling the whole family.

They took tea in the dining room before going their separate ways. Misha went to bed early, Natasha sat down to correct her pupils' notebooks. Ol'ga

Pavlovna claimed her usual seat — on the sofa in a corner of the drawing-room, — played a game of patience and knitted one of her countless blankets intended for various relatives and friends.

The prince asked Anna to play something on the piano and followed her into the salon.

"I don't feel like playing right now," she said, "I'm very tired today."

"Never mind, please just play anything." The prince was very excited and wanted some time to think. "Look, here are some preludes by Chopin, which you perform so well. Chopin was better than anyone else at infusing music with most delicate human feelings."

Anna began playing — almost mechanically. She could feel the prince's excitement. The prince leaned against the wall, tossing back his handsome mane of hair. Apparently, he was experiencing some terrible inner turmoil, but he finally mustered up the courage to speak quietly, albeit with constant pauses:

"Anna, I need to talk with you. I've being meaning to for some time, but it's so hard!" Prozorskij paused. "Has it ever crossed your mind that this old family friend could see you as anything other than a dear, sweet little girl?…" The prince's voice broke off. Anna gave a little shudder. "And to feel," he continued after the pause, "that there is nothing in life for him apart from this girl, no happiness — nothing?"

By this time Anna was trembling all over. Her delicate, cold fingers refused to obey her will, and Chopin's prelude broke off.

"Play, play!" the prince pleaded.

Anna's fingers continued to glide quietly (though nervously) over the keys, and once again Chopin's sorrowful melody could be heard.

"See, Anna, I'm not demanding anything more from you. It's just that I love you more than anyone else can in the world. Perhaps it seems funny to you to see your old friend bowing at your youthful feet. But it's not that funny to me! I have been tormenting myself all this time and, still, I would ask just one thing of you: if you feel you won't be able to love me when you are my wife, don't say anything to me, just cast me aside. Better to go through this suffering now than when you are my wife."

The prince fell silent. He looked pale and his lips slightly trembled. Yes, this was *love* — a love quite unlike the spontaneous intrigues the prince was accustomed to. In this love he felt a kind of purgatory in which all the filth of his previous sins was forgotten. And the prince rejoiced at that, though at the same time it terrified him.

Anna stopped playing. She looked at the prince, paused to think for a moment, but all at once she determinedly rose to her feet, straightened up and walked over to him.

"Yes, I shall love you when I am your wife," she replied simply and quickly, offering the prince her hand and looking him naïvely and tenderly straight in the eye. The prince realised that she was unable to lie, she was incapable of it, and that this truthful girl would certainly and simply keep her word that she gave him at that moment.

Prozorskij grasped her hands and began to kiss them.

"D'you mean it?! D'you really mean it?!" he exclaimed. She did not withdraw her hands, but calmly and joyfully watched his passionate kisses, though her face betrayed not a shadow of excitement in response to his unrestrained passion.

That night, following this important turn of events, Anna lay in bed, picturing her whole future life. There was no fear or doubt that she might somehow be unhappy with this familiar, kind, compassionate friend, who was so clever and educated, handsome and refined and, moreover, was so in love with her. She was happy to participate in his life. Indeed, she was enthusiastically ready to give her all in aid of his undertakings, which she imagined to be noble, helpful and perfect in all aspects. This helped her fall asleep with a calm, happy smile on her face.

CHAPTER 5

The next morning Anna told her mother and sister about the prince's proposal. Everyone had been expecting it and gave it its due. Ol'ga Pavlovna was concerned about her daughter's trousseau and at once set off for Moscow to get it ready. She told Anna that in five days she would take her to Moscow to try on everything that needed to be sewn.

Anna attempted to protest and begged to be spared this torment. But Ol'ga Pavlovna flew into such a state of emotion that Anna was forced to yield and promised to obey.

The prince stayed by Anna for days on end. The whole time he was terribly excited, anxious to make wedding plans, saying that no dowry was necessary. When he found himself alone with Anna, his excitement reached such a point that he could not think of what to say, silently kissing her hands and often paying no heed to her words. Several times Anna attempted to tell him about her past life and personal interests, about how hard it was to teach Misha music (as he had no ear for it), about how she had cured a little deaf girl, or how she had suddenly grasped Shakespeare and fallen in love with him — but each time the prince reacted with an air of indifference. Only one thing mattered to him: whether she really loved him and how soon the wedding would be.

Friends, relatives and neighbours arrived to offer Anna their congratulations, which she proudly and happily accepted. Never, not even for a moment, did she doubt that her happiness would be lasting.

Once, however, she received an inadvertent but irreparable blow which ruined her state of joy.

One of those congratulating Anna was a neighbour, an elderly landowner, who for some reason had no love for the prince. In conversation with Ol'ga Pavlovna, she mysteriously told her in Anna's presence (and in rather vulgar terms) that the prince was a real ladies' man, and along with this whispered something in Ol'ga Pavlovna's ear. Ol'ga Pavlovna was obviously embarrassed but said with a wave of her hand: "Well, they're all like that before marriage!"

Anna had never imagined that the prince, who was thirty-five years old, could have loved someone else before. She was terribly embarrassed, and tears ran down her cheeks. She fled to her room and sat silently by the window for a long time, trying to calm herself down.

The prince came in and quietly bent over her. She turned to face him. Taking his hand, she sat him down beside her.

"Anna, why are you so gloomy today? What's the matter with you?" asked the prince.

"I really need to talk with you. Tell me the truth, my prince, the honest truth. Before me, were there many that you loved? How many?"

Tears could be heard in her voice.

"Why are you asking me this, Anna? You are only torturing yourself and me. Of course, I can't start married life with the purity I would have liked. You see, Anna, I'm already so old, and I can't correct the past," he added with a tinge of regret. "I can only guarantee the future. But what happened in the past was not love — I can assure you that I have never loved in *that* way. This is something entirely new, unexpected, beautiful. It's something I had never imagined before and dared not even dream about."

She looked at him attentively, as though asking whether it were really true, and gave a shudder.

Prozorskij noticed this trembling, which he understood all too well, and moved closer to her. She withdrew a little, but the prince grasped her hands and started to kiss them passionately.

"You love me, Anna, don't you?"

"Yes, yes," she quietly answered.

The prince carefully bent even closer to her face. For the first time he kissed her on her lips.

Anna did not move, she was dumbfounded. A strong feeling of passion that she had not known before came over her whole body and made her feel all feverish. In her tormented imagination she pictured a whole array of different women whom *he* had loved. All at once she felt like taking his whole being into her embrace and shouting: "Don't you dare love anyone but me!" Her head was spinning, she shook feverishly all over, not understanding what was happening to her.

But the prince understood what was happening with her and smiled. He let go of her delicate, trembling hands and stepped away from her.

Anna remained seated a few more seconds, her head lowered. Sternly and calmly she said:

"You can go now, I'll be there in a moment."

When she came down to dinner, she lazily and sorrowfully took her seat, but did not touch her food. After dinner everyone went to a neighbouring farm for a carriage ride. All evening Anna avoided conversing with the prince. She fled deep into the woods, gathering fresh late-blooming flowers and breathing in the cool, refreshing air.

"How good and relaxing it is here!" she involuntarily thought. "But something is weighing heavy on my heart! If only I could forget and forget right away!"

Two days later, Anna's mother took her to Moscow to try on the trousseau. Indifferent to everything, she resigned herself to doing anything that was asked of her. She was not interested in dresses or pretty things or her fiancé's gifts. Her mother was seriously concerned, as her daughter looked rather grave and pale and was not eating anything. Her whole time in Moscow Anna was very impatient to return home. She needed the prince's presence; it was only around him that she felt even a spark of liveliness.

But they had switched roles. Now it was *he* that was talkative, tender and gentle with her. It seemed as though he were genuinely protecting her and endeavouring to calm her nerves. She sat silently beside him, listening to him tell about his travels and about life in other countries where he had gone to live, either on military duty or for his own pleasure. His voice had a calming effect, making her bend her whole will to her beloved.

On occasion, blushing and excited, Anna demanded that he tell her about his previous attractions. He avoided answering her, seeing how troubling these questions were for her, patching things over with tender words and generalities. But she kept coming back to the same thing again. These conversations aroused in her the kind of feeling which occurs when one first treats a pain in one's forehead or teeth by pressing firmly on the locus of the pain, whereby the new pain seems to alleviate the old one and makes one forget it momentarily.

This is how it was with Anna; she could not get rid of this pain the whole time up until her wedding day.

CHAPTER 6

At long last the wedding date was fixed. Anna would remember the whole day as in a dream. The prince's relations gathered, along with Anna's own extended family. A group of girlfriends helped her put on her wedding gown; Natasha and Ol'ga Pavlovna wept as they added flowers and a veil.

Ushers passed by with carnations in their buttonholes. Then came a long line of carriages, each pulled by a team of three or four horses, all decorated with multicoloured ribbons; the drivers had on their best suits. Anna was companioned by Misha, all dressed up in a white sailor's suit and holding an icon in his hands, along with her godmother (Ol'ga Pavlovna's aunt, an elderly lady-in-waiting), who had come from St. Petersburg just to attend the wedding.

The church was filled with a crowd of people. Out of the corner of her eye, she caught sight of Ljubasha, Marfa and all the familiar faces from their village. She remained unmoved by the wedding ceremony itself — her face stayed cold-looking, even stone-like.

In the house, the tables in the great hall were decorated with flowers and fruit. Several unfamiliar footmen were in attendance.

When Ol'ga Pavlovna blessed her daughter immediately before the actual wedding ceremony, Anna all of a sudden woke up momentarily and realised that something in her life was being torn apart; a chapter in her earthly existence that had lasted from the day she was born was coming to an end today, this very moment. Suddenly her sobbing reached her throat. She threw herself around her mother's neck and burst out, repeating stammeringly: "Farewell, dear Mamà, farewell! I have been so happy at home! Mamà, thank you for everything!... Don't cry, oh, my God, please don't cry! After all, you're happy, aren't you?..."

Finally it was all over. The couple's trunks had been loaded into a new large carriage called a *dormeuse*. The prince's personal servant had already taken his seat next to the coachman. Anna had changed into travelling clothes. She was about to get into the carriage together with her husband, when all at once she again heard her mother's cry of sorrow. She also heard them leading away her snivelling brother Misha. The door clapped shut, and the carriage started off.

It was September. A light rain was falling. The team of six fine horses which the prince had ordered from his estate noisily splashed through the puddles on the wide country road; the side lamps were reflected in the muddy water; it was damp and dark. After the brightly lit house, full of guests and dear familiar faces, this transition to the darkness of the night and the silence of the desolate countryside seemed particularly sharp. Anna sat in a corner of the *dormeuse*, quietly weeping.

The prince grasped hold of Anna's hand and kissed it.

"I am truly sorry, my friend, that our marriage has caused you so much sorrow," he said.

"Can't you, sir, imagine how painful it is to leave my whole family behind?"

"Why 'sir'? You don't love me; I'm still a stranger to you, my friend."

"I will get used to not saying 'sir' eventually, but for now it still sounds so unnatural!"

"At least, tell me if you love me..." the prince repeated, hugging Anna closer to him in the darkness of the *dormeuse* and passionately kissing her cold, tender cheeks.

"I think I do love you," Anna meekly replied and again remembered her mother, Misha's tears, her and her sister's room, along with all the poetry of her maiden life. She also remembered that in a few hours she would be calling a new place home, and this would be forever.

Suddenly she felt the prince tenderly embracing her. He cuddled up so close to her that she could not help noticing his unnaturally excited face up against hers. Not only that, but she could sense his intermittent, warm breathing with its odour of tobacco and spirits. Frightened and submissive, Anna leant her head back, closed her eyes and shrank into the furthest corner of the *dormeuse*. The prince embraced her and passionately kissed her.

"Yes, all that is how it is supposed to be, exactly," she thought. "Mamà said that I must be yielding and not be surprised at anything… Well, so be it… But… Oh, my God, how frightening and … how shameful, how shameful!…"

The carriage drove on. It was sixty versts to the prince's estate. At the halfway point, fresh horses were waiting for them, and they were obliged to make a temporary stop, as the prince had previously arranged, in an empty annexe of an uninhabited estate.

When they opened the carriage door for her, Anna quickly jumped out and immediately stepped into a puddle. She ran onto the unfamiliar porch, and then through an open door into a spacious, brightly lit room. Taking off her raincoat, she squatted down on the sofa, tucking her legs beneath her. She was shaking all over as she looked at the table already set with a samovar, the blazing hearth and all the furniture the room contained.

"Why are you so frightened?" said the prince, kissing her. "Make some tea, darling."

"Of course, right away," Anna replied, as though coming out of a stupor and lifting up her head, which was then hanging in shame.

"Why do I suddenly feel so strange and awkward with him?" she thought.

"But how hard it is for me to see that she still fears me so much," thought the prince. "What will be next? After all, this is the start of our glorious, celebrated honeymoon! It seems all I can get from her is fear and sad obedience — nothing more?…"

And nothing more did he get. Anna, still relatively a girl, was actually abused; she was not yet ready for marriage. Her feminine passion, momentarily awakened in a fit of jealousy, fell asleep again, pressured by shame and her protest against the prince's fleshly love. There remained only fatigue, depression, shame and fear.

Anna was aware of her husband's discomfort but did not know how to help him. She was submissive — but that was all.

It was impossible to go on with their travel; besides, the prince was not up to it. Heavy rain, darkness, bad roads — all of this prevented the newlyweds from continuing their journey and they were obliged to spend the night in this strange house.

CHAPTER 7

The next morning the newlyweds arrived at the prince's estate. His elderly mother greeted them with an icon, along with the traditional bread and salt. Anna was immediately attracted to the gentle, well-educated elderly duchess. The young woman found in her a source of tender feminine support for her future life in this house, and she right away felt at ease.

Anna ran around the whole luxurious, magnificently appointed and beautifully furnished old mansion, met the servants and asked where her room was. She began to unpack her things and arrange them in her new quarters. With her inherent artistic taste, she decorated her room with the things she had brought with her and the prince's gifts — so beautifully and originally that the prince could not help being impressed by the room's appearance. Here were girls' toys, books, portraits and études, in addition to an easel and a landscape she had begun. There were also vases full of multicoloured autumn flowers and leaves.

But it was no longer the former Anna that sat in this elegant room. For the life of her, she was unable to undertake any new activity. Neither painting, nor books, nor even walks about the marvellous gardens and forests of her new surroundings could cheer her. She felt herself beaten, sorrowful and ill.

"How did I fall asleep?" she often asked herself. "After all, I married out of love, we had so many good conversations, but now I'm afraid of him and don't know what to talk about when I am with him."

With bewilderment and some annoyance the prince followed Anna's condition. He could see that all that his distorted imagination had pictured to him in anticipation of his honeymoon with his darling eighteen-year-old bride, aroused nothing but boredom, despondency, disappointment in his young wife's tormented state of mind. Never once did he imagine that he would first have to educate that aspect of his love life with which he was so accustomed to meet the hundreds of women of all types with whom he had had previous affairs.

He did not realise that what was annoying him now was actually her charm — something that guaranteed him a quiet confidence in the face of her purity and future fidelity. Neither did he realise that the passion that would be awakened in her, even though belatedly, would remain for him alone, and that her modesty in respect to her husband would develop into an even greater modesty in respect to others, and forever ensure his honour and peace of mind.

In the meantime Anna was getting more and more accustomed to her new position, as well as more and more attached to her husband. She tried as much as possible to enter into Prozorskij's life and interests and help him. She walked or rode with him about the estate, read his articles and transcribed them for proofreading. In the evenings either Anna or the prince would read aloud from new books and journals in his mother's room.

From time to time, Anna felt in a childlike, playful mood, making the elderly duchess laugh. In need of some sort of active movement, the new bride ran and jumped, seeking an outlet for her youthful desire for fun — an outlet she had not found in her monotonous surroundings.

The prince was a good landowner and loved this activity with a passion. For a time his marriage distracted him from his managerial duties, but now he did his best to make up for lost time.

The whole household was busy. In the forest, crowds of peasants cleared away the dry underbrush; in every part of the forest, all day long could be heard blows of axes and a cacophony of voices. In the garden, they were finishing planting new trees and bushes and transplanting others to the greenhouse. In the barn, they were accelerating the harvest by using a steam thresher. All day long the prince himself supervised the planting of the young trees, which was his favourite occupation. He himself arranged everything, measured the spaces between the planting holes, and urged the day-labourers to work faster.

"Make sure you put some turf at the bottom of each hole — see, like that — keep turning over and mixing the soil," he said to one peasant woman. "Wait, not that way, you are planting the roots too deep," he told another.

Forty day-labourers — peasant women and girls — were busy setting young trees in rows. The short day was already drawing to a close and the time had come to let them go for the night.

Anna, who was expecting the prince for dinner, could not hold out and went herself to fetch him. Still a ways off, he glimpsed her delicate figure, wrapped in some sort of white garment, and flashed a joyful smile.

"You've come for me, Anna? I know, I'm late for dinner. We're just finishing. Time to let our helpers go."

"Can I lend a hand?" asked Anna as she drew closer and tried to ascertain what work was still to be done.

"Of course you can. See that they finish planting the little trees beside each hole, or the wind will damage them by tomorrow."

"I'll plant them myself."

Anna took off her raincoat and hung it on a tree. She tied on her white woollen shawl and set about planting the trees.

The prince admired her beautiful, agile movements, gave a happy sigh and headed for the other end of the planting area.

Anna went from hole to hole, working cheerfully and talking for the first time with the peasant women. One of them approached Anna and, looking her straight in the eye, addressed her boldly and brazenly:

"You see, duchess dearie, Your Ladyship, they won't take me on any more as a day-labourer at the manor house. Yesterday Avdotja washed the windows there — as if she could do it at all! That's something I used to do. You've got to have skill in everything!"

"Really, I dunno," Anna replied. "It's all the same to me. Our housekeeper, Pelageja Fëdorovna, takes care of that. Speak to her."

"All them young'uns," Arina went on, folding her arms as she kept staring at Anna, making her feel uncomfortable.

"Go back to work, no time to chat," said Anna coldly.

The woman walked away and resumed her planting. Another woman, who was working next to Anna, crept over to her and whispered:

"Look, how brazen she is, disturbing Her Ladyship that way! She was the prince's woman. Now, I s'pose, she's not with him anymore, the bitch."

A feeling of darkness came over Anna's eyes. Her hands felt heavy and began to droop. Her heart was beating so fast that for a moment it seemed to her that she was dying. Her throat was choked with spasms.

"How can it be?" she mused. "Just a moment ago I met one of those women he used to love! And she will stay living here her whole life, close to us; she will know that I, the prince's wife, am a successor to this Arina!... And who can guarantee that he will not go back to her?..."

These thoughts flashed through Anna's head all at once. She also noticed Arina's rosy cheeks and her dark temples peeking out from underneath her red headscarf with her insolent brown eyes and her clean, white gap-teeth.

Anna stood up quietly, took her raincoat and walked away from the peasant women.

She staggered at first, but as soon as she turned the corner of the old oak forest, she started to run. She wanted to run faster so that *he*, her husband, would not catch up with her, so that she would not see his face nor feel his touch, nor hear that voice which was probably at some moment whispering to Arina the same very tender words that he now spoke to her.

Her despair was deep, inexorable — the despair and horror which could not help leaving their mark for life on her young soul — not unlike the horror which might be experienced by a child upon seeing a decomposed corpse for the first time in her life.

It was not long after Anna had finally accustomed herself to her husband's way of life, when suddenly their relationship took a new and ugly turn. The thought of running away — running home to her mother — briefly crossed her mind.

"Oh, oh ... oh ... oh!" she wailed, fatigued by all her running around and giving in to wild despair.

She ran through the whole forest and garden, all the way down to the pond, and finally sat down exhausted on a bench, still weeping. By this time it had already got quite dark. After having her fill of sobbing (as only children can sob), with all her nerves stretched to the limit, she lay down on the bench, put her white woollen shawl under her head and, closing her inflamed eyes, at last fell silent.

In the meantime, the prince finished his work at the other end of the planting area and went to look for Anna.

"Where is Her Ladyship?" he asked the peasant women.

"She left ages ago," they replied.

"Did something happen to her?" he asked fearfully.

"She looked plumb tired."

Very disturbed, the prince rushed to the house. In the entrance-way, he met a steward who was anxiously awaiting the family for dinner.

"Has Her Ladyship come?" asked the prince, sensing that Anna was not in the house.

"No, sir."

The prince dashed outside again and ran to the forest near the planting area.

"Anna! Anna!" he called.

There was no answer. The age-old oak trees were already rustling with dry, but still firm leaves, while the wind blew into the prince's face sharply and penetratingly. The prince hurried into the garden.

"Anna, where are you? Answer, for God's sake!" he cried, his voice already showing signs of despair as he made his way down the allée. Anna heard his voice but did not answer. She was happy that he had come looking for her, and that he would now come and fetch her home, but the sorrow and emotion she had experienced had still not vanished, and something strange and frightening meshed in her imagination with her husband's beloved and beautiful face.

Finally he came quite close and, suddenly catching sight of her, began staring at her in surprise.

"What's the matter with you? Why did you leave?"

Anna remained silent.

"Anna, darling, what's with you?" he asked; already a tinge of horror was showing in his voice.

Instead of an answer, Anna broke out into another fit of sobbing. Her frail body trembled all over. She pushed her husband away with her arm and for a long time was unable to speak. Finally she burst out:

"Never mind, never mind! Leave me! Oh, the torture! Oh, oh … oh … oh!" she cried. "I'm going to die this moment!"

Anna again lay face down on the bench. Her whole, almost child-like body was trembling all over from shedding tears.

"I can guess…" said the prince guiltily and sorrowfully. "Calm down, my dearest, I shall do anything to calm you down. I simply can't imagine your sufferings! Anna, how can this be?! After all, I love you more than anything else in the world. Poor little girl! Say something to me."

The prince took his wife in his arms and was about to seat her on his lap, when she tore herself out of his grasp.

"No, don't, I can't… Go away, please, go away! I'll come in a moment, really, I'll come," said Anna, but she really wanted only one thing — for him to love her even more and not leave her.

Prozorskij understood this. Caressing her, he comforted her with the most tender words. She listened, still weeping quietly, and gradually calmed down. Then the prince took her by the arm and, without further questioning, led her with slow steps to the house. She walked meekly along the path strewn with dry leaves, but her whole being was overwhelmed with fatigue from the new sensations she was experiencing.

In the dining room they were met by an anxious elderly duchess. Without knowing any details, she looked at Anna, lovingly stroked the girl's head and quietly exclaimed: *"Pauvre petite!"*

CHAPTER 8

From that day on, Anna locked herself in the house and did not go out anywhere, including for a walk. The sight of a peasant skirt made her shudder, even from a distance. She began to seek both entertainment and the meaning of life in that limited, closed family circle with which she had been united by fate. Moreover, she once again turned to her favourite activity — painting. She found herself two peasant children, who made up a charming group, and worked on their portrait every morning. To keep the children from getting bored of posing, she ordered toys and treats for them from the city, told them fairy tales and played and had fun with them herself.

Sometimes the elderly duchess drifted quietly into Anna's room. She would go over to her, kiss her forehead and suggest she go for a walk. Occasionally she would sit in an armchair and, with a smile, look at Anna's work approvingly.

Anna's husband was never interested in her artistic works, which upset her very much. On rare occasions he entered her room and insincerely praised her *études* — as though they were the work of a young child. Anna got the impression that he hardly ever looked at them, even from a distance, and never actually saw them.

The prince now always managed his estate alone, while Anna, often anxiously, waited for him. Jealous thoughts often came to mind, which made her attitude to her husband seem utterly unnatural.

One time in the evening, when it was already getting quite dark and the prince had not yet returned from the threshing, Anna began to be alarmed. Her alarm soon took the form of jealous images in her mind, including that of Arina, her husband's former lover. When she could hold out no longer, she suddenly jumped up, hastily got dressed and ran to the threshing floor by a roundabout route so as not to meet anyone. Once there, she found that everyone had already left.

Anna crept through the stooks, her eyes and ears on full alert. But all was quiet. She became frightened and ran home. After running around the outside of the house, she went up to the stone terrace and began to look up at the lighted windows of her husband's study. She glimpsed Prozorskij's handsome figure; having come home by a different route, he was calmly changing his clothes for dinner.

"No, he's still mine!" she passionately thought. Her heart still beating unbearably, she became ashamed of herself. After going through the whole house, she quietly slipped into her room by way of a back entrance.

"My God! Could I believe that I would turn out like this!" she thought. "It was my dream that my husband and I would join together in our *first* pure love! But now! I'm all together infected with the poison of jealousy, and there's no escape!"

Anna began to feel sorry over her ideals and was unable to calm down for a long time. She felt sad the whole evening, and when she at last found herself alone in her room and about to get an early night's sleep, she was all at once overcome with a desire to pray.

She took off her silk blouse, tossed it on a chair, and, remembering that her husband might be coming soon, she set about praying immediately. She asked God for peace in her soul and for courage to meet all life's little challenges; she prayed for her sins, too. Tears of affection and self-pity kept flowing down her cheeks. Her bare shoulders trembled, but she was not aware of anything unusual and did not even hear her husband coming into the room. Not noticing at first that she was praying, he went over to her and passionately pressed his lips to her bare shoulders.

Anna's shoulders gave another shudder, she grabbed her peignoir from the chair and, quickly wrapping it around herself, sat down on the bed. There were still tears in her eyes. "Once again, *this* is all just leading to one thing," the thought gloomily flashed through her head. But she did not let this thought prevent her from immediately starting to justify her husband's actions. "He didn't notice that I was praying, he loves me so much!… And this is a manifestation of his love," and so forth.

The next morning the child-models came again, but Anna did not feel like painting. Bright sunlight was streaming through the windows, the first snow had fallen, and Anna ran with the children into the garden. The rustling leaves on the pathways mixed with the frosty snow. She felt light and happy — just as though she were a kid again with these children — carefree, pure and beautiful, like the Nature all around her. She wanted, even for a moment, to be her former self again: to forget her jealous fears, to forget this latest period of her husband's coarse and passionate attraction to her; to forget his subsequent indifferent attitude towards her. And, for a few moments, she did forget, though in her heart was still stirring the eternal, unresolved and tormenting question: "Why is he so tender today? Does he see only the good in me? And tomorrow, after intense caresses, is he going to blame me for everything? Will he grumpily yell at me and jab me with something particularly painful? How will I know what I am to blame for? After all, he is so clever, kind and educated… But what about me? Oh, I'm so immature!…"

Having had her fill of running, Anna was about to go home, when her husband, looking cheerful, fresh and elegant, appeared at the end of the allée. Anna was delighted and ran to meet him.

"Where have you been?" she asked.

"I was at our neighbour's. We were talking about a factory which we want to build together."

"A factory? What kind of factory?"

"A distillery. It is very profitable."

"What are you saying?! You want to make vodka?!"

"Well, yes. Why does that shock you?" asked the prince in his familiar irritated voice which he often used while speaking to his wife after the passionate period of his love for her had ceased.

"No, I'm not shocked. I just don't understand why you would want to produce something that destroys people."

"How many times have I asked you not to interfere in my business affairs?" said the prince, intensifying his pace and leaving his wife behind.

"Oh, excuse me, please!!… No need to hurry, let's walk together!"

Anna's lips trembled and she shed tears. Prozorskij gave her a surprised look and thought that she had become less pretty of late.

"You're not yourself today?" he enquired.

"Me?" asked Anna in surprise, recalling her especially cheerful mood that morning. She also remembered her husband's meek tenderness the night before, and answered him with a silent, inquisitive glance of reproach. She thought for a moment and wondered how strange it was that this person whom she loved and was ready to assist and sympathise with in everything — that this person could be involved in the production of vodka — a substance that would inebriate ordinary people! After all, is that something she could ever support him in? "And why is he so angry with me? What have I done?"

They talked no more about it. A young peasant woman passed them by at a boisterous, healthy pace, gave them a respectful greeting and — shaking her wide skirt from side to side — disappeared in the distance. Anna gave a shudder. The prince first followed the woman with his eyes. Upon noticing his wife's discontented look, he gave her a weak smile and guiltily said:

"I can't throw off the old habit of looking at every young woman from a male point of view. It is only thanks to you that I am getting better and better."

"And he admits this!" she thought to herself with horror and, blushing with anger, burst out: "What? Can you see a woman in this peasant? Phew, as if there were no other interests in the world!"

"I tell you, that was all in the past!" the prince retorted. "I'm over it now."

"I don't believe it. I don't believe it!"

"What is this, Anna? What an ugly nature you seem to have! It's quite unbearable!"

"Maybe. But I hate cynicism and immorality. I love purity, but you love the opposite."

"You have no right to say that!"

"I *do* have the right! I'm your wife."

"Oh, my God, this is terrible!" the prince exclaimed. "Terrible!"

"Terrible not for you, but for me…"

The friction went on for quite a while, though never before so tormenting. The couple did not see each other the whole evening. Anna went to bed, but the prince did not come. She was frightened and saddened by her relations with her husband; besides, she was overcome again by a devilish fit of jealousy concerning the prince's possible infidelity. She lay there, her eyes open, listening for her husband's footsteps. But he never came. Gradually her jealousy passed, and she felt she simply wanted to be a trusting friend to her husband. She wanted there to be no more obstacles to their happiness, which had been on the decline of late. She jumped out of bed, threw on a nightgown and slippers and hurried to his study.

The prince was sitting on a sofa, silently and sternly staring straight ahead. When the door opened and he saw Anna, his face took on an angry expression. She hesitated for a moment and wanted to go back, but the prospect of continuing to maintain such ugly relations with her husband prompted her to choose a path of reconciliation instead.

"Why aren't you coming to bed?" she asked.

"How can I go to bed when my heart is still beating so fast from such scenes! You're giving me a heart attack…"

Anna scowled but managed to hold herself in check.

"I'm very sorry that I upset you. Please, don't be angry."

She went over and sat beside him on the sofa. He looked at her in bewilderment, but already more tenderly. This cheered her. She took his hand and smiled. The prince drew her closer and kissed her.

When Anna realised that the reconciliation was not going the way she had so fervently hoped — that it was not going to be a pure and genuine reconciliation of the heart, but a reconciliation through kisses, — she was overcome by horror and despair.

"Oh, my dear friend, please do not kiss me! For *that* I am dead, and after such mental pain I can't reconcile *that way*. I beg of you, leave me in peace and forgive me…"

She tore herself out of the prince's arms, jumped up, opened the door and ran off. The prince listened for a long time to her receding footsteps and her lively and easy gait.

"What a strange and incomprehensible woman!" thought the prince. "And how plain-looking she is becoming — one of her teeth has already started to yellow."

Anna got worse with every passing day. The elderly duchess said that Anna's eyes had begun to turn inward, that "*la pauvre petite est souffrante*" and, indeed, Anna had great difficulty getting through her first pregnancy. For the most part, she lay in her mother-in-law's room in a state of dizziness, feeling dejected, ill and weak. She was little cheered even by thought of her future child, so strongly influenced was she by some kind of suffering apathy.

The prince, who during the first trimester had almost always stayed home, now once again resumed his former habit of constant trips to the city, to their neighbours or for hunting. He appeared to be quite bored at home and depressed by his wife's condition.

The days went by this way all through the winter, spring and the onset of summer. Anna would never forget this period of her life. Her young, immature nature found everything unbearable — she was neither physically nor morally up to the difficult position of a pregnant mother or to coping with such all-pervading loneliness. Oppressed by constant ill health and her husband's attitude of indifference, she became increasingly impatient and irritated. If the prince was late coming home from somewhere, Anna would fly into a fit of despair, weep almost to the point of hysterics and complain that she was being mistreated. Her one source of power over the prince — namely, her beauty — temporarily faded. Apparently, he needed nothing else, and this brought her into a state of even greater hopeless despair. For his part, the prince was weighed down by her uneven, tormenting mood, but, as a person of noble breeding and restraint, he was tender with his wife, though his tenderness also smacked of pretension and coldness.

How precious to Anna would have now been the presence of her mother and sister! But they had left for an extended trip abroad following Misha's inflammation of the lungs — this meant he was forbidden to spend winters in Russia.

A hot July day. In the fields the grain harvesting was well under way; it was an abundant harvest. The prince, in spite of his restlessness at home, had not dared to be apart from his wife during her last trimester. Now, however, as her due date approached, he returned to the business of managing the estate.

He spent whole days either in the field or on the threshing floor, and now, during the whole harvest time, took an active part in assembling the stooks. As he walked across the threshing floor, thinking about his wife — now thin and pale, with her deformed figure and large dark and serious-looking eyes, which often regarded him with questioning reproach — he involuntarily compared her with the young, healthy, rosy-cheeked peasant woman whom he had just seen standing on a passing wagon. He knew that only two weeks ago that same woman had given birth, but her child had died. However, she, without tears or nervousness, simply took this event in stride and now, in a cheerful blend with Nature, was working alongside her young husband.

"And what about us?" wondered the prince. He furrowed his brow and lit a cigar. "Yes, I forbid smoking on the threshing floor," he thought, and set off on the road leading into the woods.

Suddenly, upon hearing hurried footsteps catching up with him from behind, he turned around.

"Please, come home, Her Ladyship is not well," exclaimed a breathless maid, who at once turned back towards the manor house. She knew that the prince would understand what was going on. He hesitated for a moment, like someone about to undergo an operation and thinking: "Isn't there any way I can get out of this?!" However, plucking up courage and sensing there was no escape, the prince increased his pace and headed for home.

In the house everything was already bustling. They moved the beds, carried something out, brought in a small, decorated wagon with a canopy of white muslin. A woman stranger, who had recently been annoying the prince with her presence, was organising things. She was young and stylishly dressed, only with rolled-up sleeves and wearing a white apron. The housekeeper Pelageja Fëdorovna was busiest of all.

The elderly duchess, in a state of subdued excitement, went over to Anna, made the sign of the cross over her and kissed her forehead. Anna herself was indifferent to it all. She sat in an armchair by the window and, while waiting for her husband, began to pay attention to what was happening inside her. Her flushed face was solemn and serious, framed by thin wisps of hair tinged with a golden hue that fell over her forehead and temples. Beneath them peered out two large dark eyes, not seeing anyone, but curious and fearful.

When the prince came in, Anna rushed to embrace him.

"You know," she said, "it's going to be very soon, maybe even today. How strange and joyful this is — my *very own child*!… What happiness! I will come through it all, I feel very brave…"

Her words were spoken hurriedly, but all at once she exclaimed: "There, again…"

She squeezed her husband's hand and grimaced — she no longer saw anyone, and her sufferings became worse and worse. In a few seconds, though, her face resumed its former calm expression.

"It's passed again," she said with a sigh.

"Time to lie down, Your Ladyship," said the woman in the apron, whose presence was so annoying to the prince.

"You won't leave me? For God's sake, dearest, stay with me!" Anna begged her husband.

"Of course I won't leave," said the prince. "You can calm down. You're so emotional, darling," he added tenderly, using his hand to brush her wet hair away from her temples.

Anna pressed her husband's hand to her burning cheeks and joyfully thought that the child she was expecting might possibly bring her and her husband closer again and nullify the estrangement which had so troubled her this past while.

Little by little Anna lost all ability to think or feel anything. Her suffering was now becoming unbearable, continuing for a day and night already, with no end in sight. They had already brought in a doctor from the city, and everyone was terribly exhausted. The elderly duchess lit candles and lamps before all the icons and kept praying in her room, her eyes filled with tears.

The prince fled from his wife's room and threw himself on the drawing-room sofa in exhaustion, feeling that his fatigue was already reaching its final limits.

Anna's frightened, frantic cries followed him everywhere. He could not find a spot very far from her, for Anna by no means wanted to let him go. However, to stay with her was unbearable to him.

A second bright summer night had begun when, following something frantic and frightful in the bustle and the latest harnessing of their collective strength, the event occurred which everyone had been waiting so impatiently for. From Anna's room sounded first an unhuman, frightening cry of the birth mother and immediately afterwards, as though quite unexpectedly and from a different world, could be heard an unfamiliar (but always joyful for everyone) voice of an infant, a mysterious being from some place known to no one.

The prince burst into sobbing and bent over his wife. She crossed herself and exclaimed: "Praise the Lord!" Then she looked at her husband and offered him her forehead, which he kissed, and she finally lay back on her pillows in exhaustion.

When they brought Anna her son, all washed and swaddled, she spent a long time looking at the reddish, puckered up little face; then she bent over and kissed it. She did not experience the extreme joy she had hoped for, but what she did feel was something far more meaningful to her. This was *happiness*, the goal and purpose of life; this was the justification of her love for her husband, this was her future duty, and this would be no mere plaything (as it had previously seemed), but only more suffering and labour.

Taking the newborn in her arms, Anna felt that she would be unshakingly faithful to her motherly duties, just as she had unshakingly promised the prince, when he asked her to be his wife, to be faithful to her marital duties.

When the prince took his first look at his son, he was completely taken aback. He turned away from the baby in revulsion and said: "Well, that's not our role. When he grows up, that will be a different matter altogether."

Hearing this was very painful for Anna. She certainly had not expected such an attitude on the part of a father to his first-born son. "Maybe he won't love him?" Anna thought in horror, as she remembered her recent hope that the child would remove the estrangement between them and unite her and her husband again in love for their offspring.

She gave a sigh and wiped away a tear.

PART II

CHAPTER 1

Ten years passed. Anna continued to live with her family in the country as before. The only change in her life was that the elderly duchess had passed on about three years earlier. Anna was profoundly saddened by her death, for she had fond memories of her mother-in-law.

Anna herself had changed a great deal. From a thin young girl, she had evolved into a strikingly beautiful, healthy and energetic woman. Always cheerful and active, surrounded by four charming and healthy children, she appeared happy and fully satisfied with her life. The prince, whose hair had gone somewhat grey but was still as elegant, handsome and well-mannered as before, apparently continued to treat his wife well. But there was almost nothing left in common in the depths of the couple's spiritual life, and this was also reflected in their day-to-day activities.

The love the prince felt when he first married Anna could not last for long by virtue of its very nature. As a man who craved success, he needed a variety of experiences — something he was so accustomed to! A quiet family life in the country was simply too boring for him, and Anna felt that he was not to blame for that.

But this boredom frightened her. She loved her husband. Jealous, she was afraid of losing even that love which he still had for her, thanks to her beauty, cheerful character and flourishing health.

Anna felt that this was not the kind of love that she had desired. It often caused her to suffer. To compensate for the empty space in her heart, she was especially passionate in her devotion to her children and her care for them. Her husband, on the other hand, treated the children coldly. It was hard for Anna to accept his indifference to what in fact constituted the centre of both her outward and inner life. She was faced with experiencing everything alone: illnesses, doubt in her children's good and bad qualities, decisions as to medical treatment, education, nannies and governesses. She felt the need to teach the children herself, since she thought it necessary to have more personal contact with them, to get to know them better.

In response to Anna's conversations about the successes, characters and illnesses of the children, the prince either kept silent or feigned a smile, customarily answering with soft, studied phrases — as, for example, that he was very happy that his son's studies were going so well, or that it was too bad that little Jusha had been born weaker than the others, or that Manja looked surprisingly cute in her new fur coat. This Manja, now an eight-year-old girl, was the prince's favourite: she was very pretty and spoke French fluently, having acquired a genuine Parisian accent from her governess, and this amused the prince.

Prozorskij's life had not changed in any significant respect: he continued to manage his estate, go hunting and write his articles. But Anna saw that everything he did lacked energy or enthusiasm. He was simply bored, unbearably bored. Family life weighed him down. No matter how hard Anna tried to find ways of amusing her husband, no matter how often she attempted to accompany him on visits to the neighbours, to the city, to elections, to district council meetings, etc., there was never any lasting effect.

Besides, the children took up a lot of her time. She was always busy with them — either breastfeeding one or being pregnant with another or giving lessons to a third. Amidst all the household and domestic chores, she hardly ever found time to go for a walk or a ride with her husband.

As always happens in such situations, people come up with some sort of need to change their circumstances according to their feelings. The prince began to talk about his desire to collect all his articles, scattered in various periodicals, and publish them in one book. In order to do that, his personal presence was necessary, and he suggested to Anna that they spend several months in Moscow. She unhesitatingly agreed, seeing this as the only means of keeping the prince entertained.

Lately she had been noticing that the prince often tended to seek out young women and was especially lively in their company. He began to be especially fastidious concerning his appearance, and about his increasingly greying and thinning curly hair, which had formerly been so striking. Anna started to worry that the outward family decency of their home was being violated, and she embarked on an energetic struggle to preserve it — in particular, to preserve a real family atmosphere for her children.

It was decided that they would go to Moscow at the end of October. The prince said that first of all he wanted to take one more hunting trip to a distant field before seeing to his book.

On 1 September, a small but magnificent hunting party assembled in the prince's courtyard. The children saw their father off, admiring the horses and especially the dogs. Manja poked a piece of sugar into the mouth of Nochka, a beautiful slender English borzoi. The piebald, almost marble-looking Drakon was tugging at the reins and whining with impatience. The white-coloured hound Milka was running free and waiting for the prince.

Finally the prince went out, bade farewell to Anna and the children and then mounted his Kabarda horse. After announcing that he would not be returning for at least three days, he quickly left the estate.

He rode through fields to a remote estate belonging to some of his acquaintances. Anna knew that his hunting party would include their distant neighbour — a lady who had lately often flirted with the prince. There was a lot of gossip about this lady — for example, that Prozorskij had been in love with her before his marriage. All this greatly disturbed Anna. She would have gladly gone with her husband, but she was breastfeeding little Jusha at the time. Real life was furiously putting forth its claims, and Anna rejected any ugly thoughts, concentrating once more on the world of her children, full of cares, activities and love.

As soon as she had seen off her husband, Anna summoned the children for a lesson. Manja and her elder brother, the handsome Pavlik, were in the garden. They brought baskets full of acorns, and enthusiastically recounted how they found a family of young squirrels inside a hollow tree. Upon seeing their mother, however, they were struck by her morose appearance and made a serious effort to prepare their books and scribblers. The lesson lasted a whole hour. Anna had not finished correcting their scribblers, when the nanny's assistant called her into the nursery to feed the little one. Left on their own, the two oldest children started running around the table.

On her way to the nursery, Anna looked at herself in the large mirror in the drawing-room.

"Oh my God," she thought, "what do I look like?! This bulky old blouse and unkempt hair! I must see to my wardrobe and order something better from Moscow! Yesterday my husband said with disgust that I was not taking care of myself at all and had really 'let myself go'. What is there around here to dress up for anyway? I'm bored and, besides, I have no time. But, apparently, it's something required of me!" she sighed.

Anna could already hear the baby's impatient crying emanating from the nursery. She quickened her pace and began to unbutton her blouse.

"Well, well, baby, all steamed up, are we?... I'm coming, I'm on my way!" said Anna. She took little Jusha from the nanny's arms. The baby stopped crying, and soon could be heard the rhythmic sounds of his impatient sucking and hasty swallowing of the free-flowing mother's milk. Silently and lazily Anna gazed around the nursery, that familiar, calm place of refuge where all her children had passed through their infancy — a place of so many joys and sorrows, where she had often sat at night-time with a baby in her arms, wiping away tears and thinking about her husband's unexpected indifference to their children.

She also remembered nights when, after pacing the nursery floor for several hours on end in an endeavour to soothe an ill baby, she would flee to her room in exhaustion for a rest — and how her husband, not noticing her fatigue and annoyance, would open his arms in embrace, and in a beastly and passionate manner demand satisfaction of his physical inclinations — and how she, exhausted both physically and mentally, feeling hurt by his indifference, silently wept, but still yielded to him, fearing the loss of love from the man to whom she had once devoted her life.

"Could it really be that a woman's calling amounts to just this —" thought Anna, "using her body either to serve a nursing child, or to serve her husband? And this goes on by turns — *forever*! And where is my life? Where am I? The real *me*, who used to strive for a higher service — namely, to God and noble ideals?

"I am tired, exhausted, I'm dying. I have no life — neither earthly nor spiritual. And yet God has given me everything: health, strength and abilities... and even happiness. Then why am I so unhappy?..."

Anna picked up her sleeping baby's clenched little hand and kissed it. The awakened child's mouth began once again to search for his mother's breast.

However, Anna got up, gently rocked her son in her arms, placed him in his crib and went to join the two oldest children. They were both sitting under the desk, taking papers from the waste basket and scattering them all over the whole floor, looking for envelopes and tearing off the stamps.

"I'm going to have a collection of just foreign stamps," said Pavlik.

"And I have an Egyptian one, Papà gave it to me."

"What's all this? What a mess you've made here!" said Anna upon entering the room. "Have you checked what you had written of your studies?"

"Not yet."

"What are you waiting for? You still have your music to do! But first you need to clear up this mess at once."

The children got busy. From another room a knocking sound was heard, immediately followed by a girl's frightened cry. Anna rushed to the hall, where five-year-old Anja was wailing desperately in the arms of her English governess.

"Where did you hurt yourself?" asked Anna.

"*It is nothing,*" responded the governess in English.

Anna picked up her daughter and hastened to apply a cold compress to the reddish-looking lump on the girl's forehead. By the time she returned to the older children, they had already left. She could hear Manja practising scales in the corner room.

"Oh, she's missing the flat sign!" Anna exclaimed and went to correct Manja's mistake.

Then the maid came in and asked how she should sew anchors onto Pavlik's sailor outfit. Anna pointed out her error and carefully attached the anchors herself. After dismissing the girl, she sat down by the window to read an old book that she had taken from the home library: *Méditations* by Alphonse de Lamartine. She gradually forgot all that had occupied her thought a few minutes earlier and delighted in the delicate poetry of the refined French author. But her happy relaxation did not last long.

"The teacher has come," the footman reported.

"Ask her in," said Anna in a tired voice.

The schoolteacher entered — a quiet, likeable young women with a surprisingly pretty, child-like face.

"Have you come about the books, Lidija Vasil'evna? Have you made a list? Thank you. I'll definitely order them."

"You see, Your Ladyship," the teacher pointed out, "this section is for reading, and that one is for education. As far as the education section goes, I think I'll read that to them myself, as I have to explain things during the reading. It's good that you bought them a globe and some relief maps. That is extremely interesting for them, and geography lessons have gone well."

"Well, I'm very glad."

"When you leave, Your Ladyship, who will be my kindred spirit?!"

279

Anna invited the teacher to dinner, and by five o'clock the children had begun to gather in the dining room, together with the governesses and the superintendent. Anna made pleasant conversation with them all. Both the superintendent and the teacher expressed regret that the whole family was moving to the city; the former, moreover, told the duchess of the plight of the peasants that year. Anna did not like business but did like to follow the whole economic situation of the region and the population in general.

When her busy day ended and she found herself alone in her room, she felt wistful and lonely. "You know, I got married, but I don't have a husband-friend. And even as husband-lover he is drawing apart from me. What for?! What for?!"

Anna went up to the mirror and began to slowly undress. Taking off her dress and exposing her attractive arms and neck, she carefully examined herself in the mirror. With her cheek pressed against her shoulder, she examined her extraordinarily beautiful breast, full of milk, and fell into deep thought.

"Yes, *that's* what he needs…"

She remembered her husband's passionate kisses and, with eyes sparkling, decided at once that if her power were truly in her beauty, then she would be able to make use of it. Having once violated her ideals of chastity and relegating thoughts about spiritual communication with her beloved to the back burner, she determined that not only would her husband not leave her, but he would also become her slave.

She loosened her dark-golden hair, which curled around her temples and the back of her neck, lifted it up, turned her head and spent a long time examining her face in the mirror. Then she took her feathered mantelet from the chair and pressed it to her breast. The contrast between the whiteness of her breast and the dark feathers was striking.

Then Anna remembered the woman who was currently out hunting with her husband, whereupon familiar feelings of jealousy arose within her with unbearable pain.

From the nursery once more could be heard the baby's cry. Anna put off the mantelet, quickly arranged her hair, threw a lovely Persian nightgown over her shoulders and rushed to the nursery.

Taking her baby in her arms, she fervently pressed her lips to his cheek. Without realising what she was thinking, she passionately whispered: "Forgive me, oh, forgive me, my little one!"

CHAPTER 2

A couple of days after the prince's departure, Anna went for a walk with the children. Along the road leading to the town, she spotted a carriage coming toward her from the opposite direction.

"Who could that be?!" she thought. As the carriage drew closer, the children got excited and began to cry out, fascinated by the tinkling bells on the horses' manes.

Peering inside the carriage, Anna saw a man she did not recognise. He greeted her with a very polite nod but in a rather cold manner.

"I don't know who that could be," she said to herself.

The carriage went up and down a couple of hills before it entered the wide *allée* lined with old birch trees, hurrying straight to the manor house.

The visitor got out and was met by a servant, whom he asked whether the prince was at home. He was very embarrassed to learn that Prozorskij was not expecting him until the next day. The visitor paused for a moment in the hallway, contemplating his next move. At that point, the whole happy family arrived, returning home from their walk. Anna entered first and asked the stranger whom she might have the pleasure of talking with.

The confused guest hesitated on the spot for several seconds, but eventually replied, with a barely noticeable foreign accent:

"I'm very sorry, Your Ladyship, for my unexpected intrusion, but I'm an old friend of your husband's. My name is Dmitrij Bekhmetev. I have not seen my best friend for twelve years, and I'm very sorry to have missed him."

"So, you are Dmitrij Alekseevich Bekhmetev?! I've heard so much about you! We're practically old friends. Come in, come on in, please. My husband returns tomorrow. In the meantime, you can spend some time with us."

"I'd be delighted, Your Ladyship, as long as I am not imposing," said Bekhmetev in an unnatural voice, which Anna did not like at all.

"What a show-off!" she thought.

Going into her room, Anna changed her clothes, rearranged her hair very meticulously, and went out to meet the guest in the drawing-room. He was struck by her flourishing beauty and her easy, unique gait. He also noticed her little head tossed lightly back, framed by the dark fringe of her mantelet, as well as the tender pinkish colour of her freshly flushed face, and her beautiful big, dark eyes, so welcomingly regarding him.

"So, that's my friend's wife!" he thought with a touch of envy.

From their conversation, Anna quickly learnt that Bekhmetev was obliged soon after marriage to go abroad to a warmer climate for his health. That he and his wife lived in Algeria for a time, but that she was bored there and soon left for Paris. They had no children, and he, missing Russia and his relatives so much, decided to return to his homeland for an indefinite period. From Bekhmetev's hints, it was clear to Anna that he had a conflict with his wife, but she refused to have it out with him at present.

By this time Bekhmetev had moved to the country, staying with his sister, Varvara Alekseevna, whom he had not seen in more than ten years. His sister was already a widow and getting on in years. Her place was located only a dozen versts from the prince's estate, and Anna occasionally paid her a visit. She was a very well-educated woman of refined intellect, who had lost her husband and child when she was still young, and since then she had been devoting her whole life to helping peasant children. In the model school she had established, she was already raising practically a third generation of youngsters. She had set up a library, an orphanage and a children's hospital. She could not bear to see a child who was ill, cold or hungry. However, apart from the children, nothing in the world interested her nor touched her heart. Still, her appearance was stern, cold and uncommunicative.

Anna invited Bekhmetev to stay for dinner. But on this day the family meal was full of tension. The governesses, the superintendent and the children — all felt awkward in the presence of the new guest. Only Manja and Pavlik were overcome by uncontrollable laughter, for which they were even threatened with the prospect of no dessert.

After dinner, Anna invited Bekhmetev into the drawing-room, but she did not neglect her custom of gathering the children around her and keeping herself busy with them until they were ready for bed. They brought out various scrapbooks, picture-books, games and personal projects.

Everyone concentrated on their own activity. Manja was assiduously knitting a scarf for the elderly gardener, the younger girl was busy with blocks, searching for familiar letters of the alphabet, while Pavlik sat down at his easel. Anna, too, took out her sketchbook and began drawing a portrait of the English governess sitting opposite her.

Bekhmetev invited Pavlik to sit beside him, then began to draw something in the boy's scrapbook. He told him about Algeria, about the brown-skinned people there wearing huge turbans. While continuing his account, he executed corresponding pencil illustrations in Pavlik's scrapbook. The lad was in ecstasy. He took hold of the book and went to show the illustrations to his mother.

"Look, Mamà, how Dmitrij Alekseevich draws!"

"So, you are an artist?" asked Anna, recognising the hallmarks of an experienced master.

"Yes, Your Ladyship, if that word can be applied to someone who has devoted his whole life to art but never completed a single actual picture."

"That was once my dream, too — to be an artist, but you can see what consumes all my time and efforts now," she said, as she waved her hand around the table, pointing to the children.

"Mamà can draw, too!" exclaimed Manja and, tugging at Dmitrij Alekseevich's sleeve, led him over to look at one of Anna's landscapes hanging on the wall.

Bekhmetev began to praise the picture in rather glowing terms.

"He's showing off again," thought Anna.

"Why do you have such an accent, one altogether foreign?" she asked.

"I spent my childhood in England, and then lived a lot abroad. Is it really that noticeable?"

"I would have even taken you for a foreigner."

After the children had gone to bed and everyone had dispersed, Bekhmetev began to get ready to leave, but Anna demanded that he stay until the next day, since the prince had promised to be home around noon.

The next day, Bekhmetev stayed the whole morning in the annexe where he had spent the night, and Anna appreciated his consideration. The prince, however, failed to return as he had promised.

When it began to get dark, Anna became seriously concerned and got ready to go out and look for her husband. After inviting Bekhmetev to accompany her, she went to change her clothes and feed the baby.

Even though she felt burdened, she took special care in getting dressed. She knew all too well how important her external appearance was to her husband, especially in the presence of others. Besides, the thought of the beautiful, sprightly woman in the hunting party weighed her down and spurred on her disturbed imagination.

They were presented with a pair of fine English horses, freshly saddled. Anna and Bekhmetev mounted them and silently rode down the allée to the high road. They tried conversing but it did not work out. Anna was too concerned about her husband, and Bekhmetev clearly saw this.

It was now completely dark. Anna was on the point of turning home, fearing that her nursing child would start wailing without her, when all of the sudden they heard a cacophony of hoofbeats, human voices and laughter.

Anna and Bekhmetev were riding at the edge of the forest, while the hunting party, with Prozorskij and his attractive female companion in the lead, were travelling along the high road. Anna could clearly hear the woman's laughter, followed by these words:

"Non, jamais je ne me déciderai d'entrer à cette heure et dans ce costume chez vous."

"Vous voulez mon désespoir!" the prince replied, half-jokingly but fervently.

"Et que penserait votre vertueuse femme?"

At this point, Anna called out to the prince in a loud voice. He certainly did not expect to meet his wife, and their sudden encounter annoyed him.

"I was so worried about you, my friend, you said you'd be back by noon," Anna began.

"Who's that with you?" asked the prince, looking at his wife's approaching companion.

"This is your old friend Dmitrij Alekseevich. He arrived yesterday."

"Dmitrij! Where did you come from? What a surprise!"

"I came straight from Algeria. I'm so glad to see you! And with your family, too, all so happy…"

"Wait, this is all so unexpected!" the prince responded. "I am indeed happy to see you, but I must say goodbye to my companions."

Prozorskij turned his horse sharply around. Riding over to the hunters, he said a few polite words to everyone, besides tossing a choice compliment to the lady. After taking his leave, he rode off to catch up with his wife and friend.

Drawing even with his wife, he rode alongside her for several paces and then whispered angrily to her:

"I am very glad to see Dmitrij, but it is quite indecent for you to go riding at night *en tête-à-tête* with a stranger."

He looked back at Bekhmetev, who was unable to cope with his horse that kept constantly pulling to one side.

"But could it be," said Anna, "that it is more decent for a man to invite a lady — especially of the kind that should not be admitted to the house at all — as an overnight guest, without consulting his wife?"

Anna bit her lip in frustration and fell silent. She had tears in her eyes. All day long she had been so impatiently waiting for her husband, greatly concerned about him in fact, and now look at how their meeting turned out! In spite of the darkness and dampness, she struck her horse with a whip and galloped on alone. The prince and Bekhmetev galloped behind, loudly calling on her to stop.

"Anna, not so fast! The horse will take a tumble! You're crazy!" Prozorskij finally cried out in despair.

But Anna was not listening to anything or anyone. Arriving at the house, she headed straight to the nursery and then spent the rest of the evening in her room.

CHAPTER 3

Prozorskij spent the whole of the next day at home with his friend, showing him his estate and reminiscing about old times — those younger years when they often got together and lived a similar lifestyle. Bekhmetev left toward evening, while the prince, after bidding a cold farewell to his wife, went off to rejoin the hunt.

He had received news that the whole hunting party was spending the night at his neighbour's, an old bachelor landlord, and that they were expecting him to join them.

A couple of days later Bekhmetev came again. The prince had not yet returned from the hunt. Anna was alone in the house, and in a sad state of mind.

She was delighted at the guest's arrival. She blushed and was surprised herself to find Bekhmetev's visit so appealing to her.

"Excuse me, Your Ladyship, for showing up here again. I am lonely and am so attracted to your bright family home."

"We are delighted to see you, Dmitrij Alekseevich," said Anna. "But we're always busy with activities that you won't find interesting."

"They are *very* interesting," Pavlik interjected. "See how good they are — Mamà, show, please."

Anna opened a scrapbook in which were pasted a huge variety of amazingly well-dried flowers. These included bouquets, wreaths and arrangements made in the most unusual shapes and colour combinations.

"Incredibly beautiful! You're evidently an artist, Your Ladyship. Well, Pavlik, let's you and I do something incredible."

Everybody got down to work again, and the evening proceeded smoothly and joyfully.

After the children had gone to bed, Bekhmetev picked up the book he spied on the desk and marvelled that Anna was reading such ancient literature — Alphonse de Lamartine.

"How did it happen to enter your head, You Ladyship, to read de Lamartine in particular?"

"Purely by chance. I had never read him before, and now this reading gives me great pleasure. If it is not too much trouble, please read me something aloud."

"With pleasure, Your Ladyship. I had quite forgotten his writings."

Anna took up her work again and sat down beside the lamp. She had a strange feeling of being happy and at peace. She so hated to be alone! From time to time, she would look up at the serious, strained and exhausted face of her guest — at his high forehead with taut skin, with thin black wisps of hair around his temples — and thought:

"No, he's not showing off, as I thought before — no doubt he's an unhappy and magnificent human being."

Bekhmetev read:

"*La nuit est le livre mystérieux des contemplations des amants et des poètes. Eux seuls savent y lire, eux seuls en ont la clef. Cette clef — c'est l'infinie.*"

"That's where I stopped. This part is in the commentaries. I like them very much."

"And this relation of the night to the infinite — to *l'infinie* — is amazingly poetic. And if I didn't believe in this *infinie*, it would be frightening to die."

"Why all this sudden talk about death?" asked Anna and was surprised to discover a clenching feeling in her heart.

"Because they have been threatening me with it for the past twelve years, forcing me to live in warm climates foreign to me, and I decided not to do any more travelling but to go live in Russia, in the countryside."

"And we're off to Moscow for the winter," Anna responded. "My husband wants to publish his articles."

"I've heard, Your Ladyship, and very much regret that this winter, which I'll be spending in your neighbourhood, you all will be staying in the city. Luck never seems to come my way... Tell me, did you ever live here year-round?"

"Yes, for many years we did, and even now I don't really feel like going to Moscow at all... However, now it's time for supper. You had an early lunch, and I shan't let you go without supper."

Anna rang and ordered supper.

It was cozy, bright and beautiful in the dining room, as in the rest of the house. Anna sat down with Bekhmetev at the small table, which was set with flowers and on which a cold supper was served. They talked about what they had just read.

Before long the bells on the Bekhmetev's carriage could be heard from the driveway.

This was followed by the noise of an arriving carriage, and one set of bells drowned out the other. Then somebody made a noise on the porch. Anna and Bekhmetev, however, did not pay any attention and did not notice the prince coming into the room shortly thereafter. Anna jumped up in fright and asked:

"What happened?"

"Oh, nothing," said the prince. "I simply changed my mind about continuing the hunt. Hello, Dmitrij, and — goodbye. You'll have to excuse me, I'm very tired," he added, casting an angry look at his wife and offering only his fingertips (instead of a handshake) to his friend.

"You won't have supper?" asked Anna.

"No, I'm dead tired," was her husband's reply.

He then left the room, while Bekhmetev said goodbye to Anna and took his leave.

Seeing how upset her husband was, Anna ran to him at once. Prozorskij was sitting on the sofa in his study and smoking. Suspecting the truth and knowing how jealous her husband could be, Anna sat down beside him and in an unnatural voice started asking him what made him come back.

"I had to come back because I knew that you would be carrying on this *tête-à-tête* with him again. Don't you still understand how indecent that is?"

"I didn't invite him, but I couldn't chase him out either."

"You could have avoided flirting with him. Did I not see it with my own eyes?"

"Flirting? You're accusing *me*?! That's enough, my friend! Shame on you for saying that! If only you knew how much I miss you, how happy I am that you came back! Let's not quarrel, please!"

She must be guilty, the prince decided.

"Why did you look so frightened when I came in?" he enquired, becoming angrier and angrier. "What did he say to you?"

"To tell you the truth, I don't remember," said Anna, terrified by her husband's tone of voice and angry face, already with some annoyance. "We were reading de Lamartine, and talking about him…"

"And that gave you poetic feelings…" the prince observed ironically. "I don't believe anything. Can't you tell me what you were doing and what you were talking about?" he cried. He grabbed Anna by the hand and gave it a tight squeeze.

All of a sudden the nanny knocked on the door and called Anna to her baby's side.

Upset and humiliated, Anna tore her hand away and ran to the nursery. The baby was bawling impatiently.

"All these selfish men," she blurted out. "*He* is tormented by jealousy, while *I* am supposed to sit here bored and alone — and now on top of that, my agitation has probably caused my breast-milk to spoil, and now my baby won't be able to sleep through the night! Again, I'm the one who is supposed to suffer!"

Anna could not calm down. Her feeling of annoyance, along with her scorn for the man her life was tied to and whom she tried so hard to love, could in no way vanish overnight.

"He does not need anything or anyone — neither the children, nor me. He has absolutely no interest in our life. He needs me only as an object. And he is only concerned about protecting his pride! Yes, she is *his* wife! No one dare say a word to her…"

Anna became more and more frustrated. "But if he himself flirts with someone, that's nothing. My God, my God!"

Such feelings of self-pity brought tears to her eyes.

At the same time, the baby started choking and let out a cry. Anna was frightened, turned the baby on his side and with a fervent kiss comforted him with a whisper:

"My darling, my darling, calm down."

She looked deep into her boy's sleepy little face and started to talk to him mentally: "No, it's not for your father, who insulted me, but for you, little one, that I shall never leave you ashamed of your mother…"

After feeding the baby, Anna walked through all the rooms where her children were sleeping. She made the sign of the cross over each one in turn and, stopping beside the last one, began to pray. Everybody around was asleep. She stood for a long time over the child, her head lowered, concentrated and serious.

If in our paltry, everyday life there were none of these moments of deep, strict reckoning with our conscience, of stern and focused attention to our inner life, this face-to-face confrontation with our inner self in relation to God, think how impossible our existence would be!

Anna treasured moments like these. Now, feeling comforted, she went to her room.

When the prince came in, he sounded very conciliatory. He went over to her, smiled and silently embraced her. Anna reacted calmly and indifferently to his reconciliation; at that moment she felt so spiritually alone, so far from what interested her husband, that, when he reached out to her in an embrace, at first, she didn't realise what he wanted from her. Only when the reason for his sudden conciliatory gestures became clear to her, he suddenly became repulsive. She lightly pushed away his hands and cried out:

"No, I can't, no way!"

Everything about the prince seemed unpleasant: his handsome face looked coarse and stupid; his yellowed teeth, greying hair, his passionate eyes — everything put her off.

She lay down, snuffed out the candles, turned her face to the wall and pretended to have gone to sleep. After saying to herself the Lord's Prayer quickly and without thinking, she repeated it again and again so as to become consciously aware of its message. She crossed herself and, exhausted in her soul, fell asleep with trembling.

The prince's jealous outburst soon vanished. He wrote a note to his friend, inviting him to dinner, and when Bekhmetev came again, Prozorskij was fully at peace regarding his wife. Bekhmetev's calm, noble behaviour could in no way raise suspicion. His chivalrous courtesy, decency and respectful admiration toward Anna were not the kind that could arouse ugly feelings of jealousy in her husband.

In the meantime, quite imperceptibly, Bekhmetev became completely absorbed in Anna's family and inner life. He took walks with her and the children, played with them, took an interest in their affairs, telling them interesting stories or drawing pictures with them. Sometimes he would get them to sing or dance, and they ended up being so attached to him that they would be bored if he were not around for any length of time.

As for Anna, she had never felt herself so happy nor her life so full. She felt as though she were surrounded on all sides by an atmosphere of love. There weren't any tender words, nor coarse caresses — nothing that customarily went with romantic love, but everything around her breathed a kind of tenderness and all aspects of her life were full of grace and happiness. She constantly felt as though a sympathetic eye were watching over her whole life with approval and enthusiasm.

In the evenings, when everyone usually gathered around the large round table, Bekhmetev and Anna took turns using the same scrapbook to draw portraits of everyone present. They also took turns reading aloud to the children — books by Jules Verne and others, altering and clarifying passages which could be difficult or not clear to the children.

Once it happened that instead of the illustrated version they had ordered, they received a plain edition of *Around the World in 80 Days*. Bekhmetev took it upon himself to illustrate all the important scenes, which delighted the children no end. They simply could not wait for Dmitrij Alekseevich to carry on with the reading and illustrations.

Bekhmetev's care and attention to all aspects of Anna's life showed up in everything. She loved flowers — he filled her whole house with the very best. She loved reading aloud — he sought out the most interesting articles and books and spent whole evenings reading to her from them. Anna loved her school — he ordered books, drawings and various educational materials as though in an effort to please the sweet, naïve teacher whom Anna had hired.

It was only such a tender and unselfish attitude toward a woman that could have brought full happiness into her life. Never before had Anna understood so clearly why everything that used to be difficult had now become easy — why everything that had angered or frustrated her before was no longer annoying to her. All the trifles and failures of everyday life were now unimportant, everybody had become kinder. Most surprising of all — but which undoubtedly happened — her husband had become more pleasant to her. She was more tender and loving toward him, too, and this completely alleviated his feelings of jealousy.

So autumn went by, and when it came time at the beginning of November for the whole family to move to Moscow, nobody felt like parting with this happy, quiet, country life.

The prince was the only one in a hurry to leave. He was evidently quite bored at home and used any excuse to go to the city or to visit the neighbours. Everywhere he looked for amusement. This greatly disturbed Anna. She saw that her husband was gradually drifting away from both the children and her personal influence and showed his love for her less and less. She became afraid that he would leave completely, destroying the family that she had tried so hard to take care of all these eleven years of their married life. She was determined to hold on to her husband with all her might, to find ways and means of drawing him closer to her again and keeping him in the family. She had an idea of what these means would be — means personally repulsive to her, but what could possibly be better?

"Even if I lose a bit of my former purity and my virginal ideals — I shall at least have kept pure the ideal of the family. I mustn't allow my husband, the father of my children, to leave our home circle and seek impure joys outside it."

With these thoughts Anna gathered her things together and left with her family for Moscow.

CHAPTER 4

On the evening of 2 December a fleet of carriages pulled up to a wealthy and brightly lit mansion on one of the cleanest streets of Moscow.

The Duchess and Prince Prozorskij held a reception on Sunday evenings, and their drawing-rooms were always filled with a wide variety of guests. Nowhere was it as casual, cheerful, refined and interesting as in the home of Duchess Prozorskaja. Always welcoming, fun-loving and beautiful, she knew how to bring together people who liked to meet each other, and she herself made every effort to ensure that all her guests felt happy, interested and quite at home in her presence. As a result, it wasn't long before Anna had formed one of the largest and most delightful social circles in Moscow.

For a while, the prince could not help being amazed at what had happened to his previously retiring and unsociable wife. She had completely transformed herself: she was receiving visitors, going out on the town, wearing fancy clothes and coming up with a wide variety of amusements and entertainment for her guests, almost always involving her husband in the process.

"I would feel bored and awkward to be alone," she said, and the prince was always with her. He watched over her closely, over that transformation which had turned her into one of the most attractive, prolific and beloved socialites in the city. It worried him that she was suddenly showing him a brand-new side of her personality and her charm.

On this particular evening, Anna had invited a famous author — recently arrived from the provinces to publish his book — to read from his new story. A large social crowd had gathered. In the drawing-room Anna found herself in the midst of an enthusiastic conversation. It was provoked by an argument between two young women talking about the raising of children. One of them, Countess Vel'skaja, was saying that all upbringing means exercising one's personal influence on children, that the most important thing is to be present with them, to follow the development of their characters and their souls and help them in this. The other woman, the cheerful and lighthearted Baroness Insbruk, affirmed that it is best to leave children to their own devices, that everything is inherent in children, that parental upbringing is not important, and that it is better to focus one's attention on one's own life.

Everyone's temper rose, and people kept interrupting each other. One elderly general turned to Anna and said:

"As to the raising of children, you need to learn from the duchess herself. I have never seen as natural, healthy or clever children as hers."

"I think," declared Anna, "that children can be raised properly only when you yourself are fully aware of what is good and what is bad. The good needs to be developed, the bad to be snuffed out. I can only repeat Seneca's words: 'Les facultés les plus fortes de chaque homme sont celles qu'il a exercées.'"

"Where does it all come from?!" thought the prince. "What quiet self-confidence! And those diamond earrings, how beautifully they shine, even more than the brilliance of her magnificent, animated eyes!"

And the prince remembered his wife when in the evenings she would get undressed in front of the mirror, letting her dark golden hair fall on her bare shoulders, and how she would glance up at him when he entered the bedroom. He also realised that this moment would be soon approaching, and, in this happy state of anticipation, he greeted the newly arrived famous writer so joyfully that the latter had the impression that such an obvious show of enthusiasm was intended for him.

Anna also rose from the sofa to greet the famous guest. The silk train of her grey dress, bordered by a fringe of fluffy fur of the same colour, made a rustling sound. She approached the guest and welcomed him warmly.

"I know that it's hard for you, that you don't like to read in public, and thus I am especially, especially grateful to you," she said as she invited the visiting celebrity to sit beside her.

Soon the actual reading began. The story the writer read made a strong impression on everyone present. Some offered timid praise, others a simple expression of gratitude. But nobody was able to utter their appraisal so eloquently as Anna. She held out one hand to the writer, while she used the other to wipe away her tears. He realised that she had experienced the same depth of feeling as he had in writing through his own tears, and he fervently responded to her handshake.

The guests left with the impression of yet another interesting and animated evening in Duchess Prozorskaja's house.

Anna stopped a youngish-looking man with sharp Armenian features on his way out, reminding him:

"You promised to pose for me. Come by tomorrow, and afterwards we'll all go skating with the children. All right?"

"I'll be very happy to do that, Your Ladyship, and shall be at your service tomorrow."

"Don't be afraid, the sessions will be very short, and we can have some conversation at the same time. I really need your type of face for the picture I have in mind! Bye-bye for now."

When Anna found herself alone with her husband, he asked her in jest:

"What is this — another portrait of a young whelp?"

Anna laughed out loud.

"This young whelp (as you call him) has just the face I need, and I'll definitely use this sketch to paint him."

"And why go skating together?"

"Because, out of his devotion to me, he will push the younger children in strollers, so that I can skate freely."

What could possibly be malicious or distant-sounding in Anna's light-hearted and cheerful tone? Prozorskij could not understand it. Until recently, he had never seen her interact in high society, and her success and enthusiasm frightened him. In the past few weeks the prince had been completely absorbed with his wife. But she, it seemed, kept slipping from his grasp. At the same time, she had made efforts to arrange their city life so that the prince was never left bored at home and was no longer tempted to seek out other amusements.

The next morning Anna received a note from an old acquaintance of hers, urgently pleading with her to accompany her daughter to a ball. The ball was to be one of the grandest, but her friend had fallen ill and did not want to deprive her daughter of the pleasure. Anna had already received an invitation herself, but initially she had not wanted to go to this ball. Nevertheless, after thinking it over, she decided to write out her acceptance.

She did not inform her husband of her plans to go to the ball until the very last moment. She knew that he would not like her decision, but at the same time she did not want to disappoint her friend's daughter.

That evening the prince happened to be entertaining guests, reading them his articles aloud. Anna knew all the routine reasonings and conclusions set forth in his articles. She had had to copy them out so many times in drafts, which contained a lot of deliberately chosen, little-known scientific words and expressions.

Tonight she did not listen to his readings and, instead, spent the evening with the children. She couldn't help thinking of Bekhmetev and the evenings she had spent with him in the country, and this made her feel unbearably lonely and sad. After saying goodbye to the children, and putting them to bed, she began to get ready for the ball. Wearing a silvery dress with old-fashioned lace and a bright rose-pattern, all powdered up and brilliant in her beauty, by midnight she was standing in front of her dressing-table. The maid was carefully bustling about, blowing into a glass tube and sprinkling perfume on her.

Suddenly, the door opened, and Anna gave a shudder. The prince walked in and, seeing his wife in such a fancy dress, stopped in disgruntled surprise.

"Where are you off to?" he enquired.

"I'm taking Marusja Pavlovich to a ball at the request of her mother, who is ill," Anna answered calmly.

"What for? And why didn't you tell me? The mother of a family — dragging herself to attend balls..."

"What expressions are those?! *Dragging myself?*! I just wanted to do something nice for Marusja and her mother. Besides, I happen to love balls. I love the glitter, the beauty... and young people having fun... You know very well, that at balls I always sit with old women and just watch the show."

"How am I supposed to know what you do there?" the prince exclaimed passionately, not taking his eyes for a moment off his wife. "I can't help but say how very beautiful you are today," he added as he left the room, slamming the door behind him.

Anna followed him scornfully with her eyes, and for some reason the thought of Bekhmetev once again crossed her mind, along with the melancholy of the infinite space of Nature, autumn fog and a gentle, oh-so-gentle happiness.

Anna's arrival at the ball endowed the evening with an especially radiant impression. A small group of men gathered at the doors of the large ballroom. One adjutant was heard to say: "Behold, the royal entrance to the ball!"

Anna looked around. Always beautiful, sociable and composed, Duchess Prozorskaja declined to show preference to anyone, but instead seemed to promise it to all. As with almost every other very beautiful woman, Anna had a kind and gentle countenance — apparently reflecting the expression commonly shown by men admiring beautiful women.

But today Anna's thoughtful and friendly eyes, looking around at this whole cheerful, motley crowd, began more and more often to picture Bekhmetev's head bent over a book or drawing, surrounded by her fervently beloved children. She wanted to flee away from this place, from all this Moscow bustle — to the familiar, simple, tender quietude of country life. It was the only place, she decided, where she could be truly happy.

The cheerful, glittering Baroness Insbruk came over to her and asked whether she were having a good time.

Anna gave a surprise chuckle and asked how the baroness expected *her* to be entertained by a ball.

"*Mais il y a dans cette foule toujours quelqu'un qui vous intéresse?*"

"*Oui, il y a foule, mais pour moi il n'y a personne,*" Anna sadly responded.

"*Un seul être vous manque, et tout est dépeuplé,*" observed the baroness, quoting de Lamartine's verse. After a brief laugh, she disappeared into the crowd, wondering what had made Anna so happy, cheerful and brilliant. After all, never dancing or flirting with anyone — might she not be bored?

But Anna was not bored, for somewhere in the depths of her heart she had caught a spark of true happiness — the spark of Bekhmetev's love for her, with which she was so familiar and which was illumining her whole life from within. She would never admit it to herself, but she still could not help feeling it. When people admired her, she could only see Bekhmetev's admiration for her. When she was fulfilling any of her family obligations, when she was doing anything, reading or painting, she kept thinking whether he would approve of her and how he would judge her actions.

If somebody had tried to offer an explanation of the status of her heart, she would have rejected it with indignation and horror, treating it as slander or an accusation of dishonesty. But that's the way it was.

CHAPTER 5

Day-to-day life in the city meant for Anna paying heightened attention to making sure her husband didn't get bored and remained within the family circle. In addition, her renewed efforts to maintain social relations were complicated by the tasks involved in raising the children. All this exhausted her to the point where she felt she had to go off into the countryside for at least a day or two to "come to her senses," as she put it.

She was drawn to silence, to Nature, to memories of her youth, to pure impressions of country life, while somewhere in a distant corner of her heart could be felt a vague desire to see Bekhmetev. She would never allow herself to admit it, but the image of her beloved man involuntarily merged with all the other attractions of the countryside.

Anna told her husband that she had to go home to take care of some household affairs and restore order in the school — especially, to encourage and support the young teacher who had been frightened by the school inspector. Finally, she mentioned that she was so tired of the city that she absolutely had to go and gaze at the open sky unspoilt by buildings, at the pure white snow, at the frost-covered forest…, or she would inevitably fall ill.

All this seemed extremely wild to the prince, but he saw there was no use in quarrelling, that women make decisions which brook no opposition. If one tries it, he himself may get crushed, but it won't change the decision.

With the maid's help, Anna laid out a small suitcase and, so as not to waste a day on the journey, left in the middle of the night. It was terrifying for her to leave the children without their mother. For a long time she kept making the sign of the cross and kissing her little Jusha, only recently weaned from her breast. She also kissed the sleepy older children; as she did so, she was pricked by her conscience. But she could not stay — that was beyond her powers. The prince's farewell to her was condescending but especially tender. For a long time after that she still could feel the moist kisses of his lips and could picture his sensitive regard, which had lately so often rested upon her.

She achieved her goal: her husband did not leave her. But at what price! Anna remembered all that she had done to retain him and was actually repulsed by her own actions. And she, what had she turned out to be? She was drawing away, further and further from the one who had killed in her the best aspect of her personal self, and she began to be afraid.

CHAPTER 6

On her journey home, Anna wired a member of her staff to have her met at the station. She found an elderly coachman waiting at the station on a troika with bay horses. He welcomed Anna especially warmly.

When Anna first drove out into the countryside, her heart was filled with an unexpected ecstasy. The morning air was exhilarating. The bright sun shone down on the white, flat fields with blinding rays.

"Yes, this unlimited space, infinity, *l'infinie* —" thought Anna, "it's just what I wanted! I've been hemmed in by walls, fences and buildings in this terrible urban jungle! The real life is *here*. Freedom, space, God — they're all *here*!

"Yes, I am a free bird. I was born and grew up in the country, I can't live in the city..." Anna reasoned. Meanwhile the troika ran so cheerfully along the smooth snow-covered road, its sleighbells ringing monotonously. Only the occasional bump gave Anna a good shaking, interrupting her joyful and dreamy mood.

Finally they entered the old birch allée. The frost hung heavy on the branches of the centuries-old, gnarled birches, glistening with a thousand reflections of the sun and giving all Nature an especially solemn and festive appearance.

"Oh, how wonderful! How familiar everything is, how peaceful, beautiful and profound!" thought Anna, as she arrived at the superintendent's house and took in the whole estate at a glance.

The superintendent was waiting for her with a samovar and specially prepared tea. While Anna was drinking her tea, poured by an elderly servant (the superintendent's auntie), he gave her a thorough account, evidently prepared in advance, of all household affairs — the threshing, cattle, and cuttings in the forest. He then asked when she would care to take a look at the books.

"This evening," she replied. "Right now I'm going to go the barn, the school and the cattle-yard."

"Do you want me to go with you, Your Ladyship?"

"Come along, then."

Anna dutifully made a tour of the whole estate. Subconsciously for her, it was the business of the family's estate that served as an excuse for her trip. She made a concerted effort to be conscientious, even though she had little interest in the business aspect per se. It was simply that everything in this old setting seemed new and exciting to her. She paid special attention to the baby calves with their mothers as well as to the young horses newly broken in.

She took note of how much of the grain was still left to be ground and reprimanded her staff for the oversight. She even checked on the turkeys and geese (which had never interested her before). But all this was at least natural, without artifice — it was a part of Nature herself, unsophisticated and eternal!

After dismissing the superintendent, Anna went over to the school. The young teacher, looking thinner and paler than before, was standing at the chalkboard, enthusiastically explaining a problem to a young boy who was in turn regarding her questioningly and fearfully.

"Lidija Vasil'evna!" Anna called to the teacher.

"Oh, my dear lady, Duchess! What a surprise! I didn't expect you at all. What a joy!"

"How is it that you've got so thin?" asked Anna, kissing the young woman.

"We've had a lot of difficulties here, Your Ladyship. And there were some unpleasantries with the inspector. You know, you put your whole heart and soul into your work and all of a sudden it turns out you're at fault — you've read the wrong things, you have the wrong textbooks. It seems that the higher-ups are only interested in dulling people's minds, not developing them."

Anna fixed her eyes on the dear, pale face of the teacher, and suddenly it became clear to her how much better and higher than herself was this hitherto unnoticed, unsung, selfless and chaste human being, who had devoted all her young years to community service. It was something she believed in and loved more than anything, more than herself. And Anna? Wealthy, living in luxury, surrounded by her children, never content — what had she ever done to make herself useful to anybody?

This brought upon Anna a wave of self-repulsion. She started to wonder how it was possible that this dear young woman could live her dreary exist-ence without any reward while she (Anna) enjoyed all the privileges of life — with total impunity!

After her visit to the school, Anna bade a tender goodbye to the young teacher and went to check on her mother-in-law's elderly former maid, who had been struck with paralysis and lived on a pension.

The old woman was overjoyed to see Anna and began to tell her story after story (which Anna had already heard countless times) — stories about old times, about her beloved dogs, about how one night a cow had given birth to a calf which they had carried frozen into the cattle-barn, about how a chicken that had been brought to her from Moscow laid her first egg yesterday and clucked the whole night about it, and much more — all from the world of birds and animals. It was apparent that her seemingly lifeless existence was still filled with memories of the lives of others (even if they happened to be animals), and she was content with this.

"You see, my dear Duchess, on St. Nicholas day I asked that some tea might be bought for me together with some other stuff, including a small candle. So, I lit it in front of the saint's icon for the health of our master, the prince, with his wife and children. I had just lit it when I heard the foreman giving an order to go look for the prince's hunting dogs. You see, they had run off into the forest, just like young whelps. I thought right off: 'Saints alive, they'll get lost, and that would be a shame for our prince'. I started to pray to the saint: Father Nicholas, let my candle bring them back. Sinner that I am, my dear Duchess! Well, what d'you know, those damn dogs came back lickety-split."

Anna finally managed to tear herself away. She returned home, took dinner with the superintendent and his auntie and then went for a stroll alone, taking in her favourite places.

The frost hung heavy on trees, bushes, thatched roofs and every blade of grass — all incredibly beautiful. Anna walked along the pathway straight to her favourite copse. In the west, the sun had already set over the young trees. To the east, the moon was already rising over the old oak forest. The white tops of the trees — indeed, all wintry Nature — were illumined from both sides by two criss-crossing and merging shafts of light — a soft white glow from the moon and a bright pink from the sunset. The sky was still a deep blue, and pure white fluffy snow glistened especially brightly on the distant meadow.

"There's purity for you! How beautiful it is in everything, this whiteness in Nature, in one's heart, in life, in morals, in one's conscience! — everywhere it's magnificent! How I love it and how I've tried to live it everywhere, always!

"But what for?! Who needed it? Wouldn't it have been better to have memories of some passionate love-affair — even a criminal one, but one that was real and complete — would that not have been better than the current emptiness, and the utter whiteness of my conscience?... " Anna shuddered.

"Of course, no, a thousand times no! Never!" Anna was practically screaming. And suddenly, as though having washed her soul in this pure Nature, Anna felt an uplift of spiritual forces such as she had not seen in a long time.

She returned home when it was already twilight, and distractedly started to go over the superintendent's account books. She made several notations and dealt with the distribution of land to the peasants. After issuing an order to open the manor house, she headed to her husband's study to fetch some books which he had asked her to bring to him.

On entering the cold room, she shuddered and glanced around. How many memories welled up in her mind! How much joy and sorrow — not to mention disappointment — she had experienced here!

Anna sat down and began to go through her husband's things — his letters, papers, diaries. Her cold and frozen fingers leafed through a familiar book (a diary), vainly searching therein for at least some mention of herself.

All through his recent years in the country, the prince treated his wife as an empty space; she did not interest him in any respect. But then she did come across her name: "Yes, he's describing how I happened to meet him — but only with disappointment." This was followed by a description of the hunt and the lady participant. Anna's heart was racing. As she read, she was horrified at the cynicism of her husband's expressions.

"Oh, how horrible! And I loved him so much for so long!" Anna mused with a strange surge of tenderness and threw the diary on the desk. The thought vaguely crossed her mind that what she had loved about her husband was what was demanded by her pure, loving nature, and not what he had offered her in place of these demands.

Anna went to bed contemplating whether she would return to Moscow the next morning or first go visit Bekhmetev's sister Varvara (so that she could see her brother). She hardly slept the whole night. The bedding was unfamiliar — a quilt lent to her by the superintendent's auntie, who in the meantime slept on trunks, moaning and wheezing all night long.

The long December night finally came to an end, and as soon as Anna drew aside the curtains and beheld the glittering frosty morning, she at once decided that she would go see Varvara Alekseevna. She gathered her things together and ordered the horses to be harnessed.

In her imagination Anna worked out various excuses as to why she needed to see Bekhmetev's sister. She would like to check on Varvara's school, do some consultation, learn something from her during her stay. Finally — it would be simply impolite not to pay her a visit. But as Anna drove up to Varvara's estate, her heart was beating faster and faster. What would she say to her? They had never been particularly close.

Which excuse should she use? And indeed, why would she, whose place was now in Moscow with her husband and children, pay a visit to a woman she hardly knew?…

And what about the children? Yes, what would they be doing right now? Manja and her darling little Jusha?…

It was already too late for rationalisations. The sleigh drove up to the porch, and Anna nervously and timidly entered the hallway of Varvara Alekseevna's small country house.

Anna had to wait quite a long time. Eventually she heard footsteps, and Varvara Alekseevna made a stern, solemn and formal entrance into the room. She appeared quite surprised by Anna's arrival. She listened incredulously to Anna's claim that she wanted to consult with her about her school and the education of peasant children. Then she invited Anna to have breakfast with her. She did not mention her brother, but when Anna enquired about his health, Varvara frowned and said:

"He's not well. He has a terrible cough. I tried to send him to a doctor in Moscow, but he just laughed and said: 'I've had treatment by doctors for twelve years now. But isn't it all the same — sooner or later — the end is the same.' He's gone out for a walk," she added.

Anna felt a painful constriction in her heart. "The end comes sooner or later... Yes, that's the way it's supposed to be," she thought. "Nothing should ever stand in the way of my life and my conscience. Everything must turn out for the better... But how shall I go on living? What can I live on?..." Anna's inner voice cried out in horror, and no amount of reasoning about duty, husband or children, could mitigate the horror of Bekhmetev's possible death.

At that moment she could hear his voice in the hallway, enquiring as to who had come.

"Some noble lady, a duchess," replied a servant. "I forgot their name."

Not waiting for an answer, Bekhmetev hurried unto the drawing-room. Upon seeing Anna, he turned pale, and paused for a moment before the colour returned to his face and he regained control of himself.

Struck by the change that had occurred in Bekhmetev, Anna solemnly fixed her eyes on him, and this silent 'dialogue' of glances constituted their first, weighty (albeit wordless) mutual declaration of love.

"I had not expected to see you of all people here, Your Ladyship!" Bekhmetev was the first to speak, exchanging greetings with Anna. He did not enquire as to why she had come to the country — it only took a moment to understand it all — all that passionate, painfully morbid expression of her beautiful darkling eyes fixed upon him. At the moment his heart was captured by both joy and pain together.

The conversations were general. Anna talked about Moscow, about how tired she was of city life and constantly shuddered at the intermittent, cruel sounds of Bekhmetev's cough.

When Varvara Alekseevna left the room for a moment, Anna suddenly changed her tone and started asking Bekhmetev in a concerned voice:

"Are you feeling bad?"

"Yes, something's not right in the chest. It will pass during the summer."

"We'll be coming again in March." This remark involuntarily escaped Anna's lips.

"Wonderful! I've heard rumours, Your Ladyship, about your unparalleled social successes," said Bekhmetev.

"Who told you that? If only you knew how I have no friends there!" said Anna.

"Well, you may not be interested in anybody at the moment, yet everyone worships you. After all, you know that if somebody falls in love with a woman such as you, that's dangerous. When it comes to love, it is impossible to remain in the middle of the road — love will demand everything, but everything…"

Once again, Bekhmetev turned pale; he sighed, and his face darkened with a look of passionate severity. Anna stared at him in fright. These uncharacteristic words on the part of this ideal man left her with a terrible impression. She kept mum. Bekhmetev's distorted face still looked gloomy, and his restrained passion made it seem even more painful.

Anna regarded him sympathetically.

"So, that's what you think, too?" she exclaimed. "But after all, such demands on the part of love will only kill it, as it's killed every day by all, all…"

"And how, Your Ladyship, can love survive and live a long life?"

"Oh, of course, only through a spiritual connection. That kind of love is eternal, it does not die."

"D'you think it's *only* through a spiritual connection?" he asked.

"I dunno, perhaps not exclusively. But in any case, it's first and foremost, it's an undoubted source of happiness."

Bekhmetev paused to think.

"Perhaps you're right, Your Ladyship," he said quietly. "So much the better, let it be that way," he added, going over to her. He pulled up a chair so that he could sit next to her.

With enthusiasm and tenderness, he started asking her about children, about painting, about her life in general. She spoke to him in some detail — as one would talk to someone who is undoubtedly interested in absolutely everything.

When Varvara Alekseevna returned, she invited Anna to take a tour of her school. Anna tried to show full attention, but it was very difficult. After dinner, she started to set out on the return journey, so she would not miss the next train to Moscow.

"I'll accompany you, Your Ladyship, if I may?" asked Bekhmetev. "Tomorrow I have to be in the city, and I can take the opportunity of riding with you to the station."

Anna did not answer, but when they brought her sleigh, in saying goodbye, she offered:

"Dmitrij Alekseevich, it seems you would like me to drive you to the station?"

"I'm ready right now, Your Ladyship."

They did not talk along the way. The weather was overcast, a damp and warm wind was blowing. The dreary clouds hung low, snow was in the offing, and a blizzard was threatening.

"It seems we'll be running into a blizzard," exclaimed Dmitrij Alekseevich.

"Please keep quiet," said Anna. "You shouldn't be talking in such a wind."

And Bekhmetev did keep silent, but — not seeing anything outside of his own inner world even though his eyes were staring straight ahead — he was aware only of his internal happiness, the joy of being beside the woman he loved more than anything else in the world. He did not dare tell her about this, but at the same time he could feel her love as well. Anna noticed his joyful expression, and for a long, long time thereafter, at difficult and lonely moments of her life, this image would illumine her whole being from within.

And on and on they rode, both thinking about the same thing. They weren't demanding anything more from fate or even from each other. In the midst of this snowy, pure and limitless Nature, they felt only their relation to it, to God and eternity. Here, both now and forever, they would be living a shared life together, in which it would be possible to be happy and pure, and to love unselfishly and endlessly.

"I can see the lights of the station," said Anna.

"Well, Dmitrij Alekseevich," said the coachman. "It looks as though you and I are going to have to spend the night at the station. The blizzard is already upon us."

"I don't mind... We've arrived, Your Ladyship."

Upon reaching the station, Dmitrij and Anna bade each other farewell with a simple handshake.

For a long time Bekhmetev watched Anna's serpentine train as it drew farther and farther away from the station. At last it rounded a bend and disappeared under the arch of a bridge.

CHAPTER 7

As inevitably happened with Anna, when she approached the house, her concern grew moment by moment as to what she would find at home and whether the children were healthy.

"Is everyone healthy at home?" she asked the coachman who had come to meet her at the station.

"I wouldn't know, I haven't heard anything, Your Ladyship."

Impatience and anxiety reached the boiling-point when Anna finally arrived at the front entrance and a servant opened the door for her.

"Is everyone healthy?" Anna repeated her question.

"Yes, thank the Lord," said the nanny. "Only the little one has a bit of a fever."

Anna's heart still sank. "I felt it," she thought.

After warming herself up at the stove in the hallway, she ran straight to the nursery. On the way she was greeted by the cry: "Mamà, Mamà's back!"

"Jusha's got a fever," Manja triumphantly declared, hastening, as any child would, to be the first to convey the big news.

Anna ran to the baby's crib and picked up little Jusha, who started to cry with excitement upon seeing his mother.

Anna's heart was overcome with horror and despair, and she felt pricks of conscience. Her whole trip, as well as her selfish, uncharacteristic weakness seemed so repulsive to her. She looked at the weeping, feverish boy and could not bring herself to even kiss him.

"Has the doctor been sent for?"

"No," replied the nanny. "His Lordship ordered us to wait for your arrival."

Anna hastened to write a note to the doctor and then asked where the prince might be.

"His Lordship's busy in his study."

"Of course, he doesn't care whether Jusha's ill," the bitter thought crossed her mind.

The prince was still in his study when the doctor arrived. Anna intently followed the face and actions of the famous professor of children's diseases and realised that her child was in a bad way.

"There's really nothing more to say, Your Ladyship," said the doctor. "We'll know better tomorrow. He has a very high temperature. I think it could be measles, maybe with complications."

The boy was breathing with difficulty and had a wheezing cough. At this point the prince came in. After greeting his wife and the doctor, he asked Anna:

"Have you been back long?"

"Yes, two hours already."

The prince had a talk with the doctor. He made it quite clear that he did not trust medicine and bade the professor a cold goodbye.

"I'll come by tomorrow morning, Your Ladyship," the physician told Anna.

"Please do," she said as she put her boy back into his crib (as by this time he had fallen asleep). "Go and have dinner, Nanny. I'll stay here."

Prozorskij also stayed in the nursery and began to question Anna about her trip.

"Where did you spend the night?" he asked among other things.

"In the superintendent's house, of course, since there is no heat in our house."

"That was stupid and indecent."

"What?!" she asked in surprise.

"*C'est un jeune homme, et je vous dis que ce n'est pas convenable; vous manquez toujours de tact.*"

"I slept with his aunt," Anna spoke with difficulty. Then she fell silent, ruefully gazing at the sleeping boy in his crib.

"Were you anywhere else in the town?" the prince continued his questioning.

"Yes, I went to Varvara Alekseevna's to take a look at her school. I also saw Dmitrij Alekseevich. He accompanied me to the station. He's in a bad way, with a terrible cough."

"What's that? What did you say? You rode with him at night, alone?"

"Not at night, but in the evening."

Prozorskij jumped up and began pacing the nursery.

"God knows how you are carrying on?!" he screamed.

"Quiet! You'll wake the baby."

"You can't live like that! It's unheard of!" cried the prince. "You have a husband and children, yet you are ready to throw yourself at anyone who starts flirting with you!"

Anna fell silent, though tears were running down her cheeks. Feeling pressured by her pricks of conscience and concern over her child, offended by her husband's suspicions, she could think of nothing to say in her defence. Only out of the corner of her eye could she glance first at her husband, and then at the baby. She quietly whispered:

"Please, be quiet!"

Prozorskij fell silent. For a brief moment he began to doubt the correctness of his reproaches and realised that, if his wife was not to blame for anything, it was not on his account (since he had so often insulted her out of jealousy), but on account of the feverish boy whom she loved so fervently.

He left the room. For a long time he paced back and forth in his study. Lately he had been tormented more and more by jealousy. His imagination drew for him the filthiest and most cynical pictures. At one time he would imagine the superintendent entering the room of his sleeping wife at night; at others he would picture Bekhmetev, his old friend, putting his arms around her in the sleigh.

But as for her?... He hardly knew her. He had never bothered to find out what kind of woman his wife was. He knew her shoulders, her charming eyes and her passionate temperament (which he was only too happy to have finally awakened). But whether she was happy with him, whether she was a completely honest woman, and whether she loved him or not — this he did not know and was unable to determine. True, she submitted to his periodic demands, but what lay behind this acquiescence — he never could solve.

Passing his study for the umpteenth time, he recalled his pre-marital love affairs. How slyly and subtly had he deceived many a trusting husband, taking their wives away from them! How natural and even joyful was this endless courtship, these awkward devices for arranging meetings, for troika rides, when, unnoticeable to bystanders — and especially to husbands, he would squeeze ladies' warm hands under their fur mantelets or embrace their subtle waists and press them close to himself.

"Why might not others do the same with my wife? Why might not Bekhmetev take advantage of this opportunity to court such a beautiful woman who had literally thrown herself around his neck?"

More and more the prince was tormented by jealousy. His hatred toward a woman whom he considered his alone to possess, increased with fearful might. But along with this hatred also came passion — an uncontrollable, animal passion with palpable power — and that made him even angrier.

The children really did have measles. All four had to be put to bed. In the case of little Jusha, it was complicated by inflammation of the lung. Anna moved into the nursery and followed her children's condition with painful tension. Night after night she paced back and forth in the nursery with little Jusha in her arms. His face had taken on blue tinge. Bending over it, she was tortured by Jusha's laboured breathing. She blew air into his little mouth and kissed him, as though she were trying to transfer her life and health to him.

Sometimes she would stand over his crib and pray, praying as only mothers pray. Her prayer was not just a request to God to save her child. It was an admission of her helplessness before God and a yielding of herself to His power.

"Here I am, Lord, suffering, weak and obedient. Have mercy upon me, and if Thou willest, save him!"

Her husband, apparently, was weighed down by this period of children's illnesses. He said that Anna was exaggerating the danger of the diseases and poisoning the atmosphere in the home for all. He avoided meeting with the doctor, who came by every day, and was angry at Anna for her exclusive trust in this physician. But Anna did not pay any attention. Each time she would wait impatiently for the arrival of this kind and clever person. He was attentive and sympathetic to both the child and her condition. It was with such kind eyes that he always regarded this young, passionate mother who was emaciated by her suffering.

"No need to despair so, Your Ladyship," he said, as he stitched a compress on the boy's little chest. "See how much life there is in him — now that he's just a little better, he is actually playing."

And Anna, who was exhausted to the limit, was grateful with her whole heart to the person who, apart from his medical support, also comforted her at this challenging period of her life.

Little Jusha and all the rest of the children recovered. Anna once again felt lively for a time and relaxed in her heart. The prince, too, cheered up a bit. He was glad that life had resumed its former groove, that Anna had returned from the nursery to the bedroom, and that the doctor was no longer visiting. Anna understood all this and, as a result, her love for her husband experienced yet another rift. She would never forget and never forgive his indifference to the children's diseases and his lack of compassion for her suffering.

When everybody else had recovered, Anna's weakened and exhausted body all at once gave out, and she took ill. Her unbearable difficulties in looking after the children, her sleepless nights spent pacing the floor with a heavy baby in her arms, often for hours at a time, plus her constant worrying — all this induced a miscarriage, which was followed by a serious woman's disease. Anna was obliged to spend the next six weeks in bed.

At first the prince was terribly frightened. He summoned doctors himself, could not sleep at night, and contemplated the prospect that he might altogether lose his accustomed privilege of having a young, beautiful and healthy life-partner. At times he actually showed her tenderness, while at others he might have been either nervous and upset or just irritated by some careless movement on the part of his wife, reproaching her for not taking better care of herself. But after the danger had passed and the prince saw Anna, calm and pale, lying in bed for weeks with a book or some project in hand, he began to get terribly bored and sought out any excuse to be away from home. He even showed frequent signs of enmity toward her, which caused Anna to recall the proverb: *a husband loves a healthy wife…* and she sighed over her helplessness.

Little by little, Anna became accustomed to her husband's cynical attitude toward her and her loneliness. How often she would think about her mother and sister, who might have been able to comfort her at this moment. But they had long ago moved abroad for the sake of their little Misha who, it turned out, was suffering from curvature of the spine and whom they had constantly been moving around from place to place in an effort to preserve his frail existence.

Anna surrounded herself with her children and books. But the children exhausted her, and the doctors ordered them removed. Still, nobody took away her books. Rarely in her life had she enjoyed as much leisure-time as now. Before, in browsing the philosophical books in her husband's study, she had managed to read only a few and simply perused others for lack of time.

Now, however, she selected all her favourite philosophical narratives to read, copying out passages which especially appealed to her. After two months Anna took another look at her notebook and was surprised to find her greatest interest was in the subject of death — not in the sense of the end of life, but in the absence of death altogether. Her soul had been captured by a new religious feeling. She began to measure everything by her faith in immortality. In everything secular she suddenly glimpsed a point which had no limit — a point through which her heart's eye beheld infinity and immortality, and she began to feel lightness and joy.

"You see, everything that has been written on this subject in our ecclesiastical teachings also relates to immortality…" Anna mused as she leafed through her notebook. "But take Epictetus — philosopher, heathen and slave — he understood that there is no death, that death is simply the absorption of the human mind into the universal Mind…"

"Yes, we will all be absorbed into this universal Mind, this Deity, which we know with our whole being, which we love, from which we came and to whose will we submit!"

It was in this new and blessed mood that Anna left Moscow at the beginning of April and headed to the country with her whole family.

CHAPTER *8*

The prince was greatly disturbed by his wife's mood. There was something unnatural, calm and mysterious as well as self-confident in her whole being — something she was keeping from him, not allowing him to touch. He had never really understood her, now less than ever.

In the country Anna began to recover quickly from her illness. The doctor who was currently treating her warned the prince that despite this progress, if Her Ladyship were not careful, her ill health might return, possibly more than once. "Bathing in the river when it's hot, more periods of rest and avoiding increase in the family size…" the doctor added tactfully and with a little smile. The prince frowned at these words but did not say anything.

Anna also consulted with a woman-doctor she knew, and, despite the prince's evident discontent, she decided to follow all the advice she received so as to regain her health, strength and beauty.

And she managed to achieve this. The doctors' advice had its effect. Anna blossomed along with the beauty of summer, she became more lively and lovely, and all the pent-up energy within her arose with such force that now, it seemed, she would be able to harness all the human abilities that were welling up inside her.

Getting settled after the move in her customary rural surrounding, Anna right from the start gave herself fully to the joys of springtime, freedom and Nature. The prince, too, was more cheery and became calmer and more affectionate with his wife. He often asked her to go for walks with him, shared with her his thoughts about his articles and newly published book, and tried to interest her in the affairs of the estate.

"Is it still possible for us to get closer?" Anna thought joyfully. She was tender and attentive with her husband, fulfilled all his wishes and tried to bring him closer to the children. As often happens in periods of complete family equanimity, Anna put her family's happiness first and refused to entertain any doubts, nagging thoughts, or anything that might take away from the general happy atmosphere. With what simplicity and willingness Anna once more gave in to her former love for her husband! She again believed that she could be happy with him, that their discord was accidental and temporary. She behaved toward him so trustingly and compassionately! She endeavoured to banish any thoughts of Bekhmetev from the inner sanctum of her soul, where before he had surreptitiously occupied pride of place.

But the prince's loving and peaceful mood did not last very long, as it had not before. It always had its limit, it seemed.

On a rare, hot spring day in the middle of May, Anna got up earlier than usual and went out onto the terrace. Everybody else in the family was still asleep. Anna sent a servant to find out whether Manja and her governess were up yet and ordered them to be brought. But they were still in bed. Then Anna went alone to the forest. It was an unusually beautiful morning, as only happens in May when Nature has not yet given its all, but promises more and more beauty and blossoming, when everything is still fresh, bright, new and, unlike the summertime, without fear that all this mature beauty will soon start to fade and wither.

As an artist Anna was sensitive to any kind of aesthetic appeal. She delighted in all kinds of beauty and did not even notice she had reached the river a couple of versts from the house.

"I'd really love to go bathing," Anna thought and entered the recently renovated bathing station. For a moment she was afraid to get undressed and find herself alone in the river. But the bright, calm water attracted her with its freshness, and Anna hastened to disrobe and jump in.

Upon hearing footsteps and voices all of a sudden, she quickly began to get dressed again, though she still felt light and cheerful. Her direct nature had so passionately given in to this simple family and country life that nothing, it seemed, could spoil it. Quickly and lightly she started running home.

On the way she met the superintendent. She asked him where he was coming from and where he was going. He said that he had been doing his rounds on foot as his horse had an injured leg but that now he was on his way home.

"It's such a beautiful morning!" he added. "And Your Ladyship rose early."

Conversations about estate affairs, about seedlings, about the new machines which the prince had ordered from Moscow, were of little interest to Anna, but in her present kindly mood she did not feel like offending anyone and treated the superintendent's interests with attention and even some enthusiasm.

When the road came to a fork — where one direction led to the manor-house, the other to the superintendent's annexe — Anna said goodbye and right away noticed her husband coming toward her. She greeted him from a distance in a cheerful and affectionate voice but, as he drew closer, her heart sank. His face was all distorted by anger.

"Where are you coming from so early?" he asked.

"I was walking and bathing."

"*Et que veut dire cette intimité avec l'intendant?*"

"*L'intimité?* Why would you suggest that? He was simply coming back from the fields, and I from bathing," Anna explained with a light smile. "We happened to meet. Both of us were on our way home. After all, we have the same route, don't we?"

"You've always been and always will be humiliatingly tactless. This *tête-à-tête* is unseemly, *c'est presque un domestique,*" said the prince, choking with anger.

"Oh my God! Why are you always spoiling our happiness?" said Anna.

"Here you go again with sentimentalities. *Je suis trop vieux pour cela, ma chère.*"

"There's no use your torturing yourself and me," Anna went on. "I feel sorry for you. Well, take a look at me, take a look around, let's walk together," Anna tenderly persisted. The prince fell silent and ran on ahead.

"Can't you stop being angry? After all, there is nothing to be angry about! Yes, I may be tactless and stupid, but I do feel for you, in fact I love you. I really can't see such severity in you, it's simply nervousness."

She took her husband's arm and pressed up against him, as though pleading for protection and affection. But the prince brushed her off and hurried on home. Anna stopped, following her husband's receding image with dry, desperate eyes, as though bidding farewell to her last hope of happiness. After sighing heavily, deeply and loudly, she quietly made her way home as well.

From that day, the prince kept angrily picking on the superintendent and before long dismissed him from his employ without cause, depriving himself of a splendid foreman in the process.

Anna could not, did not want to admit that her husband was humiliating her. *Her*! Especially when she valued her purity above everything! When for the sake of a happy family life she would have sacrificed everything in the world if it had been required of her!

And so her good relations with her husband were interrupted once again. They became tense, distant, unnatural, and weighed heavily on her heart. Anna was not afforded much time to be carefree and happy. Once again she started to droop and, in an effort to escape from crudity, she resorted to her old favourite pastime — painting.

The next morning, taking a canvas, umbrella and paint-box, Anna went out of the house and settled down at the edge of a pond to paint a landscape. She had just got everything ready when she heard a carriage approaching. Glancing over to the road, she immediately recognised Bekhmetev's carriage and horses. He had visited only once since their arrival, and back then in a crowd of people, and she knew why he had not been coming. She had a vague guess that, above all, his unselfish love did not want to intrude on her family happiness, did not want to excite her honest heart, but this noble trait only elevated him further in Anna's eyes.

Dmitrij Alekseevich recognised Anna from afar, stopped his carriage and got out. After greeting her, he said:

"Now I see what are you up to there, Your Ladyship. As for me, I haven't painted for a long, long time."

"Let's paint together now, see who's better, all right?" Anna suggested.

"But I have no supplies with me."

"I have everything. Go say hello to my husband and then you can find everything you need in the closet in the corner drawing-room. There is the same canvas, palette and paints. I'll give you the brushes, I've got a lot of them."

Half an hour later, Bekhmetev returned with all the needed supplies and the work began.

"How is your health?" asked Anna, quickly and easily sketching the contours of peasant huts.

"Just the same, Your Ladyship, not good. But you, how much better you look, you're flourishing!"

"Yes, you're right, nothing ails me. I'm too healthy."

"God has given you everything: happiness, health, family, beauty."

"D'you think I'm *very* happy?"

"I can see it."

"Indeed?" Anna said sadly and distractedly.

They silently continued their painting.

"How encouraging this is — working together," said Anna.

"And how this brings us together, bonds us to each other — this working together," Bekhmetev quietly said.

"Let's translate something. See, I am reading Henri Amiel's: *Fragments d'un journal intime*, an amazingly good book! I would never attempt it on my own, but you have such a good knowledge of foreign languages..."

"That would be marvellous if you are serious about it, Your Ladyship."

"Me? What's so surprising here? I love a mental challenge, and you can help me."

They again fell silent. Anna all at once remembered evenings last year — her happy and calm state of mind back then in the presence of this individual, and all at once a surge of joy — a bright, quiet joy —illumined her whole existence.

She glanced over at him, and their eyes happened to meet. In their expression there was no longer that severity, that horror in the face of the possibility of a passionate, if not criminal spark between them, but there was a recognisable, joyful spiritual connection from which no evil could come, but which would brighten their life with light, meaning and eternal bliss.

From that day Anna again became calm. Once more there appeared the force of life, along with faith in everything, and meekness. Everything that used to seem important or had been disturbing to her no longer had any significance. She spent whole evenings working on translations, being carried away with them. Bekhmetev visited almost every day, helping her, and since the prince, too, was often drawn to this activity, he became fascinated by it and treated Dmitrij Alekseevich in a friendly and trusting manner.

One day after a long period of work, Anna proposed going for a horseback ride as a rest after dinner. She asked her husband if he would like to ride with her. Prozorskij willingly agreed and said to Bekhmetev:

"I hope, Dmitrij, that you'll go with us?"

"I'd be very glad to."

Three fine saddled horses were brought for them. Anna looked exceptionally beautiful with the blinding radiance of her face, dressed in her black riding habit, mounted on her pitch-black horse. The prince was riding on a palfrey, while he gave Dmitrij Alekseevich an excellent (and particularly expensive) English chestnut mare.

"I want to treat you to this horse for today — see what a beauty she is!"

"Yes, absolutely charming! And so light in her gait!"

But they had just gone no more than half a verst from the house when they were met by a distant neighbour who wanted to discuss some business with the prince.

"Oh, what a shame, I have to go back," said Prozorskij.

"What a pity!" Anna sighed.

"Well, you go on with Dmitrij. I'll catch up with you after I have a talk with my guest."

Anna hesitated for a moment as to whether she should return to the house with her husband or go on with Bekhmetev. But suddenly she was struck by the fear that the prince might notice her hesitation, and she said quite simply and naturally:

"Fine, we'll just skirt around the edge of the forest, and later you'll meet us at the brook."

The trail through the forest was very narrow. Dmitrij Alekseevich and Anna rode close together without a word between them. They were unable to talk about what was uppermost on their minds but did not feel like talking about anything else. The joy of being together was quite enough for both of them.

Finally, Bekhmetev broke the silence:

"What are your plans for the coming winter, Your Ladyship?"

"I don't know yet. The printing of my husband's books has been delayed. He is concerned — he says that the sending of the proofs is slowing things down and that this autumn we'll need to move to Moscow again. It's boring for him here in country. And I can't even think about the city. And what are your plans?"

"Probably I'll go abroad again. My health is really very bad. I need to go to a warmer climate."

"So you'll be leaving us? Temporarily or for good?"

"I dunno, Your Ladyship. It would be better for me to go — you already know that… I dare not look for happiness and I am losing my peace of mind."

"Have you tried looking for happiness?"

Bekhmetev did not answer right away. However, adopting a jocular, light-hearted tone, he began:

"Do you know your neighbour, Elena Mikhajlovna? She's tried a great deal to entertain me. A fun-loving lady!… Careful, Your Ladyship, you were not looking where you horse was walking, and she stumbled."

"Well, what about Elena Mikhajlovna?" Anna asked.

"She's held parties, gatherings — a lot of fun there — and she's been especially nice to me. I had a really wonderful time with her…"

Anna remembered this bold and carefree Elena Mikhajlovna, whom she had met with her husband during Bekhmetev's first visit and of whom she used to be very jealous. While this Elena Mikhajlovna's house was a hub of light-hearted merriment for the whole neighbourhood, decent women refused to have anything to do with her.

"Do you like women like Elena Mikhajlovna?"

"I'm a big fan of hers," answered Dmitrij Alekseevich with a kind of sinister irony. "She's a dear person and fun to talk with…"

"What's happened to him?…" thought Anna. "He's teasing me."

But he was not teasing her. He could barely keep from breaking out into the most desperate and passionate declaration of love before this woman. He could hardly breathe from excitement, he was weak, unhappy, he sputtered all sorts of stupidities — out of a sense of self-preservation. The thought that she was the only one he loved in the world practically drove him to tears. After all, here he was alone with her in this marvellous, quiet, natural forest milieu, and the combination of ecstasy and despair was enough to make him completely lose his mind. Yet he was unable to benefit from this moment, obliged as he was instead to preserve her equanimity and happiness in the company of another person.

Anna did not try again to talk to Bekhmetev. She whipped the horse with great gusto and disappeared into a copse. On the way there was the brook where the prince was to catch up with them. In spurring on her horse, Anna forgot about the brook, and by the time she noticed it, it was already too late to stop her horse. But the clever English mare remembered and came to a sudden halt. The horse's action was so unexpected that Anna was instantly thrown from the saddle. Catching up with her, Bekhmetev saw all this and let out a cry. But Anna rose to her feet and straightened up at once.

"It was a light fall," she said. "I didn't feel a thing."

"Falls like that happen only on stage, Your Ladyship," Bekhmetev said, though with a trembling voice.

"Well, then, let's ride on," said Anna as she tried to remount her horse.

"You won't get up that way, I'll help you, if you like, Your Ladyship," Bekhmetev said, extending his hand for Anna to step on.

Anna's small foot lightly brushed against Dmitrij Alekseevich's hand. Through her thin shoe she could feel his hot hand, which caused a sudden, unexpected shiver to run through her whole body. Her eyes darkened, and at the same time the image of her daughter Manja flitted across her mind.

One evening a few days ago, when she and Bekhmetev were sitting together going over a translation, the children were brought in to say good night. Her daughter Manja regarded Bekhmetev with an angry look and refused pointblank to shake his hand. She would not tell anybody why, but simply kept repeating: "Don't wanna, don't hafta."

"Oh my God!" thought Anna. "My dear, poor Manja! Don't be afraid for me, I love you too much."

"No, this is not necessary, this is not necessary!" cried Anna. "I can't do it this way, thank you very much! There is a stump here, I'll mount the horse myself."

Bekhmetev led the horse over to the stump. At that very moment Prozorskij rode up. Upon finishing his business with the neighbour, he had hastened to catch up with his wife and friend. The prince was nervous the whole way. And when he saw that Anna was not on the horse, but rather standing next to Dmitrij Alekseevich, he was overwhelmed with fearful suspicions; he turned pale and was at a loss for words. His lips trembled, and he clenched the reins tightly in his fist. His first impulse was to strike both of them with the whip that was in his hand. But he checked himself and calmly listened to his wife's account of her fall from the horse. He decided he would have it out with her at home and, moreover, would try to curtail Bekhmetev's visits.

On arriving home, Anna threw herself on the bed without undressing and burst into tears.

"I'm no good, I am a pitiful, wicked woman! I love him and hate myself for it! Lord, help me! Dear children, forgive me!"

Then she got up, crossed herself as though shielding herself from some delusion, and began to get changed. She had just taken off her riding habit when her husband walked in. With remarks all prepared, he wanted to have it out with her, but stopped in his tracks, overwhelmed by her beauty.

Her riding habit with its soft, dark folds lay next to her. Her elegant, strong, upturned hands quickly went about setting her wavy golden hair. Her shoulders and neck illuminated by the last rays of the rosy sunset streaming through the window, along with her beautiful dark eyes still filled with tears and excitement, radiated nothing but loveliness.

The prince stepped closer to his wife and, looking deep into her eyes, noticed an unfamiliar expression.

"How are you feeling?" he enquired.

"Quite well," she replied.

"It doesn't hurt anywhere?" he asked, touching her spine.

"No, no," she affirmed, pushing his hand away.

But the prince did not leave her. He stepped away for a moment, locked the door and, approaching his wife again, bent down and kissed her breast. Anna shuddered and staggered back. But the prince pressed her close to him and, embracing her, passionately kissed her on her lips and bare shoulders… She no longer resisted. Closing her eyes, not thinking of her husband, mentally blocking out everything else, she trembled all over in his embrace…

The prince was joyfully impressed by his wife's passionate submission. She gave herself to him wholly… but her closed eyes beheld only Dmitrij Alekseevich. Her imagination pictured him at moments of a silent declaration of love, but there beside him in her dream loomed the frightened, hostile eyes of Manja, who in the innocence of her soul was conscious of the danger her mother was going through…

The next day the prince was very cheerful and enterprising. His jealousy subsided for a time. He found himself making plans and thinking of various trips. He kept making jokes, and was especially nice to his friend, who had dropped by to find out how Her Ladyship was coping with the effects of her fall.

CHAPTER 9

For the first time in her life Anna felt troubled in her heart. Always firm, honest and composed, she was very self-confident and not afraid of anything. But now her strength was betraying her. She knew that in August Bekhmetev (who was already quite ill) would be leaving. She felt that the happiness that had been her mainstay all this time was coming to an end… and then what? Then she would still be left with the house, her duties and her husband's selfishness and indifference, with his crude demands — along with her inability to go on living without the light of that love with which she had been spoilt of late.

"And the children? Could I have cooled to them?" Anna asked herself in horror. "No, that's different; they have quite another place in my heart. But how tired I am! How terribly tired! And my husband? Where might I find my love for him? What has happened anyway? Why can't I love both my husband and this man who has loved me for so long and so unselfishly, simply and truly, without demanding anything in return?…"

And despite all these self-justifying thoughts, Anna felt — indeed, she could not help feeling — that what was happening was what was supposed to happen in her marital life and her love for her husband above all else — as should happen in any good marriage.

She felt bound in her heart to a man who was able — without violence, without demands, without any prerogatives — to illumine her whole life with love, and then, when this spiritual life was all full, a feeling of happiness and personal closeness to this man was awakened in her. Why could not this man have been her husband?

She had got married with such strong ideals; she so idealised her husband at first; for so long she blindly submitted to his influence; she had only a vague feeling — but never allowed herself to admit — that there was something wrong, something wrong, that she was hurt by his indifference to every aspect of her inner life and to her children, that she was humiliated by the fact that he was interested only in her blossoming beauty, her health and outward success, which not only delighted him but provoked in him that animal jealousy which had caused her so much torment and suffering.

"What will happen now? What will I now feel for my husband?" Anna asked herself, grasping in her heart like a drowning person for that straw which was supposed to save her. But she kept on drowning, drowning, clearly aware that the 'straw' was bending in her weak hands and offered no real salvation.

However, for a time fate came to her aid and deceived her, promising an escape from her difficult mental condition.

The prince, who had lately been occupied with improvements to his estate, went off to the city to purchase a new steam threshing machine. The day was very damp and cold, and, ignoring Anna's pleas to take the carriage, Prozorskij determinedly set off on horseback …

It was now late, already getting dark, and the prince had still not returned.

Anna was beginning to worry when a wagon pulled up to the house and the prince (apparently unable to walk on his own) was carried out. When Anna saw it, she screamed in horror and rushed to her husband's side. He gave her a painful smile as they carried him into the house, and hurriedly told her with a groan:

"It seems my leg is broken. Not to worry, don't be afraid."

"It's your leg, thank God! I thought it might be something worse. But we have to send right away for the doctor."

After arranging to call the doctor, she ran to her husband's room to help him into bed and to make sure his leg was as comfortable as possible. Then she quickly and deftly filled a rubber bottle with ice and applied it to Prozorskij's injured leg. After doing all this, she sat down firmly and calmly at his bedside. He groaned, tossed and turned, demanding to be waited on at every moment. Nobody else could please him. Sending everybody out, Anna tenderly and patiently took care of her husband. She was glad of this unmistakable opportunity to be of service — an opportunity which fate had imposed on her.

"Come closer," he would constantly call. Or demand: "Put a pillow under my head… Ouch, not like that!" Or: "I've exhausted you, darling," with another groan.

By morning the prince was asleep. Tiptoeing to his bedside, Anna began carefully examining her husband's face. Its beautiful but wrinkled lines had a strange effect on her. She was transported to the distant past, to a time when she trustingly, blindly and simply loved this person with neither analysis nor criticism.

"If only it were possible again! After all, he's all good inside, he loves me alone and has never betrayed me. I've been the bad one, not he … what more can I want?"

She bent over him and quietly planted a kiss on his forehead.

"Yes, he was the only one I ever loved, and he is dearer to me than anyone else in the world," Anna concluded and hastily locked away in her heart any further analysis of her innermost sacred secrets. And she was not lying in deciding the question of love for her husband. That force of love — the young, passionate, idealised love which she had given wholly to her husband in the first years of their marriage — she no longer felt such a force within her. How her husband reacted to this love was another matter, but none of this could destroy the love itself, and her love spilled over at every opportunity and fell naturally without her pushing it.

Now the prince slept, and Anna no longer heard the voice that had threatened her so crudely at times. She no longer saw the eyes which had regarded her unfairly — with either rancour or lust — she saw only the man to whom she had given herself and all her love — and loved him again …

Any woman truly loves only once. She cherishes whatever love she has been saving for the right moment. But once it has been given, she treasures it, protects it and closes her eyes to the faults of the one she has given it to. The repetition of this feeling always grows upon an old feeling, on old ideals, and if it turns out that a married woman falls in love with another man, it is almost always her husband who is to blame. It means he has failed to satisfy the poetic demands put forward by the young, pure feminine nature — instead, he has broken them, exchanging them for just the animal side of marriage. Woe to the husband if somebody else has managed to fill the place he himself had left empty, and if the same first, idealised love has been transferred to another.

Prozorskij suffered terribly the whole night, and the doctor did not arrive until the next morning. He bound up the wound and prescribed a full night's rest.

The prince's illness lasted several torturous days. He was impatient, demanding, and suspicious in the extreme. His inability to move drove him mad. He would not let Anna out of his sight for a moment. Neighbours came by to enquire as to his health. This distracted him for a time, but he was still terribly bored and constantly picked on his wife.

"Where've you been?" he would ask, when she stepped out of his room for a short time. "What have you been doing?"

"I went for a walk with the children," Anna would reply, or: "I was writing a letter," or: "I was tutoring Manja and Pavlik."

The prince checked on all these answers by questioning the children and staff, whom he seemed to inadvertently provoke into telling stories of what Mamà was doing, or whether they knew where Her Ladyship was and what she was busy with. He was not fully aware himself as to what he suspected his wife of — it was something painful, almost insane.

Bekhmetev dropped by only once to enquire as to the prince's health. He himself was feeling quite ill and was getting ready to go abroad. Anna did not go out to meet him, claiming exhaustion. After her riding adventure with him she still suffered from pricks of conscience, as though she had committed some wicked deed. The sense of self-preservation on the part of her conscience was so strong that it took all her mental strength to make her forget the sensation she had experienced at that moment.

As to fulfilling her duties as a wife and mother, she managed to achieve this. Besides, the whole material side of the life of the lady of the house inevitably sobers any passion for a short time.

"Your Ladyship," Anna's maid summoned her out of her husband's bedroom. "If it pleases you, the upholsterer is asking whether he has upholstered the furniture properly."

Anna went into the servants' room to look at the furniture and her mouth fell open. All the expensive upholstery had been applied inside out — the cross-threads of the fabric were clearly visible on the reverse side and offensive to the eyes.

"Now what have you done?" screamed Anna. "Don't tell me everything is inside out?!"

It all had to be torn up, and the spoilt fabric haunted Anna for the whole day…

Several days later, they again called Anna.

"A thousand pardons, Milady, I'm unable to cope with the cook; he's got himself drunk. It's time to bring soup up to His Lordship's room, but the cook isn't letting anybody serve it. He just stands there yelling."

Anna went down to the kitchen, quickly approached the cook and with a loud and commanding voice so unmistakably shouted at him: "Out of here, this minute!" that the cook instantly flew out of the room as though shot from a cannon, passing the soup to a pantry-man.

When Anna returned to her room, she was shaking all over and there were tears in her eyes. The whole material aspect of her life had always been hateful to her, and any kind of anger was unbearable.

CHAPTER 10

The end of August came. Autumn could already be felt in the cooler evenings, in the appearance of red and yellow leaves, shortened days, the sadness of bare fields and meadows.

The prince recovered, although he still walked on crutches and was constantly calling for a doctor, capriciously complaining about the slow pace of his recovery. Anna had grown noticeably thinner, but she had regained full control of herself and settled firmly into her familial groove of life without complaint, without wavering, with intensified energy and a joyful recognition of duty done.

For a long time now Anna had had no word of Bekhmetev. She was troubled in the depths of her heart and had no idea what his prolonged absence might mean.

One day she happened to be sitting in her husband's study and reading him the newspaper aloud. The prince lay on the sofa and anxiously looked out the window, waiting for the doctor.

"You probably haven't sent for the doctor?" he enquired.

"I did a long time ago. Anyway, what do you need him for? There's nothing he can do to help. What we need here is time. Since when have you started to believe in doctors?"

"My bandage is too tight. I know all doctors are charlatans, but this is a mechanical matter — it's something they've mastered."

"Listen, someone's arrived."

In fact, some kind of light carriage had pulled up to the porch, but it turned out to be a messenger from Bekhmetev's sister, Varvara Alekseevna, with a note.

When Anna was given the envelope, she froze on the spot. Prozorskij observed his wife attentively and waited to see what she would say. So as to hide her face, Anna turned toward the light with her back to the prince. After perusing the note, she said in a calm tone:

"Varvara Alekseevna is asking me to pay her a visit this evening. Dmitrij Alekseevich is going away, and they are giving him a farewell party. Apparently, there will be guests and some sort of celebration."

"Show me the note."

With a scornful smile Anna handed her husband the note.

"So, are you going?"

"No, I don't want to leave you... Here, the doctor's arrived."

In walked a man of about thirty years of age, medium build, rosy-cheeked, handsome, with sharp German and vulgar features, yet kind-hearted and composed.

"So, the bandage is troubling you. We'll fix that at once," he said, after greeting the prince and duchess in a rather familiar manner.

He rolled up his sleeves, washed his hands and set about his task, and Anna attentively and deftly assisted him.

"Your Ladyship," the nanny quietly called out to Anna, "please come here for a moment."

After completing the task with the doctor and her husband, Anna left the room.

The nanny asked Anna to have the doctor look at a boy whose face had been injured by a horse's hoof. It was scary to see a four-year-old whose flesh and skin hung in clumps on his face — all covered with dark spots, clotted in some places and oozing blood in others.

The pale, frightened mother regarded the doctor with pleading eyes, hoping for some kind of help for her son. After making some crying sounds, she proceeded to briefly describe some of her dreams:

"I dreamt about a red cock... I get it now! Or I see an old man going into a hut... oh, my dear... an' he beckons to me, an' I feel all stuffy and can't breathe, oh-oh-oh!"

"Call the doctor, Alexander Karlovich, at once," Anna told the nanny and ran to the household dispensary to find whatever would be needed for the suture.

They washed the child, comforted him and gave him all sorts of sweets. Anna took the boy on her knees, and the doctor went about applying the sutures, carefully pushing aside the skin. The boy was remarkably patient; the task proceeded smoothly and was soon drawing to a close.

Meanwhile, the prince eventually noticed that his wife had been gone a rather long time. With crutch in hand, he went to see what she was up to. He gave the door a sharp push, greatly startling Anna, who threw him a frightened look.

"Oh, Your Ladyship," said the doctor with annoyance, "for God's sake, hold his head, please. We almost broke a suture."

The doctor took hold of Anna's hand and showed her how to hold the boy's head properly.

At this point Prozorskij's facial expression changed dramatically.

"Give the boy to his mother; I would ask you to come and see me — I need you," he declared sharply, commandingly and maliciously.

"But first we must finish with this unfortunate lad," Anna timidly countered.

"I implore you… *Vous m'entendez!*" the prince suddenly spluttered, thumping the floor with his crutch.

But Anna was not listening and went on holding the child, while the doctor diligently and conscientiously continued his task. In adjusting the position of the boy's head, his hands constantly (though inadvertently) kept brushing against Anna's arms and even her breast, which the child was leaning against. The doctor did not notice anything and did not even hear the prince's words; he was concentrating fully on the task at hand.

But all of a sudden Prozorskij came quite close, grabbed hold of the injured boy with his hand and plopped him into the arms of his peasant mother, letting his crutch fall to the floor with a loud bang. He then proceeded to drag Anna into his study. The doctor glanced at what was happening in astonishment and, muttering "Lunatic!" under his breath, turned back to the injured lad, this time requesting the nanny to assist.

In the meantime, still grasping hold of Anna's hand, the prince threw her on the sofa. Awkwardly overturning an armchair in the process, he banged the door shut and began to pace the room, thumping the floor with his crutch and madly sputtering:

"When I ask you … you humiliate me with your behaviour toward this German bloke! … This closeness… It's all deliberate!" he cried, quite beside himself with anger.

But this time Anna, too, burst out.

"Have you gone completely out of your mind?! Think what you are saying! Where is there room for judgements like that in the presence of a suffering child?!"

"Silence!" Prozorskij shouted. "Your justifications are worse than your abominable actions! You'd better go. Go! Go!" he cried and, pushing Anna out the door, he threw himself on the sofa.

Anna left the room with a stagger. When she got to the drawing-room, she clasped her hand to her breast and simply whispered:

"There is a limit to everything! My God!"

She didn't cry. Her dry eyes stared rigidly and senselessly into space. Going into her bedroom, she sat down on a chair before the mirror and involuntarily took a look at herself. She was magnificent as a picture of indignation — her pale and proper face breathed energy and purity, her dark eyes appeared even darker and deeper with their bitter expression.

Anna did not see her husband the rest of the day. He did not come out of his study for dinner, and Anna was left alone with the children and the other members of the household. The children talked about the kite which they were going to launch after dinner. Anna all at once decided that she would go see Varvara Alekseevna after all.

"Have them prepare the four-horse carriage," she ordered in a loud voice so that her husband would hear. "And tell Dunjasha to get my white woollen dress ready for me."

"Mamà, where are you going? Don't go!" the children cried.

"Where are you going?" Pavlik persisted. "Bring Dmitrij Alekseevich to us — he hasn't been here in a long time."

Anna was sad the whole meal and hardly answered a single question.

After dinner, without going to see her husband, she went to her bedroom to change her clothes and then headed off to Varvara Alekseevna's.

Her heart froze at the exciting prospect of seeing Bekhmetev again. Even though such excitement could easily upset her, the desire to see the one whose closeness had so tenderly touched her life — in sharp contradiction to the way her husband approached her — became so great after Prozorskij's distasteful display of temper that she decided to go to Varvara Alekseevna's no matter what the cost... and see Dmitrij — quite probably for the last time.

CHAPTER 11

By the time Anna walked into the low-ceilinged (but still quite spacious) parlour in Varvara Alekseevna's house, a fairly large collection of guests had already gathered. They included neighbours, relatives and long-time friends. Two or three young ladies were grouped around the piano in the company of a young man. There was also the boisterous Elena Mikhajlovna, who had caused Anna so much sorrow.

Dmitrij Alekseevich, who had become remarkably thinner, haggard and sad looking, was sitting alone. He went over to Anna without hiding his joy or any other pretensions.

"You changed your mind and came — what a fantastic surprise! I couldn't think of leaving without seeing you."

"Why didn't you come to see us?" said Anna offering him her hand, which he kissed.

"Yes, I was of course going to come and see you tomorrow. In fact, I'll definitely come by tomorrow to bid farewell to my sick friend. But you see how frail I am…; I don't know how I'll make it to the Hyères resort," he added with a weak smile.

Anna gave a heavy sigh and went to see Varvara Alekseevna in the drawing-room. Dmitrij Alekseevich followed her.

Varvara Alekseevna exchanged a quick greeting with Anna, thanking her for coming, while continuing to supervise the setting up of the outdoor buffet which had been planned for that evening.

"Are you still determined, Dmitrij," she asked her brother, "to go and take tea with us by the lake? It's probably too damp for you."

"No, now I am more determined than ever. I want to show Her Ladyship those marvellous places which I shall probably never see again." Another smile.

"It's as though he actually delights in his inevitable and approaching death," Anna thought.

They sat in the drawing-room by the window and Bekhmetev, pointing to his chest, told Anna quietly and seriously:

"Something's gone quite wrong with me, Your Ladyship, I don't feel well."

"You'll get better when you're abroad."

"For what? To get to eternity all the sooner! It's too confining for me here."

And Anna had a feeling that, in saying this, Dmitrij Alekseevich no longer saw *her*, but that his eyes were looking somewhere far off into infinity, and she wanted to join him there, too.

A whole convoy of carriages was brought up. Varvara Alekseevna arranged who would sit with whom, reserving for herself a place with her brother in the calèche to watch over him and shield him from the dampness.

Bekhmetev, however, went up to his sister and told her quietly but firmly:

"Varvara, dear, I am asking Her Ladyship to do me the honour of riding with me."

Anna was going to object, but Dmitrij Alekseevich gave her such a stern, pleading and decisive look, that words failed her, and she kept silent.

Bekhmetev held out his hand to Anna in a knightly gesture and, after seating her, sat down beside her, covering himself with an overcoat and wrapping his legs in a plaid rug.

All the carriages then set off.

Suddenly Dmitrij Alekseevich ordered the coachman: "Turn right here!" and the calèche turned down a narrow leafy trail, which ran through an old pine forest.

"We'll take another way around," he said. "It's so beautiful here!"

All at once they found themselves alone — a situation which caused Anna to feel pricks of conscience. She was extremely moved by Dmitrij's sitting so close beside her. In fact, his deathly appearance provoked in her such despair that from moment to moment she feared she would not be able to keep from bursting into tears, or crying out, or doing something extreme. Then she closed her eyes or, alternatively, silently looked to one side, clasping her hands to her breast and heart, as though wishing to bring the life within her to a halt.

Is it possible that death — that destructive, daily feature of life — could be so majestic, lovely and meaningful? This day, the 22nd of August, became for Anna a day of triumphant, beautiful and silent termination of everything — both around her and within her. The piquant, transparent (and already autumnal) air served as a reminder of how close death actually was. The suffering heart had lost its energy of life. Death, death everywhere, so close at hand — this was terrible, and Anna began to fear it might catch her at any moment, too...

Soon they entered the heart of the old pine forest. The age-old pines, immovable and dark, barely let through the bright red rays of the setting sun, which was especially brilliant when illuminating the broad, open meadows they came upon from time to time.

"And this will be our *very last* ride together," thought Anna, glancing over at Bekhmetev.

He could feel her glance and said:

"It's marvellous here, isn't it?"

"Yes, amazingly beautiful, but why did you come? So damp and cold today!"

"No, that's nothing, let's go on... and on. Oh, so wonderful! It's never felt so good," he declared. "Remember this forest by this lake — we shall *never* see it again. Take a good look. I love these places so: the forests and the lakes — what could be more beautiful?"

"Yes, soon you will be *nowhere*, you will never have existed!" Anna said to herself, involuntarily grasping hold of Dmitrij's hand.

"Are you cold?" she asked. "What cold hands you have!"

"Could it be he is dying? And what if we never say a word to each other again? We can still love each other with the most pure and unselfish love, just the two of us — he, approaching death, and I — alas! — remaining alive — we are both obliged to sacrifice our happiness, even that very small happiness of being able to tell each other how dear we have been to each other these past years; how each of us became a relief for the other — we caused each other to forget our sorrows... in that pure atmosphere of love in which we have lived every moment of our constant spiritual communion."

Was such sacrifice justified by that suspicious coldness, that selfish and sensual attitude that she repeatedly met from her handsome but sanctimonious husband?

"But can I possibly preserve my purity for *anyone*?" Anna went on in her thought. "No, not for anyone in the world — that was a lie... I held on to the concept because I *loved* it; and I put it first, and if this man is still dear to me, it's only because he is what he is."

As if in answer to her thought, Bekhmetev all at once offered:

"This outing, Your Ladyship, will be our final farewell. I'm leaving tomorrow and, probably, we shall never see each other again." He paused.

"I wanted to tell you…" he hesitated again, "that the brightest part of my entire life has been my stay… no, truth be told… my friendship with you."

Anna wanted to say something but could not. She felt a lump in her throat. Bekhmetev continued:

"I have never met a woman with such an aureole of purity, clarity and love for all things exalted as you. Whatever happens, Your Ladyship, if God grants you just one thing — let it be to remain just the way you are."

The calèche gently rolled along the forest trail. It was getting dark, and Dmitrij Alekseevich looked so calm and happy, just as he had a year ago, when he and Anna were returning from the city in a carriage full of children whom they had driven into town to have their picture taken. This was a time when both of them knew that it was possible to be happy, and not only to love, but to love in the way one loves and delights in a clear sky or a display of marvellous summer Nature, and in the joy of being together.

This was not, however, something she could say aloud, nor could she allow anything that would provoke the slightest prick of conscience in front of these dear, innocent and beloved children. She could not even bring herself to acknowledge that joy of love — that pure, chaste and never-expressed love — that love which now, on this amazing August evening, was dying along with him, together with those ideal links with the man who had awakened in her heart all the best and highest emotions.

"And now I shall go home, and my husband will look at me with suspicion, imagining me capable of the worst and most immoral conduct, all the while kissing my exposed shoulders and arms. And all day long we, like a couple of criminals having done our deeds during the night, will not speak to each other — he with his pompous scorn and indifference to my life, and I with fear of his suspicions and in the lonely world of children and cares, torn between a fading sense of love for my husband and the budding flame within me, burning for another man …"

They kept moving ahead. Bekhmetev wrapped himself more tightly in the blanket and coughed. The cool evening air penetrated every pore with its unpleasant dampness. This journey through places unfamiliar to Anna seemed to be leading the two of them into an unknown eternity, to a transition into something that should no longer come between them…

The sun set. "And *the sun* has died as well!" thought Anna. Suddenly its last rays shone brightly on the crowns of the many trees of the garden which they were approaching. "Soon all Nature will die," Anna thought further. "And Dmitrij? No, that's impossible! What will I live by? Where will I find that pure happiness to give me strength, to make myself better, smarter, kinder... No, that's impossible!" Anna was practically screaming.

"We're here," Dmitrij Alekseevich declared quietly. Silently taking Anna's hand, he gave it a prolonged and tender kiss and again whispered: "Farewell, my dear duchess."

She bent over and kissed his forehead. The lump in her throat, which had been choking Anna the whole time, seemed to dissolve into a quiet, painful moan. Tears filled her eyes, and something broke in her heart and died — forever. Yet another facet of her life had now disappeared for good. It was finished.

But life must go on, and it had to be a good life...

A noisy crowd had already gathered in a large, round, beautiful gazebo illuminated by multicoloured lanterns. People were busy with food, tea and fruit. They were putting together seats out of boards, hanging the last lanterns in the garden, building a fire along with other frivolous but necessary makings of an outdoor buffet.

Bekhmetev was afraid of staying too late and left for home alone, after saying goodbye to the whole company. Anna was supposed to stay until the end, and, after the party was over, she found herself alone in the homeward-bound calèche in the steely cold glow of the bright August night. Then her spiritual loneliness became all too clear, and it wasn't long before sobbing sounds began to emanate from her breast. She wept painfully for a long time, as though mourning someone's passing, along with her own life which had abandoned her. It was a cry of wild despair.

Such tears were supposed to — and actually did — drive her sorrow away. By the time she approached the manor house, she had regained control of herself, and her cheerfulness and energy of life gradually returned.

The pain which had broken out in her heart upon her parting and separation from Bekhmetev all at once disappeared far away as though, after having a good cry, she had said goodbye to it forever. Long whimpering spells were foreign to her energetic nature. This pain of parting from another person seemed now criminal to her in front of her children and her husband. She was ashamed that she had left her husband while he was still feeling ill and upset. She recalled how Pavlik had pleaded with her not to go, and she was overwhelmed by the whole world of her family life pressing in on her from all sides.

The image of little Jusha was especially vivid, with his tender, intelligent-looking countenance... and the lively Manja with her quick, categorical and unexpected judgements on everything... Their lessons, too, came to mind, along with all her thoughts about the importance of home upbringing for this next generation. By the time Anna reached the house, she already felt uplifted in spirit, in the full consciousness of her duty. She walked into her house completely renewed in her mind.

She took off her coat, went first to the children's rooms, then quietly approached the door of her husband's study, where she found him still awake.

CHAPTER 12

The prince, in the meantime, as soon as he realised that Anna had left without even coming to see him as usual, began to get terribly concerned, and the wildest notions entered his head. "Perhaps," he thought, "she has left for good and won't ever come back."

He felt all constricted with mental pain upon recalling how he had pushed his wife. Nothing like that had ever happened to him before. "Oh, dear!" he groaned within himself; but all at once he remembered how he had seen with his own eyes that this fat German doctor with his lily-white hands, while adjusting the skin on the boy's forehead, had let his hands pass over Anna's breast. "Over *her* breast! And surely on purpose! And what had *she* been feeling at that moment?!"

And the prince clearly pictured before his eyes that marvellous full breast, which so many times had caused him to forget the whole world and become a slave to this woman!

In the depths of his soul, he recognised that perhaps he was wrong, that Anna's truthful eyes, her pure, almost child-like (despite her thirty years) vision could not be false. Still, the pains of jealousy were tormenting him more and more.

"And now," he reasoned, "why had she left? Bekhmetev is there, of course… Who knows — if not the doctor — perhaps my so-called friend is embracing her somewhere in the forest at this very moment? She is a stranger to me, she — more than anyone else — is mysterious and incomprehensible to me. There is something inside her that she is holding back, and that something constantly escapes me."

The prince tried reading; he went to see the children. He kept looking at his watch. But nowhere did he find peace.

The nanny brought in the two younger children — the girl and little Jusha — to say goodnight. He looked at the girl as if she belonged to someone else, took her little hands and began to examine them.

"Who knows, maybe this little girl is not *my* daughter!… Oh!… True, they say she has my hands, my manner of holding a fork, and of wiping her hands with a towel… All that is indeed true."

He looked at the boy and, drawing him close to himself, kissed him. There was no doubt that this was a genuine copy of himself.

A little later Manja and Pavlik (the older ones), too, came to say goodnight. Prozorskij cut out paper figures for them and showed how to blow on them to make it look like they were wrestling.

The children laughed, but their laughter only further irritated the prince.

"Well, go on to bed now. Is Jusha asleep already?"

"A long time ago. But before that he was crying … he was calling on Mamà to pray to God."

"Goodnight, goodnight," repeated the prince, getting more and more irritated. Meanwhile, to himself: "He called upon Mamà to pray while she is probably flirting with this wretch in her white dress."

Prozorskij lay down on the sofa, lit a cigar and began to think about his relations with his wife:

"How beautifully and patiently she had been taking care of me! Probably because she feels guilty. But what if it should turn out she really *is* guilty?" The prince drew himself a mental picture — with frightening clarity — of his wife's criminal love for Bekhmetev and a strong conviction of her guilt.

He jumped up, opened a window, looked at the round, bright moon (which appeared insolent to him), and began to listen closely to the sounds of the night. He could hear the hoofbeats of horses and the noise of an approaching carriage, coming closer and closer.

"That must be her," he thought. However, it turned out to be the doctor on his way home from the buffet. Seeing Prozorskij in the window, he stopped his carriage.

"Aren't you asleep yet, Your Lordship?" the doctor called to him. "That's not good in your condition."

"Come on in for a moment and tell me about Varvara Alekseevna's party."

"I'm sorry, Your Lordship, I can't tonight. Early tomorrow I have a surgery to perform in a village. I have to get up early and be alert."

"Is my wife on her way home? Did you see her at all?"

"Yes, of course! Well, I don't envy her. They put her in a calèche with that consumptive Bekhmetev. He took her off to show her some favourite places of his. He should not be talking at all — too cold and damp. No time here for looking at beautiful places! The man is quite out of sorts. He has less than three months to live."

"Well, goodbye, doctor. It's cold. I thank you," the prince suddenly said in an irritated tone and snapped the window shut. His face took on a frightful expression. For him there was no longer any doubt — Anna was in love, and no doubt having an affair with Bekhmetev! Prozorskij, short of breath, stood at his desk, nervously moving books, papers and other objects around, and paying acute attention to any sound from outside.

Soon Anna's carriage approached with its soft rubber tires and stopped at the main entrance. The prince heard his wife come into the house and take off her coat. She first went to the children's rooms and then, ever so quietly, with barely audible footsteps, hastily approached the door of the study. The prince remained standing fixed to the spot.

"You're not asleep yet?" Anna quietly asked.

"Dissolute deceiver!" mused the prince to himself. "She's still putting on an act!" With this thought in mind, he picked up a grey, heavy, round marble paperweight from the desk.

Anna opened the door and went over to her husband.

"How are you doing? Are you feeling worse?"

"I'm not only worse, but my heart is being torn apart, or suffering an attack. I can't tolerate your behaviour any longer."

"My behaviour? But what have I done?"

"D'you dare to tell me that you are not in love with Bekhmetev?"

Anna blushed and said:

"I love Dmitrij Alekseevich very much but…"

At this point she fell silent.

"Perhaps you are going to tell me that you did not go riding alone with him God knows where the entire evening, and in the sight of the whole company!"

"He leaves tomorrow, and I feel very sorry for him …"

"And you are in love with him — and you have been his lover for some time!"

"Not another word, for God's sake!"

"I'll kill you… you vile and dissolute woman… I've been patient for a long time, but I shan't allow… My honour, my family's honour…"

The prince was breathless with anger and emotion.

"Your honour!… Oh, no need to worry [about] your honour…" said Anna in her defence. "But calm down, for God's sake, you're only hurting yourself…"

She went up to her husband and took his hand, but her touch only inflamed him further. He again grasped hold of the heavy paperweight on his desk and lifted it in the air, bellowing:

"Out of here, or I'll kill you!"

"But what for? Haven't you known me all along? Calm down, for God's sake! Could something have been the matter?"

"It's all lies… Don't say anything! I can't vouch for my actions, go away!"

Shaking all over, he kept picking up the paperweight and putting it down.

Anna tried once more to take the prince's hand, but he instantly turned away and pushed her aside. When she ran behind the desk, he raised his arm once more in her direction.

The heavy paperweight flew across the desk and struck Anna sharply in the temple, before falling to the floor with a heavy thud.

Like a wounded bird which had let her white wings droop, bending over in an awkward position, Anna collapsed under the large desk into the soft white folds of her dress. A brief hushed groan began to emanate from her breast, and she lost consciousness.

The prince rushed over to his wife. From her bluish temple streamed a thin ooze of blood, leaving red spots on her white dress. Her face was deathly pale, her lips open, her eyes rolled into their sockets, her arms bent in an ungainly pose.

"Anna! Anna!" cried the prince, attempting to lift her. But his crutch and injured leg interfered with any movement.

He opened the door and began to call his servants. The nanny and a footman came running.

"The duchess is in a bad way; send quickly for the doctor," he ordered.

The nanny ran over to Anna and screamed:

"Look, my lady's injured herself! Oh, Lord!"

"She didn't injure herself, I killed her," confessed Prozorskij.

The nanny looked at him in shock, crossed herself and, dashing over to Anna, muttered:

"His Lordship has gone completely out of his mind. He doesn't know what he is saying."

She fetched some water from the prince's dressing room and started to douse Anna's face with it, as well as to moisten her injured temple. She tried to lift her but could not. She called the footman to help, and the two of them managed to drag Anna to the sofa and lay her down there. Then the nanny asked for some ice.

At this point, the chambermaids, the housekeeper and the Englishwoman all came running — each wearing the most outlandish variety of night attire. Manja, awakened and frightened by the commotion came barefoot in her night-dress. She stopped at a slight distance away and screamed:

"Nanny, Mamà's hurt herself? She's gonna die. Nanny, dear, where is Papà? Is the doctor coming?… There is a hole in her temple, and she is bleeding!… Oh! Oh!…"

The poor girl was shaking so much that her whole body seemed to be bouncing up and down.

"Go and lie down, Manja," the nanny comforted. "The doctor's on his way. Mamà will be fine. She fell and hurt herself, it's nothing."

However, Manja could tell from the nanny's countenance that it was far more than nothing. The nanny applied ice to Anna's temple and looked at the stiff, pale face of her mistress with a hopeless expression.

"I shan't go anywhere, Nanny, I'm afraid. I'll just sit here," said the girl, jumping into a large armchair. Tucking her legs beneath her, she sat in a squat position and kept looking at her mother and the nanny. She was shaking all over, and her teeth could not stop chattering.

All during this time the prince was absent from the room. He was sitting in the drawing-room, waiting for the doctor.

"She must have fainted," he comforted himself. "Probably by now she'll have come to. I hear voices from next door… See what her conduct has led to!" Prozorskij tried to justify himself. "How can I risk my honour? And the honour of my family name! There have never been any immoral women in our family history! I, a man, have always behaved myself beyond reproach… Shame on the children that their mother was a dissolute woman!… And the horrible possibility that she had a child who is not mine?…"

The prince went into convulsions, his face disfigured with terror. He wanted to get up but, helplessly clenching his fists, he fell back into his chair.

"Well, that's splendid, it had to be that way…" he decided.

On the table stood a bowl of plums. He picked one and began to eat it. The old-fashioned English grandfather clock rang out two chimes. By morning the cocks would begin to crow in the village. The prince looked out the window. The moon had set, but the bright stars still shone high in the night sky. Everything looked cold, and he very much felt like sleeping.

"Now what's been going on?" he suddenly thought. "Can it be that she hasn't come to yet?"

The prince hastened to his study, and the doctor came in at the same time. He rushed over to Anna and removed her icepack. As he listened to her heart and took her pulse, his countenance became gloomier and gloomier.

"What happened?" the doctor asked.

"She suffered a blow from this paperweight," replied Prozorskij, as he bent over to pick up the heavy object which nobody had noticed before.

"Yes, and the blow was right on target," the doctor observed. "Her pulse is very weak, her heart as well."

The doctor opened the bag he had brought with him and took out several vials and various medical accessories. He asked the nanny to help him, and again went over to Anna, who was lying on the sofa. Her beautiful pale head lay raised on a leather pillow.

The soft ringlets of her dark hair with golden flecks encircled her face like an aureole. Her facial expression was severe and terrified. Blood was still oozing from the deep, dark wound on her temple and flowing down her pale cheek onto her white dress.

The doctor tried to bring Anna back to consciousness, but no amount of effort could raise her out of her deep faint. The nanny took Manja away, as she had begun to sob loudly.

The prince went over to his wife. He looked questioningly at the doctor, who did not say a word, but went on with his task.

Around ten o'clock in the morning Anna started to come to. The doctor put everyone out, fearing the excitement was too much for his patient. He bound the wound, but the bandage gave Anna a pitiful, weird appearance. Finally, Anna opened her eyes and looked around with a wild gaze.

"Call His Lordship," Anna quietly muttered before closing her eyes again.

The prince came into the room and bent over her. Anna opened her large dark eyes and, with what appeared to be a great effort, began to speak in a weak, hushed voice:

"It had to turn out this way… Forgive me!… You're not to blame… But if I die, I must tell you…"

She hesitated and shut her eyes once more.

"What?… What is it?… Say something, for God's sake! Tell me at once…" he pleaded, expecting to hear some sort of an admission of guilt.

"I have to say that I have never been unfaithful to you, that I loved you as much as I could, and that I am dying with a clear conscience before you and the children… But all the better!… Oh, how tired I am!" Anna sighed and fell silent.

"I am to blame before you, Anna," Prozorskij declared. "Anna, my friend, forgive me…"

The prince began to sob. He took Anna's hand and pressed it against his cheek. Her hand was starting to cool.

"Where are the children?" Anna asked suddenly, raising herself slightly. "Call the children at once! At once!"

She fell back in exhaustion, closing her eyes. A few minutes later she opened them, but this time her eyes were no longer fixed on anyone in particular. They had a serious look which far transcended anything earthly.

"I wanted a different kind of love. Something like…" Anna raised her eyes to her husband and, as though barely recognising him, added: "You're not to blame… You couldn't possibly understand what…" She hesitated again, and finished the sentence with difficulty: "what is important in love…"

They brought in the children, terrified and weeping. Anna kissed each one of them in turn and wanted to make a sign of the cross over them, as she did every evening when she said goodnight to them, but her hand could not help drooping.

They took the children away, and in their wake something ominous, silent and frightening filled the atmosphere of the room, hovering in the air like a dark cloud.

"It's over," muttered Anna softly. "*Cette clef — c'est l'infinie…* " she muttered even more softly as though in a delirium, for some reason recalling the words of Alphonse de Lamartine, which Bekhmetev had once read to her.

The doctor came up to her. He gently shook his head and beckoned to the prince, who was still softly sobbing.

Anna never did regain consciousness. She passed away on the stroke of noon. By seven o'clock that evening she was lying on a table in the great hall, wearing a bright celebratory dress. It gave an impression of lightheartedness — in stark and awkward contrast with the seriousness and gloom of her deathly pale, petrified countenance and its pierced temple.

There was something frightening in the prince's despair. It was the helpless bewilderment of a child lost in a forest. He pounded the walls, cried out, let out groans and threw himself on the sofas and chairs, asking everyone to kill him, imprison him or execute him. He refused to eat, or drink, or sleep.

Friends and relatives shook their heads and said that he was losing his mind.

In view of his horrible condition, nobody raised any question as to the circumstances of Anna's death, and nobody listened to the prince.

"She fell and hurt herself badly," they all said.

The sad and haggard children wandered dolefully from room to room, as though looking for something. The older ones wept to such a degree of exhaustion that people became concerned for their health. On the table in the drawing-room beside Anna's work stood an art-accessory box with a needle sticking out, as though she had just been using it. On the window-sill roses were blooming, which she and the children had been watering with a small pitcher just the day before.

Here and there cardboard soldiers were scattered about which Anna had had little Jusha knock over as part of a game. They had both laughed when the prince entered... On the desk lay an unfinished letter Anna had been writing to her sister Natasha, and in the armchair beside it her white cloth shawl trimmed with dark feathers was still lying in a heap, as though it had just fallen from Anna's shoulders. Indeed, it seemed as if she might walk in at any moment...

But not only did she not come in, but on the third day they carried her out of the house to the sounds of mourning and lowered her into a deep grave. This terrible pit always evoked a feeling of horror. People inevitably wanted to retrieve — even if just for a moment — their loved ones who only recently had been buried — before the coffin was finally covered with clumps of earth.

And so Anna now merged with the Nature she loved so much, and which she now accompanied into eternity...

With the realisation that she was indeed gone, it dawned on Prozorskij not only that he had killed her in the present day with a piece of white marble, but that for a long, long time he had been killing her by his failure to recognise and appreciate her... He realised that she had been slain by the very love he had been giving her, because he had been loving her *the wrong way*... And now that her body was no more, he finally began to understand her soul... More and more he began to appreciate this loving, tender and pure soul which had recently escaped him and which, for so many years, used to animate his own life and the children's so cheerfully and in so many ways — and now he wanted to merge his own soul more and more together with hers.

The prince's friends and acquaintances began to say that Prozorskij had become a desperate spirit and that they were concerned for his mental health.

A month after Anna's death came the news that Bekhmetev had passed on abroad.

CHAPTER 5

Song without words
(A narrative)

PART I

CHAPTER 1

"WHAT ARE YOU CRYING ABOUT, MAMÀ? TELL ME, TELL ME!" pleaded the little six-year-old boy, prying his mother's hands from her wet face and looking at her with his radiant blue eyes underneath his long eyelashes. He, too, was ready to cry. Tears were already filling his eyes.

"My mother — your grandmother — is dying. I feel so bad for her, and I want to go see her. Alësha, dear, stay healthy while I am gone, don't fool around and do listen to your nanny…"

The boy threw himself around his mother's neck and was already bursting into tears.

But as soon as the doorbell rang, he at once cried out: "Papà's come!" and rushed to greet him. Aleksandra Alekseevna also got up and, with her mother's telegram in hand, greeted her husband.

"Is she worse?" he asked.

"Quite bad. I am going to pack and leave right away … I can't wait any longer. My whole heart is sick."

And again she gave into sobbing.

Alësha glanced at his mother with a frightened and tormented look. He went over to her and quietly took her hand. However, upon noticing something in his father's hands, the boy rushed over to him and broke out laughing.

"What have you there, Papà? Where did you get it?"

Pëtr Afanas'evich was holding two enormous Spanish onion bulbs in his hands. He was trying to hide them, considering it inappropriate to make a display of them at a moment which was so grievous for his wife. But Alësha had already taken hold of them and was showing them to his mother.

"These are amazing bulbs," Pëtr Afanas'evich began to explain with some embarrassment. "They were given to me by my friend — a German gardener — and I shall certainly grow this sort ... They're from Japan ... Look, Sasha dear, a pound and a half in weight ..."

But Sasha couldn't sympathise with the weight of the bulbs. Her heart was breaking from sorrow. Her mother, whom she loved dearly — her only friend in the world who always understood her completely — lay dying in the Crimea. Even after Sasha got married, she and her mother tried not to live apart and spent every summer together. But this year her mother had taken ill. She had undergone koumiss treatments during the summer and in the autumn had headed off to the Crimea along with her younger son. But neither the koumiss nor the warm climate was able to help. Sasha kept receiving the worst news, and today she decided to go to the Crimea herself.

It was time to start packing. She was obliged to say goodbye to her only son, whom she loved very much. In the meanwhile, her nerves were already weak, and every night Sasha suffered from such a bout of neuralgia that she couldn't sleep and could only look with envy on the sound, peaceful sleep of her rosy-cheeked husband.

As a rule, Pëtr Afanas'evich, after working the whole morning at an insurance company, would come home around four o'clock and head straight to his rather large urban garden, where he would start digging into the planting-beds with delight, oblivious to the whole world.

His avocation was indeed gardening. He liked nothing better than working with the soil, cultivating it and everything that came out of it. His garden attracted him even now, although it was already autumn — the flowers had been killed by the frost, all the vegetables had been dug up and the soil had been removed from the green-beds.

But today it would have been awkward to leave his wife alone. He felt sorry for her — he was a kind and good husband, unsophisticated, simple and affectionate.

"Can I help you, Sasha?" he offered.

"No, you don't have to. You don't know anything about what I need ... I can hardly picture it myself! ... My God! Mamà, my poor, dear, Mamà! She's probably waiting for me right now ... Parasha, come here! Pack my things as quickly as possible ..."

"Should I pack your black mantelet?" asked the maid.

"Yes, of course. I never know when I might need it … Put in some letter-writing paper and a travel inkwell … along with some eau de cologne … Petja, darling, I need a certificate from you; write one out as quickly as you can and send it to be witnessed by the police … Well, well …"

"Don't worry so much, Sasha dear," comforted Pëtr. "It appears the neuralgia is getting the better of you …"

"Such a grievous time! But I have to think about everything … Alësha, call your nanny!"

Moments later a relatively young, rather attractive, tallish woman came in, carrying Alësha in her arms.

"Such a big armful! Ai-ai!" exclaimed Pëtr Afanas'evich, taking his son from the nanny's arms.

"Nanny, while I'm gone, you can take Alësha for a walk as long as it's warmer than minus three, and with no wind — in case I'm delayed getting back."

"Yes, ma'am."

"And please make sure he's fed well, or Pëtr Afanas'evich will damage our child's stomach with his vegetarianism."

"And you, Sasha," countered Pëtr, "would no doubt prefer to feed him the corpse of a decomposed animal?"

"All the same, Petja may talk all he wants, but just make sure Alësha gets two days' worth of chicken … Here, Nanny, here's the money for household expenses."

The suitcase, a travel rug and pillow, along with a wooden hatbox — everything was ready.

The certificate from the police also arrived. Sasha got dressed, picked up her bag and put a book and a purse in it. Her whole body was trembling from head to foot. She had never travelled so far by herself; she had never been separated from her husband and her little son. She felt her heart being torn apart by leaving them.

Pëtr Afanas'evich tried to cheer her up, but he himself was very concerned about her. Not only that, but he was also mindful of that frightening emptiness and loneliness which he would experience in the absence of his joyful and intelligent Sasha, who filled his life in so many ways and imbued it with so much care and order.

But time went by; now there remained only three-quarters of an hour before her train departed for the Crimea, and Moscow's Kursk Station was some distance away. Sasha kissed the nanny and Parasha goodbye. Then she kissed her husband and, finally, as though drawing upon her last remaining strength, took Alësha in her arms and tearfully kissed his little eyes, his soft golden hair, the palms of his little hands and his lips. Then she made the sign of the cross over him and rushed to the door.

"Mamà, Mamà, goodbye," cried the boy. "Here, let me make the sign of the cross over you!"

Sasha came back. Alësha made a serious but awkward attempt to make the sign of the cross over his mother before calming down. Pëtr Afanas'evich suddenly realised that he was supposed to see his wife off at the station and went to get dressed. But Sasha wanted to be alone and emphatically declined his offer. Remembering that he wanted a chance to read the brochure he had just received about cultivating house plants, Pëtr was only too happy to stay at home.

"Make sure you keep Alësha's attention occupied … and comfort him," Sasha added.

It began to get dark as Sasha was leaving the house. She checked to make sure all her things had been packed in the carriage, counted them and closed her eyes. She was no longer capable of crying, nor of remembering the loved ones she was leaving at home, nor of thinking about what was awaiting her in the Crimea.

She was so exhausted from all the excitement and commotion of the last few days before her departure, and the light rocking of her carriage on its rubber tires rested her nerves.

CHAPTER 2

"Am I too late?" asked Sasha as she approached the entrance of the large new railway station which was lit by electricity.

"Are you catching the train to Kursk? It won't leave for another twenty minutes," said the porter as he took her bag. "Where are you headed?"

"To the Crimea, the express train to Yalta. What number would that be?" Sasha asked

"Eighty-six. Which class?"

"Second."

The porter, despite carrying so much weight, moved so quickly that Sasha could barely keep up with him. He dropped the luggage destined for the baggage car and went to buy a ticket for her.

"Seven poods sixteen funt to Kursk, four poods twenty-four to Tula, three poods eight to Yalta," she heard the weighmaster announce in a disconnected manner and particularly throaty voice.

But finally she found train № 86. The porter brought both the train ticket and the baggage receipt. The first bell rang, and Sasha once again hurried along the platform, trying to keep up with the porter and dashing past other passengers in a similar rush.

"Second class, ladies," she stated at the entrance to the coach.

"Please, go in; there is only one lady in the compartment so far."

"Splendid. Thank you," said Sasha, putting thirty kopeks into the porter's hand as she entered the dimly lit ladies' compartment. The porter arranged her things on the upper shelves and said with a courteous bow:

"Bon voyage!"

"Thank you. And the rug and pillow?"

"Right here."

"Please, hand them to me."

The porter got the rug down from one of the shelves. The third bell rang, and he jumped out of the coach. Then the whistle blew, the locomotive began to puff steam, and the train, after a jerk backward (as though harnessing strength), slowly started to move.

Sasha looked out the window. The crowd of well-wishers was quietly leaving the platform. Then she turned to her room-mate — a middle-aged lady, whose appearance seemed to have a calming effect on Sasha. Sasha took out a book and, after searching for a particular page, fastened her travel lamp to the wall and began to read. She was reading "*Consolation de Marcia,*" from Seneca's philosophy.

"*Quelle folie en effet de se punir de ses misères, de les aggraver par un mal nouveau,*" Sasha read Seneca's advice to Marcia in her grief, following the loss of her son. Seneca did not advise giving into grief. He cited the example of two women in ancient Rome — Octavia and Livia, who were both grieving after losing their sons. The first of these spent her whole life in a state of gloom and would not allow her son's name to be mentioned in her presence. The other, Livia, after her son's death, continued to live a vigorous existence, constantly recalling and proclaiming her son's name, through his memory making him an active (if virtual) participant in her life.

"Can either way bring comfort?" thought Sasha. "Can anyone who has lost a loved one, as I shall be losing my mother, really talk about comfort? I can't live, I can't, I can't …" Tears clouded her eyes and interfered with her reading.

"*Mais si nuls sanglots ne rappellent à la vie ce qui n'est plus,*" she read further, "*si le destin est immuable, à jamais fixé dans ses lois, que les plus touchantes misères ne sauraient changer; si enfin la mort ne lâche point sa proie, cessons une douleur qui serait sans fruit. Soyons donc maître et pas jouet de sa violence…*"

"Your ticket," demanded the ticket collector in a bass voice. Sasha gave a start — for a moment she was at a loss for words. With some haste, she rummaged in her bag and pulled out her ticket. The ticket collector read out: "Moscow — Yalta." The conductor entered it in his notebook. The open doors brought a pleasant breath of fresh air into the stuffy compartment, and once again calmness ensued.

Clickety-clack, clickety-clack — the car's wheels drummed with their monotonous iron rhythm. Sasha closed the book. The words she had just read evoked a mighty struggle of grief within her heart, along with an attack of despair over the impending death of her mother, and a desire not to suffer — a desire for someone's permission to go on living a young energetic life.

Clickety-clack, clickety-clack — drummed the wheels annoyingly. Sasha was not yet accustomed to such an unbearable din. She started listening to it, but then her thoughts gradually became confused, and she dozed off. And all at once this monotonous drumming seemed to be transformed in her mind into a kind of melody. Eventually it took on the form of a whole musical cadence, which filled Sasha's head, merging with the soft echoes of a whole orchestral accompaniment. The melody was solemn, sad and beautiful.

Sasha had a strong musical bent. She was a good pianist and could give a decent vocal performance in her pleasing and energetic, albeit not very strong, voice (while still a child her parents had thought of enrolling her in the conservatory).

But Sasha married early. Although her husband, Pëtr Afanas'evich, tried to be accommodating about her musical career, he could not hide his own lack of fondness for music. Thus Sasha would play or sing only in his absence, though lately she had given up practising entirely, on account of her nervousness and her difficulty sleeping.

Another bell rang. The melody ended, and the train stopped. Sasha's room-mate began to quickly put on her coat and hat.

"What's going on?" asked Sasha.

"A huge buffet, time to eat," said her room-mate. "Let's go."

"Yes, right away." Sasha began to hurry, and they both rushed through the door of a brightly illuminated station. They joined a bustling crowd of passengers pushing their way to the food tables. Waiting for them were waiters in tails, white-coated cooks at tables spread with a variety of dishes, and other servants in white aprons. Not terribly hungry, Sasha gulped down a bowl of thick, hot cabbage soup. After she finished paying, her eyes searched the crowd for her room-mate. Moments later she was only too happy to find herself back in her compartment on the train.

CHAPTER 3

Finally, after an exhausting two-day journey, the train arrived at Simferopol'. It was already night by the time the cabby drove her quietly through the unfamiliar city, which in the moonlight seemed to be constructed entirely of white stone without any distinguishable features. Besides, Sasha was so tired that before she knew it she found herself in a spacious hotel room which included a bed behind a wooden screen, a washbasin, a symmetrically arranged sofa and armchairs — everything exactly the same, detail for detail, as in any other Russian provincial hotel.

When the door closed behind Sasha, she felt completely alone. She became so frightened that she called out loudly for the floor attendant.

"Bring me some tea and also the timetable for coaches to Yalta."

"The coach leaves tomorrow morning at seven o'clock," a footman eventually reported, as he wiped down the table with a dirty towel.

Sasha took out a book and began to read. But she was beyond the point of understanding anything.

The clickety-clack of the train was still drumming between her ears, and once more the same unfamiliar but beautiful melody kept running through her head.

"But maybe Mother is no longer with us?! My God, if only I could once more gaze into her large, serious eyes — which so often used to look at me in such an affectionate, all-forgiving manner, as only mothers can look!"

Sasha barely slept the whole night, afraid of missing the departure of the coach. As seven o'clock approached she packed her things and walked out onto the porch of the hotel. The air was fresh and clear. The coach and horses were already waiting at the entrance.

A German passenger was talking to the coachman in broken Russian, enquiring about his bags. There was also a young cadet, taking deep puffs on a *papirosa*, shivering from the morning freshness and a sleepless night. Two other men came up, but no ladies, and this bothered Sasha. The German passenger helped Sasha into the coach and sat down beside her. He regarded her with some curiosity. Meanwhile, she curled up into a corner and dozed off.

But all at once her face brightened.

"Oh, how fantastic!" she cried involuntarily. "Mountains towering above the clouds!"

"*Die Dame reist zum ersten Mal?*" the German asked with a smile.

"*Ja,*" Sasha answered tersely, not taking her eyes off the sunlit peaks and marvelling at the wisps of cloud, lightly and airily floating below the mountain-tops. Tenderly and condescendingly, as if looking at a child, the German again fixed his eyes upon Sasha. They soon got into conversation — he was a pharmacist. The cadet, it turned out, was on his way to Yalta to see his mother, since there was a bout of diphtheria in the barracks and all the students had been sent home.

Already Sasha began to feel less lonely; she could feel the support of her companions, and the cadet chattered on so cheerfully that Sasha, too, was infected with his merriment.

"Hold on!" The coach suddenly lurched to one side, and the coachman jumped down from his driving seat.

"One wheel is broken, we can't go any further," he announced, adding: "The town of Alushta is only a verst away."

"What must be done?"

"It has to be repaired."

"Will we have to wait long?"

"About three hours …"

"I shan't make it, I shan't be able to see my mother!" was the first thought that crossed Sasha's mind. But everyone has an inherent sense of self-preservation, and Sasha did her best to overcome her sorrowful impatience. She proceeded on foot, together with all the other passengers, to Alushta, where they were served a kind of borscht.

Then, to kill time, she invited the cheerful cadet to go for a walk with her. As they were walking along the cobblestone road, they were struck by a strange noise, which caused them to stop.

Sasha had never done much travelling. The only places she had seen were Moscow and the part of the countryside where she was born. She was very curious to look around, and listened closely to the ambient sounds ... All of a sudden she cried out in a loud voice:

"The sea!"

...Yes, it was the Black Sea, noisy, boisterous, heaving its grey-blue waves as it ebbed and flowed. It was mysterious and frightening, yet at the same time curiously alluring in its grandeur and bottomless depths.

"So, that's the sea!..." Sasha ran to the very edge; the water was either retreating or lapping at her ankles with its eternal, monotonous to-and-fro action of waves, both exciting and tormenting Sasha. She found it quite overwhelming.

"The sea, the sea!" she repeated, and her heart was aflutter with a brand-new emotion.

For a long time she stood and watched the sea. The cadet, who had been gathering stones and shells, was now urging her to return to the station.

"The coach will be leaving soon, Aleksandra Alekseevna," he called out to her.

When Sasha arrived back at the Alushta station with her travelling companion, they found they still had to wait another hour, but eventually everything was ready and the coach drove on.

The closer they came to Yalta, the more anxious Sasha became. At last, the lights of Yalta loomed on the horizon — nearer and nearer ... Sasha already had butterflies in her stomach, but when the coach stopped, she heard herself addressed by a familiar voice.

"Sasha, you're here!" exclaimed her brother Dmitrij, who was with their mother in Yalta.

"Yes. How's Mamà?" replied Sasha, thinking at the same time: "He must have something to tell me ... oh-oh!"

"She's very weak, but alive."

"Thank God! Where is she?"

"At the Hotel Rossija."

"Who's with her?"

"Imagine our joy when we found Varvara Ivanovna here. Mamà is so happy. Varvara Ivanovna will not leave her side."

When Sasha arrived at the hotel, she decided not to go and see her mother right away.

Her mother needed to be warned, and Sasha to be prepared for the difficult sight of her dying loved one.

CHAPTER 4

Sasha was assigned a large, cold room — there was no other available (all the rest were taken).

The candle they lit for her dimly shed light on the small space around the table on which it stood, leaving most of the huge room in mysterious darkness. They brought in her things … In the meantime, she stood shivering, rooted to the spot in the middle of the room, without taking off her coat.

Her brother went to inform their mother of Sasha's arrival and sent to her their distant relative Varvara Ivanovna, a friend of their mother's, who normally lived in a convent but had come to Yalta for medical treatment.

"Hello, Sasha darling," said Varvara. "Don't stand on ceremony, take off your coat."

"Varvara Ivanovna dear, hello! It's so good that you're here. I'm almost afraid to see Mamà … How is she — pretty bad?"

"Just about at the end. She will be glad to see you. Now, Sasha dear, keep a stiff upper lip! Remember — God's will in everything. We need to submit and ask for His help."

Sasha's brother Dmitrij met them in the corridor. At the door of their mother's room, Sasha stopped and crossed herself. Upon hearing footsteps, the elderly maid Nastas'ja gently opened the door. Seeing Sasha, she immediately burst into tears.

"Who's there?" asked Sasha's mother in a faint voice.

With a light but firm step, Sasha went over to her mother's bedside. She looked at her, then quickly bent over and kissed her cheek and hand. After that she became motionless.

"Too bad autumn is come already, Sasha dearest," noted her mother. "It's much better here in the spring."

"Enough talk about me, Mamà dear. How are you doing?"

"Poorly. The doctor prescribed jelly with calves' knuckles, but I simply can't, I choke on it … Maybe I don't need to?" her mother added.

Sasha suddenly began to feel a kind of detachment toward her ill mother, especially when she started talking about calves' knuckles as soon as they met. With a painful heart, she realised that death was indeed almost upon them and that her mother's suffering body had already parted from her soul.

"Of course, don't you go tormenting yourself, Mamà. Where does it hurt?"

"Everywhere. Besides, it's hard to breathe … Turn me over," she said, addressing her son and Nastas'ja.

They started to help her turn onto her other side.

"Not like that! Sasha dearest, come and rub my side."

With trembling hands, Sasha rubbed her mother's side. After calming down, Sasha ran out of the room in despair, sat down next to a small table in the corridor and broke into tears.

The large, gloomy grey hall was practically empty. In the centre, a stream of water flowed monotonously from a fountain into a marble basin. Sasha mindlessly resigned herself to a state of sorrow, all the while cursing fate and whatever evil will was depriving her of her beloved mother.

Varvara Ivanovna quietly came up to her.

"Sasha darling, just submit to the will of God. You mustn't keep on punishing yourself — that's a sin."

"What sin? … What kind of God would send such suffering?"

"Oh, you, miserable and unbelieving dear! You must believe, my friend, that death can be better than life. After all, the soul still lives. It lives without the cares of our sinful body."

Sasha listened to Varvara Ivanovna's comforting words. She tried to comfort herself as well, but that proved impossible.

On the morning of the second day, Sasha's mother seemed to perk up considerably. She asked to be dressed in her beautiful robe, covered her head with a black lace shawl and, after raising herself a little from her bed, ordered tea to be brought to her room.

"Let's celebrate Sasha's arrival," she kept saying. "Open the window … that's it! How lovely the sea is! This is not a place to die."

A breath of fresh sea air swept into the room. Outside the hotel windows, some late autumn flowers were still blooming — multicoloured, motionless, frost-capped chrysanthemums glistened in the rays of the November sun. Even as this November sun cast its light on the pale face of the dying woman, it was no longer the same sun that had afforded so much growth and life in the spring. It gave the impression of being cold, offering no hope. Its rays were reflected in the shallow ripples of the peaceful sea, and it seemed as though thin gilded wires were shimmering on its surface.

Sasha's mother, lying sorrowful and motionless, gazed out at the distant sea.

"Dmitrij, come close to me," she turned to her son. "I shall be dying very soon … Take care of Sasha — watch that she doesn't do anything irrational … D'you hear, Dmitrij? I am entrusting her to you. I know her, we have loved each other too much …"

The former glint in her eyes seemed to spark up again for one last time, and she was once more enlivened by her heartfelt care for her beloved daughter.

She paused, all out of breath, and tears flowed from her eyes, which had now become lacklustre once again.

"Maybe you'll get well again … " Dmitrij started to say, but he could not lie. "You know how much I love Sasha, I won't leave her and I'll try to keep her calm … as much as I can. Don't you worry about that yourself."

They lit the candles, and all of them gathered in the mother's room. Varvara Ivanovna poured tea. While there was nothing gloomy in the whole setting, everybody sensed that death was indeed at hand, very close, and nobody felt like chatting, eating or drinking.

The next day in the evening, the mother began to toss and turn, complaining of pain in her side, and asked for the doctor. When he arrived, he surmised that the patient would not last the day. They sent for a priest. The mother made confession in a loud voice, took communion and, after the priest left, asked the doctor to try to relieve her suffering.

The doctor brought some morphine and began to prepare an injection. But suddenly he let out a gasp. The needle had broken off. He managed to pull it quickly out of her side and hastily prepared a second injection.

"What have you done to me?" the elderly woman asked.

"What do you feel?"

"I feel paralysed … Nothing … I don't feel anything … What's happening?" she suddenly screamed.

Sasha and her brother rushed over to their mother and pressed their lips to her hands. She barely managed to utter: "Farewell … " and immediately fell into unconsciousness. Varvara Ivanovna prayed quietly in a corner of the room. Nastas'ja was crying, muttering something through her tears.

The dying woman began to feel agony. An ominous silence ensued in anticipation of the great, fearful and mighty foe — death. Four hours later, Sasha's mother was gone.

With a cry and a wail, Sasha left the room in tumultuous despair. With the support of her brother, she rushed out into the stone-columned hall. The whole time while her mother's body remained in the hotel, as well as later at the funeral and afterward — Sasha was in such a terrible state that they feared for her life. She herself wanted to commit suicide, forgetting for a brief moment both her husband and her son. Only when her brother told her that they were going home, did she suddenly come to her senses and calm down.

Three days later Sasha arrived home and, taking little Alësha in her arms, she returned to real life for the first time, and to anything that could somehow connect her thereto.

CHAPTER 5

Sasha was so grief-stricken that she remained ill the whole winter. By spring Sasha, looking all thin and gloomy, kept wandering about aimlessly, like a shadow. Sometimes, out of the blue, she would burst into tears and take refuge in her room, where she would sit the whole day without food or moving about, refusing to see anyone but only repeating: "Mamà, where are you? Where are you?"

Her husband's heartfelt, guileless attempts to offer her comfort only irritated her. The noise which her son made often drove her to tears. The doctors said that Sasha's grief preyed upon her already frail nerves and that she was suffering from neurasthenia. One doctor advised her to go abroad, another suggested electric treatment, but Sasha would not listen to any of them. She only got angrier and suffered more intensely.

Spring came early that year. It always used to captivate Sasha so beautifully with renewed hopes, plans, an elevated energy and an unconscious joy. However, this time, even as the spring birds reappeared, streams of water flowed over the streets of Moscow, taxicabs rumbled through the city, church bells announced the Lenten fast — it all left Sasha cold.

Her husband suggested she take a trip to her mother's village, where she could see her brother Dmitrij and help prepare the estate for summer occupancy. At first, Sasha feared any kind of sad reminiscences, but even in Moscow — indeed anywhere — she would feel equally depressed, and so she agreed to a trip to the country together with her husband. She wanted, it seemed, to see how her strength would measure up to possible life at the estate, where she had spent every summer with her mother all her life.

At the beginning of April, Sasha and her husband Pëtr Afanas'evich were approaching the all too familiar little station located three versts from her late mother's estate. It was early morning. As the train came to a stop, many of the awakened, still sleepy passengers looked out the window and, upon seeing nothing but forests and being relieved that this was not their station, immediately went back to sleep. During the train's minute-long stop, Pëtr Afanas'evich put their bags out onto the platform. Sasha quickly alighted and started to take the bags, rugs and baskets that Pëtr handed to her. Then he, too, jumped down onto the ice-covered track, and the train went on its way with a loud whistle.

"Are there any horses coming for us?" asked Pëtr Afanas'evich at the station.

"Yes, there are," responded the station manager, whom they knew well, raising his hand to his red cap in salute. "Only the road is a disaster! Either for sleigh runners or carriage wheels … Two sleighs are coming for you."

"That's splendid! Feel the air, Sasha! I suppose they have already started work on the garden-beds and Timofeevich has already planted everything."

Sasha kept silent. She looked all around her and seemed not to recognise anything. How much she had changed during this time! Her grief was reflected in everything. But still, the morning sun felt so good and bright in the pure pale-blue sky, and the transparent brown tops of young birches seemed to disappear in the air as they merged with the pink glow of the dawn. Many of the oak-trees in the old forest preserve were still adorned by brown, dry, autumn leaves, which somehow had missed falling off through the autumn and winter. Buds ready to burst were swelling up on the aspens and willows, and birds made crazy chirping noises in the woods.

Finally they arrived at the estate. "Can it be," thought Sasha as she passed by the Great Pond, "that this is our allée, our house — just the same as when we lived here?"

Some peasant women they knew, who were standing on the dock, bowed as they squeezed out their laundry with their hands turned red from cold … Two sledges had just delivered manure to the garden-beds. Some peasants emerged from the forest with a load of brushwood. How orderly everything was! How calm, assured, necessary and important was everything that took place in the country!

Pëtr Afanas'evich was absolutely delighted.

"But why are they bringing the manure so late? …" he wondered. "Probably they've added a couple of extra beds for late planting… I still see solid layers of snow on the ground in some places … Sasha dear, look — some kind of bird, I can't make it out… How splendid, how splendid! … That's what life is in the countryside!"

"Pet'ka, Pet'ka," he called out to a little boy running by.

Pëtr Afanas'evich could no longer restrain himself. He jumped off the sleigh and ran ahead. He loved the country, along with all Nature. He loved it in a simple fashion, as might a child. He loved to work and take from the soil everything it could give.

On the porch of the house, Sasha met her brother, Dmitrij. He was excited and at the same time happy. He himself had just recently returned to their country estate — for the first time without their mother — and was extremely lonely.

He had done everything to make sure that Sasha's first impression of the house would not be gloomy but welcoming. A samovar was steaming on the table. There was coffee, along with radishes and Sasha's favourite flowers. The bright sun cast its slanting rays on the parquet floor in the main hall. Dmitrij himself had a very tender expression on his face.

However, as soon as Sasha entered the house, she experienced such an attack of despair that the very sight of her could not help but make one weep.

"But Mamà, where is she? Where?" she kept repeating in despair and horror.

This question continued to haunt her. It was the one thing she wanted most to explain to herself but could not. Wild, repressed outcries of the question: "Where… oh, where is she?" echoed throughout the house, as Sasha began to race through all rooms: her mother's bedroom, her own room next to it, the drawing-room, the terrace — all the chambers that had constituted the family nest she had loved her whole life and which had now lost its charm in the absence of her beloved mother.

"No, I can't! I can't live here! I'm going to leave today! Oh, my God, my God! …"

That evening, to her husband's great dismay, Sasha resolved to return to Moscow. Only not by way of their local station, but directly through the gubernia capital, where they could spend the night and leave the next day by express train for Moscow. It could have been dangerous to attempt a trip to the local station by night — streams might have been overflowing by the bridge during the day, and their horse could have easily got caught in the water.

Pëtr Afanas'evich was downcast. He and Timofeevich had been transplanting into garden-beds a plethora of newly opened young flowers, each blossoming with a pair of tender leaves. He also delighted in pulling up radishes and admiring the young clusters of cucumber shoots. The luxuriant, bright pink hue of peaches in the greenhouse also drove him to ecstasy, and Pëtr Afanas'evich hated to be torn away from all this.

The hotel in the gubernia capital where Sasha and her husband were staying was situated on a large urban square. Tired and heartsick, she got undressed right away and went to bed.

When she awoke in the morning, Pëtr Afanas'evich was nowhere to be seen — he had gone to find out (on behalf of his brother-in-law Dmitrij) what price oats were currently fetching in the city.

Sasha got up and went over to the window. She was quite fearful of being alone. The windows of the room overlooked the square, which was still empty at that hour. The windowsills were dotted with pigeons. Sasha picked up pieces of white bread left over from last night's tea. After crumbling them, she reached out the window and scattered the crumbs along the windowsill. The cooing pigeons first took fright and then took flight, but soon made a beeline for the bread, grabbing pieces of it out of each other's beaks.

Sasha watched them for a long time and began to feel less lonely. She remembered seeing Nikolaj Jaroshenko's outstanding painting at the Tretyakov Gallery in Moscow and quietly exclaimed: "Yes, *life is everywhere!*" She actively set about tidying up the room and collecting and packing her things.

Pëtr Afanas'evich had still not returned. Sasha began looking out the window with impatient expectation. She noticed two cows wandering about the square, picking up hay.

"Why do they let cows loose on a public square?" Sasha asked the servant preparing tea in their room.

"You see, ma'am, there is an old woman who lives here. She keeps some cows, because she can feed them here almost free of charge."

"How does she do that?"

"Well, three days a week there is a farmers' market in the square; people come bringing straw, hay and oats. Some of that gets scattered — that's when she lets her cows loose to pick it up, and it fills them up for the whole day … Sometimes she will even pick things up herself. That's how she lives — she tends the cows and sells the milk."

"That's amazing!" thought Sasha. "I would never have imagined! How little we know of real life! Indeed, *life is everywhere*," she repeated again.

Finally, Pëtr Afanas'evich returned, carrying something in a little bag.

"What have you there?" Sasha asked.

With a sly grin Pëtr opened the bag and some seeds trickled out onto the palm of his hand.

"A foreman from the Shatilovsk Agricultural Experimental Station gave them to me. These are amazing seeds … He also taught me how to graft roses. If you want black roses, you need to graft them onto a garden-plum tree, or else onto an oak … I'll definitely try this experiment … It's extremely interesting!"

Pëtr Afanas'evich kept chatting, drinking tea and chewing on a bun with a loud munching noise, which really irritated Sasha. She looked askance at her kind-hearted, self-contented husband. For the first time in her life, she saw him in an especially clear light and discovered that the two of them had very little in common. True, he did love her; he was kind, even meek … But did he really understand her? Did he ever delve into her inner life? Did he realise that his interests in the Insurance Society and the cultivation of the largest possible onions — which she had always been sympathetic to — had little actual appeal for her on the whole?

And now, in her grief, when with all the strength of her soul she was looking for something she could hold onto in life, when her soul was so highly strung and endeavouring to plumb the depths of the mystery of life and death — was he really able to help her? Could he look deeper into her soul? Was he capable of holding her interest, offering her something truly important, explaining to her the whole horror of death and the whole meaning of the life to come?… No, she knew it would not be he who would help her. Yet she herself was so weak, so nervous, so miserable …

"Anyway, our train will leave soon …," Pëtr Afanas'evich reminded her. "Are you all ready? … That's terrific, Sasha dear, you have everything packed!" he beamed, hoping to add a note of tenderness.

A half-hour later, Sasha and her husband were on the express train, heading back to Moscow.

CHAPTER 6

In the meantime, the real spring had crept in unnoticed. People were already removing their winter window-frames. City crews began to water the dusty Moscow streets. Light green fluff appeared on trees in the gardens and on the boulevards. The townsfolk had already started to take small tea-tables out to their little gardens; they were spending time on their balconies and porches in anticipation of the moment when they would move to the countryside or to their dacha.

University students, *gimnazium* pupils — indeed, the whole academic population — were tired of sweating in their stuffy uniforms, tired of waiting for the exam period to begin. The conscientious among them were busy cramming, the lazy ones could only complain as they sat by open windows with books in hands and envy the lucky people riding by on bicycles, carriages or landaus on their way out of town.

The carts of townsfolk already moving to their dachas — carrying furniture, mattresses, kiddies' wagons, plants and trunks, some even with cows attached by a rope over their horns — could be seen stretching along Moscow streets, heading for the city limits.

Caretakers, wearing waistcoats over their red shirts, after having seen their masters off to the countryside, stood cheerfully and casually by the gates, taking advantage of a moment of freedom and leisure.

Moscow's winter life had ended, giving way to a brand-new summer season.

Pëtr Afanas'evich was exhausted waiting for the move to the village. Little Alësha, pale as a result of his shut-in life over the winter, needed to have gone to the countryside a long time ago. Sasha, meanwhile, went on living in Moscow, showing no desire to relocate. On that she kept mum or complained of inertia. Finally, one fine day in May, she decisively announced to her husband that she would not go to their estate at all, since everything there reminded her all too vividly of her grief. However, she added that, if Pëtr Afanas'evich wished, she would be willing to stay the summer at a rented dacha and nowhere else …

This was a blow for Pëtr Afanas'evich, but he knew that it could not be otherwise. Moreover, his kindness was not able to go against a grieving will, and he zealously began to scour all the regions around Moscow for a dacha to let.

Finally, he came across one that seemed acceptable to him, and he asked Sasha to go have a look at it. Sasha agreed, albeit reluctantly. Taking Alësha and the nanny with her, she headed off one evening, after the heat of the day, to see the dacha her husband had found for her.

"Is it really that late in the spring?!" Sasha wondered, as the coach they had hired turned off onto a country road. The joyful feeling the spring had previously always given her once again provoked a slight shiver. "Where have I been?" she asked herself. "Oh, why all this excitement! But am I actually still allowed to feel any joy? …"

After turning off the main highway, they entered a forest. It was so calm and peaceful there. Birds were rustling in the bushes. Somewhere in the distance, drakes were exchanging their raspy calls in the swamp, underneath a rising fog. Frogs were croaking and chattering loudly in their unique, vernal style, reminding Sasha of her family estate and the old pond that they always used to pass on returning to the manor house every spring.

"I don't need memories, I don't want them, I can't suffer and cry any longer… One has to move on in life, move forward … not backward," Sasha thought, as she took in the beautiful countryside her comfortable carriage was passing through. "I want life, life … *Life is everywhere!*"

"Mamà, can I get out and run?" begged Alësha, all excited.

"Wait … we'll be there soon … very soon …"

Indeed, before long the coachman, who had previously visited this dacha with Pëtr Afanas'evich, brought them to their destination. A watchman showed them around, explaining all the features of the dacha.

The house stood on a height of land, overlooking a river below. You could see that the river was dammed up farther on, where two wooden bathhouses had recently been set up.

"And what is that small yellow cottage over there?"

"That is just a little dacha; an unmarried gentleman has rented it."

"Oh, how unpleasant that there are neighbours so close! Are there any other dachas nearby?"

"No, no others; but there are some a verst away, near the main road… Anyway, there's just the one available here. You needn't worry, ma'am. After all, both you and your neighbour have a front garden, and you will hardly see or hear anything beyond the trees. Besides, we know the gentleman who lives there — he's a gentle sort."

Alësha chased after the numerous May bugs. He delighted in picking the wildflowers, which were already in bloom, and enjoyed drinking tea in the garden. He was in ecstasy and showed no desire to go back to Moscow. However, the evening air had already started to turn cool …

Sasha liked the dacha. She put down a deposit and left.

It was a charming May evening when they arrived back in Moscow. Sunset was already on the point of merging with the next day's dawn. The air was quiet and gentle, and only when the rumble of city taxicabs on the pavement began once again to bother Sasha's ears did she lapse into her previous depressed mood. However, approaching home, she glimpsed through the transparent tree-branches a bright greenish star, beautifully casting its mysterious light over the garden.

"That's Venus! Venus — the star of love!" thought Sasha, ever the sentimentalist. "What a beauty! What can you promise me in my life with your verdant hue of hope?" Unable to keep herself from looking at the star, she again felt an overwhelming longing for some new kind of life.

Alësha had dozed off. They carried him out of the carriage and put the sleepy but ruddy boy, intoxicated with fresh air, to bed.

The next day they hurriedly packed up for the summer. A day or so later, Sasha, already feeling more cheerful, moved to the dacha.

CHAPTER 7

"Here is where I planted lettuce — we'll be having some amazing Romaine!" said Pëtr Afanas'evich, wearing an apron, with his sleeves rolled up, working on some freshly dug up garden beds. He was oh so happy, completely absorbed in his favourite earthy avocation.

"And these are radishes — eighteen varieties."

"Who's going to be eating them in such quantities?" asked Sasha, sitting on the balcony in her white dress and drying the first spring flowers in a large book.

"If there's a garden, we'll find a mouth," Pëtr Afanas'evich pronounced with a crude laugh. This bothered Sasha, and she responded with a scornful smile.

"You'd better stick to your flowers. Anything else we can buy for a farthing."

"Sure, I've planted heaps of flowers," Pëtr acknowledged. "Now we're going to water them."

"I'll go with you, Papà!" cried Alësha, carrying a small watering-can in one hand and a scrap of bread in the other.

"Come on then, we'll go water Mamà's flowers ..." his father said kind-heartedly.

"What are they delivering over there?" asked Sasha, pointing to two wagons which drove by very close.

"That's the tenant of the yellow dacha moving in," the nanny observed.

A few minutes later, an elderly footman came over from the neighbouring dacha and asked if he could borrow Pëtr Afanas'evich's caretaker and footman for a minute or so, to help move a piano for the new neighbour.

With a grunt, along with some special care and effort, they lifted the heavy instrument on large towels and carried it into the dacha. Then from the second wagon they moved in the tenant's modest belongings — trunks, chairs, a bed, baskets and so forth. The elderly footman thanked them for their help, rewarding each of them with a twenty-kopek coin, and the hubbub died down.

It all remained quiet for several days. Nobody could be seen on the terrace or through the windows of the yellow dacha. The elderly, kind-hearted footman, Aleksej Tikhonych, whose name was already known amongst the servants at Sasha's dacha, would sometimes sit on a bench and, out of boredom, watch what was going on at his neighbours'. He surmised that the owners were good people — only the master of the house was a bit of an eccentric, spending the whole day digging in the earth and growing useless flowers, lettuce (i.e., *grass*) and tomatoes, which Tikhonych would never go near.

From time to time, little Alësha would pass Aleksej Tikhonych on walks with his nanny. Once Alësha asked him his name and was delighted to discover a namesake. Another time the boy, who felt a certain connection with Tikhonych and concluded that he was lonely, invited him to go mushroom-hunting with them.

"Right away, master Alësha, just as soon as I lock up the house."

From that day on a real friendship blossomed between Tikhonych and Alësha, along with his nanny. They would often sit in the front garden drinking tea. Tikhonych knew how to make flutes out of little sticks, as well as paper cockerels. He would tell Alësha fairy tales and teach him songs that he had learnt from his master's pupils.

For a while after they moved to the dacha, Sasha felt cheerful and delighted in the spring, Nature, the forest and its nightingales and believed that she had started to experience some comfort. But from time to time she once again succumbed to a painful longing — she couldn't eat or sleep, but only sat life-lessly in a corner of the room and refused to do anything.

It was a bright summer evening, following a marvellous, peaceful day in May. Sasha had been weeping inconsolably. But now she sat alone on the balcony of her dacha and listened intently to the smallest noise. She was expecting at any moment the arrival of her husband, who had gone to Moscow that morning on business. On several occasions little Alësha came up to her — prompted by either a sad curiosity or a selfish childish annoyance over the interruption of what had been a good and happy life to date — pleading: "Mamà, when will you stop crying?"

Finally, even Alësha went to bed. Sasha then ventured outdoors and onto a sideroad. Once again, the first thing that caught her eye was the greenish star, Venus, shining glaringly and provocatively in the pure spring sky. And once again, the desire for happiness, consolation and joy momentarily awakened in her heart. She returned to the dacha but, instead of going into the house, she sat down on a bench, thinking about her late mother and recalling everything that she had read from various authors on the subject of death. Indeed, she herself had given considerable thought to this eternal and unresolved ques-tion and had even copied extracts from various essays into a little red book. She was desperately searching for some kind of escape or consolation.

"*La mort c'est l'absorption des* éléments *de l'intelligence humaine dans l'in-telligence universelle*," she remembered the words of Epictetus, aiming to com-fort herself that this *intelligence universelle* meant God and that her mother was now with God.

And further, on the question of where man goes after death, came the answer: "*Vers des choses amies et du même genre que toi — vers les éléments.*" This must mean that her mother had merged with Nature, and that was some-thing good.

And Lev Tolstoy says somewhere: "Death is nothing but the destruction of the temporary form, but this destruction will never cease …"

And elsewhere he says: "The best evidence of immortality is that no one can imagine the end of his own existence, and this very impossibility of imag-ining *death* is the evidence that it does not exist …"

But then, Mamà's gone, that's *for certain* … even though they say that the soul is immortal and that the body is its burden — "*tu es une âme, qui porte un cadavre*" — Sasha also recalled, but it would be far better at the moment if the body bearing her mother's soul were alive and sitting beside her as before in the now empty house of their estate, and everyone would be oh so happy…

"But now I'm alone, all alone …" And Sasha began to feel sorry for herself, and a simple, physical, almost child-like despair took precedence over any rationalisation; she fell with her face on her hands and sobbed, tearing her heart apart…

All at once, in the soft quietude of the May night, the melodious sounds of one of Mendelssohn's *Songs without words* in G-major distinctly resounded under the skilful hands of a master pianist. The first note of the right hand, held for an elusive moment, groaned deeply, with a drawn-out expressiveness. The left hand seemed to accompany the melody not with fingers but with a breath. After that, neither the D nor the left nor the right hand could be distinguished from each other, but all merged together and sang forth. It seemed as though this song was not only talking to Sasha about her grief, but simultaneously comforting her and promising her happiness… and life… and a new love…

Sasha was as yet unacquainted with this particular piece, nor did she want to know anything more about it at the moment. She did not even guess at first that the sound of this *Song without words* was actually emanating from the little yellow dacha next door. The performer was playing it as only one could who knew that nobody else was listening — with no self-conscious feeling in performing such a musical masterpiece in solitude, nor any distraction from the usual mutual influence between audience and performer. Only something peaceful, rational and deep, was palpable — some kind of mysterious connection between the late author and his genius of a musician. Such was the current performance of Mendelssohn's *Song without words* in G-major.

When the *Song* was finished, the invisible tenant of the yellow dacha began to play it over, repeating certain musical phrases, attempting to play them either more softly or more loudly, sometimes holding onto a single note to enhance its effect — either intensifying or diminishing a particular sound. The musician was in full control of his instrument as if it were his own voice, and the instrument obeyed his genius hands, as though it were alive and loved its master.

The whole piece turned out beautifully in every respect, and this *Song without words* conveyed something tender and caressing to Sasha's suffering soul, comforting and delighting her.

But then came the end, *pianissimo*, as though three sighs were inspiringly and tenderly voiced in one and the same phrase — and silence followed. Sasha, too, sighed, as though her heart, filled to overflowing, had all at once found relief in these sounds the piano conveyed to it.

The yellow dacha once again turned silent. Similarly, the May night was oh so quiet and warm. This silence penetrated Sasha's heart as well, filling it with joy.

"Oh, Lord, I do thank Thee!" she said under her breath. And for the first time since her mother's death, Sasha broke into a smile and felt reconciled to life.

The unseen musician once again chose several chords and soon began to play something more complex and tragic, causing it to flow into a marvellous melody in a minor key, apparently improvising. *Clickety-clack, clickety-clack* — Sasha recalled the sound of the wheels when she took the train to the Crimea to visit her dying mother, and the same melody that she heard back then in a dream was undoubtedly the very one she was listening to now.

"Yes, that's it!" Sasha suddenly exclaimed, and it frightened her. Rushing home, she ordered tea to be brought to the drawing-room. Then she shut all the doors, arranged for all the shutters to be closed and lamps to be lit. When her husband finally returned home in the carriage, which was loaded with all sorts of purchases and provisions brought from Moscow, she greeted him with a genuine burst of joy.

CHAPTER 8

Sasha did not say a word to her husband about the occupant of the yellow dacha, nor about the strong impression which she derived from his playing. She jealously guarded the secret of her consolation and waited with acute impatience for the next time she would hear any sounds from next door. But several days went by in complete silence.

The pianist led an extremely orderly life: he would get up early, go bathing, have dinner at one o'clock… Reappearing after five, he would go for a walk for the whole evening. The only person to visit him was a young man who was apparently his pupil.

A week went by. Sasha stopped taking walks so as not to miss her neighbour's practising. Nothing else interested her, and every day she went out and sat on a bench overlooking the yellow dacha, hoping once again to hear him play.

One evening, on the small balcony of the yellow dacha Aleksej Tikhonych was clearing away dishes along with the samovar. He then went back into the house, closing the door behind him. But the windows remained open, and Sasha could hear the piano lid being raised. Several chords followed. She held her breath as she recognised the beginning of a Chopin sonata. And then in the notes of this sonata she could hear the beginning of a tragic chronicle of all human existence.

At first, everything was calm and meaningful, but afterward turned sad and painful. Then followed a pause… and the sound of a funeral march, executed in a strictly classical, rhythmical style. And then came a melody of tender, emotional reminiscences, one, it seemed to Sasha, she had heard many times before in her heart … And again — the sound, gloomy, unforgiving — following a strictly prescribed rhythm.

"Oh, my!" moaned Sasha. For in this artistic masterpiece, she was able to live again with a mighty strength through all the scenes of a lost, beloved, human life. Then, like a light breeze, like spirits hovering over graves, the finale swept in… suddenly, airily and tenderly. Sasha could no longer hold out — she rushed over to the yellow dacha and sat on the steps of its veranda, listening intently to the beating of her heart, resonating in the bodice of her thin white dress — and that was the end.

At this point the pianist pushed open the door with a firm hand and came out onto the balcony. Sasha gave a shudder, but since she had not yet come to terms with the feelings that had choked her before, she did not immediately realise what was going on, and only when the musician's tall frame stood towering over her, fixing his wandering and rather wild, fast-blinking eyes directly on her, did she start to fear the consequences of her rash move. Then, suddenly taking flight like a bird and muttering in embarrassment: "Pardon me...," she bounded home at lightning speed — and feeling light as air. Her transparent sleeves and the voluminous skirt of her white dress flickered in the distance as she made her way back to her own house.

Greatly bewildered, the occupant of the yellow dacha followed this unknown slip of a woman with his eyes — a woman who had disturbed his peace and solitude. However, his aesthetic eye could not help but admire the grace and beauty which he immediately perceived in this heavenly figure. Granted, he was annoyed over the sudden intrusion into his life; rankled by the disturbance of his peace and calm; but also bothered by his own reaction — the fact that he was involuntarily excited by such an encounter and that his eyes kept peering into the darkness in search of this unexpected phenomenon.

He fell into a gloomy meditation, took off his glasses and sat down by the balcony railing. Quite imperceptibly for him, both the impression the stranger had had on him and his annoyance at her sudden appearance gradually faded from his memory. Instead, his consciousness was filled with the rich melody that he had just been improvising. This beautiful melody was becoming clearer and clearer to him — tender, bright and overflowing. It kept trilling away in his head, fluidly adaptable to the most unexpected, graceful changes, growing better and better...

His composition was gradually taking on more and more of a defined quality — it grew more and more beautiful, and the elusive white figure of the unknown woman once again clearly presented itself before the composer's eyes — equally gracious, limber, like an embodiment in the flesh of his artistic motifs. It kept disappearing, then reappearing... But it was all just like a dream.

Ivan Il'ich's feeling of annoyance quickly passed. With a joyful smile, he hurried into the house and immediately began to jot down on music paper the beautiful melody he had just improvised. It was eventually to become the principal theme of the symphony he had recently started. He kept working for quite a while before sitting down at the piano and playing his composition. Not for a long time had he experienced such inspiration from his creation.

That night, all the strength of his genius was concentrated on this brand-new work. Altering his customary order for the first time, he worked on it all night long. Only with the early morning light did he lie down to relax for few hours. By this time, the rays of the rising sun had already brightened the eastern sky and the radiant dawn was already pouring through the little windows of his bedroom.

CHAPTER 9

"Sasha dear — such a fine fellow he is, this neighbour! I went bathing with him today and promised him some radishes," Pëtr Afanas'evich declared to Sasha, coming out onto the veranda with a wet towel in his hands and dark wet hair sticking to his temples, all around his radiant face. "I'm so happy we met. He's a musician, maybe he'll play something for you. I know how much you love music."

Sasha kept mum and blushed, as though her secret were a crime of sorts. She was not happy about this mysterious musician's acquaintance with her husband. What was the point of it?

Wouldn't it have been better to have only an artistic impression of this man who brought so much joy and comfort to her, rather than an impression of his personality, which might only destroy everything.

At that very moment Alësha appeared, along with his nanny, who informed Sasha:

"Ma'am, the neighbour has sent his footman to ask if they can borrow a coffee-grinder — they have nothing to grind coffee with. Shall I lend them ours?"

"Mamà, do let him have it," pleaded Alësha. "He gave me some chocolate yesterday, he's very kind!"

Sasha smiled. So, this musical magician drinks coffee and eats chocolate!

"Of course, Nanny, give it to them — always let them have anything they ask for," Sasha replied.

"Anyway, Nanny," said Pëtr Afanas'evich. "I'll go and pull up some lettuce and radishes. Send them to our neighbour, find out his full name and send him greetings from his neighbours… and be sure to invite him to dine with us tomorrow."

"No, don't, don't start such an acquaintance!" Sasha blurted out passionately and capriciously, almost in tears. "I never see anyone here… and now all at once this complete stranger shows up!"

"You know, everyone was a stranger at one time," observed Pëtr Afanas'evich, taking offence. He was missing some company at the dacha and very much wanted to connect with the neighbour. But inasmuch as Pëtr was not in the habit of contradicting his wife, he meekly declined to pursue an acquaintance with the tenant of the yellow dacha. He added, however, that there was nothing to fear from their neighbour — after all, he was a decent and refined individual.

While Pëtr went to pull up radishes, Sasha, knowing that at this hour there would be, probably, no music (since this was the usual time of their neighbour's walk), also left the house and began to wander. Coming across a nearby grove of trees, she walked for a long time and was delighted to find herself in an unfamiliar setting.

Sasha started picking bright, fragrant violets. She picked a large bunch and ran down to a spring to rinse off the stems. Descending into a ravine, where she came across a bright brook flowing directly across her path, Sasha moistened the flowers and proceeded to take a drink out of her cupped hands. Then she sat down and began to sort the violets one by one, putting them together in a bouquet. She felt all cosy and cool in this ravine and delighted in the solitude — a silence broken only by the faint, monotonous gurgling of the brook.

But then she heard some other sounds — someone breathing, someone turning pages of a book... Sasha spied the tenant of the yellow dacha sitting on a stump, hatless and with a book in his hand. He had not heard Sasha... His face, moreover, looked pretty gloomy.

Sasha didn't know what to do. She could run, but what would be the point? That would simply be shameful.

If she stayed, a conversation could not could not help but ensue, and she did not feel up to making an acquaintance with this man at the moment. What, then, to do? But while she was deciding, the stranger got up, bowed to Sasha and said:

"You like this place, too, eh? It's not as hot down here."

"This is my first time here. I haven't got to know all the local places," Sasha replied, feeling a shiver run through her body. "I'm on my way home now..."

"D'you mind if we walk together?" the stranger said simply and calmly.

"Fine. What's your name?"

"Ivan Il'ich. And yours?"

"Aleksandra Alekseevna."

"D'you like music? I see you came by to listen the other day. Would you like me to play something for you?"

"No... I mean, yes... Thank you, some day ..."

Sasha's heart was beating with excitement. How simple and easy it was to feel this kind of happiness now, which before had seemed so unattainable...

They walked up to the top of the ravine, climbed a little hill, crossed a solid brushwood bridge over a gully, then climbed another hill, and there, lo and behold, before them unfolded a marvellous vista of a river, neither large nor small, with a bright sunset to the left and a distant old forest to the right.

"How beautiful it is here! I've never been here before. And there is a row-boat on the river, how jolly!" exclaimed Sasha. "Who does it belong to?"

"I dunno. If you like, we could go for a ride; I'll row."

"Thank you, I'd be happy to go..." Sasha agreed without thinking, as she ran quickly towards the river.

With his strong, beautiful hands, albeit ones unaccustomed to heavy work, Ivan Il'ich took hold of the boat's chain in an awkward move. He pulled the boat towards him and jumped in, then held out his hand to Sasha, and a few minutes later they were rowing calmly along in the direction of a nearby town.

The fiery glow of the sunset gradually moved towards the horizon and sank into the water. All was quiet, an evening mist descended over the river, and along its banks the lights of the town could be seen through the mist. They kept on rowing, with hardly any conversation.

Sasha felt a sense of joyful peace. The simplicity and quiet tenderness of this man at once subdued her heart and will. She had lost her own will, but the loss portended only good.

It was quite late when Sasha finally returned home in the company of Ivan Il'ich. Pëtr Afanas'evich had been worrying about his wife, he even ran about looking for her, and was delighted to glimpse her with their neighbour.

"I am really happy to see that you've met! Come and have some tea right now, get yourselves warmed up, since it's so damp out."

"It's hot, why would we need warming up?" said Sasha. "We just had a nice boat ride."

"A boat? That's great!" Pëtr Afanas'evich exclaimed in surprise.

Ivan Il'ich attacked the bread and butter and green cheese with great gusto and, after adding a goodly amount of cream to his tea, finished off three cups.

"Do you have a piano? What make is it?" he asked.

"We have one, and it's a very good one. It's a Bechstein. I myself played quite often a while back. But Pëtr Afanas'evich does not like music at all. He even suffers from the noise it makes (as he puts it) — so much so, that I've practically stopped playing altogether."

"D'you mind if I try it?"

Ivan Il'ich played something, then paused for a moment. He bowed his head, trying to remember something. Then he pushed himself slightly away from the piano and perched on the very edge of the stool. Finally he struck a chord — the opening of a Beethoven sonata, opus 31.

"What's that?" Sasha all at once asked herself, blushing all over, as though enveloped by hot steam. "Yes, I know it. But how uniquely he plays this sonata! It's all new, all new! How well — not just 'how well,' but *how incredibly well* he plays it! What a dear fellow he is, really dear! …"

Sasha was practically going out of her mind with excitement. Her whole body trembled with an inner shiver. This first *Largo*, pianissimo… and then the *Allegro*, so expressive!… And what about Beethoven himself?! Where and how had he been able to listen in on all those feelings in Sasha's heart?!

"Beethoven understood *everything*, and the pianist understood Beethoven, and I understand them both!" she mused. "I feel them both and love them both…"

Sasha watched Ivan Il'ich's face, his flitting serious-looking eyes, his intense expression, his oh so lovely hands.

But suddenly it all started to disappear.

"My God! Where has it gone to? ..." the question flashed through Sasha's mind, as though she were being dragged — weak and blind — into a completely unfamiliar world...

Under the performer's fingers, the sonata resonated with extraordinary beauty, each phrase becoming more meaningful and magnificent than the last.

"But none of this is new or unknown to me," Sasha kept thinking. "There have been times in the past when things were equally happy and good. But where was that? ... When was it? ... Was it not in the realm from where I came into this life, where everything was elusive, unlimited and timeless? ..."

Sasha tried to catch Ivan Il'ich's eye, but his serious gaze, full of meaningful expression, was still not focused on anyone or anything in particular. "What is he looking at? What is he focusing on?" Sasha kept repeating to herself — and all at once, slowly, from the very depths of her soul, a prayerful mood solemnly arose. Following a childhood habit, Sasha at once turned her gaze towards the icon in the corner of the room, and many thoughts became joyfully clear to her: thoughts of God, of spiritual happiness, of eternity, of death and immortality, of anything what was outside space and time, of her late mother, who had already passed into this very eternity. At the same time, the pain of loss, the chaos of tormenting doubts about life and death, with all their sufferings, temptations and evils — all this was brought to light like a clear sky after a storm, the sun pouring its bright rays onto the newly refreshed Nature.

Better and better, stronger and stronger, more and more meaningful, the sounds kept flowing forth from under his genius hands. Sasha felt tears starting to choke her. She jumped up and ran into the next room. Letting her countenance fall face down on her dressing table, she covered her head with her folded arms, and her internal shiver gave way to quiet sobbing.

Sasha wanted to kneel before this person and, like an ancient pagan before an idol-like embodiment of such perfect art, she felt like bowing low to the amazing power which had awakened all that was glorious within her and had brought her back to life.

"That's surely what music is meant to be?!" Sasha thought in wonderment. "Why didn't I realise it before? ..."

Ivan Il'ich finished the piece. After a moment of silence, he looked at his watch and said in a rather sleepy, ho-hum voice:

"Time for bed. Good night."

And a second later it appeared as though his whole being had suddenly shut down. The fire, the energy and strength so palpable in his playing — all that seemed to have vanished, and the valve covering the opening, the source of all these treasures, was now closed. As though on purpose, Ivan Il'ich had now become utterly prosaic, earthy and placid.

This, however, did not fool Sasha in the least. She understood his tone of voice, understood what he was trying to tell everyone: "*Leave me alone when*

*I want to be left alone, and don't intrude upon the 'holiest of holies' of my world
of art, which I love more than anything else in the world!"*

Sasha wanted to thank him but couldn't. She held out her hand to him, but
her eyes, wet and glistening with tears and excitement, told him more than
words could express. Ivan Il'ich, as though inadvertently, kept holding on to
Sasha's hand. For a moment he paused in what seemed to be a state of indeci-
sion, peering closely into her naïve, magnificent eyes with undivided interest
and even some curiosity. Then he went out onto the terrace, not completely
certain whether this new acquaintance of his was simply pretending to be an
ecstatic lover of music or whether she was actually that sensitive and responsive to it.

CHAPTER 10

The following morning Ivan Il'ich's pupil arrived, and Sasha spent the next
two-and-a-half hours listening to chromatic scales emanating from the yellow
cottage, alternating with conversation and loud youthful guffaws.

Sasha, too, began to feel happy. She, too, felt like laughing and moving
around. She made herself busy with Alësha and kept running out into the
garden and coping with various household problems. But how insignificant
seemed these everyday troubles and cares after yesterday's major event — Ivan
Il'ich's performance of the Beethoven sonata! With what simple meekness and
indifference Sasha regarded all her domestic tasks, as well as her husband's exaggerated reaction to the poor growth of the seeds! … Sasha merely shrugged her
shoulders and turned her mind back to Ivan Il'ich's performance of yesterday:

"Oh, how perfect!" she mused. "What a delight! And perhaps this same
happiness will be repeated tomorrow — indeed, the whole summer, until we
leave the dacha, and then again in Moscow! … Dear Ivan Il'ich!" Sasha tenderly thought of him, as the unidentified source of her happiness.

"However, just look at how dim and dirty our windows are in the sunlight,
but this is from dust and our lamps!" and Sasha suddenly remembered how
yesterday her husband was grumbling about that, blaming the maid. "*Parasha
must be scolded…*" he had said.

"No, no one ever needs to be scolded for anything," countered Sasha in her
mind. "*Everybody* can be happy… How wonderfully he began that *Largo* yesterday! Indeed, it's simply amazing! How marvellous, what happiness!"

Sasha took a towel and wiped off the window-panes, carefully brushing
aside the tender, transparent, feathery ferns on the windowsill. She took equal
care to avoid touching the potted roses in full bloom beside them — which
were so pleasing to her eyes.

"And Parasha needn't be scolded… Let her sleep… She was so tired yesterday… And now comes the finale of the sonata. It's more than the piano,
more than the notes — it's a whole epic poem of humanity's inner life… And
the recitative? It told me what a marvellous, all-comprehending, sensitive

soul there was in both Beethoven and his pianist-interpreter. How joyful! How good it's become to live in this world!" Her heart jumped a beat and, it seemed, could no longer bear such an awesome musical fulness.

Sasha sat down at her own piano and quietly played yesterday's sonata, trying to copy Ivan Il'ich's phrasing. She couldn't hear herself — she could hear only yesterday's music. After playing it, Sasha felt more at peace.

"Sasha dear, do have a look at these imported tomatoes!" urged Pëtr Afanas'evich, who had just entered the room and was about to offer her one. "Feel it! That's the way mine are going to be."

"What are you talking about? What tomatoes?"

Sasha didn't understand at first. But when she realised it, she took the slippery red vegetable in her hand and smiled.

And this no longer irritated her — how could everything not be just so perfect, especially when the whole world had suddenly started singing the chorus of marvellous sounds which had brought her back to life and which would now fill her entire being — now... tomorrow... a month from now... and maybe forever.

Pëtr Afanas'evich went out into his garden and began tying back his cauliflower plants. Sasha, who had never taken part in his activities, all at once cheered up and willingly began helping her husband. She did everything in spurts, not thinking seriously about what she was doing. She seemed to be listening to something with some kind of expectation.

Ivan Il'ich walked past Pëtr's vegetable garden along with a young man. He stopped at the fence for a minute or so to greet Sasha and her husband.

"Allow me introduce my pupil, Tsvetkov," said Ivan Il'ich.

Tsvetkov at once offered a smile, both with his lips and his laughing, narrow-slitted eyes — so joyfully and energetically that it was catching. He first bowed from a slight distance, then kissed Sasha's hand and began to describe the local landscape in glowing terms.

Tsvetkov was so happy and healthy; everything came easy to him. In fact, he showed such talent in everything that he apparently had no time to be shy. He was not overly self-conscious, but drank in all kinds of impressions of life with amazing speed, taking as much advantage of them as possible for his own pleasure.

"Both of you must come and dine with us," Pëtr Afanas'evich kindly invited them. "We recently obtained an enormous pike, and I bought lots of asparagus with stems as big as a huge candle — gentlemen, you should see them."

"What are you doing at the moment?" enquired Ivan Il'ich.

"Well, right now my dear Sasha and I are tying back the cauliflower plants."

"Why not come and go bathing with us instead?"

"With pleasure! Right away! I'll just fetch a towel."

Pëtr went into the house. Sasha left her task in the garden and, with a bright smile and with her cheeks all rosy, she said laughingly to Ivan Il'ich:

"Anyway, you were really practising those chromatic scales!"

"You heard them?"

"Of course I did!"

"Well, just for that, we'll play something good for you tonight."

"Well, all I can say is 'Thank you.' I look forward to it."

The men headed off, and Sasha went to see about dinner. All at once she had an urge to make everything look good — especially lovely and magnificent. She put together large bouquets from field flowers, roses, jasmine, yellow lilies and fern leaves. She herself tidied up everything in the rooms and even repositioned the furniture, endeavouring to make it all beautiful and comfortable. Motivated by a special love, she wiped down the piano keys with her fragrant cambric handkerchief before sitting down to play herself.

Then little Alësha came in.

"Mamà, come and play with me for a while!" he pleaded.

"Wait, dear," Sasha insisted, going over a prelude which Ivan Il'ich had sent her that morning.

"Aw, Mamà…"

But Sasha had just got involved in a complex passage of the prelude, trying to listen carefully to its various intertwining melodies. This capturing of the composer's thoughts afforded her particular pleasure.

But then, all at once, Alësha started to cry. Sasha was shocked by her own distraction. She picked up her son and ran out into the garden, laughing, where for a long time she played with him in a most cheerful and inventive manner. But the prelude was still ringing in her ears, and her brain was hard at work recalling the complex combinations of this musical masterpiece.

A lot of guests assembled for dinner. Among them was a friend of Pëtr Afanas'evich named Mukhatov, a great lover of opera music, a wealthy landowner, who often visited their house and harboured a secret love for Sasha. From another dacha came a recent law graduate named Kurlinskij, who had just moved there after his final exams. He appeared pale and exhausted. A distant relative of Sasha's, he was spending the rest of the summer at his auntie's dacha, where his pretty cousin Kate also lived. Ivan Il'ich showed up as well, together with Tsvetkov.

The dinner took place in the garden. Sasha's bouquets were charming. The bowls of fruit, the English place settings, the glistening silver, the bright summer sun — all of this contributed to the festive, beautiful and magnificent atmosphere.

Tsvetkov was seated beside Kate, while Sasha invited Ivan Il'ich to sit next to herself. But he kept looking with envy at his pupil and Kate, as they chattered and laughed together. Sasha was nervous, and her conversation with her neighbour turned out rather unnatural. She was also irritated by her husband, who went around offering trays of food to his guests or pouring wine for them. Mukhatov, the opera lover, felt a compulsion to discuss music with

Ivan Il'ich. The latter, who enthusiastically devoured everything that Pëtr Afanas'evich put before him, listened with a delicate but still noticeable irony to Mukhatov's elaborate praise of Wagner.

"Of course, you love Wagner, Aleksandra Alekseevna, don't you?" Mukhatov asked Sasha.

"I really don't know him at all," replied Sasha.

"You don't know him?! You must study his works — a whole new world of delight will open up to you. He is a genius! What amazing thoughts one finds in his leitmotifs, in his musical expression, all through its various phrases at each moment of the opera performance."

"It's all a big jumble to me," Sasha timidly observed. "I just find it boring."

"Oh mercy! Boring?! You must listen more closely; it's not the same flim-flam stuff as you might find in Verdi's Italian operas. It's something original, brand new: the voice acts as a link in one glorious whole, the voice blends with the entire orchestra, constituting one of its best instruments. Oh, there's nothing better in the world than those Wagner harmonies! Come spring, I shall definitely be taking my holidays in Bayreuth."

"But for me," interjected Pëtr Afanas'evich, "all this new music equates only to suffering. I think people pretend they understand something in it. But it's all just noise to me. In fact, it's painful to my ears!"

"*New music* — that's the music of the future," Kurlinskij modestly noted.

"Especially the music Ivan Il'ich composes," Tsvetkov triumphantly declared.

"Would you like me to give you a topic for an opera?" Mukhatov turned to Ivan Il'ich. "I've got an amazing one!"

"I'd be very glad to hear it," said Ivan Il'ich, again with delicate irony.

"Can a topic actually be given?" Sasha suddenly became flustered. "An opera topic can only be one's *own*... it has to be personal, springing from the unique character of its composer... If the composer is a genius, he himself will feel not only the contemporary demands arising from his art, but also the major demands of all humanity, and will respond to these demands through his creations."

"Yes, if only they had responded! ... But in reality they seldom have any success," Mukhatov, upset by Sasha's discontented expression, objected with annoyance and even some acrimony.

"Aleksandra Alekseevna is right," Kurlinskij remarked, full of admiration for the blushing Sasha.

Ivan Il'ich once again looked into Sasha's eyes with interest and curiosity. His face darkened for a moment. He winked and went on eating his strawberries.

After dinner everybody went their own way. Kate returned to her own dacha to change into her riding outfit and get ready to go for a ride with Tsvetkov, to whom Pëtr Afanas'evich offered to lend his horse.

Meanwhile, Mukhatov and Pëtr Afanas'evich discussed the question of whether or not a landowner could claim an insurance payment for a factory burned down by his workers.

Ivan Il'ich sat down to play chess with Kurlinskij. Sasha took up her needlework and began to sew silently. She felt so good and at peace. She knew that Ivan Il'ich would probably be practising some time today and was comforted in her heart by the joy of anticipation. From time to time she glanced at Ivan Il'ich's beautiful hands quietly moving the chess pieces around. She wondered what kind of a man he was. She could not understand him at all.

It began to get dark. Suddenly Sasha heard someone's voice behind her. Mukhatov, having finished his conversation with Pëtr Afanas'evich, quietly approached Sasha and began to speak to her in an emotional voice:

"Has it been a long time since you started taking an interest in music?"

"Not long. It's just that I've fallen in love with it once more."

"And who or what has caused you to fall in love with it again?"

"Why are you questioning me so?"

"Because each time you disagree with my opinion, or show some displeasure with me, it really bothers me…"

"Really?" Sasha naïvely responded.

"I would like you and me to be of one mind in everything. I would like us to love the same things. I would like…"

"Were you talking to me? …" Sasha interrupted absent-mindedly. After glancing at Ivan Il'ich, she got up and went out onto the terrace. She stood for a while in contemplation and then looked up at the sky.

"Aha! There it is, my star! All spring long it has both delighted and irritated me, yet for some reason it has also been just as meaningful to me as the comet was to Pierre in *War and peace* — the comet which he looked at with moist eyes as he was riding in a carriage and his heart began to be inflamed with a conscious love for Natasha…

"But am I in love with anyone? …" Sasha asked herself. "Pierre was ecstatic, but am I? … Yes, I, too, am ecstatic in my own way, over my new love for… *music*. And not for anything in the world would I ever give up this new and glorious love… It's not that I can expect anything special from it… But — amidst the lesser stars of common, everyday life, along with its boredom, sufferings and emptiness — it shines in my heart as clearly as this bright greenish star amidst all the other countless stars, large and small, stretching as far as the eye can reach… or as Pierre's bright comet."

A loud conversation between Tsvetkov and Kate, who had just arrived by the terrace, brought Sasha to her senses. Behind them servants were leading two saddled horses. Kate, flirting, insisted that Ivan Il'ich examine and stroke her horse.

"Now give me your expert hand and help me onto my horse," she said with a laugh.

"I'm very awkward at this," replied Ivan Il'ich as he fussed and approached Kate.

But Kate was so pretty and gave him such a winsome, disarming look that he hastened to help her mount. Admiring her slender figure and small feet, he could only envy Tsvetkov.

"My God, how naïve he is, and how banal his behaviour!" Sasha thought with annoyance. As her eyes involuntarily met Ivan Il'ich's, she immediately walked brusquely past him with her head proudly in the air and disappeared.

Ivan Il'ich was about to leave, but Pëtr Afanas'evich held him back, asking him to stay for tea and promising him some amazing melons.

Out of habit, Ivan Il'ich kept looking at his pocket-watch, then at last observed:

"It's late already."

But he stayed nevertheless.

Everyone once again gathered for tea on the terrace, and Sasha — pale and wrapped in a white shawl over her white dress — silently began to pour tea. Some kind of conflict was going on within her — she was disturbed by the episode with Kate, as well as by today's absence of music, which she was feeling a painful longing for.

"Would you like me to play for you?" Ivan Il'ich all at once asked her. Sasha gave a shudder as though she were frightened by something fearful approaching her.

"I'd like that very much!" she quickly replied.

Ivan Il'ich went into the drawing-room and began to play Beethoven's variations. Sasha immediately experienced a shiver of delight. She was especially impressed with the eighteenth variation, which was brief, calm and so expressive…

The graceful variations came to an end… Ivan Il'ich thought for a moment and then with his mighty hand played an E-flat octave.

This was the start of Chopin's *Polonaise in A-flat major*.

"Oh, my!" exclaimed Sasha and froze on the spot. Once again, some kind of invisible valve opened, and the noble, magnificent sounds tore at and excited Sasha's heart, generously embracing her (giving her no time to think rationally) with those precious, marvellous thoughts which Ivan Il'ich was absorbing from their composer and so brilliantly conveying to his listeners …

However, on this occasion the only actual listener was Sasha. She opened her heart completely to drinking in the artistic impression. She managed to catch and digest everything imparted to her by the two geniuses together — the composer and the performer. Such bliss she had never experienced before in her life.

But in this perception of bliss, so rarely encountered in life, there was something that might even have passed for criminal. The link between listener and performer was so strong that it could never again be broken. It was timeless, forever... no matter what happened next in Sasha's life, no matter how she managed to pull herself together after this evening. From that moment on Ivan Il'ich was completely in charge of her, and this possession of her soul was far stronger and more significant than any possession of her body could be.

At this point Sasha became frightened. She looked at Ivan Il'ich submissively and passionately, while he, after finishing his polonaise and casting a glance at her, suddenly became aware of his triumph and his power over this young woman that he had conquered.

"Oh, my God!" Sasha exclaimed quietly. "What was it? ... I do thank you," she said. "What a remarkable polonaise!"

"Yes, my dear friend, that was powerful indeed!" said Pëtr Afanas'evich.

Ivan Il'ich almost staggered as he rose to his feet, letting his wandering eyes focus on Sasha. Looking at his watch, he bade her good-night.

"You are a wonderful listener," he said with a smile and once more lingered as he tenderly held Sasha's hand in his.

This lingering hold was fraught with something so tender and intimate that Sasha wanted to prolong the feeling of his hand in hers, to gaze as long as she could into his kind-looking eyes, now almost asleep.

"Farewell...," Ivan Il'ich's valve once again closed, and his creative treasure-house, which Sasha only a moment ago had been peering into, shut down.

"No, not 'farewell'," thought Sasha, "but only 'goodbye'... 'til tomorrow'." Whereupon Sasha's whole heart was filled with delight and burst into song — the festive sounds of the *Polonaise* and the complex combination of voices in the prelude, along with Beethoven's variations and Mendelssohn's *Song without words* in G-major.

So that night Sasha fell asleep amid the myriad of sounds which had so completely possessed her. She dreamt about Ivan Il'ich. In her dream she could feel his closeness, his warm breathing. She saw his inspired face, transformed during his performance from its usual quiet indifference to something powerful, strong and disturbing.

CHAPTER 11

"Can I talk with you for a moment?" asked Kurlinskij, as he stepped onto the terrace where Sasha was sitting, reading a biography of Beethoven Ivan Il'ich had given her.

"Of course," Sasha replied reluctantly, "come in."

"I came to thank you for yesterday, for the pleasure afforded us by your neighbour."

"Well, you ought to thank *him*. I had nothing to do with it."

"Yes, I've already been to see him. I read him one of my poems."

"Another decadent one?" suggested Sasha.

"That's what you like to call the new direction in poetry. You are very sensitive to everything, Aleksandra Alekseevna, but on this question I see you have a prejudiced and non-impartial opinion."

"Not at all... I don't like any kind of prejudice. It's just that I'm so stupid that I don't understand and don't like the poems of Balmont or Baudelaire, nor the music of Wagner."

"May I read you *my* poems?"

"Out of friendship to you, please go ahead — I'll be listening."

Kurlinskij pulled out of his pocket a rather large notebook and began to read a series of meaningless poems in a gravelly voice.

As he was reading the last one, which was about her, he looked up at Sasha with an affectionate gaze, but immediately took fright and lowered his eyes. Ivan Il'ich (who had come to the veranda in the meantime) happened to catch these last lines.

"Splendid," he said — as usual, with a bit of irony. "I'll compose some music for you, and your cousin can sing it. Go fetch me some music paper from my cottage."

When Kurlinskij was gone, Ivan Il'ich asked Sasha whether he were disturbing her.

"Oh no, I don't have anything on at the moment. I just sent away some peasant women, who constantly come to me for medicine. Treating people's ills can be terribly challenging."

"I would have supposed it, on the contrary, to be a joyful task."

"No, not always. I know that it is undoubtedly good to wash and bind a wound, but my! how helpless I am when there is no way you can understand an illness and help — that's sheer helplessness, doubt, refusal — and all that is terribly painful."

"How vehemently you react to everything! You have to proceed more gently," suggested Ivan Il'ich.

"Thank you for your advice. I'll definitely think about it."

"Yes, I don't like to worry."

"And when you are playing or composing, are you still calm then?"

"Completely."

"But *how* do you compose?"

Ivan Il'ich pondered for a moment.

"Difficult to say. In small segments... I think it over, then one part flows from another, and it comes together all by itself. You have to study a lot and have a musical education in order to compose... you can't just sit around and wait for inspiration."

"Yes, but your education has killed the melody. In the new music, the whole aim is concentrated on harmony. But the clear expression of simple feelings used to be good for the melody."

"No, not good, boring!" countered Ivan Il'ich.

"Isn't it more boring that romance has completely disappeared from both life and music?" Sasha enquired. "Everything's started to go according to logic."

"No, everything has become more spiritual, which makes it better. Of course, this musical philosophy may be boring in the works of untalented musicians, but under the pen of gifted composers you can feel its spirituality, and so such new works impact not our nerves, but the spiritual, rational side of the human soul."

"So that's how you explain new music! … That's splendid! Well, then, play me something spiritual…"

"It's hot, maybe later. But I think we ought to choose something of just that sort."

Kurlinskij returned with the music paper, but Ivan Il'ich did not begin to write. On the contrary, all three of them decided to take a walk and watch the farmhands gathering in the hay. They took little Alësha along with them. Sasha put on a big straw hat, and they all headed down to the river. Here, on a huge flood-plain, a whole motley crowd of peasant women were raking the hay. A marvellous aroma of dry green hay treated the walkers' nostrils.

Little Alësha rushed headlong into a hay-stook and buried himself in it with a happy laugh.

"But look, clouds are gathering," said Sasha. "If it rains again, the hay will turn all black."

"Yes, but, I assume, this is not *your* hay?" Ivan Il'ich asked in surprise.

"What does it matter? Is it not all the same? Mine or yours — that's not important to me. It is always the actual work that I find interesting.

"My husband is always upset when stealing is going on in our village and the peasants have a voracious appetite for everything. As for me, I feel sorry, rather, for the beauty of an apple tree when kids break off branches or steal apples. I feel sorry when the cattle let loose by the peasants trample on a marvellous lush field of rye; I feel sorry when they cut down an old oak or birch-tree or break down young firs in a planting area… But not because it will make us any poorer — after all, the thief probably has greater needs than we do — but simply because I don't like destruction of any kind."

Ivan Il'ich once again fixed Sasha in his sight and winked.

"She is definitely unlike the others," he mused to himself. "But what have I to do with her, anyway?!" he added this thought with concern.

All at once, a helpful idea came to him, and he continued with some irony:

"Does that mean, if I fell right now and broke my arm, or even died, you would feel sorry that I could no longer play Beethoven sonatas and Chopin polonaises, but would not feel pity for me as a person — you love only the 'work' after all?"

For a moment Sasha felt burdened and plunged into thought.

"I think," she replied, "you are right that I would feel more pity for you as a musician than as a person. But this is not because you give *me* so much personal pleasure with your music, but because something good and talented would vanish prematurely and be lost."

"That means, you would never feel sorry for anyone as a person?"

"Maybe, only Alësha."

"In other words, yourself," Ivan Il'ich observed with a touch of humour.

Sasha said nothing more and walked over to the group of peasant workers.

It came to her that, if she fell in love with Ivan Il'ich as a person, she would lose her pure attachment to his art, and this would count as a failure.

"How is your son Mishka?" Sasha asked a young woman with clear blue eyes who had just removed her red kerchief from her perspiring forehead, exposing the blonde hair around her temples.

"Thank God, he feels much better from your medical drops. Thank you, dear Madame."

"Well, well, very glad. Give me your rake!"

Sasha proceeded to walk a row with the women, easily and skilfully raking the hay. How many times in her childhood she would work on her mother's estate with peasant girls and women in the happy summer harvest season... And all at once she was reminded of her childhood, and her mother, and the loss of everything she had loved so much.

Sasha threw down the rake, reached for Alësha's hand and quickly headed away from the women.

"All right if we take a rest here?" she turned to her companions, barely holding back her tears.

"Are you off home now, Aleksandra Alekseevna? Is there anything wrong?" Kurlinskij asked her with sentimental affection.

"Oh, nothing," replied Sasha. "I was just remembering the past... the estate where I lived as a child... Give me your hand, Ivan Il'ich!" she said, for some reason unconsciously seeking refuge and support from the same hand which had so powerfully comforted her soul in grief and reconciled her with life.

Ivan Il'ich took Sasha under his arm, but averted his eyes, fixing them on some distant scene, and blushed. He was amazed at the decisiveness and simplicity with which Sasha reached out for support from his hand.

Having walked up a little hill, Sasha suddenly calmed down and, choosing a spot in the shade, invited her companions to sit down. It was very hot. Alësha picked and ate berries, Ivan Il'ich lay down on the grass — lazily, but with obvious physical pleasure. He plucked a large clump of hay from the nearest stook and put it as a kind of pillow under his head.

Kurlinskij recited Tjutchev's verse:

If the Divine does not agree to this,
No matter how it suffers, being in love,
The soul cannot outsuffer joy and bliss.
Itself, though, it *can* outsuffer and improve...

In the distance, the chirping of unseen crickets could be heard on all sides, while midges swarmed about under the direct rays of the sun.

"How wonderful!" said Sasha. "Such is the power of summer, in all its glory!"

"Look, Mamà, see what bubbles are coming from the fish there," said Alësha, his eyes fixed on a little pool at the edge of the river. "Why can't we take a rod some time and go fishing?"

"Yes, good idea," Sasha said absent-mindedly.

At that moment, though, her thoughts were concentrated on remembering her recent conversation with Ivan Il'ich. She was haunted by the vexing thought that everything in life could lose its virgin purity if human influence interfered — in the form of love, for example. If you fall in love with someone, but he is not with you, will you still love Nature as much and delight in it? You won't. Everything will fail — all the beauty and joy will disappear, if your beloved is absent amidst this brilliant scene of Nature. And your virgin appreciation of Nature will fall by the wayside.

Would you be so completely in love with music, if you fell in love with someone who wanted no part in it? No, you wouldn't be able to hear it the same way as when you heard it with him or from him.

Would you go alone to an art gallery if you had not seen your beloved for a long time? But with what delight, when you were with him, you would see and understand everything together! And when this *he* is not in your life, when you are absolutely free from love — what pure, virgin, overflowing bliss appears in Nature, and music, and painting, and family pleasures!…

"Oh, my God, deliver me from this poison on my life's path!" Sasha prayed inwardly. "Preserve my purity and help me love Thee in Nature, in art, and in everything that comes from Thy pure source."

Thoughtfully and calmly Sasha rose from the ground, bade goodbye to her companions and quietly headed home.

PART II

CHAPTER 1 ❧ SUMMER PASSES

FOR SASHA, THE WHOLE SUMMER PASSED LIKE A DREAM. For her the time was divided into periods of moments when Ivan Il'ich was playing to anticipating when he would play again. During these intervals Sasha earnestly tried to keep herself busy, entertained or distracted; she became nervous, feverishly coming up with new and sometimes useless activities for herself which could help her avoid noticing the passage of time. And strangely, only in the presence of Ivan Il'ich (even when he was not playing), could she feel any peace or joy… or, for that matter, a reconciliation with her inner life.

They often took long walks as a whole group, frequently including Sasha, Pëtr Afanas'evich, Kurlinskij with his cousin Kate, Ivan Il'ich and little Alësha; Tsvetkov would show up, too.

Sometimes they would take breakfast with them, heading off for a half-day's excursion to neighbouring villages or groves and spend the whole time in the forest — collecting mushrooms, discovering new and beautiful places, relaxing, before coming home cheerfully and happily in the evening, when they would listen to Ivan Il'ich's marvellous music.

For his part, Tsvetkov, who was in love with Kate, contributed a lot of fun and youthful merriment. Nature-lover Pëtr Afanas'evich luxuriated in it just as often as he could tear himself away from Moscow and spend more time at the dacha. He generally took charge of the outings, arranging breakfasts, activities, feeding everyone generously, making sure the ladies had something to sit on, lugging jackets, baskets with provisions, and even exhausted little Alësha, caring for everyone's needs, helping the ladies across brooks and ravines. Upon returning home, sometimes laden with baskets full of mushrooms, he would sort them himself, lovingly separating their thick stems from the hard tops, and then salting and marinating them with Parasha's help. Finally, he would distribute jars with mushrooms throughout the house, showing them to everyone and offering them as a gift to friends and acquaintances.

Sasha, on the other hand, established a relationship with Ivan Il'ich that would leave her with nothing but the most poetic and serious of memories. They were quite unaware of how many things they had in common. Every strong impression of Nature had the same effect on each of them. Ivan Il'ich was finally convinced of Sasha's sincere love for and sensitivity to music and played excerpts from his compositions for her.

"How do you compose?" Sasha again questioned Ivan Il'ich. "I have always found the process of musical creativity fascinating. I am rather able to understand the art of writing, but I can't say the same at all about music."

"Indeed, it's hard to explain, Aleksandra Alekseevna. Every musical idea arises most elusively — a melody comes to mind… you make a small effort to capture it, hold it in memory, and…"

"And… and… and then…"

"Then you can no longer get rid of it. It hangs on to you, and everything else crowds around it, harmonious phrases crop up, and the farther you go, the easier it becomes…"

"Well, then, where, for example, did the drama come from in that piece you played for me yesterday?"

Ivan Il'ich smiled and did not answer right away.

"I was reading an historical piece, and I was struck by the heroism of the Scythians, who were supposed to die rather than surrender. I was in a military mood and wrote this passage…"

"Does that mean anything can inspire you?"

"Some of the time."

"But it always seems to me, looking at you, that you think up everything with your intellect. And I feel like stirring you up, inspiring you…"

"That I don't need, Aleksandra Alekseevna. Better to have peace and quiet in everything."

"Anyway, perhaps in everyday life you have peace and quiet in everything, except in music. There you are a different person, there it feels you're in a completely different place. Everything in your music is meaningful and sometimes even passionate."

All at once Ivan Il'ich put on a stern face and fell silent.

As they approached the house, Sasha turned to Ivan Il'ich and asked:

"Are you coming in?"

"Of course. I was planning on playing the first part of my symphony for you today."

"Oh, what bliss!"

"Is that really bliss?"

Sasha did not answer. Her real bliss was in this constant exchange of thoughts — an exchange built on a purely ethereal foundation.

And so the summer went on. Evenings became longer, then followed days of rain. The friendly circle of close summer acquaintances met in the evenings at Sasha's dacha for reading and chess matches, as well as for music and intimate conversations on art, often at Sasha's initiative.

Pëtr Afanas'evich, deaf to most social undercurrents, was only too happy that Sasha had cheered up and recovered. He adored Ivan Il'ich for comforting her with music. Several more days of summer heat, which the cottagers feverishly took advantage of for walks and swims, were abruptly cut short by a spell of cold and nasty weather.

Ivan Il'ich made plans to move to the Crimea, and Aleksej Tikhonych started packing everything up. The wagons came to cart away their household items, but for some reason Ivan Il'ich was slow in everything and stayed on at his dacha without his belongings (except for the piano), taking his meals daily at Pëtr Afanas'evich's dacha, at the latter's insistence.

Sasha once more became disquieted and anxious. She was so upset that she could no longer carry on with her everyday life.

CHAPTER 2 ❧ A GREY DAY

There are such days in August when, after a frightful heatwave, you wake in the morning to discover: a grey sky, a north wind blowing, a cold and depressing atmosphere. You lift the blind, are surprised at the sight and once again couch yourself in the still warm and cosy bed. And as you lie there warming up, you dream.

What is it? The end of the summer? Is it really? And so soon!…

You close your eyes again, and thoughts and memories chase through your head one after another… Yesterday was such a clear, bright and hot day, when, come evening, you could still enjoy a twilight swim in the river, peacefully opening your arms in the soft, warm water, pampering your whole being — where has it all gone to? It all seems so far away, it all happened so long ago — and it felt so good!

The soul, meanwhile, is busy tuning itself to an autumn key. You begin to decide how to spend the day, trying desperately to carry on in a summer mood. But you don't have any energy — at least not the energy that only the sun can give — that energy which yesterday prompted you to jump out of bed and exclaim with delight: "How nice and hot!..." and you ran down through the garden straight to the river. And what vigour filled your whole being! How beautifully the dew glistened on each leaf and blade of grass, playing in the morning sun!

But this cold is quite unwanted, you long for that bliss, that heat, that languor which you have been accustomed to all these past days and which you unbearably miss at the moment.

But you have to get up. It's time to adapt to a new position, to a different mood, but you still have to live, even if it's in a different way. How often the slightest change in circumstances will remind you of this simple truth — that you *have to live*. It is as though you have made a discovery and pride yourself on clarifying this thought: *you have to live*.

But had not you lived your life even before this question arose? And how do you capture what is really life as opposed to what is emptiness, misery, or, moreover, just killing time...

In his book the philosopher Seneca, among other things, exclaims with despair:

"*Hélas, la plus grande partie de notre vie n'est pas vie, mais durée...*"

Such was Ivan Il'ich's thinking and experience when he awoke on the morning of 7 August in his little yellow dacha. Aleksej Tikhonych, bringing his master's clothes and boots to his room, began to complain about the cold.

"The dacha is all cardboard, you can't heat it, and the cold here will be the death of us. Time to move back to Moscow."

"No, it's still too early, Tikhonych. Light the large lamp and put it in your room."

"What do you mean? That way I'll burn more kerosene, and that costs money. We'll just have to put up with it. After all, you have to pay rent in the city, too."

Ivan Il'ich always felt a great discomfort whenever Tikhonych was unhappy about something. He quickly got up, dressed himself and went out onto the balcony.

With his characteristic neatness, he proceeded to take his morning walk. After passing through the garden, he paused upon reaching the goat pasture, where his eyes began to search both the scenery in the distance and his immediate surroundings. Everything was cold and damp. Even the swallows were flying close to the ground, flitting past Ivan Il'ich, practically running into him. Ivan Il'ich, all shrinking from the cold and turning his face away from the piercing north wind, watched their speedy flight.

He himself did not feel like moving at all. Where would he go? What for? To do what?… It was annoying… he no longer had either yesterday's energy for work or yesterday's joy for life — there was nothing there, absolutely nothing at all, and there was certainly nothing at all he wanted.

Oooh!… hummed the wind, then some sort of loud noise, and from behind Ivan Il'ich could hear the rumble of carriage wheels. Who could it be? And so early in the morning!

The carriage drew even with Ivan Il'ich. In it he spied Sasha, all wrapped in a white Orenburg shawl. At the coachman's feet lay a suitcase, a rolled-up rug was visible behind. Parasha sat beside Sasha.

"Where are you off to, Aleksandra Alekseevna?" Ivan Il'ich asked in surprise.

"Stop, Filipp!" Sasha ordered the coachman.

"I'm going to the Troitse-Sergieva Lavra for fasting," she replied to Ivan Il'ich.

"I don't recall that being in your plans. What's gotten into your head? Or have you a lot of sins to confess?" Ivan Il'ich said with his usual humour.

"Yes, I'm terribly sinful. So, all at once I decided it's high time to fast."

"And what about Pëtr Afanas'evich?"

"He is at home with Alësha."

"Are you going for a long time? Maybe you'll end up enjoying monastery life and staying there!"

"I dunno, maybe that, too."

"Are you coming back?"

"Yes, of course."

"And when will you be going to Moscow?"

"I'm not sure … I don't know yet. I need to spend more time with Nature. Well, goodbye."

"Goodbye, Aleksandra Alekseevna. Bon voyage!"

Sasha doffed her glove and offered Ivan Il'ich her hand. And once again, as though inadvertently, his beautiful warm hand held on to hers. While Sasha did not take hers away, she did not feel excitement, but again, rather, a calm, silent sense of joy and peace.

Ivan Il'ich watched the departing carriage. He had not noticed that the sky had grown even darker, the north wind fiercer, the swallows even fussier. He very much wanted to go home to curl up in a warm, cosy corner and to let his soul immerse itself in his favourite art.

Once back home, he went straight to the piano and began to improvise. Sad chord after sad chord formed rather strange harmonic transitions. There was something tragic in their groanings, and Ivan Il'ich got carried away with his musical sensibility, which invariably but always faithfully and meaning-fully filled his whole life.

CHAPTER 3

The train arrived toward evening, just as the bells rang in the Troitse-Sergieva Lavra calling people to evening prayers. On a large square opposite the old hotel a lot of activity was going on — crowds of pilgrims and people were thronging in the shops selling toys, small icons, dishes and dried herring. Coachmen, taking people to and from trains as well as to the Khot'kovo nun-nery, the Chernigov hermitage, the priory, the theological academy and other places close to the Lavra, circled around the entrance to the hotel, ringing their bells and bargaining with their clients.

Sasha and Parasha entered the hotel and ordered a samovar to be brought to the room.

"Parasha, while we are waiting for the samovar, I am going to the monastery."

"But you ought to have a rest, Aleksandra Alekseevna."

"I'm not tired at all."

Sasha went out onto the square and headed for the gate of the monastery. All at once she heard a woman's voice behind her, speaking rapid-fire with a heavy accent, right into her ear. Sasha gave a shudder and wanted to run, but the gypsy — dark-skinned, rosy-cheeked and thin, with very dark and expres-sive eyes and unkempt hair,— so persistently demanded attention that Sasha was obliged to stop.

"You are in love with a blond man, very much in love…" the woman started. "Do you want I should cast a love-spell on him? Give me eight grivens, and, by God, I'll give you a spell. I'll give you a special herb, you can wrap it up in a hand-kerchief; once you strike it against his shoulder, he'll fall head over heels for you."

"No need! No need!" Sasha countered as she tried to break away, but the gypsy would not let up.

"Come see me — everybody knows Mar'ja Ivanovna the Gypsy. My hus-band Nikita trades in horses. Come, I have a private house. I know all the love spells… Well, it's only eight grivens… He will really fall for you, just you wait and see… At the moment, he's too timid to say anything…"

"Leave me alone!" cried Sasha despairingly, as she dashed toward the monastery gates. People were going into the church. Sasha mixed with the crowd and entered the low-vaulted nave of the church of St. Sergius. The peo-ple formed a queue to kiss the relics. Sasha took her place behind an elderly woman and then mechanically, without thinking, fell on her knees in trepida-tion and excitement before the tomb of the saint, praying for salvation.

What she was to be saved from — she did not yet know herself and did not dare to find out further details.

The priest officiating at the all-night vigil was reciting a canticle to the saint. The choir chanting in unison only made the already long monastic service seem longer. The monks moved about like shadows with soft, even steps, lighting candles and incense-burners, collecting donations and conversing with the pilgrims. Sasha was grateful to be alone among this crowd; engulfed in it, she felt a degree of security and independence — something she so desperately needed in her present state of mind.

The next day, early in the morning, Sasha again went off to the church, where once more she was captivated by the chanting, the crowd, and the overall prayerful atmosphere. She stood for mass. When they began to invite the children to take communion and the air was filled with noise and bustle, Sasha started to observe the tables being set for the holiday meal. Novices, quite accustomed to this, deftly spread the long tables with cutlery, mugs and bowls, along with large dishes with bread and kvass. One of the monks started to describe enthusiastically what kind of fish, wine and kissel would be served today, as it was a holiday. Sasha, however, did not like to be reminded of material things.

After returning to her hotel for just a few minutes for a bite to eat, Sasha once more went back to the church.

"Where are they taking confession?" she asked a group of women-pilgrims, who had been walking around all the holy places and were preparing to fast.

"Over there, with Father Fëdor, in the new church. Come with us, my dear lady, we'll confess together."

Sasha joined the women, and they took a rather long walk through stone passages and corridors until they reached Father Fëdor's door.

When Sasha started lagging behind, her fellow-pilgrims immediately called out to her and embraced her with special tenderness.

"Have a seat, good lady, sit for a while, right here... there's a nice spot here..."

Father Fëdor's cell was upstairs; its doors looked out onto a large stone balcony holding the choir stalls, with the beautiful new church below, where the all-night vigil was taking place.

At Father Fëdor's, people could be seen coming and going for confession. In the middle of the first little room one of the pilgrims was reading the Holy Scriptures.

"Go on, go on, it's your turn now," said one of the pilgrims, gently prodding Sasha. This woman had just been in conversation with her godson-monk, whom she had not seen since childhood and to whom she handed a bundle of treats from his family.

"And I shall be talking with him again. Oh my God, how he's changed!... And is it difficult for you here, Stepasha?" she enquired, addressing her godson.

"At first it seemed very difficult, but now it's better, I've got used to it. Hardest of all is chanting prayers over the dead. I am often overwhelmed by fear."

Sasha quietly opened the door to Father Fëdor's cell a little ways and entered a small, dark room, lit only by a single candle.

An ancient elder, his hair all white, sat beside a lectern and barely raised his tired eyes in Sasha's direction. His eyes no longer conveyed any significant expression. He was like a living corpse. The fatigue and struggle of a long life, along with many deprivations, had left their mark on the lines of his face, which otherwise was completely motionless, indifferent and stern.

"What's your name?" he began to take Sasha's confession in his habitual monotone. "Married?... What is your sin?... Have you betrayed your husband?... Do you believe in God?... Do you keep the fasts?... Do you have any doubts of faith?... Well, then, God forgive you."

Father Fëdor raised his epitrachelion over Sasha's head and pronounced absolution of her sins. However, could Sasha grant absolution to herself?...

After confession Sasha sat down on a bench, waiting for her companions. Then they went downstairs, where a monk was reciting tenets. Sasha, however, was so tired that she was no longer able to listen to the readings, but dozed off, rocking herself to sleep.

When Sasha got back to her hotel, she counted that she had spent nine hours at the church. She got undressed, rushed straight to bed and did not allow herself to think or remember anything. She fell sound asleep on the rather poor bed with springs sticking out and a small hard pillow.

CHAPTER 4 ❧ DRIED FLOWERS

The trip to the Troitse-Sergieva Lavra had a wonderful calming effect on Sasha, although it was but a temporary distraction from the inner turmoil of her heart. Still, when she returned to the dacha, the first thought that came to mind was: had Ivan Il'ich left, and would she hear any more of his music? Approaching the dacha, she saw that the shutters were closed on the yellow cottage and that it was enveloped in its customary silence.

"He's gone!" Her heart sank. She did not even know where he lived in Moscow, or where he had gone to, or whether he would come to see them again. "What's that got to do with me, anyway?!" she thought to herself. "Now I'll be seeing Alësha and my Pëtr Afanas'evich, and I'll be busy with my son, the house, and *music*... Music without Ivan Il'ich, without any external influence, music entirely and exclusively its own."

Sasha entered her room and gave a start upon seeing a music score and a note on her bedside table. It had all been sent by Ivan Il'ich on the day of his departure. The note bade Sasha farewell in cold, awkward terms and asked her permission to dedicate to her the romance which he had composed in her absence and would be sending to her.

"Mamà, what have you brought with you?" cried Alësha, who had just run in. "Show me!... Did you bring a little icon for Nanny?" the boy went on.

Sasha hugged her son and gave him the toys and the little icons she had brought with her. She then sent for her husband, who came running from the garden with rolled-up sleeves and dirt-covered hands.

"Well, Sasha dear, it's so good that you're back! Alësha and I have been missing you."

"What have you been up to?"

"I've been digging up the dahlias, and I wanted to snip the last coloured one."

"Yes, soon it'll be time for us to move."

"But summer's almost at an end, and it's been a good one. Pity we have to move, there are still some good days ahead."

Sasha suddenly agreed, deciding to remain 'til September.

Day followed day — monotonous and boring, but peaceful. Sasha felt herself in such a good mood that she was disinclined to take any initiative whatsoever; nor was she in a hurry to get anywhere, fearing to interrupt that even tone of life which afforded her the complete satisfaction of a duty done and a clear conscience.

It was several days before Sasha opened the romance Ivan Il'ich had left for her. But once she had got to the point where she felt completely at ease, she decided to have a look at it and even try singing it. In all his compositions it was always hard at first to fathom his musical thoughts. But the more she played or sang them, the more richly the whole beauty of his music revealed itself to her and the more easily she was able to discover the depths of his true majestic talent.

This romance, however, was nothing like his other works. Right from the very start of both the music and the lyrics, Sasha could feel so much passion, so much ethereal grace, that she understood it right off and it excited her in the extreme. Had he really written this? Whose passionate words were these? And could this unassuming man really have composed *this*? Where did it come from and for whom was it created? The boisterous accompaniment was a perfect fit for the beautiful, stirring melody, merging into the tender sound of a heart in love.

Again and again Sasha sang the passionate appeals of love, and her heart began beating faster and faster. At last she jumped up and cried out: "No more!" At the same moment she remembered the Lavra gypsy promising her a love-spell and, totally confused, she was so frightened by her own thoughts that she cried out again: "Lord save me!" Then, stepping away from the piano, she collapsed helplessly into a chair. Little by little she regained her sense of calm.

On the table beside her lay a large red book in which Sasha had pressed all the flowers she picked during the summer, pasting them in with Alësha's help, for his amusement.

Yes, in this book may be found the whole history of the summer. Here are some lilies-of-the-valley, now all yellowed and shrivelled. How lovely they were, strong and fragrant, when she picked them on a walk with her husband through their young birch forest. How tenderly careful he was with her, feeling her all too recent grief, and how comforted she felt by his simple, natural kindness.

Then the forget-me-nots came into bloom. And here they are in her book! How well they have preserved their gentle, light-blue colour, and how well preserved is the memory of that day when she picked them. It was hot, and the sky was pale-blue like the forget-me-nots. Sasha had gone to swim, but she found her husband and Ivan Il'ich already bathing there, and she was obliged to wait for them. So she continued walking along the river-bank and picking these marvellous blue forget-me-nots.

Before long Ivan Il'ich stepped out of the bath-house and asked Sasha for her flowers. Admiring them, he picked out a few of them for himself; the rest he gave back to Sasha. She could not help noticing the beauty of his hands, and then for some reason it came to her to conceal her whole face behind these marvellous fresh flowers.

The next page reveals a cluster of small blades of grass... The three of them were sitting at the edge of the forest, and Sasha picked these blades as they conversed about how good it was to live the carefree lifestyle they were now living — day after day, almost exclusively with Nature, with an unhurried, leisurely and unscripted work activity and with the scorching sun, tenderising both their body and soul... Alësha during this time ate too many berries, smearing his little chest with red juice. Afterwards he stuffed berries into the mouths of his mother and Ivan Il'ich, and his common approach to them both for some reason brought joy to Sasha's heart... And she remembered herself looking down at the ground, which was at the time crawling with countless little insects.

Sasha then turned to a new page. Here were pansies, both big and small, like some sort of little funny faces... This rich collection had been both planted and picked by her husband. She arranged them in the form of a wreath, and now all these bug-eyed flowers, like little faces, looked at her ironically — the way Ivan Il'ich sometimes looked at her — and she quickly turned the page.

Cornflowers... some had shed their petals and turned white, while others were still deep-blue. Sasha remembered the endless fields of rye all glistening in the sun and blowing in the wind. The heavy ears were bending over, the rye was already ripe, and you could feel a kind of tension in this mature summer bloom.

There were guests, whom Sasha boldly and cheerfully escorted along the narrow pathways through the fields. She could feel the presence of Ivan Il'ich behind her, who had just been complimenting her on her summer outfit — and she could now feel his admiring glance. Later he began to lag behind and picked these cornflowers.

"See how charming they are, how big and bright they are this year," he said, as he offered her a bouquet.

Sasha held out her hand to take the flowers, and her heart gave a joyful beat. That evening she dried these cornflowers, pressed them into the book and noted down the date.

Well, that's enough... But wait... there are the ferns... They were brought to her by Alësha, saying that they looked like green feathers. And now, on the very last page she saw some large barren-flower leaves, which she had recently picked from the strawberry beds. The leaves were red, and the flowers had runners but no fruit... Why then was this strawberry blooming in the early autumn, untimely and fruitless?

And why was this fruitless, unnecessary feeling of love for music and its performer blooming in her heart? Why was her heart aching so much when the music which had inspired her was gone from the yellow cottage next door? The little yellow dacha was now empty; Ivan Il'ich's remaining things, including the piano, had been removed this morning...

Was it true that it was *all* over now — the summer, and the flowers, and the music, and Mendelssohn's *Song without words*, along with her brief, crazy and carefree happiness?... Thanks to the marvellous healing sounds of music, the melody in G-major had filled her whole being with song.

But now a kind of poison was seeping into her heart. Sasha, feeling agitated and hopeless, bowed her head over her book and broke into tears.

CHAPTER 5 ❧ *LAST DAYS AT THE DACHA*

Sasha went on living at the dacha with her son for another fortnight. Pëtr Afanas'evich showed up occasionally, but his affairs at the Insurance Society required his personal presence. It was quite a catastrophe when a huge fire broke out, draining the Society's finances, and there followed a formal investigation of arson. The usually meek and mild Pëtr Afanas'evich was beside himself, shouting as he was telling Sasha about cases of fraud. He was now completely absorbed in the interests of the agency in which he had served for many a year and to which he was dedicated with his whole heart.

Sasha was not at all weighed down by loneliness. She did a lot of reading, copying out any thoughts which especially appealed to her. Besides, she continued to be closely involved with music. She enthusiastically spent hour after hour at the piano. She learnt several pieces, including one recent composition by Ivan Il'ich, which drove her to ecstasy. It represented an amazing combination of pagan beauty with the spiritual contemplation of Deity.

The accompaniment was ethereally light, so elusively quivering in its *pianissimo* that you could feel the vacillation of the prayerful soul in its contemplation of God. Then all of a sudden there entered some solemn chords, possibly indicative of God's answer to the praying soul. These chords would grow more and more majestic, more and more full, strong and meaningful, raising the soul higher and higher and, upon attaining the highest limits of spiritual tension, would suddenly cease. And in the sphere of an ethereal world, as they transitioned to *piano*, the sounds disappeared in a tender *pianissimo*, as though someone's soul were being transported into infinity and vanishing in oblivion.

It was a difficult composition. Sasha spent hour after hour on it, but the delight it afforded her fully rewarded all her efforts.

If it were not for the cold and the fear that Alësha might catch pneumonia in the poorly heated dacha, Sasha would have still held on to her tranquil life. She was not thinking of Ivan Il'ich or of what winter had in store for her in Moscow. She continued to live at one with Nature and music, and her delight in them was pure and holy. And once again she felt so truly independent, so utterly free from any troublesome human feelings, that she did not care to interrupt this mood for any other pleasure in the world.

But autumn swept in early, stormy and cold. Alësha developed a runny nose. Not being able to go outside, the boy began to be quite bored and begged to go to his Papà in Moscow. Sasha felt that it was indeed time to make the move and started to get ready. But first she wanted to go around to all her favourite places that were dear to her heart — places where she had spent the summer so meaningfully and even happily. After sorting her music sheets and precious treasures, portraits and important papers, Sasha left Parasha to pack them away and headed out for a walk.

As in the summer, the brief autumn day altered its mood several times capriciously. The morning was damp, with a nasty light rain, but then the sun came out. Sasha emerged from the forest and paused on the slope of a hill. To her right a grove of small firs had been planted, interspersed here and there with young birches. With their dried pale-yellow leaves, the latter stood out particularly starkly against both the thick green firs and the steely, dark-grey sky, which at that moment was surmounted by the full arch of a bright rainbow.

At Sasha's left could be seen a reddish-yellow stripe of the setting sun. The sun, still so summery, bright and cheerful along with its rainbow vault, seemed to contradict the dark and gloomy autumn sky. As though comforting dying Nature, it all at once shed its generous light on the crowns of the pale-yellow birches and bright green firs. Only the leaden sky stubbornly refused to yield to its warm embrace and remained enshrouded in gloom.

Sasha could only gasp open-mouthed at all this wondrous beauty and majesty of Nature. "And I shall be leaving you," she thought, mentally addressing Nature as a whole, "and I shall perish amidst human passions and temptations..."

She quickened her pace, fearful of the approaching darkness gradually enveloping the forest. It was quiet. All she could hear were the leaves falling from the trees so fast as if constantly trying to outwhisper each other. The leaves fell in little piles, and Sasha's feet drowned in this dry brown foliage rustling under her footsteps and scattering in accord with the motion of her dress.

And then she came upon the old oak tree with its gnarled roots sticking out onto the pathway. Practically all summer long she had been stumbling across it, either going bathing or meeting almost daily with Ivan Il'ich, who suddenly popped into her head. Where was he? Such a tormenting desire to see and hear him in person seeped into her heart that she practically *ran* home, straight to her room. With feverish alacrity, she packed up her remaining things, commanded a carriage and wagons to be hired, and decided to leave for Moscow early the next morning.

Before her departure, under the pretext of searching for some music scores she had forgotten in the yellow dacha, Sasha asked the concierge to unlock the door for her. Excitedly going around the small, empty rooms, she paused in the corner of the main hall where Ivan Il'ich used to sit and play the piano. Remembering him and his playing, Sasha gave herself wholeheartedly to her feelings and exclaimed in despair: "You gave me back my life, but you may also bring about its ruination!!"

CHAPTER 6 ❧ BREAKDOWN

After arriving at Moscow, Sasha immediately subscribed to the symphony concert series and began looking over her wardrobe. She loved to dress up but wore mainly black or white dresses in various combinations. In a lighthearted, restless mood, she kept busy either running around the boutiques or tidying up the house. In fact, she spent very little time at home. She did not read and began to fear the piano as some sort of enemy.

She spent the first month in this way. As to Ivan Il'ich, she eventually heard that he was in the Crimea and that he was expected to return in a day or two. Sasha was now even more bothered by his absence. The desire to see him had grown into such a painful feeling that, when, on one late October evening, Ivan Il'ich paid Sasha an unexpected visit, it almost brought on a fainting spell.

He paused at the door of her room (which was divided in two by an opaque screen) and timidly asked:

"May I come in, Aleksandra Alekseevna?"

"Yes, yes," Sasha responded. She had grown so pale that her appearance was a shock to Ivan Il'ich.

"What's the matter with you, Aleksandra Alekseevna?… Have you been ill?"

"No, I'm quite healthy, just extremely tired. I've been doing a lot of running around and rearranging some things in the house. Come on in!"

"I fear I have some bad news for you. Do you know that Kurlinskij has refused military service?"

"Poor chap! Really? Where is he?"

"He is in a military hospital waiting for his diagnosis as either physically or mentally ill. I'm sure you could have quite an influence on him... He is very devoted to you."

"All right, I'll try to talk some sense into him."

"He's been reading a lot of banned books recently, and you see the result."

"I feel sorry for him," said Sasha. "He would do better to continue writing his own poor but innocent verse. Have you been to see him?"

"No," replied Ivan Il'ich, "but I intend to."

"How have you been spending you autumn?" asked Sasha.

"It was splendid. We had marvellous weather in the Crimea... I did a lot of walking and composing while listening to the roar of the sea."

"What a lucky fellow you are! But I can't complain about my life either. I've been quite happy this autumn."

Ivan Il'ich looked over the little things that Sasha had spread out on the table, and for some reason he found all this senseless chaos of everyday feminine life particularly endearing. Along with items made of delicate, old-fashioned lace, lay Hippolyte Taine's *Philosophie de l'art*. A small wooden box held little foreign cards for the game of patience. Along with this was a bill from the tailor's as well as an amateurish drawing of Alësha's and a scattering of coloured pencils. And there was a newly copied romance score as well as a scrap of white gauze on a plush tea-rose... not to mention a red notebook...

Indeed, Sasha's whole life...

"May I have a look at your notebook?" asked Ivan Il'ich, as he took the little book into his hands and began to leaf through it with his beautiful, delicate fingers.

"I guess you can, but it's not that interesting."

"I'll take a look myself if you don't mind."

Ivan Il'ich began reading aloud with a bit of irony: "Pick up lorgnette from Schwabe's... Tsarskoe Selo, Konjushennaja Street N° 18... Length 2½, width 1½. Shoes for Alësha. Tchaikovsky's Symphony N° 5... 'Not by the might, but by the duration of elevated feelings are great people made...'"

"Who said that?" Ivan Il'ich asked.

"That, I believe, is Nietzsche."

"That's clever."

"'*Sache envisager sans frémir cette heure, qui juge la vie; elle n'est pas la dernière pour l'âme, si elle l'est pour le corps.*' Sénèque."

"Are you thinking about the hour of death, Aleksandra Alekseevna?"

"Very much so. And how beautiful and always comforting is the promise of eternity..."

"Anyway, I'll go on: 'About Semën Ivanovich, poorhouse, to petition. To study: N° 9 *Allegro assai* Étude Chopin. Paper and envelopes, gum arabic, spool of pink silk,'" Ivan Il'ich read aloud in rapid-fire. "My God, what diversity… Wait, here's something by Cicero: 'This is the rule of wisdom: to use what one has and always to act within the limits of one's own powers.'"

"It's good that you noted this down for yourself, Aleksandra Alekseevna. You always tend to overdo things, you always get so excited and waste too much energy."

"That is why I am constantly studying wisdom," Sasha replied. "Anyway, the other day I read somewhere that mental stimulation is a source of life energy and that it is needed to maintain an active body and spirit."

Ivan Il'ich put the notebook down, knocking over a ball of wool in the process. It immediately fell to the floor. The ball rolled beyond the dividing screen, underneath the bed, and no matter how much Sasha pulled on the long red thread, she could not retrieve it.

"Alësha! Alësha! Come here!" she called.

"Now, don't you fret, Aleksandra Alekseevna!" exclaimed Ivan Il'ich. "I'll fetch it."

"No, what for?…" said Sasha, embarrassed by the possibility that Ivan Il'ich might notice her bed on the other side of the screen.

But such a thought had not crossed Ivan Il'ich's mind. With awkward movements he bent down and pulled the red ball out. Likewise embarrassed, he suddenly caught sight of Sasha's white bed, covered by something light and lacy, along with her washbasin, her elegant dressing-table — all so beautiful, clean and attractive.

For a long time, ever since his youth, bachelor Ivan Il'ich had never set his eyes on such a purely feminine scene. This was an essence of the *Ewig-Weibliche* [eternally feminine], beckoning with its tender, mysterious elegance of the intimate feminine lifestyle. He frowned, his face took on a stern look, and he was overcome by a sharp change of mood.

Embarrassed, Sasha stood up, took the ball of woollen thread, thanked Ivan Il'ich and invited him to take some tea in the dining room. Passing though the drawing-room, where the piano was, Sasha stopped and timidly asked:

"Would you care to play something?"

"I haven't played for a long time… there is nothing I can play," Ivan Il'ich said abruptly.

"Come on, now, just a little…" Sasha quietly insisted, her naïve, serious eyes sparkling. She blushed, clasping her quivering hands against her breast, as though she were trying to hold something back within her. Finally, she sat down in a corner of the room.

Ivan Il'ich went over to the piano. As he played several beautiful, sonorous chords, Sasha experienced a sudden sinking feeling. Mendelssohn's *Song without words* in G-major, which she had not heard since that evening in May, sang forth more expressively and tenderly than ever under Ivan Il'ich's fingers.

Sasha pressed her hands together even more tightly as she sobbed inwardly. She suddenly realised that those very sounds, which used to bring her a sense of quietude and joy, now provoked only fright, pain and torment. They drew her whole being closer to the one who had taken possession of her through those same sounds. The art which emanated from the realm of the ethereal was now passing into one of earthly feelings. It had lost its purity and virginity.

Now it was all over! All her efforts at maintaining her composure, at keeping music separate from human passions — it all broke down on that evening. Sasha's whole inner life was to take on a completely different character.

Ivan Il'ich went on to play several variations of a Mozart sonata. Then Pëtr Afanas'evich arrived and all took evening tea together. But toward the end of the evening Sasha seemed to be not quite present — while no words escaped her lips, her expression became noticeably serious and even gloomy.

Returning home on foot, Ivan Il'ich, too, felt himself not quite in his usual state of mind. However, this whole evening with Sasha, which had indeed had a softening effect on him, proved to be but a brief episode with no impact either on his activities or on his regular habits. For Sasha, on the other hand, it was a whole epoch.

CHAPTER 7 ❧ SURRENDER

This time when Ivan Il'ich left, Sasha didn't even bother to go out and say her usual "goodbye." She remained motionless for some time, her dry, serious eyes fixed on the wall, one knee resting on the sofa where he had just been sitting. The stern expression on her face was frightening. It was as though she were pondering something important and significant with no internal struggle or fluctuation. Everything that had so recently seemed to her so distant and impossible, so sinful and disturbing — all that was now clarified as something doubtless, accomplished and inexorable.

This apparently calm and composed man, who could have such an ironic attitude both toward her and her impulses, this genius of a musician, this Ivan Il'ich, who was both weird and completely unrelated to her, suddenly turned out to be the dearest and most needful to her — no, more than that... he was actually the whole centre of her life, he alone filled her entire universe, he alone was her *all*.

"But what about the music?!" she thought. "After all, I became attracted to him because he gave me both comfort and a higher artistic pleasure, because he called me to life, because through him I was afforded so many marvellous musical ideas of composers both living and dead, because I am so full of the highest kind of art in the world.

"Could it be that this same Ivan Il'ich, this calm and collected Ivan Il'ich, who loves eating grapes and dates, who is constantly blinking his eyes and watching the clock minute by minute — could it be that he is now more important to me than his music?"

And so, like the vestal virgin who fell in love with a mortal and lost her life as a consequence, Sasha felt she had lost her *actual* life, her purity and her virginal appreciation of art — through loving Ivan Il'ich as a person.

Sasha was not a woman capable of compromises, of self-delusion or self-justification. Clearly and simply, albeit tormentedly, she surrendered and laid aside her arms. She knew that as of this day any resistance was futile, unnecessary, that she did not even want to struggle. Even if her love were laughable, criminal and sinful, even if she were a target of the whole world's scorn and condemnation, even if her husband were to break out in tears — all of that would be so much less meaningful to her, so much less tormenting than this purposeless passion which was devouring and killing her.

Her feelings of love for Ivan Il'ich had grown enormously and, given her inherent passionate nature, they overwhelmed everything else.

And when had all this taken place?… In matters of true love, one can never trace the exact moment when love began. One day you see each other, the next day you have a joyful meeting, in a week you start missing your loved one, in a month you spend a marvellous evening together with delightful conversation… And some three months later — you no longer have a life, or happiness, without him or her…

If Sasha had tried to analyse her feelings in detail, she would have remembered that they, like a dose of poison, had made their way into her heart that quiet May night when she first heard the sounds of Mendelssohn's *Song without words* in G-major emanating from the little yellow cottage.

But it had not yet been love for Ivan Il'ich himself. It was a call to love through music. And Sasha answered this call and fell in love with music. She had not yet known or seen the one who had called her back to life. It was only much later that she got to know the talented musician more closely and fell in love with him as a person. Love which is true, good and strong is always born in the ethereal world and only afterwards moves into the realm of passion.

Was she to blame for this? Was it not destiny with its inescapable fate that had blindly and persistently led Sasha to what she was now so starkly admitting in her heart?

A moment later, her realisation that she was indeed perishing drove her into a state of wild despair. With some haste she started to dress herself, threw on a warm jacket and, as if pushed by somebody else's will, made a dash for the doors, wanting like anything to run after Ivan Il'ich…

But right at this moment the nanny called out to her, reporting that Alësha had a temperature.

"Alësha? What's wrong with him?"

At first she did not understand, but when she did, she became very fearful, took off her jacket and ran into her son's room. With a remorseful heart, she pressed her lips against the sleeping child's forehead and sat in silence by his bed, thinking: "This must be the punishment for my sin…"

All night long she sat up with the boy. From time to time Pëtr Afanas'evich, in dressing-gown and slippers, carefully made his way into Alësha's room and implored Sasha to lie down and get some rest. However, she did not feel right about going into the bedroom, feeling guilty that she had already deceived her husband with her thoughts of criminal love.

Toward morning Alësha broke out into a sweat and Sasha felt relieved. But she still did not lie down to sleep. Alësha's brief illness for her was something of a distraction from that acute mental suffering brought on by acknowledging her love for Ivan Il'ich.

When Alësha awoke in the morning, once more his cheerful and active self, and his illness turned out to be just a temporary gastric disorder, Sasha's heart once again turned with frightening force to her senseless infatuation. She could not bear staying at home, there was no activity she felt like undertaking.

After feeding Alësha some bouillon with egg, she began to get dressed, without yet knowing where she should go. But again her plans were interrupted. Somebody rang the doorbell, and Sasha was informed that a visiting lady wanted to see her for a moment.

"Ask her in," Sasha said reluctantly. "Who could it be, so early?!" she wondered.

A middle-aged lady came in, wearing an old-fashioned dress — timid, quiet and sad.

"Someone asking for a favour," thought Sasha. However, upon recognising Nastasja Nikitichna Kurlinskaja, she immediately embraced her with a kiss.

"Sasha dear, hello!" she said. "Maybe you've heard that my son has been incarcerated in a military hospital for refusing army service. You must know the usual outcome of cases like that... Sasha, you've got to help me rescue him!" her voice broke off, but she managed to add: "He loves you, and he'll do as you say."

"I'd be most happy to, my dear... I feel terribly sorry for him myself... But how can we rescue him?"

"Just go to him, they'll let you through... Have a serious talk with him..."

"Are you here for long?"

"Dunno, I can't leave, but staying here in town in a furnished room is both expensive and depressing."

"All right then, come and stay with me. I'll go see him today, but d'you think it'll really work?!..."

"You know, when children grow up, you think you'll have no more cares, but it turns out that little kids won't let you sleep, and when they are older, you can't get to sleep..."

Nastasja Nikitichna broke into tears.

"Now, now there, dear, don't cry." Sasha tried to comfort her. "God willing, we'll talk some sense into him. Do stop your crying, darling!"

Sasha embraced and consoled Nastasja Nikitichna, gave her a cup of coffee and then sat and listened to the whole story of the Kurlinskij family. Like all family histories, it was fascinating and touching. Sasha then accompanied her outdoors. Nastasja Nikitichna took a cab back to her furnished room, while Sasha, in an attempt to calm her fractured nerves, chose to go on foot.

CHAPTER 8 ❧ *ON THE STREET*

It was a clear, somewhat frosty day. Streets and roofs were partially covered with a dusting from last night's snow, which lay more thickly and brightly on the lawns and boulevards of Moscow. A horse-drawn tram went squealing along the cold rails, ringing its bell at cross-streets. Sasha jumped onto a moving tram and stood on the platform 'til the next stop. Then she got off and began to wait for a tram going in the opposite direction. "I must be losing my mind!" flashed through her head.

When the tram finally came, Sasha got on and sat down. At the next stop, a woman hurriedly boarded, accompanied by a child whose eye was bandaged, and started to look for a free seat. Sasha gave up hers, having taken pity on the disadvantaged child…

Once more standing on the platform, Sasha started to observe the passengers, dividing them by class and character. Especially noticeable were their positive or negative reactions when asked by the conductor for their tickets. Some deliberately crumpled their tickets and rudely shoved them at the conductor. Others, after making an attempt to smooth them out, would hold them calmly in their hands, waiting to be asked for them. A third group, having apparently lost their tickets, fussily searched for them in their pockets and gloves. As Sasha, now standing, handed over hers, she was greeted with enthusiasm by a young man who offered her his seat.

"Tsvetkov, dear, is that you?" Sasha addressed Ivan Il'ich's pupil. Suddenly a whole summer of memories swept into her mind and she became terribly excited. "Where are you off to?"

"I'm on my way to the Conservatory," Tsvetkov replied. "And what about you, Aleksandra Alekseevna, why are you riding the tram? You must have horses of your own."

"Sometimes I like to take the tram."

"Where are you headed?"

"I'm going to see Kurlinskij, he's in a military hospital. You heard that he's refused military service?"

"I heard. That's weird!… But, aren't you going the wrong way? That hospital's in the opposite direction!"

Sasha blushed and burst out:

"Oh, dear! I must really be distracted!"

Saying goodbye to Tsvetkov, she jumped off the tram and headed for the house where Ivan Il'ich was living. Her heart was torn by the desire to see him. Before reaching his side street, however, she stopped at the gate of some other house, where she found her way blocked by a water delivery wagon. The deliveryman was making an enormous effort to wrestle a huge barrel of water into the courtyard of the house. His efforts were thwarted by a slight rise in the pavement, and the barrel kept rolling backwards.

With her strong, energetic arms, Sasha took hold of the barrel to help the deliveryman.

"All right, now, all together," she said in her gentle yet bold voice.

And all at once the barrel rolled into the courtyard, and the astonished deliveryman, together with the concierge and a smiling crowd of onlookers — everybody gazed with curiosity at this elegantly dressed young lady, who was now calmly straightening her dark golden curls slipping out from under her hat. She was smiling her characteristic smile, which served to brighten her whole face and sparked a tender, welcoming glint in her large, naïve-looking, dark eyes.

"Is it possible not to love me?" bespoke her eyes. "I myself love you, and everyone…"

And everyone felt precisely that, and everyone was ready to love Sasha…

"What is that you are doing?" asked a familiar voice, which at once caused Sasha's heart to throb.

"You saw?"

"I did. It seems you want to become a deliveryman?" observed Ivan Il'ich ironically. "In that case you'd better forget music, you'll only ruin your hands."

Sasha did not say a word, all out of breath from both her excitement and her strenuous efforts.

"Let's walk," she said quietly. "What must you be thinking of me… that I'm crazy?"

"I think that you are a woman of many contradictions in character… and many contrasts. You are like a Rembrandt painting — lots of shadow and lots of light."

"And rolling a barrel — is that light or shadow?" Sasha queried with a cunning smile, tuning in to Ivan Il'ich's mood.

"Light."

"And what would be shadow?"

"Shadow would be… instability, rash and illogical actions, jumping to conclusions, a lack of concentration…"

"You don't say! I have a lot of shadows, and I must ask you to enlighten me."

"I shan't be able to do that, Aleksandra Alekseevna. Besides, I don't have the time, I am too lazy."

Sasha blushed. Ivan Il'ich took a look at her and quickly averted his gaze. With a wink he quickened his pace. He was embarrassed by his own nervousness, his desire to somehow hurt Sasha along with the pity (almost tenderness) which he felt toward her after hurting her.

"Where are we going?" Sasha suddenly asked, frightened at her own mood.

"I'm off to enquire about my quartet — just when my musician-friends will play it for me… And where are you headed?… Truly, I don't know, and it seems that you yourself may not know either."

"No, that I do know. I'm going to the military hospital to see Kurlinskij. I'll take a cab now…"

At that moment, they spied ahead of them on the pavement a pregnant woman who was having trouble picking up a little girl, who was rather large for her age, trying to carry her across the street busy with a constant stream of carriages, trams and cabs. The girl kept capriciously acting up, even kicking her mother in the stomach. Without stopping to think for a minute, Sasha picked up the child in her arms, telling her:

"Now there, darling, don't cry, your mamà will catch up with us…" With strength and alacrity she quickly reached the other side of the street. The child, fascinated by this game of chase with her mother, who was running to catch up with Sasha, fell silent at once. Finally, she looked at Sasha and gave a hearty laugh.

"So now you've decided to become a nanny!" Ivan Il'ich called after her. But Sasha did not turn back to him. Handing the girl to her mother, she got into a cab and headed off to the hospital.

Without thinking Ivan Il'ich started to rush after her but immediately stopped himself. His face took on an expression of displeasure. He was annoyed at both himself and Sasha over the fact that it was no longer the first time that her departure provoked in him the impulse to pursue her, to not leave her alone, to look into her naïve, serious-looking eyes, which were always burning unexpectedly with either gloomy passion or a tender welcome and child-like cheerfulness.

"What spontaneity!" Ivan Il'ich consoled himself in remembering Sasha. "What energy! What distinctiveness! What simplicity!"

CHAPTER 9 ❧ THE MILITARY HOSPITAL

Sasha was none too impressed with the cabbie she got. He was a careful driver, but oh how he loved to talk! He told Sasha how his brother had detached himself from the family and married a woman from a different village, who ended up turning the whole house upside-down.

"A witch, not a woman! I drive a cab over the winter but come spring I'll be off to take part in the ploughing. It's easier now that they are leasing some land from a lady-landowner, while for the past few years we ended up having to buy bread."

"And where are you from?"

"I'm from the Kaluga region. We had such a famine last year that they had to take straw from the roofs to feed the cattle, and still they were barely alive by the summer. In fact, the cattle could not stand up without the help of a rope…

"Well, get a move on!" he shouted at his horse, jerking the reins in his hands.

Sasha listened to the cabbie and was touched by the fact that this peasant, spending whole winters alone in Moscow, was so distant in both his mind and his heart from the city, and that all his interests were concentrated on his family, on his village, on that serious, meaningful, pristine life which still attracted him, regardless of its severity and deprivations.

Soon they arrived at a red-brick building where a watchman was standing guard at the main gate. This was the military hospital. Sasha began to feel a little uneasy: she was young enough that she still feared any sign of illness, mental derangement or incarceration. At the same time the sleepless nights and excitement she had been experiencing had made her extremely nervous. Everything here was so foreign, mysterious and unfamiliar to her.

The soldier at the gate asked her whom she needed to see, and, after receiving a gratuity, let her through. He gave a jerk on the bell-pull, and a few minutes later somebody brought a key and unlocked a pass-through gate from the inside. Escorted by another soldier, Sasha went through a big iron door which led directly into a garden (or rather a courtyard planted with trees), whereupon the door shut tight behind her.

"What's this here?" she asked. "Is this where the patients take their exercise?"

"Yes, ma'am," the soldier replied with a non-Russian accent, escorting Sasha to the door of the main red-brick building. Again, a key clicked in the lock, another heavy door swung open, and they entered a dark entrance-hall.

"Anyway, I see you're well protected," Sasha observed with a smile, once again feeling the unpleasant sensation of being locked in by yet another door.

"Yes, ma'am," the soldier repeated with a dumb smile.

Sasha took off her coat in the hallway and proceeded up the stairs. The first thing she noticed was a small group of people dressed in grey cloth robes sitting on a bench against the wall, just opposite the staircase. They kept staring blankly, though curiously, at the young lady in unfamiliar garb and continued to sit motionlessly. There were about six of them. They were sitting there idly, purposelessly, only for a change of surroundings and to escape the oppressive walls of their rooms.

An easy-going soldier, evidently more civilised than her first escorts, approached Sasha and, after receiving a few silver coins (along with the answer as to whom she wanted to see), kindly showed her into a small, long room, which was also locked with a key.

Kurlinskij was sitting by a window. On seeing Sasha, he got up and went over to her, shuffling in his oversized standard-issue shoes. He was wearing a grey military cloth robe (noticeably the wrong size) which he, embarrassed and blushing, awkwardly kept trying to fit around himself. His face was pale and thin, and a pitiful, uneasy smile occasionally spread across his lips.

"Aleksandra Alekseevna, is that really you?" he exclaimed excitedly, albeit in a hoarse voice. "My friend and comrade Petrovskij," he announced, introducing the young man standing beside him.

"What possessed you to do away with yourself, Kurlinskij?" Sasha enquired.

"What makes you think I want to do away with myself?… On the contrary, I feel perfectly well, having fulfilled my duty to my conscience."

"I don't agree that it's a duty," remarked Sasha. "Tell me, what prompted you to do this?"

"I dunno. I simply couldn't do otherwise when the question was put to me straight: do I go or don't I? I can't bear arms… and I certainly could never take another's life."

"And you won't have to. But what will no doubt happen is that they will conscript somebody else in your place, somebody they would not have taken if only you had gone."

"Oh, that's a very old argument! I refuse military service because I don't accept violence against anyone."

"What childish reasoning! Let's get down to the basic essentials: even though you don't accept violence, you yourself are perpetrating it by your actions. You are committing violence against the one who will take your place in the army; you are forcing the authorities to incarcerate you here; and you are also forcing those who will be obliged to punish and torment you and to finally make you bear arms…" said Sasha, getting more and more heated.

"But that's not something they *have* to do…" Kurlinskij said timidly.

"You're wrong! Not everyone is able to refuse. We *all* live by inertia, but there is only a handful of chosen, progressive ones who lead the true path and voice the truth. Only a few will follow at first, but then more and more…

"Don't you see, my friend," Sasha went on, remembering the tears on the face of Kurlinskij's mother and imbuing her words with even greater energy and feeling, "don't you see, there has already been a lot of progress in this direction. Mankind now protests against war. The old chivalric attitude to the defence of the fatherland, as well as the honour of arms-bearing, is disappearing. There remains only the weighty feeling of necessity. You should try bearing this weight together with those who are forced to bear it. This is also its own kind of heroism…"

"Your reasoning is quite paradoxical, Aleksandra Alekseevna, and you are illogical."

"Well, let's not use destructive words, let's not be logical," said Sasha, looking at Kurlinskij more closely with her large, tender eyes. "All you have to do is hold the weapon in your hands, obey your commandant, go into the army, and…" Sasha paused. "And believe me, all your actions, words, even your very breath — all of that will only give louder voice to your anti-war protest, for thereby you will spread it around you much more effectively than being locked up here."

Kurlinskij thought for a moment.

"If I even so much as breathe such a protest, I'll be killed," he said, brushing aside with a movement of his head the grey, thick collar of his robe from his fragile young neck with its transparent white skin and delicate veins.

"And this boy is going straight into a voluntary hell!" Sasha thought with some sadness. She so desperately wanted to save him.

"Well, then... try to reconcile yourself... just try... with your internal protest against war and obey the demands of necessity... meekly and patiently. Look around you and relate tenderly, gently and beneficially to those soldiers with whom you will be in close contact — unfortunate soldiers torn from their families — and you will no longer be a soldier, but a Christian. And through your influence and attitude you will start to prove, both to them and to your superiors, that there is no place for killing where only love and meekness prevail. As for the rest of it, God will help you throw off the heavy doubts which are weighing you down at the moment..."

"You know, I'm not in doubt, Aleksandra Alekseevna, I'm ready for everything," said Kurlinskij, admiring the bold, animated expression on Sasha's face. As Sasha was about to leave, he took her hand and kissed it, adding: "Your visit has really brightened my day, thank you."

In saying goodbye, Sasha offered several touching words about his mother and her tears. On her way out, she once again passed through the series of opening and closing doors.

"Are there any healthy people here?" she asked one soldier after he let her through.

"Yes, ma'am," he replied.

"Is it really true," thought Sasha, "that all these people have been so beaten down with military discipline and are so overcome with fear that they dare not even speak?" Only "Yes, ma'am, yes, ma'am," kept ringing in her ears.

With a heavy feeling she got back into her waiting cab. Her nerves were even more on edge, her soul was languishing, and the only thing she could hear was the clicking of the keys in the locks and "Yes, ma'am, yes, ma'am."

All of a sudden the cab made a sharp turn, and Sasha was jolted awake. The whole street was torn up as they were repairing the sewer system. Clumps of earth were piled up on either side, and Sasha could see a deep pit where a man was working. She thought that this open pit gave Mother Earth at least one chance to breathe — the same Mother Earth that was covered by paving stones and asphalt, deprived of the opportunity of giving life to plants, trees and everything that feeds on this now beaten-down urban land.

A heavy sigh emerged from Sasha's chest. She sighed over her living soul beaten-down by passion... over the cabbie beaten-down by circumstances and pressured by his life in a city that he did not like and where he did not feel free... over the soldier beaten-down by military discipline... over the earth choked by stones and asphalt — and again her living soul, which could not tolerate fetters of any kind, felt a strong desire for freedom, life, air and happiness...

CHAPTER 10 ❧ *HER HUSBAND*

When Sasha returned home, she went straight to Alësha's room. She found the boy building houses of cards on the table. Wanting to spend more time with her son, she took down a book of Grimm's fairy-tales and began to read to him. Alësha was overjoyed that his mother was spending time with him, only this did not last long. Sasha's soul was still languishing unbearably. She tossed the book aside and went into the salon where the piano stood. Alësha ran after her, but she sent him outside to play. She then picked up a book of Beethoven sonatas and began to play her favourite.

Her playing was more than just playing music, it was rather a kind of suffering groan. Sasha could not bring herself to finish the piece. Her head fell on her hands pressed stiff against the keyboard, and she began to sob fitfully.

"Sasha!" she suddenly heard her husband's desperate whisper close to her ear. "Sasha, my friend, what's the matter?"

"Nothing... nothing... it's just that my nerves are frayed," Sasha quickly replied, wiping her eyes and moving away from her husband. "I was at the military hospital today, and I felt so sorry for Kurlinskij."

"No, Sasha, that's not it... You were just now playing that sonata, which you love..." Pëtr Afanas'evich said with hesitation, timidity and sadness... "and you're in love with Ivan Il'ich..."

"Not true, not true! I'm not in love with him!" cried Sasha in a despairing voice. She held her arms out, as though defending herself from something. "I'm in love with the music, I love this marvellous sonata, and that's all..."

Her voice trailed off. Exhausted, she folded her arms in a gesture of calm submission.

Her husband immediately understood it all but could not help trembling with concern. His face was pale, as though smeared with greyish lime. For a long time he kept staring into his wife's depressed countenance. All of a sudden he burst into tears.

When a woman cries, especially if she is beautiful and lovable, people take pity on her, but if a man is crying, they see it as something frightening.

Pëtr Afanas'evich wept so much, as though everything he held dear in life had been instantly torn away from him forever. He had *never* experienced jealousy over his wife; that was a feeling he did not know. Trusting, tender and kind, in a child-like way he had loved only Sasha all his life, and it never entered his head that either he or she could be in love with someone else.

This was a misfortune, a real misfortune not only for him alone, but for both of them. After he regained control of himself, he got up, walked over to his wife and quietly took her hand.

"Sasha, you don't need to say anything. I understand it all. It is a trial that has been sent to us, and we must see it through as best we can..."

Sasha's gaze was still downcast, and she fell silent.

"My dear, honest, truthful and steadfast Sasha! Poor, poor Sasha!"

Pëtr was still choked up with tears, and he paused.

"Sasha, you're a really good person after all," he boldly continued. "You're strong and full of energy. My dear friend, you and I will see this difficult experience through, only please don't shut me out of your trust and friendship."

Sasha gave her husband's hand a vigorous shake. She looked at his sullen face and said quietly:

"Yes, that I can promise you. I won't leave you, and I won't do anything bad… after all, *he* doesn't love *me*," she added bitterly, only these words hurt her husband's feelings even more. "But if, despite all my efforts, my soul involuntarily suffers a breakdown, then please forgive anything I may be guilty of… You're right, it's a grave misfortune…"

Pëtr Afanas'evich kissed his wife's forehead and went back to his room.

From that day on, he followed Sasha's condition closely. He never said another word about her feelings for Ivan Il'ich, but there was now an element of unspoken tension between the couple, and this heavy mood could be felt by the whole household. Pëtr Afanas'evich did not change his attitude toward Ivan Il'ich in the least, though he still suffered noticeably in his presence.

CHAPTER 11 ❧ THE CONVENT

"Milady," the nanny said to Sasha the next morning, "maybe you would like to go and take us, too, to the convent — today they are offering a free meal to the poor, in remembrance of the Tsar. They'll be feeding about six hundred in all."

"Yes, I heard about that, we should go," said Sasha, who was agreeable to anything that did not mean sitting at home with her own thoughts and conversing with her husband.

From childhood, Sasha loved nunneries and monasteries and even planned in her early youth, before applying to the conservatory, to enter a convent herself. The poetry of monastic life appealed to her, the idea of serving and contemplating Deity, abstention from fleshly ways, and spiritual self-perfection. Especially in her current state of mind, she very much wanted to visit a convent.

After seeing Pëtr Afanas'evich off to the Insurance Society, she got dressed and decided to go to the convent the nanny had mentioned. It was located on the outskirts of Moscow.

Sasha boarded a tram full of people. When she got to the end of the line, the view of the fields and forests across the river offered an unobstructed panorama with no houses, fences, streets or urban crowds. This at once helped Sasha regain her composure and renewed her spiritual freshness and peace.

Pausing for a short while at the gates, Sasha entered the convent enclosure and immediately saw a huge, motley crowd of women of all ages, social classes and attire — some with nursing babies, adolescents, old women, beggars, with cheerful and gloomy faces, some even well-dressed, others peasant girls in red shawls, ill people in rags — all of them women, just women…

The convent gatekeeper, keeping an approximate estimate of the number of visitors, admitted about two hundred at a time — first into the enclosure, then into a low-ceilinged stone church, where the meal was being prepared. The rest, meanwhile, awaited their turn.

In the old-fashioned church, long, narrow tables were covered with table-cloths, bordered by equally long narrow benches. At one side stood a large, separate table with whole mountains of pies and buns; there were also pots filled with cabbage soup and bowls of kissel.

Young novices, pretty and pale, with an air of reverence and seriousness about their task, quietly went around carrying huge baskets of rye bread and large cabbage-filled wheat dumplings.

The first group of some two hundred women they let in took their places at the tables in an orderly manner. Then a priest came out and recited prayers for the deceased Tsar, accompanied by a choir of sonorous nuns' voices. During the recitation of prayers, everyone stood listening reverently and crossed themselves. Then the nuns handed everyone a spoon and began to serve the soup — in such a way that several people could eat out of the same bowl.

Sasha was struck by the silence and the orderliness of the whole proceedings. It was as though the whole crowd were performing a sacred ritual. Sasha went over to a separate table where only children were seated. She felt uplifted by their cheerful mood, especially when they were given the last bowl of kissel with milk.

During the whole time, a young nun read the *Life of St. Isidore* in a loud, high-pitched voice.

Toward the end of the meal they brought around mugs of beer and honey, and an elderly nun in full habit, the convent's Procuratrix, handed every woman a five-kopek coin on behalf of the Mother-Superior.

After the meal, the priest read another prayer and the women began to leave the church. On their way out, they stopped to greet the two elderly nuns standing at the door and thank them personally. The nuns kissed the women on the lips and remarked: "Well, you are now full... thank God... well, God be with you..." And the women crossed themselves and bowed in reverence.

While the first party of diners was let out through one door and another party was let in through a different one, Sasha went up to the Procuratrix and asked her whether she had been in the convent for a long time and what had prompted her to enter.

"Oh, my dear lady," she said, "ever since I was fourteen years old, I dreamt and thought about becoming a nun. My father was a poor government worker in a provincial town. He didn't want to hear about my going to a convent — something I really longed to do. Then, at seventeen I ran away from home with just the clothes on my back, straight to Moscow."

"How did you get by without money... not knowing the city?"

"All through God's help, my dear. I managed to get there in Christ's name, and finally some kind people directed me to this convent. I went straight to see the Mother-Superior, and she was so kind to me."

"Does that mean she took you right away?"

"She said I should remain here, that God had directed me here. I was given an apprenticeship task of caring for the old and infirm in a hospital. It was hard for me at first, but never mind, I pulled through. Then the Mother-Superior praised me and assigned me an easier task. And now I have been living here for forty years already, happy and content. I thank God for everything…"

The kind smile of satisfaction on the lips of the Procuratrix so brightened her simple, peaceful, wrinkled face, that Sasha became envious of the spiritual peace radiating from the elderly nun's whole being…

However, leaning against a nearby column, stood another nun, this one taller and solidly built. The expression on her face was completely the opposite to that of the nun with whom Sasha had just been speaking. Her gloomy face reflected utter hopelessness, even though her lips were whispering a prayer. Sasha cautiously approached her and introduced herself.

"I take it you've been a nun for a long time?"

"I've been praying for a long time, praying for many years. But I have so many sins that my heart is turned to stone."

"Why do you despair so much, my mother?"

"Oh dear, my sins are so heavy, I've been praying for thirty years, there is no way I can get rid of them, I'm simply turned to stone."

"Is there a *particular* sin weighing on your soul?"

"My sin is one that nobody can redeem, it's forever unforgivable… Oh, how heavy it is, oh dear, oh dear," she said with a genuine groan, hastily crossing herself. Her stern face seemed somehow similar to her stone-like heart, and her powerful body stood firmly and motionlessly — it appeared indestructible, as though designed to be so strong as to live forever and drain to the dregs her cup of mental suffering.

Sasha left her, weighed down by a feeling of her own sinfulness. Crossing herself once more, she went out into the convent enclosure.

At the door, she again encountered the nuns with baskets of bread, while outside crowds of women were still waiting for their turn. Some of them rushed over to her, begging for alms. After Sasha had given away all the small change she had, she finally managed to make her way out of the enclosure and board a tram for home.

CHAPTER 12 ❧ A PRIEST OF ART

Upon arriving home, Sasha had no sooner entered her front door than she heard the sound of the piano.

"Who's here?" she asked, her heart beating uncontrollably.

"Ivan Il'ich come long time ago," said the servant, taking Sasha's plush jacket from her. "I tell him you are not here, and he says: 'I will wait.'"

Refreshed by her trip into town and excited at the prospect of seeing Ivan Il'ich again — especially an Ivan Il'ich waiting for *her* — Sasha flew like a bird up the stairs with a light, quick step. With a powerful arm she flung open the door and stopped in front of the piano — beautiful, blushing and passionate in her appearance.

As though silently responding to her feelings, Ivan Il'ich went on playing the loud, beautiful and meaningful passage from his symphony to the end. Only then did he get up and offer Sasha his hand.

"Our symphony!" exclaimed Sasha without thinking.

"Ours?" Ivan Il'ich echoed sarcastically. "I would be very happy, Aleksandra Alekseevna, if you were to help me compose, but this piece is all ready, and in a few days I'll be conducting it at a symphony concert."

"Yes, that was stupid of me. But I had such a strong feeling as you were composing it, when you played parts of it for me all last summer, that this symphony in some way became my own… and my favourite…" Sasha quietly said with a timid blush. "Do you find that objectionable?"

"No, it's not at all…"

"Interfering?…" Sasha interrupted.

"No, it is not interfering at all."

"And that's it?!" thought Sasha, her heart filled with despair. "And that's how it should be, it's what I deserve — and the worse, the more strictly he deals with me, the fairer I'll consider it. But, oh my God, how painful it is, how unbearably painful!! How very much I need his love! How impossible my life has become without this man!"

Sasha peered into his face, which now, after he had finished playing, was devoid of expression. She wanted to peer into the depths of his soul, to understand, after all, what kind of a person he was — but she would not understand him, either now or ever. Could it be that this genius who had turned her entire life upside down was indeed no more than a musician, and that nothing human or worldly was capable of touching him?

In fact, he was actually keeping a strict watch to make sure that nothing in life could disturb or embarrass him, and he was right in this. He maintained the whole purity and virginity of the art that was so dear to him, he kept alive the sacred fire of the temple and the deity which he served. He was so full of music in all its manifestations that there was simply no room for anything else. Everything else in life — Nature, people, their passions, events — all that, one way or another, had to serve music. Music, after all, was the centre for which everything else was merely a spoke.

In Ivan Il'ich's music, including both his compositions and his performance, could be felt the significance and the heights to which he had elevated his art. One could not help but believe in his music, one could not help but recognise the pride of place which he accorded it…

"What have you been doing all this time, Ivan Il'ich?" Sasha asked.

"I've been finishing the orchestration of my symphony. Also, my pupils have been coming to me in the evenings. Furthermore, I've been doing a lot of reading this past while…"

Ivan Il'ich looked at his watch and prepared to leave.

"You're going already?" Sasha asked with concern, peering more closely into Ivan Il'ich's eyes. With that he looked askance at her and started to move even faster.

"I really need to get home — I spent so much time here waiting for you. After all, I just dropped in to enquire about our friend Kurlinskij; I know you went to see him. I almost forgot."

Sasha proceeded to tell him in detail about her trip to the military hospital and her conversation with Kurlinskij.

Ivan Il'ich did not divulge his opinion of Sasha's actions but only remarked, upon taking his leave:

"As always, you are illogical, but you have a lot of energy. If only you could use this energy for a good cause, that would be priceless!"

"It seems you are comparing me with mill water, under which a millstone needs to be placed to make it all work."

"That sounds fine… Your work is good. Well, goodbye."

After Ivan Il'ich left, Sasha experienced a deep sense of dissatisfaction, along with a crazy desire to hold him back or to go after him. She kept feeling the urge to penetrate this closed, incomprehensible soul, but found no way she could do this.

What did he think of her? Did he understand her anguish? Maybe he was laughing at her in his heart, scorning or condemning her for her love and for everything she said or did. Oh, the painful secret of the oscillations of the human soul! — especially painful in somebody you love and whose mind you desperately want to gain access to but can't.

"If I could see just one, only one small token of his approval," thought Sasha, "of his love for me… even just one moment of happiness, just *one* moment of his love comparable to the love I feel for him — that would be enough for happiness all my life!…"

In the meantime Ivan Il'ich was slowly making his way home, thinking that he ought to walk farther for the exercise yet not arrive too late for tea or for the lesson he was to give to two poor but very gifted pupils.

Walking along the boulevard, he happened to think of Sasha.

"How come this woman has been occupying such a huge place in my life?" he thought. "This is somewhat curious and quite funny… Only I mustn't get carried away or go astray somehow. How bothersome and plain-looking she appeared today! But she was still altogether original and quite receptive… But this situation is distracting, and I should probably not come so often…"

But the thought of seeing Sasha less often was not at all appealing to Ivan Il'ich. He delighted, albeit subconsciously, in that poetic and loving atmosphere with which Sasha surrounded him by her very presence… In the meantime, without making any more decisions, Ivan Il'ich arrived at his home.

In Ivan Il'ich's small and cozy apartment tea was ready along with bread and ham on a small plate. While waiting for his beloved master, Aleksej Tikhonych spent the time chatting with two young men, pupils of Ivan Il'ich. The air was light, sweet-smelling and welcoming in this simple dwelling of the great musician. Lining the walls were several large étagères replete with music scores and books. In the middle of the room stood two grand pianos side by side. A large table was covered with symphony scores and music papers. On the wall hung portraits of Tchaikovsky and Rubinstein.

"Ivan Il'ich, they are going to publish my romance!" his favourite pupil Tsvetkov announced enthusiastically. "I just found out about it today."

"Very glad to hear it, my friend. I really like your romance…

"Hello there," he turned to the other young man, who was awkward and plain-looking, completely the opposite of Tsvetkov in every respect. "How come I have not seen you for such a long time? Are you still busy with Wagner?… Have you all had tea?… Well then, let's get down to business."

The pupils handed him their music notebooks. Ivan Il'ich sat down at the table and started correcting and explaining the mistakes in his pupils' assignments.

He was an excellent teacher. In addition to his extensive musical education, Ivan Il'ich had a pedagogical gift. He was extremely patient and logically minded and took a serious approach to his profession. In all this he was extraordinarily kind with young people and earned not only their profound respect but also such love that a private lesson with Ivan Il'ich was held to be a real treasure.

"Well, now, let's have some tea," said the teacher after finishing his corrections and pausing the session.

Aleksej Tikhonych was present almost the whole time, and it was apparent that he was very happy, after a whole day of solitude, that the house was once again enlivened by the presence of his master and the pupils… The Wagner devotee, rather plain-looking, left shortly after tea, while Tsvetkov stayed to spend the night at Ivan Il'ich's.

CHAPTER 13 ❧ *THE SYMPHONY CONCERT*

The wave of acute suffering Sasha experienced from her unexpected — and unwanted — love for Ivan Il'ich began to pass and was replaced by that state of mind when the reverse sensation occurs and love becomes a heartfelt celebration, bright, joyful, increasing one's love for the whole world and for all humanity. Everything she did was meaningful, full of fascination, radiant.

Everything was easy — Sasha had enough energy and strength for it all. Her love was enough to satisfy her need for happiness even if not reciprocated. With her whole being she longed for that reciprocation and believed in it, only for the time being she did not need it.

It was just that her imagination came up with the craziest scenes of mutual love between her and Ivan Il'ich. She dreamt of inspiring him, of serving together with him that art which they both loved so much.

It never occurred to her that she was betraying her husband — she never considered such love a betrayal — her husband always remained her husband while she remained his faithful wife and loved him in her own way. On the other hand, her relationship to Ivan Il'ich was something special, poetic and artistic, something to be celebrated spiritually, a kind of gift from above…

Upon seeing that Sasha had stopped her grieving and become joyful, even peaceful, Pëtr Afanas'evich thought that she had overcome her unfortunate passion and had calmed down. And this calmed him down, too. He was not of a jealous nature; he got upset only when his calm, trusting attitude to his wife was somehow interrupted. Now he desperately wanted to rekindle his former trust in her and to return to his former unruffled life. He knew that Sasha was terribly attracted to music, and he himself encouraged her to go to concerts, operas and other musical events of all kinds.

Sasha often met with Ivan Il'ich. Occasionally she invited him to her loge at the concert-hall or took a seat next to his. It was a treasured time for her to experience together with him the moments of aesthetic delight which resulted from the impression the music made on them both. Sometimes, without prior arrangement, they sought out each other's eyes at moments of particular musical virtuosity or upon hearing some marvellous compositions, and they both rejoiced, living by the soul of their beloved music.

From time to time, following a concert, Ivan Il'ich would accompany Sasha to her home. With his quiet, mellifluous voice, he would interpret for her some musical passage which was complex in its harmonies, or recount to her an episode from the life of one of the composers. As they walked together, she took no notice of either fatigue or the cold. On the contrary, Sasha experienced the bliss of being in love, wishing nothing more — everything was given by God, everything — and there was nowhere else to go and nothing left to be desired.

Finally the big day came, the 26th of January, when Ivan Il'ich was to conduct his own symphony. This was considered a major event in the world of music. Professors came from the St. Petersburg Conservatory to hear it. For several days before this concert Sasha did not see her musician-friend and realised he was preparing for the big evening and would be upset at any distraction from his work.

Toward nine o'clock, the Nobility Hall was the destination of all sorts of sleighs and carriages with lamps, ordinary and fancy cabs, coming from various parts of the city and driving past the mounted police. Half-frozen pedestrians were also hurrying to get inside. A special majesty could be felt in connection with tonight's concert. The public seemed nervous, on the edge of their seats and ready for that excitement which they often felt from composers and performers of musical works.

Along the staircase and walls of the side entrance which Sasha always used, could be seen working women, concierges and footmen, all chatting cheerfully.

At the main entrance two female conservatory students sat at a table covered with green cloth and with a cheerful smile hurriedly handed out concert programmes. The public in return paid with a few coins deposited on a large plate.

Crowds of people milled through the corridors, waiting for the bell inviting them to take their seats.

For this occasion Sasha had ordered a brand-new white gown to be made for her. It went well with her complexion, which was ablush with excitement, so brightly shone both her eyes and the diamonds in her tiara and earrings: her very appearance reflected the solemnity and significance of this evening's event. After greeting a number of acquaintances who were admiring her radiant beauty and gown, Sasha took her subscribed seat, all trembling with anticipation.

Ivan Il'ich's symphony was first on the programme. The orchestra members began to take their seats on the stage. At the left-hand side Sasha spotted two violinist sisters, both brunettes. The first violinist was a grey-haired, award-winning professor from the Conservatory.

The orchestra began its always discordant process of tuning. Finally, everything quieted down. With awkward, but noble, steady steps, Ivan Il'ich slowly came out on the stage to a burst of applause from the audience. After a slight bow he glanced over to where Sasha was sitting. She caught his glance and unnoticeably to others responded with a nod of her head and a smile.

And just for an instant Ivan Il'ich recalled the first moment when he caught the figure of Sasha in a similar white dress flitting away from the porch of his yellow cottage, as well as when he saw her for the first time as she was listening to his playing. It was the very same evening when, also for the first time, his head was filled with the beautiful melody which would eventually serve as the leitmotif for the whole of tonight's symphony.

This instant was inexorably brief, and Ivan Il'ich, pale but calm and totally absorbed in the cause above which nothing could exist for him, surveyed the orchestra and with a precise, energetic movement of his hands began to conduct his symphony.

"Oh my God! How wonderful, how momentous!" Sasha thought excitedly.

A roar of applause broke out even after the first movement. But then came his *Andante*, so rich in meaning; it sent forth such a powerful feeling, especially strong in the complex sounds so multi-layered in their harmonies! The leitmotif was beautifully highlighted, manifest at times in a whole variety of combinations.

The wealth of voices, interrupted unexpectedly by original transitions, was astounding. And all at once, a seemingly unquenchable flood of the most passionate emotions emerged with ever-renewing energy from some kind of an abyss and poured out in the solemn phrases of the magnificent *Andante*. Ivan Il'ich's countenance was completely transformed. His restrained excitement, seriousness and meaningfulness of expression made it seem almost beautiful. With powerful and precise movements of his marvellous hands he conducted the entire orchestra, and one could feel a sense of unity between the conductor and all these musicians, evidently enjoying performing the magnificent work of the composer-conductor.

The success was huge. The enthusiastic applause called the composer back to the stage again and again. And the success was not contrived, but genuine, sincere and fervent, from the audience infected by this genius of a masterpiece.

Sasha felt triumphant. During the interval she went to the performers' dressing-room, where she found Ivan Il'ich. He looked at her questioningly, but this time could not fix his nervous eyes on anything in particular.

"Incredible!" she exclaimed in a muffled voice full of tears. "Congratulations on your success! I never doubted it for a moment."

"But I had my own doubts and still do. The auditorium is filled with so many of my friends that I'm sure *they* contributed to my success, as you put it."

A number of musicians began approaching Ivan Il'ich to congratulate him. They surrounded him on all sides and carried him away somewhere. And Sasha would not see him again the rest of the evening.

"Why am I not his wife?" thought Sasha with despair. "Why do I *not dare* to follow him everywhere, share in his triumph, proclaim his success to the whole world?!" These were the thoughts that came to Sasha as she stood at the concert hall entrance, waiting for her sleigh, which an attendant had gone to fetch. "And why do I not dare to invite him into my sleigh and to accompany him to the place where he is off to now, expressing to him all my friendship, all my best wishes for his success, all my excitement over his genius of a masterpiece!

"And where is he? Oh, where?" Sasha tormented herself, and all at once jealousy raised its ugly head in her soul — jealousy over all those people in whose company he was celebrating tonight's triumph.

Her heart still quivering from these impressions, Sasha took her seat in the waiting sleigh, harnessed to her favourite pair of grey horses, and headed for home.

"Anyway, why do I take such pleasure in Ivan Il'ich's triumph?" she suddenly wondered. "Where is the music, where are those pure joys of comfort and artistic delight by which I used to live? I don't like this dependence; I don't want this personal love! Let art remain independent, purified of everything human — it is higher and better, and it should remain, at least for me, in the heights. Why did my feelings get involved with him, why did I not stay just as independent as Ivan Il'ich himself?! He is right, a thousand times right! I… I am the one who has gone astray," thought Sasha in despair.

The cold was bone-chilling. The frost blanketed everything with a thick layer of silvery, fluffy snow. It hung on the trees and lay on the roofs, fences, hoardings and cornices as well as people and horses, as though intentionally covering up everything that was impure, rough-edged, raggedy and unsightly — with its smooth, glistening, beautiful white counterpane. It added a touch of silver to the air, glistening far above the earth, its magnificent whiteness competing with the yellow glow of street-lamps and the reddish flame of bon-fires on Moscow street corners, around which crowds of happy lads had gath-ered to warm themselves, along with gloomy beggars in torn trousers and open-toed, worn-out shoes.

In the air above, the silvery gleam of frost-laden telegraph wires could be seen stretching in all directions — these non-human messengers informing human beings of the most acute events which concerned them — deaths, births, weddings, victories, fires, the misfortunes and the joys of human life. With a distinct sharpness these frost-laden wires cut across the dark, distant sky in different directions, beneath cold stars which, scattered through infinite space, were also extinguished by the frost.

It seemed to Sasha that the beauty of this winter's night was celebrating with her the genius and success of her most beloved companion. But it was not out of feelings of earthy love for him, but the triumph of musical art, which now seemed to Sasha to be shining in this whole silvery festive frosty blanket, glistening throughout the world — just as pure, great, eternal and beautiful as Nature itself.

CHAPTER 14 ❧ JEALOUSY

Ivan Il'ich's musical friends persuaded him to go to St. Petersburg and con-duct the same symphony there. Sasha learnt about this and was very con-cerned that she had not seen Ivan Il'ich around anywhere. She passionately gave her all to music, as she did in everything else in her life. She practised up to six hours a day with great success, but she was still overwhelmed by an inner sense of hopeless longing.

She grew thin and her whole being deteriorated so obviously that Pëtr Afanas'evich began to be alarmed and called in the doctors, who were extremely perplexed at what they found. Everything in Sasha's strong and beautiful body was fine and healthy. It was only that her large, serious-looking dark eyes showed exhaustion, nervousness and an ominous expression. The physicians prescribed her bromide, plenty of rest, daily walks, baths and relaxation. If there were no improvement, then a trip to the Crimea or abroad would be in order.

"Mamà, where is the old man Tikhonych, who was living at the dacha with Ivan Il'ich?" Alësha once asked his mother.

"He's here in Moscow, still residing at Ivan Il'ich's."

"Oh, Mamà dear, do let us go visit him," Alësha pleaded. "I really do like this dear old man with his yellow beard."

"Very good, Alësha, we'll go," Sasha agreed, well knowing that Ivan Il'ich was in Petersburg. She was subconsciously yearning to have a look at the place where her beloved composer lived and created his masterpieces.

Sasha was afraid and somewhat conscience-stricken at the thought of invading a bachelor's flat, but her excuse was that she had a child with her and, moreover, that Ivan Il'ich was not at home. Alësha brought the footman a gift of some tobacco and was delighted that, after ringing the bell, the first person he saw was Aleksej Tikhonych.

"Alësha dear, it is really you! So good of you to remember an old man," Tikhonych greeted the boy.

"This is for you, Tikhonych," said Alësha, triumphantly handing him his gift.

"Thank you, Alësha dear, come on in, I'll tell Ivan Il'ich right away."

"Ivan Il'ich?! Has he come back?" Sasha asked in horror. "Never mind, never mind, it's time to go home, and besides, Alësha's getting overly hot in his fur coat."

Sasha hastened to leave, but at that very moment Ivan Il'ich appeared in the doorway, blushing all over upon seeing Sasha. For a long time both of them said not a word. In the meantime, Tikhonych took Alësha's coat and led him into the flat, promising him some chocolate.

"I didn't know you were back, Ivan Il'ich!" Sasha was first to break the silence, offering her hand.

"Hello, Aleksandra Alekseevna, I am so very happy to see you," Ivan Il'ich said in his calm, quiet voice.

"Alësha has long been asking to go see Tikhonych, and I agreed, but…"

"I guess you must have thought I was still in Petersburg when you decided to come see Tikhonych. Naturally, I would not dare expect such an honour for myself," said Ivan Il'ich, again with a touch of irony.

"Not an honour, but…"

"But what?"

Ivan Il'ich took Sasha's hand and for a long time clasped it in his own beautiful, warm fingers.

"Are you coming in, Aleksandra Alekseevna?"

"Yes, well, what can I say? Now that I'm here, I might as well come in," said Sasha, taking off her jacket as she entered Ivan Il'ich's flat. "We haven't seen each other since the evening of your triumph, Ivan Il'ich. And how was it in Petersburg?"

"Thank you. In Petersburg they did not give me such ovations. In Moscow, my friends exaggerated my success."

"After all, your symphony is very, very good…"

Sasha felt timid and awkward. She sensed that it was not entirely decent for her, as a young woman, to spend any time at Ivan Il'ich's flat. However, her joy at seeing him was so strong and intoxicating that she could not bring herself to actually leave.

From the next room they could hear the animated voices of Alësha and Tikhonych.

"See how the old and young have come together," said Ivan Il'ich. "You can hear how happy they are!"

"I wanted to ask you, Ivan Il'ich," Sasha impulsively enquired, "where you spent the evening after conducting your symphony here in Moscow? You probably had supper with your musician friends?"

"No, getting together with people socially is not to my liking, and I try to avoid it. I wanted to go home early and go to bed, but then, at the main entrance, Anna Nikolaevna accosted me with a request to escort her home… Normally I don't like escorting ladies… but I had no choice but to go with her."

Anna Nikolaevna was a visiting soloist from a provincial opera, who had in the past flirted with Ivan Il'ich. This Sasha knew. He had admitted that at one time in his early youth he had been very much attracted to her. Sasha was suddenly overwhelmed by a feeling of intense jealousy, along with a sense of annoyance that it had all happened on the very evening of his greatest triumph — just when she was sharing his soul's excitement and joy over his great success. This feeling was so powerful that it literally took her breath away. At a moment when she was ready to give half her life just to be with him, there he was — riding together with this would-be youthful companion and listening to her vulgar and indecent conversation.

"So, you don't like escorting ladies? Is this not an indication, Ivan Il'ich, that you found it bothersome — or even unbearable — when you sometimes escorted *me* home from concerts?" — Sasha suddenly burst out carelessly and tactlessly.

"No, Aleksandra Alekseevna, I didn't mean that…"

"Maybe you didn't mean it, but you still managed to offend me," Sasha said in a tearful voice, quite unable to control herself. "I don't need any suitors to accompany me, I could have had hordes of them if I'd wanted," she continued with pride. "I counted you as a friend, somebody close… I loved conversing with you… to me you were higher than anyone else in the world… And now you come at me with these insinuations…"

Sasha became more and more heated. She spoke in a repressed voice and her sparkling wide-open eyes were no longer naïve but crazily passionate and full of tears.

"Aleksandra Alekseevna, please forgive me if I have offended you," Ivan Il'ich said calmly. "That was certainly not my intention. I have always enjoyed talking with you, and what you have just said—"

"I don't remember what I just told you…" Sasha said tersely by way of an excuse, suddenly coming to her senses. "Anyway, it's time I went home… Call Alësha, please."

Ivan Il'ich got up, his darting eyes casting a glance at Sasha. He was on the point of saying something else to her but stopped.

Alësha, with chocolate-smeared lips and a little bundle in his hands, beamed with delight, kissed Tikhonych goodbye, bade farewell to Ivan Il'ich and headed to the door with his mother.

Ivan Il'ich took Sasha's jacket from the closet and awkwardly tried to put it on her. For a brief moment his hands rested on her shoulders — she did not know whether this strange gesture was deliberate or unintentional. She turned her face toward him, their eyes met, and Sasha's countenance expressed both fright and surprise.

"Is this really happening?" she thought. Sasha's fingers were trembling so much that she could not do up her jacket.

"Let me button it for you," said Ivan Il'ich.

Sasha, once again her usual meek, loving and tender self, inclined her flexible waist toward Ivan Il'ich, who happened to touch her chin with his hands. Finally he managed to button her jacket. At once it seemed to Sasha that a bolt of lightning from the touch of Ivan Il'ich's hands passed through her entire body. She blushed all over, once more raising her eyes to her friend, and immediately fell silent.

"Goodbye," he said. "Can I come and see you some time?"

"Farewell," Sasha quietly responded.

She took Alësha's hand and, having no strength to make the journey on foot, hailed a cab and went home.

"After all, maybe he loves me, too!" This speculation momentarily flashed through her head. "On second thought, it wouldn't make me happy. Why don't I feel now the happiness I dreamt about earlier — assuming I believed in the possibility of his reciprocal love? No, that's not what I want. I don't even dare… I can't afford to get into an unhappy romance with this man. I always prize *purity* above all else. Let him remain a pure priest of his art, let him serve it faithfully, let him hang on to his soul which is virginal, calm and altogether imbued with that high art that he serves.

"Even if my life should perish, let it perish unsullied either by illegitimate love or by the sin of his love, which might only derail and ruin this genius of a composer's whole existence. Maybe he, too, was terrified at the possibility of loving me…

"Enough, enough of this tormenting desire for his love! I don't need it. It's time to wake up, time to finally realise that it is both impossible and harmful for both of us…"

CHAPTER 15

More than a month went by. March arrived with its Lenten services in all Moscow churches, along with the poetry of the anticipated spring, anxiety over upcoming student exams, and a pause in the wild, never-ending urban festivities, together with everything that comes back every year during this particular month.

But for Sasha the world had ceased to exist. She was determined to overcome in herself the feeling of love for Ivan Il'ich and, whatever the cost, to separate his person from her love for his music. Sasha began to avoid meeting with him. Day after day she would practise the piano, learning some pretty challenging pieces. And after hiring a tutor from the Conservatory, she made remarkable progress.

With the advent of Lent, the round of concerts began again in Moscow, and Sasha attended them faithfully. From time to time she would catch a glimpse of Ivan Il'ich from afar, but never again did she ask him to escort her home or ride with her or come and play something for her. Some kind of cold, distant relations developed between them; gone were the simplicity, the trust and the intimacy which had fostered the mutual confidence between them that they had nothing to fear from each other and that she could reveal her soul in all its depth.

Ivan Il'ich visited Sasha rarely and wondered (or perhaps he guessed) why Sasha had suddenly started to behave differently toward him. This caused him no suffering, so absorbed was he in his art that every moment of solitude brought him the peace he needed to carry on his musical activities.

Occasionally, however, he felt that something was missing. What was missing was that tender, beautiful atmosphere of the poetry of love with which Sasha used to surround him and which imbued him with an almost subconscious delight.

For Sasha, though, life — without the expectation that at any moment Ivan Il'ich might come and sit beside her or play something for her — became utterly unbearable and lost any trace of meaning. She kept traipsing through all her rooms like someone tormented and suffering; she kept weeping, sometimes even crying out in a pathetic voice disjointed lyrics from his romance, for example: *"Pridi, pridi ko mne..."* ["Come, come to me..."]; or she would sit down at the piano and converse with various fragments of his works:

"Here you were suffering and here you were pleading... and when you composed this marvellous piece, what were you praying about?... Here is your love... But love for whom?... And here is the calm, logical contemplation of some sort of internal spiritual process... or perhaps Nature herself... This is what is so good about music — it enables everyone to live their dreams. I have studied your entire musical soul — I know it so well and love it so much..."

Finally Sasha would leap to her feet, recalling his strange glance, while her hands kept vainly seeking the embraces which her whole young, passionate being wildly desired.

"Here, Sasha dear, a letter for you," said Pëtr Afanas'evich, to whom the postman had just handed an envelope at the front door.

"Oh, my God! It's from Kurlinskij! Where is he, the poor thing?"

Sasha began reading the letter:

You remember, Aleksandra Alekseevna, the day when you appeared to me in my prison as a guardian angel and tried to persuade me not to go against the status quo but accept military service? I have done a lot of soul-searching since then. I know that you wanted to come see me again, but this time they would not let you. Maybe it was better that way. In my solitude I thought about the evil that would inevitably follow in either case — if I refused point-blank or if I agreed to be conscripted. I realised that there was more evil in my refusal; in other words, you were right: I should both humble myself and submit to the inevitable, no matter how evil it seemed. I have now been a whole month in a soldier's uniform. In a day or two they'll be posting us to the Persian border, and before I go I wanted to say goodbye to you, at least in a letter, to thank you and tell you that I shall carry you in my memory as a bright image, and I thank Destiny for the happiness which my acquaintance with you has brought me.

May this Destiny send you the happiness which should always cast its light upon your bright and pure path of life.

Yours, Kurlinskij.

"Happiness… for me? Now the path of my life is no longer bright and pure!" thought Sasha.

"Well, thank God!" she said aloud.

"What's that for?" asked Pëtr Afanas'evich.

"He finally entered military service and is off to Persia with his regiment. He'll see a lot of interesting things there and maybe even come to his senses."

"I don't find anything particularly joyful in his decision," said Pëtr Afanas'evich drearily. "His refusal was actually more heroic."

"You're saying that his mother's grief, his own torment and suffering were better?!" Sasha bitterly objected. "You men are all alike — the more you see of evil and violence, the more you enjoy it…"

This whole past while there had been a tone of irritation and unspoken, concealed grief between Sasha and her husband. Both were suffering and looking for some kind of solution — only it never came. In the meantime their conjugal life was becoming more and more unbearable.

Pëtr Afanas'evich went over to the window and started transplanting (from one box to another) some newly blossoming plants, each of which had sprouted a couple of tender new leaves. His face was thoughtful, gone was his former cheerful carefreeness, and Sasha began to feel sorry for him. She got up and went over to her husband.

"What is it, Sasha?" he queried.

"I just wanted to be with you."

"I'm very happy, darling. See how my verbenas have come up. They are a rare variety. Wait and see what they'll be like in the summer — it will be a miracle!"

Sasha began quietly helping her husband in his work, and some of her huge tears fell on these young plants.

"Such a happy, dear and naïve person!" Sasha thought in reference to her husband. "And what about me? I shall pick these verbenas and admire them, then I'll use them to plait my hair and adorn my dress — so that I may please another person who still does not want anything to do with me."

Sasha could no longer restrain herself. She went to her own room, changed her clothes and went outdoors without a word to anyone.

It was the Feast of the Annunciation. Spring had made an early appearance, and the ice on the Moscow River had just melted. The caretakers had been sweeping away water from the streets, where it was streaming along the pavement in floods before disappearing underground.

Sasha went to the Kamenny Bridge to have a look at the river. Leaning over the bridge railing, she waited for the approaching ice-floes, which, after rising on end, broke apart against the pillars of the bridge. A throng of onlookers — working-class people, free for the holiday — crowded around her, remarking on the scene and spitting out husks of sunflower seeds. These husks were already carpeting the bridge railings and stone ledges and couldn't help but attract the eye.

Sasha watched the passing ice-floes for a long time. Her head was spinning — and it seemed to her that the whole bridge was floating. Then, afterwards, each time when she came to herself, she saw again that it was simply the ice floating down the river. But then something new occurred: it was no longer just the floes, but again the whole bridge and, indeed, she herself — together with all the onlookers from the nearby factory as well as everything else — that were being swept along under the bright, spring sun. The dark-blue sky was reflected in the muddy, polluted, swirling water… Sasha's head was still spinning.

"I'm floating… I'm going… whereto?… Indeed, whereto? And a long, long time ago, when Ivan Il'ich was playing his sonata, I had that very impression of being carried away somewhere. Isn't this the same motion, which is to carry us away into eternity, thereby answering this same question: *whereto?* — forever and ever. If this question arises, then there must also exist some mysterious realm we are all undoubtedly heading to… and which we love, since we are always delighted by this question *whereto?*"

The thought of death came to Sasha so clearly and cheerfully that she nearly threw herself into the river. Only the filthy water of the Moscow River utterly repulsed her. Sasha's passion for cleanliness stopped her even here. "I'll pull through!" she thought, like all others who are neither ready to die nor about to commit suicide.

How long she stood there, she did not notice. When she came to herself, it was already getting dark. The long spring day had come to an end, how and when — she did not know. Even now, she didn't feel like going home. Recalling that a young friend of hers, named Katja, lived close by, she decided to go see her.

Katja took one look at Sasha and gasped.

"What's the matter, Aunt Sasha? Are you ill?"

"No, I'm tired, and I have not had anything to eat today."

"Why? Did you have a quarrel with your husband?"

"With my husband?…" Sasha quite forgot that she had a husband, that she had a child and a house, and at first she did not understand her friend's question. "No, it's just that I'm very, very tired…

"Katja! Why, oh, why is everything in the world so dirty? Everything, everything…"

"What are you talking about, Aunt Sasha? You'd better have something to eat, your face is so pale. Wait here, I'll bring you a piece of chicken."

"All right, later. But listen to me, it's very curious. Haven't you noticed, everywhere there is filth, everywhere there are human passions… Let's say, you love music and fall in love with someone — and the music dies, it was besmirched by human passion… Kurlinskij loves people and he loves life — but then they go and make a soldier out of him and order him to kill…

"The water in the river is dirty, the pure earth is covered with stones and human dirt, the clear sky — with smoke and soot, people's pure love — with family betrayal… And there is no escape, not ever, and I myself am filthy, repulsive and doomed…"

Sasha sobbed to the point of fainting. Katja looked at her in horror; all at once it became clear to her that Sasha was mentally ill. She managed to calm her down and took her home, where Pëtr Afanas'evich, who had been tormentedly and vainly searching for his wife all day, met them with cries of joy. However, upon seeing Sasha, he immediately understood her emotional condition and quickly fell silent in his sorrowful concern.

CHAPTER 16 ❧ THE FINAL SIGHS OF THE SONG

Sasha awoke the next morning apparently quite calm. Pëtr Afanas'evich silently kissed his wife's forehead before heading off to the office. When he returned around lunchtime, he found Sasha playing the piano. But he had another appointment in the evening and left again.

Sasha spent the whole day in quietude. Her husband had no sooner gone than she got dressed and rushed straight to Ivan Il'ich's home. She had not seen him for a long time, and when she got to his house, she started pacing back and forth in front of the gate, hoping on a whim that he would come out on his way somewhere.

But eventually a lamp was lit in his window, and several times she noticed shadows of human figures passing by, and then someone opened the window. Sasha froze for a moment. At last her anxiety became so unbearable that she sat down on the caretaker's bench in a niche in the fence. As she listened, she kept trembling all over, fearing she might be discovered.

But all at once from the open window emanated the sounds of her favourite Chopin Nocturne in F-sharp major. She had heard this piece once during a winter concert, fantastically performed by a professor from the French Conservatory, and then proceeded to learn it herself. But to play it the way Ivan Il'ich was playing it right now — nobody in the world could manage that, save Ivan Il'ich himself.

If people can actually die of excitement, this was such a moment for Sasha. Something within her broke forever. Gritting her teeth, clenching her fists, petrified and mindless, Sasha felt attracted to Ivan Il'ich with her whole being. It seemed to her that with all her soul, with her whole existence, she had to go somewhere, to escape from her body right this moment, that she had not sufficient life-force within her to maintain her self-control. She got up and ran down the street with such loud groans and screams that passers-by stopped and stared at her.

When she got home, she found that Pëtr Afanas'evich had already returned and that Katja had come to see her. Sasha dashed right past them without so much as a word and immediately sat down at the piano.

First of all, she played the same Beethoven sonata that Ivan Il'ich had played on her birthday, at the dacha. The first chord of the arpeggio sounded forth solemnly and quietly before trailing off. But then came the allegro, and Sasha's performance became even better, more lively and more beautiful. She was undoubtedly imitating Ivan Il'ich's touch so well that at times they sounded extraordinarily similar.

However, she left the sonata unfinished and immediately started playing Chopin's Nocturne. After completing it, she looked around in a silent gaze before launching into Mendelssohn's *Song without words* in G-major.

All at once she stopped… She then began to cry out in a wild voice:

"There is no music, no… it's all muddy, filthy… it has perished…" She turned pale, and her face became distorted. She fell off her stool…

All night long Sasha felt tormented, even delirious. She kept repeating aloud that everything in the world had lost its purity, that Ivan Il'ich alone stood high, though he would not let her approach him… She would stretch out her hands, begging him to play something for her.

They sent for the doctor, who diagnosed her condition as overfatigue of the heart and extreme nervous irritation.

All day long Sasha stayed in bed, pale and quiet, only her fingers moved as though playing the piano, while her large, dark eyes betrayed such hopeless suffering that everyone impulsively averted their gaze at the sight of her.

Pëtr Afanas'evich never left Sasha's side. The next morning her mental illness became even more apparent. She kept coming back to the piano and starting into one piece after another.

She put a great deal of effort into going through a handwritten score of Ivan Il'ich's symphony. Exhausted, she began loudly chatting with someone — nobody knew with whom:

"Was that not good? Was it not the most incredible piece?… But enough… oh, how tired I am… Stop playing… there is no music, it got drowned in the mud… Oh my God, I am tormented by sounds…"

Whereupon Sasha would collapse in exhaustion and immediately fall asleep.

A couple of mornings later, after seeing her sleeping husband, also quite exhausted in the course of these past three days, she quietly got up, put on her white dressing-gown trimmed with swan's down and went to the front door. Taking her white Orenburg shawl from a little table in the hallway, she put it on her head and, unseen by anyone, hurried outside…

"Taxi! To the clinic!" she cried.

"Thirty kopeks," the cab driver calmly informed her.

"As fast as you can!" Sasha took a hurried glance around. "I'll give you something extra."

"What clinic, your Ladyship?"

"The one for nervous disorders."

As they rode along Prechistenka Avenue, Sasha was able to think about her condition rather logically. All her energy was concentrated on avoiding saying or doing something inappropriate. But her will was weakening — that she understood perfectly. Some inner moral mechanism was breaking down, and her head was filling with all sorts of wild and unwelcome thoughts.

"Indeed, I *am* going out of my mind," Sasha suddenly realised. "And now I'll ask the cabby to take me to Ivan Il'ich's, and I'll kneel before him and kiss his hands… and ask him to love me and play for me… No, *never!!* Those two things should never go together!…"

"Faster, cabby, for God's sake, faster!…"

As they passed by the Deviche Field, Sasha saw a large building on the left behind a fence. The taxi drove up to the cast-iron gates. Sasha got out and suddenly remembered that she had no money with her.

"Wait, I'll write you a note. Take it to the house where you picked me up, and they'll pay you."

While the driver muttered something in displeasure, Sasha went up to the gates and read on the sign: *University Clinic for Nervous Disorders*, and below that and to the right on the sign was an inscription (for some reason) in French: *Clinique des maladies nerveuses.*

Going up to the main entrance, Sasha began to push open the heavy door.

A soldier with many medals on his chest opened it for her and gave a surprised look at this excited figure, dressed all in white.

"What can I do for you?" he asked.

Without answering, Sasha pushed forward, surveying the building's interior.

Beyond the glass door was a long, bright corridor, all lined on either side with fresh green plants. Next to that there was a broad staircase leading up. To the left, there was another long corridor which led to a reception room. The soldier-doorman was still blocking Sasha's path, but she could not help looking around at the place where she had voluntarily come to stay.

"Please come to the reception room, your Ladyship. Here is off-limits…"

"Fine! Where is the doctor?"

"I'll announce you right away."

The reception room was empty except for the dark wooden benches lining the walls. From there an open door led into the doctor's office. One of the benches was occupied by two women — one was sobbing quietly, while the other comforted her.

Sasha pulled her shawl over her face and, closing her eyes, began to visualise the face and hands of Ivan Il'ich — indeed, his whole person.

She came to only when a hand softly touched her shoulder and a voice asked:

"Would you like to come into my office?"

"Is he really there?" asked Sasha, mindlessly staring at the doctor… "Oh, forgive me, my thoughts were elsewhere. Yes, right away."

Sasha entered the doctor's spacious office. He invited her to sit down in an arm-chair beside a large green desk, behind which he took his own seat.

"Do you wish to admit yourself for treatment or are you here on behalf of someone else?" asked the doctor, suspiciously regarding Sasha's white dressing-gown, along with her gloomy eyes and momentarily tragic beauty.

"I am asking you to admit me — you see, I am quite ill: I don't sleep, I don't eat and I've lost my self-control, I torment my family… I need rest, as well as your advice…" Sasha said hastily, making incredible efforts to sound logical and not to give the doctor any hint of her mental disorder.

"How can that be? Don't you have any relatives — a husband, maybe?…"

"Yes, I forgot. I should write to him. Can you let me have a piece of paper and a pencil?"

"Here, take this," offered the doctor. "But tell me please, what prompted you to come here? Are you unhappy?"

"No, no. I'll explain it all to you some other time… I can't right now… Is everything clean here?"

"Naturally. Where would you like to stay, in a paying ward?"

"What?"

"Can you afford to pay, say, 60 or even 90 roubles a month?"

"Yes, of course. My husband will pay for everything. D'you think you can cure me? Can you make it so that my soul no longer languishes in the muddy pool it's in? It's filthy everywhere, everywhere… My God, it's horrible!…"

Sasha began to sob. The doctor rang a little bell. The soldier with the medals on his chest came in.

"Call Marija Prokhorovna," the doctor ordered. "Open Paying Ward № 2." Then he turned again to Sasha:

"Don't worry, now we'll give you a room and send for your husband. Just jot down the address."

Sasha began to calm down. She thought for a few seconds and, making yet another strenuous effort at self-control, sat down at the desk and began writing a letter to her husband:

> Pay the cabby 80 kopeks. I've admitted myself to the clinic for nervous disorders because I have no more will, nor the strength to control myself. Please come and settle with the doctor regarding my maintenance. And send me some clean undergarments, clothes, and everything, everything clean…
>
> Yesterday I was reading Dante's *Purgatory*, and I suddenly realised that I have been spattered upon from every side, and as such I can't be accepted into the Heavenly Conservatory. Are you aware that Ivan Il'ich is no longer in Moscow? The water in the Moscow River is very dirty and there is a lot of moral filth in the Moscow Conservatory. He could not bear it, and so now he is teaching and performing in the Heavenly Conservatory, and he is calling me there, too.
>
> In the meantime, I'd like you to order me another white dressing-gown. Mine got splashed with mud today and I am in despair — still yet another black spot…
>
> I really want to cleanse my soul, but, in any case, neither you nor anyone else can touch it, since nobody has clean hands, while my soul is free…
>
> Please forgive me for disturbing you. When I am clean and healthy, I shall come home…

"You've had enough time to write," the doctor told Sasha with some annoyance. "Just put the address."

When Sasha finished, he called a female assistant, instructing her to dispatch the letter by taxi and then take Sasha to her designated room, for which she would be paying 60 roubles a month.

When Sasha found herself alone in the room, which was empty save for a bed, a table and a chair, she pulled a little notebook out of her dressing-gown pocket and took from its side-pocket a small amateur photo of Ivan Il'ich, which she had asked him for when he showed it to her.

She looked at it with excitement and pressed it to her breast.

"Now nobody can prevent me from being with you! My dearest! I feel your soul and your presence… we shall never again be parted from each other…"

She went over and lay down on the bed, closed her eyes and once more was able to catch a clear glimpse of Ivan Il'ich at the piano, with his serious, inspired gaze, not fixed on anyone in particular, and to hear his performance, which filled her whole being with happiness.

From that day on Sasha shut out everything else in her life. She grew thin and pale, and her beautiful face became almost transparent. Her delicate fingers hardly ever stopped moving as though flitting across a piano keyboard; her huge dark eyes expressed mindlessly, first bliss, then suffering.

The *song* of her love for Ivan Il'ich had been sung to the end *without words*, and this fractured her life.

Having played in her heart this whole song with all its tender and passionate phrases, Sasha still had to play the three final sighs, which concluded Mendelssohn's *Song without words* in G-major, along with her own young and beautiful life… The first sigh represented her hopeless love, the second — the repose of her cleansed soul, while the third one expressed a quiet eternal joy. Then would follow the *pianissimo*, the *morendo* — and everything would die forever…

CHAPTER 17 ❧ OBLIVION

At the end of April Ivan Il'ich sat at his large desk by an open window, going over the proofs of the musical textbook he had just finished and was in the process of publishing.

His large head with hair thinning around the crown and greying around the temples was bent over a sheet of music paper and his face appeared serious and focused. His complex textbook with its new techniques in musical education would turn out to be extremely helpful for Conservatory courses, and Ivan Il'ich was proud that he had accomplished such a useful work. Each day he devoted himself to the task at hand with extraordinary precision and pedantry for exactly two hours, before going on his usual walk. Outdoor exercise was followed by dinner and then either an evening concert, a visit to friends or a piano lesson with his pupils.

How orderly, calm and good everything was!… Complete satisfaction from fulfilling self-appointed tasks, offering help to a younger generation, keeping in touch only with men, especially young ones and primarily with musicians. No alarms, no concerns…

Occasionally Ivan Il'ich would remember Sasha, and his ego was still flattered by her love and especially by her high appraisal of his talent. But he was glad that all that was now in the past.

Today, after working his designated hours, Ivan Il'ich was about to get ready for his walk.

Handing him his coat, Aleksej Tikhonych began talking to him in a quiet monotone voice:

"Did you know that Aleksandra Alekseevna, the lady who lived next door to us at the dacha, is now in a clinic? Recently their caretaker came to ours with a request for coal. He says that she is completely exhausted and was recommended treatment."

"And how is she doing?"

"God knows! She herself went to the clinic for nervous disorders."

"She went herself!" thought Ivan Il'ich. "What a woman! Full of energy to the end!"

For a moment he had a fleeting memory of that evening when they performed his symphony, which he himself conducted — that passionate epic poem of love...

Was it really his own composition? The melody kept running through his head, along with the memory of Sasha's figure sitting in the front row, dressed all in white, with diamonds in her tiara and earrings, so joyful and majestic, keeping track of both Ivan Il'ich's symphony and his latest success with passionate excitement.

And was it really possible that this blossoming figure of Sasha's was now locked in a clinic and thus had disappeared from his life without a trace?

Ivan Il'ich went outdoors. However, something had upset his equilibrium. He walked quickly, his eyes darting here and there — he was making every effort to forget Sasha completely and concentrate on his textbook.

At the corner of the street he met his always-cheerful, rosy-cheeked favourite pupil Tsvetkov. They greeted each other. Ivan Il'ich's eyes, still darting here and there, were full of joy as he held Tsvetkov's hand and promised that this evening he would correct and play Tsvetkov's new little overture.

By the end of May the textbook was published, which brought Ivan Il'ich a goodly sum of money. This gave him tremendous satisfaction. He could now fulfil his dream and go abroad with Tsvetkov.

While Sasha was wasting away at the clinic, Ivan Il'ich was enjoying his travels in the company of his beloved young friend. He forgot all about Sasha and the whole world in a realm of epicurean bliss!

Only once more in his life did he remember Sasha. He happened to be walking by a little house somewhere in Switzerland, where through an open window he caught the sound of a violin playing Mendelssohn's *Song without words* in G-major. Ivan Il'ich stopped in his tracks and the blood rushed to his head. But he soon got over it and hurried on his walk. Never again in his lifetime did he play this piece.

"Forget, forget everything except music!" he thought. "It alone will always be my affair, my life, my interest..."

And he did forget everything except his beloved art, which he served right up until the day he died.

CHAPTER 6

Groanings: Poems in prose

THE RIVER

I FLOAT DOWN THE RIVER and try not to disturb its watery surface all around me, caressing my body…

The comfort [of the] water refreshes and strengthens me, while the caress of my loved one burns and weakens me…

The sun was shining from the blue ether, beyond time, eternal. And I kept floating, floating and carrying myself away into that same bright blue sky which was reflected in the river. All was quiet.

"Farewell, my dear land, — I have left you and do not wish to return…"

However, my peace was disturbed by the spirit of evil, the spirit of the earth; my heart skipped a beat; I shivered and began to drown. Yet the next moment I found myself on dry land: fear and the horror of death took over my body, and from the tender caresses of the river I was thrown onto the dirty shore of the land, collapsing and short of breath.

A tall reed caught in my long, thin legs; brown frogs noisily leapt into the water; a bird took flight over the meadow; a fish was alarmed and made such a commotion underwater that it caused a circular ripple effect on the surface. I walked out onto the grass, where I managed to catch my breath. I was drawn to the land. Sitting down on a prickly, recently mown meadow, I began to count my heart beats. My uneven pulse first quickened, then slowed, and finally seemed to disappear altogether… My wet arms glistened in the sun; my chest gave a heavy sigh; my whole exposed body bent over to the ground, utterly exhausted…

Oh, dear earth! I shall not soon depart from you or from this body which you have cunningly created. And I love this beautiful body, created for earthly love and now conquered by earth... But I shall eventually cast it off!...

A herd of cows mooed in the distance; they were on their way to watering, to the same river that had thrown me out. I jumped up and took refuge in a lean-to, where I had stored my clothes.

A VISION

I AM WALKING THROUGH THE FOREST. On my way I see an old oak tree. Its roots bulge out from the ground in a form of an arc... How many times my foot has stumbled over this root!... I walk and languish over the fact that someone no longer loves me and has left me. I look more closely... I see his heavy-set figure, full of energy, coming towards me. I slow my pace so as to prolong the happy vision. But now he is beside me. I put my foot on the protruding twisted root and extend my hand to him... Then, however, everything disappears. My hand, grasping hold of a dead branch of the oak, breaks it off and it falls helplessly by my side; my heart all but stops; my whole being merges with my beloved man and embraces him. The happiness of his spiritual closeness momentarily carries me away from this earthly life...

Now the moment has passed...

I walk on. I see a little mound in which ten years ago my young late son was rummaging with his thin, whitish hands, digging up mushrooms. This boy had been sent to the Earth as a pure, kind spirit. I knew this. And he later went back to his spiritual home without being touched by the Earth.

I stand on the little mound and recite the Lord's Prayer. "Thy will be done! Thy will be done!" I cry, remembering the life and death of my child. And the forest disappears, all that is earthly vanishes, and I leave — oh, bliss! — in my soul, I leave for the home of my little son, where there is neither time nor space, nor Earth, nor parting, nor sorrow, nor pain — nothing but love and unity with those spirits that I loved and blending with Him who took them from the Earth by His incomprehensible, supreme will.

О, нет сомненья, в жизни вечной	No doubt, in life's eternal art
Я встречусь с тем, кто дорог был,	I shall meet with him who was dear to me.
И связи разорвать сердечной	And to break apart the bonds of the heart
Земных уж там не будет сил!	No earthly force can there ever be!

IN THE CONVENT

DUSK. I WALK INTO THE CONVENT. It's dark and quiet in the church. A husky feminine voice, almost masculine in timbre, is reciting a prayer. I look up at this woman: she is quite tall, of a muscular build for a nun, with a stern, sullen-looking face. Standing by an interior column, she is loudly and with evident pain expressing the sufferings of her soul from the very depths of her whole being...

It became painful for me, too. I walked up close to her and asked her whether she had been at the nunnery for a long time.

"I have been praying for forty years, but I still have not extirpated my heavy sin," the old nun answered me in a husky, low, dispassionate voice full of agonising sorrow. Lowering her eyes, she once again took to praying:

"Lord, have mercy, forgive my great transgression!" she whispered.

Her face was completely oblivious to any earthly surroundings. She took no notice of me, the church, or the other supplicants. In her sorrow she had gone to the realm where only the heart lives. And God will surely look down upon the repentant sinner, who, before she died, renounced everything earthly and was able to cross into that realm of the spirit where the measure of good and evil is beyond our power.

IN THE CATACOMBS

I WAS IN A TERRIBLE STATE OF GRIEF. I fell into despair, prayed, went around to various churches and monasteries, and somehow ended up in Kiev. This beautiful city on the Dnieper, full of hills and gardens, with its ancient religious spirit, resonated in my heart.

There were five in our group. We went to the *Lavra* [monastery] and approached the entrance to the *peshchery* [catacombs]. We were not admitted immediately, as another party of pilgrims (escorted by a monk) was already inside. We awaited our turn in a long gallery, and my gaze was drawn to the frescoes on the wall. They depicted a human soul in the form of a little girl, all dressed in white, with folded arms, passing through all the ordeals and vices. Behind the girl were two angels, taller than her, with wings, while underneath them devils were shown in various poses, with horns, tails and frightening faces representing vices. In the upper part of the image, we saw the Jerusalem temple as well as Paradise, which the soul was approaching. All this was slightly naïve in style, but metaphorical, expressive and extremely impressive…

Presently an elderly monk appeared, followed by a chain of pilgrims in single file, carrying candles and showing either bright or frightened faces.

Now it was our turn. We lit our candles and proceeded into the *peshchery*. I walked directly behind the monk. We made our way, all bent over, through narrow earthen corridors and all at once I was struck by a feeling of terror.

"Go back! Go back!" I implored the fifteen people behind me. "I'm all out of breath — for God's sake!" I cried.

The monk turned around to look at me and said quietly but reproachfully:

"You ought to be ashamed, Ma'am: people lived here for years, they prayed, but were not afraid; and you're too timid to even walk through… Soon we'll be in the church which is more spacious — just you pray, now…"

And, indeed, we presently entered a spacious cavern, which at one time had served as a chapel used by a highly revered monk who had passed on. I straightened up and looked at the little, ancient icons, and vividly imagined the solitary praying elder, who had managed to leave this world of mortal, bodily fear and to step into the realm of the spirit, where his soul would be free from any external suffering or evil.

I crossed myself and all at once I felt light and easy in these *peshchery*, which had already ceased to be either a prison for my soul — now freed from fear and earthly attraction — or an obstacle to my spiritual being.

AUTUMN

DARK, GREY, WARM AND QUIET. How thoughtful Nature is — furrowing its brow, drawing deep into itself! Autumn, so deep is autumn! The leaves have fallen from the trees and covered the ground with brown foliage. How dark, deep and still is the water in the rivers and lakes! It is waiting for its winter shackles, when all life in it is frozen… Dark, grey, warm and quiet…

Fussing birds kept chirping in the bushes; all of a sudden, a woodpecker flew out of a tree and over to the window — striking its beak against the window frame, it grasped hold of some dried moss. And again — the silence and the gloom began to cover meek, moribund Nature with a thicker and thicker carpet…

Night came, and everything fell asleep. The white clouds dispersed, and the moon timidly shone through. An old man quietly rode into the forest, stopped his horse and climbed down from the wagon. He took an axe and started to cut down some young aspens. The heavy work was hard on his breathing. Afraid of the watchmen, he kept listening for any stray sound; after stopping for a moment, he would start cutting again. When the wagon was loaded, he climbed back into the driver's seat and headed out from the forest onto the main road.

The moon went behind the clouds, a strong wind blew up, some darker clouds covered the sky, trees started to sway, a swarm of leaves began to swirl; a whirlwind blew in, setting everything a-shaking and finally breaking out in huge, heavy clouds of thick, frosty white snow.

The old man's eyes were blinded; his skinny body began to freeze; his cold hands held his cap and the reins. The horse barely managed to pull the wagon; the road disappeared under the snow; it became quite dark; the air was filled with noise, frost, white fog and terror…

The old man kept crossing himself with his stiff hand; he at last threw down the reins and closed his weary eyes.

All of a sudden, the wagon with its load gave a lurch, and started to lean to one side — a moment later the whole load tipped over on top of the dozing old man, covering him completely…

Lord have mercy!…

It began to get light. The bright sun cheerfully and majestically illumined all Nature, decked out in its finest white. In this virginal purity of blanketing snow, one could sense not death, but a brand-new life.

Passing peasants came across the overturned wagon and managed to pull out the old man.

His pale face, his white beard and the snow were all of the same hue, all illuminated by the cheerful sun.

The autumn of his life had come to an end… Nature, though, was radiant in its sparkling white covering, as was this man's soul, radiantly renewed by eternal life.

FROST

WINTER… A crackling frost. Can't breathe, can't work, can't even think… You wrap yourself up, warm yourself up, yet still shiver all over… I order two grey horses to be harnessed and go to a concert. I bury my face in my fluffy arctic fox, slain for the sake of my fur coat. I feel a kind of acid taste around the lips from the fur and note something gloomy in the dark sky coming from the icy fog…

Once inside, I am blinded by the brightly lit concert-hall. I am attracted by the crowd, all decked out in their most elegant attire. The conductor gives a few raps with his baton, and the marvellous sounds of Beethoven's Fifth Symphony arouse me and carry me off to the magical world of my favourite art, in which I am to spend more than an hour.

All of a sudden, a roar from the audience assaults my ears. They rise and start leaving the auditorium… What's all the fuss? Of course, it's the interval. All these faces are now looking down at me, and the stupid, coarse and senseless expressions of most of these earthly creatures — really bother me.

I close my eyes… But all at once something pierces me deep within my heart. I shudder and look around… The man who pinned me down to the sinful Earth, the same man I love more than life itself, is stupidly laughing and making small talk with a pudgy, creepy-looking opera singer in a yellow gown. Now he is taking her by the arm, and they disappear into the crowd.

Where's the music? Where's Beethoven? I rush out of the concert-hall like a madwoman. Immersed in the soft folds of my fur coat, my lithe, earthly figure flies down the grand staircase. All the while my throat keeps choking up with sobbing, and I make a dash for my sleigh…

The sleigh runners creak as the grey horses snort their way ahead. A thick steam surrounds them as we fly along the deserted streets at frightening speed… I start to weep… my face starts to burn inside my fur. I raise my head to get some air…

What kind of a world is this? Frost, frost without end… Everything is silvery, everything is dancing and sparkling, whereas anything impure, uneven, sinful or ugly — *that*'s all covered with a pure white blanket. There's frost on the houses, on the trees, on the roofs, on the hoardings; frost on the horses, on caps and beards; frost is even flying up there, in the distant, frosty, starry sky… How perfect, how magnificent and beautiful it all is!

The broad arrays of telegraph wires covered with white, fluffy frost, stretch out in all directions, spreading to the whole world the latest news of human life: births, deaths, accidents, wars...

I forget about my earthly feelings, and my heart goes out together with these fluffy white wires into infinite space and the pure world of virginal Nature... And in my ears, I once again hear the *Andante* from Beethoven's Fifth Symphony, and the great art of music blends with Nature in my soul — it becomes as magnificent, pure and elevated as that distant sky with its flying frost in the starry, transparent ether... Gone is the Earth, gone are earthly human feelings — my soul is cleansed and awakened to God.

DESPAIR

DESPAIR, DESPAIR ALL DAY LONG!... I can't live on the Earth — my body is tormented, and my spirit wants to escape...

Dusk has fallen — and people are turning in for the night. Still awake are only ill people, night-shift workers and mothers with nursing infants. I am retiring to my room; I close the doors and sit down at my desk... Despair, despair... In a crack in the floor a mouse chews on a scrap of biscuit; my little watch ticks away fussily; a train passes by noisily in the distance. And I, a helpless earthly creature, can neither sleep, nor live this life, nor even quit it.

Bunches of beautiful fragrant flowers in two vases — field flowers on the right, garden varieties on the left — try to distract and comfort me, some with their delicate petals, others with their bright hues and distinctive features. But I don't see them, I want to see only the one I love; he is not here. He has gone away because we have not dared love each other...

I pick up a set of little, well-worn playing cards and begin predicting my fortune. The Nine of Hearts — the card of love — has fallen on the heart of the King of Diamonds, and the Queen of Clubs wearing a crown, with a fan in her hand, sadly peers down at the King from underneath her dark, meticulously drawn eyebrows and curls.

No, no, no!... Away with the devil, away with fortune-telling, away with the temptation of this tormenting, burning love!...

The cards spill onto the floor, as though I have frightened them, while I myself drop to my knees in front of a large icon of the Saviour. I bow my head to the floor and, exhausted, meekly begin to recite all the prayers I know, one after another. My arms reach out in the form of an embrace, and I pray to God for the love of the one who is far from me. I pray that his soul might visit and console me.

All at once I hear a noise... I turn my head to the door — no one there. I continue to pray with despair, tears and all the emotional forces I can muster. Once more my head is bowed down to the floor, and I fall silent, listening for any stray sounds. The window is open, and beyond the lowered curtains I suddenly hear a light, gentle rustle.

I jump up, run to the window, lift the corner of the curtain and peer out… The pitch-black night has covered everything earthly but brings the soul of the one I have been calling closer to me. So, it caresses and comforts me, it responds to my loving call, it tenderly embraces me on all sides. And I stand there motionless, watching the dark sky, while the happiness carries my sinful, earthly being far away, farther and farther from the Earth, into a realm beyond time or space.

Enough!… Our souls quickly separate, and I wake myself out of the bliss in which I have been living for the past few seconds.

A large moth strikes the upper part of the window frame. I carefully pick it up by its little wings and press it to my lips before releasing it into the nighttime mist. Below, on the windowsill, I see a cemetery of flies stuck to the sticky paper. And again — despair, despair…

The moth flies away, as has my loved one's soul. My life, too, is stuck in the grip of earthly despair. Oh God! Give me wings, let me fly into Your pure and limitless haven!

THE POET

A POET WAS BEING EULOGISED in a spacious private chapel in a Russian house. The stern face of the deceased was solemn and beautiful. While *it* was attractive, the faces of the guests with their feigned grief seemed repulsive in their hypocritical attitude.

To whom have you been singing your songs, already fallen silent? What has happened to your beautiful, graceful and responsive soul?… But you are alive by that feeling you had towards everything you loved, everything that made you sad, everything you sang about and left an immortal legacy to people who understood you.

But who here understands you? Who will now respond to your songs and give an answer?

Suddenly, a single live sound of someone's sincere sobs rang loudly throughout the church.

The beautiful, pale, thin and tall figure of a woman in a black cloud of transparent fabric quickly went up to the deceased. With a powerful gesture of her hand, she held back the lid of the casket from closing, and planted on the poet's breast a living, luxurious rose — the final gift to the poet from a loving soul.

Just one moment… one mighty breath of love… shone through the languishing lie of outward show with its artificial, cold, groaning flowers, with the just as monotonously groaning, cold speeches of hypocrites — and a burst of life broke over the dead crowd.

THE CHILD

NIGHTTIME... On a large white sofa, in a spacious room, a boy writhes and wheezes and groans. His elderly nanny's voice caresses him, comforts him and sings him a lullaby. His mother, meanwhile, sits on a low stool, her hands covering her head... Oh, mother! Who can understand this petrified, extreme, hopeless and unbearable despair to which your child's sufferings have led you?

"Mousie, mousie... Misha, catch it!" the boy sputters in a cheerful voice, but immediately again wheezes, and the child's little body writhes on the sofa, and again the nanny's hoarse voice...

In the next room can be heard the cold, mechanical sounds of somebody winding a music box, which plays a merry tune... Who would dare intrude like that?! In her madness of grief, the mother runs in, grabs the toy and takes it away. The clockwork mouse lies upside-down on the floor. Its tiny wheels shine in the light falling upon them...

"Now quiet down there — it will pass!" once again comes the nanny's hoarse voice...

The clock goes tick-tock, chimes the hour... The night becomes gloomier and more tense. The child quiets down; the mother waits, watching the feverish little face of the young sufferer. All of a sudden, the little boy's blond head gives a jerk, he opens his eyes wide and looks up...

"I see, I see..." he says distinctly and meaningfully.

"Dearest, what do you see?"

The boy looks at his mother, makes a gesture, tries to say something... and falls back on the pillow, dead...

Heaven opened itself to the departing angel. He loved his mother and tried to show her his vision but could not bring himself to.

However, at that moment the anguishing mother understood it all — the significance and sacredness of the divine will, the inevitability of what had happened, her submission to this supreme will, along with the bliss of her son's pure departed soul.

She leant her head against the back of the chair and apparently dozed off. Only this was no dream, but a momentary oblivion to everything earthly. It was the mother's farewell to the soul of her son. She helped shepherd her beloved child's tender soul from his earthly to his heavenly, spiritual home, where there are no groans, nor weeping, nor suffering... nor the sorrows of earthly evil.

Weary woman.

CHAPTER 7

Excerpts from Tolstaya's memoir My Life[1]

I.16 DIARY AND NOVELLA

HERE ENDS my little travel diary. I had kept a diary from the age of eleven right up until I got married and, unfortunately, burnt all my papers before the wedding, including a long novella based on our life. In it I wrote about us three sisters, our flirtations, our family relations, various episodes. I was sixteen when I wrote the novella. Every evening I sat by the window of our classroom and wrote enthusiastically. I wrote about my sister Tanja with a special kind of love, calling her Natasha; I did a good job with her character, and when Lev Nikolaevich began describing his heroine in *War and peace*, he took a lot, including the name, from my novella. He read it a month before my wedding and was full of praise *for the pure demands on love,* as he later put it in his proposal he wrote and handed to me. He took note of some other passages which I remember he especially liked in my novella, where I was describing a youth trip to Kuntsevo.[2]

My sister Tanja was greatly interested in my novella and gave me daily encouragement. She asked me to read to her what I had written, and questioned me ahead of time: "And did you write about me?" She was delighted to recognise herself in the sweet character I portrayed in Natasha.

1   Editor's note: Passages in some of the excerpts included in this chapter reprise shorter extracts from *My Life* cited in the critical Introduction to this volume. They are cited here in full including footnotes, as a complement to the abbreviated versions included for context in Part I.
2   *Kuntsevo* — a village and recreational park west of Moscow at the time (now within the city limits).

I should also mention *what* inspired me to write this novella. When I was fifteen, my cousin Ljuba Bers[3] came to visit us, whose sister Natasha[4] had just got married. In strictest confidence this Ljuba told me and my sister Liza all the secrets of marital relations. As a girl who idealised everything, this revelation was simply horrifying to me. I went into a fit of hysterics, I threw myself on the bed and began to cry so much that Mother came running, and to her questioning as to what was wrong with me, I could only reply: "Mamà, make me forget what I heard." I can't recall just how my mother calmed me down. I remember her cursing my cousin, and that after my tears, I fell asleep.

But somehow I had to cope with my inner feelings. I decided then and there that if I were to ever get married, it would have to be to a man who was just as chaste before marriage as I.

In my novella I described such a first, *pure* love between my hero and heroine.

In the same novella I wrote about the unattractive outward appearance of the hardened Prince Dublitskij, in whose personage I described to a small extent Lev Nikolaevich, and had him marry my elder sister Liza, who not just in the novella but in real life, too, was in love with Lev Nikolaevich and planned on marrying him. This came about because one time, in the presence of our German governess, Lev Nikolaevich said in the home of his sister, Marija Nikolaevna:[5] "If the elder daughter in the family were all grown up, I would marry her, I like the whole Bers family so much."

The governess passed this along to Liza, and it set her head spinning, and she began to dream of marrying Lev Nikolaevich. I began drawing closer and friendlier to my brother's chum, Polivanov. I idealised him as the boy who loved me *first* in his life. I wrote narratives about the ideal marriage of two poor spouses, whose home was complete with flowers and a singing canary.

None of this was destined to actually come about. I am a firm believer in *destiny*, in the inevitability of everything that happens in our lives. I even learnt not to complain about anything, and not to rebuke anyone for anything, since both the kindest and most evil behaviour of people toward me were nothing but a *tool*, the *will* of that destiny that governs my life. It was this same destiny which threw me into the life of Lev Nikolaevich. His past, however — all the impure things that I learnt about and read in Lev Nikolaevich's past diaries — never *got erased from my heart and made me suffer my whole*

---

3   *Ljubov'-Marija Aleksandrovna [Ljuba/Marija] Bers* (1835–1899) — daughter to SAT's uncle Aleksandr-Gustav Evstaf'evich Bers. Since the Bers family was of German origin [German spelling: *Behrs*], many of the Bers children born in Russia were endowed with a German first name hyphenated to their Russian one (purely Russian children were never given hyphenated first names).

4   *Natal'ja Aleksandrovna Bers* (1841–1920) — sister to to SAT's first cousin Ljubov'-Marija Aleksandrovna Bers, married (1859) to *Julij Karlovich fon Mëbes* (1819–1877).

5   *Marija Nikolaevna [Mashen'ka] Tolstaya* (1830–1912) — younger sister to LNT.

life. My grandchildren, young men — everybody who ever reads this: know that the purity of your life will be a great happiness for the beloved women you meet, and a great satisfaction for your conscience.

I.23 THE NOVELLA

THIS WAS EVEN MORE FASCINATING than photography. It was with exceeding delight that I poured into my novella my cherished dreams of a *pure* first love of my heroes. It was with considerable love that I described a profile of my favourite sister Tanja, whom I called *Natasha*.

When Lev Nikolaevich wrote *War and peace*, as I indicated earlier, he, too, took my sister Tanja as a basis for his heroine and also called her *Natasha*. I don't know whether this was just a coincidence or whether my novella had given him the idea of writing about the sweet nature of my sister and giving her the name I had thought up: *Natasha*.

Before proposing to me, Lev Nikolaevich read this novella in August 1862. Unfortunately, I burnt it the week that I became engaged. At the same time, I destroyed the diary I had kept since the age of eleven. It was silly and such a shame.

I.39 LEV NIKOLAEVICH AND THE NOVELLA

AFTER COMING TO MOSCOW WITH US, Lev Nikolaevich rented a flat in the home of a German shoemaker. At the time he was busy with his school activity, along with putting out a magazine called *Yasnaya Polyana*, whose aim was purely pedagogical, mainly intended for the peasant schools. It lasted one year.

Lev Nikolaevich came to see us at Pokrovskoe almost every day. Sometimes my father would bring him out. He and I took many walks together, had many talks, and one time he asked me whether I kept a diary. I told him I made daily entries and, besides that, the previous summer I had written a long novella.

"Let me read your diaries," Lev Nikolaevich asked me.

"No, I can't."

"Then give me your novella."

I gave him the novella. The next morning I asked him whether he had read it. He answered me — calmly and indifferently — that he had. And later in his diary I read the following notation concerning his reading of my novella: *She gave me her novella to read. What energy of truth and simplicity!* And then he told me that he had not slept the whole night and was very upset about my condemnation of "Prince Dublitskij," in whom he recognised himself, in that Dublitskij was "a prince with an extraordinarily unattractive appearance" and that he was "inconsistent in his opinions."

I recall once we were all having fun and in a rather playful mood. I kept repeating the same silly line over and over: "When I am Empress, I shall do such-and-such," or "When I am Empress, I shall issue an order to…"

Near the balcony stood my father's cabriolet, from which the horses had just been unharnessed. I took a seat in the cabriolet and cried:

"When I am Empress, I shall ride in a cabriolet such as this!"

Lev Nikolaevich grasped hold of the shaft and, taking the place of the horse, began pulling me along at a trot, saying:

"And I shall take my Empress for a ride."

This episode shows how strong and healthy he was. I was having so much fun and was glad to see Lev Nikolaevich so hale and hearty.

And then one evening we were taking tea on the balcony, and Lev Nikolaevich spoke sharply to me — I don't recall what it was. Nil Aleksandrovich Popov was there too — the one who had already shown his feelings for me. I felt offended and got up from the tea table. I called to Popov and, sitting together over to one side of the balcony, I began a quiet conversation with him. It wasn't long before Lev Nikolaevich came over to us, but I still gave him the cold shoulder. Later he told me how jealous he was of Popov at that moment.

What marvellous moonlit evenings and nights we had back then! Even now I can still see the glade all illuminated by the moon, and the reflection of the moon in the nearest pond. The nights were steel-blue, fresh and invigorating.

"What crazy nights!" Lev Nikolaevich would often say, sitting with us on the balcony or taking a walk around our dacha. There were no romantic scenes or declarations, and I didn't even have a suggestion of flirtation with anyone. Instead, I was hastening to live out some marvellous free life, a maiden's life so clear that it could not be thrown off track or contaminated. Everything was easy, everything was good, nothing was lacking, there was no anxiety to get somewhere else.

Again and again Lev Nikolaevich came to us, and it was so easy and straightforward communicating with him. Sometimes he would stay the night. But all of a sudden it seemed to my father that Lev Nikolaevich was coming so often because he was in love with my mother. She was thirty-seven-and-a-half at the time; she was still quite young and had preserved her beauty. Father, eighteen years her senior, was already jealous of almost every other man's attentions to her, and so Lev Nikolaevich's visits to us were poisoned by this jealousy of my father's.

At the same time my sister Liza's hopes were rising that Lev Nikolaevich would marry *her*. Once we went to see him off — this was at the beginning of September — and when the time came for him to leave and go home, Liza began begging me to invite Lev Nikolaevich to come on 5 September, her name day.[6] I began to call after him teasingly, but he refused, acted surprised, and asked: "Why are you asking me to come specifically on the fifth?" I didn't

---

6 *name day* [Russian: *imeniny*] — the day of the saint (on the Orthodox calendar) for whom one is named; this was celebrated as people in the West celebrate birthdays. St. Elizabeth's Day was celebrated then on 5 September (O.S.; 18 September N.S.).

dare explain. Liza told me not to. Lev Nikolaevich promised to come and he came.

At first I didn't connect Lev Nikolaevich's visits with myself. But I did start to feel a strong attraction to him.

I recall one time, in a very emotional state, I ran upstairs into our girls' room with the Italian window and the view of the pond, the church and everything which had been so familiar and precious to me right from my birth. I stood by the window, and my heart was pounding. My sister Tanja walked in and realised that I was not in a calm state of mind.

"What's with you, Sonja?" she asked with concern.

"*Je crains d'aimer le comte*,"[7] I quickly and dryly answered her in French.

"You don't say?" Tanja responded in surprise. She had had no idea of my feelings, nor of my betrayal of Polivanov.

Tanja even got angry. She knew my temperament. Back then, and ever since, *aimer* meant not being amused by this feeling, but suffering.

Between the fifth and sixteenth of September our whole family moved back to Moscow. As always, upon leaving the dacha and life in Nature, I found Moscow at first to be boring, close and suffocating, and this had a dampening influence on my spirit.

Before leaving we had a custom of *saying goodbye* to our favourite spots and going around to as many as we could in a short space of time. This year I was really bidding farewell for ever to my dear Pokrovskoe with all its maidenly life.

II.16 MY REFUSAL TO DO TRANSCRIBING

WHEN LEV NIKOLAEVICH tired of creative work and began to write his religious-philosophical essays, I got tired of transcribing them. The same intense work with the same endless corrections, but this monotonous task, all revolving around the same stubborn thought with the agonisingly flat denial of everything in the world, failed to interest me to the same extent as Lev Nikolaevich's fiction or his extremely varied subject matter of previous times. Still, I kept up the copying work. But then he began his *Criticism of dogmatic theology*, which featured such coarse, even vituperative words and phrases that they sent shock waves right through my heart. Here he was heaping abuse on the church, on the priests, on Metropolitan Makarij[8] and on everything that concerned the Orthodox faith. Everything was expressed in sharp, extreme and malicious terms.

---

7 Translation from French: "I fear I'm in love with the Count."
8 *Metropolitan Makarij* (birthname: *Mikhail Petrovich Bulgakov*, 1816–1882) — appointed Archbishop in 1862, Member of the Holy Synod in 1868; he later served as Metropolitan of Moscow and Kolomenskoe (1879–82). It was after becoming acquainted with Makarij that LNT began work on his *Criticism of dogmatic theology*, based on his own analysis of Makarij's *Rukovodstvo po izucheniju khristianskogo pravoslavno-dogmaticheskogo bogoslovija* [Guide to the study of Christian Orthodox dogmatic theology].

The essay was never published in its initial form. Lev Nikolaevich subsequently toned down his rhetoric. But as a member of the church, I did not feel or share what Lev Nikolaevich was saying in this regard, and so I endured terrible sufferings in transcribing his essays. It was no use telling him that such invective was unworthy of a wise man, that it was not convincing, that evil begat evil and would not attract any good people. Lev Nikolaevich continued his indignant tirade against the church and Orthodoxy.

Then, one fine day I gathered all the papers together — his and mine — took them to him and said that I would no longer be his assistant or transcribe his invective. And so once again he was obliged to hire a copyist.

Subsequently I returned to this work, but afterward, when my eyesight started to fail and my oculist forbade any kind of work, when I had to run all the estate business, family and publishing affairs, and my time was over-booked, each of our daughters in turn began taking over the transcribing, and our youngest daughter, Sasha,[9] is even now transcribing her father's writings on a Remington typewriter. [...]

II.50 FET

ONE TIME Lev Nikolaevich went off with my sister to see D'jakov, while I stayed alone with my little Tanja, having let the nanny go off and have lunch, and I heard carriage bells. We lived closely together. The servants were all at lunch, and everything was open. A gentleman soon entered and announced himself right off, as though he were a stranger:

"Fet,[10] an old friend of your husband's. Allow me to present myself to you once again."

I didn't recognise him at first, and was terribly embarrassed. I said my husband wasn't home and invited him to take a seat. But, alas, it was time for me to breast-feed my little girl. I was holding her on my lap, and she was trying with all her might to unbutton, or rather, to tear open, my delicate white nainsook[11] dress. I was embarrassed to tears. Finally, Fet said with a smile:

"Your little maid is presenting her legitimate demands. Please don't stand on ceremony with me."

And I went off to feed her. Then I handed the baby to a nanny and went out to Fet, who later wrote about us:

"Here was a charming, blushing mother, like a Madonna, with a charming baby in her arms..."

In any case, as a poet he tended to idealise everything, but in his everyday life he was altogether a prosaist.

---

9   Aleksandra L'vovna [Sasha] Tolstaya (1884–1979) — the Tolstoys' youngest surviving child.
10 Afanasij Afanas'evich Fet (real surname: Shenshin, 1820–1892) — Russian lyrical poet and translator of poetry from German and Latin; a close friend of the Tolstoy family. See Illustration 13.
11 nainsook — a fine, soft cotton fabric, originating in India.

II.70 THE CHRISTMAS TREE — 1867

AT CHRISTMASTIDE IN 1867 the English girl Hanna and I very much wanted to put up a tree. But Lev Nikolaevich had no use for Christmas trees or any kind of decorations, and strictly forbade us buying any presents for the children. But Hanna and I managed to wangle his permission for a tree, and for buying Serëzha just one toy horse, and Tanja just one doll. We decided to invite the children of the servants and local peasants. Apart from various sweets and gilded nuts, candies, and so forth, we also bought them undressed wooden skeleton-dolls and clothed them with a wide variety of outfits, to the great delight of our children.

II.71 THE SKELETONS

LEV NIKOLAEVICH used these skeletons as a basis for a children's story about how these skeleton-dolls were lying dead and then came to life and started living with the kids of Yasnaya Polyana. He used these dolls as a pretext to describe the reality of peasant life, especially the life of peasant children, in the hut where each recipient of one of the dolls lived. Unfortunately, the first part of this story was lost, and the story was never written.

I tried using this theme to write a children's Christmas story, but I found myself quite unable to describe rural life, and so I left this story unfinished.

Hanna and I got the tree ready, and we enjoyed ourselves just like children. By the time Christmas day came, Hanna had made a plum pudding, a tradition in her homeland, and asked for roast beef and turkey, which I ordered for her pleasure. At the dinner table the plum pudding flared up when the flaming rum was poured on, and Hanna and the children were thrilled.

About forty youngsters had gathered from the servants' and village families, and the children and I were delighted to hand out all the goodies from the tree. My little ones, though tired from all the bustle, were happy with their gifts — the toy horse and the doll — which were the very first presents they had ever received.

As I was placing the candies, toys, nuts and other things into the peasant children's hands, I was surprised to see clumps of skin coming off some of these little hands, just like gloves.

"What is that?" I asked.

"You see, some kind of disease is going round the whole village," the adults answered. "First they throw up, then they get hot and a rash breaks out."

I still didn't realise that they were talking about scarlet fever, since I had never seen any victims of scarlet fever, and there was none in our family.

II.83 NIKOLAJ NIKOLAEVICH STRAKHOV

THE FIRST REVIEW OF THIS WORK [*War and peace*] was written by Nikolaj Nikolaevich Strakhov[12] and published in the journal *Zarja*.[13] This review, replete with high praise for the author, served to initiate our acquaintance with Strakhov, this clever man who was so well versed in all branches of learning.

According to Lev Nikolaevich, Strakhov's review imbued *War and peace* with the high significance which the novel would come to enjoy many years later, and which it continued to enjoy forever thereafter. All the more so since Saltykov (Shchedrin),[14] who at that time was living in Tula, gave a very negative review of this work, saying that *War and peace* reminded him of the chatterbox tales of old nannies and grannies. Even though Saltykov had been earlier acquainted with Lev Nikolaevich, he never came once to see us during his posting in Tula.

If I had thought about it earlier, there is so much more I could have said about this dear man, Nikolaj Nikolaevich Strakhov. My whole fascination for his personage was linked, of course, to his intellectual and spiritual life. To outward appearances he was a quiet, taciturn and unassuming old bachelor. He had a large, marvellous library of books he had chosen for himself; he acquired *the very best* (as he himself believed) work by each author. He left his collection to the Petersburg Public Library, where he had served for many years as a librarian.

He was the son of a priest and a graduate of the University of St. Petersburg. He was a master of the natural sciences and possessed tremendous knowledge in all branches of learning. During our walks together I might ask him about this or that and he would give me a detailed but brief, clear and logical account of anything I wanted to know. In just a few words he could outline a fine explanation of Darwin's[15] theory, which I had not read up on myself, for lack of time. And another time he told me all about the stars, and a better lesson in astronomy was not to be had.

He was a great lover of literature and wrote many reviews, but by the bent of his mind he was above all a philosopher. Lev Nikolaevich often told him verbally or in a letter that he should devote himself exclusively to philosophy. To which Strakhov would occasionally reply to Lev Nikolaevich that, yes, he was right, but "what can I do when I *like* to write reviews so much?"

12 *Nikolaj Nikolaevich Strakhov* (1828–1896) — Russian philosopher, librarian, literary critic and long-time editorial associate of LNT and SAT. For his correspondence with both Tolstoy and Tolstaya (reproduced in Russian only), see Donskov 2000 and 2003. See Illustration 15.
13 *Zarja* — a Slavophile journal published in 1869–1872, founded in 1869 by *Vladimir Nikitich Kashpirëv* (1839–1879), a Russian writer with moderately conservative, Slavophile leanings. Publication ceased in 1872 for lack of subscriptions.
14 *Mikhail Evgrafovich Saltykov-Shchedrin* (real surname: *Saltykov*, 1826–1889) — Russian satirical writer and political commentator; he frequently criticised Russia's historical backwardness in relation to Western Europe. He and LNT had frequent encounters from 1856 to 1858.
15 *Charles Robert Darwin* (1809–1882) — English naturalist who promoted the theory of natural selection. His most famous work was *On the Origin of Species*, published in 1859.

Visiting us for the most part in the summertime, coming only occasionally for special holidays during the winter months, Nikolaj Nikolaevich was always extravagant in his praise for life at Yasnaya Polyana, always expressing his gratitude for the benefits he derived from this life. Thus, for example, on the 17th of August 1877 he wrote Lev Nikolaevich:

"I feel like another person, as though I had found that norm of vigour and seriousness which I am destined to hold onto for ever."[16]

He endeavoured with all his might to be helpful to Lev Nikolaevich and when it came to the second edition of *War and peace* he offered to do the necessary corrections on typographical and other errors. Apart from that, he conducted negotiations with publishers about the publication of *War and peace*. While he did bargain with them, he never came to any agreement with them.

When it came to publishing *A primer* and *Readers*, once again Nikolaj Nikolaevich endeavoured to play an active role in helping Lev Nikolaevich. He himself undertook the proofreading and correction of *A primer* in 1872. This is what he wrote about it from Mshatka, from Danilevskij's[17] [estate]: "I haven't yet got around to proofreading *A primer* — Danilevskij's children are eagerly reading it."[18]

He also wrote Lev Nikolaevich, saying that there had been too few announcements [in the press] about *A primer*. Later he was upset that he had done a poor job of proofreading and that there were still many uncorrected typographical errors.

In 1874 he showed *A primer* and *Readers* to the Scholarly Commission and said that they subjected it to a point-by-point criticism. In his letter of 22 September 1874 he wrote:

"No matter what you propose, it will be rejected because it contradicts what has already been accepted and proved."[19]

Lev Nikolaevich loved Strakhov and always had respect for his opinions and his tremendous education.

Strakhov had also endeared himself to my sister Tat'jana Andreevna Kuzminskaja, with whom Nikolaj Nikolaevich had dinner in Petersburg on Tuesdays. My children, too, especially Serëzha, treated Strakhov with love, trust and respect, and he loved them as old bachelors with no families love the families of their dearest and closest friends.

---

16 Strakhov's letter to LNT of 16–17 August 1877, reproduced (in Russian) in Donskov 2003: I: 356.
17 *Nikolaj Jakovlevich Danilevskij* (1822–1885) — Russian sociologist, economist, natural scientist, political commentator and a promoter of *pan-slavism*. His estate, *Mshatka*, was located not far from Simeiz in the Crimea. Tolstoy made a memorable visit to Danilevskij at Mshatka in March 1885 (Donskov 2003: II: 678).
18 Strakhov's letter to LNT of 4 December 1872 (Donskov 2003: I: 83).
19 Strakhov's letter to LNT of 22 September 1874 (Donskov 2003: I: 179).

Nikolaj Nikolaevich Strakhov visited us for the last time in 1895,[20] follow-ing my son Vanechka's death. He had just had an operation on his tongue. They had cut out a tumour, but the poison remained in his blood, and some-how got into his brain. Nikolaj Nikolaevich passed away in Petersburg the following winter [on 24 January 1896], quite suddenly.

III.26 BEGINNING OF [LEV NIKOLAEVICH'S] RELIGIOUS WRITINGS
SOON [...] he began writing his comprehensive treatise on religion. For this he picked up a large notebook and told me:

"What I write in this large notebook reflects my aim of proving the absolute necessity of religion." But at that time Lev Nikolaevich still had not included in his philosophical-religious writings that spite for the church, its rituals and clergy, which he would later spew forth so vehemently in his *Criticism of dog-matic theology*. At this point it was still just in its beginning stages, and much of the malice and acrimony was eventually expunged.

Back then his mood was good and meek, he was searching for God and an escape from faithlessness and doubts.

I wrote about him in my diary:

> Lev Nikolaevich's character keeps changing more and more. Even though he has always been modest and undemanding in his habits, now he is becoming even more modest, meek and patient. And this eternal struggle, which began in his youth, with moral self-perfection as its goal, is being crowned with complete success.

At that time Lev Nikolaevich read quite a number of books on religion. He became interested in Renan,[21] and in December Nikolaj Nikolaevich Strakhov sent him Renan's *Les Apôtres*, saying that, as far as he was concerned, this was the best of all Renan's books.

III.38 TURGENEV AND URUSOV
IN AUGUST we were expecting a visit from Turgenev,[22] with whom Lev Nikolaevich had a longstanding disagreement. I made a note about this as follows:

20 Strakhov's visit lasted from 4 July to 9 August 1895.
21 *Joseph Ernest Renan* (1823–1892) — French philosopher, writer and historian. His insistence on scientific objectivity in examining the Bible and its personages brought him into conflict with the Roman Catholic Church and resulted in his dismissal as professor of Hebrew from *Le Collège de France* in 1862. He is known especially for his popular work *Vie de Jésus* (1863), written from the standpoint of historical biography rather than theology. His work *Les Apôtres* was published in 1866.
22 *Ivan Sergeevich Turgenev* (1818–1883) — Russian classical writer and poet, his most famous works being *Otsy i deti* [*Fathers and children*] (1862) and *Zapiski okhotnika* [A hunter's notebook/A sportsman's sketches (the book is known in English under various translations of the title)] (1852). See Illustration 14.

Getting more and more into a religious mood, Lev Nikolaevich became saddened by the thought that there was someone he seemed to be on inimical terms with, and that spring he had written a letter to Turgenev in Paris which included the sentence: "Forgive me for what I am guilty of in your eyes." Turgenev responded: "I am happy to shake your extended hand."

And on the 8th of August Turgenev came to see us for a couple of days, to try and persuade Lev Nikolaevich to take part in the celebrations being organised in Moscow in memory of the poet Pushkin.[23] Lev Nikolaevich was not favourably disposed to any kind of ceremonies, celebrations, speeches or dinners. He never took part in them and refused Turgenev on this occasion, too.

Turgenev came by to see us again in September.[24]

Lev Nikolaevich engaged in a good deal of philosophising and arguing with Turgenev. I recall one day the dinner hour had come, but both Turgenev and Lev Nikolaevich were nowhere to be seen. I followed a hunch and headed out to search for them in the Chepyzh forest, in Lev Nikolaevich's new little cabin. I went in, and there, indeed, stood the imposing figure of Ivan Sergeevich, his face all red, arguing something and gesticulating, and Lev Nikolaevich, also in a heated mood, trying to prove something to his interlocutor. Unfortunately, I was not able to hear what this *something* was.

In the evening the arguments took on a purely religious-philosophical tone.

Another guest at that time was Prince Leonid Dmitrievich Urusov,[25] an avid follower of Lev Nikolaevich's teachings on Christianity, a frequent visitor to Yasnaya Polyana and a tremendously loyal friend to all its residents. Later this Prince Urusov did marvellous translations — first, *Les Méditations de Marc Aurèle*[26] [into Russian] and then Lev Nikolaevich's work *V chëm moja vera?* [*Ma religion*][27] into French.

23 *Aleksandr Sergeevich Pushkin* (1799–1837) — universally acknowledged as Russia's greatest poet of all time. The celebrations in question, to be held 26 May (6 June N.S.) 1880 (the poet's birthday) included the unveiling of sculptor Aleksandr Mikhajlovich Opekushin's (1838–1923) statue of the poet on Strastnaja Square in Moscow (renamed Pushkin Square on the centenary of the poet's death in 1937). Laudatory speeches were given at the 1880 celebrations by both Turgenev and Dostoevsky.

24 In fact, LNT continued his meetings with Turgenev up until July 1881, when they met for the last time at Turgenev's Spasskoe-Lutovinovo estate. (See: Pokrovskaja and Shumova 1978: 129).

25 *Prince Leonid Dmitrievich Urusov* (1837–1885) — deputy governor of Tula Gubernia (1876–85) and family friend of the Tolstoys, with whom he became acquainted in early 1878. He was also known for his literary translations between French and Russian. See Illustration 16.

26 *Marcus Aurelius Antoninus Augustus* (121–180 CE) — Roman Emperor (161–80), known also as a stoic philosopher. He was known in French as *Marc Aurèle*. His *Méditations* [Russian title: *Izrechenija Marka Avrelija*] were written ca. 167 CE.

27 *V chëm moja vera?* — English title: *What I believe*.

Urusov was fond of any religious-philosophical works and ideas. At that time, he got me interested in reading the philosophers: Seneca,[28] Marcus Aurelius, Plato,[29] Epictetus[30] and others. With great enthusiasm I set about reading all of them at once, copying passages and literally drinking it all in. This was a field nobody had ever opened up to me, except in my youth, when I was sixteen years old, I read a lot of philosophical materialists — such as Büchner and Feuerbach[31] — at the recommendation of my Russian teacher.[32] Now, when Urusov enlightened me and showed me the beauty, depth and importance of philosophical questions, I devoted myself completely, with my customary fervour and energy, to the joy of reading, especially the ancient thinkers, and made copious notes and even memorised certain passages.

He and I often talked on all sorts of subjects connected with people's spiritual life in both ancient and modern times, and when he later translated *What I believe* [*V chëm moja vera?*][33] we checked the translation together, and the Prince reminded me of all the grand thoughts of my husband's and predicted that in time they would spread throughout the world. Once when he and I were working together, he suddenly said to me:

"Isn't it true, Countess, that nothing brings or ties people together more than joint intellectual work?"

III.39 THREE SIGNIFICANT PERIODS

THERE WERE THREE SIGNIFICANT PERIODS in my life that had a considerable influence on me. The first was the reading of Lev Nikolaevich's *Childhood* and *Boyhood*, which revealed to me the beauty of the *word*, the beauty of literary creativity. This is how I fell in love with literature, how I got started studying it. All during my early youth, at thirteen, fourteen and fifteen, I read my fill of all the Russian *literati*, along with many foreign writers, both in the original and in translation. But as for Lev Nikolaevich, who had opened up the treasure of literature to me through his *Childhood*, I naturally began to poeticise him, to love him as a human being. And, despite all the ups and downs in our lives, I have never stopped loving him.

28 *Lucius Annaeus Seneca (Seneca the Younger,* ca. 4 BCE–65 CE) — Roman Stoic philosopher, dramatist and statesman, tutor and advisor to the Emperor Nero; also the author of 124 essays known as *Epistulae morales* and a number of tragic dramas.
29 *Plato* (ca. 429–ca. 348 BCE) — classical Greek philosopher, whose work, along with that of his mentor Socrates and student Aristotle, underlies much of current Western philosophy.
30 *Epictetus* (ca. 55–ca. 135 CE) — Greek stoic philosopher, who rose from slave status to teaching positions in philosophy in Rome and Greece, eventually founding his own school of philosophy at Epirus (Greece).
31 *Friedrich Karl Christian Ludwig Büchner* (1824–1899) and *Ludwig Andreas von Feuerbach* (1804–1872) — German materialist philosophers.
32 See *My Life,* Chapter I.18 ("Study and the teacher").
33 Also known as *Where happiness lies.*

The second significant period in my spiritual life was the time when I learnt to know the beauty of the philosophical thinking of the sages, who afforded me so much by way of spiritual development and even helped me live, simply through their wisdom. It was L. D. Urusov who set me and later guided me along this path. I became quite attached to him, and loved him for a long time because of this, — in fact, I have never really stopped loving him either, even though he has been dead a long time. Besides, we were united in our love for Lev Nikolaevich, as well as by [Urusov's] interest in religious studies.

My acquaintance with the prince began at the Samarins'[34] home in Tula. We were having dinner there together and, when Urusov was introduced to me, I didn't like him at all.

Artificial, even to the point of putting on airs, naïve and less than clever, speaking exclusively in an unnatural French — this is how Urusov appeared to me back then. At that time he had just been appointed deputy governor of Tula, where he settled down. But all these outward failings of the prince's disappeared once I got to know him better. He was unhappy with his wife, whom, apparently, he never stopped loving. But his wife Monja,[35] *née* Mal'tseva, was a very unpleasant woman, who had lived almost all her life in Paris, and with a poor reputation to boot. I knew her, she was at our place, and when I asked why she wasn't living with such a good husband and was depriving their father of his three little girls and his boy Serëzha, she said, amidst other cynical arguments:

"*C'est un amant fort ennuyeux, mon mari!*"[36]

Another time, during her time at Yasnaya Polyana, she sat smoking with her hands down at her sides, and I sat opposite her. She fixed her glittering, malicious-looking and smart dark-grey eyes on me and said with a malevolent grin:

"*J'ai grande envie de dire au comte que ce ne sont pas ses principes que mon mari aime, mais que c'est* sa femme!"[37]

She put great emphasis on the last word and burst out into raucous laughter. I attached the most mundane sense possible to this last phrase, telling her calmly that I was certain the prince was a bit fond of me, just as I was of him, that we were on quite friendly terms, and that the one did not interfere with the other.

This was true. We were both always happy to see each other whenever we met or when the prince came to spend a weekend with our family.

34 *Pëtr Fëdorovich Samarin* (1830–1901) — a Tula landowner, who served as the Gubernia representative for the nobility in the latter half of the 1870s; an old acquaintance of LNT's.
35 *Marija Sergeevna [Monja] Urusova (née Mal'tseva, 1844–1904)* — daughter to *Sergej Ivanovich Mal'tsev* (1810–1894), a factory owner in Brjansk Uezd of Orël Gubernia (which would later become part of Brjansk Gubernia).
36 Translation from French: "He's a very boring lover, my husband is."
37 Translation from French: "I have a great desire to tell the Count that it's not his principles that my husband likes, but his wife!"

His relationship to me was gentlemanly and courteous, albeit occasionally a little on the ecstatic side. But we never, either in word or gesture, hinted at anything in the way of a romance between us.

At one time somebody told the story of a lady who left her husband and ran off with her lover, but was unhappy with him, while in the meantime her family life had been ruined. Urusov leant over to me and said quietly:

"*On ne détruit pas le bonheur d'une femme qu'on aime. N'est-ce pas, comtesse?*"[38]

And in his voice I could detect a kind of sad tenderness. And if in each of our hearts there was a slightly exaggerated feeling of attachment, we might have said in the words of Paul Bourget:[39]

"*C'est une liaison indéfinissable, où il ne se prononce jamais un mot trop tendre — et tout y est tendresse; où il ne se hasarde jamais un geste caressant, et tout y est caresse...*"[40]

And Prince Urusov spread this tendresse over my whole family — including me, and my children, and my sister Tanja, with whom he passionately played croquet for hours on end, and whom he loved to hear sing.

Most important of all, the prince simply adored Lev Nikolaevich. He played chess with him, talked a great deal with him on religious topics, and kept up an active correspondence with him. He would often say to me that we would live to see the day when Lev Nikolaevich would be renowned throughout the world.

The prince was loved in our house by the children and even the staff. Only Tanja was abrupt with him and did not like him. For Prince Urusov I always ordered a tastier dinner, put on a prettier dress, rehearsed what I planned to talk about with him, and occasionally flirted with him — more mentally than physically, trying to please him. But that was all.

The prince would bring me huge bouquets of flowers. He would arrive with candy and books, and loved to shower our whole family with presents. He gave me a rather fine pair of scissors, as well as a Saxon porcelain doll and a fan to Tanja, etc., etc. He had a rare knack for bestowing gifts simply and cheerfully.

In my subsequent life-story Prince Urusov's name will crop up quite frequently, and that is why I have written about him here.

---

38 Translation from French: "One does not destroy the happiness of a woman one loves. Isn't that so, Countess?"

39 *Paul Bourget* (1852–1935) — French poet, novelist and critic, who used the pen-name *Claude Larcher.*

40 Cited from: Paul Bourget, *Physiologie de l'amour moderne. Fragments posthumes d'un ouvrage de Claude Larcher recueillis et publiés par Paul Bourget, son exécuteur testamentaire* (Paris, 1891). Translation from French: "It is an elusive liaison where one is ever careful not to utter a word too tender, and yet everything is [infused with] tenderness; where one never risks a caressing gesture, and yet everything is [infused with] caressing."

I shall conclude my confession by talking about the third period which significantly influenced my life. I shall write about it in more detail, if I live long enough, when I come to 1895. For the moment I shall offer but a brief sketch.

This was the time following the death of my little son Vanechka.[41] I was in a state of extreme despair — the kind that happens only once in a lifetime. Such a state of sorrow is usually fatal, and those that survive are not in a condition to endure such heart-wrenching suffering a second time. But I did survive, and for that I am obliged to chance, as well as to the mysterious medium of... *music*.

At first after the death of my beloved boy I kept praying, went around to various monasteries and churches and lived completely in God. In one church I caught cold, took seriously ill and almost died.

In the spring I managed to pull myself together and my health began to improve. I decided to go see my sister in Kiev, again in the same prayerful mood.

One day in May, after recovering and returning to Moscow, [where we were living at the time,] I was sitting on the balcony. It was a warm day, and the whole garden had already turned green. Sergej Ivanovich Taneev[42] dropped by — someone I hardly knew and felt rather uncomfortable with. To make conversation, I asked him where he would be spending the summer. He replied that he didn't know, that he was looking to rent some kind of *dacha* [cottage] on a country estate.

And then all at once it came to me that our annexe at Yasnaya Polyana was empty, and I offered it to him on the condition that I must first consult with my family. I myself was morally reaching out for anything that would take my mind off my life with Vanechka, and the presence of someone who was completely oblivious of my sadness to date — and was a pretty good pianist to boot — seemed quite desirable to me.

But fate has a hand in everything, and our own will counts for so little in comparison with God's.

And so, one way or another, Taneev came to us at Yasnaya Polyana and took up residence in the annexe along with his dear old nurse, Pelageja Vasil'evna.[43] He did not want to impose on us and insisted that we rent the annexe to him and that he pay us in full. He and Tanja agreed on a payment of 100 roubles for the summer, and I at once put this sum aside for the poor — it was too hot for me to hold for any length of time.

41 *Ivan L'vovich Tolstoy* (1888–1895) — affectionately known as *Vanechka*.
42 *Sergej Ivanovich Taneev* [also spelt: *Taneyev*] (1856–1915) — Russian pianist and composer, professor (and later director) of the Moscow Conservatory. His most famous composition is the opera *Oresteia* (1894). Taneev was a frequent visitor to the Tolstoy home and made a particular impression on SAT. See also Chapter VI.117 ("Sergej Ivanovich Taneev") p. 492 in this volume, as well as Illustration 17.
43 *Pelageja Vasil'evna Chizhova* (1825–1910) — nanny to Taneev in his youth; later cook, housekeeper, secretary and caregiver.

Taneev had quite a bit of contact with the young people. You could often hear his strange, jolly laugh when [the residents of Yasnaya Polyana] went for walks all together or played tennis. He studied Italian along with Tanja and Masha, played chess with Lev Nikolaevich, and they had a wager: whoever lost a match was obliged to carry out his opponent's wishes. In other words, if Taneev lost, he would have to play something suggested by Lev Nikolaevich, while if Lev Nikolaevich lost, he would have to read something he had written, according to Sergej Ivanovich's request.

I recall the strange inner awakening I felt upon hearing Taneev's wonderful, deep playing. My sadness and heartfelt longings somehow disappeared, and my heart was filled with joy and serenity. Each time the playing stopped, my heart was once more overwhelmed by sorrow, despair and a lack of desire to go on living.

But then Sergej Ivanovich would lose a match, and start playing a Beethoven sonata, or Chopin's *Polonaise in A-flat major*, or the *Freischütz* overture,[44] Mendelssohn's *Songs without words*, variations by Beethoven and Mozart and many, many more wonderful pieces. As I listened, I felt more and more often a tinge of delight within me, and my heartaches would grow lighter, and I would wait for the healing music with agonising anticipation.

And then Taneev might invite us to his rooms in the annexe to hear his opera *Oresteia*, which he played and tried to sing, even though he did not have a voice, but this came across as rather strange and not very pretty. And I gladly listened to this music, which exuded so much beauty, as I sat serenely in my chair and allowed my sadness to dissipate.

Sometimes Taneev would play over a particular scene time and again, unaware that I was listening, while I sat on the annexe's porch, listening to him play through the open windows, and I felt at ease.

This went on for two summers, and for part of the winter, too. I became intoxicated by music and got so accustomed to hearing it that I found myself no longer able to live without it. I subscribed to concerts and listened to music wherever I could, and even started taking lessons myself.

But Taneev's music affected me most and best of all. It was he who first taught me, through his marvellous playing, to listen to and love music. I made every effort to hear his playing wherever and however I could, and would arrange to meet him just for this purpose — just so that I could ask him to play. Occasionally, when I did not manage to do this for some time, I felt sad, tormented by the burning desire to hear him play once more, or even just to see him.

His presence had a beneficial effect on me whenever I started feeling a longing for Vanechka. I would weep and feel the energy drain from my life. Sometimes all it took to calm me down was to meet with Sergej Ivanovich and

44 *Der Freischütz* [*The marksman*] — an opera composed between 1817 and 1821 by the German composer *Carl Maria von Weber* (1786–1826) — German composer of the early Romantic school.

hear his quieting, dispassionate voice. I had already got accustomed to being calmed by his presence and especially his playing. It was a kind of hypnosis, an involuntary influence on my aching soul — one he was completely unaware of.

It was not a normal state to be in. It happened to coincide with my change of life. For all my moodiness I remained virtually unaffected by Taneev's personality. Outwardly he was nothing to look at. He was always even-tempered, extremely closed in, and an utterly inscrutable person, as far as I was concerned. One often imagines that behind a person's inscrutability lies something deep, special and significant, and, indeed, that was how Taneev could sometimes appear to me. It seemed as though in his daily life he repressed any trace of the impulse and passion which his music bestowed so beautifully, irrepressibly and fascinatingly upon his listeners, revealing the inner world of the performer. I shall be writing more about my relationship to him and our further acquaintance when I come to the year 1895 in my memoirs.

For healing my sorrowful soul unintentionally through his music — he didn't even know about it — I have remained forever grateful to him, and I have never stopped loving him. He was the first to *open* the door for me to an *understanding* of music, just as Lev Nikolaevich led me to the understanding of the literary arts, just as Prince Urusov gave me an understanding of and love for philosophy. Once you enter upon these scenes of spiritual delight, you never want to leave them and you constantly come back to them.

What feelings I experienced during those twelve years of profound delight from concerts and listening to music! How many times, when tormented by various unpleasantries at home, complications in family and business affairs, etc., I would go to a concert and hear fine music, or even play myself, and I would all at once feel a sense of peace, joy, serenity, and come to terms with life's challenges.

As far as any kind of romantic relationship to the *performers* of musical works was concerned, I refused to entertain such a thought. I would always deny it and was actually afraid of it, even though there was one time when the influence of Taneev's personality was very strong. Once that kind of feeling surfaces, it kills any sense of importance in the music and art. I wrote a long piece on that.[45]

III.40 TURGENEV AND URUSOV (CONTINUED)
I SHALL NOW GO BACK to my description of the year 1878, from which I digressed after mentioning Ivan Sergeevich Turgenev's visit to Yasnaya Polyana. My reminiscences of him I published in the *Orlovskij vestnik* of 22

---

45 The narrative "Song without words" was written by SAT between 1895 and 1898 and revised in 1900, but never published. This is to be distinguished from Leah Bendavid-Val's 2007 publication *Song without words: the photographs and diaries of Countess Sophia Tolstoy* (see Bibliography, latter part of Section I).

August 1903, after hastily writing down in fragmentary form (at the request of Mikhail Aleksandrovich Stakhovich[46]) a few words on Turgenev,[47] in which I made a few mistakes in reference to the years and months.

On the evening which I had been describing earlier there were some rather heated arguments, and Prince [Leonid Dmitrievich] Urusov, while trying to prove a point to Turgenev, suddenly flew back from the table on his chair and fell, landing at once in a sitting position on the parquet floor. He went on sitting there, practically under the table, still continuing his heated argument with expressive gestures, which provoked general laughter in the room, while Turgenev, deliberately distorting Urusov's name, backed away from the table with a wearisome look and said:

"Oh, this Trubetskoj[48] has me completely worn out; he'll drive me out of my mind with those arguments of his!" During this visit Turgenev described to us with amazing artistry his impressions of Antokol'skij's[49] statue, as well as about *Pegas the Dog*.[50]

III.73 STUDYING THE GOSPELS — LEV NIKOLAEVICH'S DIFFICULT DISPOSITION

AT THAT TIME Lev Nikolaevich had surrounded himself with all sorts of books on religious themes and continued working on studying the Gospels. He became oblivious of life and was delving wholeheartedly into *thought*. I wrote about him (I don't recall whether it was in my diary or a letter):

> Lev Nikolaevich has become quiet, concentrated and taciturn. He is by no means as happy as I would have wished. That lively, cheerful spirit that he had

46 *Mikhail Aleksandrovich Stakhovich* (1861–1923) — poet and writer from Orël Gubernia, who switched from his liberal views to being an arch-conservative and in the 1900s participated in the first and second State Dumas as a right-wing deputy. Following the February 1917 revolution he served as Governor-General of what was then the Russian province of Finland for the Provisional Government.

47 Note by SAT: "See the end of Book 3 of my autobiography." In this case it appears that she may actually be referring to *My Life* — see Chapters III.115 ("More about Turgenev") below, as well as III.143 ("More on Turgenev and censorship") in *My Life*. But SAT did write a separate *Autobiography* (see Introduction).

48 *Trubetskoj* — no specific reference. In this case it appears that Turgenev is simply teasing Urusov by substituting a different princely name for his.

49 *Mark Matveevich Antokol'skij* (1843–1902) — Russian sculptor born of Jewish parents in Vilnius (then part of the Russian Empire), who in the 1870s was working in Rome and Paris. He won top honours at the Paris World's Fair in 1878 and was awarded the French Legion of Honour. The statue mentioned here is Antokol'skij's *Khristos pered sudom naroda* [Christ before the people's court]. A bronze version, made in 1874, is housed in the State Russian Museum in St. Petersburg, while the marble variant (1876) is in the Tret'jakov Gallery in Moscow.

50 *Pegas the Dog* [Russian: *Sobaka Pegas*] — the title of a painting by the artist and memoirist *Il'ja Efimovich Repin* (1844–1930) — celebrated Ukrainian-born Russian artist and memoirist. The painting is housed in the Ekaterinburg Museum of Visual Arts. Repin, a close friend of LNT's, had many discussions with him about art, and did quite a few portraits of the writer using various media.

when he was writing his fiction hardly ever breaks through any more. When he was describing a ball, or hunting, for example, he would catch the experience himself and come alive…

All this weighs heavily upon me. Life does not wait, and its demands pour in from all sides…

His health also started to go, he lost weight and aged, and his hair went grey over that winter. Never again would Lev Nikolaevich display that cheerful liveliness which had always attracted and infected all of us around him.

And I felt sad about his works, about how his inner view had completely turned in the direction of poverty, suffering, malice, people's injustice, oppression, war, prisons etc.

I couldn't help thinking: "Aren't there any happy people?"

Concerning his perception of the world, Lev Nikolaevich said that he had changed his whole view of people. Before there was a small, known circle of people close to *him*, whereas now millions of people had become his brethren.

Everybody at the time was decidedly interested in Lev Nikolaevich's change of heart and looked for the reasons behind it. They were upset that he had abandoned his fiction writing.

Countess Aleksandra Andreevna Tolstaya[51] wrote to Lev Nikolaevich, saying that Dostoevsky[52] was very interested in Lev Nikolaevich's mood and asked him to let him have whatever religious articles he had recently written. But Dostoevsky never had a chance to read Lev Nikolaevich's latest writings, since he unexpectedly died that same year, 1881. Back on the 3rd of February I wrote that while Lev Nikolaevich did not know Dostoevsky [personally], he was saddened by his death.[53]

I also recall that Sergej Andreevich Jur'ev[54] came to see us and questioned me in some detail on how Lev Nikolaevich had got into that state of religious seeking in which he found himself at the time, and why he had quit writing

51 *Countess Aleksandra Andreevna Tolstaya* (1817–1904) — daughter of *Andrej Andreevich Tolstoy* (1771–1844), whose brother, *Il'ja Andreevich Tolstoy* (1757–1820) was LNT's paternal grandfather. In 1846 she was appointed lady-in-waiting to the Imperial Court and in 1866 governess to *Grand Duchess Marija Aleksandrovna*.

52 *Fëdor Mikhajlovich Dostoevsky* (1821–1881) — one of Russia's greatest novelists, probably best known in the West for his novel *Crime and punishment* [*Prestuplenie i nakazanie*] (1866) and *The brothers Karamazov* [*Brat'ja Karamazovy*] (1879–80). See Illustration 33. Fëdor Mikhajlovich Dostoevsky passed away on 28 January 1881 (O.S.; 9 February N.S.).

53 SAT is evidently referring to her letter to her sister *Tat'jana Andreevna Kuzminskaja* of 2 February 1881, in which she wrote that LNT was "terribly shocked" by the news of Dostoevsky's death. See Pokrovskaja and Shumova 1978: 129.

54 *Sergej Andreevich Jur'ev* (1821–1888) — a prominent Russian literary figure, who trained and worked as an astronomer before devoting himself to literature. He also translated a number of Shakespeare's plays into Russian, as well as Goethe from German. From 1880 to 1885 he served as the first editor of the journal *Russkaja mysl'*, and subsequently (1886–88) as chairman of the Society of Russian Drama Writers.

and abandoned his interest in *The Decembrists.*[55] It was difficult for me to explain it all to Jur'ev. I had lived too closely with Lev Nikolaevich to take note of the moment when the change happened. I told Jur'ev as much as I could, from my point of view, about Lev Nikolaevich's spiritual journeys and seekings in the area of religion. He liked what I had to say, and even asked me to write it down, which I did.

Regarding S. A. Jur'ev, Strakhov would later write: "He worked out a philosophical formula [to account for] Tolstoy's development and explained to me the stage of development he was currently at."[56]

While people on all sides were analysing and discussing him, Lev Nikolaevich was going his own way, seeking, tormenting himself, and listening to all sorts of religious beliefs. For example, he asked my sister's husband, Aleksandr Mikhajlovich Kuzminskij, to find out in Khar'kov, where he was currently serving, whether there were any *Stundists*[57] there, what their situation was and whether or not there really was such a sect there. He was even prepared to go to Khar'kov At the same time Lev Nikolaevich asked him to find out whether a certain Garshin[58] (a writer, still little known back then) were possibly being held in a Khar'kov insane asylum, and how he was doing.

To this my brother-in-law [Aleksandr Mikhajlovich] Kuzminskij replied from Khar'kov on 14 February 1881 that there were no Stundists there, and that Lev Nikolaevich was probably confusing them with the *Sabbatarians,*[59] who were quite numerous in Khar'kov.

III.88 REMINISCENCES ABOUT TURGENEV

I REMEMBER Ivan Sergeevich Turgenev from back in my father's home — he had known my father since childhood.

My father had been a household doctor to the Turgenev family, and Turgenev's mother was especially well disposed toward my father. In one of his letters to me, my father mentioned that in 1831[60] he went to Paris by carriage, along the highway, with Ivan Sergeevich Turgenev. The return journey with him from Paris to Moscow took twenty-eight days and he was so tired

---

55 *Decembrists* — a secret group of élite officers from noble families whose plans for a revolt to overthrow autocracy and serfdom and institute either a republic or a constitutional monarchy culminated in an uprising on 14 December (26 December N.S.) 1825. For LNT's literary interest in this movement, see *My Life,* II.13.

56 From Strakhov's letter to LNT dated 6 March 1881, reproduced in Donskov 2003: II: 594–95.

57 *Stundists* (or *Stundobaptists*) — an evangelical movement of German Baptists in Ukraine, named for the *Bibelstunden* [Bible hours] they organised.

58 *Vsevolod Mikhajlovich Garshin* (1855–1888) — Russian writer who wrote his first drama at five years of age. Several of his stories were written in the spirit of LNT's "stories for the people" (e.g., *Skazanie o gordom Aggee* [Tale of the proud Aggej], 1886; *Signal,* 1887).

59 *Sabbatarians* [Russian: *subbotniki*] — an offshoot of the Molokans, who insisted on observing Saturday [*subbota*] as their day of worship, in contrast to the *voskresniki,* who worshipped on Sunday [*voskresen'e*]. See Donskov 2008a: 24.

60 Probably not the correct date, as Turgenev was born only in 1818.

that he fell ill.

Whenever Turgenev came for a stay in Moscow from abroad, he would always pay us a visit. I have a vague recollection of how distant Turgenev's face seemed to be when I threw back my little head and delighted in looking up at the kindly eyes and the black braid of long hair falling from [the head of] this huge man.

He would lift us up in his giant arms, kiss us and say something tender or tell us a brief but interesting story.

After that he didn't come around for a long time. We grew up, and the next time we chanced to see him, his hair had already gone grey.

"The little girls have become young ladies," he said. "Now I can no longer kiss you, but please do offer your hand."

My sister was fifteen back then, and I was fourteen. He kissed our hands, shook his head and said:

"Pity that the little girls have grown up."

When I got married, I found out that there was some kind of misunderstanding between my husband and Turgenev, and they hadn't seen each other for a long time. This bothered me, but I was glad to see this work out over the years, and Turgenev twice visited us at Yasnaya Polyana. [61]

The first time was in 1878. He came to invite Lev Nikolaevich to take part in the ceremonial unveiling of a monument to Pushkin and was very upset at Lev Nikolaevich's refusal. [62]

Ivan Sergeevich did not stay very long with us this time, but the memories of his visit remain very pleasant. His reconciliation with Lev Nikolaevich was cherished by both men, and Ivan Sergeevich (as I recall) took delight in everything: Russian nature, the village, our family life, and even Russian food.

It was spring. [63] Knowing Ivan Sergeevich's love for Nature and gun hunting, Lev Nikolaevich invited him and all of us to [accompany him on] a woodcock hunt. In the dusk we harnessed the longwagon, and we all headed off into the young birch forest on the edge of the government preserve [*Zaseka*]. It was a lovely spring evening, but the hunt was unsuccessful. Someone took a shot at a flying woodcock, but we couldn't find the [fallen] bird.

Turgenev stood with me beside a huge oak tree which had not yet been dressed in foliage and was fiddling with his rifle, when I asked him:

"Why have you gone so long without writing anything, Ivan Sergeevich?"

Turgenev looked about him and smiled a guilty smile, which I found

61 Earlier in Part III SAT describes three visits by Turgenev to Yasnaya Polyana: August 1878, September 1878 and spring 1880.
62 SAT earlier describes this visit as taking place in August 1878. See Chapters III.38 ("Turgenev and Urusov") and III.40 ("Turgenev and Urusov (continued)") above.
63 SAT inadvertently switches to 1880, here, as she also describes the following conversation in Chapter III.59 ("Practical matters — Spring 1880 and Turgenev's arrival") in *My Life*.

especially charming in this physically huge man, and said:

"Nobody can hear us. Well, I'll tell you that whenever I was about to write anything, I would be shaken by a feverish influx of *love*. That's gone now, I'm old, and can no longer either love or write."

When I asked Turgenev that evening what I could offer him tomorrow in the way of food, he asked me to prepare a "purely Russian dinner": soup with semolina, flavoured a little more with dill, a round chicken pie and something else besides (I don't recall).

My memories are fragmentary and surface only in the form of isolated, brief episodes. I do not have on hand either diaries or notes of those times when fate brought me together, albeit for brief periods, with Ivan Sergeevich.

I remember a few scenes at Yasnaya Polyana when Turgenev visited us for the second time — 1881, as I recall.[64] When the time came for supper, neither Turgenev nor Lev Nikolaevich was anywhere to be seen. Finally, after a rather long time went by, a thought came to me as to where they might be. Not far from the house, amidst the tall oak trees in an oak grove, stood a small hut which Lev Nikolaevich had built for himself to withdraw to in the summer and find a secluded refuge from flies, children and visitors. Off I ran to this hut, built on four pilings, climbed up the stairs and through the open door I could see the two writers, hotly arguing about something.[65]

That evening my children and nieces decided to dance a quadrille. The children's happiness infected the elderly Ivan Sergeevich, too. He went through the quadrille with my nieces, then took off his jacket, put both hands behind his waistcoat and, to the children's delight, began to execute strange movements with his legs, saying that "this is how they dance the can-can in Paris."

He was full of fun that evening, offering praise to everyone and everything. With an affectionate glance at me, he told Lev Nikolaevich:

"What a good thing you did, my friend, when you married your wife!"[66]

At this point he went on to talk about French women, describing with a tone of sad sympathy the deficiencies in their education.

"How much better, and better educated, are the Russian women and girls than the French!" he said. "It is like coming out of a dark room into a bright one when you come to visit a Russian family."

I recall one time Ivan Sergeevich coming to see us in Moscow all exhausted and telling us how different girls would approach him in huge numbers and ask for his autograph.

"I've been sitting the whole day signing my name. There's no way I can

---

64 See Note 62, p. 443.

65 SAT describes this incident above as taking place in September 1878 — see Chapter III.38 ("Turgenev and Urusov") above.

66 Again, this incident is connected above with Turgenev's visit in the spring of 1880 — see Chapter III.59.

refuse these dear, educated Russian girls," Ivan Sergeevich said.

In telling about one Russian actress whom he was quite excited over, he suddenly stopped, seemingly embarrassed, and asked:

"And today I kissed her hand. What do you think, my friend?" he asked Lev Nikolaevich. "D'you think that was all right?"

Ivan Sergeevich's naïveté and almost child-like timidity were quite unexpected and touching in him. But even dearer was his malice-free and outreaching attitude toward everyone. It was sad for me to see one time in him his fear of death.

We were sitting at the table, and the conversation turned to the subject of death. Turgenev naïvely and sincerely admitted that he was afraid of death, that one could not help being afraid of it and that many, no doubt, were of like mind. All at once he raised his hand and said in French:

"*Qui craint la mort, lève la main!*"

Nobody raised their hand. Turgenev sadly and timidly lowered his hand, and his head, and said quietly:

"*Je suis le seul.*"

After he had taken quite ill, he sent me a little photographic card with his signature and wrote me a kind, affectionate letter. At the same time Ivan Sergeevich sent me his charming story "Perepëlka" [The quail], which he gave me for a collection of children's stories my brother was about to publish.

I always found Ivan Sergeevich extremely friendly, and I regret that I had so little occasion to get together with this dear, sensitive, refined and talented man, who loved refinement and beauty in everything.

Countess Sofia Tolstaya

10 August 1903. [67]
Yasnaya Polyana.

III.115 MORE ABOUT TURGENEV BACK IN MAY

LEV NIKOLAEVICH had written me in passing that after learning about Ivan Sergeevich Turgenev's illness, he had written him a letter of encouragement. I noticed over my lifetime that Lev Nikolaevich in his heart of hearts had a genuine liking for Turgenev, despite any quarrels they happened to have. He was glad about Turgenev's reply, telling me: "Today I received a pleasant letter from Turgenev. He was very touched by my letter and says he's getting better, he's out of danger, but there's little chance he'll come back to Russia." That same autumn [1882] I received a very nice letter from Turgenev along these lines. Still desiring to help my brother Petja financially, Lev Nikolaevich gave him his stories *What men live by*, *God sees the truth* and several others, for

---

67 This is the date given by SAT on which she reached this point in writing *My Life*. Earlier in Chapter III.79 ("Gloomier and gloomier") she mentions writing in 1907, probably indicating a later addition to her memoirs.

which he asked artists to contribute pictures. This they did without requesting compensation, and [Lev Nikolaevich] suggested that my brother put out a deluxe children's edition. I then wrote to Turgenev, asking him to send me one of his children's stories for this book. Turgenev sent me his story "Perepëlka" [The quail], along with a very lovely letter. His story was included in this edition, splendidly illustrated. That was in the autumn of 1882.

III.116 PRINCE LEONID DMITRIEVICH URUSOV AND PHILOSOPHY
OUR FRIENDSHIP with Prince Leonid Dmitrievich Urusov was still going strong back then. A student of philosophy, which he loved, Urusov was translating at the time Marcus Aurelius[68] from the French and read the translation to Lev Nikolaevich in May while visiting Yasnaya Polyana. The book is amazingly interesting and instructive, and I read it, as soon as Urusov gave it to me, while Lev Nikolaevich had written me earlier about it:

> May 1882. In the evening we read Urusov's translation of Marcus Aurelius. The translation was strange and not quite accurate, but I, for one, cannot tear myself away from this book. Christ was right when He said: "Before Abraham was, I am."[69] And Marcus Aurelius knew this Christ, which was before Abraham, better than Makarij (the metropolitan[70]) and others know Him.

That same summer, I recall, Urusov brought me Epictetus and Seneca,[71] with his favourite places marked in pencil.

At the time I was terribly attracted by the reading of these philosophers. Not having the time during the day, I read them late into the night, copied out the thoughts which particularly impressed me, memorised them, and simply *studied* the wisdom of various philosophers. Prince Leonid Dmitrievich Urusov and I would often talk about these books, pointing out to each other the parts we liked, the parts that especially struck us or begged discussion. I can honestly say that both back then and since then, the reading of the philosophers has, in many respects, helped me get through life. Apart from the wisdom that filled the pages of these philosophical books, I was enchanted by their conciseness, along with the high (albeit sub-conscious) religiosity of the pagans and of Epictetus — a slave [in his youth] — as well as the eloquence, brilliance and flexibility of expression with Seneca, the quiet wisdom of Caesar Marcus Aurelius, and so forth. Then I tried reading the German philosophers too, including Schopenhauer,[72] but the German thinkers no longer delighted or satisfied me.

68 *Marcus Aurelius* [Marc Aurèle] — see Note 26, p. 433.
69 John 8:58.
70 *Metropolitan Makarij* (birthname: *Mikhail Petrovich Bulgakov*) — see Note 8, p. 427.
71 *Epictetus, Seneca* — Stoic philosophers (Greek and Roman, respectively) — see Notes 28 and 30, p. 434.
72 *Arthur Schopenhauer* (1788–1860) — German philosopher, author of the 1819 landmark book *The world as will and representation* [*Die Welt als Wille und Vorstellung.*]

III.119 PRINCE LEONID DMITRIEVICH URUSOV AGAIN

I AM NOT ABOUT to take on the task of tracking the course of my husband's inner life — a task much too complex and difficult. I know that this inner life was all very beautiful right from Lev Nikolaevich's youth, it was all majestic, but fate has put us into such complex situations, too, [arising from] a large family, that both of us have had to suffer on more than one occasion. In any case, may God's will be done in everything!

Lev Nikolaevich was greatly comforted and cheered by the bond he shared with the like-minded Prince Leonid Dmitrievich Urusov.[73] They kept up a constant correspondence, and when Lev Nikolaevich wrote *What I believe*, Urusov made a splendid French translation under the title of *Ma religion*.

There was one thing I always wondered about: how could [Urusov] go on being the Deputy Governor and Lev Nikolaevich continue to live in his own surroundings if they were so deeply convinced of the sinfulness of such a life? We all paid numerous visits to Urusov in Tula. He lived surrounded by books, engravings and very beautiful pieces [of art]. I even wrote a satirical poem in French about this for our letter-box. Here is one stanza from it:

> Entre les fleurs et les gravures
> Et tout ce qui élève l'âme
> Il passe ses heures de loisir
> *Ignorant la vie et ses drames...*[74]

Later on I suggested that this temple wherein he fashioned his seclusion remained empty, and people were chasing after something else — after an idol that they were so attracted to:

> Ce dieu qui donne la passion et l'amour,
> *Qui brûle, qui tue, qui assomme*
> *Mais qui fait oublier tous les jours,*
> *Leur sort fatal — aux hommes.*[75]

One time Urusov invited us all over for breakfast. Always the gentleman, polite and courteous with ladies, he took the dish holding the pie from his servant's hands and began serving us himself. My sister Tat'jana Andreevna was there, as well as my daughter Tanja, and someone else besides (I don't remember).

When Urusov served the pie to me, I smiled and said, reminding him that he had the imperial rank of a *Kammerherr* [chamberlain/*chambellan*]:

---

73 *Prince Leonid Dmitrievich Urusov* (deputy governor of Tula Gubernia) — see Note 25, p. 433.
74 Translation from French: "Amidst th'engravings and the flowers / And everything that lifts our hearts, / He spends his quiet leisure hours / Oblivious of life and its dramatic parts..."
75 Translation from French: "This god, this giver of passion and love / Which burns, torments and slays, / But which makes men ever oblivious of / The fateful end of their days."

"Mon Dieu! [C'est] le chambellan de Sa Majesté qui nous sert."

"Comtesse, chacun a ses impératrices," Urusov replied, with what seemed to be an ultra-special bow and an ultra-refined smile. Indeed, that was how he always treated me, as though placing me on a pedestal and standing on his knees before me. And I enjoyed it. I always did like him, even though I saw in him some rather absurd (*ridicule*[76]) aspects, too.

In August of that summer Urusov's wife Monja arrived from abroad along with their elder daughter, fifteen-year-old Mèri,[77] and their son Serëzha. She paid us a visit, too, staying with her husband in Tula before going off to see her father, Mal'tsev,[78] in the Crimea. Her relations with her husband were terrible: she insulted him at every turn, scoffed at him, while he tried to be meek, calling her *dushka* [darling], which grated us all the wrong way. According to all indications, they hated each other. She thanked me on behalf of her husband, saying that we had given him everything she was not in a position to give: a family, affection and happiness. And this is when she tossed that declaration at me:

"J'ai grand envie de dire au comte, que ce ne sont pas ses principes, que mon mari aime, mais que c'est sa femme."[79]

Nevertheless, her children were charming. Mary played the piano brilliantly, especially Beethoven, and both of them — she and Serëzha — impressed us with their endearing spontaneity, naïveté and purity.

We were all very fond of the prince's children and felt sorry for him being separated from them by a malicious wife.

Lev Nikolaevich would often send peasants to Urusov with their requests, which the prince always tried his best to respond to. He was very sensitive to the needs of the common people.

IV.5 PRINCE URUSOV'S ARRIVAL AND MY RELATIONSHIP TO LEV NIKOLAEVICH

WHILE LEV NIKOLAEVICH was away, around the 1st of February I received an unexpected visit from Prince Leonid Dmitrievich Urusov. I was very glad to see him, and the two of us spent the whole evening together, each of us filling the other in (by turns) on what had been going in our lives since we had last parted. Our mutual relationship was indeed very friendly, trustful and straight from the heart. We weren't afraid to speak the whole truth to each other, not concealing either our feelings toward events or our families, nor the heartfelt care we felt for each other, which came through in our conversation.

---

76 *ridicule* — French word added here in parentheses by SAT.

77 *Monja* — Marija Sergeevna [Monja] Urusova; *Mèri* — a representation of the Cyrillic transliteration of the English name *Mary*.

78 *Sergej Ivanovich Mal'tsev* — see Note 35, p. 435.

79 Translation from French: "I have a great desire to tell the Count that it's not his principles that my husband likes, but his wife!" SAT also quotes this statement in Chapter III.39 ("Three significant periods").

Urusov had a bad cough, and said he wasn't feeling well. I recall buying him a splendid respirator and begged him to wear it in severe cold weather.

Urusov only spent a day in Moscow and promised to stop by on his way home.

On the 5th of February he came by once more to see me, and again the two of us spent the whole evening in wonderful conversation, in which there was not a single word that needed to be concealed or which the whole world could not hear. But such a conversation could only take place with someone whose meaning you could catch in the blink of an eye, all based on purely abstract concepts, on Lev Nikolaevich's new teachings, on readings in philosophy, an appreciation of philosophical wisdom and its application to daily life. Refined and affectionate, with his outwardly impeccable behaviour and manners, he embodied the exact opposite of the image Lev Nikolaevich deliberately projected of himself at that time. His brother Sergej Nikolaevich[80] recounted to me the following incident after one of his visits to Yasnaya Polyana:

> There was Lëvochka sitting in his shirt and dirty woollen stockings, all dishevelled and disgruntled, together with Mitrofan (the estate manager),[81] sewing boots for Agaf'ja Mikhajlovna,[82] and a schoolteacher — reading aloud the *Lives of saints*.[83] He won't go to Moscow unless Sofia Andreevna (that's me) summons him, or unless something happens in our lives.

This account of Sergej Nikolaevich's greatly disturbed and angered me, and I selfishly made up my mind that I wouldn't summon [Lëvochka] for anything and wouldn't even write to him. I told my sister in a letter:

"Such rot and indifference to the family I find so repulsive that I shall no longer write to him. He fathers a heap of children, and then he is unable to find any substance or joy or even simple obligations in connection with his family…"

But these sparks of annoyance faded, and once again I felt an influx of the love I used to have for my husband. Then, on that same day, 4 February, I wrote to him:

"Finding myself eagerly anticipating your letters, I know how dear you are to me, and how I am nothing without you."

While Lev Nikolaevich was away, I used the few leisure hours I had left over to read a book by La Boétie,[84] an eighteenth-century thinker, and I asked

---

80 *Count Sergej Nikolaevich Tolstoy* (1826–1904), elder brother to LNT.

81 *Mitrofan Nikolaevich Bannikov* — see Chapter III.112 ("Lev Nikolaevich at Yasnaya Polyana in the spring") in *My Life*.

82 See Chapter III.100 ("Agaf'ja Mikhajlovna") in *My Life*.

83 *Lives of saints* — (Russian: *Zhitija svjatykh*) — biographies of Christian saints and others canonised by the Christian church, beginning with the early Christian martyrs in the Roman Empire, and including a number of Slavic saints canonised by the Russian and other Eastern Orthodox churches.

84 *Étienne de La Boétie* (1530–1563) — French writer of the sixteenth century (not the eighteenth, as SAT states), and a close friend of Montaigne's.

Lev Nikolaevich to bring me the Montaigne[85] book he was then reading at Yasnaya Polyana and had high praise for. I had a great need at the time for serious books, searching in them for support, edification and comfort — but, most of all, a distraction from life, which invariably I found to be a burden more exhausting than I could bear.

In my letters to Lev Nikolaevich I was no longer as open and carefree as before. He wrote me, for example:

> In your letter I see reflected for me not only your own mental state, but the children's too — our whole household. I may be mistaken, of course, but through your letter I can follow, as on a thermometer, what I always meticulously follow — the moral temperature of the family — has it gone up or down?

Sometimes he would write: "I got your two marvellous letters." Or he might say: "I see by your letter that you're out of sorts..." or something along this line.

I was already too mature to be marked on my letters, and these indications of approval or disapproval caused me to be not completely sincere in my letters. Occasionally I would write with a deliberately provocative tone.

IV.37 FET

I LIKED BEING THERE only when Fet and his wife came, along with [LNT'S] nieces Varja Nagornova[86] and Liza Obolenskaja.[87] One time I happened to come across a book lying on the table at Sergej Nikolaevich's. It was *Le Pessimisme du xix siècle* by Caro.[88] I started reading it and couldn't tear myself away from the book the whole evening.

Fet's witticisms could be quite amusing and engaging. Moreover, he was so often overenthusiastic in his praise of me that I could not help indulging in the pleasure of provoking such outbursts. When I sent him in the spring a new photographic portrait that had just been done of me and was attracting many comments to the effect that it was not a good likeness, too flattering, and so forth, Fet sent me a poem he had dedicated to me:

> And here's the portrait: so like you, yet unlike you...
> What likeness or unlikeness can we find?

85 *Michel de Montaigne* (1533–1592) — French Renaissance writer, credited with popularising the *essay* as a literary genre.
86 *Varvara Valer'janovna [Varja] Nagornova (née Tolstaja 1850–1921)* — elder daughter to LNT's sister, Marija Nikolaevna Tolstaya (1830–1912).
87 *Elizaveta Valer'janovna [Liza/Lizon'ka] Tolstaja (1852–1935)* — second daughter to Marija Nikolaevna Tolstaya and Valer'jan Petrovich Tolstoy — married to *Prince Leonid Dmitrievich Obolenskij (1844–1888)*.
88 *Erasmo María Caro (1826–1887)* — French writer and philosopher, inspector-general of the Academy of Paris, defender of Christianity against encroaching materialism and positive thinking.

That's not our lot, O Lord, but is it likely
We'll find one that more joyfully will shine?

Where beauty reigns, there's no room for dissenting.
Who knows wherefrom the star its flame derives?
A mere young bride? Let them keep on pretending!
Our own true goddess we've not recognised…

But all of us, on bended knee together,
Should fall and worship here before your feet,
As you, in modest charm that lasts forever,
Sit and observe our own grey hair retreat…

With a boldness which makes me blush today, I responded to Fet with some poor verse of my own:

Why all this fuss and adulation
Of me — so ugly, old and bland,
Why stir the soul to consternation
By dint of mighty poet's hand?

In a world of different light I be,
Wont to retreat within the shadows…
Oh, poet, do not stir in me
A feeling I should be afraid of![89]

S.T.

There was nothing flattering about me in Fet's poem, but I was grateful to him just for including the word modest, as well as for another poem he had written long before, in which he stated (among other things):

And here, all filled with fascination
Before you, on this country knoll,
I see, Illustrious Creation,
The utter *pureness of your soul.*[90]

One time he got everybody laughing with a conversation later related to me by Sergej Nikolaevich. Fet spoke more or less as follows:

89 The original Russian versions of Fet's poem and SAT's response are reproduced in *My Life,* Poetry Appendix, IV.37.
90 This is the second stanza of one of several of Fet's poems entitled "Grafine S.A. Tolstoj" [To the Countess S. A. Tolstaya] (the third stanza is quoted in VIII.6 in *My Life*). This poem is cited in a dramatisation of Sofia Andreevna's relationship with Fet in Act II of a modern Russian play by Vladimir Jurovitskij, *Sof'ja Andreevna — drama v chetyrëkh dejstvijakh s prologom* [*Sofia Andreevna — drama in four acts with a prologue*]. For the full Russian text of the poem along with an English translation, see the Poetry Appendix in *My Life,* IV.37.

Lev Nikolaevich, along with Chertkov,[91] wants to draw pictures that will stop the common folk from believing in miracles. But what's the point of depriving the people of this happiness of believing in the matter they love so much that they eat up their God in the form of bread and wine and get saved that way? That's like asking a barefoot peasant to go into a cave with a tallow candle end to find his way in the dark cave. And then asking him to snuff out the candle end and use the wax to grease his boots, but he's barefoot.

Not being a lover of either gypsy songs or card playing, I often stayed home alone. Apart from my proofreading, I also did a translation, though I no longer recall what it was. I know that the book contained a chapter entitled "The enigma of the Sphinx," which Lev Nikolaevich had been explaining to me earlier. But I had to leave off the translation for want of time, as I wrote Lev Nikolaevich:

"Pity I have no time — I feel terribly happy when I'm translating! When one's own intelligence fails, one feels the need of revolving in some friendly intelligent sphere, even if it happens to be someone else's intelligence."

During this time I continued giving lessons to Andrjusha and Misha, but that was actually more of a relaxation for me than a job. How interesting and delightful these lesson times were! If I were running late, Misha would come after me and ask: "Mamà, do come and teach us!" One time when I was explaining subtraction to Andrjusha, Misha listened and listened and all at once his face beamed.

"Oh, what fun that is!" he said. "Teach me, too, how to take away!" He was six at the time.

IV.45 THE LAST RIDE

I DON'T RECALL how many days we spent at Djat'kovo,[92] but I remember that on our last day there the prince ordered two carriages harnessed and insisted we all go for a ride. The air was fresh and he was coughing a great deal. He wrapped himself in a tartan blanket and was extremely serious.

When they brought the carriages to us, he turned to me and said:

"I hope the Countess will do me the honour of riding with me."

Of course, I agreed. My heart was wrenched as I watched his all but extinguished figure, his face staring straight ahead with no expression but concentrated seriousness. Along the way he complained to me about his wife, that she would not agree to taking a trip to see his mother and showing the elderly woman her grandchildren.

Then he ordered the coachman to turn off somewhere, and we parted from the larger carriage in which his wife and children were riding along with my

91 *Vladimir Grigor'evich Chertkov* (1854–1936) — a close friend and adviser to LNT, who in exile set up his own publishing house in Britain, known as *Svobodnoe slovo* [Free Word] to publish works by Tolstoy and his followers.
92 *Djat'kovo* — Urusov's brother-in-law Nikolaj Mal'tsev's estate in Brjansk Uezd.

daughters, and we began to make our way through the woods alone. I asked the prince to go back, saying it was cold and that he had had enough of a ride, but he kept giving the coachman new instructions — he seemed to be in such a frightful hurry — meanwhile drawing my attention to the beautiful scenery.

I tried to keep him from talking too much, but he replied that he was feeling ill in any case, and this was our last ride together.

When we got back to the house, he took my hand, and as he kissed it he began to thank me both for the ride together and for everything I had given him in life. At the end he added that he wished me happiness, and most of all to always the stay the same as I was.

IV.46 THE DEATH OF PRINCE URUSOV

WHEN WE PARTED, something was painfully wrenched from my heart for the rest of my life. Soon after this, his wife and daughters went to the princess's father's in the Crimea, while the prince stayed behind with his son Serëzha and a doctor. On the 23rd of September [1885], in the presence of his son and the doctor, Prince Leonid Dmitrievich Urusov passed on from an aortic or cardiac rupture (I can't recall which). We received a telegram informing us of his death, and the 23rd was exactly the day of my wedding [anniversary]. Everybody was sad. I wrote my sister:

"There is some kind of terrible emptiness in my heart: I have one less friend in the world, and there is something unfinished in my relationship with him."

Nikolaj Nikolaevich Strakhov, who had often seen Urusov at our place, wrote us upon learning of his death:

"Urusov's death is a real tragedy for those who understood him. He radiated a purity which was a joy and a treasure to behold… I wish you… gladness and happiness forever."[93]

Yes, if I loved Urusov, it was precisely for his radiant purity and love for ideas, for everything non-material.

It is only men such as these that I could love and idealise in my life, men in whom shone either God's spark through religion or God's spark through some particular talent.

IV.106 FET AND TOLSTOY ON WOMEN

IN ONE OF HIS LETTERS TO ME, [Fet] took a strange twist in respect to his communication and conversations with me. He wrote:

Women by nature are not very practical in major undertakings, and it is difficult to be practical at the very centre of idealistic views. Shouldn't we be looking to the harmonious coming together of two spiritual aspects to find the solution to this sense of joy which is awakened within me by my discussions with you?

93 From Strakhov's letter to SAT dated 30 September 1885, reproduced in Donskov 2000: 189.

Everywhere in Fet one can notice his love for women in general and his admiration for women. With Lev Nikolaevich, on the other hand, it is rather *lack of love*, even scorn.

Here are some thoughts from his notebook:

A woman views a man's accomplishment *only* through [the eyes of] others. Women use words only for the purpose of *charmer*[94] and to attain their own goals…

Women as such use words only for [their own] purposes, and that's how they think about others too.

There is the question about equality for all: the women's question is part of that question.

A woman can be free only if she is a Christian. A liberated woman who is not a Christian is a terrible beast.

It is useless to reason with women because they are not motivated by reason. No matter how judiciously they might reason, they will still live by feeling.

IV.129 BIRTH OF VANECHKA

BY THE MORNING OF THE 31ST OF MARCH [1888] I was already feeling quite ill. The ever-loyal Marija Ivanovna Abramovich,[95] who had helped me bear my children for the past twenty-five years and was now quite advanced in age herself, was staying with us in anticipation of the forthcoming childbirth. She, as usual, announced to Lev Nikolaevich and me with great solemnity that the labour process had begun. We hastened to make all the necessary preparations, while in the meantime, downstairs, my dear young people were getting concerned. [The composer] Sergej Ivanovich Taneev[96] had dropped by to see them, quite unaware of what was going on. He kept asking where I was and what was the matter with me. Tanja told him that I had eaten too much cabbage the night before and had a stomach ache.

Taneev stayed the whole day, conversing and joking with the children, and when at eleven o'clock at night little Andrjusha came running down to announce that Mamà had just had a little boy, Sergej Ivanovich was so embarrassed that for two whole years he wouldn't come to see us.

The labour was challenging. Lev Nikolaevich stayed beside me the whole time and wept. The child of a sixty-year-old father and a nervous and life-weary mother (albeit still healthy, energetic and young-looking) was born weak, thin, and so frail that he was a pitiful sight to behold.

The question of breast-feeding arose. I feared that because of my advanced years I might not have enough milk and that the boy might die of starvation. Lev Nikolaevich and, strange to say, especially the children, urged me to feed

94 *charmer* — here the French verb ["to charm"], given by SAT in French.
95 *Marija Ivanovna Abramovich* — SAT's midwife; see Chapter II.24 ("Birth of my first son") in *My Life.*
96 *Sergej Ivanovich Taneev* — see Note 42, p. 437.

the little one myself. He [Vanechka] seemed to arouse in everyone a feeling of sweetness and tenderness.

We decided to send for the pediatrician Dr Pokrovskij,[97] who also advised me to breast-feed. I gave in, but how I suffered physically from painful cracks [in my nipples] and mentally from the fear that the baby would starve! What can I say that is interesting about this period? My whole life was focussed on caring for this weakly, sickly Vanechka. Oddly enough, I called the boy Ivan, even though I really wanted to name him Jurij. My older sons, the first letters of whose Christian names spelt out a word, decided that the letter *i* was missing, so that the letters would spell SILAMI:[98]

S — Sergej
I — Il'ja
L — Lev
A — Andrej
M — Mikhail

The girls' names, on the other hand, spelt TMA:[99]

T — Tat'jana
M — Marija
A — Aleksandra

And so the boys kept clamouring that they had conquered the darkness [TMA] with their strength [SILAMI] and so insisted on the name Ivan. For some reason even the girls were in favour of this, as well as Lev Nikolaevich.

Vanechka was christened by my brother Sasha and cousin Vera Shidlovskaja.

Lev Nikolaevich was getting more and more depressed by life in Moscow. He again began to suffer from liver complaint attacks, he was constantly sick in the pit of his stomach and he often sat depressed, gloomy and completely inactive in his chair and his appearance showed signs of age and exhaustion. I felt sorry for him: he felt put out by our whole family life; he had immersed himself so deeply in the negating of everything that there was no room left for a positive life. I often thought of Amiel's dictum:

97 *Dr Egor Arsen'evich Pokrovskij* (1834–1895) — Moscow pediatrician and professor, physician-in-chief at the Sofijskaja Pediatric Hospital in Moscow. During the 1870s he had made a trip abroad to study pediatric hospitals in Berlin, Vienna, Paris and other European cities. In 1890 he published his book *Fizicheskoe vospitanie detej u raznykh narodov, preimushchestvenno Rossii* [The physical education of children among various peoples, particularly in Russia]. He was also editor of the magazine *Vestnik vospitanija* [The Education Herald].
98 SILAMI — instrumental case [an indirect case in Russian] of the plural word *sily* [strength], indicating "by (one's own) strength." See Illustration 28 for a photo of the Tolstoys' five elder sons (1904). For Vanechka's portrait, see Illustration 18.
99 TMA (in standard Russian: *t'ma*) — the Russian word for "darkness" or "gloom."

"Malheur, si la négation domine, car la vie — c'est une affirmation."[100]

Masha was sitting her exams, but Lev Nikolaevich did not approve.

Lëva was preparing for a Grade 8 entrance exam, but, again, no support from Lev Nikolaevich.

Serëzha was working for the Peasant Bank, but again, to Lev Nikolaevich's displeasure.

Andrjusha and Misha were fasting, gently and zealously, by their own will, though this time not with me, but with the Nagornovs,[101] while Lev Nikolaevich, a denier of the church, was suffering on account of the faith of his little ones.

My passionate maternal affection for the newborn separated me for a time from my husband, and this, too, proved harmful.

V.5 FET'S JUBILEE

THAT JANUARY a number of people were raising the question about celebrating the 50th-anniversary jubilee of Afanasij Afanas'evich Fet's[102] literary activity. He himself was greatly desirous of such [a gesture], and made his desire known in every way he could. I considered Fet a close and long-time friend of our family. I was grateful for his unswerving adoration of me, for the high esteem with which he always treated me and which I had done little to earn. And so I zealously promoted the celebration, set for the date of 28 January.

I was in touch with Gol'tsev, Grot and Solov'ëv, and asked various suitable acquaintances to participate, and before long we opened a subscription to the dinner, and prepared speeches, articles, tributes and garlands. I also wrote to Nikolaj Nikolaevich Strakhov,[103] inviting him to come and also to write an article. He did oblige with an article, but declined to come in person. He was still quite angry that Fet had pushed so hard for a chamberlainship, which he won through the offices of Grand Prince Konstantin

---

100 Quoted from Henri-Frédéric Amiel (1821–1881), *Fragments d'un journal intime, précédés d'une étude par Edmond Scherer* (Paris: Sandoz and Thuillier, 1884).

101 *Varvara Valer'janovna Nagornova* (née *Tolstaya*) — see Note 86, p. 450.

102 *Afanasij Afanas'evich Fet* (real surname: *Shenshin*) — see Note 10, p. 428.

103 *Nikolaj Nikolaevich Strakhov* — In a letter dated 28 December 1888, SAT wrote Strakhov: "The purpose of my letter to you, Nikolaj Nikolaevich, is to ask your co-operation in celebrating this old fellow [Fet]. After all, you are one of the *generals* of literature and have some clout in Petersburg... So, perhaps you could coax another literary stalwart to come, too, and congratulate and celebrate Fet, and couldn't you yourself write at least a brief review of his literary activity? — after all, nobody could do it better" (Donskov 2000: 210). Strakhov's "clout in Petersburg" was considerable. A corresponding member of the Russian Academy of Sciences, he sat on the Pushkin Prize adjudication committee. He was acknowledged to be one of the most prominent literary critics of his day. By the time he reached retirement, Strakhov had achieved the civil rank of state counsellor [*statskij sovetnik*], which corresponded to a rank just below that of major-general. Hence SAT's military metaphor was quite apt. See Illustration 15.

Konstantinovich.[104] The Grand Prince was a writer of poetry himself and on this common ground had become quite fond of Fet.

On the subject of the chamberlainship, Strakhov wrote that Fet wanted one, but Polonskij[105] became suspicious and as a result of this broke up with his old friend. Strakhov cited Polonskij's words addressed to Fet:

> Just imagine, there are rumours spreading abroad that you are pushing for a chamberlainship. I keep telling everyone it's all silly slander, that you cherish above all the title of poet — a title which nobody can confer and nobody can take away.

I remember that part of Fet's petitioning was for the Tsar to legitimise him as Shenshin's son and confer this name on him. Turgenev himself wrote to Fet:

"You had a *name* (as a poet), and you have changed it to a *surname*."[106]

But if people understood how someone can be tormented their whole lifetime by the burden of their illegitimate status and shame for their mother, they would forgive Fet's weaknesses, too.

Strakhov, Polonskij, et al., were unwilling to comprehend this, and Strakhov even complained that he himself had been awarded a medal he had absolutely no need of.

There was another unpleasant incident that happened around this time: on the 5th of January Fet's wife broke her arm, and they feared it would not be mended by the end of the month. They sent to me for a bag of ice, and even here Fet did not waste the opportunity to write me these grandiloquent lines:

> The heavenly Sun, merely by its own enlivening nature, makes its presence to be joyfully welcomed everywhere, regardless of whether it brings out the gaily coloured orchids in the tropics or glances down upon Greenland and releases the ice-floes, summoning the frozen moss to new life. Your welcoming Sun has illumined and enlivened even our poor Greenland.

Fet's appeals to me in his letters kept increasing in intensity, probably in gratitude for my supporting his jubilee celebration. He wrote:

104 *Grand Prince Konstantin Konstantinovich Romanov* (1858–1915) — grandson to Emperor Nicholas I, who was also a poet; in 1889 he was appointed president of the Imperial St-Petersburg Academy of Sciences.
105 *Jakov Petrovich Polonskij* (1819–1898) — a contemporary of Fet's, who wrote stories, poems and epics in verse.
106 Turgenev's actual wording was slightly different: "...as Fet you had a name, [while] as Shenshin you have only a surname" (I. S. Turgenev, *Polnoe sobranie sochinenij i pisem v 28 tt.* [*Complete collected works and letters in 28 volumes.*], 10: 339). On 26 December 1873 Fet's patrimony had been restored by order of the Tsar, including the right "to the lineage of his father Shenshin with all the rights appertaining to his title and lineage." See Pokrovskaja and Shumova 1978: 130.

"Incomparable, golden Countess! I use this epithet, although you are much more deserving of words like *sparkling* or *brilliant*."

As for me, I simply found it a pleasure to organise and take part in the event. As a rule, I am quite fond of celebrations, glamour, fun, beauty, the company of pleasant people, although, apart from the latter (i.e., I do have the company of pleasant people), I was destined to live my life completely outside of that whole [sphere]. On this occasion, too, fate robbed me of the very celebration I had organised.

v.8 VANECHKA'S RECOVERY AND FET AGAIN

GOD HEARD MY PRAYER, and my little Vanechka recovered back then. God left this angel on the earth for another six years. But, as Emerson[107] says, such children are sent to earth to remind people of love, and God takes them back to heaven because they are not strong enough to stand up to earthly life, and they are not created for it. I always seemed to have the same feeling and so I was crazy about this baby.

And even as a baby he was beloved by everyone, and everyone brightened [from being around him].

Fet came to thank me for my support of his jubilee and stayed to dinner. After dinner he was engaged in such a passionate conversation with Lev Nikolaevich that there was no way they would listen to me when I invited them into the drawing-room for coffee. So I grasped Lev Nikolaevich by one arm and Fet by the other and led them into the drawing-room myself. On the following day Fet sent me a letter and a poem dedicated to me. This is what he wrote in the letter:

> Here is the latest offering by one of the two old men you honoured yesterday, taking them by the arm into the drawing-room. I didn't want anybody else's hand to touch my "baby," and so I am copying it myself in my illegible handwriting:

> *To Countess Sofia Andreevna Tolstaya*

> It's time! Through global dew I follow…
> Into a new world I step forth.
> And then, with tender, heartfelt sorrow,
> I look upon my cherished North.

> I know! Upon a wave I'm carried,
> The bright North Star within my gaze,
> Far off you burn for me, all starry,
> In your fair beauty and bright rays…[108]

107 *Ralph Waldo Emerson* (1803–1882) — American essayist, poet, abolitionist and philosopher.
108 Poem *Grafine Sofii Andreevne Tolstoj* [To Countess Sofia Andreevna Tolstoy], written 19 February 1889 (to be distinguished from a poem he wrote in 1866 with the same title — see

After Fet's jubilee, on 5 February 1889 a very nice article about him appeared in [the weekly newspaper] *Nedelja*. It wasn't signed, and I don't know who wrote it. Here's an excerpt:

> Fet's significance is not universally acknowledged. Even today there are a lot of people who do not appreciate the charm of his verse. That takes quite a refined taste...
>
> As a purely lyrical poet, Fet is altogether free in his artistry. He knows only his own inner world, and is subject only to his feeling and dreams...
>
> A sincere, free and simple [poet] is Fet, yet at the same time a poet of extraordinary elegance.

I don't remember where N. N. Strakhov's article on Fet[109] was published. Strakhov was, evidently, quite proud of it, since he later wrote Lev Nikolaevich:

> I am very pleased with my brief article on Fet, and I'm quite put out that neither did Fet offer me any special thanks, nor has Sofia Andreevna, who was actually the one that got me going on it, given me any indication that she is satisfied or that she forgives me for my criticisms of Fet. But I couldn't do any more than that, and if you can believe my own self-esteem, I thought that my brief article would bring Fet no less joy than a chamberlainship.[110]

Both Strakhov and Lev Nikolaevich were quite critical of Fet for his weakness in desiring to celebrate his jubilee, and I felt sorry for him. Lev Nikolaevich's dropped by Fet's place on the 30th of January, when there was a grand dinner for Fet's well-wishers. Lev Nikolaevich criticised it as follows:

"Everybody's terribly silly, overeating, overdrinking and singing. Even gross!"

And in his diary he wrote concerning Fet:

"Vainglory, luxury, poetry — it's all quite enchanting when one is filled with the energy of youth, but without youth or energy, with only the dullness of old age permeating everything, it's gross!"

For some reason, however, I myself did not find it gross. I was happy to bring what might have been a final pleasure to this elderly poet. Life is so hard, grey and complicated that it's good when one sees flaring up in it from time to time, if not sunlight, then at least a tiny star!

Chapters IV.37 ("Fet") above and VIII.6 ("Student evening at the Conservatory...") in *My Life*. When the poem was subsequently published, the last stanza was slightly changed: "I know! Upon a wave I'm carried" [*Ja znaju! unosim volnoju*] became "Upon a cruel wave I'm carried" [*Zhestokoj unosim volnoju*], while "Far off you burn for me" [*Chto ty vdali gorish' za mnoju*] was changed to "I know you burn for me" [*Ja znaju, ty gorish' za mnoju*]. For the full text of the published poem in Russian with English translation, see *My Life* Poetry Appendix, V.8, p. 1038.

109 Strakhov's "Jubilej poèzii Feta" [Jubilee of Fet's poetry] was published in *Novoe vremja*, N° 4640 (28 January 1889).

110 From Strakhov's letter to LNT dated 13 April 1889, reproduced in Donskov 2003: II: 784–86.

V.44 AGAIN *THE FRUITS OF ENLIGHTENMENT*
AND *THE KREUTZER SONATA*

ON THE 22ND OF APRIL I received a letter from my dear elderly friend, Baroness Mengden,[111] saying that at the Chinese Theatre[112] in Tsarskoe Selo[113] an amateur company was staging the comedy *The fruits of enlightenment*, and that the play was a dazzling success. The Tsar himself attended, along with his whole family; indeed, the whole élite of society was in attendance. The Tsar laughed unrestrainedly, but there were some genteel people there who were less than pleased by what they saw as an overall poking fun by servants at their masters. Such an appraisal provoked mockery [of the critics themselves] in other quarters. Human opinions are rarely unanimous; there are always going to be protesters, even if they are only a minority.

Concerning *The fruits of enlightenment* Nikolaj Nikolaevich Strakhov wrote the following:

"I managed to hear *The fruits of enlightenment* at Tat'jana Andreevna's (my sister Kuzminskaja's), and I greatly admired it. It was funny, dramatic and instructive."[114]

N. N. Strakhov also wrote Lev Nikolaevich concerning *The Kreutzer Sonata* in April 1890, after the story was banned once and for all by the censors:

What is striking is that, more often than not, no notice is taken of the moral aim, nor of the condemnation of egotism and wantonness — so accustomed have people become to these habits of egotism and wantonness, that they feel offended directly by you, [wondering] why you attack the inevitable, attack what we manage to get along with very well. It is only the smart young people, only the smart, keen women who have fathomed your exposé, recognised the evil you are protesting against, and support your preaching of chastity. I was amazed at Countess Aleksandra Andreevna Tolstaya's reaction — she blurted out simply: "What?! Does he want to put an end to the human race?" As though it were somebody's responsibility to argue for the continuation of the human race. Maybe start up some breeding stables?[115]

---

111 *Baroness Elizaveta Ivanovna Mengden* (née *Bibikova*, 1821–1902) — a writer who had briefly attracted LNT's attentions in 1857. She maintained her friendship with the Tolstoys throughout the rest of her life. She was married to *Baron Vladimir Mikhajlovich Mengden* (1825–1910), a state counsellor and secretary to the senate.
112 *Chinese Theatre* [Russian: *Kitajskij teatr*] — a theatre built and decorated with Chinese motifs in 1778–79, formerly known as the *Stone Opera House* [*Kamennaja opera*].
113 *Tsarskoe Selo* [lit., 'Tsar's Village' — the name of the town of *Pushkin* from the 1780s to 1917] — a town about 24 km south of St. Petersburg where the Russian Imperial family maintained one of their summer residences. Following the revolution, the Bolsheviks renamed the town *Detskoe Selo* [lit. "Children's Village"]. The name *Pushkin* was bestowed in 1937, in honour of the centenary of the poet's death.
114 From Strakhov's letter to LNT dated 24 April 1890, reproduced in Donskov 2003: II: 813–15.
115 Strakhov to LNT, 24 April 1890.

In Petersburg, as everywhere else it was put on, *The Kreutzer Sonata* stirred up considerable reaction. It was the talk of the town and everyone, upon meeting their relatives or acquaintances, would ask right off: "Have you read *The Kreutzer Sonata*?"

On the 30th of April Baroness Mengden, whose husband was on friendly terms with Pobedonostsev,[116] wrote me, saying that Pobedonostsev was surprised that *The Kreutzer Sonata* had been banned, and that this had been done at the request of the Tsar.

Stakhovich, on the other hand, wrote me exactly the opposite. In these governmental spheres everybody lied to each other, [he said,] and the truth was barely recognisable. In any case, *The Kreutzer Sonata* caused a furore not only in Russia, but in [Western] Europe as well.

Fet wrote Lev Nikolaevich about the criticism and praise of Lev Nikolaevich's works by a Mr. Edwin Bauer. The following year Vogüé, who had translated *The Kreutzer Sonata* into French, wrote a review of the story saying that Tolstoy was suffering from his own analysis — *"analyse creusante"* [scathing analysis], as he put it — and that this analysis [had the effect of] killing in him any personal or literary life. In this there is indeed a grain of truth.

At the beginning of May Lev Nikolaevich took ill at Pirogovo and sent for me by telegram to come to him. He was unable to write himself and dictated the following diary entry (of 9 May 1890) to me concerning *The Kreutzer Sonata*:

> Many of the thoughts I have expressed of late belong not to me but to people who have turned to me with their questions, perplexities, thoughts and plans. For example, the underlying thought — or, rather, the feeling — of *The Kreutzer Sonata*, belongs not to me, but to a certain Slavic woman, who wrote me a letter — comically phrased but significant in content — on the subject of the sexual abuse of women. She later came to see me and left me with a powerful impression.

V.52 WOMEN IN LEV NIKOLAEVICH'S EYES

I DON'T REMEMBER the details of our life with the Kuzminskijs, with our little children — there's no record of that anywhere. That life was always clear, simple and happy. The love of little children is pure and joyous, not like men's love. When I happened to read in Lev Nikolaevich's diary, for example, "I behaved myself *well* this night, so as to misbehave tomorrow…," I felt a disturbance rippling through my whole soul. This *misbehaving*, in my husband's eyes, was the possession of a woman, a wife. His passionate attachment to her sometimes made him weep as he kissed her breast. This living woman, or wife, full of intellectual and heartfelt questions, became, in her husband's

---

116 *Konstantin Petrovich Pobedonostsev* (1827–1907) — senior procurator of the Holy Synod of the Russian Orthodox Church.

eyes, a kind of *object*, an excuse for some kind of *misbehaviour* and therefore, as it were, an accessory to sin. And what did she experience and endure as a result of such treatment, just in yielding to her husband's desire? Who would even care?

This lack of either love or respect for a woman as a human being showed through with Lev Nikolaevich constantly, everywhere, in his diaries, and this both offended and distressed me.

Once again Mme Helbig (*née* Princess Shakhovskaja)[117] and her daughter came to visit us that summer. We talked a lot together on various subjects; she was not very much inclined toward Tolstoy's ideas, his haycutting and agricultural labours. She was a strong supporter of European cultural sensitivity, especially any form of art, music and civilisation. Married to a German professor, she was a pupil of Liszt's and spent all her time in Rome. She played [the piano] magnificently, and had made a special study of Wagner, and there was no accommodation in her mind for deprivations, manual labour and the absence of a cultured or artistic life.

Lev Nikolaevich wrote in his diary:

Conversations — boring, difficult. Idleness, stuffing, music…
The principal trait of women is disrespect for thought…
If men weren't bound to women by sexual feelings and the condescension that arises therefrom, they would clearly see that women (at least the majority) do not understand them, and they wouldn't [bother] talking with them. (With the exception of virgins.)

Why he made this exception I have absolutely no idea. Virgins, for the most part, are abnormal and hysterical, while women, satisfied with a normal human life, always have a clearer view of everything. Lev Nikolaevich wrote further:

"You begin to understand women through your wife, and fathom them completely through your daughters… The same old depression, koumiss and haycutting…"

First Lev Nikolaevich would cut hay for a widow and then he and [our daughter] Masha would haul it to her [on a wagon]. They would go with the wagon, and my heart simply ached watching them. There was Masha — thin, sickly and pale, and a tired, frail old man — both so serious, exhausted and utterly miserable. I felt a kind of estrangement between myself and them, all the more so after I found out that Masha was still corresponding with Birjukov against my wishes — a fact she and her father both concealed from me.

---

117 *Nadezhda Dmitrievna Helbig* (née *Shakhovskaja*, 1847–1922) — married to *Professor Wolfgang Karl Helbig* (1839–1915), deputy secretary of the Prussian Archaeological Institute in Rome (1865–87), later a researcher and art dealer in Rome.

I myself began manifesting symptoms of some undetermined disease, and it soon turned out that I was pregnant again. This caused Lev Nikolaevich shame and distress. Here I was 46, and he 62. Everyone was amazed at my youthful appearance, but my body was still worn out by frequent births, breast-feeding and life in general.

I had considerable pain in my uterus, and both the doctor and the midwife diagnosed inflammation of the uterus. Despite my oncoming pregnancy, Dr B. prescribed internal uterus leeches. My midwife had the prescription filled in Tula. This caused me unbearable pain and resulted in a miscarriage.

Neither Lev Nikolaevich nor I admitted to being happy about this result, but such a feeling most certainly was stirring in each of us. We kept mum about it in front of the children, we were both so ashamed.

My health quickly recovered, and Lev Nikolaevich was greatly helped by drinking koumiss. After some improvement, he began bathing daily [in the stream], mowed oats in July, and in the artistic and intellectual domain took to writing *Father Sergius*. Lev Nikolaevich kept thinking about this story the whole summer and would constantly go back to it. It was also at that time that his treatise *Why do men stupefy themselves?*[118] was written, and Lev Nikolaevich revised the proofs.

Occasionally in the evening he would take up boot-sewing, but not with the same zeal as before.

V.65 *THE KREUTZER SONATA* AND MY STORY

WHILE I WAS PROOFREADING *The Kreutzer Sonata* for Volume XIII — a story I had never liked on account of its coarse treatment of women on the part of Lev Nikolaevich, it made me think about writing my own novel on the subject of *The Kreutzer Sonata*. This thought kept coming to me more and more frequently, to the point where I could no longer restrain myself. I did write this story, but it never saw the light of day and is now lying among my papers at the Historical Museum in Moscow.

Concerning Lev Nikolaevich's story, on the other hand, I wrote the following in my diary:

"Some kind of visible thread connects Lev Nikolaevich's old diaries with his *Kreutzer Sonata*, while I am caught by chance in this spider-web like a buzzing fly, from which the spider is sucking blood."

I wrote this under the influence of Lev Nikolaevich's extremely changeable mood regarding me. When [the first] signs of my new pregnancy appeared, he seemed to take fright, since *The Kreutzer Sonata* was just then in press. But the pregnancy ended in ill health and a miscarriage. At that point Lev

---

118 *Why do men stupefy themselves? [Dlja chego ludi odurmanivajutsja?]* — sometimes translated in English as: *Why do people intoxicate themselves?* (1890). It was also published as a Foreword to Pëtr Semënovich Alekseev's book *On drunkenness [Predislovie k knige Petra Semënovicha Alekseeva «O p'janstve»]* (Moscow, 1891).

Nikolaevich was affectionate and attentive to me, and I felt overjoyed and wrote in my diary:

"Oh, if only we could have the same kind of relationship without *this*! But that rarely happens with him... And when he is kind to me, I feel so happy..."

At the same time, Lev Nikolaevich, too, was probably in a good mood, since Strakhov responded to one of Lev Nikolaevich's letters:

"You write to me that you have a happy life ..."[119]

And Strakhov went on to write [in the same letter] about [a couple of] articles:

Two articles about you have now come out... one by Volynskij,[120] [the other by] Vogüé... In reading Volynskij's whole review, I saw that he is more involved in his own thoughts and says rather little about you. Vogüé's article[121] is intelligent, and people here [in Petersburg] are reading it enthusiastically; still, he has no idea as to what Christianity is all about, and that's why he can't understand you either.

V.92 INVITATION TO THE PALACE

AT 11 O'CLOCK THAT NIGHT, no sooner had I lain down than I received a message from Zosja to the effect that the Tsar was inviting me, through Sheremeteva, to meet with him the following day, at 11.30 in the morning, at the Anichkov Palace.[122]

My chief joy in those initial moments was that within twenty-four hours I would be able to be on my way home. Immediately I started packing up everything, wrote various essential memos, sent a message to my acquaintance Mme Auerbakh, asking for the carriage and coachman which she had offered to me earlier for my trip to the palace. I was terribly excited, and it was after 2 a.m. by the time I lay down to sleep. But sleep I could not, as I kept going over and over and consolidating in my mind what I would say to the Tsar.

In the morning, I quickly arranged to pay anything I owed, and asked my sister Tanja to pack up the rest of my things. I got dressed and sat down to

---

119 This and the following quotation are from Strakhov's letter to LNT of 2 January 1891, reproduced in Donskov 2003: II: 849–51.

120 *Akim L'vovich Volynskij* (real name: *Khaim Lejbovich Flekser, 1861–1926*) — Russian literary and ballet critic. His major book publications were: *Leonardo da Vinci* (1900), *F. M. Dostoevsky* (1906) and *Kniga likovanij. Azbuka klassicheskogo tantsa* [The book of rejoicing: an alphabet of classical dance] (1925). The article referred to here is "Nravstvennaja filosofija gr. L'va Tolstogo" [Count Lev Tolstoy's moral philosophy] (Flekser 1890).

121 E. M. Vogüé, "Po povodu 'Krejtserovoj Sonaty'" ["Concerning 'The Kreutzer Sonata'"] (Vogüé 1890).

122 *Anichkov Palace* [Russian: *Anichkov dvorets*] — a palace built from 1741 to 1753 by Empress Elizabeth, designed by architects *Mikhail Zemtsov* (1688–1743) and *Bartolomeo Rastrelli* (1700–1771). It is located on the Nevsky Prospekt at the point where it crosses the Anichkov Bridge over the Fontanka River.

await the appointed time to leave. I had sewn myself a black mourning dress, along with a black lace hat with a mourning veil.

At a quarter past eleven I started out. My heart was beating a bit faster than usual as we entered the courtyard of the Anichkov Palace. At the gates and on the veranda everyone saluted me, and I bowed in turn from the carriage window. When I entered the hallway of the palace, I asked the porter whether the Tsar had issued a command to receive the Countess Tolstoy. "No," he said. They asked someone else, with the same answer. My heart sank.

Then they summoned the Tsar's personal runner.[123] A fine-looking young man appeared in a bright red, gold-trimmed uniform, wearing a huge three-cornered hat. I asked him:

"Is there an order from the Tsar to receive the Countess Tolstoy?" He replied: "Of course, Your Ladyship! The Tsar has just come back from church and he has already been asking for you."

That day the Tsar had been at the christening of Grand Duchess Elisaveta Fëdorovna,[124] who had converted to Orthodoxy.

The runner ran up a steep staircase adorned with a rather ugly bright-green rug. I followed him. The "runner" did justice to his title and literally flew up the straight, steep staircase at lightning speed. Not accounting for my breathing capabilities, I, who was quick and strong on my feet, dashed up the stairs after the runner, fearful of lagging behind. And when the runner finally bowed to me and departed, leaving me in the drawing-room, I felt such a rush of blood to my heart that I thought I would die right then and there on the spot.

My condition was terrible. The first thing that came to my head was that this business was not worth the cost of my life, that when the runner came to summon me to the Tsar's presence, he would find my corpse, or, if I were alive, I wouldn't be able to say a word. My heart was beating so fast that it was literally impossible to breathe, speak or cry out.

After sitting for a little while, I wanted to ask somebody for some water, but I couldn't. Then I remembered that after [coachmen] drive their horses fast, they start walking them slowly. I got up from the sofa and began to walk about quietly. But for a long time it was no better. I carefully and surreptitiously reached in and undid the fasteners on my corset underneath my bodice. Then I sat down again, massaging my breast with my hand and thinking about my nine children and how they would react to the news of my death.

Fortunately, the Tsar, upon learning that I had not yet come, gave audience in the meantime to a general from the Caucasus, which allowed me enough time to rest and recover my composure.

123 *runner* [Russian: *skorokhod*, lit. "fast-walker"] — a messenger retained by the Tsar to run quick errands.
124 *Grand Duchess Elizaveta Fëdorovna Romanova* (1864–1918) — granddaughter to Britain's Queen Victoria (1819–1901) and wife to *Grand Prince Sergej Aleksandrovich Romanov* (1857–1905). She was a devoutly religious believer, known for her charity work.

I did recover and was finally able to breathe more freely. Shortly thereafter the runner appeared again and proclaimed in a loud voice:

"His Majesty invites Her Ladyship the Countess Tolstaya into his presence."

I followed him, and as we walked across a huge, almost empty room, in which three adjutants (probably guards on duty) were standing by the window, I heard my name being called and could sense curious stares in my direction. In my external appearance, I could feel the immaculate elegance of my whole mourning ensemble, as well as my youthful look and lightness of step, and this gave me a degree of confidence and composure.

V.93 EMPEROR ALEXANDER III

IN THE TSAR'S STUDY stood two black Africans[125] in native uniforms. The runner once again bowed to me, opened the door and left.

The Tsar met me right at the door and offered his hand. I curtsied to him, and he began with the words:

"You must pardon me, Countess, for making you wait so long, but circumstances made it impossible for me to receive you earlier. I hope the stairs didn't wear you out? They're pretty steep."

And I responded to the Tsar:

"I myself am deeply grateful that Your Majesty has extended this courtesy to me by receiving me."

The Tsar gestured to an armchair beside his desk, while he himself sat down at the desk. He began talking (I don't remember his exact words) about Lev Nikolaevich, and asking what I specifically wanted from him. Since Feoktistov had already allowed me to publish Volume XIII of Lev Nikolaevich's writings, the only thing left for me to petition for was *The Kreutzer Sonata*, and perhaps this reason might seem too insignificant a request for an audience. But I showed no sign of embarrassment and began speaking altogether firmly and calmly from the start. The Tsar's kind, pale-blue eyes looked at me so gently, then he himself showed such a touching bashfulness that it was quite easy for me to talk with him. And I began:

"Your Majesty, in recent times I have begun to notice in my husband a disposition to write in his former, belletristic genre. He recently told me that he has retreated from his religious philosophical works to the point where he can write fiction [again], and that something has been coming together in his head on the order (and of the magnitude) of *War and peace...*" (This was the honest truth.) And I went on:

125 Africans had been included in the service of the Imperial Court ever since Peter the Great first brought them to Russia in the early eighteenth century as part of his modernisation campaign (following the trend in a number of Western European nations). One of the earliest, *Abram Hannibal* (1697–1782), was not only one of Peter the Great's most trusted guardsmen (under Empress Elizabeth I he rose to the rank of lieutenant-colonel of artillery), but also a maternal great-grandfather to Russia's best-loved poet, *Aleksandr Sergeevich Pushkin* (see Note 23, p. 433).

"Nevertheless, warnings against him are still springing up. You see, for instance, Volume XIII of his writings has been detained. Just the other day they managed to clear it, for some reason. They also banned *The fruits of enlightenment*, yet now an order has been issued to stage it at the Imperial Theatres…"

"Yes, *The fruits of enlightenment* will now be staged," said the Tsar. "This was put on by an amateur troupe at Tsarskoe Selo,[126] and I laughed my head off. It was a splendid performance. But there's no serious motif there, it's just a farce."

"Excuse me, Your Majesty, the serious motif lies in the fact that for us of the nobility, land is an amusement, a toy, but for the peasants, it constitutes their daily bread."

"Yes, but the farce lies in the fact that the chambermaid outwitted her noble masters and turned out to be smarter than they."

After a brief pause, I then began speaking about the detention of *The Kreutzer Sonata*. On this point the Tsar said to me:

"You see, the way it's written, you probably would not want to give it to your children to read. After all, the Count is writing against marriage."

And I said:

"How could the Count write against marriage, when he has been proving by his entire life that he is in favour of marriage? We have nine children. It is unfortunate, though, that this story is written in such an extreme form, but the underlying thought is that the ideal is forever unattainable. If extreme chastity is held up as the ideal, people in a wedded state can only be pure."

I also recall that when I told the Tsar that Lev Nikolaevich seemed to be [now more] disposed to writing fiction, the Tsar exclaimed:

"Oh, how good that would be! He's *such* a good writer, such a good writer!" He put special emphasis on the word *such*.

After my definition of the ideal in *The Kreutzer Sonata*, I added: "How happy I would be if the ban on *The Kreutzer Sonata* in the *Collected works* were lifted! This would be a clear sign of favour toward Lev Nikolaevich and, who knows, it might even encourage him to work [on his fiction]."

Whereupon the Tsar replied:

"Yes, it could be cleared for the *Complete collected works*. Not everyone's in a position to afford them, and there could be no talk of wide distribution."

I don't recall just where in our conversation, but the Tsar twice repeated his regret that Lev Nikolaevich had cut himself off from the church, and added further:

"And so much heresy is being aroused among the common people and it is having a harmful effect on them."

To which I responded:

"I can assure you, Your Majesty, that my husband never preaches anything, either among the common people or anywhere else. He does not say a word to the peasants and not only does he [himself] not circulate his manuscripts on

126 See Chapter V.44 ("Again *The fruits of enlightenment*…") above.

the religious question, but often expresses despair that they are being circulated. The thoughts he writes down are not always for publication, but for his notebooks. But quite often people secretly copy his manuscripts and appropriate them for themselves. For example, one time a young man stole a manuscript from Lev Nikolaevich's briefcase, copied something from his diary and a couple of years later began making lithograph copies and distributing this essay."

I was thinking then, without naming him, of Novosëlov,[127] and this behaviour of his greatly disturbed me. He had secretly taken Lev Nikolaevich's *Nikolaj Palkin*,[128] then later printed and distributed it.

The Tsar was surprised and expressed his disapproval.

"You don't say?! How awful! That's just terrible! Anyone should be able to write what they like in their diaries, but stealing a manuscript — well, that's a really bad deed!"

At this point the Tsar said that Lev Nikolaevich had a huge influence on the common folk, as well as on young people, whom he was converting to his own faith and drawing them away from the church. But I told him that the young people whom Lev Nikolaevich was influencing had already fallen away from the church a long time ago, and the majority of them were on the path of political evil, and his turning people's attention to the land, to loving one's neighbour, to non-resistance to evil, to the teachings of Christ, could only be viewed as something desirable, as it had already saved many from bad deeds, violence and evil. And even if these people weren't in the truth, at the very least they were on the side of order.

The more we talked, the more our mutual trust grew, along with that elusive sense of affinity which made our conversation easy and pleasant. The Tsar spoke meekly, in a very pleasing, slightly sonorous voice. His eyes showed tenderness, his smile was bashful and kind. He was quite tall with a broad-shouldered figure. He was on the stout side, apparently quite strong and powerful. His head was pretty much devoid of hair, and the space between his temples seemed too narrow, with a bit of a squeezed look.

Then the Tsar asked me what the children thought of their father's teachings. I replied that they could have nothing but respect for the high moral rules their father preached, but that I felt a need to raise them in the faith of the church, that I had fasted with the children in August, only in Tula, not in the village, since our priests, who were supposed to be our spiritual fathers,

---

127 *Mikhail Aleksandrovich Novosëlov* (1864–1938) — a Tolstoyan, who after his father's death used the land he inherited to set up a Tolstoyan commune in 1888 at Dugino in Tver' Gubernia. In 1892, however, he would subsequently renounce Tolstoyism and return to the fold of the Russian Orthodox Church, becoming a theologian and religious writer.

128 *Nikolaj Palkin* — a nickname derived from the word *palka* [stick] (LNT's work of this title is sometimes translated "Nicholas the Stick"). The story was banned in Russia for many years but was finally published posthumously in 1917.

had been turned into spies and had been writing false reports about us. I was probably thinking of the Synodal report to which my sons had written a reply, as I mentioned earlier. [129]

To these words the Tsar replied with a tone of sadness:

"I've heard about that."

And he then proceeded to ask me what my children were doing. I told him that our eldest son was the head of a *zemstvo* [district council], the second had married and was busy with his estate, the third was a student, while the remaining six [children] were at home.

I also forgot to mention that when we were talking about *The Kreutzer Sonata*, the Tsar said:

"Couldn't your husband revise it a bit?"

I responded:

"No, Your Majesty. He can never revise his works once they are completed and concerning this story he has said that he has started to find it repulsive, that he can't stand even hearing of it."

Another thing the Tsar asked me was whether Lev Nikolaevich's banned works were being reproduced secretly in typo– litho–... At this point the Tsar stopped short, clearly unable to distinguish the difference between the words *lithographic*, *typographic*, etc. I hastened to prompt him and, of course, I flatly denied this assumption.

"Oh, no! Lev Nikolaevich could never do anything *secretly* or illegally. He writes down his thoughts, and lets people do what they like with them."

Then the Tsar asked:

"Do you often see Chertkov, [130] the son of Grigorij Ivanovich and Elizaveta Ivanovna? [131] He's one your husband has completely converted, after all."

This question I was not at all prepared for, and I was momentarily stuck for an answer. But then it came to me and I replied:

"Chertkov we haven't seen in more than two years," I said. (This was true.) "His wife is ill, and he can't leave her. The ground where Chertkov and my husband came together was not religious at first, but something else. My husband noticed that when it came to literature for the common people, there were a tremendous lot of idiotic and immoral books. He gave Chertkov the idea of transforming literature for the people by giving it a moral and educational direction.

"My husband had written by then several stories for the people. Chertkov put up the money for publishing them. But after being sold in several millions

129 See Chapter V.49 ("Our sons' letter on the Synodal report") in *My Life*.
130 *Vladimir Grigor'evich Chertkov* — see Note 91, p. 452.
131 *Grigorij Ivanovich Chertkov* (1828–1884) — adjutant-general, deputy head of the Senior Committee on Military Equipment and Training (1874–84). *Elizaveta Ivanovna Chertkova* (1834–1923) — wife of Grigorij Ivanovich and a follower of Lord Radstock (English religious activist).

of copies, they were then determined to be harmful, non-ecclesiastical, and they, too, were banned. In addition, a whole lot of scientific, philosophical, historical and other books were published. The venture was a good one, and was making good progress, but then it came up against harassment, too."

To this the Tsar had no answer.

Finally, I decided to state what should have been the reason for my visit and what the Tsar expected to hear me say, although this was the most difficult of all for me:

"Your Majesty, if my husband should again write in the belletristic genre and I publish his works, it would give me the greatest happiness if the fate of his writings were to be decided by the personal will of Your Majesty."

To which the Tsar answered me:

"I shall be most happy to do so. Send his writings directly to my attention."

I had just been thinking that this would never be possible, and I felt awkward and ashamed.

I don't recall exactly whether anything else was said. I think I've written everything down [just as it happened], in good conscience. I do remember the Tsar adding:

"Don't worry, it will all work out. I'm very pleased."

Whereupon he rose to his feet and offered me his hand. To my great joy, I had achieved what I wanted. I had *possessed* the Tsar spiritually, and he had fallen under my influence. I felt triumphant in my soul over the fact that the strength of both my outer and inner energy had not failed me on this occasion. Our conversation lasted fifty minutes.

V.94 EMPRESS MARIJA FËDOROVNA

IN CURTSYING TO THE TSAR, I said to him:

"I'm very sorry that I wasn't able to request a presentation to the Empress.[132] I've been told she's not well."

"On the contrary, the Empress is in good health today and will receive you. Just ask to be announced."

I was already in the doorway leading out of the little room next to the Tsar's study when he stopped me with a question:

"Are you going to be staying long in Petersburg?"

"No, Your Majesty, I'm leaving today."

"So soon? But why?"

"I have a baby at home who's not all that well."

"What's wrong with him?"

"He has the chicken-pox."

"That's not dangerous at all. Just don't let him catch cold."

---

132 *Empress Marija Fëdorovna (née Dagmar, Princess of Denmark, 1847–1928)* — daughter of King Christian IX of Denmark (1818–1906); she married Russian Emperor Alexander III in 1866.

"That's just it — I'm afraid that without me there they will let him do just that. We've been having such freezing temperatures."

We were conversing like good friends, in a simple and heartfelt manner. I was later told that the Tsar expressed considerable regret at my leaving, and said he was going to ask Sheremeteva to invite me to dine at her place along with him.

Whereupon I left, after yet another curtsy. After a warm, extended hand-shake from the Tsar, I went out into the drawing-room while he went off through some interior passageways to the Empress' chambers. My feeling toward the Tsar was: *What a glorious and kind person he is! God grant him the very, very best and all happiness!*

Finding myself alone in the drawing-room, I began to look about me. The furniture was covered in red silk. The centre of the room featured the statue of a woman, flanked by two statues of little boys. There were two mirrors on the side walls of the archways which divided the drawing-room from the parlour. Plants and flowers were everywhere in profusion. I shall never forget that enormous tree with its azaleas in a luxuriant deep-red hue — the one I had looked at an hour earlier, when I thought I was going to die. The view out the windows was none too interesting — just the paved courtyard where two carriages were standing and soldiers were moving about.

A middle-aged servant with a foreign face and accent stood at the door of the Empress' reception room. On the other side stood an African in his native uniform. I asked the servant to announce me to the Tsaritsa, adding that this was with the permission of the Tsar.

He said that there was a lady already with her, and that he would announce me once she left. I waited about fifteen to twenty minutes. A lady came out. The servant told me that the Tsar had spoken to the Empress and told her of my desire to be presented to her.

I went into her room. As the Empress Marija Fëdorovna came toward me, [I noticed] her slender form and how quick and light she was on her feet. Her face was of a very beautiful colour, her hair was groomed with amazing neatness, as though stuck on, and bore a lovely chestnut hue. Malicious tongues had it that the Tsaritsa wore a wig. She had on a black woollen dress, and her waist was long and very slim, as were her hands and neck. She wasn't all that tall, but not all that short either. Her voice was impressive with its loud, guttural sounds.

She offered me her hand, and just like the Tsar, invited me to take a seat.

"*Je vous ai déjà vue une fois, n'est-ce pas?*" she asked.

"*J'ai eu le bonheur,*" I replied, "*d'être présentée à Votre Majesté, il y a de cela quelques années à l'Institut St-Nicolas, chez Madame Schostak.*"[133]

---

133 *Ekaterina Nikolaevna Shostak* (née *Islenèva*, ca. 1814—1904) — director (1863–92) of the Nicholas Institute in St. Petersburg and first cousin to SAT's mother. L'Institut St-Nicolas was founded in 1837 in St. Petersburg for daughters of slain military personnel.

"Ah! Certainement. Et votre fille aussi. Dites-moi, est-ce vraiment possible qu'on vole les manuscrits du comte, et qu'on les imprime sans lui demander sa permission? Mais c'est une horreur, c'est très mal, c'est impossible."

"C'est vrai, Votre Majesté, et c'est bien triste, mais que faire!"

Then the Empress asked how many children I had, and what they did. I expressed to her my joy that her son, Georgij Aleksandrovich,[134] was feeling better. I told her I felt great compassion for her, knowing how hard it must be for her to be apart from her two sons, one of whom was so ill.[135]

She said that he had now completely recovered, that he had had inflammation of the lungs from a cold he had caught at sea, because he had not wanted to put on a jersey (against the advice of Count Olsuf'ev);[136] the illness had then been allowed to fester and she had become very alarmed.

It was not so much an Empress as a mother standing there before me, and this made it easier and more pleasant for me.

I expressed my regret at not seeing her children, to which she replied that they were all at Gatchina.

"Ils sont tous si heureux, si bien portants," she said. *"Je tiens qu'ils aient des souvenirs heureux de leur enfance,"* she added touchingly.

"Dans une famille comme celle de Votre Majesté tout le monde doit se sentir heureux," I said flatteringly. She went on:

"Ce petit Michel[137] aux joues roses, il joue toujours avec Olga. Et Ksenija est déjà une grande fille, elle a seize ans."

Then she rose, offered me her hand and affectionately said:

"Je suis très contente de vous avoir revue encore une fois."

I curtsied and left. Mme Auerbakh's carriage took me back to the Kuzminskijs' home. With a sense of contentment, I bounded up [to their apartment], not even noticing this time the four flights of stairs. I was greeted by my sister Tanja and her husband and children, Vanichka Èrdeli (Masha Kuzminskaja's

134 *Grand Prince Georgij Aleksandrovich Romanov* (1871–1899) — second (surviving) son of Tsar Alexander III and Empress Marija Fëdorovna. Because their elder (surviving) son, *Nikolaj Aleksandrovich* (1868–1918) was childless at the time he inherited the throne (as Nicholas II) upon Alexander III's untimely death in 1894, Georgij Aleksandrovich was proclaimed *Tsarevich* (heir to the throne) but died a childless bachelor himself (allegedly from tuberculosis) in 1899.

135 In late 1890, Georgij Aleksandrovich accompanied his elder brother Nikolaj (the future Nicholas II) on a trip to Japan, travelling by way of Greece, Egypt and India. During a stopover at Bombay [Mumbai], Grand Prince Georgij fell ill and was obliged to return home early.

136 *Count Aleksandr Vasil'evich Olsuf'ev* (1843–1907) — a high-ranking officer in the Imperial Court, brother to the Tolstoy family's close acquaintance *Count Adam Vasil'evich Olsuf'ev* (1833–1901).

137 *Grand Prince Mikhail Aleksandrovich Romanov* (1878–1918) — youngest son of Tsar Alexander III and Empress Marija Fëdorovna. In 1917 Nicholas II abdicated in favour of his brother Mikhail, but the latter refused the throne. There were also two sisters: *Grand Duchess Ksenija Aleksandrovna Romanova* (1875–1960) and *Grand Duchess Ol'ga Aleksandrovna Romanova* (1882–1960).

fiancé),[138]as well as Zosja, Manja and Misha Stakhovich. I felt obliged to tell them the whole story; everybody warmed to me and congratulated me. I wrote two telegrams — one to Lëva in Moscow, the other to Yasnaya Polyana. Happy to be going home, I had lunch and headed off to the station.

By three o'clock that same afternoon I was seated in the train. These same people came to see me off, and I was terribly sad at bidding farewell to my sister Tanja, especially when I looked into her worn face and recollected how much trouble I caused her and how much I had to involve her in my affairs…

V.95 SUCCESS

AFTERWARD PEOPLE FROM ALL SIDES recounted to me the Tsar's description of the impression I had made on him, and this — alas! — flattered my self-esteem. He was ebullient with praise for me in talking with [Countess Aleksandra Andreevna] Tolstaya, and Sheremeteva, and Zhukovskij. He said I was sincere, truthful and likeable. He even said he had not expected to find me so youthful-looking and beautiful.

Countess Aleksandra Andreevna Tolstaya wrote to me, saying that the impression I had made on the Tsar was *superb*. And then, jokingly, she asked me:

"*Qu'est-ce que vous avez fait pour enticher tellement l'Empereur?*"

Then Zosja Stakhovich said in a letter to me that "the Tsar was very sorry, but an urgent matter prevented him from continuing the conversation with you longer, and he said several times how pleasant and interesting it was for him."

All Petersburg began talking of my audience with the Tsar. Many were upset and jealous. Nikolaj Nikolaevich Strakhov reported that Pobedonostsev,[139] upon meeting him on the Nevsky, took hold of him by his coat-button and said disapprovingly:

> Who does this Countess Tolstaya think she is, that over and above all the presentations and visits by society ladies and others she manages to worm her way into an audience with the Tsar and wangle *The Kreutzer Sonata* out of him?! When I suggested it should be cleared, nobody listened to me, but here a biddy asks, and he obliges.

VI.42 MY STORY AND MY SON LËVA'S REACTION TO IT

JUST AS IN THE COUNTRY, so too in Moscow, where I was living, I filled my long, lonely evenings with writing the long story I had started in response to

---

138 *Ivan Egorovich [Vanichka] Èrdeli* (1870–1939) — a distant relative of LNT's, a Russian calvary general, who would later participate on the side of the White forces (against the Bolsheviks) in the Civil War (1918–22), in which he helped establish a volunteer army.
139 *Konstantin Petrovich Pobedonostsev* — see Note 116, p. 461.

Lev Nikolaevich's *Kreutzer Sonata*.[140] My son Lëva, upon hearing of its contents, strongly criticised me for it and even wrote to me from Petersburg on 27 November 1892:

> As Papà's wife, as the mother of us all, someone who couldn't possibly carry out her appointed task better than she does and is still not finished with it, you have earned the right to high praise indeed. But if you should begin to corrupt this position of yours through various outpourings of your groundless and unfair annoyances in [the form of] a poorly written story, you will be departing from your chief, exalted purpose as a wife and mother, since there will no longer be any love here, and you will knock yourself off track.

I don't know whether my son was right or not. I do know that I began writing this story because, without any provocation, all eyes of the public, from the Tsar's right down to Lev Nikolaevich's brother Sergej Nikolaevich's, were focused on me. They began to feel sorry for me as the victim of a jealous husband, and a few of them began to suspect something. I wanted to give a more accurate portrayal of an honest woman and her ideals of love, in sharp contrast to male materialism.

More than any of the other sons, Lëva had a better overall understanding of and love for his father. He even gave me advice on how to gain a wiser perspective on Lev Nikolaevich's life in the country and his unwillingness to come to Moscow, as well as on his indifference to the children and their education.

I could also sense his father's influence on him in the matter of compulsory military service. He wrote to me:

"This whole rigmarole they made me go through today — turning on the spot, like a wolf cub, saluting and falling into line, and how to answer one's superiors — all that is disgusting, repugnant and stupid — it makes me cringe."

Upon noticing that Lëva was so reluctant to serve, and that his health was so poor, the company commander of His Majesty's Infantry Battalion Ozerov said right from the start that Lëva would probably be discharged altogether in a couple of months, and this was how it actually turned out.

And Lëva began filling his head with all sorts of life plans which he never got the chance to realise, so exhausted and overwrought was he — he had got so ill and was unable to recover for a very, very long time.

Apart from writing my story and other things to attend to, I was very busy that autumn with a new edition of the writings of Lev Nikolaevich, who was, at the time, not in favour of publishing too many of his portraits. He wrote me:

---

140 This story of SAT's was eventually published under the title *Ch'ja vina?* [*Who is to blame?*], given in this volume in a new translation by John Woodsworth and Arkadi Klioutchanski.

"It's not a good idea to publish different variants of my portrait in the new edition. It's shameful and indecent when someone's still alive. What do you think?"

Now, however, in 1909, Lev Nikolaevich is quite agreeable to having all sorts of portraits made of him and was especially willing to have V. G. Chertkov[141] take hundreds of photographs of him.

Upon learning about my [projected] new edition, Nikolaj Nikolaevich Strakhov offered me his help in editing the text and gave me a lot of good advice.

VI.43 FET AND HIS PASSING
IN THE AUTUMN OF 1892 Fet's[142] health began to take a noticeable turn for the worse. Despite that, he still kept up his correspondence with me. Back in September he dictated a letter to me:

> Above all, please give our love to our dear friends Sashen'ka and Vanechka (my children) and tell them that these old folks, along with our mynah bird [a talking bird who lived with Fet], send our greetings to them on the occasion of Mamà's name day.[143]
> I've been very ill the whole week. I'm not afraid of death, but I hate suffering.

Fet still had the same high appreciation and love for Lev Nikolaevich, who at that time was reading Faust[144] in Fet's [Russian] translation. He wrote to me about it on 23 October 1892:

> I've now started reading Goethe's *Faust* in Fet's translation. Please give him my very best. Tell him not to think, as he sometimes does, that we've parted ways. I sometimes get the feeling, and especially with him, that people have the impression that I am supposed to alienate myself from them, and they end up alienating themselves from me.

Fet's struggles were often very hard. He was breathing oxygen, and still found himself coughing and short of breath.

One day when I was visiting the Fets, he told me:

> Tell Lev Nikolaevich that back when I read *War and peace*, I used to criticise him for Andrej's gruff attitude toward Natasha on his deathbed. But now I realise that this is surprisingly correct. When someone is dying, his love dies too.

141 *Vladimir Grigor'evich Chertkov* — see Note 91, p. 452.
142 *Afanasij Afanas'evich Fet* (real surname: *Shenshin*). For a portrait of Fet, see Illustration 13.
143 *name day* — see Note 6, p. 426.
144 *Faust* — an epic play in verse by the celebrated German poet *Johann Wolfgang von Goethe* (1749–1832), considered to be one of the finest works of German literature. It is based on the classic German legend about a man who sells his soul to the devil in return for superior knowledge — a legend which has served as a basis for a great many literary and musical works.

My heart is wrenched in two by suffering and helplessness — helplessness in everything, it seems, including love.

Afanasij Afanas'evich [Fet] was vivacious and firm in spirit. He was dying gradually, [his attention] concentrated and serious. There was something very majestic and fascinating and touching in this patient, sober process of dying.
     Another time he told me:

> Here I've been dying during this time and remembering in *The death of Ivan Il'ich* how a healthy peasant sat with him and held his feet, and it made him feel better. And if at this moment Tolstoy should walk in, I would prostrate myself at his feet. Someone who has understood and written such a thing is not a mere man, but a whole unit, a leviathan.

He further told me that nobody was able to calm him down like the simple woman that had been living with them for some time. She would sit beside him and comfort him in a calming voice:
     "Don't worry, sir, have patience. The 12th of December[145] is coming, the sun will turn towards summer, the winter will turn to frost, and all illnesses will then get easier."
     And this Akulina had the kind of effect on Fet that the kitchen peasant did on Ivan Il'ich in Lev Nikolaevich's story.
     At Fet's I met up with an employee of *Moskovskie vedomosti*, Govorukha-Otrok (Nikolaev) and began reproaching him for the article against Lev Nikolaevich. He said that he was not a participant in that, and added his regret that Lev Nikolaevich was writing articles instead of fiction. Fet stopped him and said:
     "In Africa we came to a desert, all white, covered with sand, and there was nobody around. And all of a sudden we looked and there was this mighty *Lev*[146] a-roaring. And he was all alone, with just emptiness around."
     And that *Lev*, of course, was Lev Nikolaevich.
     Even though seriously ill, Fet was still reading Lev Nikolaevich's writings. He wrote me (dictating to his secretary) on 14 November 1892:[147]

> I've been reading over *Childhood* and *Boyhood*. I don't know of any book where the line between decency and indecency is as sharply defined as in *Childhood* and *Boyhood*. Lev Nikolaevich once said: "A man wants to reform the world, and yet he doesn't know enough to behave himself decently in my room — but sits there with his legs crossed."

145 12 December (O.S.; 24 December N.S.) — the date traditionally associated with the winter solstice in the Julian calendar.
146 *Lev* — here used as the common Russian word for "lion."
147 The actual date of this letter was 14 September 1892. Pokrovskaja and Shumova (1978: 133) point out several minor inaccuracies in SAT's citing of Fet's letter.

Fet set great store, on the whole, by the quality of aesthetic appeal, both external and internal. His wife, kind, simple-minded and loyal, having grown up in a merchant family (the Botkins), was fond of observing any kind of celebration, entertaining and stuffing people to the gills. She was now talking of [baking] a pie for Fet's birthday, the 23rd of November. I happened to drop in on this conversation and Fet asked my opinion, whether it was necessary to entertain guests and relatives and serve them pie. I said I wouldn't advise, in view of his ill health and frailty, entertaining guests, chatting and spoiling the air with stuffiness.

"Smart woman!" he said to me as he blew me a kiss. "You always have been," he softly added.

But Fet did not live to see his birthday and passed away on the 21st of November 1892. I shall cite a few passages from my letter to my husband concerning his last days:

> *20 November 1892.* I was at Fet's last night. He sat there breathing heavily, unable to utter a word, hadn't eaten anything for three days. He beckoned me to his side, and when he took my hand and pressed it to his lips, I felt an eeriness at how cold, like a corpse, his hands were, as well as his forehead, which I touched with my lips. I thought he would die that very night. But when I came to see him [the next day], he was sitting up in his study, was able to talk a little, and had slept the night.
>
> His was a measured dying: a spark flares up, and goes out again. Once more it brightens, and then is extinguished for good. An intelligent man dies intelligently, too — calmly, steadfastly and wisely. He is not afraid of death, he desires it. He does not spare his life, but as long as he lives, what was firm before in it is firm still within him…
>
> And you recall his ode to death, and his attitude toward it. Here's one excerpt:
>
>> You still, I know, perforce, my will are heeding,
>> You're a shadow at my feet, a faceless ghost unseen.
>> My thought you are, and nothing more, as long as I'm still breathing,
>> A flimsy plaything fabricated by deep depression's dream.[148]

On the very day of Fet's death I told Lev Nikolaevich of his passing:

> Today at twelve o'clock noon, after a sleepless, tormenting night, Fet himself walked from his study to the dining room and lost his breath. For ten minutes he kept breathing heavily, then more and more quietly, and then stopped breathing altogether. Before this he had been begging (his wife) Mar'ja Petrovna to go

---

148 Final stanza from Fet's 1884 poem "Smerti" [To Death]. Note that the first line is truncated in SAT's version: "You still, I know, perforce, my will are heeding" [*Ty vsja eshchë pokorna moej vole*], whereas the published version reads: "And still each moment you, perforce, my will are heeding" [*Eshchë ty kazhdyj mig moej pokorna vole*]. For the full text of Fet's poem in Russian with English translation, see Poetry Appendix, VI.43, p. 1042 in *My Life*.

bring him some champagne and drop in to the doctor's to ask him whether he might take a drink. All these past few days he had been sending her on errands, thinking up pretexts — he needed cologne, or something else.

After Mar'ja Petrovna had got dressed [to go out], Fet called her over and said: "Farewell, my dear Mamochka, farewell, take care." He kissed her hand, and she his.

Just yesterday morning he sent me a note criticising me for leaving his place on foot instead of sending for a cab, and for being unfriendly to him for the first time in my life. He asked whether I had arrived safely and whether I was in good health. He was attentive and solicitous with those he loved, right to the end.

I attended Fet's funeral, which was held in the university church. There were not that many mourners or wreaths. At his own request, Afanasij Afanas'evich was buried in his chamberlain's uniform. It was strange to see this comic-looking, gold-braided outfit in the coffin, along with the pale, severe face of the deceased, with its humpbacked nose and sunken lips, and that special, unearthly expression of his whole appearance.

I went right up to the coffin and placed a living, luxuriant rose on Fet's chest, and they buried it with him. "Then go give this sweet rose to a poet..." I recalled his verse.[149]

I was sad to see that the coffin was metallic, and that it was closed tightly. I am always bothered when someone's body is not allowed to fulfil its natural law of returning to the earth, but this decomposing body is kept in its own decomposed state. Why? And I am always pleading with my family to bury me in the cheapest wooden coffin or, best of all, directly in the earth, as the Tatars, the Caucasus dwellers and other peoples do.

Upon learning of Fet's death, Nikolaj Nikolaevich [Strakhov] wrote me:

"For Fet death was, of course, a deliverance, and I am prepared to repeat his verse: *You're suff'ring's o'er, while my own joy's still fading!..*[150] He was a powerful man... and he achieved all that he wanted."[151]

149 This is the fourth line of Fet's 1887 poem "Esli raduet utro..." [If you're cheered by the morning...]. The full text of Fet's poem, along with an English translation, is given in the Poetry Appendix, VI.43, in *My Life*.
150 The first line of a three-stanza poem by Fet, "Ty otstradala" [Your suff'ring's o'er] written in 1878. For the text of Fet's entire poem in Russian and in English translation, see again Poetry Appendix, VI.43 in *My Life*.
151 Strakhov's letter to sat, dated 28 November 1892 (from which this passage is taken), is worth quoting at length: "It's more and more difficult for me to think of Fet's death. The first blow, the telegram from [Fet's widow] Marija Petrovna [Shenshina] on the actual day of his death didn't seem too hard to take, but ever since then I can't help remembering the deceased and there is no let-up to my grief, it is only getting worse... He was a powerful man, he struggled all his life and achieved all that he wanted: he earned himself a name, riches, literary fame and a place in society, even at the Court. He appreciated and enjoyed all this, but I'm sure that his poems were dearer to him than anything else in the world and that he knew that they had an incomparable charm — the very height of poetry. As time goes on, others will come to realise this, too... Forgive me! I very much wanted to share my grief with someone, and I know you felt a great attachment to the

At Strakhov's request I wrote him the details of Fet's death, and he sent me this reply on 10 December:

> I received your letter telling about Fet's death. A precious letter, indeed! It has given me so much pause for thought and sheer amazement at his energy! He didn't eat anything for six days — meaning, he couldn't, or didn't want to? In any case, [his] death is a magnificent one. His life, too, in its own way, was really good...
>
> [As to] his verses... their charm is incomparable, the very height of poetry. The more time passes, the more he will be understood by others, too... Fet was a clear and unmistakable reality.
>
> In his relations with others he was a firm and lucid individual, harsh only in his words. [152]

Strakhov was very involved at the time in helping me publish Lev Nikolaevich's writings. He carefully corrected the mistakes in the text, doing so quite willingly. He wrote me, saying that he kept finding new charm in Lev Nikolaevich's writings. On 19 December 1892 he wrote me concerning *The Cossacks* and *The raid* [*Nabeg*]:

> What amazingly serious pieces of writing! What's Turgenev [by comparison], who is constantly primping and shuffling his feet?
>
> Of course, you do a terrific job of proofreading, but I am concerned about your eyes. Four printers' sheets (68 pages) a day — are you joking? [153]

Even before that Strakhov had advised me not to do the proofreading myself. He had written to me, saying: "All that expenditure of energy I'd hardly call taking care of yourself!" [154]

Strakhov also sent me his booklets and an article on Fet, a very good article, and after reading them I sent him my reaction. Not long after that I received a reply from him, in which he wrote, among other things:

"I thank you for your attention to my booklet, and the poetry, and the narrative. How dangerous it is to write in any case! I have a feeling someone else will now see all my faults, all my weak heart, in which, perhaps, the only good thing may be the feeling of an ideal." [155]

---

deceased poet, and I am sure you are saddened no less than I." (Reproduced in Donskov 2000: 244–45).

152 Quoted from Strakhov's letter to SAT dated 10 December 1892 (reproduced in Donskov 2000: 253–54), except for the penultimate paragraph, which is taken from one of Strakhov's earlier letters to SAT, dated 28 November 1892 (Donskov 2000: 244–45), and interpolated here.

153 Donskov 2000: 258.

154 Donskov 2000: 253.

155 Donskov 2000: 253–54 (again, Strakhov's letter of 10 December). SAT's "reaction" (or "attention to [Strakhov's] booklet, and the poetry, and the narrative") appears to have been expressed in her letter to him of 1 December 1892 (Donskov 2000: 246–48) where she wrote in part: "I thank you, Nikolaj Nikolaevich, for the books you sent. [Your] poetry I had read

On 26 December 1892 he wrote further:

"Has anyone noticed that my article on Fet is imbued with sadness?"[156]

Not long afterward I learnt of two other deaths: Il'ja's little son Nikolaj died, as did Pavel Dmitrievich Golokhvastov,[157] an acquaintance of ours with whom Lev Nikolaevich corresponded when he was studying Russian *byliny*.[158] Golokhvastov was a real expert on and lover of *byliny*.

VI.94 A PERFORMANCE

IN THE MIDDLE OF JULY, the fun-loving and eternally enterprising Tanja decided to put on a play with the peasant kids by way of entertainment for Andrjusha and Misha. During a single afternoon Lev Nikolaevich dictated to his daughter Masha a whole five-act play drawn from peasant life. I don't recall its content, and I don't know where this brief little play is today. It probably remained with Masha.[159] I was charged with coming up with some kind of special effect for the ending. The preparations went on all day long, and the performance was being readied in the spacious and empty kitchen in the annexe.

The performance came together quite well, but I should say, without boasting, that the presentation I thought up had a much greater success with the audience. My original composition was more suited to everyone's ability.

On stage a bandit met an old man in the woods, who steered the bandit into living a good life, and at the end of the play there was an apotheosis: two angels with wings (one of them was my little Vanechka, the other a huge doll), and as sparklers went off, both costumed angels proclaimed God's forgiveness to the repentant bandit.

Bored as I was without my sister in the stuffy atmosphere of the Chertkovs and various "dark ones," I planned to take a trip with Vanechka (and, if I recall correctly, with Misha, too) to Il'ja's at Grinëvka, to Serëzha's at Nikol'skoe, and from there to my brother's[160] in Orël. The Kuzminskijs were staying that summer at his dacha near Pesochnaja Station. I was glad to stay with members of

earlier; Fet and I were still talking about it, and I am surprised at how little [poetry] you have written, seeing how good you are at it." (Strakhov's poem "Kometa" [The comet], which particularly appealed to LNT, is reproduced in Donskov 2000: 248–49.) However, SAT evidently did not receive Strakhov's article on Fet until a few days later; she thanked him for that in a letter of 13 December 1892 (Donskov 2000: 255–56), noting: "I must also convey to you my great excitement over your article on Fet. What a fine and elevated appraisal you give of poetry!" A pertinent excerpt from Strakhov's article is reproduced (in Russian) in Donskov 2000: 256, Note 1.
156 Donskov 2000: 259.
157 *Prince Pavel Dmitrievich Golokhvastov* (1838–1892) — Russian writer, historian and researcher on Russian folk legends, and an active participant in Slavophile circles.
158 *byliny* — Russian medieval heroic folk poems or songs.
159 The Tolstoys' daughter *Masha* (*Marija L'vovna*) passed away in 1906.
160 *Aleksandr Andreevich [Sasha] Bers* (1845–1918). See Chapter IV.43 ("Work in the fields") in *My Life*.

my family, who greeted me with love and understanding. Besides, I felt lonely [at home]. I later wrote my sister:

> Lëvochka is never around, after all. He's either writing or sleeping or taking a walk, and he spends all his evenings at the Chertkovs'. I was so overwhelmed today by depression. Naturally, I thought of you right off and felt like simply crying: "Tanja, Tanja!" I climbed into the summer house the children call "Mamà's Tower," and sat there for a long time.

VI.109 DEATH OF VANECHKA

SEVERAL DAYS BEFORE HIS PASSING Vanechka surprised me by starting to give away his things, attaching a note in his own hand, such as "In memory, to Masha from Vanja," or: "To the cook S. N.[161] from Vanja" and so forth. Then he took down various pictures in frames from the walls of the children's room and put them in the room of his brother Misha, whom he was passionately fond of. He borrowed a hammer and nails from me and hung his pictures in Misha's room. He loved Misha so much that if, after a quarrel with Misha, his brother wasn't ready right off to make up with him, he would mope to the point of despair. To what extent Misha loved little Vanechka, I don't know. But later on he named his first son[162] after him.

One time, shortly before his death Vanechka looked out the window, suddenly had an idea and asked me:

"Mamà, is Alësha[163] (my little deceased son) an angel now?"

"Yes, they say that children who die before the age of seven are angels."

To which he replied:

"Then, Mamà, it would be better for me, too, to die before I'm seven. Soon it'll be my birthday, and I'd be an angel, too. But if I don't die, Mamà dear, let me fast so I don't have any sins."

These words acutely tugged at my heartstrings.

On the 20th of February Masha volunteered to assist the nanny in taking Vanja to see Professor Filatov at his clinic for a scheduled appointment. They came back in cheerful spirits. Vanechka was thrilled to announce to me that he was allowed to eat everything, do lots of walking and even go for [horseback] rides. After lunch he went for a walk with Sasha and then enjoyed a hearty dinner.

After being worn out from the sight of Vanechka's illness, everybody in the house was greatly relieved. Not having families of their own, Tanja and Masha brought all the power of their maternal love to bear upon their little brother.

---

161 *Semën Nikolaevich [Sëmka] Rumjantsev* (1867–1932) — son of Nikolaj Mikhajlovich, who filled his position as the Tolstoy family cook after his father's death in 1894.
162 *Ivan Mikhajlovich Tolstoy* (1901–1982) — first son born to *Mikhail L'vovich Tolstoy* (1879–1944).
163 *Aleksej L'vovich [Alësha] Tolstoy* (1881–1886).

On the evening of the 20th Sasha and Vanechka asked their sister Masha to read them the story of Dickens' *Great expectations* as adapted for children under the title *Doch' katorzhnika* [*The convict's daughter*]. When the time came to go to bed, Vanechka came to say goodnight to me and I was shocked to see how sad and tired he looked. I asked him about the reading.

"Don't even mention it, Mamà. It's so sad, terrible! Estella didn't marry Pip."[164]

He and I went downstairs to the children's room. He yawned and spoke to me with such sadness and with tears in his eyes:

"Oh, Mamà, it — it's back again, the fever."

I checked on the thermometer, and his temperature was 38.5. Vanechka complained about a pain in his eyes, and I thought it might be the onset of measles. When I was convinced that Vanechka was falling ill again, I started crying. Upon seeing my tears, he said:

"Don't cry, Mamà, this is God's will."

Not long before that, Vanechka had asked me to explain the Lord's Prayer[165] to him, and I put particular emphasis on the words "Thy will be done" and what they meant. Then he asked me to finish reading one of Grimm's fairy tales which we had recently begun — I think it was the one about the crow.[166] I carried out his request. My son Misha came into the children's room, and I went out to my bedroom. As I found out later, Vanechka told Misha:

"I know I'm going to die now."

During the night he was very hot, but he slept. In the morning we sent for Dr Filatov, who immediately diagnosed scarlet fever. Vanechka's temperature was already up to 40 degrees, and this was coupled with stomach pains and severe diarrhoea, resulting, he explained, from the scarlet fever being complicated by intestinal diphtheria.

At three o'clock in the morning Vanechka awoke, looked at me and said:

"I'm sorry, Mamà dear, that you had to be woken up."

I told him:

"I've had my sleep, dear. We're taking turns staying with you."

"And now whose turn will it be — Tanja's?"

"No, Masha's."

"Then call Masha and go to bed."

My dear, sweet boy lovingly sent me off, and began to kiss me with big and tender kisses, pursing his little dry lips and pressing them against me. I asked him:

"Where does it hurt?"

"Nowhere."

---

164 *Estella, Pip* — two of the main characters in Charles Dickens' three-volume novel *Great expectations*, which he completed in 1861.

165 Matt. 6:9–13..

166 Possibly a reference to the Grimm's fairy tale known as "The seven crows," on the theme of sibling love and forgiveness.

"What is it then, depression?"

"Yes, depression."

After that he hardly ever regained consciousness again. The following day the fever had reached 42 degrees. Filatov wrapped him up in a sheet that had been soaked in mustard water, and even placed him in a warm bath, but nothing helped. His little head drooped helplessly to one side as on a corpse. Then his little hands and feet grew cold. He opened his eyes once more, as though surprised by something, and then lost consciousness.

This was at eleven o'clock at night on the 23rd of February [1895].

Lëvochka, my husband, led me into Tanja's room, sat with me on the daybed, and I fainted, resting my head on his chest. We were in such despair we couldn't move. Vanechka's last moments were attended by my daughter Masha and [Lev Nikolaevich's sister] Marija Nikolaevna (the nun), who kept praying the whole time. The nanny, like me, beside herself with grief, lay on the bed and sobbed intermittently, as I was told later. Tanja kept going in and out of the children's room.

After they had dressed Vanechka in a white jacket and combed his long, fair and curly hair, Lëvochka and I dared to go into the children's room. Vanechka was lying on the daybed, and I placed a little icon on his chest. Someone lit a wax candle and placed it near his head.

It wasn't long before our relatives and friends learnt the news of the death of Vanechka, who was so loved by everyone. So many flowers and wreaths were sent that the whole children's room was like a garden. Nobody even thought of [the possibility of] contagion. Dear, kind-hearted Safo Martynova,[167] who had four children of her own, came over at once, wept with us and actively joined us in our mourning. And all of us clung together with particular passion, united by our love for the deceased Vanechka. Marija Nikolaevna stayed with us and gave us such heartfelt, religious comfort. In his diary Lev Nikolaevich recorded the cry of his heart:

"*26 February*. Vanechka buried. Terrible! — No, not terrible, but a great emotional event. I thank Thee, Father! I thank Thee."

On the third day, 26 February, we held a burial service for Vanechka, nailed the coffin shut, and at twelve o'clock noon his father and brothers, along with Pavel Ivanovich Birjukov, brought the coffin out and hoisted it onto our four-seater sleigh. My husband and I sat across from each other, and set off quietly, while our friends saw us off.

I subsequently described all the events of Vanechka's death in a letter to my sister Tanja:

---

167 *Sof'ja Mikhajlovna [Safo] Martynova* (née Katenina, 1858–1931) — wife of *Viktor Nikolaevich Martynov* (1858–1915) — Gubernia secretary.

And so, Tanja, all during Vanechka's service, without shedding a single tear, I held his ice-cold head in my hands, warmed his deathly cheeks with my hands and kisses. But I did not die of grief, and now, even though I am weeping over this letter, I am alive, and shall, no doubt, live a long time with this stone resting on my heart.

Lëvochka and I silently rode along with our last beloved child, our bright future. As we began to approach the Pokrovskoe cemetery near the village of Nikol'skoe, where we were taking Vanechka to be buried alongside his brother Alësha, Lëvochka started reminiscing about the time when he was [first] in love with me. He used to walk or ride along this same road to Pokrovskoe, where we were staying at the time at our dacha.[168] He became emotional and wept, and comforted me with words and reminiscences, and I felt so comforted from his love.

VI.110 THE FUNERAL

THERE WAS QUITE A CROWD in the village of Nikol'skoe near the Pokrovskoe cemetery, made up of both local residents and those who had come for the funeral. It was a Sunday, and schoolchildren were walking through the village, admiring the wreaths and flowers. Once again, it was Lev Nikolaevich and [our adult] sons who carried the coffin. Everybody wept at the sight of the elderly father, all bent over, stricken with sorrow. Apart from our family, the funeral was attended by Manja Rachinskaja, Sonja Mamonova,[169] Kolja Obolenskij, Safo Martynova, Vera Severtseva,[170] Vera Tolstaya[171] and many others. All wept loudly.

As the coffin was being lowered into the grave, I fainted. It felt as though I had fallen into some kind of oblivion. They said later that our son Iljusha blocked this terrible grave from my gaze, and someone was holding me by the arms. My husband, Lëvochka, put his arms around me and held me to his chest, and I remained a long time in some kind of daze.

I came to upon hearing the cries of the throng of peasant youngsters, to whom our nanny, on my instructions, was giving out various sweets and buns. The children laughed, dropped and picked up their *prjaniki*[172] again. I remembered how Vanechka loved to treat everyone and celebrate just about anything — and I cried for the first time after his death.

168 See Chapter I.1 ("Birth and childhood") in *My Life*.
169 *Sof'ja Èmmanuilovna [Sonja] Dmitrieva-Mamonova* (1860–1946) — an artist and friend of Tat'jana L'vovna's.
170 *Vera Petrovna Severtseva* [also spelt: *Severtsova*] (married name: *Istomina*, 1870–1900) — daughter to SAT's first cousin *Ol'ga Vjacheslavovna Severtseva* (née *Shidlovskaja*).
171 *Vera Sergeevna [Verochka]Tolstaya* (1865–1923) — third child born to LNT's brother *Sergej Nikolaevich Tolstoy* (1826–1904).
172 *prjaniki* — traditional Russian honey-cakes.

Right after the funeral the artist Kasatkin[173] came to the grave after every-body had gone and painted two études of the fresh gravesite. One of them he gave to me, the other to [our daughter] Tanja, and in conjunction with this wrote a very dear, heartfelt and poetic letter full of love for Vanechka, whom he called "transparent."

We returned like orphans to our empty house, and I recall how down-stairs in the dining room Lev Nikolaevich sat down on the sofa, which had been previously brought in for the sick Lëva, and, breaking into tears, said: "I thought that Vanechka, of all my sons, would carry on my mission on earth after my death.

And at another time he repeated essentially the same [thought]: "As for me, I dreamt that Vanechka would continue God's work here after me. What do I do now?"

And watching his deep sorrow was even harder on me than my own suffering.

I wrote to my sister [Tat'jana Kuzminskaja] concerning Lev Nikolaevich:

> Lëvochka's all bent over, he's aged, he walks around sad, with pale-tinged eyes, and it's evident that the last bright ray of his old age is still kindling in him. On the third day after Vanechka's death he sat weeping and saying: "For the first time in my life I feel a sense of hopelessness."

Of all the children, Vanechka most resembled his father in the face. The same deep, thoughtful and sparkling eyes, the same seriousness of his inner spiritual essence. One time, while combing his curly hair in front of a mirror, Vanechka turned his little face toward me and said, smilingly:

"Mamà, I myself feel how much I resemble Papà."

VI.111 AFTER THE FUNERAL

THE FIRST NIGHT after Vanechka's death I jumped up in the middle of the night in a fit of horror from the hallucination of a particular aroma, and this aroma haunted me for a long time afterward, even though my husband, who was sleeping with me at the time, assured me that there was no aroma, that I was just imagining it. And then all of a sudden, I heard Vanechka's voice, tender and affectionate. It seemed as though I was praying to God together with him, we made the sign of the cross over each other, and he told me:

"Kiss me tighter, place your head next to mine, blow on my little chest so that I can fall asleep with your breath."

There is no love purer, stronger or better than the love between a mother and child. Vanechka's death brought an end to the dear child-oriented world

---

173 *Nikolaj Alekseevich Kasatkin* (1859–1930) — an artist of the Itinerant School, with whom LNT became acquainted in the late 1880s.

in our home. Sasha walked around the house like a lonely orphan, not knowing where to find peace for her soul. She had a wild and uncommunicative
nature. Vanechka, by contrast, liked people, he liked writing letters, entertaining, celebrating, giving, and how many people loved him!

Even the cold-hearted Men'shikov[174] wrote of him:

"When I saw your little son, I thought that he was either going to die or end
up a greater genius than his father."

I received many, many marvellous letters of condolence over Vanechka's
death and about Vanechka himself. N[ikolaj] N[ikolaevich] Strakhov wrote
to Lev Nikolaevich:

"He was full of promise. It is possible that he would have inherited not
only your name but your fame, too. As to how dear he was, there's no words
to describe that!"[175]

A certain writer named Zhirkevich[176] wrote:

> One writer from Petersburg who is not personally acquainted with either you
> or Lev Nikolaevich or Vanechka, has written an article about Vanechka, a rave
> review, calling him a marvellous creature, full of hope and promise. All mothers
> and fathers grieve with you today, and my own voice is drowned out in the roar
> of universal sympathy.

Here is M[ikhail] A[leksandrovich] Stakhovich's reaction:

> It's too bad about Vanechka himself, such a dear, touching and interesting child,
> whom I didn't see much of, but who unwittingly made himself memorable in
> that he was different from common children, in his persistent, serious gaze, and
> the meaningfulness inherent in his child's talk and actions.

O. A. Golokhvastova[177] wrote of Vanechka:

"Dear, clever, sensitive, pale Vanechka!"

S. A. Filosofova[178] tried to comfort me, assuring me that I was dear and
needful to so many people, adding:

"You still have a lot of good to give through your clear, sincere and suffering heart."

---

174 *Mikhail Osipovich Men'shikov* (1859–1918) — Russian thinker, journalist and political writer.
Initially sympathetic to LNT's ideas, he later changed his mind and wrote articles in *Novoe vremja*
critical of LNT.

175 From Strakhov's letter to LNT of 2 March 1895, reproduced in Donskov 2003: II: 988.

176 *Aleksandr Vladimirovich Zhirkevich* (1857–1927) — military jurist, literary activist and philan-
thropist, a close friend of the artist Repin. He wrote under the pseudonym of *A. Nivin*.

177 *Ol'ga Andreevna Golokhvastova* (1840–1897) — Russian writer, wife of *Pavel Dmitrievich
Golokhvastov* (1838–1892) — writer, historian and researcher on Russian folk legends, and an
active participant in Slavophile circles.

178 *Sof'ja Alekseevna Filosofova* (née Pisareva, 1847–1901) — wife of *Nikolaj Alekseevich Filosofov*
(1838–1895) — director of the Moscow School of Painting, Sculpture and Architecture and mother
of Il'ja L'vovich's wife, *Sof'ja Nikolaevna [Sonja] Tolstaya* (née Filosofova, 1867–1934).

A. G. Dostoevskaja[179] had seen little of Vanechka, but wrote to me about him: "He was a richly endowed being with a tender, sensitive heart."

Peshkova-Toliverova, who published Vanechka's story in [her magazine] *Igrushechka* [The Little Toy],[180] wrote:

"Oh, how alive he is standing there before me, pale, modest, but with inquisitive eyes."

Our old friend Prince Sergej Semënovich Urusov[181] had a calming effect on me, firmly assuring me of the blissful, Paradise state of Vanechka's soul. He was such a firm and religious Orthodox believer that he infected me with his faith.

Many people prayed for Vanechka and for us in churches and homes. We felt special sympathy from fathers and mothers who themselves had lost children, such as Aleksandra Alekseevna Chicherina (*née* Kapnist), who had lost her only daughter, or Baroness Mengden,[182] whose two adult sons had died, etc. I described in a letter to her something of what I was feeling at the time. I wrote to her on 3 March 1895:

> On this occasion, too, your sensitive heart has responded to my sufferings. Thank you. It is a great comfort to me that all my close relatives and friends have shown such kindness and compassion toward me. I dare not complain to you of my grief, as you have experienced incomparably worse, but my God! What terrible torture, heart wrenching and hopelessness my present suffering is! No matter how much I tell myself that it was too difficult for an infant with such a refined nature as Vanechka's to live, no matter how often I try to affirm all day long "Thy will be done!," I find no escape from my situation. It's just as though, after this dear, loving being was taken away from me, my whole soul has been taken from me and my body is perishing in hopeless agony.
>
> I pray to God and ask whoever can, to pray for me, so that I may be able to find some kind of holy purpose in my life, capable of filling that pure, bright spot in my life left vacant by the absence of my angel.
>
> Please forgive this painful cry of my heart and love, as before, one who passionately loves you and is devoted to you,
>
> S. Tolstaya

I kept up my correspondence with this dear baroness, E[lizaveta] I[vanovna] Mengden, until the end of her life. She was extraordinarily kind to me. After

---

179 *Anna Grigor'evna Dostoevskaja* (née *Snitkina*) — Dostoevsky's widow (1846–1918).

180 *Igrushechka* — an illustrated magazine for children edited and published (beginning in 1888) by *Aleksandra Nikolaevna Peshkova-Toliverova* (1842–1918). Vanechka's story was published in issue Nº 3 (1895): 39–43. Peshkova-Toliverova also put out a literary journal under the title *Zhenskoe delo* [Women's Forum]. She first met LNT in 1892.

181 *Prince Sergej Semënovich Urusov* (1827–1897) — a veteran of the Sevastopol' campaign in the Crimean War, where he became lifelong friends with LNT. He was also known as a champion chess master.

182 *Baroness Elizaveta Ivanovna Mengden* — see Note 111, p. 460.

my visit she wrote, for example, in her diary (which her daughter [later] kindly gave to me to read):

"I was very happy about Countess S. A. Tolstaya's arrival. She is a charming woman. Her honesty is astounding and constitutes her principal charm."

But is honesty a quality? Is it possible to be otherwise?

VI.112 LEV NIKOLAEVICH'S REACTION TO VANECHKA'S DEATH

MORE THAN ANYTHING ELSE, Lev Nikolaevich displayed *artistry* in every aspect of his life. The artistry of the moment, the situation, people's words, Nature — everything in the realm of both life and thought. He was often deaf to people's sufferings and yet would shed tears over a book, or music, or what people said aloud. Since everyone who comes across these memoirs will, of course, be most interested in how Lev Nikolaevich reacted to Vanechka's death, I shall cite a few examples of his diary and his letter to Countess Aleksandra Andreevna Tolstaya.[183]

From his diary of 12 March 1895. Vanechka's death was for me like Nikolen'ka's death — no, to an even greater extent — a manifestation of God, an attraction to Him. And so not only can I not say that it was a sorrowful, difficult event, but I shall say openly, that it was... an event of mercy from God, breaking the lie of life and drawing [us] closer to Him.

Sonja can't possibly see it this way. For her the pain is almost physical — like that of a rupture, hiding the spiritual import of the event. But she surprised me. The pain of the rupture at once freed her from everything that was overshadowing her soul. It was as though the doors had been flung open (and *I* said it was as though the heavens had been temporarily opened for me), and the divine essence of love which constitutes our soul had been revealed. She surprised me in those first days with her amazing capacity to love: whatever violated that love, even in the slightest — whatever hinted at a condemnation of someone or something, even a hostile thought — all that offended her and caused her to suffer, and caused the exposed sprouting of love to undergo painful contractions.

But time has passed, and that sprouting of love has closed up again, and her sufferings have ceased to find satisfaction... in universal love, and have become inconsolable and torturesome... I have been trying to help her, but I can see that to date I have not been able to help her. But I love her, and it is both difficult and comforting to be with her. She is still physically weak... We are all very close to one another...

I look upon the death of children objectively this way: Nature tries to give the best, and upon seeing that the world is not yet ready for them, takes them back. But she must keep trying in order to go forward. This is the demand. When swallows try to migrate too early, they freeze. But they still have to come. So did Vanechka.

183 *Countess Aleksandra Andreevna Tolstaya* (1817–1904) — daughter of *Andrej Andreevich Tolstoy* (1771–1844). See also Note 51, p. 441.

The English [*sic*] writer Emerson[184] says somewhere that he has found an answer, more or less, to every question of life, but for a long time he couldn't understand why [some] children are born to die. The only solution he could come up with is that God sends children to earth to remind people of love.

Lev Nikolaevich also wrote:

"Sonja, through these weighty sufferings, is making a transition to a new stage of life. Help her, Lord!"

Lev Nikolaevich never wanted to see anything religious in me, since I did not want and simply was not able to walk away from the church as had he. At the time I wrote to my sister:

> I am seeking comfort in the fact that through suffering I am making a transition to eternity, and that these sufferings are necessary for the purification of my soul, which ought to join together with God and Vanechka, who was here nothing but love and joy, and I am crying out: "Thy will be done!" — if this is necessary for my transition to eternity. But despite this constant uplifting of the spirit and the genuine cry of my heart to submit to God's will, I find no comfort in this, nor in anything, not in anything.

For some reason Lev Nikolaevich denied any kind of religiosity in me. It irritated him that I kept constantly going to churches and monasteries and cathedrals. I recall that by way of a fast I once spent nine hours straight in the Arkhangel'skij Cathedral [in the Moscow Kremlin], either standing for the service or sitting on the entrance steps with petitioners, pilgrims and an educated woman who, as I, had lost a son (already an adult) and was seeking comfort in prayer and God's temple.

One time it rained all the way home as I walked back from the Kremlin to Khamovniki Lane. I got soaked, caught cold and was ill for a long time. But before then Sasha and I were fasting, which was probably not something dear to Lev Nikolaevich's heart. He wrote in his diary of 27 March 1895:

"Sonja is still suffering the same way and is unable to rise to any religious height... The reason is that she has focused all her spiritual forces on an animal-like love for her wee one."

Why an *animal-like* love? I had many children, but it was with Vanechka, in particular, that spiritual love prevailed in our affection for each other. He and I lived with a common soul. We understood each other, and, despite his age, we would go off into a spiritual or abstract realm.

Even though Lev Nikolaevich's letter to Countess A[leksandra] A[ndreevna] Tolstaya had already been published, in a book put out by the Tolstoy Museum entitled: *Perepiska gr. L. N. Tolstogo s grafinej A. A. Tolstoj* [L. N. Tolstoy's

---

184 *Ralph Waldo Emerson* (1803–1882) — see Note 107, p. 458.

correspondence with Countess A. A. Tolstaya],[185] I shall cite an excerpt from it here as a living illustration of Lev Nikolaevich's mood at the time. I had actually started the letter myself, but I fell ill.

> *29 March 1895.* My sincerely esteemed, dear Granny![186] We have thought of you many times in our sorrow as a loving heart always open to compassion and love, and your letter delighted us, just as though we had been expecting it from you the whole time. The sorrow which has overtaken us is far more than could ever be imagined. Regardless of our unlimited love for Vanechka, we ourselves were not fully aware of what a tremendous role this tender, loving seven-year-old boy played in the life of our whole family. He was just a month shy of his seventh birthday when he died of a bad case of scarlet fever, which he had had for two days. The case was further complicated by a serious intestinal stomach disorder. He did not experience any more suffering, since the high 42-degree fever made him lose consciousness.

I did not finish the letter, as this was the day that I caught cold upon [return-ing from] confession and was confined to bed for a long time. Lev Nikolaevich continued:

> *31 March 1895.* Sonja began writing this letter a couple of days ago. She didn't finish, and has come down with influenza, and now is still not well and has asked me to take over. And I am most happy to do so, my dear, sweet old friend. It seems Sonja's physical condition is not dangerous or onerous, but her inner pain is extremely heavy to bear, though I think it is not only not dangerous, but is actually beneficial and joyful, like giving birth, like being born to a spiritual life. Her sorrow is tremendous. From everything that was difficult, unexplained, and troubling in her life, she has sought refuge in this love, a passionate and mutual love for a boy who was indeed extraordinarily spiritual and lovingly blessed. (He was one of those children whom God sends prematurely into a world not yet ready for them, one of the harbingers, who freeze [to death] like early-migrating swallows.)[187] And then all of a sudden he was taken from her, and, despite her motherliness, she seemed to have nothing left in the secular world.
>
> And so she was involuntarily led to the necessity of rising into another, spiritual world, in which she had not lived hitherto. And it is remarkable how her maternal qualities have kept her pure and capable of perceiving spiritual truths. She amazes me with her spiritual purity — especially her humility. She is still seeking, but so sincerely, with all her heart, that I am confident that she will find [what she seeks].

185 See in the bibliography: Aleksandra Andreevna Tolstaja 1911.

186 *Granny* [Russian: *babushka*] — an affectionate name by which LNT was wont to address his first cousin, once removed — *Countess Aleksandra Andreevna Tolstaya* (1817–1904). He would tease her that she wasn't old enough to be called "Auntie" (their age difference was but eleven years), so he should call her "Granny" instead.

187 Note by SAT: This precise artistic thought was recorded in Lev Nikolaevich's diary around the same time.

What is good in her is that she is submissive to the will of God and only asks Him to teach her how to live without the being to which she had been applying the full force of her love. Yet still to this day she has not found an answer.

This loss is painful to me, too, but I am a long way from feeling the way Sonja does about it: first, because I have had and still have another life — the spiritual, and secondly because her sorrow tends to obscure my own deprivation — instead, I see what great things are happening within her, in her soul, and I feel sorry for her and am anxious over her condition. On the whole I can say that I feel fine.

These last few days Sonja has been fasting with the boys and Sasha, who is so dearly and seriously praying, fasting and reading the Gospel. She, poor thing, has been most acutely affected by this death. But I think it's for the better. Now she has been taking communion, while Sonja has not been able to on account of her illness. Yesterday she went to confession with the very intelligent priest Valentin[188] (a friend and mentor to [Lev Nikolaevich's sister] Mashen'ka), who was right in telling Sonja that mothers who lose their children always turn to God initially, but then later turn back to their earthly cares and again withdraw from God, and he warned her about this. And so, it seems, this will not happen in her case…

How many times I have asked myself before (as have many): why do children die? And never have I found an answer. Lately, however, not thinking at all about children but about my own life and human existence in general, I have come to the conclusion that the only goal for any individual in life lies exclusively in increasing love in one's self, and in doing so, infecting others similarly, thereby increasing love in them. And now when life itself has posed to me the question as to why this little boy lived and died before living even a tenth of a normal human life, the answer I have come to, not thinking exclusively about children, applies not only to this death, but what happens to all of us thereby confirms its own validity.

He lived to increase this love in himself, to grow in love, since that was what was required by Him Who sent him, and for the purpose of infecting all of us around him with this same love, so that when he left [this] life to go to Him Who is love, he might leave the love that grew in him in us, to unify us with it. Never before have we been so close to each other as now, and never, either in Sonja or myself, have I felt such a need for love or such a repulsion toward any kind of disunity or evil. Never have I loved Sonja so much as now. And this makes me feel good.

Farewell, dear, sweet friend. Forgive me for writing only about myself and my family. Write us a few words about yourself. Hugs from Sonja, me and all the children.

L. Tolstoy

Since I have entitled this book *My Life*, I felt it was very important to include this marvellous letter, which gave me the joy of recalling that love with which

---

188 *Father Valentin* (birth name: *Valentin Nikolaevich Amfiteatrov*, 1836–1908) — well-revered archpriest, known for his excellent preaching, recognised as a 'miracle-worker' [*chudotvorets*].

my husband comforted me at that time. Indeed, he was touchingly tender in the overall way he treated me then. I remember him asking me [to go with him] to visit his sister Mashen'ka [Marija Nikolaevna] on her name day, 25 March, and we talked over what we should give her. I recall her wanting an alarm-clock, so as not to miss church services, and the two of us bought an alarm-clock and gave it to her, which, like our visit, delighted her.

I also recall that under the pretext of buying books for prisoners Lev Nikolaevich asked me to go to the Palm Sabbath celebrations. He thought that it would amuse me. I bought some artificial white flowers — a branch of white lilacs — which even today hangs over a large portrait of Vanechka.

After visiting his sister Marija Nikolaevna, Lev Nikolaevich wrote in his diary:

"Mashen'ka has become kinder since she entered the nunnery. What does that mean? How can paganism be joined together with Christianity? I can't fully clarify [*ujasnit'*] it for myself."

He considered me the same kind of "pagan" only because, like [his sister] Mashen'ka, I did not renounce the church. And I always thought that a faith relying so much on form and circumstances was pretty poor. And how could my faith be interfered with by the place where people for centuries have gathered in God's name, preserved this idea of Deity, brought to the temple their sorrows, joys, spiritual moods, hopes, doubts — i.e., everything mankind has lived by and still lives by.

VI.117 SERGEJ IVANOVICH TANEEV

BACK IN THE SPRING I was lying in semi-pain on a daybed on the balcony of our Khamovniki home when Sergej Ivanovich Taneev[189] came to see me. During our conversation I asked him where he was planning to spend the summer. He said that usually he spent his summers with his friends, the Maslovs,[190] in a village in Orël Gubernia, but this year they had a sick child with them and he didn't feel right about imposing on them, so he was looking to rent a private room somewhere on a nobleman's estate. At once the thought came to me of renting him our Yasnaya Polyana annexe, but we didn't yet know whether it might be occupied by our sick son, Lëva, as he had proposed earlier, or whether he would stay at Hanko.[191] In any event I offered Sergej Ivanovich the annexe on condition that Lëva declined to spend the summer there.

189 *Sergej Ivanovich Taneev* — see Note 42, p. 457, also Illustration 17.
190 *Fëdor Ivanovich Maslov* (1840–1915) — Russian lawyer and jurist, chairman of the judicial service for the Moscow area. He was an acquaintance of the composer Pëtr Ill'ich Tchaikovsky (1840–1893). The Maslovs often spent summers at their Selishche estate in Orël Gubernia.
191 *Hanko* [the Russian variant used by SAT here is *Gange*] — a port city on the Gulf of Finland, 130 km west of Helsinki on the Hanko Peninsula, which features many sandy beaches. During World War II it briefly served as a Soviet naval base, under the 1940 Moscow Peace Treaty.

It seemed that my proposal was very much to Taneev's liking. We parted with the agreement that he would think it over, and that I would talk about it with my family and get in touch with Lëva. The upshot was that Sergej Ivanovich, along with his elderly nanny, moved into the annexe for a total payment of 125 roubles. I didn't want to take any money, but Taneev would not agree to live at our place rent-free. This money I donated to a charitable cause, since Taneev's stay and his amazing piano playing gave us nothing but joy.[192]

After dinner he would usually play chess with Lev Nikolaevich, and later, in the evenings, he would do a lot of practising on the piano, and everybody was in ecstasy at his playing. Lev Nikolaevich and he had an agreement: if Sergej Ivanovich lost a game of chess, he was to play for Lev Nikolaevich whatever Lev Nikolaevich desired. And if Lev Nikolaevich lost, he would have to read for Sergej Ivananovich from his latest writings. This agreement was most advantageous for all of us, since we all were an audience and our evenings were greatly enriched.

I recall the feverish impatience with which I waited for these evenings and Taneev's marvellous playing, which relieved my acute emotional struggles for a time. Sometimes I would go to the annexe where Taneev was staying, and sit unnoticed on the porch and listen through the open windows while Sergej Ivanovich was rehearsing a Chopin polonaise that Lev Nikolaevich had asked for, or a Beethoven sonata or some other piece. During these moments I would be oblivious to my grief, carried away as I was into another realm, relaxing in my soul and acutely anticipating again and again the repetition of this blissful condition.

Truth be told, it was not until that moment that I had a clear understanding of what music was all about. I rarely went to concerts and was not acquainted with any good musicians, especially pianists. Taneev's playing was special. When it came to music, he was a philosopher, too. Sometimes he performed with such passion that it was eerie — all the more so since in life he was rather placid, and seemed to be completely devoid of passion. He liked jokes and satire, he liked to eat, and in his outward appearance he was plain to the extreme. One had to get to know him more closely to understand his inner substance and the very essence of his nature and spiritual life. One thing was for certain: more than anything else in the world, he loved music and his old nanny Pelageja Vasil'evna.[193]

Sometimes I would go for walks with Taneev, Sasha and her dear English [governess], Miss Welsh,[194] but frequently, if something should remind me

---

192 Taneev's stay at Yasnaya Polyana in the summer of 1895 was described earlier by SAT (with a few variations) in Chapter III.39 ("Three significant periods") pp. 434–439.

193 *Pelageja Vasil'evna Chizhova* — see Note 43, p. 437.

194 *Anna Welsh* [known in Russia as *Anna Lukinichna Vel'sh*] — proprietor of a small music school in Moscow, who spent her summers at Yasnaya Polyana tutoring the Tolstoys' daughter *Aleksandra L'vovna [Sasha]*. In her reminiscences Aleksandra L'vovna wrote of her: "At first I tried

directly of Vanechka, I would run off alone home in tears. It was even harder to go for walks with my immediate family. I recall one time Lev Nikolaevich inviting me to go for a walk with him, and I felt such joy at his tender invitation, but along the way I burst into tears and upset my poor husband, who said rather depressingly:

"There's nothing out there, there's no real summer. It's as though a new era in life [has begun] which is altogether unfamiliar and, in my view, extremely difficult."

All day long each of us would stay in our respective corners and come together only at dinnertime [lunch], supper-time and tea-time. I was often sad, too, over the absence of my sister's family, with whom we had spent almost twenty-five consecutive summers together.

As I describe these facts, I greatly regret not having noted down Lev Nikolaevich's conversations at the time, or anything about his spiritual life. Personally, I was always interested in his career and his mood. It's just that it never entered my head to write it down. At the time I had no idea that in my advanced years I would be writing the whole story of my life.

VI.118 NIKOLAJ NIKOLAEVICH STRAKHOV

OUR CLOSE FRIEND AND CONSTANT VISITOR, N. N. STRAKHOV,[195] took seriously ill at this time. It turned out he had cancer of the tongue, probably from excessive smoking. Lidija Ivanovna Veselitskaja (whose pen-name was Mikulich)[196] wrote to us that Nikolaj Nikolaevich was in the Nicholas Hospital[197] and that they were cutting the cancer out of his tongue. The operation had gone well, and he was already on the road to recovery. From the hospital he wrote me a letter, thanking us for the invitation we had sent him. Thinking only of how I could live a better, kinder and worthier life after Vanechka's death, the thought that I might be able to look after and care for our recovering old friend was a joyful one to me. He wrote to me, among other things:

"It pleases Him (God) for you to go on living and taking steps to be helpful, as before, both to those close to you and to those further removed from you. You need to calm down and get a hold of yourself."

I was surprised that when I asked Lev Nikolaevich whether I might invite N. N. Strakhov to spend the summer with us, he replied in the negative. But later he agreed, though rather reluctantly.

to play tricks on her just as I had done with other governesses, but this didn't work, and I became attached to her." (A. L. Tolstaja 1930: 26).

195 *Nikolaj Nikolaevich Strakhov* — see Note 12, p. 430.

196 *Lidija Ivanovna Veselitskaja* (pseudonym: *Mikulich*, 1857–1936) — Russian writer (especially of children's stories).

197 *Nicholas Hospital* — an old military hospital in St. Petersburg, opened in 1840 at the behest of Tsar Nicholas I. The name *Nicholas* was added in 1865 by Emperor Alexander II in honour of Nicholas I.

On the 1st of July[198] Strakhov arrived at Yasnaya Polyana and spent most of his time with me, chatting about the most varied subjects. One time he would be explaining Darwin's[199] system to me. Another time we might go for a night-time walk and he would point to the stars and share the mysteries of astronomy with me. He was knowledgeable about so many things and explained things so clearly, calmly and understandably. These conversations, too, took me away from my burdensome thoughts and recollections, and to this day I feel gratitude in my heart to my two friends, Taneev and Strakhov, for helping me at this difficult time.

Strakhov changed little after his operation, only his diction suffered. For example, he could not pronounce the letter *r*. He could not eat any hard food and was always touched when I ordered some especially soft cutlets for him, or pap, or something else. So he stayed with us quite a while, after which he headed off to Kiev and somewhere else, besides.

My grandchildren were brought to me that summer — Il'ja's children Annochka and Misha.[200] I loved my grandchildren, though nobody could ever replace the refined, all-understanding and tender soul of my Vanechka — he was incomparable and irreplaceable.

VII.16 CROWDS AND TANEEV

OUR SUMMER OF 1896 was quite busy and crowded. Let alone the tutors for Sasha and Misha — the Russian teacher Kursinskij,[201] the Swiss woman[202] for German, the Englishwoman[203] for music — there were a tremendous lot of visitors. The Chertkov family was staying close by. Chertkov himself, with his customary lack of courtesy, not only came by almost every day, but frequently brought five or six others with him. This greatly exhausted Lev Nikolaevich, who was very wrought and burdened by everyone and everything as it was. I was glad when a persistent fever obliged Chertkov to try a change of climate and he and his whole family left.

Lev Nikolaevich also began to get irritated by Taneev's presence, even though in the evenings he continued to play chess with him and listen to his music. Whenever they talked, Lev Nikolaevich would get irritated and once even told Taneev: "Only peasants or very stupid people would ever reason like that!" Taneev got up and walked out without saying a word, and later Lev Nikolaevich apologised to him.

---

198 Other sources give the dates of Strakhov's 1895 stay at Yasnaya Polyana as 4 July–9 August.
199 *Charles Robert Darwin* — see Note 15, p. 430.
200 *Anna Il'inichna Tolstaya* (1888–1954) and *Mikhail Il'ich Tolstoy* (1893–1919) — children of the Tolstoys' son Il'ja L'vovich. For a sample of SAT's drawings for her grandchildren, along with a dedicatory message, see Illustrations 42 and 43.
201 *Aleksandr Antonovich Kursinskij* (1872–ca. 1919) — poet, translator and literary critic. He spent the summers of 1895 and 1896 at Yasnaya Polyana as tutor to Mikhail L'vovich Tolstoy.
202 *Mademoiselle Aubert* — Swiss governess employed by the Tolstoys to tutor Sasha.
203 *Anna Welsh* — see Note 194, pp. 493–494.

Subsequently he wrote in his diary that he didn't like the fact that Taneev had become *le coq du village* in our home. Indeed, everybody liked him, and everybody had a good time with him. He studied Italian together with Tanja and Masha. We would all go for walks together or take a carriage ride. I was friendly with Taneev, too — I was very excited about his piano-playing.

All this did not go over well with Lev Nikolaevich, and he was especially angry at me. I couldn't put it down to jealousy; at first that never even entered my head. I was already fifty-two, and men as such could not possibly exist for me. Besides, I was too firmly and fervently in love with my husband, and there was absolutely no point in comparing anyone with such a being as Lev Nikolaevich, who was unique in terms of his spiritual beauty and elevation. I also recall being especially happy at Taneev's purely friendly relations with the Maslovs, and I wanted the same kind of relationship with all of them, including Taneev.

A great deal of fuss and bother, but also vivacity, was contributed to our home by the boys — Misha and his chums Mitja D'jakov,[204] Sasha Bers,[205] [and] Jusha Pomerantsev[206] (a pupil of Taneev's). They were all dear and happy lads, but Lev Nikolaevich seemed to feel burdened by them.

The 28th of June was our son Serëzha's birthday and name day, and I went to see him at his Nikol'skoe estate, where he was living at the time with his wife, Manja. I could sense even then that this young woman didn't feel at home here. As the only daughter of a single father, she had been spoilt, she loved luxury, and had graduated in mathematics from Cambridge University. She wasn't accustomed to the countryside and had no love for it, besides being sickly and weak.

VII.25 MUSIC AND SHATTERED NERVES

I WASN'T FINDING SATISFACTION in any aspect of life, especially without Lev Nikolaevich around, and more and more I kept retreating to my musical interests, exploring and discovering more and more aspects of beauty I had overlooked and not comprehended earlier. I trained myself to listen for them, often following each instrument in the orchestra and even all the subtleties of musical technique. But I knew that music was only a form of *entertainment* [*razvlechenie*], and not a *serious activity* [*delo*] to which I was accustomed, and so even music didn't always satisfy me. I wrote to Lev Nikolaevich at the time:

204 *Dmitrij Dmitrievich [Mitja] D'jakov* (1880–1943) — son to LNT's friend *Dmitrij Alekseevich D'jakov* and school chum to the Tolstoys' son Mikhail L'vovich [Misha].
205 *Aleksandr Aleksandrovich [Sasha] Bers* (1883–1907) — SAT's nephew, son to her brother *Aleksandr Andreevich [Sasha] Bers* (1845–1918).
206 *Jurij Nikolaevich [Jusha] Pomerantsev* (1878–1933) — (in adulthood:) composer and Bolshoi Theatre conductor.

October 1896. You enquire, dear friend, as to my mood. I am burdened by idleness in the sense that I find myself unable to look upon hanging curtains, ordering dinners, selling books and such like, as serious activities. They do not interest me in the least; everything works by inertia, and only rarely requires of me any direction or effort. I don't have any real or serious activities at the moment, like raising children or helping you, even by way of transcribing. I have never been able to invent anything for myself; I have just been living for the moment. My attraction to music has come too late, and yet still it is the only thing that I find interesting and entertaining right now…

I might have been able to find a measure of interest and joy in communicating with and bringing up Sasha, if only she had been like Vanechka. But Sasha had a very difficult nature. She was extremely stubborn and secretive. She had no need of drawing close to people, even her mother or her brothers, and no interest in spiritual or religious matters — [this was true] right from early childhood and afterward as well. At fourteen she refused to fast any longer with me and her brothers, remaining utterly faithless and only scornful of all of us. She was a poor student and so, in the hope that other people might succeed where I had failed, I entrusted Sasha's instruction to good schoolteachers. But even they had a hard time with her, and often turned their lessons into more cheerful conversations.

On the 20th of October Sasha, Misha and I took a trip to Yasnaya Polyana, returning on the 23rd. It was a place we always wanted to go to, any time, with our whole heart.

I recall how on the way back Lev Nikolaevich was seeing us off at Kozlova-Zaseka, and some sort of confusion arose over the arrival of the train. I was terribly frightened of something (I can't remember what), but I shall never forget the way Lev Nikolaevich treated me. I wrote to him later from Moscow:

> Once in the carriage I remembered everything — how I stupidly lost control of myself, and how you put your arm around me as though I were a child, and right away I felt a sense of peace. I remembered how I submitted myself to your care, after losing my own will. Pity that I had so little opportunity in my life to submit to your will like that — it's so joyful and comforting. But you responded awkwardly, feverishly and not consistently. You either treated me with passion or you completely forgot about and abandoned me, angry at one moment and tender the next…

Lev Nikolaevich wrote me similar letters of moral support in Moscow. I sincerely thanked him for them and said that I did not deserve his kindness, and felt so far inferior to him that I could never come up to his spiritual level. "But I shall try," I wrote, naïvely thinking I might be able to. At the end of my letter I wrote him:

"Farewell, and forgive me for anything in me that you find distressing."

On the 28th of October I wrote to my sister Tanja:

Lëvochka has become unusually affectionate and patient with me (as though he's afraid of losing me). Especially lately I have felt his influence on me, in the sense of spiritual protection. He understands the loss of my inner equilibrium and is constantly helping me, kindly and tenderly.

We had a good, fun stay at Yasnaya Polyana. Lev Nikolaevich was riding once again, both bicycle and horseback, and got in a lot of tennis-playing with the young folks. But afterward Dora and Lëva came to see me in Moscow for a week or two and stayed with me, which I was very happy about.

I took out subscriptions to both symphony and chamber music gatherings, I joined the Conservatory as an active member and went to various concerts. But by the end of November they had worn me out to such an extent that I was no longer quite so enthusiastic about attending them.

And I had a lot of purely material tasks to take care of. Our son Andrjusha, who in November had gone off to his regiment in Tver', asked me to send him all sorts of household utensils. On several occasions Dora and Lëva sent me to the customs office and everywhere else to petition for the clearance of Dora's things which had been forwarded from Sweden. Our daughter-in-law, Sonja (Il'ja's wife), asked me to get her clothes and dresses for the children, which Tanja and I later sewed. Misha was in a hurry to get into the Lycée and order his coat and uniforms. I got a letter from Yasnaya asking me to send Lev Nikolaevich his half-length fur coat and other things. All these activities I found quite a bother, quite exhausting. How on earth could I live an exclusively spiritual life here?

VII.50 THE ARTICLE *ON ART* — DOUKHOBORS — MUSIC AGAIN
LEV NIKOLAEVICH'S MAIN INTERESTS over the course of the winter of 1898 were his article *On art* and the resettlement of the Doukhobors[207] from Russia to Canada. While I was away Lev Nikolaevich received a visit from an American[208] proposing to resettle the Doukhobors on the Hawaiian Islands.

207 Tolstoy's connection to the *Doukhobors* (a religious group dating from the seventeenth century who rejected violence and the official Orthodox church, believing that God was to be found only in individual thinking) actually began in 1895 (the year of their burning of their weapons in the Caucasus), when he initiated a correspondence with the Doukhobor leader *Pëtr Vasil'evich Verigin* (1859–1924). In the late 1890s LNT was motivated to complete his novel *Resurrection* so that he could use the profits therefrom to help finance the Doukhobors' emigration to Canada in 1899. Verigin was first exiled in the Far North and Siberia and then allowed to join his Doukhobor émigré flock in Canada in 1902. See Donskov 1995, 1998, 2005, 2008a and especially 2019.
208 *Nicholas Russel* [birthname: *Nikolaj Konstantinovich Sudzilovskij*] (1850–1930) — radical student activist at Kiev University, who fled Russia in 1874 to escape political persecution. Two years later he obtained his doctorate in medicine at the University of Bucharest in Romania. In 1887 he emigrated to America, first to San Francisco and five years later to Hawaii. He idealised the native

Everything he said about the locale, its beauty and facilities, was very tempting. Unfortunately, however, it was too late, since it had all been arranged by that time for the Doukhobors to go to Canada. Only the procedure was stalled for lack of money. And on the 19th of March 1898 Lev Nikolaevich wrote his *Letter to society* [*Appeal*], asking for help for the Doukhobors.

Lev Nikolaevich's move to Moscow in February of 1898 was prompted mainly by the publication of his article *On art* in the journal *Filosofija i psikhologija*, published by N[ikolaj] Ja[kovlevich] Grot. I transcribed this work many times; somewhere I mentioned that I transcribed the "Conclusion" of this article first seven times, and later: nine.[209] This article left a strange impression on me: Lev Nikolaevich's undoubted love for any kind of art, along with his acute denial of it. This struggle was especially evident in the case of music: he loved this form of art best of all; but for personal reasons he decried it, too.

The religious censorship board kept throwing up barriers to the publication of *On art* in its pure form. They made changes everywhere, distorted it, cut out [the equivalent of] two whole printers' sheets before finally, begrudgingly, allowing it to go to press. Lev Nikolaevich was very unhappy about all this and said that the key meaning of his article had been distorted and lost. And then he wanted to get it translated into foreign languages as soon as possible.

To this end he rode on horseback over to see Emily Shanks[210] on Pokrovka Street (daughter of the proprietor of the English Shop) and negotiate with her over an English translation. The translations of Tolstoy's works were being looked after then, as later, by a Mr Maude,[211] who was married to one of [Emily]

Hawaiians and deplored their exploitation by continental Americans, especially the missionaries. He encouraged the use of Hawaiian in the local schools. After annexation of the Hawaiian territory by the United States in 1898, Russel joined the "Home Rule" party and was elected a territorial senator, later senate president. During the Russo-Japanese War in 1905, Russel was persuaded by American diplomat George Kennan to go to Tokyo and preach liberal government for Russia among the Russian prisoners of war in Japanese labour camps. Always on the lookout to attract more Russian immigrants to Hawaii, upon learning of the Doukhobors' need to emigrate, he wrote to and visited LNT in person, urging him to facilitate their relocation there. But by this time the decision had already been made in favour of Canada. See: Ronald Hayashida and David Kittelson, "The Odyssey of Nicholas Russel," *The Hawaiian Journal of History* 11 (1977): 110–24; B. S. Elepov and S. A. Pajchidze, *Geopoliticheskij kharakter rasprostranenija russkoj knigi: k postanovke voprosa* [The geopolitical nature of Russian book distribution: toward a formulation of the question] (Novosibirsk, 2001): 33.

209 See the fourth paragraph of Chapter VII.43 ("Departure of our daughters…") in *My Life*.

210 *Emily Shanks* (known in Russia as *Èmilija Jakovlevna Shanks*, 1857–1936) — an Anglo-Russian artist who attended the Moscow School of Painting, Sculpture and Architecture. She was the first female member of the Itinerant [*Peredvizhniki*] movement. One of her sisters, Mary Shanks, was also an artist, and produced illustrations for Tolstoy's story *Where love is, there God is also* [*Gde ljubov', tam i Bog*]. Their father, *James Stewart Shanks* (1826–1911), was a partner in a Moscow jewellery concern which included the *Magasin Anglais* [English Shop].

211 *Aylmer Maude* (1858–1938) and *Louise Maude* (née *Shanks*, 1855–1939) — a husband-and-wife team who were the principal translators of LNT's works into English during his lifetime.

Shanks' sisters. At the beginning of July this article was translated by Maude and he sent me two copies [of the translation] under the title *What is art?*[212]

Life for me was quite difficult at that time. I wrote in my diary:

"It's hard to live under any kind of despotism, but under the despotism of jealousy, it's horrid!"

As a fifty-four-year-old woman, I did not want to — could not — accept being treated that way.

I amused myself at the time by skating with all my children at the Patriarch Ponds,[213] where we would run into the much older and rather comic Count Aleksej Vasil'evich Olsuf 'ev.[214] I was jokingly told that he was my permanent cavalier.

In spiritual terms I was in a surprisingly good mood. In my diary of that period I wrote:

"The need has arisen [for me] to pray, and for that I thank God."

And again, on 2 February, I wrote:

"A highly religious mood. It's as though I had lifted a curtain and took a serious look into the next world — i.e., that incorporeal, purely spiritual state, by comparison with which everything earthly is made insignificant."

My love and passion for music frequently attracted musicians to our home who appreciated Lev Nikolaevich's *understanding* of music and his love for it, and valued his opinion.

Thus, on the 6th of February, Sergej Ivanovich Taneev[215] and A[leksandr] B[orisovich] Gol'denvejzer came and played us a four-handed [variant of] the symphonic overture to Taneev's opera *Oresteia*.

The listeners had little understanding or appreciation for it. Lev Nikolaevich cautiously said that he liked the theme. Of Taneev's music he always said that it was undoubtedly very *noble*, but often boring.

And so Lev Nikolaevich once again expressed his opinion about Taneev's symphony which [the composer] played for us on the 12th of March 1898. At Taneev's request, he stated his opinion seriously and respectfully, and began outlining his impressions, namely:

They were both part of a thriving British community in Moscow. In 1897 they moved permanently to England, where they were associated with the Society of Friends (Quakers) as well as the Tolstoy-influenced Brotherhood Church. The Maudes were also instrumental in facilitating the Doukhobors' resettlement in Canada.

212 *What is art?* [*Chto takoe iskusstvo?*] was the title LNT gave to his final variant in a series of articles and attempted articles on the subject, published in *Voprosy filosofii i psikhologii* in 1897–1898.

213 *Patriarch Ponds* [*Patriarshie prudy*] — a series of three ponds in the centre of Moscow dating from the seventeenth century on the estate of the Patriarch of the Russian Orthodox Church.

214 *Count Aleksej Vasil'evich Olsuf 'ev* (1831–1915) — Russian cavalry general.

215 *Sergej Ivanovich Taneev* — see Note 42, p. 437.

...in this symphony, as in all modern music, there is no consistency in anything, neither in the melody, or in the rhythm, or even in the harmony. You just start to follow the melody when it breaks off. You just get a feel for one rhythm and it switches over to another. There's always a feeling of dissatisfaction. Besides, in works of true art you get the feeling that it can't be *any other way*, that one flows from the other and you think that you yourself would probably have done the same thing.

Sergej Ivanovich listened to Lev Nikolaevich attentively and respectfully, but it seemed to me he was still distressed that his symphony did not appeal to Lev Nikolaevich the way he would have liked. Another time Taneev brought his four-voice composition *Voskhod solntsa* [Sunrise] and played it for us. Two elements were beautifully juxtaposed here: the anticipation of the sun and its appearance.

A similar thought was expressed by Godard[216] in his work *Au matin*.

On multi-voice music Lev Nikolaevich declared:

"It is important that a voice has something to say. Or else, there may be many voices, but each one ends up saying nothing."

In line with my musical interests, I began reading biographies of various composers. I was fascinated with Beethoven's biography. I recall copying excerpts from this book; I no longer remember the name of the author. And Beethoven's music became even dearer and more interesting to me. How sorry I felt for this genius when I read of his miserable, difficult life!

For some reason even my reading of Beethoven's biography irritated Lev Nikolaevich. It seemed then as though he always felt threatened by anything I loved. I loved refinement in any form, I loved purity in everything, in both the inner and outer world, I passionately loved any kind of art. This was not what Lev Nikolaevich needed. He needed a *woman*, but one who was passive and healthy, without a word or will of her own.

"And now," I wrote in my diary, "my music bothers him, he condemns my flowers, my love for any kind of art, and he makes fun of my reading of Beethoven's biography or Seneca's[217] philosophy..." He called Seneca a pompous, stupid Roman, a lover of fancy words.

"Poor, poor me!" I wrote in my diary as a cry from my heart. "See, my life is over, there is no point in stirring up all the painful memories in my heart."

I was still upset at Lev Nikolaevich's attitude to my activities and amusements. There was still much in the way of a youthful quality in my nature — a sensitiveness, a zest for work, an ability to feel both love and distress, and a passion for music, for any kind of art, and even for fun, for skating...

216 *Benjamin Godard* (1849–1895) — French violinist and composer of the Romantic school. His creative output included eight operas, three symphonies, three string quartets, two piano concertos, a number of piano pieces (including *Au matin*) and many other works.
217 *Lucius Annaeus Seneca* (Seneca the Younger) — see Note 28, p. 434.

And at home, in my husband's study, there appeared more and more often people utterly alien to me, a crowd of people of all social strata. They exhausted Lev Nikolaevich, who was often ill that winter.

I began to feel frequently overwhelmed by my former depression and acute memories of Vanechka's death. It was only in music that I could drown all my sufferings. The less music there was, the greater my depression. Taneev's playing, especially, had a calming effect on me, and I made efforts over and over again to hear this amazing playing.

In spite of the visitors and his ailments, on the 16th of February Lev Nikolaevich opened his black, oilcloth notebook in which, I knew, he wrote his belletristic compositions, and began to write. This gladdened me, as usual.

Then P. A. Sergeenko[218] came, that unfortunate *literator*, and for some reason asked Lev Nikolaevich to sketch out the plan of his old house,[219] which now no longer exists. Lev Nikolaevich touchingly sketched out the plan of the house, adding:

"Here was the nursery, here was Praskov'ja Savishna's[220] room, and here was my father's large study, the large parlour, the unmarried servants' quarters, the sitting room, and so forth."

How Lev Nikolaevich loved his childhood memories! In the spring of that same year our son Lev, too, went with Sergeenko to the village of Dolgoe to look at the large house which had been transported from Yasnaya Polyana, in which his father had been born. The interior of the house was all in ruins, but on the outside it had not lost its former appearance, and Sergeenko took a picture of it. Now, in 1915, there is no trace of the house left.

I am writing this on the basis of fragmentary notes and adding a few details from memory, and that's why it's not so good.

We had an acquaintance named Rusanov,[221] a landowner, a jurist by training, who adored Lev Nikolaevich. In Lev Nikolaevich's writings and ideas he found peace and comfort to relieve his sufferings from spinal-cord disease. He had a wonderful wife, and one time Lev Nikolaevich and I set off together to see the Rusanovs.

218 *Pëtr Alekseevich Sergeenko* (1854–1930) — Russian writer and literary critic, who was acquainted with LNT for many years. He authored several books on Tolstoy, and was the first to publish a compilation of LNT's correspondence.

219 A reference to the house at Dolgoe where LNT was born — see Chapters V.55 ("Fasting with the children") and VII.45 ("Return of our daughter Tanja...") in *My Life*.

220 *Praskov'ja Savishna* [first name and patronymic] — housekeeper to the Tolstoy family during LNT's childhood. Tolstoy described her (fairly accurately) in *Childhood* under the name *Natal'ja Savishna*. As a child he would love to sit in her room and listen to her stories of the past.

221 *Gavriil Andreevich Rusanov* (1846–1907) — member of the Khar'kov District Court until 1884; a close acquaintance of Tolstoy's, who shared his views.

I was struck at the time by Rusanov's opinion of Chertkov, whom I didn't know very well back then. He said he didn't like Chertkov, that he wasn't a decent person, that he had attacks of insanity, as manifest in suspicion, verbosity, despotism and fussiness. All in all, there wasn't much kindness in the man. Everything Rusanov said turned out to be quite true and justified, and I personally was on the receiving end of all the wrath and shallowness of this man [Chertkov] who was so hateful to me, whom I was slow to understand.

VII.64 OUR SON ANDRJUSHA'S WEDDING — CHICHERIN — IN MOSCOW

ON THE 1ST OF JANUARY 1899 we were still staying on at Yasnaya Polyana. In the country I had more leisure time, and I used it to transcribe Lev Nikolaevich's diaries and sew him a shirt. I was glad to see him in his good spirits and even friendly to our guests who had arrived: M. A. Boldyreva[222] and Prince V. Volkonskij.[223] I was quite put out that I had to go to Moscow, to take Sasha's friend Sonja Kolokol'tseva,[224] whom we had brought to Yasnaya Polyana for the holidays.

The 8th of January marked Andrjusha's wedding to Ol'ga Diterikhs[225] in Tula. My son Il'ja and I gave our blessing to him at the hotel, and after the wedding ceremony the reception was held at the home of General Kun,[226] the head of the Tula Arms Factory, as his wife was a relative of Ol'ga's.

Everybody's mood, especially mine, was less than joyful: I had a premonition that there would be no happiness in this marriage. It wasn't [good] for someone of Andrjusha's nature to choose a wife almost six years his senior.

All our sons gathered for the wedding. Lev Nikolaevich went straight to the railway terminal on horseback to see the newly-weds off [on their honeymoon]. A large crowd had gathered to see "Tolstoy and the Wedding" — an extraordinary spectacle and one that had caught the public's fancy. This time, apparently, Lev Nikolaevich was quite amused, since he greeted the crowd with a cheerful smile.

---

222 *Marija Aleksandrovna Boldyreva* (née *Cherkasskaja*) — an estate owner at Vorontsovo in Tambov Gubernia (southeast of Moscow) who was fond of hunting, dogs and horses.

223 *Prince Vladimir Mikhajlovich Volkonskij* (1868–1953) — grandson to the Decembrist *Sergej Grigor'evich Volkonskij* (1788–1865), chamberlain, head of nobility for Shatsk Uezd. In 1892 he married *Anna Nikolaevna Zvegintsova* (1870–?).

224 *Sof'ja Nikolaevna [Sonja] Kolokol'tseva* (1884–?) [also spelt: *Kolokol'tsova*] (married name: *Perfil'eva*) — daughter to *Nikolaj Apollonovich Kolokol'tsev* (1848–1920) and sister to *Nikolaj Nikolaevich [Kolja/Kol'ka] Kolokol'tsev* (?–1918).

225 *Ol'ga Konstantinovna Diterikhs* (1872–1951) — sister to Vladimir Chertkov's wife, *Anna Konstantinovna Diterikhs* (1859–1927). In 1899 she married the Tolstoys' son Andrej L'vovich but divorced him in 1906. Even after the divorce she stayed on at Yasnaya Polyana, helping LNT in his correspondence.

226 *General Aleksandr Vladimirovich Kun* (1842–1916) — one of the managers of the Tula Arms Factory.

The newly-weds headed off, while we — Lev Nikolaevich, Sasha, Marusja Maklakova (who was then visiting Yasnaya Polyana) and I — returned to Moscow on the 10th of January.

Delighted that Lev Nikolaevich did not stay on in the country but went with us to Moscow, I was especially affectionate toward him, so customarily simple and friendly was our relationship [at the time]. *If only it could always be this way!* I thought to myself.

I recall how one evening Lev Nikolaevich came to me and offered to read me aloud Chekhov's story "Dushechka."[227] He always read superbly, but this time it was with special emotion, as he liked this story very much, and wrote a foreword to it.[228]

Apparently Lev Nikolaevich's work on *Resurrection* was not yet quite complete. He kept coming back to it again and again. On the 17th of January he invited the warden[229] of the Butyrka Prison to come see him, who furnished him with various indications regarding the conditions and lives of inmates. At the same time Lev Nikolaevich hastily (in time for the printing of the novel) sent to the editorial offices of *Niva*[230] an epigraph taken from the Gospels,[231] which he asked to have included in the novel (I'm not sure before which chapter).

I was most upset that so much of *Resurrection* had been excised at the censors' discretion (though there were parts which even I would have deleted). *Niva* editor Marks promised he would give us three copies of the novel intact, but he did not carry out this promise.

While I did wish to have a more complete copy of *Resurrection*, there was much in this novel that I regarded not only negatively, but with acute annoyance. For example, regarding the communion bread and wine, Lev

227 "Dushechka" [Darling] — a story written in 1899 by *Anton Pavlovich Chekhov* (1860–1904) about a woman who had a need to give love to many people, whom she instantly won over, but had no children of her own and was never satisfied herself.
228 This was written in February 1905 and was of considerable length. Sources vary in identifying it as a foreword or an afterword.
229 *Ivan Mikhajlovich Vinogradov* — warden of Butyrka Prison. These visits took place over three consecutive evenings. See: I. M. Vinogradov, "Iz zapisok nadziratelja Butyrskoj tjur'my" [From the notes of the warden of Butyrka Prison] in the collection: *Tolstoj i o Tolstom* [Tolstoy and concerning Tolstoy] (Moscow, 1927): 48–53. *Butyrka Prison* [Russian, formally: *Butyrskaja tjur'ma*] was the principal transit prison in Imperial Russia, built in 1879 on the site of an earlier prison dating from the reign of Catherine the Great. Among its more famous political prisoners were two twentieth-century writers: poet *Vladimir Vladimirovich Mayakovsky* (1893–1930) and novelist *Aleksandr Isaevich Solzhenitsyn* (1918–2008).
230 *Niva* (subtitled: *Zhurnal litratury, politiki i obshchestvennoj zhizni* [A journal of literature, politics and social life]) — an illustrated, middle-class-family-oriented journal published in St. Petersburg from 1869 to 1918 by *Adol'f Fëdorovich Marks*. Marks was given the first right of publication of LNT's novel *Resurrection*, with royalties set aside to help fund the Doukhobors' emigration to Canada.
231 LNT's four epigraphs at the beginning of *Resurrection* are drawn from the following Gospel verses: Matt. 18:21, 22; Matt. 7:3; John 8:7; Luke 6:40.

Nikolaevich called it *okroshka*,[232] and instead of the crucifixion of Jesus Christ, he described Jesus as being "executed on the scaffold." There were a lot of other phrases, too, which I vehemently objected to. Lev Nikolaevich himself later expressed a desire to delete these words from the novel, which had offended his sister Marija Nikolaevna as well. But the stupid and stubborn despot Chertkov, contrary to Lev Nikolaevich's wish to delete them, went ahead and published them in a foreign edition.

On the 18th of January we received a visit from Boris Nikolaevich Chicherin.[233] He was one of the few friends Lev Nikolaevich knew on informal terms of address right to the end of his (Chicherin's) life. He read us his article on two unjustly accused elderly *Khlysts*[234] in the place where he lived in Tambov Gubernia. At court Boris Nikolaevich was unjustly excluded from serving on the jury, which greatly disturbed him.

At this time Lev Nikolaevich was not completely healthy; he was suffering from back-aches. This was on account of the fact that while living in the country, even before the holidays, he had gone on horseback to Pirogovo to see his brother Sergej Nikolaevich.[235] From Pirogovo to Yasnaya Polyana is a distance of 35 versts, consequently Lev Nikolaevich had ridden 70 versts in the space of twenty-four hours. And he was then already seventy-one years old. The doctors prescribed daily massage, for which I hired a masseur. But the pain did not easily go away.

I had just begun to miss my son Serëzha, who had gone off with the Doukhobors to Canada, and was complaining in my diary about my loneliness of heart, when I received a comforting telegram from Serëzha. That same evening, the 20th of January, Sergej Ivanovich Taneev came and dissipated my melancholy with his music. He gave a superb performance of a Bach fugue, Lev Nikolaevich's favourite Chopin polonaise, a rondo by Beethoven, along with two waltzes and an impromptu by Chopin. It was a whole magical concert, which Lev Nikolaevich listened to with delight, often with tears in his eyes, even though at the time he was just as often cursing music [in his diaries and writings].

I was told by Modest Il'ich Tchaikovsky[236] (Pëtr Il'ich Tchaikovsky's brother), when I ran into him at the Maslovs,[237] that Lev Nikolaevich

---

232 *okroshka* — a cold soup made from kvass, cucumber and other vegetables.
233 *Boris Nikolaevich Chicherin* (1828–1904) — Russian law professor, philosopher and historian, appointed honorary member of the Petersburg Academy of Sciences (1893).
234 *Khlyst* — a member of a Christian sect originally known as *Khristovery* [Christ-believers]; this term was corrupted to *Khristy* and eventually to *Khlysty*. Like the Doukhobors, they renounced the priesthood in favour of finding God within each person. They were rumoured to have practised self-flagellation (the word *khlyst* is also the Russian word for "whip").
235 *Count Sergej Nikolaevich Tolstoy* (1826–1904) — see Note 80, p. 449.
236 *Modest Il'ich Tchaikovsky* [Russian: *Chajkovskij*] (1850–1916) — Russian dramatist and writer of opera librettos, younger brother to the famous composer.
237 *Fëdor Ivanovich Maslov* — see Note 190, p. 492.

had written a letter to Pëtr Il'ich, saying that he recognised music as the highest of the arts, and accorded it first place in the world of art — and I quite agree. In music the dream always remains, without spelling out its thoughts in full, while in pictures and literary works everything is clear, fully spelt out.

We often had interesting, idea-oriented conversations on various topics. I remember one time in conversation with some visitors Lev Nikolaevich maintained that it was possible to perfect one's self spiritually, even if a person's behaviour were weak. Personally, I did not agree. If one's behaviour is faulty and weak, there can be no spiritual progress — it is stultified.

VII.70 MY ACTIVITIES AND TRIPS

MY EVERYDAY LIFE was then full of photographic and musical activities. Sometimes I would play for four hours at a time. I would often retreat to the empty annexe [at Yasnaya Polyana] where even at night I would not fear loneliness, as I would get carried away studying a Beethoven sonata, or a Chopin scherzo, or Mendelssohn's *Song without words*.

My photographic snapshots I gave away to many people. I sent them to our daughter Tanja in Vienna and they gave my family members pleasure, although, whenever I asked anyone to pose, they almost all declined.

In late June I went to see our sons Serëzha at his Nikol'skoe [estate], and to Il'ja's family at Grinëvka. I had been so worn out with illness that for a long time afterward I was weak and very nervous. But Lev Nikolaevich, too, was then often suffering with his usual gastrointestinal attacks. Around the 5th of July he had sharp pains in his liver and stomach, accompanied by fever and vomiting.

This happened for two reasons — from bathing and from eating a lot of potatoes and berries [just before going to bed] for the night. I was able to help Lev Nikolaevich fairly quickly, since I knew from experience how to relieve his sufferings.

My main activity that summer was the transcribing of all Lev Nikolaevich's letters to me over thirty-seven years. Later I added to this, transcribing all the rest he had written right up to the end of his life. And now they have all been published.

When Lev Nikolaevich had fully recovered, I planned to go to Kiev with Sasha again. I also decided to respond to a very precious standing invitation from the Maslovs to go see them at their estate in Karachevskij Uezd.

Like the preceding one, this trip [to Kiev] was both successful and joyful. I wanted very much to see my sister after the difficult illness she had gone through in February, [to see her] once again as healthy and full of life as ever.

Upon returning to Yasnaya Polyana, I found quite a few visitors there: two Frenchmen, the sculptor Gintsburg,[238] the D'jakov brothers,[239] the young Count Bobrinskij,[240] Marusja Diterikhs[241] and others.

This constant throng of visitors, from which there was no relief even in the country, greatly exhausted us. I was the least to blame for this. The majority of the visitors came to see Lev Nikolaevich, and the next largest group was for the children. I was left, as the housewife, to take care of everything and everyone.

In August our son Misha[242] announced to me that he would no longer go to the Lycée, but had decided to enlist voluntarily in the Sumsk cavalry regiment[243] and, after completing his military service, was going to marry Lina Glebova. I didn't feel I had any right to interfere in his decision, even though I could sense how difficult it was for Lev Nikolaevich to see his sons in the very military service he so fervently deplored — in his life, in his letters and in all his articles, such as *Do not kill* [*Ne ubij*], *On the war in the Transvaal* [*Po povodu Transvaal'skoj vojny*],[244] *On the conference in The Hague* [*Po povodu konferentsii v Gaage*][245] and others.

Twice that autumn I had to go to Moscow on book business, in which I was greatly helped by N[ikolaj] N[ikolaevich] Ge Jr, that dear person who lived with us on friendly terms for two years. He helped me establish the subscription option for Lev Nikolaevich Tolstoy's writings and their sale on a solid footing.

238 *Il'ja Jakovlevich Gintsburg* [also spelt: *Ginzburg*] (1859–1939) — a prominent Russian sculptor. He would later serve as dean of the Faculty of Sculpture at the St. Petersburg Academy of Arts. He sculpted a statuette of LNT in 1891, and several monuments to Tolstoy in St. Petersburg in 1911, following the writer's death.

239 *Dmitrij Dmitrievich [Mitja] D'jakov* (1880–1943) — son to LNT's friend *Dmitrij Alekseevich D'jakov* (1823–1891), younger brother to *Aleksej Dmitrievich D'jakov* (1878–1919) and school chum to the Tolstoys' son *Mikhail L'vovich [Misha]*.

240 Possibly a reference to *Count Vladimir Alekseevich Bobrinskij* (1867–1927) — political activist, three-term member of the State Duma, leader of the Neo-Slavic Movement.

241 *Marija Konstantinovna [Marusja] Diterikhs* (married name: *de Ferran*, 1866–1924) — sister to *Anna Konstantinovna Chertkova* (née *Diterikhs*) and *Ol'ga Konstantinovna Tolstaya* — see Note 225, p. 503.

242 *Mikhail L'vovich [Misha] Tolstoy* (1879–1944).

243 *Sumsk Hussar Regiment* — formed in 1651 in Ukraine by the Cossacks of *Sumsk Sloboda* and designated a Hussar regiment in 1765. It distinguished itself, in particular during the War of 1812 against Napoleon.

244 The war in the Transvaal is usually associated in English with the First Boer War (1880–81), although it is evident here that LNT, writing in December 1899, had the Second Boer War (October 1899–1902) in mind. His remarks on this subject were published in the journal *Svobodnaja mysl'* [Free thought], Nº 4 (1900), under the title *Who is right? (On the war in the Transvaal)* [*Kto prav? (Po povodu Transvaal'skoj vojny)*]. See: Golinenko and Shumova 1998b: 191. It is also known as LNT's letter to Prince G.M. Volkonskij of 4 December 1899 [16 December N.S.].

245 Published under the title: *On the peace congress. Letter to the Swedes* [*Po povodu kongressa o mire. Pis'mo k shvedam*] (1899).

Lev Nikolaevich was still living at Yasnaya Polyana, apparently observing a uniform daily schedule: in the mornings he would write, at two o'clock he would take dinner, then he would have a nap, go for a walk or a horseback ride, and then read in the evenings. Our relationship was even and peaceful, and his jealousy over S[ergej] I[vanovich] Taneev had completely vanished. He had finally come to terms with the understanding that my relationship with Taneev was extremely innocent, friendly, trustworthy and simple. After all, I was fifty-five years old already.

It is likely that Taneev had not even an inkling of jealousy on the part of Lev Nikolaevich, whom he loved, of course, much more than me. He was very kind, and apparently an utterly dispassionate and naïve individual, not to mention a first-class musician. All my children were very fond of him, and he, for his part, treated our family with great tenderness, and paid us frequent visits, especially when Lev Nikolaevich was gone from Moscow, along with all the commotion which he [Lev Nikolaevich] introduced into our lives, courtesy of his visitors.

VIII.16 LEV NIKOLAEVICH'S EXCOMMUNICATION — MY LETTER
TO POBEDONOSTSEV AND THE METROPOLITANS — OVATIONS
FOR LEV NIKOLAEVICH ON LUBJANKA SQUARE
THE STUDENT PROTESTS coincided with Lev Nikolaevich's excommunication from the [Russian Orthodox] Church, as announced everywhere [in the press] on 25 February.[246] That day Lev Nikolaevich took his usual walk, and on Lubjanka Square, which he had to cross to get where he was going, he was all of a sudden surrounded by a crowd, which began to press in on him. Many doffed their hats with shouts of *Hurrah!* One could hear the constant roar from the crowd: *Tolstoy! Tolstoy!*

Lev Nikolaevich had a hard time making his escape. He hastily jumped into a [horse-drawn] cab. Someone (I don't remember who it was) then escorted Lev Nikolaevich and helped him climb into the cab and escape the crowd. Such a crowd is often frightening and dangerous.

In the meantime, while Lev Nikolaevich was out, I opened up the papers and read about Lev Nikolaevich's excommunication. I immediately felt so disturbed and annoyed by this action of the Synod that I wrote a letter to Pobedonostsev[247] on the spot. The following day, after realising that the Metropolitans, too, must have signed it, I sent a similar letter to them.

I was particularly surprised at Pobedonostsev's participation in the excommunication. In 1900, in a conversation with Countess Aleksandra Andreevna

246 According to other sources, Tolstoy's excommunication from the Russian Orthodox Church occurred on 24 February. Especially in this final part of *My Life*, it is evident that SAT did not always record or remember dates accurately.
247 *Konstantin Petrovich Pobedonostsev* — see Note 116, p. 461 above and Illustration 19.

Tolstaya, Pobedonostsev had expressed the opinion that Lev Nikolaevich should not be deprived of a church funeral, as nobody could know what might happen in the soul of a dying man even two minutes before his death.[248] This was actually said in connection with both the description of the mass in the novel *Resurrection* and the [resulting] threat of excommunication.

When Lev Nikolaevich came back from his walk on the 24th (or the 25th), the letter to Pobedonostsev was already in the post. I read him the draft of the letter, whereupon he smiled and said:

"There have been so many books written on this subject that they wouldn't even fit into our house, and here you want to teach them with your letter!"

Nevertheless, that letter of mine practically flew around the world. It was translated into all sorts of languages, and garnered flattering reviews of my action and praise for my boldness, though the Synod and clergy kept mum. The most intelligent article on the subject came from Metropolitan Antonius.[249] He was reported as being against excommunication.

Subsequently, Lev Nikolaevich himself wrote his famous *Reply to the Synod* [*Otvet Sinodu*].[250] But it didn't resonate with the same effect as my impromptu action of a woman defending her husband, which took everyone by surprise. Later, when we were living in the Crimea, the young lady in charge of the library at Koreiz[251] told me how she and those around her kept reading my letter to the clergy over and over for several days and made copies [to share with others]. It was praised even by non-Russians.[252] I append this letter herewith:

Having read in the paper the cruel decision of the Synod regarding the excommunication of my husband, Count Lev Nikolaevich Tolstoy, from the Church, with the signatures of the pastors of the Church, I could not remain indifferent. My sorrow and displeasure [at this decision] know no bounds. And not from the standpoint that this decree might mean the spiritual death of my husband — no, that is not for men to decide, but for God. From the religious point of view, the life of the human soul is unknown to anyone and, thankfully, not subject to anyone. But from the point of view of that Church to which I belong and from which I shall never stray, which was created by Christ for the blessing, in God's name, of all the significant moments of human life: birth, marriage, death, people's joys and sorrows… a church that ought to be loudly proclaiming the law of love, universal forgiveness, love for one's enemies and for those who hate us, and prayer for all, — from that point of view the Synod's decision is

248 See the last few paragraphs of Chapter VIII.7 ("Birth of Sonechka…") in *My Life*.
249 *Metropolitan Antonius* (birth-name: *Aleksandr Vasil'evich Vadkovskij*) (1846–1912) — appointed Metropolitan of St-Petersburg and Ladoga in 1898, senior member of the Holy Synod in 1900.
250 *Reply to the Synod* — completed 4 April 1901. See *PSS*, 34: 245–53.
251 *Koreiz* — a historical town not far from Yalta in the Crimea, the site of the palace of *Grand Prince Pëtr Nikolaevich Romanov* (1864–1931), built in the mid 1890s.
252 *non-Russians* [Russian: *inorodtsy*] — this could refer, alternatively, to *inovertsy* (i.e., people outside the Russian Orthodox faith).

incomprehensible to me. It will evoke not compassion, but displeasure among people and an even greater love and compassion for Lev Nikolaevich. We are hearing of such declarations and there will be no end to them, [they will come] from all over the world.

I cannot refrain from mentioning the sorrow I have experienced on account of that nonsense I heard about earlier, namely, the Synod's secret directive to its priests not to hold a funeral service in church for Lev Nikolaevich in the event of his death. Whom do they want to punish? The deceased person, who no longer can feel anything, or those around him — believers who are close to him? If this is a threat, then who or what is being threatened? Do they expect that to commemorate my husband and pray for him in church, I would not be able to find either a reputable priest who does not fear people before the true God of love, or a disreputable one who can be bought for a high price to perform such a service? But even this is not something I need. To me, the Church transcends material concepts, and I recognise as its priests only those who truly understand the significance of the Church. On the other hand, if the Church is recognised as made up of people who dare to violate, through their malevolent attitudes, Christ's higher law of love, then all of us who truly believe and attend Church would have left it long ago.

And those guilty of sinful departure from the Church are not the errant ones seeking the truth, but those who proudly proclaim themselves to be its leaders and in the place of love, humility and universal forgiveness have become the spiritual executioners of those whom God forgives for their humble life full of renunciation of earthly goods, full of love and assistance to others, even if outside the Church, more certainly than those who wear diamond-studded mitres and stars, yet punish and excommunicate — [and here I'm referring to] its pastors.

These words of mine may well be refuted with hypocritical arguments. But no one can be deceived by a deep understanding of truth and of people's true intentions.

Countess Sofia Tolstaya
Moscow. 21, Khamovniki Lane
26 February 1901

My letter appeared in the papers on 25 March.[253] Almost at the same time, i.e., on 15 March, Lev Nikolaevich wrote an article entitled *To the Tsar and his associates* [Tsarju i ego pomoshchnikam].[254] In it he gave all sorts of advice and directives as to how to govern Russia. I published this letter in the twelfth edition of L.N. Tolstoy's *Complete collected works*, but it was subsequently removed [by the censors].

253 SAT's letter to Pobedonostsev was first published in the Russian Orthodox paper *Tserkovnye vedomosti* [Church News], which had published the original excommunication decree. In so doing it apparently violated an order from the official church press office forbidding any discussion of Tolstoy's excommunication in the media.
254 *To the Tsar and his associates* — sent to the Tsar 26 March 1901. See PSS, 34: 239–44.

On the 17th of March I held a charity concert in aid of the shelter I mentioned earlier (in my description of 1900 and of how I became a trustee of the shelter). At the end of March I fasted with the children and employees of the shelter. Under the influence of her father, Sasha[255] did not attend church, which greatly distressed me.

VIII.20 AFTERWORD

I HEREWITH CEASE MY NOTATIONS, and I shall probably not have the opportunity to continue them. As I never intended to write them out, I *did not prepare* the materials, and when I started these notes, the materials I had appeared meagre and not even all that interesting. On the other hand, the absence of any biased forethought [means that] everything here is true and sincere.

I do not have Lev Nikolaevich's diaries of the last years of his life. They are with our daughter Sasha. There is my diary from 1901 and 1902 in the Crimea — it may serve as a continuation of these notes.[256]

255 *Aleksandra L'vovna [Sasha] Tolstaya* (1884–1979).
256 See Illustration 40.

CHAPTER 8

Selected poems by Sofia Andreevna Tolstaya

A WITTICISM (1850S)

Рубашка грязная спустилась	A filthy dirty shirt hung clearly
С её прежирного плеча,	From her fatty shoulder down.
И перед зеркалом садилась	And so she sat before the mirror
Она зевая и ворча, и т. д.	And yawned and yawned and grumbled on, etc.

A DITTY DEDICATED TO DAUGHTER TANJA (1881)

Какие нужны выраженья,	Now what expressions so endearing
Чтобы в стихах сказать тебе,	Need I in this my verse create
Что о твоей со дня рожденья	To say: From the time of your appearing,
Скорблю душой я о судьбе.	My heart has grievèd for your fate.

Что нет мне в свете больше горя,	To tell you I've no greater sorrow
Как если горько плачешь ты,	Than when you weep so bitterly,
Что больно быть с тобой в раздоре,	Or when we're caught in painful quarrel,
И страшны мне твои мечты…	And when your dreams strike fear in me…

CONCLUDING STANZA OF A POEM ADDRESSED TO LEV NIKOLAEVICH ET AL.

Но мир без ваших слабых рук	The world without your feeble hands
Стоять всё будет так же твердо,	Will go on standing just as soundly,
Хоть жалкий лишний свой досуг	In spite of all the time and plans
Ему бросаете так гордо.	You waste and throw at it so proudly.

A DITTY (1882)

Вечер чудный был и ясный	What an evening, clear and gorgeous —
Алый с запада закат,	Western sunset's rosy glow —
Был у нас пикник прекрасный,	This day's picnic was so glorious,
Всякий ехать был так рад.	Everyone was glad to go.
«Ну, мамзель Софи, пойдёмте,	"Ma'm'selle Sophie, shouldn't we, rather,
Надо нам костёр зажечь,	Get going and light a roaring fire?
Листья, сучья соберёмте,	Leaves and twigs and branches gather,
Будем мы картошки печь».	And fry potatoes midst the brier?"
Рыбки Лёля три поймал	Lëlja he caught fishes three,
И пустил их в лужу.	But let them go — too easy.
Вот костёр наш запылал	Campfire flares up bold and free —
Хоть бы в зимний день и стужу.	Just as if it were cold and freezing!
Самовары закипели,	Samovars began to gurgle,
Собралися мы в кружок,	Everyone sat down to eat
Чинно рядышком все сели,	Side by side, we formed a circle
Стали кушать все пирог.	All had pie — oh, what a treat!
Только вдруг Илья схватил	Then all at once Il'ja did snatch
Из огня горящу палку,	A burning stick right out of the pyre.
Бросал в воздух и ловил,	He'd toss it in the air and catch,
Даже рук не было жалко.	No thought for hands being burnt by fire.
Чуркой долго он махал,	He waved the stick in magic spells,
Всё мамзелей удивлял,	Amazing all the demoiselles,
Прозевал пирог и чай,	Missing out on pie and tea —
Сам виновен — не серчай.	'Twas his own fault, so don't blame me!

Response to Fet's poem (1885)

За что такое восхваленье,
Мне скромной, старой и дурной,
Зачем будить в душе волненье
Поэта мощною рукой.

Живя в среде, иной где свет,
В тени привыкла я спасаться…
О не буди ж во мне, поэт.
Того, чего должна бояться!

Why all this fuss and adulation
Of me — so ugly, old and bland,
Why stir the soul to consternation
By dint of mighty poet's hand?

In a world of different light I be,
Wont to retreat within the shadows…
Oh, poet, do not stir in me
A feeling I should be afraid of!

My farewell (1886)

Прощайте, милые друзья,
Я покидаю вас с тоскою,
Хоть не надолго еду я,
Но дух тревожен, нет покою.

Не властны все мы над судьбой,
Быть может, мне не возвратиться;
Друзья, с одной теперь мольбой
Хочу я к вам всем обратиться:

Коль уж не быть мне среди вас,
Простите всё, чем огорчала,
Порывы злобные подчас,
И всё, чем жизнь омрачала.

Несправедливость, горечь, гнев,
Забудьте всё, что больно было…
И каждый вспомнит пусть, что всех
Так нежно, долго я любила…

Farewell, dear friends, I'll soon be gone:
It is with longing that I'm leaving…
And though I shan't be gone for long,
I have no peace, my spirit's grieving.

We are not masters of our fate:
Perchance for me there's no returning;
My friends, I have one plea to make
To all for whom my heart is yearning:

When I'm no longer with you here,
For being so mean I ask forgiving,
Forgive my bursts of anger, fear,
And any act that's spoilt your living.

Unfairness, sorrow, anger, aye,
Forget all said or done unduly…
And let each one recall how I
Loved all of you so deeply, truly…

THE PROPHET (1886)

Да, не признали вы пророка
В семье, в отечестве своём,
Но нет тяжеле в свете рока
Как быть непризнанным вождём.

«Я вам о счастии вещаю,
Поймите, вас же всех любя,
И Царство Божье обещаю,
Взгляните только вы в себя».

«Вы погибаете в обмане,
В роскошной праздности живя,
Вы счастье ищете в тумане,
Но горечь сердца лишь тая».

И молча все внимали
Пророка праведным речам,
Но призрак свой не отдавали…
Он ясен лишь пророческим очам.

И вот с главой поникшей
Посыпав пеплом он главу,
Отшёл туда, где мир был высший,
Где не слыхать людей молву.

This prophet you have not accepted
In his own land. There's no worse shame
Than being a leader once rejected,
Unrecognised, without a name.

"I love you all — I mean it, honest:
I'm telling you of joy and wealth,
God's Kingdom here — that's what I promise:
You need but look within yourself."

"You perish in your vain illusion,
You live by luxury's idle art,
You seek for joy in vague confusion,
But hide the wrath within your heart."

Yes, silently they've been intaking
The prophet's words true and sincere,
But phantoms they've not been forsaking:
Only to prophets' eyes they're clear.

And with his head bowed low in sadness,
With ashes sprinkled o'er his head,
He's gone to a world of peace and gladness,
Where human words are not heard said.

Ode to Yasnaya Polyana (1886)

Тебе писать хочу я оду,
Поляна Ясная моя.
Твою воспеть хочу природу,
Твои прелестные края.

Ты колыбель людей мне милых,
Ты счастье жизни мне дала;
И дней весёлых и унылых
Безмолвным зрителем была.

Ты гения нам в мир дала,
Художника для русской славы,
Тебе и честь же, и хвала,
Что рос в тени твоей дубравы.

Люблю тенистые аллеи,
Куда спасалась я в тоске,
И всё мне делалось милее,
В твоей таинственной листве.

Люблю Чепыж я тёмный
С его столетними дубами,
Люблю с балкона, в полдень знойный,
Я вид с златистыми полями.

Люблю окрестности с лесами,
Посадки с чудными грибами,
Проспект с заросшими прудами,
И ёлки, росшие веками.

Свободу, радость, красоту
В тебе всегда я находила,
Задач житейских суету —
Всё в жизни ты мне разрешила.

От преступлений и соблазна
Ты младость раннюю мою
Безмолвно, твёрдо и не праздно
Хранила свято, как в раю.

Прими ж на склоне моих дней
И душу грешную мою;
Чтоб среди простых людей
Мне умереть в родном краю.

To write an ode to you I'm wanting,
My Yasnaya Polyana dear.
To sing and praise your Nature hauntings,
The charms that permeate your sphere.

You've cradled those I hold in gladness,
You've given joy for me to share;
In days of fun and days of sadness,
You've been a silent witness there.

You bore a genius to the world,
An artist for our Russia glorious,
All praise to you who a life unfurled
Beneath the shade of your old oak forest.

I love your shady allées, clearings,
Where I sought refuge from my grief,
And all was made e'en more endearing
By each and every hidden leaf.

I love Chepyzh, so dark and shady,
With oak trees that are centuries old…
From sunny balcony at midday
I love the view o'er fields of gold.

I love the woods in our surroundings,
And mushroom forests so astounding,
The lane and ponds with reeds abounding,
And firs with rings of ages mounting.

Delight and freedom, joy and beauty
In you I have forever found —
The tasks of living's daily duty —
My life with everything you've crowned.

So calmly, firmly, never idly,
You kept my young days free from vice,
From yielding to temptation wildly,
Kept holy, as in Paradise.

Now take, in my declining years,
My sinful soul by your firm hand,
That I might die midst all those dear
And simple folk in my native land.

INDEX OF NAMES

A

About, E. — 51
Abramovich, M. I. — 454
Agaf'ja Mikhajlovna — 150
Aksakov, I. S. — 13, 51, 184
Albertini, L. G. — 141
Alekseeva, G. — x
Alekseev, P. S. — 463n
Alexander II — 102, 108, 494n
Alexander III — 32, 53, 108, 116, 119, 466, 470n, 472n
Ambrosius (Father) — 108
Amiel, H-F. — 19, 308, 455–456n
Amoursky, E. — 10, 157
Andersen, H. C. — 73
Antinous — 110
Antokol'skij, M. M. — 440
Apollo — 110
Arenskij, A. S. — 6, 140
Aristotle — 19, 434n
Arkhangelov, S. A. — x
Arnautov, I. A. — 109
Artsimovich — see Gorjainova, E. V.
Asquith, C. — 9, 176
Aucouturier, M. — ix
Azarova, N. I. — 6n, 101n, 156, 164, 166

B

Bajkova, Ju. G. — see Shumikhina
Bakunin, P. — 6, 19
Bannikov, M. N. — 449n
Barbanjaga, E. — 159, 176
Basinskij, P. — 9, 75, 80, 159
Bauer, E. — 461
Bers, A. A. [Sasha] (brother) — 111n, 480n, 496
Bers, A. A. (cousin) — 104n
Bers, A. A. (nephew) — 123
Bers, A. E. (father) — 102, 104
Bers, E. A. [Liza] (sister) — 104n, 128

Bers, E. I. (grandfather) — 50
Bers, E. I. (grandmother) — 102
Bers, L. A. [Ljuba] (cousin) — 59, 424
Bers, L. A. (mother) — 113n
Bers, M. D. (sister-in-law) — 111n
Bers, N. A. [Natasha] (cousin) — 59
Bers, S. A. [Stëpa] (brother) — 104
Bers, T. A. (sister) — 59, 103
Bers, V. A. (brother) — 143n
Beethoven, L. von — 54, 81, 84, 93, 125, 134, 355, 357–358, 362–363, 365, 391, 409, 419–420, 438, 448, 493, 501, 505–506
Belin (professor) — 109
Bendavid-Val, L. — 10, 156, 439n
Bergman, V. — 117n
Birjukov, P. I. — 45, 123, 146, 462, 483
Bobrinskij, V. A. — 507
Boldyreva, M. A. — 503
Bonaque, M.-L. — 10, 157
Borisov-Musatov, B. E. — 142
Boudreau, C. — xi
Büchner, F. — 19, 247, 434
Bulgakov, M. P. — see Metropolitan Makarij
Bulgakov, V. F. — 147, 152, 154
Bulygin, M. V. — 148

C

Caro, E. M. — 450
Catherine the Great — 106n, 504n
Chekhov, A. P. — 118, 140, 504
Chertkova, A. K. — 507n
Chertkova, E. I. — 469n
Chertkov, G. I. — 469n
Chertkov, V. G. — 9, 33, 39, 45, 52n, 55, 97, 111, 123, 127, 141, 144–147, 150n–151, 452, 469, 475, 495, 503, 505
Chicherin, B. N. — 19, 503, 505
Chirkov, V. V. — 109
Chizhova, P. V. — 437n

Lightning Source UK Ltd.
Milton Keynes UK
UKHW020931240322
400547UK00005B/22